the **psychology** companion

Palgrave Student Companions are a one-stop reference resource that provide essential information for students about the subject – and the course – they've chosen to study.

Friendly and authoritative, **Palgrave Student Companions** support the student throughout their degree. They encourage the reader to think about study skills alongside the subject matter of their course, offer guidance on module and career choices, and act as an invaluable source book and reference that they can return to time and again.

Palgrave Student Companions – your course starts here

Published
The MBA Companion
The Politics Companion
The Social Work Companion
The Psychology Companion

Forthcoming
The Cultural Studies Companion
The English Language and Linguistics Companion
The Health Studies Companion
The Literary Studies Companion
The Media Studies Companion
The Nursing Companion
The Theatre, Drama and Performance Companion

Further titles are planned

www.palgravestudentcompanions.com

the **psychology** companion

bridget adams

your course starts here

palgrave
macmillan

First published 2009 by
PALGRAVE MACMILLAN

Palgrave Macmillan in the UK is an imprint of Macmillan Publishers Limited, registered in England, company number 785998, of Houndmills, Basingstoke, Hampshire RG21 6XS.

Palgrave Macmillan in the US is a division of St Martin's Press LLC, 175 Fifth Avenue, New York, NY 10010.

Palgrave Macmillan is the global academic imprint of the above companies and has companies and representatives throughout the world.

Palgrave® and Macmillan® are registered trademarks in the United States, the United Kingdom, Europe and other countries

ISBN-13: 978-0-230-00818-2   paperback
ISBN-10: 0-230-00818-6   paperback

This book is printed on paper suitable for recycling and made from fully managed and sustained forest sources. Logging, pulping and manufacturing processes are expected to conform to the environmental regulations of the country of origin.

A catalogue record for this book is available from the British Library.

A catalog record for this book is available from the Library of Congress.

10 9 8 7 6 5 4 3 2 1
18 17 16 15 14 13 12 11 10 09

Printed and bound in China

Contents

List of figures

Acronyms

ACTH	adrenocorticotrophic hormone or adrenocorticotrophin
AI	artificial intelligence
ANS	autonomic nervous system
APA	American Psychological Association
ASC	altered state of consciousness
BACP	British Association of Counselling and Psychotherapy
BPS	British Psychological Society
BSRI	Bem Sex Role Inventory
CAT	X-ray computed axial tomography
CEP	BPS Consciousness and Experiential Psychology Section
CNS	central nervous system
CT	X-ray computed tomography
DCoP	BPS Division of Counselling Psychology
DNA	deoxyribonucleic acid
DSEP	BPS Division of Sport and Exercise Psychology
DTRP	BPS Division for Teachers and Researchers in Psychology
ECS	electroconvulsive shock
ECT	electroconvulsive therapy
EEG	electroencephalograph
EI	emotional intelligence
EQ	emotional intelligence quotient
EV	evoked potentials
GABA	gamma-amino butyric acid
GAS	general adaptation syndrome
GSR	galvanic skin response
hGH	human growth hormone
IQ	intelligence quotient
IT	information technology
IT	inspection time
LOP	levels of processing
LOT	language of thought
LTM	long-term memory
LTS	long-term (memory) store
MOPs	memory organization packets
MRI	magnetic resonance imaging
NLP	neurolinguistic programming
NMR	nuclear magnetic resonance

NMRI	nuclear magnetic resonance imaging
NVC	non-verbal communication
PCP	personal construct psychology
PET	positron emission tomography
PM	procedural memory
POWS	Psychology of Women Section of the BPS
QAA	Quality Assurance Agency for Higher Education
REBT	rational emotive behaviour therapy
REM sleep	rapid eye-movement sleep
SGCP	Special Group in Coaching Psychology
SMG	Student Members Group of BPS
SNS	sympathetic nervous system
SPSS	a comprehensive package for statistical calculations
S–R	stimulus–response
STM	short-term memory
STS	short-term (memory) store
SWS	slow wave sleep
TABP	Type A behaviour pattern
TAT	thematic apperception test
TENS	transcutaneous electrical nerve stimulation
TOPs	thematic organization points
ZPD	zone of proximal development

Acknowledgements

The author would like to thank the BPS and QAA for allowing items from their websites to be reproduced, Professor Noel Entwistle for permission to reproduce his categories of approaches to learning, and Dr Nick Adams at Edinburgh University for helping with the metaphysics. All the material from QAA is extracted/reproduced with permission from *Subject benchmark statement: Psychology 2007.* © The Quality Assurance Agency for Higher Education, 2007.

Thank you also to the editors at Palgrave Macmillan who were enthusiastic in asking me to take on this project and who continued to give support and encouragement throughout the long process of writing.

Thanks also to the reviewers at each stage of production, particularly the proposal stage and draft manuscript, who gave positive comments as well as excellent suggestions for improvement, and kept me going.

Thanks are also due to all colleagues who shared, over the years, teaching suggestions and material that could be adapted to suit this book.

Introduction

The Palgrave *Psychology Companion* is primarily intended for students planning to embark on a degree course in psychology but it is also suitable for anyone who is interested in finding out about psychology, either as a career or as an academic course of study at A-level, Access, Diploma or undergraduate level. This will include prospective students, new students, returning students and experienced professionals who are undertaking a course of study in psychology, health psychology, counselling or interpersonal skills or any psychology-related course. No previous knowledge of psychology is assumed. The book is also invaluable as support for students during their study.

The Table of Contents shows that there are seven parts, in line with the generic structure of the Palgrave Companion Series.

Each section, where appropriate, includes the relevant specifications from the *Subject Benchmark Statement: Psychology 2007*, published by QAA, and extracts from the BPS qualifying examination syllabus for 2008.

QAA, the Quality Assurance Agency for Higher Education, reviews standards and quality, and provides reference points that help to define clear and explicit standards. All undergraduate psychology courses will include the topics they list.

The Qualifying Examination of the BPS (British Psychological Society) is intended for people who are graduates but who do not hold an honours degree in psychology recognised by the Society and who are therefore not yet eligible for the Graduate Basis for Registration. The syllabus indicates the kinds of topics that will be included in typical BPS accredited undergraduate courses (see also Part 7).

Part 1 deals with general information about psychology, including ethical standards and values, applying for courses and developing the kind of approach to higher-level study that will help you get the most out of your course.

Part 2 looks at the many different approaches to investigating and understanding human minds and behaviour: from the traditional, split into biological, behavioural, cognitive, social, humanistic and psychodynamic psychology, to more modern additions of lifespan development, human diversity, evolutionary, cultural, forensic, political, lesbian and gay, military, political, sport and transpersonal psychology and other applied fields.

Part 3 presents a wide range of over 400 terms and concepts in psychology, arranged alphabetically, with a brief definition in most cases and a fuller account where this is needed to explain a particular concept. Many concepts in psychology are named using invented words. These are sometimes common words to which a special meaning applies. For example, the word 'complex', which usually means complicated, is used in psychodynamic literature for an unconscious mental state or pattern such as 'Oedipus complex'. The word 'iconic', which may be familiar to you from religious icons such as paintings or statues, or computer icons that indicate the buttons for open, save, or print, is used in psychology to refer to a style of thinking in visual images. Other terms may be derived by combining words or parts of words, from Greek, Latin or other languages. For example, the word psychology combines *psyche* with *logos* (see Part 1.1). The text is as simple and plain as possible and illustrates applications to practice with examples.

Part 4 provides a brief overview of the history of ideas relating to human mind and behaviour in philosophy and psychology, followed by an alphabetical listing of some of the most well-known theories and studies, both historical and current, with brief biographical details of the theorists. This helps you see them in their proper context as real people, some of whom use their websites for you to see them in action and to invite you to contact them.

Part 5 covers the essential ideas in psychological research methods, indicating the kinds of experimental design that can be used and the relevant statistical tests. It is beyond the scope of this book to describe experimental designs or statistical tests in detail. Only a few of the simpler mathematical formulae are included. Tables of significance are not included.

Part 6 gives information about pursuing a career as a chartered psychologist or following a psychology-related career.

Part 7 comprises a bibliography of all references mentioned in the text, and other useful texts for further reading, together with useful general websites and specific sites relating to items in the book. Brief details are given for useful psychology and education organisations.

Psychology is one of the most popular subjects in UK higher education. We hope that the *Psychology Companion* will help you understand what psychology is about, and help you get the most out of your psychology course and prepare for the career you would like.

How to use this book

The *Psychology Companion* can be used in many different ways: as a directory that will lead to information about different kinds of psychologists and careers in psychology, and as an introductory text that will tell you something about the subject and provide a stepping stone to standard psychology textbooks, specialist textbooks and journals, and a starting point for searching the Internet. It can also serve as a glossary for quick reference to individual terms or as a study guide or revision aid.

As far as possible the QAA and BPS terms are defined and explained. Where possible, the terms used by the pioneers in this vast study are defined, and the meanings of concepts that can seem difficult at first are made clear. Throughout the book, an indication is given of the main arguments or debates and this is perhaps one of the most important features.

Reading the whole book cover to cover is highly recommended at some stage in your development, but the *Psychology Companion* is designed for dipping into and as you follow the cross-references you may find you are led into new areas and down new avenues.

Different pathways through the text may be useful for different purposes and some ideas crop up in different contexts, for example as a key term or as a key study. There is some repetition but mostly the discussion in Parts 2, 3 and 4 builds as you move (forwards or backwards) through the book, so that following up cross-references gives you a fuller picture. Cross-references are given where the same, or a similar, item appears elsewhere. Where a word is given in italics this means that it is defined elsewhere in the book. In Part 2, in each of the sections referring to a particular approach, a list of relevant items in Parts 3 and 4 is given at the end of the section.

All terms are also listed in the index and this may be a useful place to start when seeking information about a particular word or person or locating cross-references.

You will be guided where to look for information but some primary sources may be difficult to obtain. There are extra references where the topic may be found in more readily accessible secondary sources, if this might be helpful or where criticisms and applications are included. However, you are encouraged to unearth the primary sources when undertaking an in-depth study. A guide to using a library has been included in the study skills section in Part 1. A guide to the Internet and list of useful websites are given in Part 7.

If you are new to study or are moving to a higher level of study you may find some sections of Part 1 particularly helpful. Part 1.3 looks at ways of approaching study and helps you become more aware of how you study, and how you can develop and make the most of your abilities. It then covers the basic elements of the skills of writing, referencing and giving a presentation.

If you want to think about what to do when you finish your course, Part 6 describes the procedures for qualifying as a chartered psychologist and describes some psychology-related careers.

The 'Handy headings' on the next page give a quick summary of many of the key ideas in psychology.

Handy headings

PSYCHOLOGY IS:

The scientific study of behaviour and mental experience
A vast collection of individual studies
A rich mixture of contrasting and contradictory approaches
Often integrative, eclectic or multimodal, according to level of enquiry
• time dimension • scope • level of generality • meta-level

Influenced by:
Art • magic • superstition • myth • religion • science • politics •ethics • economics • law
• culture •environment • evolution • history • philosophy • healing • medicine

Following or integrating different schools, approaches or perspectives:
Behaviourism and social learning theory
Biopsychology, neurological, ethological, comparative and evolutionary approaches
Cognitive psychology and cognitive-behavioural approaches
Humanistic (phenomenological) psychology
Psychodynamic (including psychoanalytic) psychology
Social, environmental and cultural psychology
Lifespan development and human diversity

Involving analysis and integration of the domains of the:
AFFECTIVE – feelings and emotions
COGNITIVE – beliefs and understanding
CONATIVE – intentions, will
BEHAVIOURAL – observable activity

Using quantitative and qualitative research methods
Project justification • choice of paradigm
General, pilot or preliminary work • detailing and categorising
Selection of variables • formation of hypotheses or research questions
Project design • collection of data
Analysis of data • theories, laws and models
Publication and debate • application

Answering the questions:
Who, when, where, what, why, how, so what, what next?

Meeting the criteria of:
RELIABILITY AND VALIDITY

In order to:
DESCRIBE – EXPLAIN – PREDICT – CONTROL

and concerned with issues such as:
Mind–body interaction, integration and reductionism
Conscious and unconscious mental processes
Free will and determinism • nature–nurture interaction and integration
The individual within society • language and communication
Mental and physical health and illness • death and dying

APPLIED PSYCHOLOGY IS:
the application of research in a particular field:
*Clinical • coaching • consciousness • counselling • educational • forensic • health
• lesbian and gay • military • occupational • political • women • psychotherapy •
social • sport and exercise • teaching • transpersonal*

1 studying psychology

1.1 Context of psychology

What is psychology?

In the ordinary sense, psychology is anything to do with understanding and influencing human minds. That is, all of our behaviour and experience: what we do, think, feel or say; and why; and how we can change.

In the academic sense, psychology is the scientific study of all this. Rudyard Kipling's six serving men or fundamental questions cover most things we need to know, tackled according to scientific principles and methodology:

> Who?
> When?
> Where?
> What?
> Why?
> How?

And we just need to add;

> So what?
> What next?

The word psychology literally means the study of the mind, from psycho and logy. Psycho is from the Latin *psyche* for soul, mind or breath, from the Greek ψυχη and ψυχο. And logy is from *logos*, the Greek λογος for knowledge or discourse.

Psyche (pronounced sigh-key) was also the name given to a beautiful woman in Greek myth who fell in love with Cupid, possibly as a metaphor for love and soul, a story told in *The Golden Ass* by Lucius Apulius in the 2nd century AD.

Psychology, as an academic discipline, developed initially as a branch of philosophy and gradually adopted the methodology of the natural sciences, and is now usually defined as the science of mind and behaviour, or the scientific study of behaviour and experience, or similar expressions.

Some definitions of psychology

William James (1890/1981): Psychology is the science of Mental Life, both of its phenomena and of their conditions. . . .The phenomena are such things as we call feelings, desires, cognitions, reasoning, decisions and the like.

Wright et al (1970: 20, 25): Psychology is the application to human behaviour, including speech, of the observational and experimental methods of science; and its aim is to locate the antecedent conditions associated with particular forms of behaviour, and to explain these relationships through theories which may or may not take account of what are ordinarily understood as mental processes. . . . Psychology is a group of specialisms [but] the boundaries between them are far from distinct.

Atkinson and Hilgard (1990): The scientific study of behaviour and mental processes.

Richard Gross (1992): The science of mind and behaviour.

BPS: Psychology is the scientific study of people, the mind and behaviour. It is both a thriving academic discipline and a vital professional practice. (http://www.bps.org.uk, accessed June 2008, with permission).

Alec Gill: Psychology is simply common sense dressed up in quasi-scientific jargon. (http://www.hull.ac.uk/php/cetag/2apsycho.htm, accessed June 2008).

Wikipedia: Psychology is both an academic and applied discipline involving the scientific study of mental processes and behavior. Psychologists study such phenomena as perception, cognition, emotion, personality, behavior, and interpersonal relationships. Psychology also refers to the application of such knowledge to various spheres of human activity, including issues related to daily life – for example family, education, and work – and the treatment of mental health problems. Psychology is one of the behavioral sciences – a broad field that spans the social and natural sciences. Psychology attempts to understand the role human behavior plays in social dynamics while incorporating physiological and neurological processes into its conceptions of mental functioning. Psychology includes many sub-fields of study and application concerned with such areas as human development, sports, health, industry, law, and spirituality. (http://en.wikipedia.org/wiki/Psychology, accessed June 2008).

Pinker (1998): Psychology is engineering in reverse. In forward engineering, one designs a machine to do something; in reverse engineering, one figures out what a machine was designed to do.

The emphasis in all academic and experimental psychology is on using scientific research procedures and presenting findings for debate. See also Parts 2 and 5.

In many contexts, the term psychology also encompasses psychoanalytical, psychodynamic or depth approaches and person-centred or humanistic approaches in interpretation of art and in psychotherapy and counselling. These are based on clinical studies not experimental research, but many psychology courses include some reference to them for completeness and to open up these areas for debate.

Two things academic psychology is not:

> Psychology does not include psychiatry.
> Psychologists do not read minds and most do not interpret dreams as part of their professional training or practice.

Many hospital and community mental health care teams include a psychiatrist and a psychologist, together with some form of psychotherapy or counselling.

A psychiatrist is a medical doctor who specialises in diseases of the brain and mental illness and who usually has not studied psychology. The focus is on medication or surgery to treat recognised symptoms. In practice the psychiatrist is normally the consultant who leads the team.

Psychologists have followed a degree programme in psychology and post-graduate training in a particular branch of applied psychology (see Part 6). In the health care context this would be clinical, health or counselling psychology.

Psychotherapy and counselling are loosely defined terms for many different kinds of 'talking' or behavioural approaches to mental health or lifestyle problems and may be provided by psychiatrists, psychologists or other trained personnel.

Psychoanalysis is not normally included in health care but can be sought privately. A psychoanalyst undergoes many years of training and analysis in a particular 'school' such as Freudian, Jungian or Kleinian and qualifies to offer analysis (which may include dream analysis) to anyone who seeks it, whether out of interest or because of mental health problems. Psychoanalysis is not, of itself, a therapy. It is a way of exploring the unconscious mind, which may or may not have therapeutic benefit.

Psychoanalysts, psychotherapists and counsellors (apart from counselling psychologists) have not usually studied academic or experimental psychology to any extent.

If you do an Internet Google search for 'psychology' you will get over a hundred million entries, before you even attempt to look at the subdivisions. Many entries refer to psychology courses, others to ways in which you can change your life or influence other people. Similarly, if you look at the psychology section in a bookshop or library you will find everything from popular self-help psychology through introductory textbooks to advanced specialist books. Topics range from reducing anxiety and depression through improving management techniques to communicating effectively with your partner.

All of these are concerned in one way or another with what makes us tick, and most are concerned with solving problems and improving us and the human condition either individually or generally.

However, as with all human endeavours, there is a great difference between the amateur, untaught, largely intuitive kinds and the trained, professional, scientific, research-based approaches. Self-help programmes that are not supported by research are not generally considered worthy of academic study or debate. Academic and professional psychology is based on systematic scientific research and aims to be replicable and reliable.

Psychology courses help you distinguish between the reliable and unreliable sources.

Psychology is a complex discipline that encompasses many different approaches, which complement and often contradict each other. These different approaches have arisen for historical reasons and are to do with the different kinds of answers that different psychologists are looking for. See Part 2.

See also the introductory pages for a list of handy headings that set out some of the inter-relating aspects of psychology.

QAA Benchmark Statement: Psychology 2007

Psychology is one of the most popular subjects in HE in the UK. It is the largest scientific discipline and the second largest discipline overall. The most recent statistics indicate that there were nearly 70,000 students studying psychology at all levels in UK HEIs in the academic year 2004/05. Psychology appeals to students from a wide range of backgrounds. Some 80 per cent of students are female, 47 per cent are mature students and 11 per cent have non-traditional qualifications. There are also significant numbers of ethnic minority students (14.5 per cent).

All indications show that psychology students are well taught. In its *Subject Overview Report*, published in 2000, QAA stated that 'the quality of teaching is high' and noted the 'high progression and completion rates'. It emphasised for specific commendation 'the supportive and friendly environment created by departmental staff', and also commented on 'the high added-value achieved by students with non-traditional entry qualifications in psychology'.

http://www.qaa.ac.uk/academicinfrastructure/benchmark/statements/Psychology07.pdf (accessed 08 July 2008) with permission from *Subject Benchmark Statement: Psychology 2007*. © The Quality Assurance Agency for Higher Education, 2007.

Like John Radford (Brody et al, 1982), I am glad I chose to study psychology. My best subjects at school were physics and mathematics and I was automatically channelled into science A-levels, but my favourite subjects were art, music and literature. At 16 I was fascinated and absorbed by an introductory undergraduate psychology textbook that my parents found for me; it was not then available as a subject for A-level. Undecided about whether I wanted to be a physical scientist, I opted for a degree in psychology, at first with physics and maths, and later with philosophy and sociology, returning to physics at postgraduate level.

Specialisation did not appeal to me. I preferred, and still prefer, to be a 'Renaissance' person, equally well versed in the arts, humanities and sciences. Psychology has enabled me to do this as I have explored psychological aspects of many different things in my teaching and writing. One exciting project was helping to design a degree course for adult 'returners' to education in which psychology was combined with art history, literature, media studies, politics and sociology in order to approach themes such as creativity from all possible angles.

In contrast, other psychologists enjoy a specific and narrow form of specialisation in research or practice. Psychology, more than any other subject perhaps, is all things to all people. You can make of it what you want because of its breadth, its different levels of enquiry and its unique approach to study.

Psychology is more about enquiring than acquiring knowledge. Moreover, we ourselves are part of the enquiry – as the things to be enquired about as well as the enquirers. There is a wealth of accumulated data (some of which you will need to learn, or at least be familiar with) and a multitude of theoretical explanations (for you to debate), but few set answers or 'laws'. If something does not seem right to you, then maybe it isn't right and you may have the opportunity to help find a better explanation. There is no limit to the scope of psychology: it concerns every aspect of what it means to be human, from biology to philosophy. You can choose whether to maintain a breadth of enquiry or channel your exploration in one particular direction. Furthermore, as you think and learn and talk about psychology, you can engage in finding out about how you think and learn and what it makes sense to say.

Alongside psychology, you can study pretty well anything from animal welfare, anthropology, art history and architecture, through dance, drama and design, to urban studies, visual arts and zoology.

Psychology is about developing skills and competences: in scientific method, in philosophical debate, in communication, in logical and creative thinking and problem-solving.

Studying psychology provides for at least four major outcomes:

> an avenue for students to become more self-aware
> better understanding of the behaviour of others
> basic knowledge and principles of human behaviour for students preparing for careers in social services, business, education, medicine, or law
> a sound foundation for graduate work and careers in psychology.

The relative emphasis on these four outcomes varies from course to course – and from student to student.

Some students enter psychology expecting that it will help solve personal problems. However, this is not what either an academic course or a career in psychology is intended for. If you have personal problems, seek professional help – you may well find that it is a psychologist who helps you best.

One other small word of warning before you fill in your application forms; you will need a certain measure of mathematical competence, or a willingness to learn, as you will have to get to grips with statistics. These days, you can get your computer to do the hard work but it helps enormously if you understand the concepts and can follow the steps.

The social and political context of psychology

BPS Paper 3 Section 2 – conceptual and historical issues

The syllabus is structured around a number of key questions: . . . To what extent is psychology socially and culturally constructed? Can psychology be politically neutral? Can psychology be morally neutral? . . . (with permission)
   (See Part 7.3 for the BPS Qualifying Examination.)

The content of any academic field and the way it is taught are influenced by the people who are involved in publishing in that field, and in particular by those who design and examine courses for education and training.

Looking at the history of psychology will reveal significant differences in the ways in which behavioural psychology developed in Russia and the United States of America. It can be said that early Russian psychology focused on physiological processes (for example Pavlov) and the United States on measurable behavioural components (for example Skinner). See also Part 4. One suggestion is that would be interesting to speculate how psychology would have developed if it had started in Confucian China.

Even when contributors come from many different social and cultural backgrounds there is usually a dominant influence, particularly when the majority of contributors have been raised within the dominant culture and if they are not aware of this to any great extent. Where contributors become aware of their own backgrounds and of others, they are more able to make efforts towards approaches that are less culturally bound.

Although these aspects are usually considered more relevant to less scientific academic areas, particularly sociology, it is important not to allow psychology (or any science) to become an 'ivory tower' discipline, detached from its impact on society.

Even in the most scientific of physical sciences, cultural bias influences the kinds of research that will be undertaken and the ways in which funding is allocated. University psychology cannot escape this.

In the practice of psychology cultural bias will also affect how clients are regarded and treated. Areas of concern include:

> Inclusion/exclusion: for example racism, ageism, sexism.
> Political dissenters and other 'inconvenient' people risk being labelled as mentally incompetent and 'sectioned' or otherwise detained.
> 'Recovered' memories that arise during hypnosis may not be as true as they seem.
> Cultural and language bias in psychometric tests may result in unfair testing.

One area where cultural bias is significant is the design of intelligence and educational aptitude tests. All early tests were heavily dependent on extensive knowledge of the English language and English myths and customs. When testers realised that this gave unfair disadvantage to people from different cultures, test items became more varied but even today, the 11-plus selection tests rely on knowledge of things like the English names of flowers for items testing logic skills unrelated to a specific language. Various psychometric tests for mental ability or confusional state expect knowledge of English names for the days of the week, months and seasons, prime minister and so on. This tends to go unnoticed until a newly arrived immigrant fails to answer and the tester is faced with having to find alternative means to assess the true level of ability.

It is generally agreed in the humanities, arts and social sciences that the dominant ideology in the Western world (North America, Europe, Australia and New Zealand) is white, male, middle-class capitalism. We can also add able-bodied and heterosexual. The majority of people in positions of power and influence in politics, business and higher education fit that description and their views on what is good, desirable and the right way to do things prevail. Everyone else is 'other' and at a disadvantage. Opposing ideologies include multiculturalism, feminism, gay rights and Marxism.

Psychology as an academic discipline and in applied fields finds itself in a somewhat contradictory position. On the one hand, it has grown out of the dominant system with the majority of practitioners male and white and keen to make money, but on the other hand is concerned with understanding and improving the human condition. Universities need to make money and attract funding. Research has to be approved by the funding bodies. To work with the contradictions, psychology needs to be critical, both of the dominant system and alternative ideologies, striving to make sense of human nature and find the best possible solutions to problems.

Professor Mark Burton at Manchester Metropolitan University (MMU), Head of Manchester Learning Disabilities Partnership, argues forcibly that some psychologists have aligned themselves with dominant power structures that are harmful to 'oppressed' people, notably in propaganda and persuasion, exploitation of workers, and selling (http://homepages.poptel.org.uk/mark.burton/global3.doc, accessed 06 July 2008).

Ethics and Code of Conduct

All members of the British Psychological Society and all chartered psychologists are required to keep to the Society Code of Ethics and Conduct.

This Code covers all aspects of professional and personal relationships, standards of practice, confidentiality and research issues, and anything that might bring the Society into disrepute. Examples include working with animals, advertising services, equal opportunities and sexual harassment at work. It is based on the four principles of

> respect
> competence
> responsibility
> integrity.

The full Code can be found at:

http://www.bps.org.uk/document-download-area/document-download$.cfm?file_uuid =5084A882-1143-DFD0-7E6C-F1938A65C242 &ext=pdf.

Alternatively, go to www.bps.org.uk and follow the links The Society>Code of Conduct and ethical guidelines>download Code of Ethics and Conduct.

See also 'Research ethics' in Part 5.

1.2 Your psychology course

Get the most from university

Decide when to start

If you are at school, your chief decision will be whether to take a gap year before starting at university. Many colleges and universities encourage a gap year as it gives you time to mature and decide how committed you are to higher education. You will be expected to do something worthwhile during the year so you will need to choose carefully whether to work (paid or voluntary), shadow someone at work, travel, take a further education course, read extensively or develop yourself in some other way relevant to the course you choose. Your next decision will be whether to apply for a course before or after the gap. It is simpler to apply in advance as you can use the school application procedure, but applying the following year means you will know your examination results.

If you are a mature student returning to study you may find you have a choice of part-time or full-time courses and with some modular courses you may even have a choice of the time of year for starting. If you like studying independently then the Open University gives the greatest flexibility. If you do not think you have sufficient qualifications to start an undergraduate course, or do not feel ready for higher education, enquire about an Access course, see Part 7 for websites.

Apply for financial help

Full-time higher education students could be eligible for a student loan to cover the cost of tuition fees and a student loan to help towards accommodation and other living costs. The interest is linked to inflation and you do not have to start repaying until you are earning a reasonable wage.

As well as student loans, you may be able to get a maintenance grant or special support grant to help with your accommodation and other living costs. You do not have to pay this back. Whether you can get one depends on your income and your household income.

You may be able to get extra help from the university in the form of a bursary or scholarship or other award that is based either on income or academic ability.

Extra help is available for students with a disability, mental health condition or specific learning difficulty, and for students with children or adult dependants.

All the information you need is available at the website listed in Part 7, with special links for overseas students.

Choose the right university

If you have not yet chosen where to study then there are various guides to help you choose. Guides are normally available through public libraries. The websites listed in Part 7 provide useful information, or you can do a search for 'choose university'.

Your choice will depend on various factors such as whether you want to live at home or away, whether you prefer a city campus or out of town, a traditional or new-style university or a college of higher education. If you do not yet know your A-level (or equivalent) results when you apply you might want to put a selection of universities that require different examination results.

Your choice will also depend on whether the course you want is available.

Choose the right course

This can be a difficult choice as it is impossible to know all the factors involved. A key factor is whether the course is approved by the BPS. You will need this if you wish to go on to become a chartered psychologist.

Your other main decisions will be about the combination of subjects, the structure of the course and assessment procedures (integrated or modular, mainly exams or course work), the quality of the course and the cost. See Part 7 for the need for National Curriculum subjects if you want to go into teaching or educational psychology.

One thing to watch out for is whether the course leads to an arts (BA), science (BSc) or social science qualification. This may reflect the emphasis of the course and the part of the university it is located in, as well as your choice of subsidiary subjects.

You will generally find that if you make a bad choice you can later transfer to something more suitable. Websites in Part 7.2 will give assistance.

Get the most from your course

What to expect from your psychology course

The jump from A-level to undergraduate work is huge. At A-level, you may have found yourself channelled into learning by rote and demonstrating your learning in short written answers and course work according to some methodical and predictable system. You will most likely have been given regular homework and chased until you gave it in. Feedback will tell you how to do better next time. Even if your teachers were not psychology specialists, they will have been trained teachers and relatively skilled in presenting material in a readily digestible form. You may have had most of your notes dictated, written on the board or given to you as handouts. Your textbook will have been geared, chapter by chapter, to the examination.

All this changes dramatically at degree level. Your aim, and that of everyone concerned with your education, is to transform you into an independent learner as quickly as you reasonably can.

Most lecturers are not trained teachers. They are researchers and, in many cases, much more interested in their research than in struggling students. They are usually happy to impart their knowledge to you, but some do not want, or expect to have to, help you study. Mostly, they believe that it is better for you if they do not help. You will become a better student if you have to work things out for yourself. Of course they are right and you will come to appreciate that, but you probably won't agree with it at first.

It is possible that no one will tell you what to do, or when to do it. You will be expected to have read the notices on the bulletin board. Maybe no one will chase you for essays or experiment reports or tell you when or where the exams will be held. You will have a lovely time until you are sent a letter informing you that you have failed.

Support: academic and pastoral

If you are lucky, you will be given detailed course handbooks with more or less organised content setting out the course requirements, the assignments and examination structure, a timetable of lectures and seminars, and a map of the site. From time to time, you will probably be given updates or contradictory information. Various lecturers and tutors will barrage you with handouts, lecture notes and other sundry pieces of paper. You will do your best to take notes in lectures and from books. It is your first task to get on top of all the paperwork by sorting it into files and keeping these where you will not lose them and where you will remember to consult them occasionally. For most courses, you will be assigned a personal tutor who can help you make sense of it all.

In addition to an academic tutor, you may be assigned a pastoral tutor who can help you with personal worries such as accommodation, money and sickness, or just feeling miserable. If you happen to find that you cannot get on well with your tutor please ask if you can change.

If you do not know who your tutors are check in the office. If no one is available try the student services.

Typical structure and content of undergraduate courses

Psychology degrees usually last for three years (four years in Scotland). Most institutions offer single honours degrees in psychology, but it is also common to combine psychology with another subject as a subsidiary or minor area of study, or to study psychology as one component of a joint honours degree where both subjects carry equal weight.

The *Subject Benchmark Statement: Psychology 2007*, published by QAA, includes the following:

> scientific understanding of mind, brain, behaviour and experience, and interactions between these
> understanding of different approaches or perspectives in a way that fosters critical evaluation
> real life applications of theory
> the role of empirical evidence
> research skills and methods
> ability to appreciate and critically evaluate theory, research findings and applications. (http://www.qaa.ac.uk, accessed 03 July 2008, with permission from *Subject Benchmark Statement: Psychology 2007*. © The Quality Assurance Agency for Higher Education, 2007.)

1.3 Study skills for psychology

Make the most of your abilities

As you study you need to get to know yourself and the best ways in which you could study. This section looks at how to approach your learning.

If you are new to independent learning, you may find it particularly helpful to look at the following educational models of learning styles and strategies and try to see what approaches you normally take and how you might improve. All of these models take the point of view that our abilities are not fixed and that we can all learn and improve as soon as we are pointed in the right direction. Useful websites are given in Part 7.2.

Felder and Solomon's learning styles and strategies

As shown in Figure 1.1, Professor Richard M. Felder and Barbara Solomon at North Carolina State University have identified four dimensions of learning, in each of which they see learners tending towards one end of each spectrum.

In the first dimension, the contrast is between an active approach, preferring to try things out first to see what happens, and a reflective approach, wanting to think things through first. Either extreme has its dangers, as a purely active approach may take a lot of trial and error before a solution is found, while a purely reflective approach may get bogged down with planning and never get off the ground.

Secondly, the comparison is between a sensing approach, preferring to learn facts, use familiar methods and be patient with details, and an intuitive approach, wanting to understand concepts and work out relationships, impatient or careless with details.

The third dimension shows a preference for either visual diagrams and spatial arrangements or verbal explanations in written and spoken forms.

Fourthly, sequential and global approaches are contrasted. A sequential approach follows linear steps, each one leading to the next. A global approach is more concerned with trying to get an overall picture before seeing the connections.

ACTIVE AND REFLECTIVE LEARNERS
SENSING AND INTUITIVE LEARNERS
VISUAL AND VERBAL LEARNERS
SEQUENTIAL AND GLOBAL LEARNERS

Figure 1.1 Felder and Solomon's learning styles and strategies

In each dimension, a score between the extremes is usually most effective, indicating that the learner can move between different styles as needed. The website provides questionnaires that aim to enable you to sort out your normal way of approaching problems and find out how you might help yourself to develop.

Sternberg's theory of triarchic intelligence

Professor Robert J. Sternberg is Director of the Center for the Psychology of Abilities, Competencies, and Expertise at Tufts University, relocated from Yale. As shown in Figure 1.2, Sternberg promotes a theory of three types of intelligence, suggesting that all people have all three types to some degree but most are strongest in one type.

Analytical Intelligence
Metacomponent
Performance component
Knowledge acquisition

Creative Intelligence
Experience continuum
Novelty to automaticity

Practical Intelligence
Adapt
Shape
Select

Figure 1.2 Sternberg's theory of triarchic intelligence

Analytical intelligence is the traditional kind, concerned with abstract thinking and reasoning and verbal and mathematical skills, and may also involve a 'meta' component of self-awareness and an understanding of how you are solving problems. Problems requiring these skills tend to have one correct solution (see *convergent* thinking in Part 3).

Creative intelligence is freer, more suited to situations that need *divergent* thinking with a willingness to deal with novel situations and come up with new ideas.

Practical intelligence is about being 'streetwise', applying knowledge in the real world and having the ability to change the environment or choose a new one.

Sternberg stresses that intelligence is affected by culture and is trainable. Various websites explain his approach in more detail and describe ways in which to strengthen the different types.

Carol Dweck's ITIS

Professor Carol S. Dweck at Stanford University provides us with a clear model that stresses the way in which we approach the world, in particular whether we believe our intelligence and other abilities are inborn and fixed, or whether, like Sternberg above, we believe we can grow and change.

Figure 1.3 shows the continuum from believing all our assets are inborn to believing everything can be developed.

Figure 1.3 Dweck's 'growth' and 'fixed' mindsets

A questionnaire ITIS (Implicit Theory of Intelligence Scale) has been devised to help students identify where they come on the continuum. Then those who find they have always believed their abilities to be limited can begin to take a new approach and think more positively about development. This is particularly important in relation to attitudes towards making errors while learning. Those with a fixed mindset tend to be defeated by errors, seeing themselves as failing and unable to improve. With a growth mindset, errors are seen as a positive and necessary part of learning.

Entwistle's ASSIST

Professor Noel Entwistle at Edinburgh University has been involved for many years in sorting out the different ways in which students approach learning. He has identified three main approaches: surface, strategic and deep. The student who takes only a surface approach shows little interest in the subject matter but wants only to scrape through with the minimum of effort.

A strategic approach provides the structure within which a student can aim to achieve the best possible results. With a deep approach a student can fully engage with the subject matter and gain the inner satisfaction of understanding. Successful academic performance is usually associated with a combination of the strategic and deep approaches.

Figure 1.4 shows the bare outlines of the three approaches from Raaheim et al, 1991. Later (Tait et al, 1998) the diagram was further developed to show a more complex interaction between the three approaches, derived from the Approaches and Study Skills Inventory for Students (ASSIST) and further information can be found at a number of websites including those given in Part 7.2.

You may find it helpful to work out which approaches you have normally taken in the past and what you could try to do to achieve more satisfaction and better results.

Competence and capability

Capability (as used in several university learning programmes) is having justified confidence in your ability to:

> take appropriate and effective action
> communicate effectively
> collaborate with others
> learn from experience.

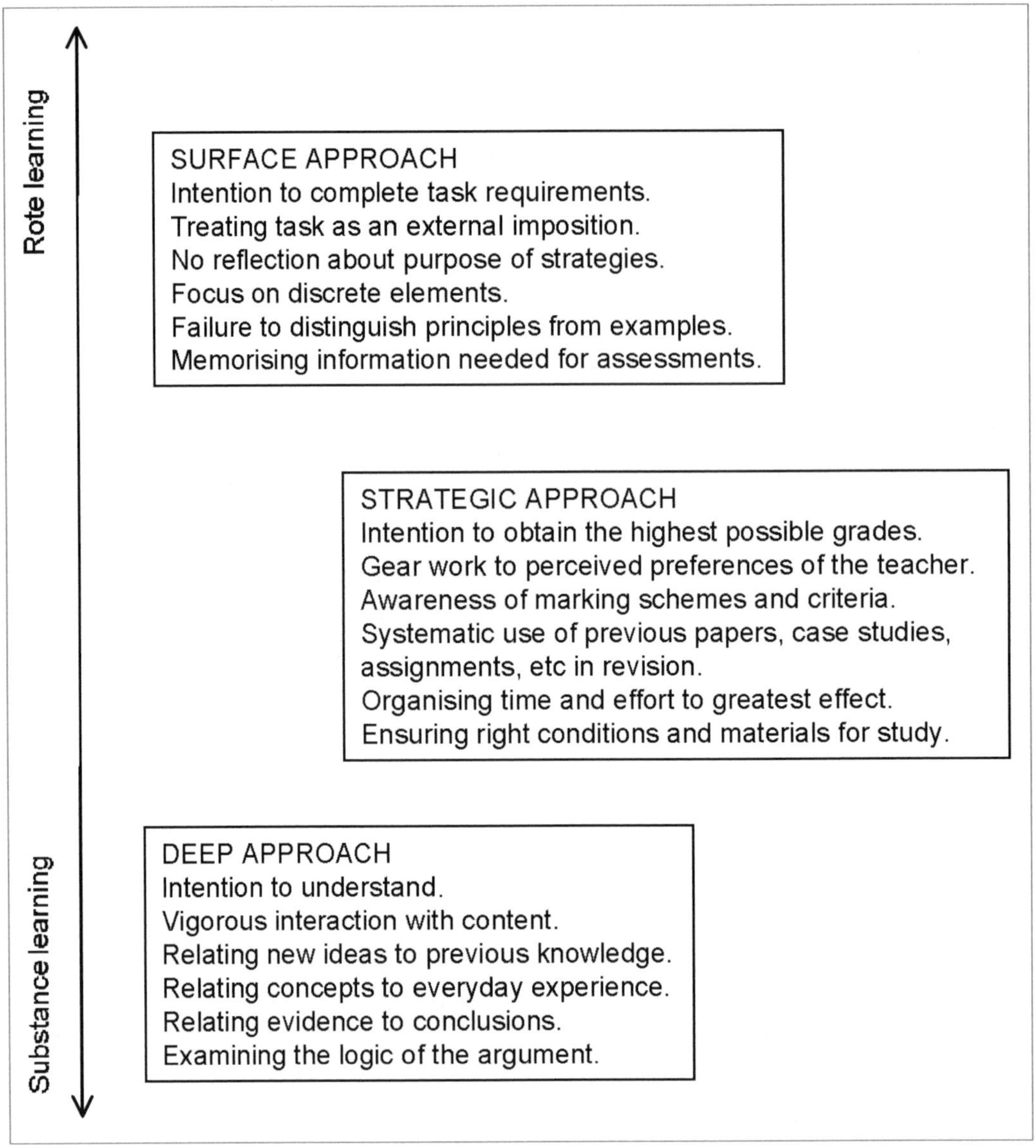

Rote learning

SURFACE APPROACH
Intention to complete task requirements.
Treating task as an external imposition.
No reflection about purpose of strategies.
Focus on discrete elements.
Failure to distinguish principles from examples.
Memorising information needed for assessments.

STRATEGIC APPROACH
Intention to obtain the highest possible grades.
Gear work to perceived preferences of the teacher.
Awareness of marking schemes and criteria.
Systematic use of previous papers, case studies,
assignments, etc in revision.
Organising time and effort to greatest effect.
Ensuring right conditions and materials for study.

DEEP APPROACH
Intention to understand.
Vigorous interaction with content.
Relating new ideas to previous knowledge.
Relating concepts to everyday experience.
Relating evidence to conclusions.
Examining the logic of the argument.

Substance learning

Figure 1.4 Entwistle's categories of approaches to learning

If this seems daunting at first, do not worry; think of this as your goal and plan some small steps in that direction. It helps to make a distinction between familiar and unfamiliar problems in familiar and unfamiliar contexts, as shown in Figure 1.5. Your target is to move gradually from being able to solve familiar problems in familiar contexts (position A) to increasing the unfamiliarity (B and C) and eventually to tackling unfamiliar problems in unfamiliar contexts (position D).

Develop a portfolio or transcript of personal development

As you progress through your course, you may find it extremely helpful to keep a record of your work and activities that demonstrates your ways of working, your experiences and your abilities. This will enable you to present evidence to prospective employers or for further

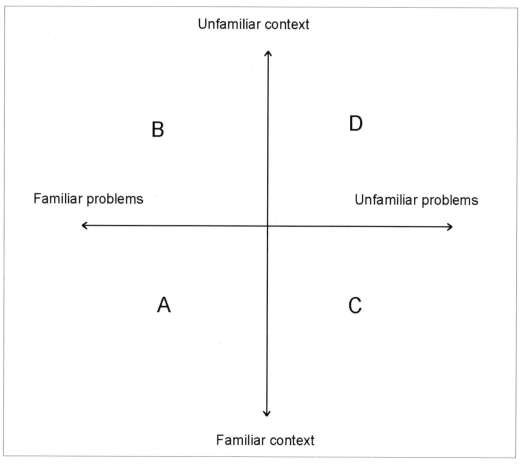

Figure 1.5 Capability and competence

courses. Moreover, as you review your records you will be able to identify your strengths and the areas where you need to improve. You may have the opportunity to discuss your portfolio with your tutor. The kinds of skills that people are looking for include:

> willingness to learn/independence as a learner/self-reliance
> communication skills in speaking, writing, reading and listening
> teamwork and being able to contribute ideas effectively, show leadership, delegation, adaptability
> analysis and problem-solving with planning, critical evaluation and creativity
> IT and numeracy, including being familiar with the Internet and able to use standard word-processing systems, databases and spreadsheets etc.

The sorts of examples you might want include are:

> a goal that you set yourself and the obstacles you overcame in order to achieve it
> a complex problem that involved analysing data, developing opinions and implementing solutions.

Something to try might be searching the Internet for application forms for companies and seeing if any include this kind of information. You could start with http://www.mypgcareer.com/application/interview.html, for example.

Understand the nature of academic writing and critical thinking

After A-levels, writing is not merely about showing that you know certain facts, gaining credits or passing examinations. Academic and professional writing enables you to share your thoughts with colleagues and contribute to the growing body of psychological knowledge.

Although you must not copy from books and websites, you are not expected to write purely from your own imagination. You will need to read widely and deeply and gather data about research and the debates concerning scientific explanations and theories. Your ability comes into play in the construction of an argument. Note that in academic work an argument is not a quarrel but a debate. In particular, a psychology essay requires gathering of scientific evidence to support or refute an argument.

For many course work assignments you will be asked to produce a piece of written work. This may be an essay, a report, a literature review, a dissertation or some other piece. You may be asked either to choose a question from a list of alternatives, or to design your own question on a topic of your choice. You may be required to do some of this writing under time constraints or examination conditions. You may also want to go on to develop your work for publication.

Course assignments give you an excellent opportunity to investigate a topic thoroughly, develop your skills of reading and research, master the art of planning and organising material into a coherent discussion, improve your ability to reason, argue and question, and help you to express yourself clearly in writing. The assignments also give tutors an opportunity to help you assess your skills and understanding, and identify areas where help or guidance is required.

Writing an essay or preparing for a seminar usually involves reading a wide range of research papers, articles or books on a particular topic, analysing and discussing the ideas in a critical way, and drawing conclusions from them to enable you to formulate and put forward your own ideas on the subject.

It might help you help to assess your own views on a topic and think about how to argue or debate more effectively if you break down the early part of the process, before you start to write, into three stages:

> The first stage involves identifying and stating in your own words the arguments for and against a proposition. As with all academic work it is necessary to be able to identify the source of an idea and therefore you need to document the references in your notes.
> The second stage requires you to consider to what extent the sources presented can be considered to be authoritative and reliable. If you have several articles on a topic, which articles do you consider to be:
> - the most authoritative
> - the least authoritative.
>
> Give reasons for your decision. Factors that might influence your decision could include the nature of the publication in which the article is printed, the type of peer review involved, the qualifications of the author, the research methods, style of writing and the use of supporting references.
> In the third stage you have to decide which of the arguments you find most persuasive. What arguments persuade you? Why? Is it because those arguments:
> - reinforce your own previously held opinions on the subject
> - are more clearly and rationally stated

- are more forcibly presented
- are presented in a more emotive way
- are supported by research evidence
- other reasons – state what they are.

Are these equally valid reasons for being persuaded by an argument?

Reference your sources

When preparing academic work, you are expected to use the ideas and evidence contained in the published work of others to contribute to and support your own ideas, and you are expected to give credit to the authors of this work. Any time you refer to something you have read, whether as an exact quotation, or in your own words or just a brief mention then you must identify the source.

There are at least three main reasons for clear and accurate referencing:

> It supports and substantiates your points and arguments.
> It directs readers to the source of the information, enabling them to gain further details and check the accuracy of the information.
> It acknowledges and gives credit to the original source of the idea, argument or finding.

Without clear referencing, the reader may have difficulty distinguishing between your ideas and those of others and this may lead to suspicions of plagiarism. Apart from this, it is important that tutors reading your work know when you are offering your own opinion and when you are offering that of someone else.

Plagiarism

Plagiarism is the use of another author's work without due acknowledgement and/or permission, and can be seen as literary theft. Plagiarism is a very serious offence – it is important not to copy material out of books and journals. Nor can you mention someone else's ideas without clearly indicating the source. If it is essential for you to give direct quotations it is important to keep to APA guidelines (see below and Part 7). Penalties for plagiarism can be severe. Work will most likely be disqualified and in severe cases a student may be asked to leave the course. Fees may be forfeited.

The main problem for new students is accidental plagiarism. At school you may have been permitted, or even encouraged to copy material out of books or from websites for your projects. At higher levels this is simply not allowed. Leach (2008), like many other tutors, recommends that you never make notes or write essays with the reference book open in front of you. Read a section, close the book and write a summary in your own words. Check back to make sure you have not used the same words inadvertently (and that you have not missed something important). Cottrell (2003: 133–4) gives a clear explanation of how to detect plagiarism and avoid it. See also paraphrasing, below.

Referencing systems

There are several accepted systems of referencing in common use in publications in Britain and in international journals. Two which are most widely used are the Harvard system and the Vancouver system, although not everyone uses these names or adheres strictly to a set of rules.

The websites http://www.apastyle.org/ and http://www.liu.edu/cwis/cwp/library/workshop/citapa.htm give information about referencing. You should check these for the most recent APA guidelines.

The Harvard system uses names and dates within the text of the article or book whereas the Vancouver system uses names and numbers. The Harvard system is used throughout most scientific disciplines, including nearly all psychology publications and many other social science, medical and nursing works. Vancouver-style numbering systems are used in arts and humanities books and journals, including art history, literary theory, philosophy, theology, some political and sociological texts, some science journals such as *Nature*, and some medical and nursing journals.

The Harvard system (author–date)

You will probably be asked to use the Harvard system in all your psychology assignments. There are two main aspects of referencing:

> citations within the text
> reference list or bibliography (see below for details).

The Harvard system uses names and dates within the text of an article or book, or in your essay, every time a work is mentioned. Only the last name or surname is given; no first names or initials, with the year of publication, for example 'Gross (1996)'.

Numbers and abbreviations, which are used extensively in the Vancouver system, are not used in the Harvard System.

Full details are given, once only, in the reference list of bibliography. Examine your course textbooks and this book for examples.

Citations – paraphrasing, quotations and ellipses in your essay

To cite something means to mention it or refer to it. You can refer briefly to an idea or you can give some details. There are a number of different places you can position the reference in a sentence depending on your style of writing and whether you have paraphrased or copied a word-for-word quotation.

Paraphrasing

If you take the main points and rewrite in your own words this is called paraphrasing. Paraphrasing usually involves working out the essential ideas and the point that the writer was making and then re-wording it to fit with your style and what you are arguing. You can put the source reference at the beginning or end of your sentence. For example:

Springer and Deutsch (1981) suggest that . . .
It has been suggested that . . . (Springer and Deutsch, 1981).

Note that in the first style where the sentence begins with the name the date goes in parentheses (brackets), and in the second style, where the reference comes at the end of the sentence, the name and the date are in parentheses and placed *in* the sentence before the full-stop.

Quotations

If you repeat the exact words that another author has used, this is a quotation. In most academic work, it is nearly always better if you can paraphrase rather than quote word for word. Certain quotations can sometimes be very effective, but it is important not to overdo them.

Dramatic use of quotations is more suited to popular magazines than serious academic work. It is usually distracting (and disliked by tutors) in a formal essay, to start or end with a vivid or dramatic quotation. This might be useful for a seminar presentation or a journal article if you can justify this with an appropriate discussion of its relevance. (This, of course, does not apply in literature studies where quotations are essential for illustration.)

If you feel the author's exact words are essential and you quote word for word then check the latest APA guidelines to avoid plagiarism. See http://www.apastyle.org/electext.html.

Usually, the page number or chapter must be given with the date, i.e. Surname (Date: page number): for example 'Springer and Deutsch (1981 p214)' or 'Springer and Deutsch (1981: 214)'.

Ellipses

If you omit part of a quotation, this should be indicated with three spaced full stops (ellipses). Use three . . . to indicate material omitted from within a sentence, then add an extra full stop if the omitted words come at the end of the original sentence.

Using citations from secondary sources.

If you are using a secondary source such as a textbook, where the author is talking about or citing someone else's work, you will need to give the names and dates of the primary and secondary sources in your essay, making it clear who is doing the citing. In your bibliography or reference section you normally need give only the full details of the secondary source – the one you have read. However, if you are required to list both sources you will need to look for the details of the cited source in the bibliography of your secondary source.

For example:

i. *May (1991) cites Melzack (1973) who found that . . .*
ii. *It has been found that . . . (Melzack, 1973, cited by May, 1991).*

Note again that in the second style, where the reference comes at the end of the sentence, the reference goes *in* the sentence before the full-stop.

Reference list

As with all published material, at the end of your essay or project, you must give a list of the works you have mentioned or cited in your text. It must be possible to match every name and date in your essay to an entry in your list of references. For each reference you give the full details of the source.

The list is then given in alphabetical order, each one starting with the surname.

If you are using a word processor, you might like to find out how to use the 'sort' function, often found in the menu under Table. Do *not* number them. Do *not* give the surname in CAPITALS, or arrange the details in columns. Use the bibliography in this book and your main psychology textbooks for examples of best practice.

If you have already given a reference section, then an additional bibliography is usually optional and less specific than the reference list. It is placed after the references and contains all those other works which you have used for background reading and which helped influence your assignment; it may include annotated notes on those works. It is very handy for future study, when you need to remind yourself which books and journal articles were useful. It is particularly helpful if you have kept a card index system with brief notes about each source (see later). Check with each tutor to find out their individual preferences with regard to bibliographies.

On some courses, you will be required to give a bibliography only, which will then include all your references plus any additional material.

This book, for example, gives a bibliography that contains all the works cited in the text plus additional material that the author thinks will be helpful.

Citing books in the reference list or bibliography

You give:

> the author's surname
> initials
> year of publication
> title of book
> city of publication and the publisher.

This information can be found at the beginning of a book. If there is more than one place of publication then give the one nearest to where you are. For example if a book is given as New York and London, then if you are in the UK you give London. The date of publication refers to the year of the edition, not necessarily the latest year of printing. It is important to state which edition you used because page numbering and other details will have been changed. You put the date in brackets and the title of the book in italics. For example:

Banyard, P. and Grayson, G. (2000). *Introducing Psychological Research, 2nd edn*. Basingstoke: Palgrave.
Bee, H. (1997) *The Developing Child, 8th edn*. London: Addison-Wesley.

Citing chapter of book

If you are citing work from a chapter of a book for which the individual chapter authors are different from the editor(s), then you give the chapter author and chapter title first, for example:

Janis, I. L. (1983). Stress inoculation in health care: Theory and research. In D. Meichenbaum and M. E. Jaremko (eds), *Stress Reduction and Prevention*, pp.67–99. New York: Plenum.
May, B. (1991) Pain. In M. Pitts and K. Phillips (eds), *The Psychology of Health: An introduction*. London: Routledge.

Note that the *book title* is in italics (not the chapter). It is not necessary to repeat the date and there can be slight differences in the name/initial order according to preference.

Citing journals

You give the author's surname, initials, year of publication, title of article, title of journal, the volume and issue numbers, with full date if known, and page numbers. The title of the journal is given in italics. For example:

Holmes, T. H. and Rahe, R. H. (1967). The social re-adjustment rating scale. *Journal of Psychosomatic Research*, **11**: 213–18.

Note that it is always the title of the publication that is given in italics: that is, the *title of the book*, or the *name of the journal*. When handwriting or using a typewriter that cannot produce italics, you can underline the titles.

Citing two or more authors

If there are two joint authors of a piece of work, give both names in your essay for example 'Springer and Deutsch (1981)'. Where there are more than two, give only the first name in your essay, with 'et al' (short for 'et alia' meaning 'and others') for example 'Nisbett et al (1973)'. Give the full details, with *all* the names, in the reference section, as follows:

Nisbett R. E., Caputo C., Legant P. and Maracek J. (1973) Behaviour as seen by the actor and as seen by the observer, *Journal of Personality and Social Psychology*, 27: 154–65.

Note that where there are two or more authors for a book, the order in which their names are given usually shows seniority or the relative importance of their contribution to the book. Different editions may have a different order. Two authors may write several books jointly and put their names in a different order on each one, for example;

Burton, G. and Dimbleby, R. (1988) *Between Ourselves*. London: Edward Arnold.
Dimbleby, R. and Burton, G. (1985) *More Than Words*. London: Methuen.

You should not alter this order.

Citing two publications by same author

Where you refer to two publications by the same author they should be listed chronologically, starting with the oldest. If they were published in the same year then label them a, b and so on. For example two books by Peter Jarvis published in 1983 would be given as 'Jarvis (1983a)' and 'Jarvis (1983b)' in your essay as appropriate and then given in full chronologically in your reference list.

The month of publication can be found with other details at the beginning of the book, so it is not usually difficult to discover in which order they were published.

Jarvis, P. (1983a) *Professional Education*. London: Croom Helm.
Jarvis, P. (1983b) *The Theory and Practice of Adult and Continuing Education*. London: Croom Helm.

Citing Internet websites, blogs, emails and other electronic sources

There are several different guidelines, for example MLA (Modern Language Association) and APA (American Psychological Association). Guidelines are similar, but look for the format that is closest to the Harvard System.

You need to give enough information for someone else to find the same source. It is very important to make a note of the format of the item, as this determines how you reference it.

For example, give the full website and the date that you accessed it. Your access date is important as websites change.

See Part 7 for websites that give details of how to reference all electronic sources.

If these are no longer available, then doing a search for 'citing websites' or 'citing emails' and so on will produce lists of possible sites.

Citing newspapers

> author(s) of the article
> date of publication
> full title of the article (include subtitle if present)
> title of the newspaper in which the article appears
> section and page numbers.

For example:

Tabor, M. B. W. (1999, July 11). Despite low prestige and pay, more answer the call to teach: College students are increasingly showing interest in teaching profession. *The New York Times*, p. N1.

This example is taken from http://tutorial.lib.umn.edu/infomachine.asp?moduleID=10 andlessonID=74andpageID=237 (accessed 14 August 2007).

Citing television, radio, films, DVDs and videos

> producer and/or director
> date of broadcast or publication
> title of programme or publication
> type of production
> place of production or availability.

For example:

Le Chat, F. (Executive Producer). (1999, September 25). *Purrrfectly Wild* [Television broadcast]. New York: Felis Broadcasting Service.
Fudd, E. (Producer), and Leghorn, F. (Director). (2002). *Nothing to Crow About: Chicken exploitation in America* [Motion Picture]. (Available from Looney Productions, 12 Egg Drive, Suite 12, Albuquerque, NM).

These examples are taken from http://www.unf.edu/library/guides/citationguide.pdf (accessed 14 August 2007).

Citing lecture and seminar notes

It is not usually advisable to cite material from lectures and seminars but check with your tutor about this.

Vancouver system (author–number)

You will not be required to use this system in psychology. However, you may come across it in your reading in other disciplines such as ethics and philosophy, and in some science journals such as *Nature* and some medical and nursing journals. If you are combining psychology with courses from the arts and humanities, such as philosophy, art history or literature, you must be careful to use the appropriate system in each discipline. If in doubt, ask the relevant tutors.

References within the text in the Vancouver system

Instead of putting the author's name and date in the text, a small number is given as a 'superscript' above the line of text.

Bibliography for the Vancouver system

The list of references is always referred to as a bibliography and may or may not include any additional material. Items are given in the numerical order in which they occur in the text. Where the same source is referenced more than once abbreviations will be used, such as *ibid* meaning the same (as the previous entry) or *op. cit.,* which is short for opus cited, meaning the work already cited.

Converting from Vancouver to Harvard

If you wish to use references from a source given in the Vancouver system, you will need to convert them to the Harvard system in your writing. Replace all the superscript numbers with names and dates in the text. Rewrite the references in full for your reference list and give these in alphabetical order by surname. Do not number items in your reference list or use any abbreviations.

Use the library and Internet

Find published material

Research evidence is the most important part of an essay that relates to psychology as research-based practice. Try to find a selection of different research papers that give a range of supporting and conflicting evidence. It is most useful if you obtain the primary sources (the research articles) particularly as you progress through your course. You should be able to order these through the library or locate them on the appropriate website. If they are not available, it is acceptable to use a secondary source such as a textbook or discussion article to indicate the research, provided you make this clear. You may also want to refer to some of the discussion in the textbook or article, which you would then treat as a primary source for that author. (See also the section on Referencing above.)

You may want to refer to theories or models that illustrate your argument. It is not normally necessary to describe these in any detail. Aim to summarise the main point that is useful and reference a good source. If the information is difficult to obtain and you think it would help your reader to see it, you could put it as an appendix.

It is often useful to illustrate a point or argument with an example from professional practice but this also involves dangers. Avoid excessively long, elaborate examples that might unbalance your essay and detract from the main thread of discussion. Ensure that the example makes the point you intend it to make. You can draw examples from your own experience but avoid numerous anecdotes. You can use examples to illustrate a point, but never to establish a generality.

It is normally preferable to paraphrase material, that is, put everything in your own words, rather than quote word for word. If you want to quote from a client you must ask the client for permission and, to preserve confidentiality, you must invent a name (and make it clear that you have done so).

Never copy sections out of your source books: even if you reference this and make it clear it is copied. It is not your work and therefore cannot be used towards your grade and is likely to be seen as plagiarism. If it includes something the reader needs as background, it could be added as an appendix.

Primary and secondary sources

In psychology, a primary source is an original published piece of work, for example an account of a piece of research or theory, written by the researcher(s), usually an article in a specialist journal or a specialist book. Other examples include sets of data, such as census statistics, diaries, autobiographies, works of literature and original documents.

Secondary sources are based on primary sources and are a discussion of research or theories by someone else. They may include generalisations, analysis, synthesis, interpretation or evaluation. In psychology these may be articles in popular journals or magazines or textbooks. Also, most primary sources for research begin with an overview, thus serving as a secondary source for other research in the area.

Some writers also refer to tertiary sources which list, index, organise and compile citations and show you how to use primary and secondary sources. Examples would include almanacs, dictionaries and encyclopaedias, guidebooks and manuals, but these may also simply be regarded as secondary sources. A fuller account can be found at http://www.library.jcu.edu.au/LibraryGuides/primsrcs.shtml (accessed 13 November 2007).

Figure 1.6 summarises primary, secondary and tertiary sources.

Primary sources
researchers reporting their own work

Secondary sources
someone discussing other people's work

Tertiary sources
works that index and organise primary and secondary sources

Figure 1.6 Primary, secondary and tertiary sources

Primary sources are preferable to secondary sources wherever possible. However, secondary sources are useful for comparing different primary sources, research and theories, and for providing critical debate and discussion. It is often a good idea to start with secondary sources. They will usually also be a good source of other references and show you where to find the primary sources.

In most articles, the authors include a literature review or discussion of previous research in their area. This can be a useful secondary source for the previous research as well as being the primary source of the new research.

Library cataloguing systems

Most public libraries in the UK use the Dewey Decimal Classification System but many colleges and universities have their own system. Where an alternative system is employed, guidance should be available. The Dewey system has numbers 000, 100, 200, 300 and so on for the major divisions into subject areas. A summary of the hundreds is given in Figure 1.7.

000	Communication theory
100	Philosophy and parapsychology
150	General and developmental psychology
300	Social psychology
360	Special needs
370	Education
610	Nursing
612	Brain and nervous system
613	Health psychology
615	Complementary therapies
616-618	Psychotherapy, counselling, substance abuse, family and play therapies

Figure 1.7 Summary of useful sections in the Dewey Classification System

At the time the Dewey system was devised, psychology was in its infancy. It was regarded principally as an offshoot of philosophy and had not yet acquired its scientific credibility. For this reason, most general and introductory psychology texts are classified alongside philosophy. This section now also includes most cognitive psychology, covering perception, memory, cognitive development and so on. Books that deal with areas of psychological interest that overlap considerably with philosophy, such as mind and consciousness are close by, as are psychological approaches involving the paranormal, occult, telepathy and so on that are given the general name of parapsychology ('alongside psychology').

Social psychology developed somewhat separately from cognitive psychology and can be seen to relate more closely to other social sciences such as sociology, politics, economics and education.

The chief problem for librarians lies in deciding the best place for a particular book. The tendency is to go by title and general impressions of content. This means that books may be differently classified in different libraries. It also means that books of related content may be in quite separate sections. For example, cognitive therapy may be found either with cognitive psychology or as therapy. Titles such as *Health Psychology* or *Psychology for Health Care* may be in different sections. Books on stress may be found variously in general, lifespan, social, biological, medical, nursing or survival. Given sufficient time, browsing along shelves is often the most successful way of finding relevant material. Some of the best research has been triggered by serendipity or chance finding.

Journals are normally located separately from books and tend to be shelved in alphabetical order and by date. The most recent issues may be displayed in a reading area.

If the title or author of a book or article is known, it can be located quickly and easily via the library cataloguing system. Apart from the Internet, bibliographies and computer databanks can be used for tracking down books and articles relating to topic areas. Three useful CD-ROM data banks for psychology and health psychology are PSYCHLIT, CINAHL and MEDLINE.

For Internet search engines, websites and blogs, see Part 7.2

Make notes from books and journals

Reading a book. It is rarely necessary to read whole books from cover to cover. Check the list of contents and look for items of relevance. Use 'post-its' or bookmarks to mark pages of interest. If you own the book you may want to make notes in the margins – otherwise make notes elsewhere.

Gather material for an essay. Try to start your research early. This gives you time to order articles from the library and gives you thinking time so that your ideas can mature, and enables you to revise your first attempts. Gather a range of source materials, which could include:

> lecture and seminar notes for organising your ideas and planning what to look for
> general textbooks for background, breadth and context
> specialist textbooks for a coherent in-depth account of the topic
> popular journals for easy-to-read digested accounts of relevance to practice, and references to useful primary sources
> refereed journals for reliable up-to-date research evidence and yet more citations and references.

Look for sources that give opposing views. Discuss the question with friends, colleagues and team members. Never follow one source too closely, especially if this is an introductory text or summary. Most important of all, *never plagiarise*.

Read selectively, picking out that which is directly relevant to the essay question. To do this you need to know what you are looking for and the following procedure is advised:

1. Start by jotting down what you know already about the topic in a brief, itemised list. This will get your mind thinking about the question and provide a guide to areas you need to study further.
2. List those questions/topics that you think may be relevant to the essay question, even if you know nothing about them.
3. As you read you will inevitably discover new topics and questions. Make a list of these as you go, and follow them up later.
4. Keep a notebook or file cards for your notes. When taking notes, do not rewrite the

book – just jot down the vital points. Try to separate key issues and concrete examples. If you are marking up a photocopy, try using different colour highlighters for these, one colour for the key issue(s) in each paragraph, another for the examples. Aim for a minimum of highlighting. You could even practise spotting the *transition* words (see below). Always record the source, including page number, for future reference.

Keep a card-index system. This can be done on a word processor or on cards that can be filed in a box. You need one card for each book and article, including those you have found on websites. Figure 1.8 shows one possible layout that might be suitable to start with.

```
FRONT

•   Author of Book          or          Author of  Article
•   Date                                Date
•   Title of Book                       Title of Article
•   Place: Publisher                    Title of Journal, Vol. No. Pages

•   Where to find it:   e.g. own copy, town library, college library,
        order from British Library, photocopy available, friend (name), website

•   Rating of usefulness
•   Relevance to course work
•   Cross-reference to other notes
```

```
BACK

•   Pages used

•   What is it about? – brief summary

•   Main idea(s)

•   Key words and concepts

•   References to other sources

•   Types of evidence or examples

•   Main conclusions
```

Figure 1.8 Card for a card index system

Take notes in lectures and seminars

Taking notes is a very individual process so there are no exact rights and wrongs. As with making notes from written material, the format you choose can vary between bulleted lists, columns, boxes or spider diagrams. The following questions are designed to help you think about what you do and how you might improve so that your notes are more useful to you and you get more out of the lectures and seminars.

> Why do you take notes during lectures and seminars?
>   - Will this help you to stay awake?
>   - Will it help with essays or revision?
>   - Will it help you to follow the main points the speaker is trying to make?
>   - Will it help you to make sense of the material?
>   - Will it help you to see if there are any gaps?
>   - As you read through your notes, do questions spring to mind?
> What do you do before a lecture or seminar?
>   - Do you regularly refer to the module outlines or plans?
>   - Is there a diary showing titles or content of lectures?
>   - Does the lecturer provide handouts in advance, or put lecture slides or notes on the intranet or in the library?
>   - Do you ever arrive at a lecture or seminar without any idea of what it will be about?
>   - Do you ask yourself, 'what do I already know about this subject?'
>   - Do you do any reading before a lecture or seminar so that you have an idea of the topic?
>   - How might a small amount of pre-lecture preparation help with note taking?
> What do you do during the lecture or seminar?
>   - Do you use the first few minutes, while waiting, to read through your notes from the previous lecture?
>   - Do you try to write down everything on the screen, or everything the speaker says?
>   - Could you listen more and then summarise the main points in your own words?
>   - Could you devise a system of abbreviations or learn some shorthand?
>   - Could you fill in detail later, using materials from your reading list?
>   - Could you write down questions as they occur to you and then find out answers to them at the end, or later on?
>   - Could you leave gaps in your notes so that you make additions later?
>   - Could you use the seminar to clarify points?
> What do you do after the lecture or seminar?
>   - Do you take rough notes and then write them out neatly?
>   - Summarise under main headings?
>   - Summarise on cards?
>   - Use boxes, colours etc. to highlight important ideas?
>   - Add notes from further reading?
>   - Use notes to generate questions for further exploration of the topic?
>   - Make links between different lectures and seminars?

Write an essay, report, dissertation or article

Essay writing skills are important throughout the course and so, whether you have recently completed other studies or have not undertaken any formal academic work for some time, it might be worth spending a little time thinking about the nature of the task and the best ways to tackle it. The following pages outline some simple guidelines for writing essays. The same basic rules apply to all kinds of writing. Where there are some essential differences, these are given under separate headings.

Understanding what you should be aiming to achieve when writing essays, and the best ways of going about it, will help to ensure that as well as achieving good marks you derive maximum benefit from the task which will help you promote good psychology practice.

Different tutors have different ideas about what makes a good essay. These are my ideas that have arisen from many years of working with beginning and mature students. They may not suit you or your tutor.

What is in the title question?

It is essential to start by having a careful look at the title or question. What exactly are you setting out to do? Is a broad survey or a narrowly focused discussion appropriate? What are the assumptions behind the question? What are the limits to the topic? Does it require you to consider one, or more than one, issue? Higher education usually involves getting to grips with a small well-defined area of interest and dealing with it in depth. Essays are most effective if they focus narrowly on a specific concern but there will be a difference in the balance of breadth and depth between, say, a general introductory essay and a critical debate about a particular theory.

In focusing on the assignment task, it is often useful to underline the key command words in the title – those that specify the kind of essay required. Figure 1.9 lists some examples.

Sometimes an assignment topic will include more than one of these key words. In this case it is important to take account of all and not just one of them. For example if you are asked to *Describe* a theory and *Justify* its application to practice, you would need to set out a clear account of the theory and then show adequate grounds (through research evidence and personal experience) for using it, together with the main objections to doing so. If you only focus on one of the key words, you will only have completed half of the task. If you are given a general question or topic area, you may be expected to invent your own title or sub-title.

Design a question

If you are designing your own question, you should try to include key words that encourage an argument or debate, not just a description. For example, the title *Caring for Confused Patients* is merely descriptive, it does not give any indication of what needs to be debated. There would be a temptation to write a descriptive, anecdotal account of various patients with, perhaps, some descriptions of research studies. Such an essay is likely to be superficial and uncritical. In contrast, the titles *A Discussion of the Use of Reality Orientation with Confused Patients* or *Do Confused Patients Benefit from Reality Orientation?* give a particular focus. They indicate that there may be advantages and disadvantages of something called Reality Orientation which may not be widely known or understood and which needs to be debated so that each practitioner or carer can make an informed choice about whether to use the method or not. These titles encourage explanation and debate with in-depth evaluation of the research and its relevance to practice. Titles for experiment reports and dissertations will almost always have a title relating to a special field of study. These need not be in the form of a question.

Title page

It is usually necessary to include a title page with relevant administrative detail and your assignment title. A possible essay layout is shown below. Please note that most universities now mark assignments 'blind to identity' to avoid bias. If you are given an ID number you should use this, not your name. The word count must be given and should normally come within 10 per cent either side of the stated limit. Your course and module guidelines may set out precise details of what is needed. Almost certainly, there will be precise requirements for dissertations. Check these first. If no information is given, ask your tutor if there are any specific requirements. If there are not, then the title page given in Figure 1.10 may be useful.

Compare:	Look for similarities between; and perhaps reach a conclusion as to which is preferable.
Contrast:	Set in opposition, in order to bring out differences.
Criticise:	Give your judgement about the merits of theories, or opinions about the usefulness of research. Back your judgement by a discussion of evidence or reasoning involved. Criticism includes positive and negative aspects, not just negative.
Define:	Set down the precise meaning of a word or phrase. In some cases it may be necessary or desirable to examine different possible or often used definitions.
Describe:	Give a detailed or graphic account of.
Differentiate or Distinguish:	Explain the difference.
Discuss:	Investigate or examine by argument; sift and debate; give reasons for and against. Also examine the implications.
Evaluate:	Make an appraisal of the worth of something, in the light of its truth or usefulness. Include, to a lesser degree, your personal opinion.
Explain:	Make plain; interpret and account for; give reasons for.
Illustrate:	Use a figure or diagram to explain or clarify; or make clear by use of concrete examples.
Interpret:	Expound the meaning of; make clear and explicit, usually giving your own judgements also.
Justify:	Show adequate ground for decisions or conclusions; and answer the main objections likely to be made to them.
Outline:	Give the main features or general principles of a subject, omitting minor details and emphasising structure and arrangements.
Relate:	Show how things are connected to each other, and to what extent they are alike, or affect each other.
Review:	Make a survey of, examining the subject carefully.
State:	Present in brief, clear form.
Summarise:	Give a concise account of the chief points of a matter, omitting details and examples.
Trace:	Follow the development or history of a topic from some point of origin.

Figure 1.9 Key command words in essay title questions

NAME OF UNIVERSITY OR COLLEGE

FACULTY (OR DEPARTMENT)

ID Number /Name. . . . .   Course Title. . . . .

Intake year/Level. . . . .   Module Title. . . . .

Submission Date . . . .   Module Leader. . . . .

TITLE OF ASSIGNMENT

and

YOUR TITLE OR SUB-TITLE
(if different from above)

Number of words . . . . (requested word limit = ...±10%)

Figure 1.10 Title page for essay

Plan

A plan is vital for good writing and provides a structure that helps you to write: you are not expected to invent or imagine what to write about from your own experience or let the essay emerge spontaneously as a stream of consciousness.

Planning shows the reader that you are in command of the topic and that you understand what is behind the title; it gives fluency and helps to avoid irrelevance and repetition. Your plan could consist of a series of brief headings or notes, either in logical linear order or as a 'spider' diagram (mind map or pattern notes). If you are handwriting, it may help to arrange your points on separate pieces of paper that you can move around. If you are using a word processor or computer, you can cut and paste on screen, but you may also find it helpful in the early stages to print out and cut the paper. Never let your sources dictate your plan – use your plan to help you find the best sources. Following too closely the approach taken in source material may amount to plagiarism, but in any case makes it difficult for you to demonstrate that you have understood the material and developed your own ideas about it.

Your plan is your guide to the finished essay, but you need not set about writing it in the order in which it will finally appear.

Draft

Whenever possible, write a first rough draft and leave it for a few days before reading it through again. You will then find it far easier to be objective and critical about your own work. Deal with each point in turn, discussing each one fully before passing to the next. Avoid repetition and irrelevance. If appropriate, extract any sections of purely descriptive material, lists or diagrams and put these in appendices. Summarise the main points in a sentence or two in your essay and refer the reader to the appendix for the detail. Try reading the draft out loud, record it and play it back, or read it to a friend – better still to an enemy!

Essay structure

For a standard academic essay, the most common basic structure is:

> Introduction: perhaps one tenth.
> Discussion: at least three major debating points with evidence.
> Conclusion: perhaps one eighth.

This is a natural division, and normally there is no need to use any subtitles or subheadings.

It helps to keep the introduction to about one tenth of the essay length. This is where you indicate the breadth and scope of the topic area, and how or why the essay will take one aspect to discuss in depth. You might want to comment on the title and explain your interpretation of the question in relation to psychology practice. You could indicate the main debate and any problem areas that need discussing. It might be useful to say what aspects will be covered and those that will not be discussed and why. It is often appropriate to outline the order of your discussion to help the reader through your debate. It may be necessary to define some terms – especially if these may be unfamiliar to your reader, or there are conflicting definitions in common use, or some confusion about meanings. Many people find the introduction is the most interesting or difficult part to write and leave it until last. It can certainly be helpful to write the introduction and the conclusion at more or less the same time, so that you ensure that they relate to each other and to the question and to your debate. Although this will be your personal approach, it is still (usually) more appropriate to use the third person (see below) when outlining your intentions.

When planning the main body of discussion of your essay, put down your key points in a sensible order – one that will enable your discussion to flow and which avoids repetition. A useful rule-of-thumb for beginning students is to choose three key items for debate, with arguments for and against and supporting evidence. Look for connections between the points. You may want to put all the arguments in favour, followed by all the opposing arguments, or alternate views relating to specific points. Use connecting words or phrases such as: however, although, on the other hand, nevertheless, in addition, in contrast, finally. Where appropriate, expand on the points with examples or illustrations. Check that your discussion answers the question. If the question has two or more parts, make sure you keep these distinct, and allow the proper amount of space to each.

The conclusion could be about one eighth of your essay length. Summarise your main ideas or arguments and draw a conclusion if possible. Ensure that your conclusion corresponds to the question asked, and to what you set out in the introduction, and that it follows from the discussion in the main body of the essay. It is not always possible to give a firm answer to a question; instead you may need to explain your uncertainties. Do not include any new arguments or material here, but it may be appropriate to suggest the wider implication of your discussion, or point to future trends, or areas that are worthy of future research. Some students like to end with a pithy quotation but this is more appropriate to an informal or popular article than a formal academic essay.

References

This list comes after the conclusion and before any appendices. You may also be asked for a full bibliography of all the sources that you consulted, even if you did not use material directly. You could keep this in your files, even if not requested. (See above for details on how to reference your sources.)

Appendices

You may like to use appendices to provide detailed information, such as lists, models and diagrams, which would interrupt the flow of your discussion but are needed as background information. They are not normally assessed and are not included in the word count. Make sure that you indicate the appendix at the appropriate point in your essay. For example if you mention, say, Maslow's (1962) hierarchy of needs, and include this as your second appendix, put 'see Appendix Two', at the appropriate point in your essay.

The references, bibliography and appendices need headings.

Subheadings

Some writers like to guide the reader through their work by using subheadings. There is lively debate amongst academics as to whether subtitles are suitable in essays. Traditionally, subtitles in psychology essays have been viewed as inappropriate as they break up the flow of a discussion, and it is felt that the structure alone should be sufficient in demonstrating the area of concern in each section of the essay.

In the absence of other subtitles, there is no need to subtitle the introduction and conclusion, as these will be self-evident.

However, in some circles there seems to be a growing trend to use subtitles, perhaps to assist the student in focusing on the key issues and in line with a general trend towards 'packaging' information in small units for quick and easy access. If you have identified the issues and believe it would be helpful to yourself and the reader to make these explicit, and your tutor approves, then you may want to make this choice, but you are advised to use the subtitles sparingly in order to maintain the integrity of the whole essay.

Different expectations apply to books, journal articles, report-writing, seminar presentations, dissertations and projects, which would normally make full use of subtitles and sub-headings. In this book paragraphs are deliberately short and items are arranged with bullet-points wherever possible for easy reference and recognition.

Flow

The flow and coherence of your discussion will depend on the order of your issues, and hence your paragraphs and the way you link them. You will help your reader if you arrange a continuous thread of argument or discussion throughout your essay with each point leading on to the next.

You may want to put all the evidence in support of an idea first, followed by all the contrary evidence. Or you may choose to alternate between support and contradiction for each point. One useful approach is to put contrasting points in adjacent paragraphs: for example, for and against; cause and effect; positive and negative; merits and demerits and so on.

Deal with each point in turn, discussing each one fully before passing to the next. To move from one paragraph to the next, it helps if you use transition words or phrases, for example 'however', 'it follows that', 'consequently', 'furthermore', 'on the other hand'. But be careful to use these properly. For example, do not use 'therefore' unless what follows is implied by the previous point or really does follow from it. Try not to overuse the same few transition words: starting each paragraph or new point in the same style does not make for an essay that reads well. It is helpful to distinguish between phrases that introduce a point that you want to make and those that help you draw to a conclusion. The first can be called 'reason indicators' and include: because, for, since, the reason being, firstly, secondly, however, furthermore, on the other hand. . . . The 'conclusion indicators' are: therefore, hence, so, thus, which proves/ shows/ implies/ demonstrates/justifies the belief that, it follows that, consequently . . .

Personal style

You will develop your own special style, but this need not be fixed and can always be open to experiment and improvement. Always aim to be clear and succinct. A good, varied, fresh vocabulary is attractive, but try to use short words and simple straightforward language where possible. It helps if you keep most of your sentences short so that you do not risk muddling up several ideas. Use very short sentences where you want to make a clear, powerful point. Longer sentences can give a pleasant contrast to these, but avoid a jungle of subordinate clauses.

Register and jargon

You will need to use the special language, or 'register' of psychology. However, do not try to impress. Make sure you fully understand special terms and use only those technical terms that are essential for precision. Be careful that you do not slip into casual jargon, using words and phrases that psychologists use in speech amongst themselves but which do not come across well in writing. Moreover, even though you are writing chiefly for other psychologists, you will develop a more useful style if you can be widely understood. As with all good writing, avoid abbreviations, contractions, slang, colloquialisms, clichés and hackneyed phrases.

The style must be appropriate to the subject matter and discipline. That which is suitable for a literary creation, religious tract or political pamphlet will not be suitable for academic essays. Essays demand evidence and rational argument, coherently and concisely stated. To develop a 'feel' for different styles, read as widely as you can and compare the style of different journals.

Use of standard English

Ambiguities, muddled sentences, spellings that do not exist in dictionaries or mean something else, all slow your readers down and involve them in hard work in deciphering what you are trying to say. Be particularly careful with specialist words that sound the same but have different meanings, such as, cite and sight, counsel and council, discrete and discreet, affect and effect, complimentary and complementary.

Be aware that although it is not particularly helpful to be pedantic about 'right' and 'wrong' grammar, the meaning of a sentence can be completely changed by small alterations to spelling or punctuation.

For example, 'Psychologists who are stupid cannot help their clients,' does not mean the same as 'Psychologists, who are stupid, cannot help their clients.'

The established rules of standard English are there to help us get our meaning across effectively. Make sure your sentences are clear and that you are using standard spelling and grammar because if you do not your readers may not be able to interpret correctly and *your* meaning may be totally lost.

Choice of person and voice

Psychology essays are traditionally written in formal style, using the 'third person'. Tutors do not usually recommend use of the first person (I, we, us) or the second person (you), except in reflective work. For example, instead of saying '*I have noticed . . .*' it is better to say, '*It is sometimes observed in practice . . .*'. However, there is a danger that this will give a vague and woolly impression. It might be preferable, simply to write, '*In practice, . . .*'. It is also preferable to avoid substituting 'one' or 'the writer' for the first person, when attempting to refer to your ideas, as these give an artificial stilted style. There is no need to say 'I think . . .' or 'One thinks . . .' or 'The writer thinks. . .'. Your ideas and discussion will be obvious if you have referenced other writers correctly.

Traditionally, scientific papers have used the passive voice predominantly – for example the liquid was poured into the test tube – because the results will be the same whoever pours the liquid. However, popular journals and magazines now prefer the active voice, both to acknowledge who is performing the action and to give a more up-to-date, punchier style, and you will find that your computer grammar-checker will query passive usage. Person and voice are summarised in Figure 1.11.

Final appearance

Reading an essay is, to a large extent, influenced by factors other than content and structure. It may not always be fair but illegible handwriting, scruffy presentation or poor layout will all detract from the impression given by your essay and slow the reader down.

It is always easier for the reader if the essay is typed, on one side of the paper only, with double spacing between the lines. This is particularly important where a tutor may want to write comments. If you are using a word processor you can set the line spacing to double. Leave generous margins on both edges and check that when the essay is in its binder, the typing does not disappear behind the clip. To help your reader see your paragraphs easily, you may indent the first line of a paragraph, and then there is no need to put an extra carriage return between paragraphs. If you prefer a block layout, with no indent, you will need to separate paragraphs with an extra carriage return. If you hand-write your essay, you may find narrow-lined paper more suitable for double spacing than wide-lined.

Avoid using correcting fluid as this nearly always looks messy. It is normally better to correct an error by putting a neat line through the word and re-writing it. If you find several sentences that are incorrect, your only choice is to re-type or re-write the page. The final script should not have more than a few last-minute proof-reading corrections.

	Singular	Plural
First Person	I, me, my, mine E.g. I am going to write about Piaget's theory of cognitive development because it is important.	we, us, our, ours
Second Person	you, your, yours	you, your, yours
Third Person	he, his, she, her, hers, it, its, the topic. E.g. Piaget's theory of cognitive development is important because . . .	they, them, their, theirs

Active voice – The 'subject' of the sentence is doing the action.

E.g. The psychologist helped the client. The dog chewed the slipper.
Have you finished the essay? Have you handed it in?

Passive voice – The 'subject 'of the sentence is having the action done to it.

E.g. The client was helped by the psychologist. The slipper was chewed by the dog.
The essay is finished. It has not yet been handed in.

Figure 1.11 Person and voice

In general you will be expected to present written work in a protective cover which makes marking and handling easy. The marker may need to handle individual pages, or to makes notes on them, so do not put each page into an individual plastic sleeve unless asked to do so. Lightweight transparent plastic covers that can be opened flat are usually preferred to a sleeve, from which the essay has to be removed. Hard files are not usually liked, particularly where a pile of essays will be posted to external examiners. You may be asked simply to staple your pages in one corner and leave uncovered. Always check with each tutor to see what is preferred.

Pages should be numbered and, preferably, include your ID and course on each page. A word processor can be set to give page numbers and a header or footer.

A checklist is given in Figure 1.12

Scientific report structure

As part of your undergraduate work you will probably have the opportunity to carry out practical research projects. As with A-levels, the first year practicals may be simple

Have I read the course/module/publisher's instructions?
Have I consulted the tutor about specific preferences?
Have I identified the key words in the title?
What is the debate that corresponds to the title?
Have I answered the particular question that was devised?
Does the introduction set out the purpose and focus of the essay or article?
Have I arranged the material logically?
Have I covered all of the main aspects and covered these in enough depth
     and weighed all the evidence?
Have I presented a convincing argument that I could justify in a seminar
     discussion or interview?
Is the content accurate?
Does the writing move smoothly from one section to the next, from
     paragraph to paragraph?
Are the paragraphs a good length?
Can I clearly identify the key issue in each paragraph? Is each issue
     discussed in depth?
Is each point supported by evidence, examples and evaluation? Have I
     weeded out all unnecessary description?
Have I distinguished clearly between my own ideas and those of others?
Have I acknowledged all sources and given references?
Does the conclusion summarise the main points of the discussion and
     match the intentions of the introduction?
Does each source (name and date) cited in the essay match a full entry in
     the reference list?
Is the reference list accurate, in alphabetical order with all details?
Is the essay or article the right length?
Have I written plainly and simply?
Have I read it aloud to sort out clumsy and muddled phrasing?
Have I shown it to a friend for a second opinion?
Are the grammar, punctuation and spelling standard so that they convey
     my meaning easily?
Is the essay neat and legible, with good margins, and double-spaced?
Have I used the type of cover specified in the course requirements?
Is the title page correct, according to requirements?
Have I proof-read scrupulously?
Have I made a copy for my records?
Is it ready to be handed in on time?

Figure 1.12 Essay checklist

reproductions of well-established research but as you progress through the course you may be invited to design your own variations.

The report structure for psychology practicals may vary from course to course but most use the following format:

> Title.
> Abstract.

> Introduction.
> Method:
>   – design
>   – participants
>   – apparatus
>   – procedure.
> Results.
> Discussion.

The abstract is a brief (100–150 words) summary of the whole report that covers the topic, method, variables, experimental hypothesis and results.

The introduction gives the background to the area you are investigating with a critical summary of related studies, with a link to the key emphasis and aims of your experiment. Ethical considerations may be given here.

The design section states:

> type of experiment of observation, for example, correlation or inferential
> design, for example repeated measures, independent measures
> explanation of choice of design
> variables (dependent and independent)
> experimental hypothesis
> null hypothesis.

The participants section states:

> number; type (for example sex, age); how selected (for example random, opportunist).

The apparatus section gives:

> materials and equipment
> diagrams if needed

The procedure section gives:

> experimental conditions
> details of controls
> instructions given to participants
> responses to unforeseen problems.

The result section gives a summary of the data (not all the raw data) presented clearly in relation to the hypothesis, usually as tables and graphs or diagrams, together with interpretation. See Part 5.

The discussion is the most important part. With published work in journals many readers go to the abstract and then the discussion in order to make a judgement of whether to read more.

You will need to cover:

> statement of results
> statistical test, calculated and critical values, significance level
> whether experimental or null hypothesis has been rejected
> other features such as trends, key results, features in graphs or diagrams

> notable results
> relation of your results to background as given in your introduction
> critical review of the strengths and weaknesses of your method
> suggestions for improvements and further study
> brief conclusion restating the hypothesis that was supported.

See Part 5 for more information.

Dissertation

A dissertation is a long piece of work, often required towards the end of a degree course at undergraduate or masters' level. An undergraduate dissertation may be about 10,000 to 12,000 words, compared with a normal essay of 1,500 to 2,000 or a long essay of 5,000 to 6,000 words. The dissertation is a more in-depth exploration of the topic than either an essay or a normal practical and usually involves your own original research.

Detailed information is usually supplied and requirements vary so you will need to check with tutors. You will normally be able to choose your own topic, within limits, and research question (see above for designing your own question). You will then need to carry out a literature review and collect and analyse evidence.

Be careful how you choose your topic as it needs to be something you are interested in and for which you can readily find material, and for which you can design a suitable piece of scientific research using approved methodology.

Be careful with the word limit, also. The limit you are set is not a minimum or a maximum but the required length, usually with a 10 per cent margin either way.

Even more than with an ordinary essay, you need to prepare well in advance so that you can order published material and start the background reading. It also helps enormously if you can submit some sort of plan or draft (according to regulations) in the early stages so that you can get as much feedback as possible.

Writing for publication

If you think your work would be useful for others, spend some time looking at different publications to find one that fits your work and your style. If necessary adapt your style to suit the publication. Each publisher or journal has its own house style and will send you their guidance for contributors on request.

If you want to post your material on the Internet then you can start your own website or blog or other available system. The Internet is changing all the time so you will need to watch out for new developments.

If you wish to subscribe to Wikipedia you will be able to write articles for that site.

You may also find that your university or college has an Intranet that you can use to share material with other students.

Give a presentation

Much of the following is applicable to any kind of presentation, including classroom presentations at school. The emphasis here is on seminars as these are likely to be the first presentations you will be faced with at university.

Seminars are intended to offer you the opportunity for discussing and developing your own ideas in a small group and to handle debate.

Students can find seminars difficult at first, especially since many students can be shy about saying what they think. It is all too easy for most students to sit back and take notes without participating more actively in the seminar. Everyone has a different learning preference and style and it is recognised that non-participation does not mean that learning is not taking place, but the success of a seminar depends on as much participation as possible of all members of the group.

Seminars are not meant to be a forum where one or two students (or the tutor) take over the discussion. Tutors are often accustomed to working hard to find ways to draw people out. Moreover, the tutor may feel solely responsible for the success of the seminar and assume the familiar role of leader of a class and fill in awkward silences. However, such a pattern does not benefit the students' development, either as presenters of a seminar or participants. It is therefore important for all members of the seminar group to regard themselves as having a responsibility for encouraging others to take part and for the tutor to take a minimal role.

The main aim of a seminar is to generate discussion. When presenting a seminar, you are in a teaching position and should prepare your material accordingly.

As a general rule the presentation should:

> have a title which asks a question and indicates a debate, not just one word or just a descriptive phrase
> last no more than half the total time available
> aim to set out issues and arguments supported with research evidence but not reproduce facts for their own sake
> include an indication of all the sources you have used
> conclude with a summary and two or three questions which the group could address

You will need to chair the discussion addressing the questions which you have identified, then summarise again and end the session.

Preparation

As you may have found in the past, presentations by individual students to a group are often dull and boring because they are not planned and co-ordinated. They take too long, and the audience is usually more interested in their own presentation than in yours.

Plan

Define the purpose. Why are you giving this seminar and why have you chosen this particular topic and debate?

Define aims and objectives. What do you want to achieve for yourself and what do you want your audience to know or be able to do that they couldn't do before?

Know who your audience is. How many are there? Do you know them well? Have they already studied this topic? Do they know as much as you? Do they respond well in seminar and discussion situations? People think more if they can relate what you are saying to what they already know. Find out what people have read and what they are familiar with and adjust your presentation accordingly.

Know the setting and conditions. What is the room like? What facilities are there? Can you re-arrange the seating and layout?

Framework

> Identify the key points and sub-points of the topic that you want to put across.
> Identify key words and phrases.
> Use examples and illustrations to support the message and clarify unfamiliar ideas.
> Choose a starting point.
> Find a clear pathway through the material.

Your appearance

> Find out if there are formal dress requirements.
> Choose your clothes to suit the situation.
> If you are nervous and blush easily, wear cool fabrics that cover you well, such as with a high collar and long sleeves.
> Wear comfortable shoes that are least likely to make you stumble or trip.
> Pay attention to your hair and general appearance so that you feel good.

Content

Inexperienced presenters almost always have too much material to present and rush through it, overburdening their audience and still taking too long. About 15–20 minutes uninterrupted listening is the limit on most people's concentration even when the presentation is riveting. Cut down your content and slow down on your rate of speaking. Break your talk into sections with intervals for activities or discussion. Have a practice and time how long it takes. If you are worried about running out of material, give yourself time-fillers such as extra examples, something for the audience to read, or questions for the audience to answer and discuss part-way through. Think about what might intrigue, puzzle or contradict expectations. Be controversial or entertaining.

Notes

Inexperienced presenters often write out their presentation in full and read it out word for word. This can be very dull for the audience and it isn't much fun for the presenter either. Experienced presenters rely on much briefer notes which give them an overview and a way of seeing very quickly what they are supposed to be talking about and what is coming next. Methods include:

> Microsoft PowerPoint notes pages to accompany slides
> index cards which each contain one key idea or sub-section of the presentation
> a handout for the audience which the presenter uses as a framework for the talk
> transparencies which summarise the key points and which the presenters use to remind themselves
> very brief skeleton notes, containing only single words or phrases which provide clues about the content.

Support materials

It is hard to just listen to a presentation. It is easier when you have something to look at. Have a clear purpose for the material. Make sure that the material is clear and legible. Make sure you write the title of your talk and all unfamiliar terms and names.

Display

> Microsoft PowerPoint slides; on screen, direct from the computer. You could use this for pictures, charts and graphs. You should be able to scan in pictures from textbooks. Experiment with enlargements. Many word processors now have packages that make preparation very easy. Experiment with different sizes and styles of lettering until you find something which suits you and your subject matter and projects well. Keep to a simple, unfussy style which can be read quickly. Keep information to an absolute minimum – just key words, not lots of text. A useful rule of thumb is one ppt slide per minute. Use advanced computer technology to insert animated clips or video extracts. Ask for help in the computer department and explore how to present graphs and to use slides to reveal or hide different sections.

> Interactive whiteboards are used with a computer and projector to create a touch-screen display. Special software is available for various demonstrations and exercises. Try an Internet search for the latest materials.

> If the automatic PowerPoint equipment is not available you can use the software and create acetate transparencies of your main points to use with an overhead projector. If you handwrite or draw, make sure you have the correct pens, which may be washable or permanent. It is possible to photocopy from books directly onto acetates. Always ask for help with unfamiliar technology and make sure you use the correct type of acetate – the wrong kind will melt and wreck the photocopying machine. These can be used with PowerPoint notes pages and handouts as above. Paper strips can be used to reveal or hide different sections. Turn off the projector or cover the screen with a blank sheet of paper when you are not referring to the slide.

> Other handouts (containing a summary of your case study or extracts from texts or crucial passages from your central sources).

> Whiteboard or chalkboard to summarise your points or illustrate what you are talking about. Special whiteboard pens enable writing to be erased with a dry cloth.

> Flipcharts you have prepared beforehand which provide an overview, a map, or a diagram. Flipcharts require broad nib felt pens.

> Slide projector with a set of prepared slides.

> Video.

Try everything out well in advance – so you have time to make another set if writing is too crowded, too small or pale etc. Remember that with a slide projector, the lights will have to be dimmed and blackout is usually necessary.

Activities

It is more interesting for your audience if they have something active to do. This might involve reading a passage, analysing a text, solving a problem, suggesting alternative ways to interpret or analyse a passage or historical event, suggesting examples of a phenomenon, and so on. You can ask for volunteers, select victims or split people into small groups for a few minutes to prepare something.

Handouts

People can't join in, or even think very much, if they are busy taking notes. Provide a handout so that your audience can concentrate on what you have to say. Your handout can help to structure and link the contributions of the members too. If your slides have complicated diagrams with lots of boxes, give your audience either a paper copy or a partial copy with the outlines of the boxes which they can fill in with words as you speak. PowerPoint handouts give a miniaturised version of the slides with space for notes.

Practice

> Time yourself.
> Try out all the materials.
> Learn to project your voice. Find a singing teacher to help you.

Examine your fears

> What makes you feel nervous?
> How likely is it to happen and what will you do if it does?

Before the presentation

> Check location of power points of extension leads.
> Check that all equipment works and that there are no trailing leads or other hazards.
> Get spare bulbs, pens, pads, chalk etc. Make sure you have the right pens for the screen.
> Arrange seating
> Check that presentation notes are to hand
> Check that all your samples, diagrams and handouts are available.
> Make final preparations.

Delivering the seminar paper

Starting to speak

> Focus on your breathing.
> Relax your face and neck muscles.
> Establish eye contact.
> Occupy your hands.
> Start your opening words.
> Introduce yourself and team.
> Speak slowly and clearly.
> Try to address yourself to the whole audience.

Voice control

> Keep your breathing even.
> Project your voice, do not shout, mumble or gabble.
> Vary the pitch, tone and loudness.
> Do not fade out at the ends of words and sentences.
> Do not turn your back on your audience while you are speaking.

Speaking techniques

> Use pauses for punctuation.

> Use questions.

Look confident

> Stay in control.
> Use facial expressions consciously.
> Use gestures and body language appropriately.
> Use your position in the room consciously.

Use the support material

> Know when to use the material.
> Make sure that everyone can see the material.
> Use your additional materials to the full.

Where the screen shows a short list of key words, you could show the whole list to establish what you will be talking about, then cover up the list, revealing each term in turn as you talk about it. Do not rush. Allow time for the group to read and make notes. If you do need to include lots of information on one screen, or have included a diagram, talk the group through it – do not leave them to read it, or make sense of it, on their own. Do not display one set of information and then talk about something else. Turn off the projector or cover it when you are not directly referring to it. Shift your eye contact to different people as you are talking. Your aim should be to be able to look at the audience most of the time, and to give the impression of thinking while you are talking.

Have fun

Presentations do not have to be straight-faced and deadly serious. There will be more energy and involvement if people are enjoying themselves. Give yourself permission, and your audience permission, to relax and have a laugh.

Respond and be flexible

Things do not always work out the way you thought. If you are way over people's heads or boring them to tears by going too fast, don't just plod on regardless. Although you may be tempted to rush through your paper, remember that in many cases the material you are presenting will be new to the group. Look around all the time and be alert to signs of non-comprehension. Be prepared to pause and digress from your prepared script occasionally to answer questions and explain more fully.

Invite questions

If you talk non-stop, especially if you avoid eye contact with your audience, they are unlikely to ask you questions, even if they have questions in their mind. You need to invite questions. You can do this by saying at the start: 'Please stop me to ask questions or seek clarification.' Don't forget to stop and invite questions: 'Before I go on, is there anything you'd like to ask or for me to clarify?' You can stop and look around, inviting interruptions with your body language. Leave plenty of time even though the silence may feel threatening – it takes time to formulate question. If none of these work, stop and ask people to write down two questions they would really like answered, give them a minute, and then let each person in turn read out their questions.

Ask questions

Involve and challenge your audience by asking them questions. Prepare questions in advance. Don't ask *closed* questions, to which there is a right and wrong answer ('Who wrote . . .?' 'Did . . . write this before or after . . .?') but *open* questions which can start discussion ('What might be the problems of this way of looking at things?' 'Is this the only way of seeing this?' 'What is your opinion on this?').

Summarise

When you have finished, don't just suddenly stop and say: 'Well . . . that's it really.' You will need a conclusion or overview. Summarise what you have said and make it clear what the key points were. Make sure your audience leaves with a clear impression of what you discovered or what your views are.

After the seminar

Writing up the final version of your paper for assessment

A seminar paper is not necessarily exactly like an essay so you may be permitted to be flexible. Subtitles are probably useful and you could include copies of your visual material where appropriate, perhaps as appendices. Referencing should follow the standard guidelines for the Harvard system. Your paper should include the material you prepared in advance and the discussion that occurred in the group, with any further thoughts you have had. Check with the tutor first.

Learn from your presentation

In order for you to monitor your own progress and development, ask for feedback from the group – students and tutor – at the end of the session. The following comments have been made by lecturers:

> what they tend to do is to write an essay and read it out loud, usually at breakneck speed, with the other students frantically scribbling notes. All of this takes about 15–20 minutes which leaves three-quarters of an hour. I haven't found a way to handle that kind of seminar and persuading them that this is not a good approach is difficult.

> I had this student who sat there week after week and didn't say anything. Then one day, I could see he wanted to say something and, you know, I gave him all the signs to come on. Anyway, he made his point, and his friend sitting next to him turned round and said 'Don't be so wet!'

It takes patience and practice to get a group to reflect on the effectiveness of their presentation and give each other honest feedback without feeling discouraged or belittled. But after a few attempts they can usually see what works and what does not, even if they cannot yet do it well. Like all skills, learning to lead a seminar takes time and effort.

Manage time

There is never enough time. You will always have tasks left over at the end of each day but the trick is to make sure these are the least important ones.

Each day, or week, you need to distinguish between urgent and important tasks and sort these out from the trivial, non-urgent and unimportant ones. Urgent tasks have a short deadline and need to be done as soon as possible. Select the ones that have a serious outcome if they are not done. Important tasks may not be urgent but if you do not plan for them they could become crises. Make a list.

If you feel that your time is mainly controlled by others, remember that other people's lack of planning does not mean an emergency for you. Sort the tasks you have been given into urgent and important, set realistic deadlines and work through them in order.

Deal with interruptions (enquiries, telephone calls, visitors) as swiftly as possible, arranging a time to deal with them later when you are free.

Be able to say NO (politely and sympathetically).

Recognise your time-wasting activities.

If you are a mature student with a family, returning to study, try to plan support well in advance. It will not be easy to study but you need to sort out time and a place for yourself that the rest of the family understands and honours. That's the ideal anyway! Discuss problems with student services before they develop into crises.

As part of your strategic approach to learning (see Entwistle above) you will need to keep track of time. You need to know when and where you should be for lectures, seminars, practicals and examinations. You need to know when work has to be handed in and keep to the deadlines.

You will find it helpful if you become more self-aware about the best time of day to read, study and write, and if you can arrange your personal schedule to allow for your best times. Think about whether you usually tend to be early or late for events. Are you relaxed or do you tend to rush around? Do you leave things to the last minute? Do you forget to do things? Cottrell (2003) suggests keeping a diary and learning from it.

One useful suggestion I came across a long time ago refers to the times of examinations. If, like me, you tend to droop after lunch but find you have an examination at that time, it can help to spend the previous days practising to study after lunch and try to interrupt your habitual pattern.

Revise and prepare for examinations

The purpose of examinations or supervised assignments is to demonstrate under time constraints:

> clear and logical development of an argument
> powers of analysis and debate
> application of knowledge
> drawing together of relevant material
> effective use of references
> succinct writing
> parity between course work and examination performance.

These are the formal reasons. You may find in preparing that you suddenly get to grips with all the material you have been faced with all semester and suddenly realise how to write an essay. There is nothing quite like having to memorise something to sharpen the mind. If you find you are getting too anxious go and see your tutor or students services. Do not forget that it often helps if you imagine you are writing your essay in order to explain the material to a friend who missed that bit of the course (but keep it in formal style not conversational).

There are various kinds of exam, including:

> unseen
> open book
> seen question
> short questions
> multiple choice.

Planning for examinations needs to start well in advance. You will need to find out what sort of exams to expect and the dates. Ask whether there will be any mock papers. Past papers can sometimes be purchased from the university bookshop. If not, ask your tutors. For essay papers, work out your timing so that you allow a suitable proportion of time for each question, according to the marking scheme. You will normally pick up most marks in the first part of the time so do not waste time trying to finish something you find you know little about but go on to the next topic. Allow your plan to show clearly, so that if you do not have time to finish at least your plan will show what you intended.

With unseen papers, where you do not know the questions in advance, you will probably have been given an indication of the topic area, or can tell from past papers.

Prepare notes of the key issues, arguments and evidence, and prepare typical essay plans that you can adapt. You will need to arrange your notes in easily memorised format. Remember the magic seven plus or minus two (Miller, 1956) and practise with a friend to discover your personal optimum for memorising lists and arrange bullet points or spatial diagrams within your range: three or five points are often the best.

With an open book examination, you do not need to memorise all the details but make sure you make notes and use markers so that you can find relevant material quickly. You will not have time in the examination to find new material.

With seen questions, you can prepare your answer in advance. You can write out a whole essay if you like, but as it is unlikely that you can memorise it all, a plan with short lists of the main points is best.

With short answers make sure you get all the key points in a few words.

With multiple choice papers do not forget to fill in an answer for every question as you might get it right by chance.

Make sure you have good equipment such as your ID card and examination number if applicable, several pens and pencils, ruler, eraser, wristwatch, calculator if relevant, drinking water if allowed. You will probably have to leave your bag at the back of the room so make sure you do not have a lot of items. If scrap paper is allowed it will be provided, but it is usually sensible to write your notes on the examination paper and then cross through neatly anything you do not wish the examiner to read.

You will probably not be allowed to use white-out to cover up errors. Cross through neatly.

Try to keep your handwriting neat and legible and use standard spelling and grammar so that you do not slow down the examiner or make your work difficult to understand and mark.

If you have a recognised condition such as dyslexia it is up to you to discuss this with your tutors well in advance so that you can have extra time or whatever the regulations permit. (If you know people who are dyslexic please remind them of this – they may have had difficulty reading this!)

If using a calculator, check that it is the permitted kind. Programmable calculators are often disqualified.

Cottrell (2003) gives useful advice on revision and examination preparation.

2.1 Ways of looking at the behaviour and minds of people

Scientific nature of enquiry

Like all methods of enquiry, in history, philosophy, literature and so on, the purpose of scientific research is to increase our knowledge and understanding. All science is concerned with similarities between things in the search for the underlying 'oneness' of the universe (see Metaphysics below) and in defining the differences that enable us to label and classify.

Some definitions of science

Allport (1947): [Science provides] understanding, prediction and control above the levels achieved by unaided common sense.

Wright et al (1970): The term 'experimental psychology' has been used for several decades to refer to scientific psychology, which uses mainly experimental methods, as opposed to kinds of psychology based mainly on philosophic or therapeutic considerations. . . . Psychology bridges the gap between the biological and the social sciences.

Searle (1989: 11): All sorts of disciplines that are quite unlike physics and chemistry are eager to call themselves 'sciences'. A good rule of thumb to keep in mind is that anything that calls itself 'science' probably isn't – for example, Christian science, or military science, and possibly even cognitive science or social science. ... There is only knowledge and understanding . . . . some disciplines are more systematic than others, and we might want to reserve the word 'science' for them .

Collingwood (1998: 4): The word 'science', in its original sense, which is still its proper sense not in the English language alone but in the international language of European civilization, means a body of systematic or orderly thinking about a determinate subject matter. . . . There is also a slang sense, unobjectionable (like all slang) on its lawful occasions . . . in which it stands for natural science.

What makes an enquiry scientific is the attention paid to being systematic, controlled, replicable, unbiased, objective and reliable. The natural sciences (physics, chemistry, biology and so on) also use experiments in laboratory conditions. This means that any piece of research that is repeated in exactly the same way will give the same results: the data are independent of the person conducting the research. Each researcher must write a report that gives sufficient information for someone else to be able to repeat the procedures. In this way, we can accumulate a reliable body of data. Psychology, as far as possible, uses the methodology of the natural sciences and when psychologists define psychology as a science they are referring to natural science.

approaches

The next steps involve interpreting the data: looking for relationships, similarities and differences. and explaining why they occur (see also research process and quantitative research in the section on 'Approaches in psychological research' in Part 5). Explanations grow from hunches and hypotheses that are tested and retested until the researcher is able to put forward a *theory* or *model* that adequately explains why an observed relationship occurs and is able to predict what will occur in carefully controlled circumstances. The same researcher, or anyone else, should then be able to set up circumstances in order to achieve desired effects. This process can be summarised as:

> describe
> explain
> predict
> control.

See also Part 5. Figure 5.1 summarises some of the possible steps in the research process, or scientific method.

The theoretical explanations are usually the interesting part but they are not actually necessary to the scientific process. It is possible to collect reliable data and be able to establish *laws* that predict outcomes without being able to explain what is happening. This occurs in physics, for example. Since the days of Isaac Newton, physicists have been able to describe gravitational effects and devise laws of gravitation that accurately predict what will happen. Partial explanations for particular effects have been put forward but no one has yet been able to explain why gravity exists or how it works.

Scientists compete to find the best explanations for existing data and seek new data that either upholds a theory or contradicts it. Theories can never be 'proved'; they only remain in currency until disproved or improved. Explanations, then, are not wholly objective. They are based on observable and measurable data but they also depend on the perceptions and conceptions of the theorists and are restricted to available data. Publication and debate are vital to the scientific process.

Without comparisons and new approaches that draw attention to how the world works, our perceptions and conceptions cannot develop. Most people without an experimental approach to gravity believe, like Aristotle, that light objects fall more slowly than heavy ones. They have never noticed that this is only true for certain objects like feathers or crumpled sheets of paper that float down, supported by the air. We tend to see what we expect to see and happily ignore anything else. Not many people take the trouble to observe, say, an apple and an apple-sized iron ball being dropped together. Systematically dropping a selection of heavy and light objects of different materials and shapes and sizes, and timing their fall, leads to new perceptions and new understanding.

When comparing with the physical and biological sciences, there is a great deal of argument over whether psychology can be truly considered as a science since it is virtually impossible to control conditions so that results are completely replicable. People are not identical and what happens with one individual or group may not happen with another, however carefully the experimenter tries to match characteristics and provide identical experimental conditions.

However, by using scientific procedures, psychologists can be reasonably certain that the data are reliable for the circumstances that were tried and that the descriptions are true for a certain percentage of the participants. It would be expected that if the circumstances are reproduced as closely as possible, then a similar percentage of people will achieve the same outcomes. Publication and debate and competition between psychologists and their institutions, ensures that everyone continues to strive for the best data and the best explanations and predictions.

Level of inquiry

Researchers choose a particular level of enquiry, from a reductionist biological approach to cognitive psychology or a philosophical point of view, depending on the kind of questions they want to ask and the kind of answers they want to find.

For example, in memory studies some researchers will be involved in looking at the areas of the brain involved in storing and processing memories, others in looking at the way in which the nervous system carries the information. These neuropsychological approaches are seen as fundamental and reductionist. Cognitive psychologists look at the kinds of mental processes we consciously employ, for example in order to remember things, and at how long it takes to learn (and then forget) certain items. They develop complex theories to explain the mental experience of memory. Psychodynamic approaches look at the hidden or unconscious mental processes that give meanings and significance to memories and forgotten events.

Similarly, we need a different kind or level of explanation if we ask 'Why did Mary cross the road?', 'Why did Mary run across the road?', and 'Why didn't Mary run across the road?'. For the first question we can ask Mary or observe her behaviour. She may say that she went across to the shop to buy bread. We might also observe that she chatted animatedly to the shop assistant and infer that she likes to buy her bread at that particular shop because she likes the assistant. These answers belong at the cognitive level and involve social issues. Further investigation would be needed for full answers. For the second question we are not interested so much in why she went across the road but why she ran. We might observe that Mary ran in order to catch a bus, or avoid the traffic or heavy rain, and this too involves choices and is at the complex cognitive level. If there is no bus or traffic or rain then we would look for other explanations such as Mary's mood or disposition that leads her to run. This might involve biological or genetic explanations. And, finally, if she does not run and we can see traffic coming and she is in danger, then we might investigate at the neurological level to see whether Mary can perceive movement or whether she is suffering from depression, and so on.

Time dimension

Studies can be static and independent of time, concentrating on particular events, or they can follow a developmental approach, comparing people of different ages or following people through a given period of time. For example, Piaget used a developmental approach, first by observing how his own children changed as they grew older and then by comparing other children of different ages. Another study of children's behaviour, such as Bandura's Bobo doll studies of 'modelling', might look at one particular age group and compare how different circumstances affect how the children behave. Static studies of memory might look at differences in learning lists of real and nonsense words. Longitudinal or developmental studies might look at the changes that occur with age.

Scope

This refers to how broad or narrow the extent of the study is, and what factors need to be taken into consideration. In particular, studies vary according to whether or not they consider an individual independently of the social context, or whether they view people as individual agents or social beings. Cultural, cross-cultural, environmental and political psychology all take into account the cultural and social context and, in this way, differ considerably from traditional approaches. Lesbian and gay psychology and the psychology of women look specifically at disadvantaged groups and seek to understand and influence attitudes.

Level of generality

Some studies remain specific to the conditions of a particular experiment; others can be generalised to a wider context and, at best, compared with real life situations.

A division can be made between 'process' and 'holistic' approaches. Biopsychology, behaviourism and cognitive psychology are concerned with separate processes which do not need to take into account the whole person. Social psychology and humanistic psychology are more inclined to view the person as a whole, although much research in social psychology concentrates on one particular aspect at a time. Psychodynamic psychology can be seen as viewing people holistically, but is sometimes accused of making interpretations of hidden dynamics in a way which seems detached from real life.

'Meta level' of enquiry

This involves thinking about how we enquire, how we look at people and plan and do research, and getting some idea of exactly *why* there are so many approaches and perspectives on psychology. Metacognition involves examining our own cognitive processes; this includes metamemory or awareness of our memory processes, and metacommunication. These help us direct our enquiry towards the most important areas and help us decide which approaches are best suited to particular problems.

At some point, if we wish, we can stand back from the plethora of studies, try to get a fuller picture and move into the realm of metaphysics.

Metaphysics

It is important to keep asking what we should be studying and why and how. Much of the reasoning behind scientific enquiry depends on common sense and intuition. These are not the end result but part of the process of deciding what to do and why and working out what are our problems and priorities. Much of the time decisions are based on who can attract funding and other pragmatic issues. Metaphysics is concerned with deeper reasons for enquiry, and what it makes sense to do.

The term metaphysics comes from the title of a collection of Aristotle's writings that 'come after physics' (Collingwood, 1998). Aristotle used three different names for a particular type of systematic enquiry, all of which contribute to our modern use of the term metaphysics:

> first science
> wisdom
> theology.

First science means the science with logical priority over other sciences, even though it is studied last. Here, science means 'a body of systematic or orderly thinking' (Collingwood, 1998: 4), not only natural science. Hence it includes logic, ethics, philosophy, mathematics and so on. In this sense metaphysics is beyond or contains all other sciences in a logical system, in the same way as mathematics contains arithmetic, geometry, algebra and other subdivisions. Metaphysics has to be studied last, when the other sciences have been understood to some extent, just as tackling an understanding of mathematics as a whole can only be attempted after getting to grips with arithmetic, algebra and geometry.

Wisdom is the thing for which all science is the search.

Theology is the science that describes and explains the nature of God. In this sense, God means the logical ground of everything else or the underlying 'oneness' of the nature of the universe and everything in it, not a powerful super-human being.

Philosophy is particularly concerned with finding ways of 'repairing' systems of enquiry that appear to be failing. A leading metaphor in this 'repairing' or reparative reasoning is that of medicine (Adams, 2008 and personal communication). We can substitute psychology for medicine as follows:

Consider how a psychologist treats a patient or client who presents an account of her suffering. Three alternative outcomes can be identified.

1. The psychologist recognises symptoms of an identifiable problem.
   At this level the psychologist may know of an appropriate treatment that will lead to an ending of the suffering.
2. The psychologist does not recognise symptoms of an identifiable problem.
   At this level the psychologist needs to identify where the problem lies. Does the psychologist lack knowledge that another psychologist might possess? Is there a lack of trust with the client? Is the psychologist insufficiently skilful in diagnosis, or lacking in flair? If it is any of these then 'the healer needs healing' (Ochs, 1998: 254).
3. There is nothing in the body of psychological knowledge that can help. The inability to find a suitable treatment is attributed to a failure of psychology, rather than the individual's practice of it.
   At this level it is not the individual practising psychologist who determines where the problem lies, but someone who can ask about the 'science of psychology'. This will be a philosopher or a psychologist who takes a philosophical approach.

Thus, there is the failure of the client's ability to cope; the failure of the psychologist's skill; the failure of psychology. Each of these three kinds of failure is deeper than the previous one and requires a deeper kind of repair. A psychologist can repair a client's ability to cope; a better psychologist can repair a poor psychologist's failure; a philosopher can repair psychology's failure. Psychology is a system of repair. 'Philosophy is a system of repair of systems of repair' (Adams, 2008: 453, reproduced and adapted with permission).

There is a fourth level concerning who can repair philosophy. The answer must lie in metaphysics, often approached through theology.

Any psychologist can study philosophy or metaphysics and take a metaphysical point of view, but in practice this is rare. Many psychologists would consider that they do not have time, or that they do not want to, or cannot understand it, or argue that metaphysics is irrelevant or even damaging to psychology.

Sorting into approaches and perspectives within the overall discipline

Psychology covers such a wide variety of subject areas, topics, fields, domains and interests that it is extremely difficult to sort these into meaningful categories and approaches.

Beginning students sometimes ask which is the right approach as if there were only one right approach and a heap of wrong ones. However, at higher levels of education and in practice, it is much more exciting to think in terms of searching for all possible solutions (see *divergent thinking*) and then selecting the most appropriate ones for particular situations.

How can we start to sort?

Within and across all the topics, we can consider four principal domains. These were introduced by Immanuel Kant (1724–1804) and have since been used in various educational classification systems including Bloom's taxonomy (1956):

> affective domain (feelings, *mood* and *emotions*)
> cognitive domain (perception, *thinking*, understanding and other mental processes)
> *conative* domain (will, desire, intention, striving or choosing to do something)
> behavioural domain (observable activity) or psychomotor (manual or physical skills).

Linked to these domains, we can identify a list of seven traditional types of explanation:

> behavioural
> biological
> cognitive
> comparative
> humanistic
> psychodynamic
> social.

These have different historical and geographical backgrounds and look at different aspects of human experience.

Then we find that some topics like intelligence and personality are not easily tackled from any of these perspectives, either separately or together, and seem to need a different kind of approach.

To cope with these, we arrive at two newer theoretical approaches or perspectives:

> developmental psychology
> human diversity or individual differences.

Further, we can add other theoretical approaches that address the level of enquiry and scope, such as cognitive neuropsychology, and cross-cultural, ecological, environmental and evolutionary psychology. Studies of mind and consciousness, that went out of favour with the arrival of behavioural and cognitive science, have returned as a separate approach.

Now we can make a distinction between theoretical perspectives and applied divisions. In general, the theoretical approaches or perspectives form the basis of academic psychology courses. The applied divisions relate to careers in psychology and make use of one or more of these theoretical perspectives in a particular context.

As with all classification systems the distinction is often blurred, with some approaches occurring both as theoretical construct and application. See also Part 2.2 and Part 6.

Altogether, this gives rise to over 20 different categories that encompass the different theoretical perspectives and applied divisions. Figure 2.1 lists theoretical perspectives and applied divisions and their relation to the BPS categories. See also BPS divisions, sections and special groups in Part 7.3. The APA lists American divisions on its website, see Part 7.

These lists are not exhaustive and you may find other approaches as you study.

You may notice that the schools of psychodynamic and humanistic psychology do not appear as key perspectives in the BPS syllabus but they are included within other sections, particularly 'Individual differences'. Similarly, behaviourism and comparative psychology are no longer included in the basic list but knowledge of these is expected; for example, animal cognition is included under biopsychology.

To avoid duplication between theoretical and applied approaches and divisions, all of the key approaches are outlined in this chapter. Further details of registering as a chartered psychologist and information concerning psychology-related careers are given in Part 6.

Traditional theoretical perspectives or 'schools of thought'	BPS approaches and applications as indicated in: qualifying examination topics, options and papers, divisions, sections and special groups
Behaviourism	Topic within individual differences
Biological psychology	Paper 1, BPS Section (Psychobiology)
Cognitive psychology	Paper 1, Paper 4 Option 5, BPS Section
Comparative (animal) psychology	Topic within psychobiology (animal cognition)
Humanistic psychology	Topic within individual differences
Psychodynamic psychology	Topic within individual differences
Social psychology	Paper 2, Paper 4 Option 6 and BPS dection
Newer perspectives in psychology	
Developmental psychology	Paper 2, Paper 4 Option 7, BPS dection
Individual differences or human diversity	Paper 3

Figure 2.1 Theoretical perspectives and applied divisions: showing emphasis within BPS

Additional approaches and applications	
Clinical psychology	Paper 4 Option 2, BPS division
Coaching psychology	BPS special group
Consciousness and experiential psychology	BPS section
Counselling psychology	BPS division
Cultural psychology	Paper 4 Option 9 and within social psychology
Ecological psychology	Topic within Psychobiology Paper 1 and Paper 4 Option 4
Educational and child psychology	Paper 4 Option 1, BPS divisions, BPS section (education)
Environmental psychology	
Ethological psychology	
Evolutionary psychology	Topic within Psychobiology Paper 1 and BPS division
Forensic psychology	Paper 4 Option 4
Health psychology	Paper 4 Option 8, BPS division
History and philosophy of psychology	Paper 3, BPS section
Lesbian and gay	BPS section
Mathematical, statistical and computing	Paper 5, BPS section
Military psychology	
Neuropsychology and cognitive neuroscience	Topics within Psychobiology Papers 1, 4, Cognitive Psychology Paper 4, BPS division
Occupational psychology	Paper 4 Option 3, BPS division
Political psychology	
Psychologists and social services	BPS special group
Psychotherapy	BPS section
Psychology of women	BPS section
Qualitative methods	BPS section
Sport and exercise psychology	BPS division
Teachers and researchers	BPS division
Transpersonal psychology	BPS section

Figure 2.1 continued

2.2 Core approaches

In each of these core approaches outlines are given from the *Subject Benchmark Statement: Psychology 2007*, published by QAA, and the BPS syllabus for the qualifying examination (2008), reproduced with permission. These regulations are updated annually; see Part 7 for further information and websites.

2.2.1: Biological or physiological psychology/neuropsychology

Biological psychology combines biology and psychology and is the perspective that helps us to understand behaviour and mental experience by examining what is happening physiologically in the body, particularly in the brain and nervous system.

This approach has several different names, each of which links biology or physiology with psychology, such as biopsychology, psychobiology, neuropsychology, psychophysiology and 'the biological basis of behaviour'.

Biopsychology may also be combined with social psychology to give a biosocial or biopsychosocial perspective, often referred to in relation to health care.

Topics include the endocrine system and principles of genetics, some ideas about stress and pain and the relationship between brain functioning and mental experience and what is known or believed about different or altered states of awareness; in particular: sleep, dreaming, hypnosis, hallucinations, dementia and the effects of psychoactive or psychotropic drugs.

Some definitions of biological psychology

Glassman (1979): The biological approach emphasises the physical (or physiological) basis of behaviour and the interactions between mind and body. The interactions work both ways: body can affect mind . . .and mind can affect body.

Green (1994): Biopsychology studies . . . those changes in physiological systems that occur whenever behaviour changes. It has concentrated on individual psychological processes such as memory, attention, emotion and motivation, and attempts to demonstrate how, for instance, learning a particular task is correlated with a particular change in activity in the brain.

Pinel (1997): Biopsychology is the study of the biology of behaviour . . . . [It] covers more than the neural mechanisms of behaviour; it also deals with the evolution, genetics and adaptiveness of behavioural processes. . . . [The term] denotes a biological approach to the study of psychology rather than a psychological approach to the study of biology.

QAA

BPS PAPER 1 SECTION 2 – PSYCHOBIOLOGY

Basic neurochemistry and neurophysiology of nerve transmission; the structure and organisation of the CNS; behavioural genetics; hormones and behaviour. Psychopharmacology, the brain and reward, drug action and behaviour. Biological aspects of learning, memory, motivation and emotion, sleep and arousal. Evolutionary explanations of behaviour; primatology, Socio-biology, animal cognition and comparative psychology. Human neuropsychology, cortical localisation of function, biological basis of psychological abnormalities.

BPS PAPER 4 OPTION 4 – PSYCHOBIOLOGY

Basic neurochemistry; neurotransmitters; the brain and reward; drug action on behaviour. Human neuropsychology; problems of localisation; perceptual memory and cognitive disorders following brain lesions; rehabilitation. Evolutionary explanations of behaviour; primatology; behaviour genetics and socio-biology. Animal cognition. Biological bases of psychological abnormalities. (With permission.)

Biological approaches to psychology began in the 17th and 18th centuries with the work of Willis, Galvani, Bell and Magendie (see Part 4.1) that increased our knowledge of the brain and nervous system and the relationships between parts of the brain and behaviour. This was considerably extended in the mid-19th century with Darwin's theory of evolution, which justified comparisons between humans and other animals. Broca's discovery of speech centres in the brain, together with Marshall Hall's work on the nervous system in relation to voluntary movements and Helmholtz's measurement of the speed of nerve impulses firmly established the biological basis of behaviour. Gustav Fechner (1801–1887) can be considered to be the founder of experimental psychology through his attempts to apply the laws of mathematics to the physiology of sensation and develop psychology as a science with a mathematical base.

The appearance of psychology as a subject discipline in its own right is generally dated at 1879, when Wilhelm Wundt (1832–1920) founded the first laboratory for experimental psychology at Leipzig. (See also Parts 4.1 and 4.2.)

Many mainstream psychologists today consider an understanding of biological processes fundamental to understanding psychological processes. The most comprehensive psychological theories, for example in learning, memory, emotion, sleep, pain and stress, are those which can be shown to relate psychological experience to known physiological mechanisms. This does not mean that biopsychology is necessarily 'reductionist', that is attempting to explain behaviour *only* in terms of the biology or reducing complex mental experience to a set of physical laws, but that for the psychological explanations to make proper sense there should be a good match between what is observed psychologically and physiologically with no significant contradictions.

Neuroscience is the scientific study specifically of the brain and nervous system and of the links between brain activity and behaviour. Neuropsychological studies include measurement of brain activity, using EEG, CAT, PET and MRI scans corresponding to different states of consciousness. Theories try to provide neurological explanations for how and why we sleep and dream; what happens in the brain and nervous system during hypnosis; the effects of drugs on the nervous system and how and why hallucinations occur; and alterations in brain functioning in conditions such as schizophrenia, autism and dementias. The motor nervous system is regarded as under voluntary conscious control, but not the autonomic nervous system (ANS). There are exceptions to this as voluntary control can be gained over the ANS through hypnosis, yoga and biofeedback and lost in the motor system due to damage in the central nervous system (CNS).

The BPS Special Group in Clinical Neuropsychology was redesignated the Division of Neuropsychology in June 1999 following a vote by the membership of the Society. The Division provides a forum for psychologists engaged in the assessment and management of brain-damaged patients and those who teach and undertake research in the field of clinical neuropsychology.

The biopsychosocial model is a model of health and illness that suggests that links among the nervous system, the immune system, behavioural styles, cognitive processing and environmental factors can put people at risk for illness.

Animal cognition, comparative psychology and primatology are discussed in Part 2.3.4. Ethology and evolutionary psychology are in Part 2.3.9.

See also:

Part 2.3.4   Comparative (animal) psychology and ethology.
Part 2.3.5   Consciousness and experiential psychology.
Part 2.3.9   Evolutionary psychology.
Part 2.3.11   Health psychology.

See Part 3 for: After-image; Arousal systems; Auditory location; Autokinetic effect; Autonomic nervous system; Basal nuclei ; Blindsight; Brain; Brain damage; Brain imaging; Cerebellum; Cerebral cortex; Chaos theory; Chromosome mutations; Chromosomes; Colour vision; Dark adaptation; Diurnal/circadian rhythms; Dopamine; Dreaming; ECT; EEG evoked potentials (EV); Fight or flight mechanism; Galvanic skin response (GSR); Gate control theory; General adaptation syndrome; Genes; Genetic counselling; Genotype; Habituation/sensory adaptation; Hearing; Hemispheric specialisation; Heterozygous; Hippocampus; Homozygous; Hypothalamus; Kinaesthesia; Language centres; Limbic system; Mid-brain; Myoclonic jerk; Narcolepsy; Nerve fibre; Nervous system; Neuro-transmitters; Phenotype; Pineal body; Proprioception; Psychoneuroimmunology; Psycho-tropic drugs; Resting potential; Saccadic eye movements; Sensation; Senses; Sensitisation; Sensory memory; Serotonin; Sex; Smell; Split-brain; Synaesthesia; Synapse; Taste; Thalamus; Touch; Topography; Twins; Twin studies; Vestibular sense; X-rays and Gamma rays; Zygote.

See Part 4 for: Blakemore, Cannon, Damasio, Friedman and Rosenman, Hebb, Hubel and Wiesel, Luria, Mollon, Olds, Oswald, Penfield, Rose, Sacks, Selye, Sperry, Tulving, Weiss, Wundt, Yerkes, Young, von Helmholtz and Maxwell.

See Part 6 for neuropsychology as a career.

approaches

2.2.2: Cognitive psychology

Cognitive psychology, as part of cognitive science, represents one of the three most important mainstream perspectives in psychological enquiry, alongside biopsychology and social psychology. It has largely replaced behaviourism or behavioural science as the dominant approach in the United Kingdom. Areas for enquiry include attention, perception, memory, thinking, problem-solving, intelligence and language.

To avoid duplication, thinking and problem-solving are discussed under cognitive development in Part 2.2.3.

Some definitions of cognition and cognitive psychology

Drever (1964): Cognition. A general term covering all the various modes of knowing – perceiving, remembering, imagining, conceiving, judging, reasoning. The cognitive function, as an ultimate mode or aspect of the conscious life, is contrasted with the affective and conative – feeling and willing . . . .

Eysenck (2003: 24): Cognitive psychologist look at topics such as memory, perception, thought, language, attention and so on. In other words they are interested in mental processes and seek to explain behaviour in terms of these mental processes.

Wagner (2008): Cognitive psychology is the branch of psychology that studies mental processes including how people think, perceive, remember, and learn. As part of the larger field of cognitive science, this branch of psychology is related to other disciplines including neuroscience, philosophy, and linguistics. The core focus of cognitive psychology is on how people acquire, process, and store information. There are numerous practical applications for cognitive research, such as ways to improve memory, how to increase decision-making accuracy, and how to structure educational curricula to enhance learning. (http://psychology.about.com/od/cognitivepsychology/f/cogpsych.htm, accessed 12 June 2008).

Cognitive psychology is chiefly concerned with experimental investigation of those mental processes to do with knowing and understanding which can either be brought readily into consciousness or revealed experimentally through careful manipulation of variables.

Cognitive science is a global term for an approach to understanding cognitive processes which includes cognitive psychology, neurological approaches, philosophy, linguistics, artificial intelligence (AI) and other aspects of cybernetics and computer modelling. Leiber (1991) argues that cognitive science approaches questions about thought and thinking, about consciousness and computation, according to the assumption that whatever the human brain does can be done by other materials.

Cybernetics is the science of systems of control and communications. The applications within cognitive science involve modelling of cognitive processes using special purpose models which can be analogue, mathematical, statistical or other kinds which can be carried out by computer programmes. Automata or robots may also be used.

Cognitive neuropsychology focuses on the way in which the brain and nervous system behaves during cognitive thought processes. One of the most useful approaches has been in the use of neural nets which parallel the interactions between neurones. This can assist in exploring the possible effects of having different numbers and types of synapses. Each system to be studied is said to be 'complex, dynamic, capable of "learning" and has feedback, feedforward or both' (Paritsis and Stewart, 1983: xi).

QAA

Cognitive psychology, e.g. perception, learning, memory, thinking, language, consciousness and cognitive neuropsychology. (Reproduced with permission from *Subject Benchmark Statement: Psychology 2007*. © The Quality Assurance Agency for Higher Education, 2007.)

BPS PAPER 1 SECTION 1 – COGNITIVE PSYCHOLOGY

Perception; visual information processing, auditory perception and speech recognition. Attention. Visual and spatial imagery. Comprehension. Conceptual knowledge. Learning. Skill acquisition and expertise. Memory; encoding and retrieval processes, working, autobiographical, episodic and semantic memory, implicit and explicit memory, memory improvement. Thinking and reasoning, problem solving, decision-making. Language; structure, comprehension, production, reading. Connectionist models. Emotion and cognition.

BPS PAPER 4 Option 5 – Cognitive psychology

Current accounts of perception, cognition, memory and language understanding. Human cognitive neuropsychology. Emotion and Cognition. Artificial intelligence and computational models of cognition (including connectionist models). Applied problems, for example eye-witness testimony, human–computer interaction, cognitive failure. (With permission.)

Cognitive approaches began with the Gestalt school of psychology (see Part 4.1 and below) in the 1920s and 1930s, formed in Austria and Germany and then spreading to America. Also in the 1920s interest in child development became important, with mental testing, the problem of 'backwardness' in schoolchildren, and Piaget's theory of cognitive development (see Parts 4.1 and 4.2). At first cognitive psychology was considered mostly as a reaction to the deterministism of psychoanalysis and behaviourism but took over as the dominant experimental approach in psychology after behaviourism passed its peak in the 1960s.

Cognitive approaches form the main perspective for the study of perception, which covers all the mental processes, conscious and unconscious, involved in paying attention and in recognition and interpretation. Studies of particular note include inverting goggles, impossible and ambiguous figures, illusions, perspective, constancy, depth perception, selective attention, perceptual *set*. Debates centre on the type of information processing involved in perception and the comparison of these processes with memory.

Understanding the processes of perception helps in appreciating the similarities and differences between people. In one way the individual's interpretation of surroundings is unique, depending on individual past experiences, needs and interests. On the other hand, there are recognisable patterns of perception which can help us to anticipate people's responses and plan accordingly. For example the colour scheme of a room can influence mood. Background sounds can invoke fear or reassurance depending on how they are organised and explained.

If something cold and wet touches your back while you are sunbathing, you are likely to react with a primitive response, either leaping up and away in a startled fashion or 'freezing' until the danger passes. The sense receptors in the middle of your back cannot tell you whether you have been attacked by a monster from the deep sea, a friendly dog, a bunch of seaweed or the hand of a friend. If you were brave enough to put your hand round behind your back without looking, the sense of *haptic* touch in your fingers could give more detailed information. Vision provides a much more comprehensive picture. Vision and hearing can give advance warning of an event which is about to happen and the opportunity for evasive action if necessary.

Vision seems instantaneous. We do not appear to have to 'feel round' an object with our eyes in the same way as we would with our hands, it seems as if we simply look and we know (see also *Affordances*). However, other evidence seems to indicate that we do have to go through a similar process of sorting out the outline, distinguishing an object from its background, assessing texture, colour, distance, patterns or special features and matching these up with previous experience. We pay attention to things that have importance for us individually, depending on our needs and interests. One of the current debates in cognitive psychology is whether perception involves mainly *top-down* or *bottom-up* information processing.

Emotion and cognition: Traditionally, emotion and cognition have been regarded as separate entities or domains. In the 19th century, Kant suggested that all psychological processes could be classified as *cognitive, conative* or *affective*, that is: thoughts; acts of will, volition or choice; and emotions. This classification has dominated psychology and has led to conceptions and theories of cognitions and emotions as separate processes, somehow influencing each other, rather than as different aspects of the same processes. Common sense suggests that cognition comes first. Faced with a dangerous situation such as encountering a bear, we know it is dangerous and then we feel afraid. Conversely, the James–Lange approach (from William James and Carl Lange independently in 1884) suggests that emotion comes before cognition: we see the bear, feel the *'fight or flight' arousal* and hence know we must be afraid. Lazarus (1982) proposes that faced with the stimulus, a mixture of unconscious processes and conscious awareness both of the stimulus and the emotional arousal lead to *cognitive appraisal*, which in turn, with further unconscious and conscious processes, leads to the emotional experience and the ability to name it.

Current thinking (for example Damasio, 1994, 2000) is moving towards an integration of emotion and cognition with the argument that we cannot have thoughts which are free from, or detached from, our emotional responses and it is the emotional association or quality that gives the thought *value* or gives a sense of urgency. This is sometimes referred to as emotional colouring or flavouring.

This approach allows a more complex analysis of cognitive restructuring than the *cognitive appraisal theory* suggests. *Cognitive therapy* may give rise to the introduction of new cognitions with a different emotional colouring. These do not automatically replace previous cognitions but need to be taken into the individual's scheme of looking at things.

Gestalt psychology is a school of thought in cognitive psychology that introduced the notion that 'the whole is greater than the sum of its parts'.

The German word *Gestalt* means an organised whole or pattern. This approach argues that in order to make sense of something we have to pay *attention* to the parts and integrate this information into a whole. The key elements identified are:

> similarity
> proximity
> continuity

> closure
> *figure-ground*
> part-whole relationship.

This means that when we look at a picture or diagram, we pay attention to marks that are similar to each other, we notice where things are close together, and we look to see whether there are any continuous flowing lines or shapes, even if these have gaps or spaces in them. In this way we can pick out a figure from its background, identify familiar shapes and see how each part relates to the whole picture. Moreover, for example, when we recognise a face we see the person, not a simple arrangement of eyes, nose and mouth. Furthermore, in order to analyse and understand the various components of a particular issue or event, it is important to understand the context of the event and put the components in perspective. An artist painting a portrait must know something of the person, not merely copy the features, in order to create a meaningful likeness. These processes are automatic and unconscious, and perception is spontaneous. Although the Gestalt principles do not provide the whole story, they provide some basic ideas for understanding perception. The Gestalt theory of *forgetting* says that memories are not lost but instead undergo qualitative changes over time, bringing them more into line with a cleaner, more streamlined view of the world. (Baddeley, 1976).

See Part 3 for; Abstract thinking; Accessibility; Acoustic store; Affordances; After-image; Ambiguous figures; Amnesia; Artificial intelligence; Attention; Availability; Beliefs; Bottom-up processing; Central executive system; Chunking; Cognitive appraisal; Cognitive map; Colour constancy; Colour of surroundings; Colour vision; Complexity theory; Computational theory of mind; Convergent thinking; Creativity; Cue dependence; Deduction; Depth perception; Dichotic listening; Divergent thinking; Dynamic memory theory; Efforts after meaning; Emotion; Enactive representation; Face recognition; False memory syndrome; Figure-ground reversal; Flashbulb memory; Forgetting; Frame problem; Grammatical representation; Hierarchical network model; Iconic representation; Iconic store; Identity constancy; Induced motion; Information processing; Insight; Interference; Lateral thinking; Levels of processing; Lightness constancy; Long-term memory; Means–end analysis; Memory span; Memory; Mental modules; Mentalese; Metacognition; Metamemory; Modality-specific; Motion parallax; Movement illusions; Muller–Lyer illusion; Multi-store (dual process) model; Necker cube; Overlearning; Paired-associate learning; Paradoxical figures; Parallel processing; Pattern recognition; Perception; Perceptual constancy; Perceptual disorders; Perceptual set; Phi phenomenon; Phonological loop; Phonological suppression; Preconception; Primacy effects; Problem-solving; Procedural memory; Prospective memory; Recall; Recency effects; Recognition; Reconstruction; Redintegration; Rehearsal; Relearning; Reminiscence; Remote memory; Retention; Retrieval; Semantic memory; Serial processing; Serial reproduction; Shape constancy; Short-term memory; Signal detection theory; Size constancy; Slave systems; Structural components; Subliminal perception; Syllogism; Symbolic representation; Synthesis; Thinking; Top-down processing; Transfer; Value; Visual distortions; Visual fictions; Visual illusions; Visual images; Visuo-spatial sketchpad (Scratchpad); Working memory; Triggers.

See Part 4 for Atkinson and Shiffrin, Baddeley and Hitch, Bartlett, Blakemore, Broadbent, Craik and Lockhart, De Bono, Deutsch and Deutsch, Ebbinghaus, Gibson and Walk, Gregory, Hebb, Kahneman, Loftus, Miller, Pinker, Shiffrin, Sperry, Treisman, Wason and Johnson-Laird.

2.2.3: Developmental and lifespan psychology/educational and child psychology

Developmental psychology and educational psychology are separate disciplines with considerable overlap. Traditionally developmental psychology considered only babies and children but has moved on in many places to consider development throughout the lifespan. With our ageing population there is growing interest in developmental changes in later years. Educational psychology draws on developmental theories in applications to teaching and learning.

The study of thinking and problem-solving has been traditionally considered to be largely the province of cognitive psychology and the cognitive development of children. Other psychological perspectives had little formal relevance but it is now recognised that all perspectives can be seen to be important in terms of social interaction, communication and emotional content and, as with most psychology, the trend is towards integrating ideas under the umbrella of lifespan development.

Some definitions of thinking, problem-solving and creativity

Thomson (1959: 11–20): We all think from time to time. . . . We know very well how some of our thinking sticks to the point and moves steadily to its conclusion while other thinking runs round in circles or drifts off into blind alleys or gets bogged down. Some answers to problems come in a flash, while at other times we are confused and befuddled in spite of hard efforts. . . . Thinking can be regarded as a disposition – a complex co-ordination and integration of specific activities . . . . There are typical operations and systems or groups of operations examples of which can be recognised in any thought process. . . . The psychologist is interested in describing what people actually do when they are thinking and what conditions determine the precise pattern of their performance.

Barron (1965: 6): A man may think a thought which for him is a new thought, yet it may be one of the most common thoughts in the world when all thinkers are taken into account. His act is a creative act, but the 'something new' that is produced is something new in the population of thoughts he can claim as his own, not something new for mankind as a whole.

Runco and Albert (1990: 9, 266): There is a growing awareness of the complexities of the field of creativity, both conceptually and methodologically. . . . It would be helpful to teach all persons that failure is intrinsic to creative behaviour, and that continuous effort tailored to the lessons of failure, rather than the emotions of it, . . . would help remove, or at least reduce, a sense of helplessness and a passive belief and reliance on inspiration, chance, or blind luck as necessary elements of creativity.

Bransford and Stein (1993: xiii): an ideal problem solver is someone who continually attempts to improve by paying attention to his or her processes and by learning from any mistakes that are made.

A number of different ways of thinking can be identified: inner speech, mental images, thoughts without recognisable speech or images, logical processes, lateral connections, insight, intuition, acting out or doing, visual representation in writing, pictures and models, talking through. Some of these process can be clearly linked to activity in different

Developmental psychology, e.g. childhood, adolescence and life-span development, development of attachment, social relations, cognitive and language development, social and cultural contexts of development. (Reproduced with permission from *Subject Benchmark Statement: Psychology 2007*. © The Quality Assurance Agency for Higher Education, 2007.)

BPS PAPER 2 SECTION 2 – DEVELOPMENTAL PSYCHOLOGY

Research methods appropriate to the study of development. Nature of perceptual, motor and cognitive development during infancy. General theories of the nature and nurture of psychological attributes. Development of general representational abilities; especially language, drawing and number. Nature of cognitive change in the school years. Comparative analysis of constructivist, socio-cultural, and information processing theories of development. Development of self and identity. Gender socialisation. Emotional development.

BPS PAPER 4 OPTION 7 – DEVELOPMENTAL PSYCHOLOGY

Cognitive and social development during infancy. Inter-subjectivity and theories of mind during childhood. Constructivist, socio-cultural and information processing concepts of cognitive development. Literacy and schooling. Child abuse and family psychopathology. Ageing. Developmental research methodology. (With permission.)

BPS PAPER 4 OPTION 1– EDUCATIONAL PSYCHOLOGY

Psychological models and methods of assessment in educational settings. Psychological interventions with pupils with special educational needs, including learning and behaviour difficulties. Evaluation of classroom process, teacher effectiveness, school and organisational factors; social psychology of groups and organisations in education. Educational strategies relating to ethnic groups, gender and the role of parental involvement. (With permission.)

parts of the brain and there is evidence that the left and right hemispheres of the cortex process information in different ways (for example, Springer and Deutsch, 1993).

Each individual may use many or all of these methods, according to mood, interests and the type of task. Problem-solving abilities may depend on specialised knowledge in a particular discipline. The same individual may be both good and poor at problem-solving, depending on the sort of problem.

Some people may notice they have a preferred method of working, with a tendency to neglect other methods. It is suggested by various authors, for example, de Bono (1971), Buzan (1988), Bransford and Stein (1993), that all types of thinking and problem-solving can be regarded as skills which can be practised and improved and that awareness of one's own processes (metacognition) greatly assists development.

The psychology of child development began in the early 20th century as an outcome of the focus on childhood in Freudian analysis and on genetic inheritance in Darwin's theory of evolution. In the UK and United States, mental tests were developed that used statistical methods to correlate mental traits and give normative data for the population. These were used extensively in schools to try to address the problem of backwardness, and in job selection and the armed forces. While working with these tests, Piaget formed his theory of cognitive development. His notion of the stages of development and the need for 'discovery' learning rather than rote learning greatly influenced the nature of the early school years. (See also Parts 4.1 and 4.2.) Later theories, such as those of Bruner, Vygotsky and G. H. Mead, while contradicting his findings, are indebted to his radical ideas.

Piaget identified what he saw as stages in development as children moved from giving 'incorrect' to 'correct' answers to questions. He believed that children could not think logically and must have experience of events before they can develop the language to describe them and thus learn best through unaided discovery. Conversely, Bruner argued that children use different styles of problem-solving and increase the number of styles as they develop, moving back and forth between these for different problems, as adults do. Bruner asserted that children need language before they can properly perceive and understand events, and learn best when instructed. Vygotsky supported the common-sense view that children and adults need a mixture of experience of events and appropriate language when learning new concepts and that we learn more quickly and extensively when assisted by someone who can already solve the problems. George Herbert Mead stressed the social aspects of children's learning.

Subsequent research builds on this debate and focuses on helping learners of all ages and abilities develop a positive attitude to learning and become independent and productive. There has been a shift away from convergent or closed problem-solving to divergent and creative thinking. There is fierce debate as to whether rote learning of 'rules' such as multiplication tables, spelling and grammar are essential tools or detrimental to creativity and self-esteem. School assessments are shifting away from essays to multiple choice and short answers, delaying the more advanced skills to later in the education system. Educational debate centres on when and how to introduce particular concepts and skills, drawing on psychological research on cognitive change and social and cultural aspects.

Other aspects of lifespan development involve socialisation, the development of social skills and language, acquisition of moral values and reasoning (see Kohlberg), emotional development, sex and gender identity (see Bem) and lifestyle choices.

See Part 1 for Felder and Solomon, Sternberg, Dweck and Entwhistle.
See also:
Part 2.2.4   Individual differences and human diversity.
Part 2.2.5   Social psychology.
Part 2.3.7   Cultural psychology.
Part 2.3.14   Lesbian and gay psychology.
Part 2.3.19   Psychology of women.
Part 2.3.22   Teaching and researching in psychology.
See Part 3 for Abstract thinking; Accommodation; Ageing; Altered body image; Animism; Assimilation; Attachment and bonding; Attitudes; Broken information games; Centration; Concept; Concrete operations; Conservation; Creativity; Discovery learning; Egocentric; Enactive representation; Equilibration; Face recognition; Fantasy play; Formal operations; Formative years; Frame problem; Group of displacements and reversibility; Iconic representation; Metacognition; Metamemory; Motivation; Object concept; Parenting; Play; Preconception; Schema; Sensori-motor; Seriation.

See Part 4 for Ainsworth, Bandura, Bem, Bowlby, Bernstein, Bruner, Bryant, Burt, De Bono, Donaldson, Elliot, Erikson, Freud, Gibson and Walk, Gilligan, Harlow, Kohlberg, Piaget, Rutter, Vygotsky.

2.2.4: Individual differences or human diversity

This approach draws together a wealth of information that allows us to look in some depth at the individual and the differences between individuals. The main topics are emotion, intelligence, motivation and personality, together with notions of mental health or abnormal development. Research involves both idiographic and nomothetic studies (see Part 5), covers all the levels of enquiry (see above in Part 2.1) and encompasses behavioural, biological, cognitive, developmental, humanistic, psychodynamic and social psychology principles.

Some definitions of emotion, personality and self-image

Drever (1964): [Emotion is] a complex state of the organism, involving bodily changes of a widespread character – in breathing, pulse, gland secretion, etc. – and, on the mental side, a state of excitement or perturbation, marked by strong feeling, and usually an impulse towards a definite form of behaviour.

Rubin and McNeil (1983): Emotions set the tone of our experience and give life its vitality and, like motives, they are internal factors which can energize, direct and sustain behaviour. (Cited in Gross, 1996.)

Stratton and Hayes (1993): [Emotion is] the experience of subjective feelings which have positive or negative value for the individual. . . . Most current theories regard emotions as a *combination* of physiological response with a cognitive evaluation of the situation. . . . Some definitions would reserve the term emotion for fairly intense and fairly brief experiences. . . . [Affect is] a term used to mean emotion, but covering a very much wider band of feeling than the *normal* emotions. Affect includes pleasurable sensation, friendliness and warmth, pensiveness, and mild dislike etc., as well as the extreme emotions such as joy, exhilaration, fear and hatred. Broadly speaking, affect refers to any category of feeling, *as distinct from* cognition or behaviour. [My italics.]

Williams et al (1988): Discussions of the relationship between cognition and emotion tend to focus either on the effects of emotion on cognitive processes or on the role of cognitive processes in the genesis of emotional states.

Robinson (1996): Cognition and affect are not separate processes but all cognitions are emotionally coloured which gives a sense of urgency to the cognition.

Peck and Whitlow (1975: 10): Some psychologists have defined personality very widely so that it covers virtually everything a person does, from how he solves problems and how he deals with incompatible thoughts, to changes in physiological functioning in response to emotion-rousing situations.

Ryckman (1989: 3): Despite the plethora of definitions, there is basic agreement among investigators that personality is a psychological construct: that is, a complex abstraction that includes the person's unique learning history and genetic background . . . and the ways in which these organized and integrated complexes of events influence his or her responses to certain stimuli in the environment. Thus, many investigators see the study of personality as the scientific study of individual differences that help to account for people's unique ways of responding to various situations.

approaches

Eysenck (1947: 2): Character denotes a person's more or less stable and enduring system of conative behaviour (will); temperament, his more or less stable and enduring system of affective behaviour (emotion); intellect, his more or less stable and enduring system of cognitive behaviour (intelligence); physique, his more or less stable and enduring system of bodily configuration and neuroendocrine endowment.

Millon and Everly (1985: 3): Personality . . . refers to the pattern of deeply embedded and broadly exhibited cognitive, affective, and overt behavioural traits that emerge from a complex biological–environmental formative matrix. This pattern persists over extended periods of time and is relatively resistant to extinction. Temperament, on the other hand, may be viewed as a biologically determined subset of personality . . . [and] character may be thought of as the person's adherence to the values and customs of the society in which he/she lives.

Price (1990: 12): We should like to believe that our self-image is congruous with, and is an expression of, our personality. Yet we also guess that our self-image is strongly affected by what other people think of us. Self-image then, is our own assessment of our social worth. It is composed of ideas of whether we are 'true unto ourselves' and whether others think we are worthwhile people. Self-image is important for our confidence, our motivation and our sense of achievement.

Rogers (1961): Self-concept includes self-image, ideal self and self-esteem.

The topics within this perspective were treated separately until the late 20th century, so it is a recent development to draw them together in a balanced consideration of the similarities and differences between people and move away from older notions of normal and abnormal. The shift in title in some establishments from 'Individual differences' to 'Human diversity' indicates a further desire to regard everyone equally.

QAA

Personality and individual differences, e.g. abnormal and normal personality, psychological testing, intelligence, cognitive style, emotion, motivation and mood. (Reproduced with permission from *Subject Benchmark Statement: Psychology 2007*. © The Quality Assurance Agency for Higher Education, 2007.)

BPS PAPER 3 SECTION 1 – INDIVIDUAL DIFFERENCES

Key assumptions of, and sources of evidence for, the main approaches to emotion, motivation, the self and normal and abnormal personality development, including; psychoanalytic, behavioural, cultural, social learning, social cognitive, radical behaviourist, humanistic-existential-phenomenological, lexical-trait, neo Darwinist, biological and behavioural genetic. Influence of genetic, environmental and cultural factors on individual differences. Temporal and situational consistency of individual differences. Influence of personality on other behaviours including; health; education; culture; relationships; occupational choice and competency. History of mental and psychological testing. The nature of intelligence, contemporary approaches to intelligence and their implications for educational and social policy. (With permission.)

Emotion, intelligence and motivation are core concepts. Arguments include whether emotion can be separated from cognition (see Part 2.2.2 and *cognitive appraisal theory* in Part 3), to what extent personality can change and to what extent intelligence can be learned.

Studies of personality, self-concept and person perception are usually presented in different chapters or sections of textbooks even though the subject matter overlaps considerably. They generally include consideration of how we see ourselves, how others see us, how we think others see us and how we see others. Approaches are derived from social psychology, cognitive psychology and from humanistic and psychodynamic therapies. Although the definitions above point towards personality as consisting of stable and enduring characteristics, most people are aware of their own fluctuations and variations with mood and with the situation and the other people who are present. Attribution theory illustrates how important the context is in determining what we notice about a person and how we interpret our own and other people's behaviour. Studies of groups show how adherence to group norms and expectations influences behaviour irrespective of individual differences. The effectiveness of psychological interventions and therapies is dependent on certain characteristics being amenable to change, and it is open to debate whether the constructs of personality which have developed during the 20th century are really the most useful ways of describing individuals.

Many approaches to the study of self-concept and person perception involve descriptions of personality traits such as friendly, warm, withdrawn or shy, but there is considerable controversy over whether such traits can be measured systematically, and whether they occur in clusters which can be identified as 'personality types' or are essentially individual. As with other aspects of self-concept, we may gain an awareness of our personality through feedback from others and by comparing ourselves with others. In addition, we may choose to fill in questionnaires purporting to assess personality, either from a professional psychometric agency or from a popular magazine, or even accept descriptions given by astrology. When we look at other people, we use all our social and personal understanding of how people think, feel and act in order to make sense of their personalities.

Mental health is not a single topic but covers a range of issues from diagnosis to treatment and care. Mental health practitioners, nurses, counsellors and psychotherapists often try to take a positive, humanistic and holistic view of the people in their care, focusing on the person rather than on the diagnosis of an illness. Psychology tends to approach this area from the medical point of view of abnormality or mental disorders or psychopathology.

As with other approaches to individual differences all levels of enquiry are pursued and all behavioural, biological, cognitive, developmental, humanistic, psychodynamic and social psychology principles can be involved.

See also:
Part 2.2.3   Developmental psychology.
Part 2.2.5   Social psychology.
Part 2.3.1   Behaviourism/behavioural science.
Part 2.3.7   Cultural psychology.
Part 2.2.8   Ecological and environmental psychology.
Part 2.3.9   Evolutionary psychology.
Part 2.2.11   Health psychology.
Part 2.3.13   Humanistic psychology.

Part 2.3.18   Psychodynamic psychology.

See Part 3 for Abnormal; Affect; Affective disorders; Aggression; Anger; Anxiety; Attachment and bonding; Attitudes; Authoritarian personality; Autism; Catharsis; Character; Cognitive appraisal theory; Congruence; Container for emotions; Creativity; Defence mechanisms; Dissociative disorder; Dissociative identity disorder; Emotion; Emotional intelligence; Empathy; Extroversion; Facial expressions; Factitious illness; Five-factor model of personality; Freudian slip; Gender; Gender identity; Grief; Hardiness; Implicit personality theory; Inspection time; Intelligence; IQ; Introversion; Leakage; Learned helplessness; Limbic system; Mood; Motivation; Non-verbal communication; Personal construct theory; Personality traits; Personality types; Personality; Play; Pleasure principle; Power; Projective techniques; Psychogenic illness; Psychosexual stages; Psychosomatic; Rationalisation; Reaction formation; Repertory grid; Schizophrenia; Self-concept; Self-efficacy; Self-esteem; Self-fulfilling prophecy; Self-image; Sensitisation; Sex; Sexuality; Sublimation; Subjective; temperament; Thematic apperception test; Transference; Type A behaviour pattern; Unconditional positive regard; Value.

See Part 4 for Adler, Adorno, Ainsworth, Allport, Bandura, Baron-Cohen, Berne, Bion, Bowlby, Burt, Cattell, Ellis, Erikson, Eysenck, Fromm, Harlow, Horney, James, Jung, Kelley, Kelly, Klein, Kraepelin, Lacan, Laing, Maslow, Perls, Rogers, Rorschach, Sacks, Seligman, Sheldon, Winnicott.

See Part 5 for idiographic, nomothethic.

2.2.5: Social psychology

Social psychology covers all those areas of human behaviour concerned with interaction and communication in everyday social settings and can be considered to be an academic discipline in its own right as well as a subdivision of psychology. The main topics are language and communication, person perception and attributions, attitudes and attitude change, conformity and obedience, group structures and processes, and organisations (see Part 3). Social psychology may also be combined with biology to give a biosocial or biopsychosocial approach. A related approach is cultural psychology and allied to all these is ethnography, the qualitative study of a group of people, including the language and cultural norms. This kind of study aims to describe and analyse the ways in which people use their language to represent concepts and categorise the meaning of their world in a cultural context.

Some definitions of social psychology

Tajfel and Fraser (1978: 19) state that the aim of social psychology is to analyse and understand human social behaviour. 'Social behaviour, as we observe it, is the product of [a] balance between the "universal" and the "culture-specific"; this is true both of individual behaviour and of certain features of social organization which affect masses of people sharing a common cultural setting of their lives'.

Argyle (1983: 11) suggests that 'it looks as if social behaviour is the product of at least seven different drives ... biological needs, dependency, affiliation, dominance, sex, aggression, self-esteem and ego-identity'.

Abraham and Shanley (1992: 1) say that social psychology is about understanding people and what they do. 'It is the study of how people behave in everyday social settings. It focuses upon what happens between people; how they interact. It attempts to discover patterns in this interaction and thereby poses questions about the kinds of beings we are; questions about what controls and regulates our everyday activity'.

Aronson (1992) states that social psychology is about social influence.

In the mid-1920s social psychology research began to take a firm hold in psychology. An important publication was *Social Psychology* by Floyd Allport (1924), see Part 4.2.

Most social psychology books are not classified in the library with general psychology (which developed from roots in philosophy) but catalogued alongside other social sciences, such as education, sociology and politics. There is considerable overlap with sociology, but whereas sociology provides a wide perspective of groups and organisational structures, patterns and development, social psychology focuses on the individual's day to day behaviour within these structures. Moreover, social psychology, unlike the other social sciences, adopts experimental techniques and quantitative research methods wherever relevant.

Studies of groups show how adherence to group norms and expectations influences behaviour irrespective of individual differences. The study of groups is central to social psychology and of importance to professional psychologists who are likely to become involved with, or participate in, a variety of groups during their career. Examples of these include: families, training groups where members learn from the group leader and from each other, professional groups which exist to accomplish particular goals, and therapeutic groups where members attempt to help each other in some way.

A group is generally considered as two or more people who have something in common which links them in some way in a particular context such that they can be seen, either by themselves or by others, to belong to a group. It is usually argued that a group is more than just a collection of individuals and that each individual may behave very differently when in it or outside it. Brown (1988) says it is hard to imagine a group in which its members do not at some stage mentally classify themselves as actually belonging to it. In psychology, this has interesting implications and may be strongly linked to the concept of *labelling*. When a person is diagnosed as, say, having agoraphobia, the professional may have a mental classification of 'agoraphobics' as a group with certain characteristics. An individual may not at first share this conception and not have any sense of belonging to a group. However, continued exposure to the label 'agoraphobia', media-expressed stereotypes and the awareness of self-help groups may bring about identification as an 'agoraphobic'. It can be argued that such group identification has some advantages and some disadvantages. Behaviour of group members tends to become uniform and this can lead to stereotyping and expectations concerning the group label.

There are probably almost as many definitions of communication as there are writers on the subject but accounts agree that communication is a basic non-stop human activity for getting and giving out information. This information is conveyed through organised systems or codes. These codes may consist of a relatively unstructured collection of signs or a more elaborate language.

A distinction can be made between *primary representation* of the world, which is our immediate perceptual experience, and *secondary representation,* which is how we communicate about that experience. Bandler and Grinder (1975) demonstrate that there is always a 'slippage' between the two.

Within therapy, much of the therapeutic process in concerned with developing a shared means of communication between therapist and client and finding ways for communicating thoughts and feelings which have hitherto been inaccessible to the client's conscious awareness or are difficult for the client to express or articulate.

See also

Part 2.3.7   Cultural psychology

Part 2.3.8   Ecological and environmental psychology

See Part 3 for Aggression; Altered body image; Altruism; Anger; Anger management; Animism; Assertiveness; Attitude development; Attitude questionnaires; Attitudes; Attribution theory; Attributions; Bales interaction process analysis; Body boundaries; Body image; Cognitive dissonance; Conformity; Crowds; Depersonalisation; Desensitisation; Discrimination; Empowerment; Eye-witness testimony; Facial expressions; False consensus; False consistency; Fundamental attribution error; Gender identity; Gender; Group development; Group initiation rituals; Group processes; Halo and horns effects; Ideal self; Instrumental; Person perception; Leadership; Leading questions; Leakage; Modelling; Non-verbal communication; Norms; Obedience; Paralanguage; Parenting skills; Parenting styles; Peer group; Power; Punishment; Recency effects; Reward; Self-concept; Self-efficacy; Self-esteem; Self-fulfilling prophecy; Self-image; Social constructionism; Social learning theory; Social roles; Sociograms; Symbolic interactionism; Vicarious learning; Weapons effect.

See Part 4 for Adorno, Allport, Aronson, Asch, Bales, Bandura, Bernstein, Chomsky, Elliot, Ebbinghaus, Festinger, Kelley, Labov, Lacan, Lacan, LaPiere, Latané, Milgram, Osgood, Sapir and Whorf, Schachter, Sherif, Tajfel, Triandis, Zimbardo.

2.3 Other approaches

2.3.1: Behaviourism/behavioural science

Behaviourism developed in the 1920s as a reaction to other early types of psychology, such as introspection, and reached its heyday in the 1960s. Psychology, particularly in the United States, was sometimes referred to as 'behavioural science'. It has now largely been superseded by cognitive science.

Behaviourism proposes an objective approach to the study of human behaviour and aims to explain, predict and control behaviour by exploring the extent to which environment determines behaviour, including speech. This school of thought, or perspective, considers only observable, measurable phenomena and does not take account of accompanying thoughts or mental activities, regarding mental processes and the mind as unknown and unknowable (a black box) whose presence can only be inferred.

A key assumption of the school of behaviourism is that learning takes place by conditioning and that this learned behaviour can be described in terms of stimulus–response units (S–R units). That is, learning can be seen to have taken place whenever a particular response predictably follows a particular stimulus without the need for conscious effort or will.

There are two types of conditioning, one which just happens passively through repeated exposure to associated stimuli (classical conditioning, associated with Pavlov), the other in which actions are reinforced (operant or instrumental conditioning, associated with Skinner). Both of these can also be thought of as 'trial and error' learning.

A related approach is social learning theory (associated with Bandura), which is an extension and development of behavioural principles that takes social interaction into consideration. Other aspects of animal behaviour such as instincts and imprinting are covered in comparative psychology.

Various interesting results emerged from the early studies with animals. For example, behaviour learned in connection with intermittent reinforcement takes much longer to extinguish than behaviour that has been conditioned by regular reinforcement. Punishment, which is often naively assumed to be a deterrent, does not necessarily lead to extinction of previously learned actions and may be found to reinforce unwanted behaviour.

If we extend these findings to people, we might say that when 'socialising' children, it is likely that predictable *rewards*, such as sweets or regular praise for good behaviour (or good school results), will be less effective in reinforcing that behaviour than an irregular and unpredictable assortment of attention, occasional treats and the child's own evident pleasure in the activity. Reinforcement is more successful if it meets intrinsic rather than superficial or extrinsic needs and interests. If sweets come to be expected, then good behaviour may not be forthcoming without them. Regular praise can sound empty and patronising and, if too predictable, may not leave anything to strive for. Genuine pleasure that erupts occasionally and spontaneously in response to new actions may be a better reinforcer. Ignoring mildly naughty behaviour and diverting the child to desirable activities and giving added attention is likely to be more effective than punishment. Frequent predictable punishment, even if painful, frustrating or humiliating, may well provide much-needed attention and act as a reinforcer.

One of the main problems with applying many of the behavioural principles to human behaviour lies in the difficulty in identifying what needs are likely to be met by the available reinforcers. It can be helpful to refer to Maslow's *(1962) hierarchy of needs* (see Part 3) to see that an extensive range of psychological needs exists beyond the basic needs for food and freedom investigated by Skinner and Thorndike.

Behaviourism is no longer considered an adequate explanation for human behaviour. Opposition to behaviourism comes from cognitive, social, humanistic and psychodynamic perspectives, in all of which it is argued that most learning does not occur in isolation from social interaction, emotional and cognitive processes.

Evolutionary psychology argues that many patterns are inherited, having been established through natural selection, for example natural fears of snakes, thunder or open spaces. Adult phobias are more likely to be a persistence of these fears, not a conditioned response or acquired through social learning, while many people have 'unlearned' the fears through social interaction.

Today, where behavioural principles are applied in therapy, they are nearly always used in a way that acknowledges the clients' cognitions, emotions and lifestyle. Behavioural programmes are often combined with cognitive therapy. Moreover, since conditioning is seen as being beyond conscious control, the principles of behaviourism offend anyone who holds that humans, if not other animals, can exercise free will and are not just automata responding mindlessly to reinforcement of basic needs. Behaviourism does not leave any room for notions of freedom or free will and cannot adequately explain artistic practice.

One type of criticism comes from asserting that behaviourism states that complex behaviour such as stopping at a red traffic signal is the result merely of classical conditioning or operant behaviour shaping. It is easy to see that this cannot be true in any simplistic way since we are able to choose whether or not to stop on any particular occasion. However, it may well be true that some of the steps of learning that lead to complex behaviours are, at least to some extent, conditioned.

See also Part 3 for Anger; Anger management; Behaviour therapies; Behaviour shaping; Blank slate/*tabula rasa*; Classical conditioning; Cognitive map; Extinction; Learning theory; Mediators; Operant conditioning; Punishment; Reinforcement; Reinforcement schedules; Reward.

See Part 4 for Bandura, Pavlov, Skinner, Tolman, Watson.

2.3.2: Clinical psychology

The BPS describes clinical psychology as aiming to:

reduce psychological distress and enhance and promote psychological well-being. A wide range of psychological difficulties may be dealt with, including anxiety, depression, relationship problems, learning difficulties, child and family problems, and serious mental illness.

BPS PAPER 4 OPTION 2 – CLINICAL PSYCHOLOGY

Concepts of psychological health and ill-health. Theoretical understandings of the causes of, and maintaining factors in, psychological problems. Psychological therapies including behavioural, cognitive, social, humanistic, systemic and dynamic. Psychological interventions with adults, children, older adults and people with learning disabilities. Work with individuals, groups and families, in a range of health care settings. Rehabilitation, community psychology and health promotion. (With permission.)

To assess a client, a clinical psychologist may undertake a clinical assessment using a variety of methods, including psychometric tests, interviews and direct observation of behaviour. Assessment may lead to therapy, counselling or advice.

Clinical psychologists work largely in health and social care settings, including hospitals, health centres, community mental health teams, child and adolescent mental health services and social services. They usually work as part of a team with, for example, social workers, medical practitioners and other health professionals. Most clinical psychologists work in the National Health Service, which has a clearly defined career structure, but some work in private practice.

The work is often directly with people, either individually or in groups, assessing their needs and providing therapies based on psychological theories and research. Clinical psychology is a rapidly developing field, and adding to the evidence base through research is very important. Some clinical psychologists work as trainers, teachers and researchers in universities.' (Reproduced with permission from the BPS booklet *So You Want to Be a Psychologist,* available on their website.)

To achieve these aims, clinical psychology draws on all the core approaches of biological, cognitive, developmental, individual differences and social psychology as well as behavioural science, counselling, health psychology, humanistic and psychodynamic approaches and all other relevant research.

See Part 3 for: Affect; Affective disorders; Ageing; Aggression; Altered state of consciousness (ASC); Amnesia; Anger; Anger management; Attitude; Anxiety; Arousal systems; Autism; Behaviour (or behavioural) therapies; Brain damage; Brain imaging; Cognitive distortion; Cognitive impairment (dysfunctional cognition); Cognitive therapy; Dementias; Depression; Dissociative disorder; Dissociative identity disorder; ECT (electroconvulsive therapy) EEG (electroencephalograph); Empowerment; Factitious illnesses; False memory syndrome (recovered memories); Groups; Learned helplessness; Motivation; Parenting styles; Power; Rorscharch psychodiagnostic test; Schizophrenia; Visual neglect.

See Part 4 for Baron-Cohen, Kraepelin, Rutter, Sacks.
See Part 6 for becoming a chartered clinical psychologist.

2.3.3: Coaching psychology

Coaching psychology is a relatively new applied branch of psychology that applies psychological principles and research in coaching and mentoring in a number of contexts. There is a wealth of information on the Internet. Below are a few useful sites.

The BPS website (http://www.bps.org.uk/coachingpsy/coachingpsy_home.cfm) says:

> The term 'coaching' has become one of the popular names now used for the application of psychologically focussed techniques for both life and business improvement. The SGCP [Special Group in Coaching Psychology] has now been established to provide psychologists who are members of the British Psychological Society with an easy and effective means of sharing research as well as practical experiences that relate to the psychology of coaching . . .
>
> The SGCP is committed to demystifying the services offered by Psychologists within the Coaching marketplace. We aim to provide easier access to psychological resources to assist HR Directors, Non-psychologist coaches as well as individual purchasers of coaching services to both find and use psychological services more effectively. [With permission.]

The Australian Psychology Society (APS) (http://www.groups.psychology.org.au/igcp/) states that:

> Coaching Psychology . . .can be understood as being the systematic application of behavioural science to the enhancement of life experience, work performance and well-being for individuals, groups and organisations who do not have clinically significant mental health issues or abnormal levels of distress.

The Coaching and Mentoring Network (http://www.coachingnetwork.org.uk/resourcecentre/WhatAreCoachingAndMentoring.htm) defines both coaching and mentoring as 'processes that enable both individual and corporate clients to achieve their full potential', and suggests that:

> The key difference between coaching and the therapies is that coaching does not seek to resolve the deeper underlying issues that are the cause of serious problems like poor motivation, low self-esteem and poor job performance. Coaching and mentoring programmes are generally more concerned with the practical issues of setting goals and achieving results within specific time-scales.

Their website gives information on what coaching and mentoring entail in business, management, performance, skills, sport, job roles, personal 'life' coaching and other contexts.

The Centre for Coaching, established in 2001, (http://www.centreforcoaching.com/) has a Faculty of Coaching Psychology with chartered psychologists who teach and supervise in an International coaching training centre and consultancy for coaches, managers, trainers, psychologists, health and HR professionals in the United Kingdom.

The Coaching Psychology Unit at City University, established in 2005 (http://www.city.ac.uk/psychology/research/CoachPsych/CoachPsych.html) focuses on encouraging research into all aspects of the developing field of coaching psychology and coaching.

2.3.4: Comparative psychology

Comparative psychology is the study of non-human animals in order to compare them with humans. Areas of interest include:

> problem-solving
> tool use
> language (including teaching human language to animals)
> memory
> culture
> emotions
> morality
> personality
> theory of mind.

Related disciplines include ecology (particularly primatology), which is the comparative study of animal behaviour in its natural setting, dating back to the 1930s, and evolutionary psychology.

We used to think we were entirely separate from other animals with special and unique traits. However ethology, captivity and laboratory studies are revealing that different species exhibit many of our attributes in one way or another.

Primatology is the study of primates. These include monkeys, gibbons, gorillas, chimpanzees, bonobos and orang-utans. (N.B. The term is often miss-spelled as primotology – even by the BPS – but that spelling is normally used to refer to mystic studies.)

Since the 1960s and chimpanzees like Washoe (see Fouts, 1997) we have known that chimps can learn sign language. Research demonstrates that they, like gorillas and other apes, use natural gestures with visual and auditory signs, both in the wild and in response to humans. Although apes have a range of meaningful vocal sounds and can use these in different combinations they do not have recognisable speech and it is not clear why this is so. Chiefly it is thought that it is because they do not have a well-developed or 'descended' larynx that would enable a wider range of different vowel and consonant sounds. However, the larynx is not unique to humans and cannot be given as an evolutionary explanation for speech. Some other animals such as lions and koalas do have a permanently descended larynx and other animals such as dog, goats, pigs and monkeys can pull the larynx into a lower position in order to vocalise (*New Scientist*, Vol. 198, No. 2657, 24 May 2008: 28–34).

The study of problem-solving in animals dates back to the early 20th century with Gestalt psychology. Apes were found capable of discovering the solution to a practical problem such as using a stick to reach a banana that was out of reach or setting a rope swinging in order to catch it from a distance. Gestalt explanations favoured 'insight' or a sudden 'aha' experience but it is argued that solutions may come from previous experience or trial and error. Ethology shows that many animals use tools in a range of contexts and can teach each other how to use them. For example, it has long been known that thrushes find a flat stone on which to smash snails, birds have been seen to place nuts at an intersection and wait for cars to drive over and crack them open, and one kind of crow can use intricately shaped leaves to hook insects out of crevices (*New Scientist*, as above).

Evidence of group patterns of behaviour that we can describe as culture are found not only in primates but also in cetaceans. For example, killer whales have distinct ways of greeting each other and other ways of communicating according to which group they belong to and can teach their offspring (*New Scientist*, as above).

Animals show behaviour that we can describe as 'moral' in the ways that they share food, defend resources, groom each other and give care. Elephants, baboons, whales and chimps all show varying kinds of emotional response. Variations between animals within a species indicate characteristics that we might label as temperament or personality: that is, whether they are adventurous or retiring or are easily startled, features that have long been known to animal trainers and pet owners and are now being researched systematically.

To test whether an animal has 'theory of mind' – that is, if it has a sense of self as distinct from others and can appreciate that others may not share the same beliefs – we can observe whether it can recognise itself in a mirror or deliberately set out to deceive others. One mirror test involves putting a blob of red paint on the ape's (or human baby's) nose and seeing if it reaches up to touch its nose. Animals are known to demonstrate deceit but it is not yet clear whether any of this is explicit and deliberate in the same way as human behaviour.

See also:

Part 2.2.2   Cognitive psychology (for Gestalt theory).

Part 2.3.1   Behaviourism.

Part 2.3.9   Evolutionary psychology.

See Part 3 for Aggression; Altruism; Appeasement gesture; Attachment and bonding; Emotion; Gesture; Insight; Instinct; Motivation; Personality; Problem-solving; Temperament; Theory of mind.

See Part 4 for Goodall, Harlow, Hubeland Wiesel, Kohler, Lorenz, Thorndike, Tinbergen.

2.3.5: Consciousness and experiential psychology

Consciousness was the original focus of psychological research and is once more a central topic of enquiry. The growth of interest and research over recent years has been explosive, and to foster this development a new section of the British Psychological Society, the Consciousness and Experiential Psychology Section (CEP) was formed in 1997. Its purpose is to advance our understanding of consciousness, to bring scientific research on consciousness closer to other traditions of inquiry into the nature of mind, and to explore how this research can be used to improve the quality of life.

(http://www.bps.org.uk/conex/consciousness-experiential_home.cfm, accessed September 2007, reproduced with permission)

The study of consciousness is an area of psychology very much interrelated with and dependent on philosophy and biological physics, and the concept of consciousness is one that has occupied and puzzled philosophers and scientists throughout history.

It is difficult to relate our perceptions of awareness of ourselves and our mental processes to what is known about the functioning of the central nervous system. There is a need to know whether our mental experiences bring about changes in our brain functioning, or whether changes in brain functioning bring about certain experiences, or whether there is always a mixture of both, or whether both are created by something else, at present unknown.

Some definitions of Cartesian dualism and consciousness

Ayer (1963: 82) quotes Descartes' view that a person is a combination of two separate entities, a body and a mind or soul. Only the mind is conscious; the physical properties that a person has are properties of his body. The two entities are separate in the sense that there is no logical connection between them.

Dennet (1991) says that we must abandon the dualism of mind and body that is our legacy from Descartes and the idea that there is some part of the brain that is the seat of consciousness.

McGinn (1993) suggests that neural transmissions just seem like the wrong kind of materials with which to bring consciousness into the world, but it appears that in some way they perform this mysterious feat. The mind–body *problem* is the problem of understanding how the miracle is wrought, thus removing the sense of deep mystery.

Pinker (1998) argues that the mind is not the brain itself but what the brain does. He advocates a *computational or information-processing theory of mind* (see Part 3) and suggests that evolution led to a mind that consists of a number of separate entities that perform separate functions.

Gregory (1981: 499) argues that we would expect theories of consciousness to be related to theories of *perception*. . . . [T]hen we may suspect that our knowledge of ourselves is a construction; perhaps very much as perceptions are hypotheses of the physical world.

Chalmers (1995) distinguishes between what he calls the 'easy problems' and the 'hard problem' of consciousness. The easy problems are those to do with how a person integrates information and responds appropriately, including talking about what is happening; the hard problem concerns what we actually mean by subjective experience. Chalmers suggests that some philosophers are addressing only the easy problems and that consciousness may be a fundamental in itself, not reducible to anything more basic, and requiring new principles to explain it.

Social psychology looks at the ways in which we communicate our ideas and feelings and how we influence each other. This includes study of the language which we use to try to convey our inner experiences and by which we infer what another person is experiencing. This language-based awareness seems to be at least part of what we mean by consciousness.

We are aware that we can shift from one state of consciousness to another and that our experience of ourselves and of the world varies according to mood, drowsiness, sleep, hypnosis and the effects of drugs. Increased awareness of what to look for and awareness of our own processes (metacognition, metamemory, metacommunication) can lead to greater access to processes which otherwise remain under autopilot.

We can compare the mind/brain activity with the Internet. There is a great deal going on, of which we can become aware of a tiny amount when we choose to or when it pops up, and there is no one in charge! We might think we are in charge of our mind as we direct our attention from one matter to another and order our thinking and planning, but we are certainly not in charge of all of our brain activity.

The main philosophical debate appears to be whether the Cartesian mind–body dualism is still an appropriate way of talking about consciousness, and if not what *paradigm* should now replace it. The Cartesian *dualists* talk in terms of the mind being quite separate from the body, others, the *reductionists*, in terms of mental activity arising from (or capable of being reduced to) the biological activity, and yet others, *monists* or *identity theorists*, that mind and brain are not separate at all but identical, with the concepts of mind and brain being simply two rather different descriptions of the same thing. So-called *'mysterians'* (Chalmers, 1995) assert that we will never understand consciousness at all. Gregory (1981, Ch 17) gives a useful review of some of the different approaches.

There are now many consciousness research groups, for example the Association for the Scientific Study of Consciousness, the Science and Consciousness Review and the Tucson Conferences. Not only psychologists but individuals from many different disciplines study consciousness, including philosophers, neuroscientists, physicists, engineers working in artificial intelligence, anthropologists and artists. Social psychology research can be contrasted with art, which endeavours to 'express the inexpressible'. Creative arts therapies explore different means of communicating about emotions and experiences, including dreams and altered states of consciousness, using methods which are not dependent on words, or which use words in special ways. There are also many ancient traditions for investigating consciousness that have developed in the East.

See also
    Part 2.2 1   Biological psychology.
    Part 2.2.2   Cognitive psychology.
    Part 2.2 5   Social psychology.
    Part 2.3.1   Behaviourism.
    Part 2.3.9   Evolutionary psychology.

Part 2.3.13 Humanistic psychology.

Part 2.3.18 Psychodynamic psychology.

See Part 3 for Altered state of consciousness (ASC); Apparition; Clairvoyance; Coma; Dreaming; EEG; False awakening; Hallucinations; Hypnosis; Lucid dream; Metachoric experiences; Out-of-the-body experiences; Paranormal; REM sleep; Sentience; Sleep cycles; Sleep.

See Part 4 for Baron-Cohen, Gregory; Kraepelin, Luria, Oswald, Pinker, Sacks.

2.3.6: Counselling psychology

On the whole, the term counselling is used in relation to clients with social, occupational, family or other situational problems, whereas the term psychotherapy is used when clients have serious mental health problems. However, in many contexts the terms psychotherapy and counselling are used interchangeably or according to the context or establishment in which the therapy takes place, rather than its form or the nature of the client's interests or problems.

Counselling psychologists are chartered psychologists who work in many different contexts, using a range of different psychometric, counselling and psychotherapeutic approaches.

It can be argued that although there are more than 400 distinct models of counselling and psychotherapy, there are three 'core' approaches; humanistic, cognitive-behavioural and psychodynamic, as shown in Figure 2.2. These represent fundamentally different ways of viewing people and their emotional and behavioural difficulties (McLeod, 1993).

The BPS Division of Counselling Psychology (DCoP) is the organisation devoted to furthering the development of counselling psychology, as a body of knowledge and skills and as a profession.

http;//www.bps.org.uk/dcop/dcop_home.cfm (accessed June 2008)

http;//www.bps.org.uk/careers/areas/counselling.cfm#what%20they%20do

The British Association of Counselling and Psychotherapy (BACP) distinguishes between counselling and counselling skills, and provides a separate code of ethics for practitioners who are not trained counsellors but who wish to use counselling skills in their workplace. http://www.bacp.co.uk/(accessed June 2008).

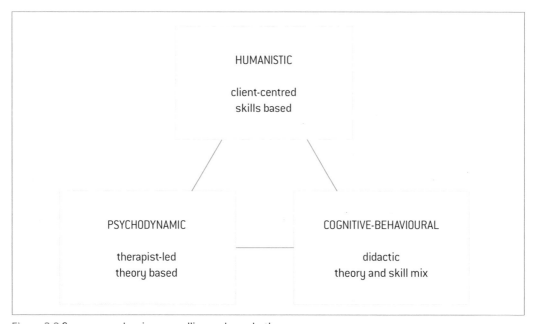

Figure 2.2 Core approaches in counselling and psychotherapy

This diagram exaggerates the extremes to enable different elements to be identified. In practice, many counsellors or therapists integrate styles and some cannot always say precisely what approach they are using at any one moment.

See also:

See Part 3 for Affect; Affective disorders; Altered body image; Altered state of consciousness (ASC); Amnesia; Anticipation; Anxiety; Arousal systems; Assertiveness; Attachment and bonding; Autism; Avoidance behaviour; Behaviour therapies; Body boundaries; Body image; Brain damage; Brain imaging; Catastrophising; Cognitive appraisal; Cognitive distortion; Cognitive impairment; Cognitive therapy; Colour of surroundings; Coping styles; Depression; Dissociative disorder; Dissociative identity Disorder; Dreaming; Empathy; Factitious illnesses; False memory syndrome; Grief; Hypnosis; Ideal self; Learned helplessness; Loss; Mood; Motivation; Post-traumatic stress disorder; Psychogenic illness; Secondary representation system; Self-concept; Self-efficacy; Self-esteem; Self-fulfilling prophecy; Self-image; Silence; Touch; Traps.

See Part 4 for Adler, Berne, Bion, Ellis, Erikson, Freud, Holmes and Rahe, Horney, Jung, Kelly, Klein, Lacan, Laing, Perls, Rogers, Rorschach, Seligman, Winnicott.

See Part 6 for becoming a chartered counselling psychologist.

2.3.7: Cultural psychology

Cultural psychology is a relatively new force in the field of psychology that takes psychology out of laboratory studies and controlled settings.

Hazel Markus argues that in early American psychology cultural factors may not have been as obvious and there was a certain 'uniformity' to social psychologists who tended to be white, middle-class men with similar training and perspectives. Only when students from different backgrounds began to enter psychology did the dominant culture become noticeable (http://www.learner.org/discoveringpsychology/26/e26 expand.html, accessed 22 August 2007).

The core principle of cultural psychology is that people's minds are products of their social communities and that there are different ways of being human.

BPS PAPER 4 OPTION 9 – CULTURAL PSYCHOLOGYY

Cognitive and social practices as mediated by various cultural resources. The role of tools, technologies and symbol systems in organising human action; interpersonal co-ordinations and psychological development. Learning under various formal or informal circumstances for guidance and teaching. Patterns of inequality and their psychological significance. Psychological influences of institutional cultures. Distributed cognition. (With permission.)

See also:

Part 2.2.5   Social psychology.

Part 2.3.8   Ecological and environmental psychology.

See Part 4 for Bernstein, Chomsky, Labov, Sapirand Whorf, Vygotsky.

See Part 7 for websites for information on activity theory and cultural-historical psychology that relate to new *paradigms* introduced by Vygotsky in the 1920s, and on distributed cognition, which is a branch of cognitive science developed in the 1990s by Edwin Hutchins that proposes that human knowledge and cognition are not confined to the individual but distributed by placing memories, facts or knowledge on the objects, individuals and tools in the environment.

approaches

2.3.8: Ecological and environmental psychology

Ecological psychology and environmental psychology are sometimes regarded as separate disciplines, sometimes as different names for the same or similar areas of research. Some see environmental psychology as an offshoot or subdiscipline of ecological psychology.

Other titles include environmental social sciences, architectural psychology, socio-architecture, ecopsychology, behavioural geography, environment–behaviour studies, person–environment studies, environmental sociology, social ecology and environmental design research.

The various names reflect the particular emphasis of a department or organisation and there is considerable overlap between them. All draw on work in a range of scientific and non-scientific disciplines, including ethology, anthropology, geography, sociology, psychology, history, political science, engineering, planning, architecture, urban design, ekistics (the scientific study of human settlements, from dwelling design to community, city and regional planning), philosophy and aesthetics.

Ecology is usually considered a branch of biology and is the scientific study of the distribution and abundance of living organisms and how these are affected by interactions between the organisms and their environment. The environment of an organism includes both physical properties and other organisms that share its habitat.

Ecological psychology focuses on the relationship between people and their environment and has a number of early strands. The two main ones are attributed to the writings of J. J. Gibson (see *affordances* in Part 3), and the work of Roger G. Barker, Herb Wright and associates at the University of Kansas in Lawrence (for example Barker and Wright, 1955). The latter is sometimes given as the forerunner of modern environmental psychology.

Departments of ecological psychology have varied histories of development and tackle the complex topic in different ways. For example The Ecological Psychology Research Group that was established in the Psychology Department at the University of Portsmouth in 1995 is in the process of merging with the Language, Culture and Mind Group, to form a new Research Centre for Ecology, Culture and Communication.

Ecopsychology is an alternative approach with its roots in Buddhism and other religious and philosophical traditions. This has the central Gaia theme of interdependence or connection that serves to sustain the balance of life on the planet.

Clinical ecology is a field of psychology that relates disorders such as anxiety and depression to environmental irritants and sources of trauma.

Environmental psychology takes as one of its key concepts the notion that all psychological processes are 'place-related' and 'place-dependent' and focuses on the effects of environmental conditions on behaviour and the ways in which an individual perceives and acts on the environment. This includes all that is natural on the planet as well as social settings, built environments, learning environments and informational environments. Research is problem-oriented.

According to the Environmental Psychology Research Group at Surrey, many of society's problems result from a 'breakdown of the relationship' between people in an environmental context, or 'between people and the physical environment itself' (http://www.surrey.ac.uk/Psychology/EPRG/, accessed 9 June 2008).

If we want to make sure that there is enough food, clothing, housing, employment and security, and that quality of life is good, then we need to go on investing in the planning, design, construction, management and use of the physical environment.

The Environmental Psychology Department at the University of Michigan proposes that environmental design and management should be based on 'a model of human nature that predicts the environmental conditions under which humans will behave in a decent and creative manner' (http;//www-personal.umich.edu/~rdeyoung/envtpsych.html, accessed 9 June 2008).

See Part 3 for Attention; Cognitive maps; Environmental stress and coping; Perception.

Other key concepts include Preferred environments; Participation, Conservation behaviour; Synomorphy (the shape and design of the places where group members interact shape their dynamics), Sociofugal (moving away from others/achieving privacy) and Sociopetal (moving towards/being able to see and interact with others).

See Part 7 for other useful websites.

2.3.9: Evolutionary psychology

Evolutionary psychology applies evolutionary theory to psychological phenomena and contemporary social issues.

Evolutionary psychology brings together two scientific revolutions. One is the cognitive revolution of the 1950s and 1960s, which explains the mechanics of thought and emotion in terms of information and computation. The other is the revolution in evolutionary biology of the 1960s and 1970s, which explains the complex adaptive design of living things in terms of selection among replicators (Pinker, 1998: 23).

Evolutionary theory

As biological organisms replicate (sexually), the resulting offspring contain chromosomes and genes (see Part 3) from each parent that encode a mix of characteristics that is different from either parent. Moreover, from generation to generation, mutations (alterations) in the genes can occur spontaneously so that new characteristics emerge.

In the natural world all organisms compete for food, safety and the ability to mate and reproduce. Those with the best characteristics survive and go on to have more offspring; the less successful variations die off. In this way new varieties of animals and plants develop, each with characteristics that are most suited to their environment. When some animals (or plants) find themselves in a new environment, only those with suitable characteristics will survive and reproduce. Hence different varieties will emerge in different environments.

This process is known as natural selection or 'survival of the fittest'. Everything that exists now has had the same chance. Successful things go on reproducing.

Misinterpretations

There are three main misinterpretations of evolutionary theory that tend to confuse people, particularly when they are not sure whether to believe the theory. The first two errors are known as Lamarckian, after Darwin's predecessor Jean Baptiste Lamarck:

> Use and disuse – Lamarck believed that characteristics that animals use will be reproduced and those that are no longer used will not continue. This suggests some kind of design or intention and cannot be explained properly by natural selection. There is no design in natural selection, only increased reproduction of successful varieties. For example, there is no reason to suppose that humans will lose the appendix in the future simply because it is no longer required for digestion. The only way it could disappear is for some humans to be born without an appendix, due to a natural mutation, and for those humans to reproduce much more prolifically than others and then kill off everyone with an appendix. Even then, in subsequent generations there would be 'throwbacks' as children would be born with the previous appendix-making configuration of genes. As it happens, the appendix is not useless but is used by the immune system so it is an advantage to keep it.

> Inheritance of acquired characteristics – Lamarck thought that if an animal succeeded in learning successful behaviour, or suffered some mishap that resulted in a bodily change such as the loss of a tail, this would be passed on to future generations. However, there is no mechanism by which this could occur. For example, giraffes did not develop long necks in order to reach higher branches, or by practising reaching up higher and higher. Natural selection resulted in giraffes that happened to be born with longer necks being

able to reach higher branches and hence survive when food was scarce; giraffes with shorter necks starved and died without producing any offspring. This process would have continued over thousands of years until the length of the giraffes' necks matched the height of the available trees or until the advantages of having a longer neck were outweighed by the disadvantages.

> Thirdly, natural selection does not give rise to behaviour directly. Some writers explain the way organisms adapt to their environment by talking about the 'selfish gene' (for example Dawkins, 1989), arguing that genes 'strive' to reproduce and will ensure that the organism will do everything possible to mate and reproduce so that the genes will be replicated. However, this should not be interpreted as implying intention, and having 'selfish' genes does not imply that we must be selfish in our behaviour. Our minds evolved to enable behaviour that would have been adaptive in our ancestral environment. Again, this can be explained by saying that our ancestors enjoyed doing those things that replicated the genes and avoided those things that did not. We have inherited the same tendencies for enjoyment and avoidance. This does not mean that we are compelled by our genes, only that we have desires and fears. How we make use of those desires and fears depends on how we chose to adapt to our modern environment.

Evolutionary psychology uses knowledge and principles from evolutionary theory in research on the human mind and behaviour. It is a *way of thinking* about psychology that sees the mind as a set of information-processing machines that arose by natural selection to solve adaptive problems faced by our hunter-gatherer ancestors.

When we look at current behaviours, therefore, we can look at evolutionary development to see why that behaviour occurs and evaluate whether the behaviour is adaptive or not in the current environment.

Unfortunately, many evolutionary psychologists fall into one or more of the traps described above and talk about human minds being 'designed' to solve certain environmental problems, rather than arising from chance mutation and surviving by natural selection because they happened to solve the problems. Moreover some writers assert that all our behaviour must have had some useful purpose at some time in our evolutions; they do not allow for chance mutations or random behaviours that survived without specific usefulness.

Evolutionary Psychology is an open-access peer-reviewed journal that aims to foster communication between experimental and theoretical work on the one hand and historical, conceptual and interdisciplinary writings across the whole range of the biological and human sciences on the other. (http://www.epjournal.net/, accessed on 23 September 2008).

See Part 3 for Emotion; Frame problem; Grammatical representation; Intelligence; Mental modules.

See Part 4 for Pinker.

2.3.10: Forensic/criminal psychology

Forensic psychology, formerly known as criminal psychology or criminological and legal psychology is the application of psychology in the criminal and civil justice field.

Forensic psychologists can work for academic institutions, prison services, the National Health Service, probation services, police services and social services. The range of work includes occupational and clinical elements, working with offenders, victims, criminal and civil justice staff and managers.

Forensic psychology examines psychological theories, methods and processes within the context of the legal, criminal and civil justice systems. In particular it looks at the treatment and assessment of offenders, especially those who are mentally disordered, contributes to the investigation of crime by examining issues such as identification of suspects, investigative interviewing, psychological profiling and detecting deception.

Forensic psychologists work in collaboration with criminal justice practitioners such as police and probation officers as well as other psychologists within the special hospitals and the prison service.

Two key areas of development in recent years have been 'risk assessment' procedures with offenders and interventions with sex offenders in particular, with a focus upon reducing the risk of re-offending. Also, forensic psychologists are increasingly becoming involved in child protection work with social services.

Forensic Psychology Practice Ltd is a private practice of forensic and clinical psychologists, which has national coverage and provides a wide range of services. Their website (http://www.forensicpsychology.co.uk/, accessed June 2008) explains the nature of forensic psychology in some detail and lists the following clients and issues:

Clients include:	Issues addressed include:
People with learning disabilities People with mental illness Sexual offenders Violent offenders Other offenders Children and adolescents Adult survivors of sexual abuse	Parenting and contact Therapeutic needs Domestic abuse Substance abuse Criminal behaviour Political asylum Brain injury Suicide and self-injury

See Part 3 for Aggression; Brain injury; Cognitive distortion; Colour of surroundings; Conformity; Crowds; Depersonalisation; Desensitisation; Eye-witness testimony; Factitious illnesses; False memory syndrome; Power; Punishment; Vicarious learning; Weapons effect.

See Part 4 for Loftus, Zimbardo.

2.3.11: Health psychology

The emergence of health psychology as a rapidly growing discipline in its own right offers health-care professionals a vehicle with which to explore the concept of health and the many factors that influence health along the continuum from wellness through impaired health to dysfunctional health and ultimately to death.

The BPS Special Group in Health Psychology was redesignated the Division of Health Psychology in December 1997.

BPS PAPER 4 OPTION 8 – HEALTH PSYCHOLOGY

Biological mechanisms of health and disease. Health and illness related behaviours and cognitions. Individual differences (e.g. personality) and emotional correlates of health and illness. Stress and coping. Hospitalisation. Living with chronic conditions. Lifespan, gender and cultural issues. The applications of health psychology (e.g. in health promotion). (With permission.)

The concept of health is a complex one. A person's health is commonly understood to have a number of dimensions, such as physical, psychological, social, cultural, environmental and spiritual. The origins of many health problems are found in the lifestyle of the sufferer, linked to the person's beliefs about herself or himself.

By emphasising health promotion and illness prevention through the identification of health risk factors and the development of strategies to cope with life crises, health psychology provides health care professionals with a supplement to the traditional medical approach to health problems.

Some definitions of health psychology and health

Matarazzo (1980), cited in Pitts and Phillips (1991: 3): Health psychology is the aggregate of the specific educational, scientific and professional contributions of the discipline of psychology to:

> promotion and maintenance of health
> prevention and treatment of illness
> identification of etiologic and diagnostic correlates of health, illness and related dysfunction
> analysis and improvement of the health care system and health policy formation.

Kasl and Cobb (1966): Health behaviour is ... an activity undertaken by a person believing him/herself to be healthy for the purpose of preventing disease or detecting it in an asymptomatic stage.

Kiger (1995): Health represents a condition of mastery in which the extent of growth and the direction of potential lie with the individual.

It is easy to assume that if the lifestyle risk factors associated with health problems can be identified, those at risk will be motivated to change their behaviour in order to prevent the occurrence or deterioration of the health problem.

However, simply encouraging those at risk to change their behaviour may be ineffective, as the links between a person's health beliefs and health behaviour is a complex one.

Although health beliefs can be influential in determining health behaviour, a number of factors beyond the control of individuals can hinder them in taking responsibility for their own health.

Such factors include the social, cultural, environmental and economic framework around which the lifestyle of an individual is based. The individual may be powerless to influence these factors, but such factors can exert a profound influence over the choices available to people and may be regarded by them as having priority over the attainment and maintenance of health.

Additionally, and perhaps more importantly, it has recently been realised that many decisions relating to health and lifestyle are not based on rational choices but are linked to an individual's *self-concept* and *self-efficacy*.

See Part 3 for Affect; Affective disorders; Aggression; Altered body image; Altered state of consciousness (ASC); Amnesia; Anger; Anticipation; Anxiety; Arousal systems; Assertiveness; Attachment and bonding; Autism; Avoidance behaviour; Biofeedback; Body boundaries; Body image; Brain damage; Brain imaging; Cognitive distortion; Cognitive impairment; Colour of surroundings; Coma; Container for emotions; Coping styles; Dementias; Depression; Dissociative disorder; Dissociative identity disorder; Diurnal/circadian rhythms; ECT; EEG; Empathy; Factitious illnesses; False memory syndrome; Fight or flight mechanism; Gate control theory; General adaptation syndrome; Grief; Ideal self; Learned helplessness; Loss; Mood; Motivation; Pain; Placebo effect; Psychogenic illness; Psychosomatic; Relaxation training; Self-concept; Self-efficacy; Self-esteem; Self-fulfilling prophecy; Self-image; Schizophrenia; Sensory deprivation/ overload; Sleep; Stress; Toughness; Type A behaviour pattern.

See Part 4 for Cannon, Damasio, Friedman and Rosenman, Holmes and Rahe, Lazarus, Seligman, Selye, Yerkes.

2.3.12: History and philosophy of psychology

This topic is fundamental to a study of psychology and its importance is reflected in the formation of the BPS History and Philosophy Section and History of Psychology Centre.

The Section provides an opportunity for those interested in the history of psychology or in various philosophical aspects of the subject to exchange ideas and promote the discussion of these interests within the Society.

The History of Psychology Centre is responsible for the British Psychological Society's archive and library activities, for supporting and promoting research and teaching in the history of psychology, and for public engagement activities in the history of psychology.

They are planning to develop their website into a major resource for history of psychology research, devoted primarily to British psychology with a detailed online catalogue of the archive holdings, with links to other major catalogues.

BPS PAPER 3 SECTION 2 – CONCEPTUAL AND HISTORICAL ISSUES

Critiques of traditional methods in psychology; the significance of the standpoint from which values are understood.

Paradigms and research programmes: Kuhn, Lakatos and Feyerabend. Lessons from the history of psychology: reductionism, structuralism, functionalism, relativism and the nature of consciousness.

Critical psychology and subjectivity: the critical psychological view of subject and subjectivity. The origins of ethical issues to psychology; moral underpinnings of theory, research and practice of psychology; psychologists and community members as partners in the construction of ethically responsible practices. (With permission.)

See Part 2.1 for the scientific nature of enquiry.

See Part 2.3.5 for the nature of consciousness.

See Part 3 for Functionalism; Identity theory of mind (monism); Nature–nurture debate; Ontological insecurity; Paradigm; Reductionism; Relativism; Sentience; Structuralism; Subjectivity; Teleology; Theory of mind.

See Part 4 for a brief overview of the history of psychology and Adler, Adorno, Ainsworth, Allport, Asch, Bartlett, Bettelheim, Broadbent, Burt, Cannon, Damasio, Dennett, Ebbinghaus, Eysenck, Feyerabend, Harlow, Hebb, James, Kuhn, Lakatos, Mead, Pavlov, Turing, Watson, Wundt, Young, von Helmholtz and Maxwell.

See Part 5 for scientific process.

approaches

2.3.13: Humanistic psychology

Humanistic approaches are also known as phenomenological, person-centred, client-centred, non-directive and facilitative (see Part 3).

Humanistic psychology is primarily an applied field concerned with counselling and psychotherapy, and developed in the first half of the 20th century in response to dissatisfaction with the extremes of the psychodynamic and behaviourist approaches. Although there is a wealth of clinical experience, the absence of systematic, quantitative data based on hypothetico-deductive methods, means that the approach remains outside mainstream psychology.

Some definitions of humanistic psychology

Rogers (1961: 11): It is the client who knows what hurts, what directions to go, what problems are crucial, what experiences have been deeply buried. It began to occur to me that unless I had a need to demonstrate my own cleverness and learning, I would do better to rely upon the client for the direction of movement in the process.

Burnard and Morrison (1991: 104): In client-centred counselling, the counsellor is not an expert in other people's problems but someone who enables or facilitates the problem-solving capacity of the other person.

McLeod (1993: 2): Humanistic psychology has always consisted of a broad set of theories and models connected by shared values and philosophical assumptions, rather than constituting a single, coherent, theoretical formulation. . . . The common ingredient . . . is an emphasis on experiential processes. . . the here-and-now.

Silverstone (1993: iv): The theory is concise. The theory is so easy to understand intellectually, so difficult to incorporate into one's way of being. Very few of us have experienced a model in our upbringing in which the person knows best. So, it is like learning a new language.

Phenomenological approaches concentrate only on observable phenomena: that is, objects and events. Behaviour and events are explored only from the point of view of the client. Phenomenological therapy focuses on the wholeness of experience and emphasises the searching for personal meanings and essences of experience as they appear to an individual. Therapy is not concerned with theory-driven interpretations of hidden or unconscious emotional dynamics or quantitative measurements of behaviour.

Humanistic or person-centred approaches, based on the phenomenological *paradigm*, involve the application of psychological knowledge, awareness, intuition and counselling experience in working with clients in such a way that the relationship between therapist and client is one of an equal partnership.

Prominent figures in humanistic psychology have been Carl Rogers, Charlotte Buhler, Abraham Maslow and Sydney Jourard. These practitioners share a vision of therapy that will facilitate the human capacity for growth, creativity and choice. The image of the individual in humanistic psychology is of someone striving to find meaning and fulfilment in the world.

In the client–carer relationship, the client is encouraged to take control and the therapist encourages and assists the client in finding a sense of direction and moving towards whatever the client perceives as desirable.

Rogers (1961, 1980) argues that there are three basic principles of the client-centred or person-centred approach:

> *congruence*
> *unconditional positive regard*
> *empathy.*

Rogers believes that the actual method or style used in counselling or psychotherapy may be a matter of preference for therapist and client but that no method can be successful unless it is based on the three basic principles. Moreover, in practice, only these three are needed; that is, they are the 'necessary and sufficient' conditions for effective therapy. Murgatroyd (1985) says that other researchers agree that they are necessary but argue they are not sufficient and he mentions Robert Carkhuff, who identified three more basic conditions of helping:

> concreteness
> immediacy
> confrontation.

This identification of essential elements can be usefully compared with neurolinguistic programming (NLP), which also purports to have found what makes therapy work – what is called the 'magic' of therapy (Bandler and Grinder, 1975, 1976).

The chief drawbacks with a person-centred technique are that it takes time and that a counsellor who never asks questions or gives suggestions may be perceived by the client as unengaged or uninterested in the process. Such difficulties are most likely to result from a lack of understanding of the technique, or because a poorly trained counsellor is not using the techniques well, the method has not been explained to the client, insufficient time has been given for the client to move towards a position of control, or the technique is not suited to the client or the problem. Person-centred approaches tend to be most successful with educated, highly motivated people who have a natural tendency towards self-examination.

See Part 3 for Congruence; Empathy; Human-potential movement; Individuation; Motivation; Unconditional positive regard.

See Part 4 for Ellis, Maslow, Rogers.

approaches

2.3.14: Lesbian and gay psychology

The Lesbian and Gay Psychology Section of the British Psychological Society aims to provide an integrative forum for those involved in research, teaching and applied work in the United Kingdom. The Section aims to serve members whose work is relevant to lesbian, gay, bisexual and transgender issues. The section is strongly committed to developing non-heterosexist and gender-inclusive forms of research, theory and clinical practice in British psychology.

The interests and activities of the Section focuses on research and theory on a wide range of issues relevant to the lives of lesbians and gay men, including: lesbian and gay development across the lifespan, especially lesbian and gay identity development; the establishment and maintenance of lesbian and gay relationships – including couple, family and social relationships – and relationship problems; attitudes towards lesbians and gay men and implications for psychosocial functioning and well-being; lesbian and gay parenting, including lesbian pregnancy, childbirth and child rearing practices; and ethnic and cultural diversity among lesbians and gay men. As well as these content areas, theoretical concerns are also be pursued at both a macro-level and at a topic-specific level.

The Section represents psychologists who work in all areas, including clinical psychology, community psychology, counselling psychology, critical psychology, developmental psychology, experimental psychology, health psychology, history of psychology, the psychology of women and social psychology.

The Section aims to provide an integrative forum for those involved in research, teaching and applied work that is relevant to lesbian and gay psychology but who, at the moment, are diversely located. It publishes the *Lesbian and Gay Psychology Review* three times each year (http://www.bps.org.uk/lesgay/lesgay_home.cfm, accessed June 2008).

See also:

Part 2.3.7   Cultural psychology.

See Part 3 for Abnormal; Altered body image; Anima; Archetype; Attitude development; Body image; Conformity; Discrimination; Formative years; Gender, Gender identity; Intersexuality; Nature–nurture debate; Norms; Self-concept; Self-esteem; Self-image; Sex; Sexuality; Social roles; Transgender/transsexual; Transvestite.

See Part 4 for Bem, Gilligan.

2.3.15: Military psychology

Military psychology can include a vast array of activities in psychological research, assessment and treatment. Military psychologists may be either soldiers or civilians. The field can encompass every aspect of the human mind that interests the military.

Research is focused on the psychology of military organisation, military life and combat.

Military psychologists are involved in testing recruits for intelligence and aptitude for military specialisations, and helping to find more effective ways of training them, including identifying and optimally training officers and other leaders.

The American Psychological Association (APA) Division 19 – Society for Military Psychology promotes research and the application of psychological research to military problems. Members are military psychologists who serve diverse functions, including research activities, management, providing mental health services, teaching, consulting, work with Congressional committees and advising senior military commands. Members receive the quarterly journal *Military Psychology* and the newsletter *The Military Psychologist*, published twice a year (http://www.apa.org/about/division/div19.html, accessed 31 August 2007).

At the time of writing there did not appear to be any undergraduate or graduate courses in military psychology in the UK but the armed forces employ psychologists in various capacities, see Part 7.

approaches

2.3.16: Occupational psychology

Occupational Psychology is a Division of the BPS and as such is regarded as one of the most important applied approaches in psychology in the UK.

Chartered occupational psychologists are concerned with the performance of people at work and in training, with developing an understanding of how organisations function and how individuals and groups behave at work. Their aim is to increase effectiveness, efficiency and satisfaction at work.

BPS PAPER 4 OPTION 3 – OCCUPATIONAL PSYCHOLOGY

Assessment of individual, group and organisational effectiveness. Psychological methods and models for careers counselling. Selection and assessment. Job design. Task analysis. Cognitive ergonomics. Stress in work organisations. Factors affecting the quality of working life, unemployment and retirement. Motivation. Employment relations. Organisational change. (With permission.)

Occupational psychologists can appear under many different guises, working in organisational psychology, ergonomics, applied psychology, industrial psychology, personnel management, time and stress management and management consultancy. However, the majority of occupational psychologists work as general problem-solvers or facilitators across broad areas such as organisational consultancy, assessment and training, or ergonomics, health and safety.

Occupational psychologists:

> identify abilities and potential
> motivate
> assess performance both on and off the job
> help people and organisations adapt to change
> design effective organisations.
  http://www.bps.org.uk/sub-sites$/dop/about-the-division/about-the-division_
  home.cfm

See also
    Part 2.3.3   Coaching psychology.
    See Part 3 for Motivation; Stress.
    See Part 5 for Psychometric tests.

2.3.17: Political psychology

Political psychology examines various individual factors of political figures such as traits, motives, decision strategies and non-verbal communication, and their relation to success or failure in the political sphere. The term 'political' is used broadly to cover virtually every situation where decisions must be made 'for the many on the part of a few' and is not limited to high-level politicians such as prime ministers, presidents and members of parliament.

The last 15 years has seen a renaissance of interest in the field of political psychology in both Europe and the United States. This reflects dissatisfaction with increasing specialisation, splits between social science disciplines and changes in expectations since the origins of political psychology in the 1960s. Political psychologists attempt to integrate political scientists' interest in social change and institutional development with psychologists' interest in cognition, emotion and personality. Graduate programmes tend to adopt the perspective of either political science or psychology. Within this context they then tend to emphasise either theoretical issues or empirical ones. Some courses may be interdisciplinary.

The emphasis is different in different universities. Courses may include: social change and democratisation, ideology, altruism, social and political identity, voting behaviour, mass media effects and international integration, intra-organisational interactions, group decision-making, leadership styles, leaders or political organisations during times of crisis or other critical decision-making points, war against terrorism.

As with cultural psychology, political psychology focuses on the interrelationship between political organisation and culture and individual thought and emotion.

See also
> Part 2.2.5   Social psychology.
> Part 2.3.7   Cultural psychology.
> See Part 3 for Altruism; Emotion; Leadership; Groups; Motivation; Non-verbal communication; Personality traits; Power.

approaches

2.3.18: Psychodynamic psychology

Psychodynamic psychology is based on the belief that it is possible to interpret what is going on in the unconscious mind, using theories of the structure and dynamics of emotional development.

Some writers regard all in-depth therapeutic approaches as psychodynamic, including humanistic and cognitive strategies. In this book, the term psychodynamic is reserved for those therapies which are based on a coherent theory of unconscious processes and are inclined towards a medical or therapist-centred model of the therapeutic relationship, such as Freudian and post-Freudian psychoanalysis, Jungian analytical psychology and Adler's individual psychology (see Part 4).

Psychodynamic theories attempt to explain all experiences, but in particular why people sometimes behave irrationally or in ways which are (or appear to be) dangerous or unpleasant for themselves and others.

Conscious awareness is viewed as only the tip of the iceberg of the mind. The whole of the rest of the mind is not conscious and is perpetually processing thoughts, emotions and behaviour without conscious awareness or control.

This is a view which is shared to some extent by all psychologists, but psychodynamic theories go further than the mainstream perspectives in attempting to create a comprehensive interpretative structure based on the dynamics of emotional development. Psychodynamic theories are not normally considered to belong within mainstream scientific or experimental psychology as they are based on speculation derived from qualitative data and individual case histories and are not seen to be supported by objective, statistically quantifiable research.

The most prominent theory is that of Sigmund Freud (see Part 4), who over a period of many years proposed and continuously refined an elegant psychoanalytical theory of the mind which was intended to explain all the vagaries of human experience. Freud's books are fascinating to read but can be difficult to understand. Much of what he says seems odd, or even stupid or irrelevant to current lifestyles. Many secondary sources paint lurid pictures of Freud's psychosexual models while missing the point of what he was suggesting. Psychodynamic terms are frequently used and evoke powerful associations but are little understood.

Psychodynamic approaches indicate that our emotional experience seems to be influenced, or even governed, by deliberately hidden or *repressed* unconscious activity. Freud talked as if the mind were structured in terms of three distinct layers; the conscious, the pre-conscious and the unconscious. The unconscious part contains the deliberately repressed material, kept hidden through defence mechanisms. Some of this may leak accidentally into consciousness in a symbolic way through dreams but the symbolic coding usually prevents total awareness so that the dreamer remains protected from disturbing thoughts and memories. Therapies address this hidden or repressed unconscious mental activity. The symbolism is believed to be decodable through inferences concerning which defence mechanisms are operating and a systematised analysis of the reasons behind them. Analysis of dreams may assist with understanding and may lead to more effective coping mechanisms. Comparisons may be made with symbolism found throughout the visual arts.

A key assumption is that who we are at any stage in our lives, and how we feel, depends entirely on all our previous experiences and that the first few years of life are crucial in determining what follows. Each new experience builds on the ones before as our expectations shape our new perceptions. What we take notice of, and how we interpret it, depends on what we have met before and what happened in a similar situation last time.

Put like this, psychodynamics doesn't sound very different from behaviourism, which suggests that all behaviour is determined, or conditioned, by the outcome of previous experiences. Both perspectives are deterministic. What makes the difference between the two approaches is that behaviourism ignores the workings of the mind (the black box), concentrating solely on visible actions, whereas psychodynamics examines the inner mind and focuses particularly on emotional experiences. In psychodynamics, emotions, particularly anxiety, are what matter, more so than overt cognitions or behaviour.

The psychodynamic approaches also support a belief that detailed and thorough analysis can trace the ways in which previous experiences have shaped the current state of the person. Analysis of an individual's experiences will lead to that person having a better understanding of himself or herself and hence a greater ability to cope with problems. However, even Freud admits that his style of psychoanalysis does not necessarily make a person feel happier, it just helps with understanding the causes of unhappiness.

There are now many different psychodynamic theories or styles. Most can be seen to have been influenced by Freud in one way or another but each theory is based on different sets of beliefs or interpretations of behaviour, each adding something new to our overall understanding.

Case studies make very compelling reading and are illuminating, but the data are not replicable and the results cannot be generalised because each individual case is unique.

See Part 3 for Anima and animus; Archetype; Asceticism; Catharsis; Cathexis; Collective unconscious; Compensation; Complexes; Container for emotions; Counter-transference; Death-wish; Defence mechanisms; Denial; Displacement; Dreaming; Ego; Fixation; Free association; Freudian slip; Id; Identification; Individuation; Intellectualisation; Libido; Mandala; Manifest content; Persona; Pleasure principle; Preconscious; Principle of opposites; Projection; Projective techniques; Psychodrama; Psychosexual stages; Rationalisation; Reaction formation; Regression; Repression; Resistance; Rorscharch; Subconscious; Sublimation; Superego; Thematic apperception test (TAT); Transactional Analysis (TA); Transference.

See Part 4 for Adler, Ainsworth, Berne, Bettelheim, Bion, Bowlby, Erikson, Freud, Fromm, Horney, Jung, Klein, Lacan, Perls, Rorschach, Winnicott.

2.3.19: Psychology of women

As indicated in Part 1 and under 'Cultural psychology', much of established psychology follows the dominant ideology of white, middle-class, male capitalism. Until at least the 1980s most of the experimental and observational work was carried out and interpreted by men, and most participants (then called subjects) were men. It is strongly believed that this has led to a biased and skewed psychology that does not sufficiently include and has little relevance for women. The psychology of women seeks to address topics related to women that are not necessarily covered in mainstream psychology.

Topics of concern include: education; lifespan role development and change; sexuality and sexual orientation, career choice and training; management and performance variables; physical and mental health and well-being; physical, sexual and psychological abuse; violence and harassment; prejudice and discrimination; and therapeutic processes.

The Psychology of Women Section (POWS) was set up as a subsection of the British Psychological Society in 1988 in order to draw together all those working in different areas of psychology who share an interest in the psychology of women, and to provide a forum within which issues in this field may be debated. The aims of the section are to:

> bring together everyone with an interest in the psychology of women
> provide a forum for the psychology of women in research, teaching and professional practice
> increase awareness and action around gender and inequality issues within the BPS, the psychology profession, and the teaching of psychology.

POWS is open to all members of the BPS. The majority of members are women who work in the various areas within psychology: clinical, educational, social, developmental, health, occupational, and lesbian and gay psychology. POWS produces a periodical and newsletter: see http://www.bps.org.uk/pows/pows_home.cfm.

The American Society for the Psychology of Women was established in 1973 as Division 35 of the American Psychological Association. *Psychology of Women Quarterly* (http://www.apa.org/divisions/div35/quarter.html) is a feminist journal that publishes research related to the psychology of women and gender. http;//www.apa.org/divisions/div35/

See also
Part 2.3.7   Cultural psychology.
Part 2.3.17   Political psychology.
See Part 3 for Ageing; Anima; Archetype; Attachment and bonding; Attitude development; Authoritarian personality; Body image; Cognitive distortion; Conformity; Discrimination; Empowerment; Formative years; Gender, Gender identity; Nature–nurture Debate; Norms; Parenting styles; Power; Self-concept; Self-esteem; Self-image; Sex; Sexuality; Social roles.
See Part 4 for Bem, Gilligan.

2.3.20: Psychotherapy

The term psychotherapy implies for many people a focus on psychodynamic approaches to therapy, based on the theoretical models of Freud, Jung or other 'schools' of psychoanalysis. In practice, psychotherapists may use humanistic, behavioural or cognitive approaches or a personal blend of different approaches without adherence to one particular school.

On the whole, the term psychotherapy is used when clients have serious mental health problems, whereas the term counselling is used in relation to clients with social, occupational, family or other situational problems. However, in many contexts the terms psychotherapy and counselling are used interchangeably or according to the context or establishment in which the therapy takes place, rather than its form or the nature of the client's interests or problems. The different types of psychotherapy and counselling are given above under 'Counselling psychology'.

BPS Psychotherapy Section (formerly Medical Psychology)

The Section is the main forum within the Society for psychologists and others who share an interest in psychotherapeutic psychology. One of the oldest specialist groups within the Society, it has a long and distinguished history as a meeting ground for discussion of psychotherapy and related issues. It is concerned with the relationship between psychotherapy and psychology, and seeks to further an understanding of how social and cultural factors have a bearing upon psychotherapeutic theory and practice. The approach tends to be medically oriented with particular focus on mental illness (http://www.bps.org.uk/ps/ps_home.cfm, accessed October 2007, with permission).

Psychology and Psychotherapy: Theory Research and Practice is an international journal concerned with recent developments of clinical activities in the areas of psychology and psychotherapy, with a focus on the psychological aspects of mental health difficulties and well-being and psychological problems and their psychological treatments. The journal publishes original, high-quality empirical research and rigorous theoretical contributions on cognitive, interpersonal and other psychological aspects of mental health and the psychological therapies See also

Part 2.3.2   Clinical psychology.
Part 2.3.6   Counselling psychology.
Part 2.3.13   Humanistic psychology.
Part 2.3.18   Psychodynamic psychology.

2.3.21: Sport and exercise psychology

BPS Division of Sport and Exercise Psychology (DSEP)

Sport psychologists work with sports participants across a range of both team and individual sports and from amateur to elite levels of competition. The aim is predominately to help athletes prepare psychologically for competition and to deal with the psychological demands of both competition and training. Examples of the work sport psychologists carry out include counselling referees to deal with the stressful and demanding aspects of their role, advising coaches on how to build cohesion within their squads of athletes, and helping athletes to deal with the psychological and emotional consequences of sustaining an injury.

An exercise psychologist is primarily concerned with the application of psychology to increase exercise participation and motivational levels in the general public. Examples of the work they do include optimising the benefits that can be derived from exercise participation and helping individual clients with the implementation of goal-setting strategies.

Sport and exercise psychologists work in a wide range of sport and exercise settings and with a diverse range of clients. Most sport psychologists combine consultancy work with teaching and research or psychological consultancy in other areas such as the clinical and occupational domains. Some sport psychologists do hold full-time positions with professional sports teams or national governing bodies and opportunities to work as a full-time sport psychologist are constantly increasing in number.

A similar scenario exists for exercise psychologists, with most practitioners combining consultancy with teaching and research careers. The work of exercise psychologists might involve GP exercise referral and setting up and evaluating exercise programmes in employment, prison and psychiatric contexts.

The work of a sport or exercise psychologist is centred on people and can be extremely varied. Although consultancy work may be office-based it is equally likely that consultants will work in field settings such as team premises, competition venues, clinical rehabilitation and recreational exercise settings (http://www.bps.org.uk/careers/areas/sport.cfm, reproduced with permission).

2.3.22: Teaching and researching in psychology

BPS Division for Teachers and Researchers in Psychology

The Division for Teachers and Researchers in Psychology of the British Psychological Society aims to be the professional home for any psychologist whose principal activities include research, teaching, or a combination of both. It was formed to address the practitioner development issues that concern those members of the Society and their colleagues who teach psychology in schools, colleges and universities and/or conduct psychological research in public or private establishments, or are undergoing training to equip themselves for careers in these settings.

The work of research psychologists and teachers of psychology provides and disseminates essential elements of the knowledge base on which a substantial range of professions rely, both the specialised practice areas within psychology and those other professions with expertise that can be founded in psychology. Best practice in the professions of psychological teaching and research themselves is now based on extensive specialist training and continuous professional development. The Division's members acknowledge that their activities in support of learning can have direct psychological impact on individual clients including pre-degree and degree students, graduate trainees and the readers of research reports in both fundamental and applied psychology.

The Division is the only body that looks to the interests of all psychologists in teaching or research, from teachers in schools and colleges, through contract researchers in public or commercial services, to the academic staff of old and new universities. DTRP was formed in December 1997 to subsume the functions of the former Special Group for the Teaching of Psychology, but we aim equally to support the needs and priorities of research psychologists.

The Division's members seek to serve those who teach psychology or conduct psychological research and the individuals who learn from their activities. Thus DTRP endeavours:

1. To promote the individual continuing professional development of psychologists working in research and/or teaching.
2. To encourage, sustain and promote the development of psychological understanding and its dissemination through the activities of individuals.
3. To promote the highest standards of excellence in both teaching and research.
4. To ensure that the essential mutual relationships between teaching and research – so special within psychology – are sustained wherever psychologists are engaged in teaching.
5. To promote the application of psychological knowledge in the settings where psychological research is conducted and psychology is taught.
   (http://www.bps.org.uk/dtrp/about.cfm, accessed 28 Sept 2007 and reproduced with permission)

See also:
Part 6 for qualifying to teach as a chartered psychologist.
Part 7.3 for psychological organisations and institutions.
Part 7.4 for educational organisations and institutions.

approaches

2.3.23: Transpersonal psychology

The BPS Transpersonal Psychology Section

The word transpersonal means beyond (or through) the personal. It refers to experiences in which there is an expansion beyond our ordinary sense of self and a feeling of connection to a larger, more meaningful reality. Religious or spiritual experience is often seen as central to the transpersonal agenda, although the transpersonal can also be about extending our concern for (or our sense of identification with) other people, humankind, life, the planet or nature.

The BPS Transpersonal Psychology Section was established in 1996. It provides a forum for members who share an interest in psychological research and perspectives on the transpersonal.

The section also seeks to develop and maintain links, both nationally and internationally, with other scientific bodies concerned with transpersonal psychology, and to mobilise psychological expertise to cope with the exponential growth of lay interest in transpersonal issues.

The aims of the Transpersonal Psychology Section are to examine:

> The nature, history and purpose of transpersonal psychology.
> The influences of transpersonal experiences and beliefs upon the behaviour, performance and psychological well-being of individuals and groups.
> The relationship between personality, motivation and such emotions as love, empathy and compassion – particularly in the context of personal growth and the development of transpersonal aspirations, beliefs and experiences.
> The role of transpersonal psychology in exploring; (a) mystical, transcendental, meditative and peak experiences; and (b) the psychological factors that may contribute to these experiences.
> The effect of permitted and non-permitted drugs on the presence and nature of transpersonal experiences.
> The efficacy or otherwise of transpersonal therapeutic practices and techniques in healing, and in the enhancement of human potential and psychological well-being.
> The role of meditation in self-exploration and self-development.
> The psychology of religion.
> Eastern psycho-spiritual traditions.

In addition, the Section will seek to develop and maintain links, both nationally and internationally, with other scientific bodies concerned with transpersonal psychology, and to mobilise psychological expertise to cope with the exponential growth of lay interest in transpersonal issues. (http://www.transpersonalpsychology.org.uk/, reproduced with permission.)

The Centre for Transpersonal Psychology (CTP)

http://www.transpersonalpsychology.co.uk.

The Centre for Transpersonal Psychology (CTP) is a registered charity and an accrediting member of the United Kingdom Council for Psychotherapy (UKCP), founded in 1973 by Ian Gordon-Brown and Barbara Somers.

See also Part 2.3.5 Consciousness and experiential psychology.

See Part 3 for Altered states of consciousness; Archetypes; Collective unconscious; Paranormal; Self-actualisation.

See Part 4 for James, Jung, Maslow.

Abnormal [123] ¦ Abstract thinking [123] ¦ Accessibility (memory) [124] ¦ Accommodation [124] ¦ Acoustic, auditory or echoic store [124] ¦ Affect [124] ¦ Affective disorders [124] ¦ Affordances [124] ¦ After-image [124] ¦ Ageing [125] ¦ Aggression [125] ¦ Altered body image [125] ¦ Altered state of consciousness (ASC) [125] ¦ Altruism [126] ¦ Ambiguous figures [126] ¦ Amnesia [126] ¦ Anger [126] ¦ Anger management [126] ¦ Anima and animus [126] ¦ Animism [126] ¦ Anticipation [127] ¦ Anxiety [127] ¦ Apparition [127] ¦ Appeasement gesture [127] ¦ Archetype [127] ¦ Arousal systems [127] ¦ Artificial intelligence [128] ¦ Asceticism [128] ¦ Assertiveness [129] ¦ Assimilation [129] ¦ Attachment and bonding [129] ¦ Attention [129] ¦ Attitude [130] ¦ Attitude development [131] ¦ Attitude questionnaires [131] ¦ Attribution [131] ¦ Attribution theory [131] ¦ Auditory location [131] ¦ Authoritarian personality [131] ¦ Autism [132] ¦ Autonomic nervous system [132] ¦ Availability (memory) [132] ¦ Avoidance behaviour [132] ¦ Bales interaction process analysis [132] ¦ Basal nuclei (previously known as basal ganglia) [133] ¦ Behaviour shaping [133] ¦ Behaviour (or behavioural) therapies [134] ¦ Beliefs [134] ¦ Biofeedback [134] ¦ Blank slate/tabula rasa [135] ¦ Blindsight [135] ¦ Body boundaries [135] ¦ Body image [135] ¦ Bottom-up processing [135] ¦ Brain [135] ¦ Brain damage [137] ¦ Brain imaging [138] ¦ Broken information games [138] ¦ Catharsis [138] ¦ Cathexis [139] ¦ Central executive system [139] ¦ Centration [139] ¦ Cerebellum [139] ¦ Cerebral cortex [139] ¦ Chaos theory [139] ¦ Character [140] ¦ Chromosome [140] ¦ Chromosome mutations [140] ¦ Chunking [140] ¦ Clairvoyance [140] ¦ Classical conditioning (also known as associative, contigual or contiguous conditioning) [140] ¦ Cognitive appraisal [141] ¦ Cognitive appraisal theory [141] ¦ Cognitive dissonance [141] ¦ Cognitive distortion [142] ¦ Cognitive impairment (dysfunctional cognition) [142] ¦ Cognitive map [142] ¦ Cognitive therapy [142] ¦ Collective unconscious [143] ¦ Colour constancy [143] ¦ Colour of surroundings [143] ¦ Colour vision [143] ¦ Coma [144] ¦ Compensation [144] ¦ Complexes [145] ¦ Complexity theory [145] ¦ Computational theory of mind [145] ¦ Conation [145] ¦ Concept [145] ¦ Concrete operations [146] ¦ Conformity [146] ¦ Congruence (genuineness) [146] ¦ Conservation [146] ¦ Container for emotions [147] ¦

3 key terms and concepts

concepts

Convergent thinking [147] ¦ Coping styles [147] ¦ Creativity [147] ¦ Crowds [148] ¦ Cue dependence (memory) [148] ¦ Dark adaptation [148] ¦ Death-wish (Thanatos) [148] ¦ Deduction or deductive reasoning [148] ¦ Defence mechanisms [148] ¦ Dementias [149] ¦ Denial [149] ¦ Depersonalisation [149] ¦ Depression [149] ¦ Depth perception [150] ¦ Desensitisation [150] ¦ Determinism [150] ¦ Dichotic listening [150] ¦ Discovery learning [150] ¦ Discrimination [150] ¦ Displacement [150] ¦ Dissociative disorder [150] ¦ Dissociative identity disorder [151] ¦ Diurnal/circadian rhythms [151] ¦ Divergent thinking [151] ¦ Dopamine [151] ¦ Dreaming [151] ¦ Dynamic memory theory [152] ¦ Electroconvulsive therapy (ECT) [152] ¦ Electroencephalograph (EEG) [152] ¦ Efforts after meaning [152] ¦ Ego [152] ¦ Egocentric [152] ¦ Emotion [153] ¦ Emotional intelligence (EI) [153] ¦ Empathy [154] ¦ Empowerment [154] ¦ Enactive representation [154] ¦ Episodic or autobiographical memory [154] ¦ Equilibration [154] ¦ Evoked potentials (EV) [154] ¦ Extinction [154] ¦ Extroversion (or extraversion) [154] ¦ Eye-witness testimony [155] ¦ Face recognition [155] ¦ Facial expressions [155] ¦ Factitious illnesses [155] ¦ False awakening [156] ¦ False consensus [156] ¦ False consistency [156] ¦ False memory syndrome (recovered memories) [156] ¦ Fantasy play [156] ¦ Fight or flight mechanism [157] ¦ Figure–ground reversal [157] ¦ Five-factor model of personality [157] ¦ Fixation [157] ¦ Flashbulb memory [157] ¦ Forgetting [158] ¦ Formal operations [158] ¦ Formative years [158] ¦ Frame problem [158] ¦ Free association [159] ¦ Freudian slip [159] ¦ Functionalism [159] ¦ Fundamental attribution error [159] ¦ Galvanic skin response (GSR) [159] ¦ Gate control theory [159] ¦ Gender [160] ¦ Gender Identity [160] ¦ General adaptation syndrome (GAS) or adaptation level theory [161] ¦ Genes [161] ¦ Genetic counselling [161] ¦ Genotype [161] ¦ Glia cells [162] ¦ Grammatical representation [162] ¦ Grief [162] ¦ Group development [163] ¦ Group initiation rituals [163] ¦ Group processes [163] ¦ Group of displacements and reversibility [164] ¦ Habituation/sensory adaptation [164] ¦ Hallucinations [164] ¦ Halo and horns effects [164] ¦ Hardiness [165] ¦ Hearing (auditory sense) [165] ¦ Hemispheric specialisation [165] ¦ Heterozygous [166] ¦ Hierarchical network model [166] ¦ Hippocampus [166] ¦ Homozygous [166] ¦ Hypnosis (hypnotism) [166] ¦ Hypnotherapy [167] ¦ Hypothalamus [167] ¦ Iconic representation (iconic imagery) [167] ¦ Iconic store [168] ¦ Id [168] ¦ Ideal self (ego-ideal or idealised self-image) [168] ¦ Identification [168] ¦ Identity constancy [168] ¦ Identity theory of mind (monism) [168] ¦ Implicit personality theory [168] ¦ Individuation [168] ¦ Induction or inductive reasoning [168] ¦ Induced motion [169] ¦ Information processing [169] ¦ Insight [169] ¦ Inspection time [169] ¦

concepts

Please note that the length of each item is not related to its importance: some items require more information for clarity. The information is not sufficient for undergraduate work but is intended as an introduction or quick reminder and stepping stone to understanding lectures and more rigorous textbooks.

Abnormal: this is perhaps one of the most varied and interesting terms in psychology and one that is likely to give rise to misunderstandings since labelling something as abnormal or not normal usually attracts negative attitudes. The following types of definition of abnormal characteristics are in common use:

> statistically uncommon
> medical diagnosis
> personal distress
> maladaptive behaviour
> social norm violation
> socially disruptive behaviour.

A characteristic is usually considered statistically uncommon if it occurs outside about two *standard deviations* either side of the *mean* in a *normal distribution* (see Part 5). The 95 per cent of the population that fall within this range are normal; the other 5 per cent are not normal but either abnormally low or abnormally high. If we consider that IQ (*Intelligence quotient*) produces a normal distribution around a mean of 100, and a standard deviation of 16, then we can say that the average IQ is 100 and that 95 per cent of the population come between 68 and 132. Anyone higher than 132 can be said to be abnormal – which covers quite a few people in university.

Medical diagnosis of mental illness (for example DSM-IV) involves classification according to the presence or absence of symptoms, either separately or as part of a syndrome. Generally speaking, a person is considered to either have or not have a particular illness, perhaps along a continuum from mild to severe.

There is ongoing heated debate as to whether conditions such as autism should be considered abnormal, and thus unwanted, since some conditions bring special benefits. In one view, research and funding should be directed towards treatment that brings as much normality as possible, or directed towards publicity with a view to changing attitudes in favour of acceptance or even celebration of the variations, and recognition of lesser forms of the conditions in the apparently normal population. Person-centred approaches to therapy tend to avoid the concept of abnormality, preferring to give equal respect to everyone.

Personal distress such as depression or anxiety may be regarded as abnormal if it is interfering with 'normal' or desirable lifestyle. In this sense, the use of the term abnormal seems less upsetting than medical labels of abnormality. The worries are outside the normal, acceptable range and therefore need to be resolved but the person is not labelled as abnormal.

People may engage in behaviour that is damaging to themselves, such as excessive drinking, smoking, eating or drug taking that results in disruption to their lifestyle, inability to reach goals or adapt to the demands of family or job. As with personal distress, there is usually a clearer distinction between the person and the behaviour than with mental illness, and it is therefore easier to label the behaviour as abnormal (and undesirable) rather than the person, but this may vary according to how socially undesirable the behaviour is and whether it presents problems for other people.

We often have difficulty relating to people who do not follow social conventions and norms or expectations about the right or wrong way to do things. This can involve quite small things such as dressing in an unusual way, not observing the conventions relating to gender or age, avoiding eye contact or failing to take the proper 'turns' in conversation. If we do not understand people's motives or background we may regard them as abnormal or as the local 'weirdo'. In many cases this may include wanting to avoid them.

Social deviance that is disruptive and dangerous to others can also be regarded as abnormal behaviour and deserving of 'treatment' rather than criminal justice. Historically, this has resulted in repressive regimes labelling unwanted dissenters as abnormal and subjecting them to the kind of inhumane treatments given to mentally ill people at the time.

Abstract thinking: thinking about things which are not actually present or which do not exist in material or concrete form. This sort of thinking may be iconic, in visual or other sensory images, or symbolic, in words or other symbols such as mathematical notation. In order to cope with adult problem-solving, children must learn to make the transition from concrete, common-sense reality to coping with abstractions.

This process of moving beyond the bounds of common sense does not appear spontaneously but is made possible through education based on the product of long ages of culture. In practice only a small minority of people develop intellectually to a high level of competence in abstract thinking and the question for educationalists is whether they should accept this as inevitable or seek new teaching methods. See also *Concrete operations*, *Formal operations*, and Part 4, Piaget, Bruner, Donaldson.

Accessibility (memory): the extent to which we can retrieve information stored in memory. That is, whether we can actually 'find' something in memory that we believe we learned. It depends on the way we encoded information and is to be distinguished from availability, which depends on whether the information has been stored at all.

Accommodation: a term used by Piaget and others to describe the process by which children adapt existing schemas or conceptions when they assimilate new information that contradicts previous notions. Bruner extended the ideas behind this concept and suggested that children (and adults) learn most effectively when confronted with contrasting evidence and have to develop new mental representations in order to make sense of the contradictory data. In the absence of contradictions, new learning may only take place at a superficial level. The term accommodation also refers to the process by which the ciliary muscles change the thickness of the lens of the eye to permit variable focusing on near and distant objects.

Acoustic, auditory or echoic store: the short-lived memory store of perceptions of sounds. Some writers use this term for the sensory store, implying that storage takes place in the sense organ before the cortex interprets and processes the sounds. Other writers suggest that even the simplest storage involves cortical organisation.

Affect: when used as a noun, affect is a general term that refers to all levels of *mood*, *emotions*, or feelings from mild to strong. Since emotions are often defined in terms of *facial expressions*, affect can be a more useful word when referring to inner feelings, particularly where people do not display any facial or other *non-verbal* clues to indicate their feelings or where there is a discrepancy between what they feel and what they display. Positive affect includes feelings of pleasantness or well-being and negative affect refers to unpleasant or distressing feelings.

Affective Disorders: disorders of *mood* and *emotions*. This medical diagnosis usually refers to *depression* or negative affect but can also be used for mania, bipolar mood disorder, seasonal affective disorder (SAD), *anxiety,* and other affective or emotional states.

Affordances: this term was used by Gibson (for example 1950) in his theory of visual perception to refer to properties of objects that give meaning to the visual information available to the eyes. The affordance of an object is related to its perceived function. For example, the affordance (or function) of a hammer is to hit nails or other objects. Gibson argued that we only have to look at an object to know its affordance and we do not need to use *top-down processing* in order to decide what an object is, or is for. Most objects can have more than one affordance which may depend on the observer's needs at the moment of perception; for example, a hammer could be used as a doorstop or a weapon. This concept has been extremely influential in ecological and environmental psychology and in the field of design and ergonomics.

After-image: there are two kinds of visual after-images, positive and negative. Bright lights tend to persist as a positive after-image after the source is removed. This is also known as persistence of *vision* and is an example of perseveration. For example, if we wave a 'sparkler' or fluorescent strip around in the darkness we can write our name in the air. A negative after-image may appear when people have been staring for a few moments at a stationary image and then look away to a blank surface. For example, after staring at a black square on a white background, the negative after-image is a white square on a dark background. With coloured images, the complementary colours are seen. The image may be faint or ghostly and not everyone gets this effect readily.

concepts

Ageing: an extensive area of study that covers the whole lifespan but with particular emphasis on later years. Early models of ageing (for example, Bromley, 1966) that assumed that peak performance was achieved in early adulthood, after which all faculties were thought to decline, are known as 'decrement models'. It is now acknowledged that development continues throughout life, which has given rise to a 'personal growth model' (for example Rapoport and Rapoport, 1980). Even when some *short-term memory* and *attention* processes deteriorate in old age this does not prevent a continued improvement in 'wisdom' or crystallised *intelligence* and overall *cognitive appraisal* of the world.

Aggression: any form of behaviour that is directed at living or inanimate objects with the intention of causing physical or psychological harm or to gain an advantage. It may take the form of a physical and violent attack but is more commonly expressed as a verbal outpouring of emotion. Aggression can be:

> physical or verbal
> direct or indirect
> active or passive
> *instrumental* or hostile
> impulsive or planned (see also *Weapons effect*)
> overt or subtle.

Verbal aggression can take the form of insults, threats, sarcasm, gossip, graffiti or any other spoken or written activity intended to cause harm.

Passive aggression is withdrawal from a situation or refusal to co-operate with intention to annoy or produce an outcome undesirable or harmful to the other person (Buss, 1961). This can be in the form of refusing to attend planning meetings, or not offering help, or deliberately *'forgetting'* to do something. In relationships, there may be sulky *silences* and unspoken resentments.

Adult bullying (Randall, 1997) may include ridicule in front of others, subjection to bad language and getting unpleasant substances through the letterbox or actual physical assault. It is a systematic or repeated use of aggression and may involve an abuse of *power*.

Berkowitz (1983) argues that aggression is transmitted between generations so that people who are exposed to violence when young develop an aggressive tendency themselves (cycle of violence or intergenerational transmission of *aggression*).

Retterstol (1990: 75) suggests that 'women, more than men, use the act of suicide as an aggressive weapon, as a defensive weapon or as a means with which to manipulate their environment.' It appears that if women are socialised into acting in a restrained way and not showing violence, they are likely to retain this behaviour even when desperate and take out their aggression on themselves. Hendin (1964) has argued that aggressive antisocial behaviour, when accompanied by puritanical and pious *attitudes*, may lead to a moral form of suicide. Suicide and deliberate self-harm can also take the form of martyrdom or *instrumental* self-harm, as when protesters starve or burn themselves to death in order to bring about social reform.

Altered body image: a change in the *perception* of one's appearance, bodily functions or state of health with the potential for a change in *self-esteem*. This may be triggered by an actual physical change such as injury, surgery, illness, effects of drugs, loss or gain in weight, increase or decrease in exercise, maturation and ageing. In some cases, however, an altered perception can arise with no actual change of appearance or state but from a situation or event that simply leads the person to view his or her body differently.

Altered state of consciousness (ASC): Ornstein (1973: 43) defines an ASC as:

> a qualitative alteration in the over-all pattern of mental functioning, such that the experiencer feels his consciousness is radically different from the way it functions ordinarily. ... An SoC [state of *consciousness*] is thus defined not in terms of any particular content of consciousness, or specific behaviour or physiological change, but in terms of the over-all patterning of psychological functioning.

Ornstein lists as ASCs: *dreaming*, hypnogogic (falling asleep) and hypnopompic (waking) states, alcohol intoxication, effects of marijuana and LSD, meditative states, so-called possession states and autohypnosis. We can add *hallucinations* and the effects of other psychoactive or *psychotropic* drugs, and even view conditions such as *autism*, *dementia*, bipolar mood disorder and *schizophrenia* as altered states of consciousness. Autogenic training aims for an altered state of consciousness or awareness.

Altruism: unselfish *attention* to the needs of others, sometimes at some disadvantage to oneself. Vaillant (1977) identified altruism as a healthy defence mechanism directing attention away from one's own *pain* and *anxiety*. Examples might include that of a grandparent coping with the death of a grandchild by becoming a volunteer at a children's hospital. In contrast, some interpretations of Maslow (1943) suggest that altruism is the highest in the hierarchy of needs, addressed only when a person achieves self-actualisation. Some animals demonstrate what looks like altruism, which can be explained in evolutionary terms as being beneficial to the species as a whole.

Ambiguous figures: popular illustrations of visual illusions in which the drawing can be interpreted in more than one way. The most commonly known one is the old woman/young woman, illustrated in many introductory psychology textbooks.

Amnesia: inability to remember, either total or partial. Retrograde amnesia is impairment in recalling events that occurred before the onset of illness and anterograde amnesia refers to difficulty in recalling or recognising events that have occurred since the onset of illness. Both conditions may appear together. *Brain damage* may result in severe effects on *long-term memory*. Critical lesion sites in the *limbic system* give rise to a global amnesic effect. Other evidence suggests an alteration in the active processes of *retrieval*, rather than passive *reminiscence*.

Analysis of amnesia has contributed to active information-processing models of memory.

A period of loss of *memory*, when the individual withdraws for a time from the normal lifestyle is known as a fugue.

Anger: a natural human emotion of displeasure, often passionately felt. People may express anger in a variety of ways including *aggression*, or not at all. Some researchers believe anger is important in health and illness-related conditions, particu-larly when it is repressed or inhibited (Spielberger et al, 1988; Eysenck, 1985, 1994). Most research lists anger as one of the basic *emotions* associated with characteristic *facial expressions* and postures and linked to fundamental physiological processes, in particular the *hypothalamus* of the brain.

Anger may be a response to confusion, frustration or fear, all of which may be associated with other health problems. Anger is one of the most commonly found emotional responses to *loss*, and listed in most 'stages' models of bereavement.

Anger may be associated with guilt and blame and directed towards the self. Alternatively, it may be directed towards others. According to psychoanalytical approaches, it acts as a defence mechanism, protecting the person from *anxiety*, guilt and blame by involving the *displacement* or *projection* of anger towards anyone seen as responsible for the loss, such as family members, health care professionals, God or the deceased. Some 'stage' models indicate that a person may move from internally-directed anger to externally-directed anger.

Anger management: a range of activities and techniques used to enable an individual to manage provoking situations. Anger management training may be helpful both for people who find it impossible to show their *anger* and for those who flare up too easily. Approaches include cognitive and behavioural therapies, *psychodynamic* therapy, group therapy and creative arts.

Anima and animus: the feminine and masculine *archetype*s, which form a complementary pair of complexes. Jung was one of the main theorists to argue that individuals have both masculine and feminine characteristics and refers to 'transpersonal' traits. Jung suggests that all people have both anima (unconscious beliefs and feelings relating to femininity) and animus (unconscious beliefs and feelings relating to masculinity), but that the anima is predominant in women, the animus in men. See also *Gender identity*.

Animism: treating inanimate objects as if they are alive and have intentions towards the person. We make the assumption that other people have beliefs and desires and it appears that we see all behaviour as intentional, and we like to look for intentions. Cartoonists make use of this, and the effect has been studied systematically (Heider and Simmel, 1944). Children are particularly noted for imbuing toys with personality and judging them to be blameworthy or praiseworthy for their actions.

This tendency is utilised in such experiments as Bandura's work on aggression towards an inflatable hobo doll (Bandura, 1965), and McGarrigle and Donaldson's (1974 use of the 'Naughty Teddy' in exploring cognitive development. However, not only children indulge in animism. Many adults like to refer to cars by personal names and praise or blame them for their performance; others get angry with objects that get in their way and blame the traffic lights for changing to red just as they approach, as if the lights had done it deliberately. Other examples include blaming the rain for re-wetting the dried washing on the line or blaming a cup for falling and breaking.

It could be argued that a simple belief in a supernatural or super-human god or gods is an extension of animism. If there is too little or too much rain and the crops fail, it is a small step from blaming the rain to blaming something or someone that controls the rain, perhaps as part of some larger plan. See also *Theory of mind*.

Anticipation: a healthy conscious type of defence mechanism identified by Vaillant (1977). It involves anticipating *problem*s and finding solutions for them before they happen. An example of a healthy anticipation is planning for interviews or examinations. Anticipation can become unproductive if the person worries so much that plans are incomplete or inadequate and the additional worry outweighs the benefits.

Anxiety: one of the basic *emotions*, a term used in preference to fear in most contexts. It can range from mild to severe, is generally unpleasant, usually accompanied by heightened autonomic *arousal*, and sometimes by a characteristic facial expression. Anxiety may constitute a warning and can be seen as useful in helping a person cope with threatening situations, but in excess may interfere with coping. Writers often use the terms anxiety and stress interchangeably when referring to the emotional distress experienced in a new situation and we need to use both words in literature searches.

Apparition: an imagined appearance of something as if it was there. This can involve any one of the *senses* or a combination of senses. Most people describe apparitions solely as visual but this is likely to be because *vision* is normally the prominent sense and other sensory experience is ignored. Green and McCreery (1989: 1) suggest that we think of an apparition as a figure of a person who 'isn't really there' superimposed on the normal environment. They distinguish between apparitions and waking dreams, in which the person perceives the whole environment as different from normal and there is a temporary loss of awareness of the normal physical surroundings. Note that apparition refers to the object and *hallucination* to the experience.

Appeasement gesture: a term used in ethological approaches for an *instinct*ive act by a victim that inhibits the victor's *aggression* and thus prevents a dominant animal from killing the victim. To avoid further conflict, humans may adopt appeasement or conciliatory behaviours by making concessions in conflict situations, for example giving in or admitting defeat, or by looking submissive.

Archetype: a term used by Jung, among others, for a symbol that represents a universal theme or ideal. In Western history, the archetypal or ideal male is seen as the warrior, bold and strong, and the ideal female as soft, pliant and nurturing. The gods of ancient Greece and Rome exemplify these extremes. The medieval symbols for iron ♂ (a hard, strong metal) and copper ♀ (a soft, pliable and decorative metal), adopted as symbols for male and female, represent the same characteristics.

Jung's notions of archetypes are quite likely to be described today as culturally determined stereotypes that are by no means universally accepted.

Arousal systems: as shown in Figure 3.1, two fundamental patterns of physiological arousal are the:

> closed loop of sympathetic nervous system – adrenal medulla (see *Fight or flight*)
> open loop of pituitary – adrenal cortex (see *General adaptation syndrome*).

Technical advances in hormonal analysis have made it possible to go beyond these two and

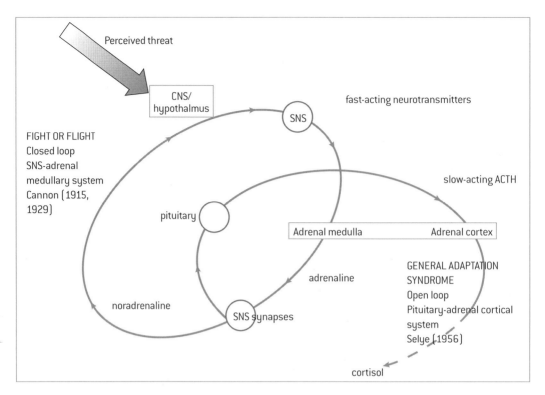

Figure 3.1 Physiological arousal systems

study a broad spectrum of hormones and endocrine systems, including the pituitary-gonadal, growth hormone and insulin systems (Mason, 1975; Ursin et al, 1978). It seems there is no *single* stress hormone but that all endocrine systems are responsive to psychological stress. Work in the field of *psychoneuroimmunology* suggests that the immune system, too, is responsive to psychological demands (Ader, 1980). The physiological response to stress is a complex and interrelated patterning of *autonomic*, hormonal and immune systems. See also Cannon and Selye in Part 4.

Artificial intelligence: the use of 'thinking machines' and computer modelling to copy or simulate human behaviour in an attempt to increase understanding. Turing (1936/37) compared the typed responses of a machine with those of a human given the same question. He argued that if an observer could not tell whether the response came from the machine or the person, then the machine could be said to be thinking. See also Part 4. Whether or not that conclusion is valid, the early work has given rise to some interesting speculations. Through analysis of the questions and

answers that are typical of a diagnostic interview, various computer programmes have been devised which simulate a clinician's responses and assist in diagnosing a client's main areas of concern. Naturally enough, this is increasing in use as it saves money. Happily, clients report some satisfaction with the arrangement and sometimes feel more at ease typing in responses at a keyboard than talking to a therapist. Other lines of investigation simulate *problem-solving* behaviour and seek greater understanding of neural nets and processes. Artificial intelligence is an important and growing area of cognitive psychology.

Asceticism: denying oneself pleasures. Anna Freud suggested that adolescents sometimes deny themselves self-indulgent behaviour, for example by refraining from eating certain foods, because of their uncertainties in growing up. This is one explanation given for the early stages of anorexia nervosa. Some writers describe food fads and vegetarianism as examples of asceticism. It is possible that asceticism forms part of many disorders where an individual feels guilty about over-indulging. Prior to *psychoanalysis*, the term referred mainly to religious sects who observe strict lifestyles.

Assertiveness: putting forward one's point of view in order to achieve desired goals; behaving positively and forthrightly without being combative or causing harm. Contrary to common incorrect usage, assertiveness and *aggression* are not synonymous: assertiveness is associated with self-confidence and tact, speaking out in a spirit of co-operation, negotiation and compromise rather than competition or hostility. See also *Traps*.

Assimilation: a term adopted by Piaget to refer to the process of taking in new information. If new evidence contradicts what has been previously learned according to the person's individual *schemas* or pre-conceptions, the person may do one of three things:

> reject the new information and soon forget it
> assimilate the new data at a superficial level alongside the previous schemas with no shift in understanding
> accommodate the new data by developing more effective schemas.

Assimilation of contradictory ideas, without *accommodation*, can lead to *cognitive dissonance* and in turn to distortion of one of the ideas, or later rejection, *forgetting* or *denial*.

Attachment and bonding: Bowlby (1988) believes attachment behaviour stems from the need for safety and security and is intended to maintain bonds. See also Ainsworth and Bowlby in Part 4. A threat to the bond, such as impending *loss* through absence or death, may activate attachment behaviours such as crying, clinging, loss of independence and activity. Bowlby (1951,1969) asserts that mother love in infancy and childhood is important for mental health and that any kind of psychiatric disorder always shows a disturbance in social relationships/affectional bonding, in many cases caused by disturbed bonding in childhood. However, it can equally be argued that a child's difficult behaviour may be caused by biologically determined factors and will result in disturbances in bonding if the parents cannot cope. Bonding is defined as 'selective attachment' and although it is now recognised that the mother is not the only person to whom children form attach-

ments, it is considered important for children to have regular contact with a few significant adults. This enables long-term relationships to form and avoids repeated episodes of loss.

Kennell et al (1979) gives evidence from the point of view of the care-giver and suggests that skin-to-skin contact is important for a parent soon after birth and needs to occur within a critical period of 6–12 hours after birth for a firm bond to be established. However, Rutter (1979) argues that bonds build up slowly over many months and that 'maternal *instinct*' is not automatic or immediate. See also Harlow in Part 4.

Attention: a term usually linked to *perception* that covers research in cognitive and *psychodynamic* psychology concerned with how and why we direct our attention towards one thing rather than another. One of the problems for theories of *attention* and *perception* is working out how the *brain* and *nervous system* process incoming stimuli and make decisions about which bits to pay attention to. We can deliberately direct conscious attention towards any of the *senses* at any time, but the greatest part of the selectivity takes place automatically at an unconscious level of processing. *Habituation* plays a part in this as the nervous system stops responding to repeated stimuli after a while, but this still leaves a great deal of other incoming information to sort.

Current ideas (known as filter models, for example Broadbent, Deutsch and Deutsch, Treisman, see Part 4) are that all the information is taken in and then filtered by some process that identifies and selects only those items of interest and importance. The *thalamus* in the centre of the *brain* acts as the chief interchange of neurones in the brain, routing information from the senses and passing it on to the relevant areas of the brain, and may play a part in the selection of material in response to signals from the cortex.

All approaches indicate how the conscious awareness of incoming information is limited to a tiny fraction of what is available in the world (both externally and internally) and that limits are essential in order to protect from 'information overload'. Only information relevant to the current problem should be allowed in from the perceptual field and from memory.

There appear to be four main components of attention:

concepts

> initial unconscious parallel processing that labels each location in the perceptual field
> a conscious serial stage that examines each location (often obstructed by bottlenecks that constrict the flow of information)
> emotional colouring of experience that attaches value
> funnelling of control to an executive process that we experience as the self or 'I', or our will.

Attitude: a settled or fixed way of responding to people and objects in the environment. Attitudes can be stuck in a rut or can change in response to new experiences or persuasion. Psychological study is concerned with how attitudes are expressed and how they develop and change throughout the lifespan. Triandis (1971; see also Part 4) gives the following reasons for holding settled attitudes. They:

> help us understand the world around us, by organising and simplifying a very complex input from our environment
> protect our self-esteem by making it possible for us to avoid unpleasant truths about ourselves
> help us to adjust in a complex world by making it more likely that we will react so as to maximise our *rewards* from the environment
> allow us to express our fundamental *values*.

Attitudes help us to function with least effort. Once we have established a pattern of reactions to a given category of attitude objects, we are saved from having to decide again, starting from first principles, what our reaction should be. Our previous experience is a guide. Moreover, we can adjust socially by making it easier to get along with people who have similar attitudes (Newcomb, 1953).

In most usage, an attitude is regarded as having two components (cognitive and emotional), which then lead to behaviour. From this point of view, questioning a person about *beliefs* and feelings is thought to give direct information about the attitude.

However, a significant early theoretical approach is the three-component model from Rosenberg and Hovland (1960), see Figure 3.2, which suggests that our behaviour is actually part of our attitude. This model is based on behavioural principles with equal emphasis on each component, helping to make a clear distinction between:

> *belief*
> opinion, which consists of stated beliefs and values
> attitude, which includes beliefs, feelings and actions.

Observation of all outcomes leads to inferences about the attitude. The attitude itself is defined as an 'intervening variable' or abstract *concept*,

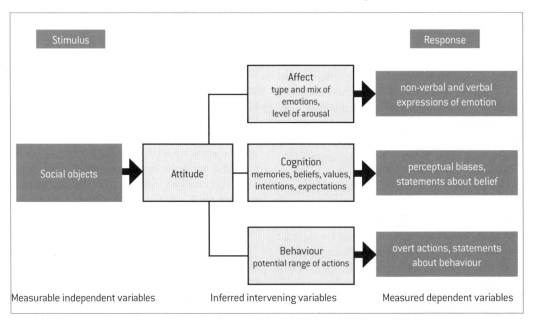

Figure 3.2 Three-component model of attitude (after Rosenberg and Hovland, 1960)

between the stimulus and the response, that cannot be measured directly.

The main debate is whether attitudes can be measured directly by questionnaire or only indirectly, by observing all responses. See also LaPiere in Part 4.

Attitude development: Niven (1994) identifies three main ways in which *attitudes* are formed:

> *operant* (or instrumental) *conditioning*,
> *modelling*
> direct experience.

The principles of *operant conditioning* are based on the *reinforcement* of responses to stimuli. A child's parents, teachers and friends will often provide reinforcement for expressing the 'right' attitude and criticise the 'wrong' one. The reward may be only slight, such as a nod or continued attention.

Modelling refers to copying others who may or may not realise they are being used as 'role-models'. Many *attitudes* are learned by children acting out in *play* things they have seen their parents do or have watched on television. *Attitudes* acquired through direct experience with an attitude object, or person, tend to be stronger and more vivid that those acquired 'second hand' through *conditioning* or modelling (for example, Fazio and Zanna, 1978).

Attitude questionnaires: the simplest way of directly measuring *attitudes* is through questionnaires. These may use the Q-technique (see Stephenson, 1953; Brown, 1986) and usually consist of a set of questions or statements to each of which the respondent assigns a score on a Likert-type scale (see Part 5). Designing an attitude questionnaire usually involves the following steps:

> Define the topic, attitude object and participants.
> Sort out the aspects – cognitive, affective, behavioural.
> Choose the dimension, such as favourability/unfavourability.
> Select the statements and test them for validity (see Part 5).
> Construct a Likert-type scale (see Part 5).

One limitation of questionnaires is that they tend to measure what people think they believe, rather than what they actually do. See LaPiere in Part 4.

Attribution: how people explain events such as an accident or why they become ill: what they attribute the event to.

Attribution theory: attribution theory, from Heider (1958), includes a basic assumption that people tend to see the social environment as predictable and controllable according to what is perceived as the cause of events or behaviour. A number of effects can be identified:

> *fundamental attribution error* (which varies with the seriousness of consequences)
> *animism*
> *actor–observer* effect (see *Fundamental attribution error*)
> *self-serving bias*
> *false consensus*
> *false consistency*
> *primacy/recency* effects
> *halo and horns effects*
> *self-fulfilling prophecy*
> *stereotyping*.

Some of these effects can be viewed as *person perception* errors that can be corrected through increased awareness and the development of interpersonal perceptual skills.

Auditory location: picking out the direction from which a sound is coming. The ability to do this accurately depends on having similar *hearing* in both ears as the *perception* of direction depends on an evaluation of the differences in timing and loudness of the sound arriving at each ear. An interesting illusion is often noted where a sound is directly behind or in front of the listener. Since the signal arrives at both ears simultaneously, it may not be possible to tell whether the sound is coming from front or back.

Authoritarian personality: a term derived from work by Adorno et al (1950) to refer to people who favour an authoritarian and hierarchical social structure and are particularly prone to stereotyping and prejudice against minority groups. The term 'authoritarian personality' does not necessarily mean 'in authority' but can apply to a person anywhere in a hierarchy, in either a low or a high position. See also *Parenting styles* and *Power*.

concepts

Autism: Anthony Clare and Lawrence Bartak (in Williams, 1992) describe how people with autism have difficulty in understanding other people's *facial expressions*, emotional reactions and conversational tones, and find it hard to process information dealing with people and relationships. Bartak asserts that this is not caused by bad parenting, as was once thought (for example Bettleheim), but by brain development. There may be a link with Vitamin B12 metabolism.

Baron-Cohen (for example, 1989; see also Part 4) describes how many autistic children have difficulty appreciating what someone else might be thinking and cannot see that someone else might have a different point of view from their own (see also *Theory of mind*).

Hobson (1993) describes autism as a profound disturbance in interpersonal relatedness and gives examples of people with autism who cannot grasp what is meant by friendship or what it means to have a friend.

Oliver Sacks (for example 1985, 1996) gives detailed descriptions of people with autism.

Autonomic nervous system: the autonomic nervous system (ANS) is the part of the peripheral nervous system responsible for governing the activities of:

❭ glands and hormones of the endocrine system
❭ muscles of the organs or viscera:
  – in the skin (around hair follicles; smooth muscle)
  – around blood vessels (smooth muscle)
  – in the eye (the iris; smooth muscle)
  – in the stomach, intestines and bladder (smooth muscle)
  – of the heart (cardiac muscle).

There are two inter-related systems and a third sub-division:

❭ sympathetic nervous system (SNS)
❭ parasympathetic nervous system
❭ enteric nervous system.

The SNS increases *arousal* and the parasympathetic nervous system restores to normal. The SNS originates in the spinal cord and is not generally under conscious control, but techniques such as *biofeedback*, autogenic relaxation training and yoga can help a person gain some control. The

enteric nervous system is a meshwork of *nerve fibres* that innervate the viscera (gastrointestinal tract, pancreas, gall bladder). See also *Arousal*, *Fight or flight*, *GAS*, the *Nervous system* and Figures 3.1, 3.3 and 3.13.

Availability (memory): the extent to which information has been stored in the *memory* and is available for *retrieval*.

Avoidance behaviour: it is important not to confuse avoidance behaviour, where the people recognise a loss or unpleasant memory but do not talk about it, with unconscious *denial*. Hinton (1980) suggests that dying patients remain quiet to avoid hurting their families, and families tend to avoid the issue in order not to upset the dying person. Avoidance may be important in critical situations where there is a possibility of recovery. See also *Grief*.

Bales interaction process analysis: a tool developed by Bales (1950) for examining the interaction that takes place when a group is engaged in accomplishing a task. Interaction is classified according to whether it is task-orientated or socio-emotional.

Coding categories are subdivided into problems of:

a) communication
b) evaluation
c) control
d) decision
e) tension reduction
f) reintegration.

These can be seen in terms of four main groups: (A) positive reactions, and (D) negative reactions, which are socio-emotional, and then (B) attempted answers and (C) questions, which are task-orientated. See also Part 4.

Bales and Cohen (1979, cited in Brown, 1988) further refined the analysis to include aspects of status and friendliness, and developed SYMLOG – a system for the multiple level observation of groups. This separates three dimensions:

❭ friendly–unfriendly
❭ dominance–submission
❭ towards–away from goal direction.

Analysis can reveal the patterns of communica-

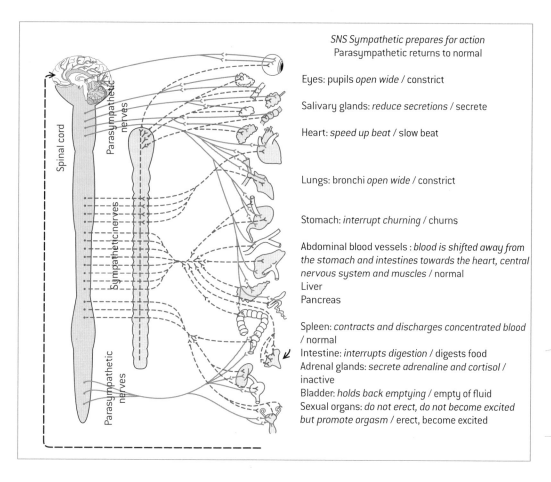

SNS Sympathetic prepares for action
Parasympathetic returns to normal

Eyes: pupils *open wide* / constrict

Salivary glands: *reduce secretions* / secrete

Heart: *speed up beat* / slow beat

Lungs: bronchi *open wide* / constrict

Stomach: *interrupt churning* / churns

Abdominal blood vessels : *blood is shifted away from the stomach and intestines towards the heart, central nervous system and muscles* / normal
Liver
Pancreas

Spleen: *contracts and discharges concentrated blood* / normal
Intestine: *interrupts digestion* / digests food
Adrenal glands: *secrete adrenaline and cortisol* / inactive
Bladder: *holds back emptying* / empty of fluid
Sexual organs: *do not erect, do not become excited but promote orgasm* / erect, become excited

Spinal cord

Parasympathetic nerves

Sympathetic nerves

Parasympathetic nerves

Figure 3.3 Autonomic nervous system and target organs

tion that take place, individual styles and the triggers that lead to certain behaviours. For example, it can be seen whether anyone tends to take the lead in asking questions or making suggestions, who tends to be more focused on the task in hand, and who engages in social interaction (such as telling jokes or encouraging others to speak). It can be seen whether this helps the group in the task or hinders it, or whether individuals withdraw by *silence* or unhelpful suggestions.

Brown (1988) points out that SYMLOG is limited in its usefulness by applying only to certain kinds of groups and neglecting intergroup relations. In a classroom or seminar situation, a simplified form of the Bales IPA can be used with *broken information games* and *sociograms* in order to give an introduction to the basic ideas and help members to improve *metacommunication*. See also *Group processes.*

Basal nuclei (previously known as basal ganglia): these consist of several clusters of cell bodies or nuclei (plural of nucleus) deep within the cerebral hemispheres. The basal nuclei receive impulses from different parts of the *cerebral cortex* and are thus supplied with information relating to thoughts. The command signals sent out from the basal nuclei pass first to the *thalamus* and from there to many areas of the *cerebral cortex,* including the motor control area. They are important in co-ordination of movement and in related aspects of Parkinson's disease. The term nuclei is now preferred for structures within the central nervous system; the term ganglia is used for those in the peripheral nervous system.

Behaviour shaping: the alteration of behaviour or the production of new behaviour through the systematic use of *reinforcement*, based on the principles of *operant (instrumental) conditioning.*

Although the terms 'behaviour shaping' and 'behaviour modification therapy' are often used interchangeably, behaviour shaping is sometimes reserved for a 'purer' form of therapeutic programme in which success does not rely on the participant having cognitive awareness of the aims of the programme. The term 'behaviour-shaping' is also used where there is no therapeutic attempt, and to refer to the training of animals to perform complex tasks.

Shaping is linked to trial and error. Animals engage in a range of behaviours, some apparently intentional, some random. When a certain item of behaviour is followed by a *reinforcement* (that is a desirable outcome, such as food), that item of behaviour is likely to be repeated. The trainer, with an end goal in mind, waits until a bit of behaviour occurs that, with luck and further training, will lead toward the end goal and then gives another *reinforcement* or *reward*. When that item of behaviour is established, the trainer withholds *reinforcement*s until new behaviour occurs that is a little closer to the target behaviour. The behaviour gradually becomes closer and closer to the required goal until the goal is finally reached.

Behaviour (or behavioural) therapies: a global term for all treatment approaches that apply *classical* or *operant conditioning* techniques or other aspects of *learning theory* to the analysis of behaviour problems in an attempt to change the problem behaviour. In some texts, the term 'behaviour therapy' is used only for techniques based on *classical conditioning* (see Gregory, 1987), but the term is used in the wider sense here. There are various types, including:

> behaviour modification or shaping
> avoidance learning
> response prevention
> aversion therapy
> graded exposure
> progressive desensitisation
> implosion and flooding.

Behavioural techniques may also be combined with cognitive therapy to provide a *cognitive-behavioural* programme. See also Adams and Bromley (1998).

Beliefs: Morgan and King (1971) define a belief as 'the acceptance of some proposition'. It can be argued that most knowledge consists of beliefs rather than facts, in that many so-called facts are simply widely held beliefs for which there is consistent empirical evidence. Plato distinguishes between three types of knowledge or belief:

> things for which there is little or no empirical evidence or rational argument and which require faith, such as confidence in the efficiency of free market economics or the existence of fairies or Father Christmas
> things that are true according to widely held belief, perhaps because they always happen that way, or can be shown to happen through scientific investigation, such as that the sun will rise tomorrow or that *touch* is an important aspect of communication
> things whose truth is a matter of irrefutable knowledge, for example 'by definition', such as that a triangle has three sides.

It is argued that some scientific findings can be considered irrefutable, provided the conditions under which things always occur can be precisely defined. Later philosophers make this kind of distinction by talking of 'grammar' (Wittgenstein) or 'sense' and 'reference' (Frege). That is, the choice of words used to refer to things and the 'rules' for putting words together determines how the truth about those things is communicated. Putting free market economics next to fairies in the sentence above, possibly suggests something about the writer's beliefs.

Biofeedback: a set of techniques for helping people gain some control over processes which are normally outside conscious awareness and control, such as muscle tension, heart-rate, blood-pressure and epileptic seizures (Phillips, 1991). The chosen process is monitored, usually by an electronic device, and connected to a computer or television screen that can give the person a visual or auditory signal of some kind. Through practice, a person learns to associate changes in the signal with something that he or she is doing, and may eventually be able deliberately to create desired changes. In many cases, the person does not actually know exactly what causes the changes, only that feeling a certain way or willing the changes to happen will have the right effect. This is similar to the way many activities are learned through natural feedback from the surroundings,

concepts

like walking, swimming or riding a bicycle. Maybe it was not obvious how it was done, but it worked, and improved with practice.

Blank slate/*tabula rasa*: Watson (1930) is often quoted for his reference to a child being a blank slate or *tabula rasa* that can be trained in any required manner. See also *Frame problem*, below, and John B. Watson in Part 4.

Blindsight: if a person has damage to the visual cortex, this may result in a large blind spot in the visual field. The person said to have blindsight will deny seeing anything there, but if asked to guess can guess correctly well above chance levels. This can be interpreted by saying the person's brain has access to the objects but the person is not sentient, that is conscious, of them. This also occurs in some *split-brain* patients.

Body boundaries: we seem to have quite distinct boundaries between self and non-self. Much of early child development is concerned with learning these boundaries and identifying what things in the world belong to 'self' and what are 'other'. There are recognisable developmental changes in knowing and understanding limits of bodily self.

As adults, we are not usually aware of these boundaries until something happens to upset them. Allport (1955), cited by Gross (1996), points out that bodily fluids we accept comfortably while in the body cause different reactions after elimination; he describes the difference between swallowing saliva while it is still in the mouth and when it has been spat out into a cup. The change in acceptance of blood, urine and faeces from inside to outside the body is considerably greater.

Body image: perceptions of self (*self-image* and *self-concept*) that relate specifically to the body. These can include anything to do with appearance and also the physical state or state of health or bodily functions. Thus body image might include a description of facial features, or the current position in the menstrual cycle or pregnancy, the extent of a suntan, fitness, or whether one is constipated or has any other condition. In most usage, the term 'body image' covers both description and evaluation, together with the associated *self-esteem*: that is, how people feel about how they look or what they can do.

Price (1990: 11) identifies three aspects of *body image*:

> Body reality – the way in which our body is constructed, namely the way it really is. This is affected by both nature and nurture factors.
> Body ideal – how we think we should look. We hold a personal body ideal that may also affect how we think other people 'should' look. Body ideal is constantly changing and susceptible to a variety of influences.
> Body presentation – how we present our body appearance (dress, pose and action) to the social world. We are able to control body presentation within certain limits and to reflect actively on how body presentation was received by others. See also *Persona*.

One limitation of this approach is the reliance on the notion that there is an absolute 'reality'. All perceptions are coloured by previous experience, knowledge and beliefs, and it can be hard to be absolutely objective about what a person is 'really' like.

Price (1986) also lists the following factors that contribute to body image formation:

> genetics
> socialisation
> fashion
> mass media
> *peer group* pressure
> culture/race
> health education.

Bottom-up processing: a term that has a variety of meanings, depending on the context.

In general it means working upwards from basic information or raw data towards a higher mental process. This can be compared with notions of induction in *thinking* and *problem-solving*. In *perception*, this refers to awareness of the world that is determined solely by the incoming sensory information. This is also known as data-driven processing and involves initial *recognition* of all the basic elements in order to match the incoming stimuli with previous experience. These elements can then be *synthesised* into a complete whole.

Brain: the brain fits closely inside the top of the skull and is described as having the consistency of soft cheese or mushroom enclosed in a fine skin. There are four main sections:

> *cerebral cortex* (sometimes called just the cortex), the outer layer, greyish in colour
> *mid-brain*, the inner part, whitish in colour
> brain-stem that leads down into the spinal cord
> *cerebellum*, at the back.

The brain consists mainly of two types of cells:

> *neurones*
> *glia.*

A baby is born with all the neurones in the brain and central nervous system. As the baby grows, the neurones enlarge and grow, the dendrites extend and spread further and the axons grow, and more connections are made between nerves via *synapses*. This kind of *structural change* can continue throughout life and can be seen to correspond to the activities that a person undertakes.

It used to be believed that brain cells do not divide and reproduce, and are not replaced when lost through accident or disease. However, Weiss (Reynolds and Weiss, 1992, see Part 4) discovered neural stem cells in the brains of adult mammals and his research has lead to new approaches for brain cell replacement and repair.

The brain is active all the time with signals passing from place to place along well-established routes that have grown and developed according to the person's individual experience. Most of this activity takes place automatically without conscious awareness, as the brain monitors incoming information, matches it with previous patterns, assesses it for importance and activates relevant *autonomic* and motor systems or, occasionally, makes new connections between previously unconnected data. Snippets of data reach *consciousness* as we interact with our environment or we become aware that we are hungry or aching or we have an idea.

See also *Basal nuclei, Glia cells, Cerebellum, Cerebral cortex, Computational theory of mind, Evoked potentials, Hearing, Hemispheric specialisation, Hippocampus, Hypothalamus, Language centres, Limbic system, Mid-brain, Pineal body, Nerve fibre, Neurone, Sleep switching mechanism, Smell, Synapse, Thalamus, Topography, Touch, Vision.*

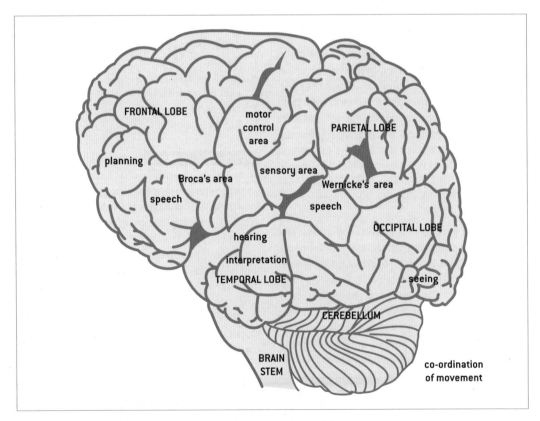

Figure 3.4 Outside of the brain, showing the left hemisphere of the cerebral cortex

concepts

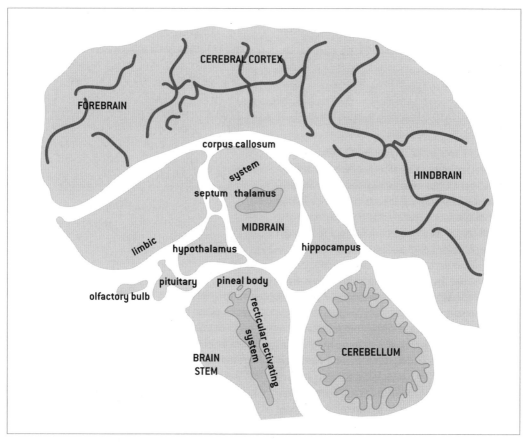

Figure 3.5 Inside the brain, showing the mid-brain and brain-stem of the left hemisphere

Brain damage: damage can be caused by direct injury or loss of blood supply in a stroke, or other means. Areas of damage can be identified with loss of particular functions. This does not necessarily imply that all the processing for a particular function takes place within that area, only that an essential piece is missing. This piece may simply be a significant part of the communication from one area to another. This can be compared with removing one component from a circuit board in a television, radio or computer. When the component is removed, the function of the set is altered but it cannot be said that the lost function resided in that component, only that the component was necessary as part of the whole process.

This comparison further enables us to regard the *brain* as a very special instrument. In most computers, a particular 'chip' will need to be replaced before function can be restored, whereas in the *brain* other parts sometimes seem to be able to take over functions so that if one part is damaged, skills can be relearned by using other parts. However, some functions are hard-wired and not changeable, see Sperry in Part 4.

The implications for caring for people following a stroke are that repeated practice of an activity may eventually result in some improvement, even if the brain is locally badly damaged. More research is needed to help indicate when it is worthwhile persevering. An alternative approach is to look for a related function that will achieve a similar purpose. For example a person who loses the ability to read because the part of the brain that processes visual *recognition* of letters and words is damaged, but who can still see, may learn to read in a new way. By tracing out the shape of letters with a finger, it is possible for muscle or *procedural memory* in the fingers and hand to associate a pattern of movements with the name of each letter, using a previously unused and undamaged area of the brain. This method is slow and requires the same sort of continuous practice as playing a violin in order to produce sufficient *structural change* but might be worthwhile. See also *Blindsight, Split-brain, Visual neglect*.

Brain imaging: there are a number of techniques, such as CT, PET and MRI, for scanning the *brain*, each of which gives a different kind of information.

> CT or CAT images (X-ray computed tomography or X-ray computed axial tomography) are computer-generated images of tissue density produced by measuring the absorption of *X-rays* in body tissue. The *X-rays* pass through the *brain* tissue as a fine beam sweeping through many different angles. This provides a succession of pictures or representations of slices of the tissue. The word tomography comes from the Greek work 'tomos', meaning 'cut', as in appendectomy.

> MRI (magnetic resonance imaging) is also known as NMR (nuclear magnetic resonance) or NMRI (nuclear magnetic resonance imaging). Like CT X-ray images, MRI images give anatomical data of the *brain*; finer detail is possible than with X-rays, but both techniques are needed for a full picture as different structures show up. The technique was first discovered in the 1940s (see Gregory, 1987) and came into widespread medical use in the 1980s. Nuclear magnetic resonance is based on the observation that the nuclei of some atoms behave like miniature magnets when placed in a magnetic field. They can be lined up in a magnetic field and then manipulated by a controlled radio signal. As they recover from the radio disturbance, they emit radio frequency signals that give information about the surrounding atoms. This provides a picture of how all the atoms in a particular region are arranged. In the *brain* tissue, the abundant hydrogen nuclei (which are simple protons) respond the most strongly to the magnetic and radio disturbance; for this reason the technique may also be referred to as 'proton NMR'.

> PET (positron emission tomography) scanning gives functional information; that is it shows what is actually happening chemically in the *brain*. The technique involves giving a person a radioactive substance such as radioactive glucose, and then detecting where that substance goes in the *brain*. Since brain activity depends on using glucose, regions which show up as having a high level of radioactivity can be assumed to be most active. The radioactive atoms in the glucose have very short half-lives of a few minutes and the radiation consists of positrons which can be thought of as positive electrons or positive beta (β) rays. When an emitted positron interacts with an electron in the *brain* tissue, photons of gamma (γ) radiation are emitted which can be picked up by the detectors which are usually arranged around the head in a circular fashion. PET images show areas of abnormal *brain* function and illustrate real-time brain activity during *perception* and *problem-solving* activities.

When this information is processed together by computer all these images can be combined to give very detailed 3-D models of the brain or other organs of the body. Computer operators can rotate the 3-D image on the screen, explore different aspects of it, cut it open, look inside, and roam through it. This has provided highly accurate data on the location of specific areas of injury affecting human function. Surgeons can simulate the effects of different approaches and, in effect, practise different cuts or techniques on a particular patient's organ and work out the best technique before the actual surgery. Computers are also available to many surgeons during surgery so that they can follow their actions on the screen. This enables surgeons to work deeply inside an organ without making a large incision. See also *EEG*.

Broken information games: games which have been devised for education and training which involve the group in solving a task for which each member has only a small piece of information. Only by sharing the information and working together can the group work towards the solution. An example is solving a crime, in which each member has only one or two clues. Analysis, using *Bales IPA* or SYMLOG or other tool, can reveal some of the processes of interaction. These simulations can be compared with occupational situations such as ward rounds or conferences.

Catharsis: a sudden powerful release of pent-up emotion with a subsequent feeling of calm and well-being. This term was used by Aristotle in relation to the 'purging' of strong emotions of fear and pity through tragic poetry and is an important *concept* in *psychodynamic* approaches where discussion or expression of *emotions* is encouraged in order to reduce *stress*. It is an important feature of *psychodrama*, primal integration therapy and some aspects of *anger management*.

Cathexis: a term used in *psychodynamic* theory to refer to investment of energy in a particular object. Anticathexis is restraining of energy.

Central executive system: this is a sub-system suggested by Baddeley and Hitch (1974), see Part 4), used for processing *short-term memory* tasks. When concurrent or *parallel processing* is required the central executive helps to co-ordinate these tasks in the *slave systems*. If there are too many items for the slave systems to cope with, some items can be transferred to *long-term memory* which acts as a back-up. See also *Working memory*.

Centration: a thought pattern common during the beginning of the preoperational stage of cognitive development, characterised by the child's inability to take more than one perceptual factor into account at the same time.

Cerebellum: the cerebellum, or little brain, is at the back of the brain and can be distinguished by the fine grooves. It is concerned with *procedural memory*, learning and reconstructing skilled movements.

Cerebral cortex: the outer layer of the brain where most of the so-called 'higher' functions of the brain take place: *thinking*, *perception*, interpretation and so on. This outer layer has many folds in it, rather like a sheet that has been crumpled up, and consists of four distinct regions called the frontal lobe, parietal lobe, temporal lobe and occipital lobe (see Figure 3.4).

Within these lobes, the different folds have been given names and are associated with different functions (see *topography*). It is estimated that if it were spread out, it would be like a sheet of foam rubber, three to four millimetres thick and about half a square metre in area. The nerve cells, or *neurones*, are arranged throughout this layer rather like the circuit boards in a computer. Estimates of the number of neurones range from a thousand million (10^9) to about a million million (10^{12}). It is as if the circuit board has been crum-

pled up into a ball, giving maximum area within minimum volume.

The cortex consists of two cerebral (cortical) hemispheres or 'half spheres', often referred to as the 'left brain' and 'right brain'. There is a fissure separating the hemispheres, running from front to back, but the two halves are connected by thick cables of fibres, in particular the corpus callosum, towards the centre of the *brain*. The upper components of the brain grow outwards from the brain-stem.

Chaos theory: also known as catastrophe theory, this is an approach to solving complex scientific *problems* that began in the mid-1970s with the work of Feigenbaum (cited by Gleick, 1988). Classical physics had provided useful solutions for ordered processes but these could never quite be applied to situations that appeared to be disordered, such as when smooth water flow suddenly becomes turbulent when the speed is increased. Feigenbaum and others began to see similarities in the ways that different complex systems developed into disorder and found a way of expressing the disorder, or chaos, in mathematical terms. The most familiar items from this approach are the 'butterfly effect', 'fractal curves' and 'strange attractors'. It is suggested that chaos effects can be compared with a butterfly flapping its wings in one part of the world and setting in train a sequence of events that can create a storm somewhere else. Strange attractors, through minute influences, affect how the next tiny change will take place. Fractal curves produce beautiful and intriguing pictures.

Chaos theory has been applied to various biological processes and to certain aspects of conditions such as *schizophrenia*. Gleick (1988) describes how Huberman (*c.* 1986) examined the eye movements of schizophrenic patients, and found a mixture of order and chaos that pointed to a genetic explanation for schizophrenia and can be linked to further discoveries of the unusual processing of *dopamine* now associated with schizophrenia. The ways in which nerves and blood vessels branch into successively smaller and smaller channels, with each branch seemingly random, but the overall effect following a recognisable pattern, can be analysed using 'chaos' mathematics.

Character: a term that is difficult to define in a way that distinguishes it from personality. Often, no such distinction is made or attempted. Millon and Everly (1985) define character as a person's adherence to the values and customs of the society in which he or she lives. Eysenck (1947) sees character more as a matter of will or volition (*conative* behaviour). In common language, it is often associated with moral qualities, and we can talk of having a 'good' or 'bad' character and of activities being 'character-building'. Such aspects as willpower, strength of character and cultural values may be seen as contributing to notions of *self-efficacy* and the kinds of lifestyle that are valued. In a more general sense, it may be useful to think of character as being that part of personality that is learned, in contrast to *temperament or disposition*, which may be seen as inborn. However, as with the whole nature–nurture debate, it is the interrelationship of genetic inheritance and experience that is important.

Chromosome: a complex molecule containing *genes* that are responsible for the way in which characteristics are passed down from parents to children. The chromosomes are situated within the nucleus of each cell in an organism. The same arrangement is found in all cells. There are normally 46 chromosomes in humans that occur as 23 pairs, one chromosome in each pair inherited from each parent. Each pair may be associated with particular characteristics such as hair and eye colour, but many characteristics are governed by a variety of *genes* in several different chromosomes. They are numbered in order of length (starting with the longest) from 1 to 22 (autosomes) with the last pair being the *sex* chromosomes XX or XY. Chromosomes are a combination of protein and DNA (deoxyribonucleic acid). The DNA consists of very long molecules coiled in a double helix. The strands are made of sugars and phosphates and the two lines are joined by cross-bridges, which are bases. There are four principal kinds of base: adenine, cytosine, thymine and guanine. Along the whole chromosome, individual sections of DNA can be identified, each of which is a discrete amino acid, which can consist of up to 1,000 pairs of bases. These individual sections are the *genes*. The order in which the bases are arranged in each gene is known as the genetic code and is important in heredity, and in what is known as genetic engineering.

Chromosome mutations: in some cases of abnormalities, an alteration to the whole chromosome, or part of a chromosome, can be identified. Down's Syndrome is associated with an extra Chromosome 21, so that the person has three of these *chromosomes* instead of the usual pair. This occurs during cell division where an extra division takes place. Unlike inherited genetic codes, this abnormality can occur without either parent having any family history of Down's syndrome. In other instances, fragments of chromosomes can become lost, attached to the end of another chromosome, inverted, or inserted into another chromosome. Mutations of the X and Y chromosomes give rise to unusual sexual characteristics, see *Sex*.

Chunking: a mnemonic process or strategy of remembering a long list of items in a series of groups or chunks, such as remembering a telephone or credit card number in chunks of three or four digits (Miller, 1956, see Part 4). It is most helpful if the number of chunks is within the person's *memory span* and sometimes a hierarchy of chunking is used where each set of subdivisions is within the span.

Clairvoyance: popularly defined as foreseeing the future. Green and McCreery (1989) argue that clairvoyance can be regarded as particularly vivid hallucinatory *perception*s in which details are 'seen' or 'known' that would not be perceived under normal visual conditions.

Classical conditioning (also known as associative, contigual or contiguous conditioning): the first kind of *conditioning* to be described. This shows how learning takes place when an association is made between two stimuli. To establish a conditioned response, it is necessary to start with a natural unconditioned response such as a reflex. After repeated exposure to two stimuli together, the natural response to one stimulus is found to occur also in response to the other stimulus. Pavlov (see Part 4) found that if he rang a bell whenever a dog was eating and salivating, after a few times the dog salivated in response to the bell even if no food was given. Classical conditioning is usually summarised as follows:

> Unconditioned stimulus (US) – A stimulus which elicits an innate reflexive response, for

which no learning is assumed. For example, food in the mouth.

> Unconditioned response (UR) – The reflexive response elicited by the US. For example, production of saliva.
> Conditioned stimulus (CS) – A neutral stimulus which does not initially elicit the UR but which becomes paired with the US during the experiment. For example: the sound of a bell.
> Conditioned response (CR) – The response occurring to the CS as a result of paired presentations of the US and CS. Note that this may differ in some ways from the UR. For example: production of saliva (possibly of a different composition from the UR).

Classical *conditioning* may account for some of a baby's learning of rooting and sucking in response to the appearance, feel and *smell* of the mother (or other carer). Rooting and sucking are natural in-born reflexes that occur in response to anyone or anything touching the baby's cheek or putting anything in the baby's mouth. The sucking reflex is strongest immediately after birth and may fade considerably within a few hours if the baby is not fed. If fed, these responses, after a few days or weeks, occur more strongly in the presence of the regular feeder than any other adult. Responses to other adults may, however, occur, and it is not unusual for a visiting man, holding a new baby for the first time, to find the baby hunting enthusiastically for the breast. Further associational learning leads to finer discrimination between stimuli, and older babies learn which carers provide food. Similar processes may account for much of what is learned by children and adults, but it is usually difficult to distinguish between classical and *operant conditioning* and to separate this kind of learning from *cognitive* and social learning.

Clinical observations may be interpreted as examples of classical conditioning, such as when a person develops a fear of going outdoors following a mugging attack. An unconditioned response of fear to being mugged can become a conditioned response of going outdoors when this is repeatedly associated with memories of the attack. The process by which emotions become associated with particular objects or events is also known as *sensitisation*. In some cases this may involve *cognitive* elements and social learning as well as conditioning. Counterconditioning methods such as progressive desensitisation may be used to reduce fear.

Cognitive appraisal: a mental summing up of a situation that takes into account all knowledge, *beliefs*, memories and *perceptions*, and the *value* placed on the experience and expectations. This process can be a mixture of conscious and unconscious mental activity. The term is commonly used in relation to *emotion, stress, aggression* and *pain*.

Cognitive appraisal theory: a model from Lazarus (1982; see also Part 4) for the relationship between *emotion and cognition* which suggests that the ability to put a name to an emotion and talk about it, and hence the emotion itself, follows *cognitive appraisal*. This appraisal includes both the situation (primary appraisal) and awareness of the state of physiological *arousal*.

If emotion depends on cognitive appraisal then the emotion will alter if the cognitive appraisal alters, and this assumption forms the basis of *cognitive therapy*. That is, if a person can be persuaded to view the situation in a different light then a change in emotional state will automatically come about. The level of arousal may stay the same but interpretation of the situation will change whether the arousal is judged as positive or negative.

For example, if someone is approached from behind and kissed, without being able to see who it is, he or she might experience a sudden rush of adrenaline but will not know whether to be pleased, disgusted or angry until the perpetrator is known. Initial pleasure might soon turn to dismay on fuller cognitive appraisal. When clients with bipolar disorder experience a sense of arousal, they tend to interpret the arousal according to environmental rather than personal cues. *Cognitive therapy* seeks to help people alter their *perception* of themselves and of events so that they can reinterpret their emotional *arousal* in positive terms.

Cognitive dissonance: personal conflict between ideas or *beliefs*. For example, a person may hold humanistic *beliefs* that every individual has the right to be self-determining but also have religious beliefs that certain actions such as euthanasia, *suicide* and abortion are morally wrong. Festinger (1957, see Part 4) developed cognitive dissonance theory based on the proposal that there is a basic need or drive for consistency of beliefs. If a person

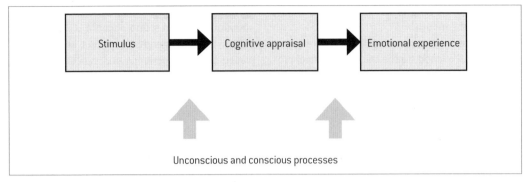

Figure 3.6 Cognitive appraisal theory

holds two ideas that are inconsistent, this is likely to result in discomfort, so the person is motivated to remove the inconsistency. The person may do this by changing one of the ideas or by ignoring or repressing one of them.

The concept of dissonance also refers to inconsistency between *beliefs* and behaviour. Where behaviour is inconsistent with a belief, either the behaviour or the belief could be changed to reduce the dissonance. In practice, most people are more likely to change their beliefs than their behaviour. For example, someone who 'knows' that increased exercise would promote health but does not want to exercise may justify the lack of exercise by finding reasons to suggest that exercise can be harmful.

Cognitive distortion: negative or distorted thoughts and *beliefs*, often associated with problem behaviour or feelings of low *self-esteem*. These may include:

> Dichotomous reasoning: seeing things in terms of two extremes, for example, 'I need to completely hide my anger, because once I start getting angry, I'll totally lose control'.
> Selective abstraction: selecting or abstracting some parts of a situation and ignoring others, such as thinking 'If only I had thinner thighs, I would be more attractive'.
> Arbitrary inference: a conclusion is drawn from irrelevant or insufficient evidence, for example, 'Everyone is avoiding me because I have a pimple on my face'.
> Overgeneralisation: concluding from one negative event that another negative event is likely to follow, such as 'I was late for my appoint-

ment last week, so something is bound to go wrong next time'
> Catastrophising: thinking the very worst of a situation, for example, 'I've failed my first assignment – I'm obviously hopeless at study'; 'I've eaten a chocolate and ruined my diet'.
> Excessive reliance on the words should and must: such as 'I must exercise for at least an hour each morning', 'I should take the children to the park every day' and 'I must not eat chocolate'. Failure to achieve such self-imposed targets may generate pressures.

Cognitive impairment (dysfunctional cognition): 'inability to think straight'. The prefix 'dys' is used to mean not functioning properly or presenting a problem. Dysfunctional cognition is a term associated with *brain damage* following an accident or stroke, or with a patient's inability to take in new information because of *anxiety*, *depression*, lowered *self-esteem* or information overload.

Cognitive map: a mental representation of physical space. Tolman (1948) introduced this term to refer to what rats had learned when they had found their way through a maze to obtain food. We now use the term, or a similar one, for many kinds of mental representations of spatial relationships; for example, in *artificial intelligence, cognitive neuroscience, ecological and environmental psychology* and even for the mind maps suggested by Buzan (1993) for creating a spatial diagram (or pattern notes) of relationships in a topic for discussion.

Cognitive therapy: one of the main 'talking' therapies, cognitive therapy is concerned with analysing clients' *beliefs* and understanding of themselves and their situation. It is based on the assumption that problems are often caused or exacerbated by limited or inaccurate knowledge and distorted *perceptions* and *beliefs*. It is a didactic or teaching approach aimed at improving knowledge and restructuring *beliefs*. Cognitive therapy has always been concerned with confronting reality rather than simply substituting positive thinking for negative or distorted thinking. Where reality is itself bad (as with a serious illness), therapy becomes concerned with making the negative thoughts explicit so that they can become accepted rather than hidden or associated with shamefulness or contributing to feelings of low self-esteem. Cognitive therapy tends to be best known as an effective method for treating *depression*, but is also used with patients who are anxious, distressed by physical ill health, suicidal, obsessional or hypochondriacal, or as an alternative to cognitive-behavioural programmes for clients with smoking, eating, drug or alcohol problems (Scott et al, 1991). Derivatives of cognitive therapy include rational–emotive therapy, solution-focused therapy and neurolinguistic programming (Bandler and Grinder, 1975, 1976).

Collective unconscious: Jung (see Part 4) gives various ambiguous descriptions of the collective unconscious. He suggested that because people throughout the world have so much in common in dreams and art there must be an underlying factor common to all humans. He called this commonality the collective unconscious. He regarded it as genetically inherited to some extent. He also seems to have held the belief that the *archetypes* expressed through creative arts indicate that humankind is in some state of communion with a divine or world mind.

Colour constancy: one type of *perceptual constancy*, this is the tendency to see objects as unchanging in colour even though the light source changes. As we move from sunlight into artificial light, we do not usually perceive a change in colour, but photographers have to adjust their cameras because the light is actually rather different. We only notice changes when the light source is dramatically different, such as sodium or mercury street lighting. See also *Colour vision*.

Colour of surroundings: colour in our surroundings is very important to us, even if we are only vaguely aware of it. Certain colours, usually bright or zingy combinations, invigorate us; quiet colours, such as pale green, are soothing; dull colours can be depressing, sapping us of energy. When designing a room in terms of colour, we also need to consider the lighting since artificial light contains a restricted range of frequencies and alters the way we perceive objects. If rooms with a specialist use, such as counselling after rape, intensive care and children's wards, are carefully designed they can provide the optimum conditions to promote a feeling of well-being. Schauss (1985) describes how one shade of pink, called Baker-Miller Pink, has been nicknamed 'drunk-tank pink' because of its use to calm violent prisoners.

Colour vision: the retina of the eye contains cells called cones that respond to different frequencies (or wavelengths) of light. The colour that an object appears will depend on how the cones respond to the range of frequencies of light that the object reflects from the light source into the eye, as shown in Figure 3.7.

Early research (see Young–Helmholtz in Part 4) described three main types of cone (trichromacy) and it is still convenient to refer to these as blue-sensitive, green-sensitive and red-sensitive, respectively, since blue, green and red, are defined as primary colours in colour physics. However, the cones are not sensitive to only one colour each but to a range of frequencies as shown in Figure 3.8.

Mollon (see Part 4) has described a variety of different cones that account for colour vision variations (commonly misnamed colour blindness), involving either two types of cone (dicromacy) or three types of cone (trichromacy), or even four types. See also Sacks (1993).

Sunlight (white light) contains the whole range of frequencies. A white object reflects all these frequencies into the eye and stimulates all types of cones simultaneously.

Coloured objects do not present all these frequencies to the eye. A red object reflects only the red components and absorbs the others, and stimulates mainly the red-sensitive cones. In the same way, a green object reflects only the green components and stimulates green-sensitive cones and so on.

White light contains all colours. The colour that an object appears to be depends on the components of the light that are reflected into the eye and stimulate the cones in the retina.

A red object reflects only red, a green object only green and so on.

Figure 3.7 Colour of objects

The colour of the light also determines which frequencies reach the eye. If blue light illuminates a red object, which can only reflect red, the object appears black. Mercury street lighting has this effect so that all red objects, including blood after an accident, appear black.

Coma: prolonged period of unconsciousness. The depth of coma can be assessed according to the Glasgow Coma Scale, which assigns a numerical value to the amount of eye opening, verbal/vocal response and motor response to *pain*. Early *beliefs* about coma are exemplified by Glaser and Strauss (1965: 29):

> As an interactant, the comatose person is what Goffman has called a 'non-person'. Two nurses caring for him can speak in his presence without fear that, overhearing them, he will suspect or understand what they are saying about him. Neither they nor the physicians need to engage in tactics to protect him from any dread knowledge.

However, it is now realised that, as with anaesthetic, some people in a coma are responsive to the environment. Families may bring in favourite music or read aloud in the hope that such stimuli will help the patient regain *consciousness*. Helpers are advised, as with anaesthetised patients, not to discuss patients in their presence, or say anything they would not wish them to hear.

Compensation: an unconscious defence mechanism that shows itself in finding an alternative pleasure to compensate for missing emotional love, comfort and security.

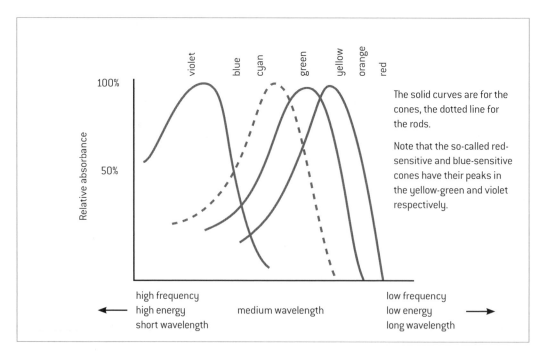

Figure 3.8 Relative sensitivity curves

Complexes: a word coined by Jung, but also used extensively by Freud, to refer to an important group of unconscious associations, or a strong unconscious impulse lying behind an individual's otherwise mysterious condition. There are many kinds of complex, but at the core of any complex is a universal pattern of experience, or *archetype*, that may be related to traumatic experience, or not. Many Jungian complexes appear in complementary pairs for example, the *anima and animus*, the puer and senex. Only when a complex results in destructive behaviour would it be seen as pathological; otherwise, a Jungian view of psyche accepts the presence of diverse complexes in ordinary health. Freud held that the Oedipus complex was universal and the central complex in psychopathology as well as explaining normal sexual development.

› Freudian:
  - Oedipus complex
  - castration complex
  - Electra complex.
› Jungian:
  - anima
  - animus
  - puer or eternal youth (for example, an individual's unconscious dread of growing up, of losing one's romantic ideals or freedom)
  - senex or archetypal old man (for example, acting out an 'old man' role, in creative or destructive ways)
  - father.
› Other:
  - inferiority complex
  - superiority complex
  - Napoleon complex
  - Messianic complex
  - God complex.

Complexity theory: a mathematical theory that looks for principles of order underlying complex systems – cells, organisms, brains, ecosystems, societies, weather patterns, crystals and so on – that is thought to help to explain the mechanisms of evolutionary natural selection. See also *Chaos theory*.

Computational theory of mind: this approach to the mind is based on information processing or computation and helps to explain the mind–body problem (see *Consciousness*). Pinker (1998) describes how information and computation are held in patterns of data and are independent of the physical medium that carries them. Pinker gives the example of telephoning another person. The information in your message remains the same as it goes from your lips to the receiving person's ears even as it physically changes its form from vibrating air (sound) to electricity in a wire, to charges in silicon, to flickering light in a fibre optic cable, to electromagnetic waves and then back again to sound in reverse order.

Beliefs and desires about things in the world can be seen as information, held by the neurones in the brain in an arrangement that has been triggered by those world things via the sense organs. Electrical activity in the neurones allows 'messages' carrying information to travel between different parts of the brain, triggering other beliefs or memories or triggering muscles giving rise to behaviour.

All brains are built up out of the same kinds of neurones but the content of the thoughts and actions lies in the pattern of combinations of neural activity. This can be compared with saying that all books are physically just combination of the same letters and punctuation but the content of a book lies in the combinations of the patterns of ink marks. Moreover, as a book may be arranged in meaningful chapters, the mind is arranged in a system of entities with different functions. See also 'Evolutionary psychology' in Part 2.

Conation: a term used by Immanual Kant and others to refer to the *concept* of volition or our will to do something or the freedom to make choices about what to do. This is associated with the issue of 'why' and may cover all conscious aspects of *motivation*, desire or willingness to do something, but would not normally be used to refer to unconscious needs or drive states. It is the personal, intentional, deliberate, goal-oriented, planning or striving component of *motivation*, the proactive (as opposed to reactive or habitual) aspect of behaviour (Baumeister et al, 1998; Emmons, 1986). See also *Self-efficacy*.

Concept: an *abstract* idea, mental image or word picture (Talbot, 1995: 652), usually derived by looking at a set of examples and working out what it is that they have in common. For example, a carrot, a parsnip and a cabbage have something in common which gives rise to the concept of vegetable. Apple, orange and peach contribute to the concept of fruit. Concepts often give rise to classification systems and precise definitions. The accurate identification of similarities and differences forms the basis of much scientific work. We can classify items differently for different purposes, depending on what concepts come to mind or are useful. We can call a tomato a fruit or a vegetable, according to whether we are thinking about botanical definitions or food.

Many concepts are difficult to grasp or define precisely, such as justice, *pain*, *stress*, *intelligence* or *personality*. One way to understand a new concept is to look at lots of different examples and learn by trial and error to recognise when a particular example belongs to a given class. In everyday contexts, we do not need to give a precise definition of what examples have in common or what makes them different from items that do not belong. By sharing experiences and comparing examples over a long period, a culture invents words to stand for concepts and gradually builds a more and more useful language.

Concrete operations: the second main stage of intellectual growth described by Piaget, lasting from about 18 months to 11 years (see also *sensori-motor* and *formal operations*). According to Piaget, thinking during this stage is restricted to concrete or real objects and examples, without any facility for *abstract thinking* or *formal operations*. Piaget believed that a child in this stage was unable to think logically or cope with abstract ideas. Some writers sub-divide the stage into pre-conceptual, intuitive and operational. As children move through these sub-stages, their thinking becomes clearer and more systematic; *concepts* such as *conservation* become established and the children can describe and manipulate observations.

Conformity: a measure of the willingness of an individual to fit in with or adopt the behaviour of other members of a group despite a difference of opinion or *values*. A number of classical studies of conformity have been carried out, including those by Sherif (1935) and Asch (1956), cited in most general psychology texts. In controlled studies, it is usually found that participants justify their conformity by saying they did not want to spoil the

experimenter's results or that they doubted their own judgement, thinking that there was perhaps a trick of the light or other illusion.

Festinger (1957) and others give three main reasons for conformity:

> We rely on others to help us formulate our beliefs and develop an understanding of the world.
> Achievement of group goals depends on having agreement and uniformity.
> Approval is more likely to be achieved by not seeming different.

See also *Saccadic eye movements* below and Asch, Milgram and Sherif in Part 4

Congruence (genuineness): Rogers (1980: 115) defines genuineness or congruence as: 'the therapist openly being the feelings and attitudes that are flowing within at the moment'.

The therapist makes himself or herself transparent to the client, the client can see right through what the therapist is in the relationship, and experiences no holding back on the part of the therapist. As for the therapist, what he or she is experiencing is available to awareness, can be lived in the relationship and can be communicated if appropriate. Thus there is a close matching, or congruence, between what is being experienced at the gut level, what is present in the awareness, and what is expressed to the client.

A counsellor or therapist who is perceived as honest and genuine may help clients to feel more trusting of their own feelings, and may encourage their honesty and genuineness in relation to others.

One of the aims of the person-centred approach is to provide training which enables the counsellor to explore personal feelings and develop awareness. The more the counsellor can accept himself or herself, the more likely he or she will be able to respond in a personal, honest way to the client. See also *Empathy* and *Unconditional regard*, Rogers in Part 4, and Part 2.3.13 'Humanistic psychology'.

Conservation: a term used by Piaget (see Part 4) to describe whether children have reached a stage in their development when they can correctly answer questions relating to changes in the appearance of objects, but not the quantity. Using tasks related to length, area, volume, number and mass, Piaget identified the order in which children develop *concept*s of conservation. That is, they understand that the quantity is conserved (remains the same) while the appearance changes.

According to Piaget, children in the pre-conceptual stage respond to all tasks incorrectly and therefore cannot conserve any quantities. During the intuitive stage, children begin to conserve length and area. For example, they can tell that a piece of string stays the same length when it is curled up and straightened out. But these children cannot tell if liquid poured into a different shape container is still the same amount. They appear distracted by either the height or width of the container and do not seem to be able to pay attention to both dimensions at the same time. Conservation of volume and weight or mass develops during the operational stage.

Alternative explanations of the faulty answers are given by Bruner (1964), Donaldson (1978) and Bryant (1982), who suggest the questions are misleading, that the children do not understand what they are being asked, they do not understand words like more and less or they cannot remember what has taken place.

Container for emotions: a *concept* associated with Melanie Klein and W. R. Bion. They illustrate how a parent or other carer can provide a safe environment for a child who is experiencing ambivalent feelings of love, hate, fear and concern during the difficult period of growing from a position of total dependence to independence. Parents can help in this development by allowing a child to express *emotions* safely in a warm and secure environment and fluctuate between being independent one moment and dependent the next. This is a useful concept in professional care where patients are forced into a position of dependence. They may experience feelings of hopelessness and powerlessness coupled with rage. The carer can help to provide a safe 'container' for the expression of these *emotions*.

Convergent thinking: a style of problem-solving that is intended to reach one particular solution and all efforts are directed towards that. See also *Divergent thinking, Lateral thinking, Problem-solving, Thinking*.

Coping styles: a tendency for a person to deal with a *stress*ful event in a particular way. Miller and Mangan (1983) and Miller (1987, 1989) studied the information-seeking behaviour of patients and identified two coping styles: monitoring and blunting. 'Monitors' use information-seeking strategies to gain a sense of control over the stress-inducing situation and will ask many questions about their health *problem*, prognosis and treatment options. In contrast, 'blunters' will ask few questions preferring not to be reminded of the stress-inducing situation. Similarly, Roth and Cohen (1986) proposed two types of stress-coping style, approach and avoidance, which differ according to the amount of *attention* given to the stressor. People who adopt an avoidance style tend to use strategies such as selective inattention and *defence mechanisms* to avoid thinking about the stressor. People who favour an approach style tend to use strategies such as seeking information to confront and cope with stressors.

Creativity: the ability to generate ideas or products that are both novel and appropriate to the circumstances. However, this is a difficult *concept* to define precisely, as ideas about creativity range from regarding a creative act as one in which an individual produces something new only to the individual, to something which is new to the culture or the world as a whole. The study of creativity is concerned both with attempting to measure personal attributes and with examining the processes by which people are able to produce novel solutions to *problem*s, whether on an individual or global basis.

Most researchers add 'appropriate to the circumstances' since being unusual or eccentric is not necessarily creative, even if statistically it is uncommon.

Evans and Deehan (1988: 11) argue that common conceptions of creativity derive from *beliefs* in a divine Creator and a conviction that creative people are 'gifted' or 'touched with genius' and that this leads most people to think they cannot be creative.

Early models, for example Wallas (1926), which seek to outline the stages in the creative process can be compared directly with those of Thomson (1959) and Bransford and Stein (1993) for *problem-solving*. No differences are found between creativity in art and science and it is now widely held that, although the end products are different, the processes involved in achieving them are the same. Like all thinking and problem-solving, the creative process may involve a combination of conscious rational processes and flashes of inspiration derived from unconscious connections.

Other approaches have reviewed biographies and autobiographies in a attempt to isolate the features of a specially creative personality. In both of these approaches researchers now look for the skills involved and how these can be developed. This change has shifted the emphasis away from considering creativity as an in-born special ability, available only to a select few, towards a belief that creativity can be taught. See also Dweck in Part 1, and Part 2.2.3.

Crowds: crowds can be considered either as primitive or as elementary forms of groups. In order to explain how crowd behaviour can lead to riots, it is argued that within a crowd, either people feel anonymous or become 'deindividuated', losing their sense of personal identity and returning to primitive, barbarous behaviour (Le Bon, 1896; Zimbardo, 1969; both cited by Brown, 1988), or there is a change of identity towards greater cohesion, pride and a sense of defending the territory against outsiders (Reicher, 1982, 1984, cited by Brown, 1988). In the latter case, new group *norms* may be quickly established, and where two groups are in conflict, these norms may become polarised towards opposite extremes (seen in, for example, rioters in conflict with police).

Most riot scenarios involve more than one group. In some cases, it is possible to identify an 'in-group' and an 'out-group', and point to behaviour by the out-group that may have served to trigger the defensive behaviour of the in-group and later the whole crowd. This may be interpreted as behaviour becoming more regulated and cohesive rather than primitive and chaotic.

Cue dependence (memory): *recall* is sometimes enhanced if the participant re-creates or imagines the physiological *state* or the context in which material was learned. This is sometimes noticed in everyday life when one forgets what one went to fetch but can remember it by returning to where the idea first occurred.

Dark adaptation: as a person moves between

areas of dim light and bright light, the eye has to adapt to the varying conditions. This happens by the iris expanding or contracting to let in varying amounts of light and by the retina responding to the different levels of illumination. When going from a bright area into a dark one, the eye is insensitive so that hardly anything at all can be seen at first, but improvement begins rapidly for most people. It can take half an hour to reach full dark-adapted sensitivity. The iris responds quickly to the change and the pupils enlarge but the pigments in the retina are bleached by strong light and need time to be naturally restored. People working in an environment that requires frequent changes may learn to compensate. They need to be aware that a newcomer will take longer to adjust.

Death-wish (Thanatos): Freud, and many analysts following him, point to the existence in people of dark and destructive qualities. This is sometimes viewed as an unconscious wish to seek nirvana, the extinction of individual existence.

Deduction or deductive reasoning: the reverse of *induction*, such that thinking progresses from general principles to individual examples. That is, if a person knows how things work and wants to predict what will happen in a particular situation, that person can use the knowledge to deduce the answer. It is sometimes helpful if such thoughts are written as *syllogisms*.

Defence mechanisms: conscious or unconscious mental strategies adopted by an individual when faced with emotional experiences that are too painful or difficult to be faced directly:

> Unconscious mechanisms:
  - denial
  - reaction formation
  - repression
  - transference and counter transference.
> Conscious defence mechanisms:
  - *anticipation*
  - avoidance
  - suppression
> Mainly unconscious but which can sometimes involve some conscious awareness:
  - *altruism*
  - *asceticism*
  - *compensation*

- *displacement*
- *fantasy*
- *identification*
- *intellectualisation*
- *projection*
- *rationalisation*
- *regression*
- *sublimation*.

Where the mechanism is completely unconscious, the person involved cannot see what is happening, although it may appear obvious to others.

Defence mechanisms often form part of a healthy, beneficial process for protecting from *anxiety* and give the individual time to adjust to a new, painful or frightening experience. It may be important to distinguish between defences that arise in response to new changes, and those lingering from early-established and deep-seated anxieties. Simple uncritical acceptance and respect may be all that is necessary to provide support and allow time for healing but if defence mechanisms persist or interfere with daily living, then specialist counselling or psychotherapy may be recommended.

Dementias: Stuart-Hamilton (1991) defines dementia as the 'global deterioration of intellectual function resulting from atrophy of the central nervous system (CNS)'. He states that dementia can occur at any age and although the probability of becoming demented increases with age, it should not be considered a disease of older people. The psychological abilities of patients with dementia are quite different from those of normal elderly people and dementia is not a natural part of the normal ageing process. Haase (1977), cited by Stuart-Hamilton (1991), has identified about 50 different causes of dementia, with the commoner ones being classified according to five main types: Alzheimer's disease, multi-infarct dementia, Pick's disease, Creutzfeldt-Jacob disease (CJD) and Huntington's disease. The progression of the disease is different in each type, depending on the order in which different parts of the *brain* are affected. Parkinson's disease and syphilis can also cause dementia or dementia-like symptoms. Severe *depression* in elderly people may result in low *motivation* and poor scores on psychometric tests of *memory* and other cognitive functions. This may be known as pseudodementia. However, these people are usually well oriented. Their level

of activity tends to vary through the day and they are usually well aware of their poor performance.

Denial: inability to believe something distressing is true, even when faced with evidence that everyone else accepts; continuing to act as if something is not true even when others try to convince one that it is. Examples include the belief that a person who has been declared brain dead will eventually recover, searching for a baby who has died, continuing to expect to recover the use of limbs even after tests confirm permanent damage to the spinal cord. Within the caring professions, denial is the most commonly mentioned *defence mechanism* and there is ongoing debate over how best to be supportive: that is whether to confront the patients with their denial and try to coax them into acceptance. Most short-term forms of denial are part of a healthy, beneficial process for protecting from *anxiety* and give the individual time to adjust to a new painful or frightening experience. When denial appears to persist, it is important to distinguish between a genuine inability to come to terms with reality that is hindering normal living, and rituals that are comforting, or healthy avoidance strategies.

Depersonalisation: the sense of a loss of personal identity often felt by people who are subjected to labelling as members of a readily recognised sub-group of society. This is particularly noticeable for people who use wheelchairs or those with a disfigurement, who may be viewed as non-persons and find that others do not know how to approach them or may regard them as unable to communicate. As with any visible form of discrimination, an affected person may be advised to try to take the first step in establishing communication with others who appear hesitant (Rumsey, 1991). Compare with deindividuation; see *Crowds* and *Individuation*.

Depression: a diagnosis of depression or depressive illness is made where a person has a persistent or pervasive condition characterised by low mood, pessimism, feelings of low self-worth or self-esteem, loss of interest and reduced energy level. Clinical use of the term needs to be distinguished from ordinary low *mood* or sadness. Regular bouts of depression in winter months, or seasonal affective disorder (SAD), is thought to be

concepts

associated with low levels of *serotonin*. Depression and *anxiety* are often linked (Montgomery, 1990).

Depth perception: the *perception* of objects and the space around them in three dimensions. This occurs with solid objects even though the retinal image is only two-dimensional. Commonly the term is used to refer to vertical depth and the most well-known experimental work is that of Gibson and Walk and the 'Visual cliff' apparatus (see any introductory psychology text such as Cardwell et al, 1996; Gross, 1996; Bee and Mitchell, 1984). Clues to depth perception are given by relative size, texture, partial hiding of further by nearer objects, geometrical perspective, accommodation of the lens, *motion parallax* and the difference between the two images received by the two eyes. It is not yet known exactly to what extent depth perception is inborn or learned. Babies have many months of visual experience before they can move independently, so it is not possible to test them before they have had time to learn.

Desensitisation: used in the social sciences to refer to a complex process during which a person becomes less sensitive to social stimuli. For example, the more people are exposed to aggressive behaviour the less likely they are to be disturbed by it. In relation to television violence, it is argued (for example, Drabman and Thomas, 1974) that repeated exposure to violent programmes reduces emotional impact and greater violence is then needed to produce an emotional reaction. See also *Habituation*.

Determinism: the doctrine that all events – physical, behavioural and mental – are determined by specific and potentially knowable causal factors, often used in relation to behaviourism and psychodynamic theories and linguistic determinism.

Dichotic listening: listening to two different messages simultaneously, one relayed to each ear. Experiments of this kind contribute to understanding of *attention* processes and *levels of processing*.

Discovery learning: a learner-centred, self-directed approach to learning which is associated with Piaget (1926, 1929, see 1989, 1990) and

with Bruner (1960; 1964). This approach requires learners of all ages to take an active role in the teaching and learning process, drawing upon their own experiences and researching information. Discovery methods favour experimentation by the learner. The methods present learners with problems and challenges and allow for learners with different kinds of knowledge to work at different speeds. Questions that contain an element of controversy or contradiction may prompt the learner to reflect on the subject matter. Simulation exercises present the learner with imaginary *problems* designed to mimic those they faced in reality. This can promote debate and understanding and may encourage the learner to adopt a *problem-solving* approach.

Discrimination: a term used to refer to the observable behavioural component of prejudice, in which people express or demonstrate unfavourable *attitudes* towards an individual or group. Allport (1954) proposes five levels or strengths of discrimination:

> Antilocution: hostile talk, verbal insults, racial or sexual jokes.
> Avoidance: keeping a distance without inflicting any harm.
> Discrimination: exclusion – from housing, civil rights and employment.
> Physical attack: violence against persons or their property.
> Extermination: violence against an entire group.

Displacement: finding a socially acceptable activity for the expression of *psychosexual* energy, for example using sport to channel *aggression* and competition. When the activity is highly regarded by society, as in artistic expression, the term *sublimation* may be used. The term displacement is also used to refer to *emotions* that are displaced. Destructive feelings towards someone or something that cannot be expressed may be redirected on to someone or something else. People who have unresolved or unexpressed feelings of *anxiety* about their health problems may develop feelings of aggression towards health care workers, and distress related to death or *loss* may be displaced as *anger*.

Dissociative disorder: a personality disorder

concepts

marked by a disturbance in the integration of identity, memory, or consciousness.

Dissociative identity disorder: originally known as Grande Hysterie and until recently as Multiple or Dual Personality, this is an extremely rare condition, in which a person apparently has the experience of being a different person on different occasions, sometimes with, sometimes without, awareness of this change. Schreiber (1974) describes Sybil who would suddenly find herself in strange surroundings without any understanding of how she came to be there, and who gradually came to realise that she was living part of her life as one person, part as another. During her treatment, various other personalities emerged, some of whom were aware of the other 'selves'. A very disturbing account is given in *When Rabbit Howls* by Truddi Chase (1987), where the author describes her multiple personalities that developed to enable her to cope with severe sexual abuse. Another well-known, and controversial, account is *The Three Faces of Eve*, made into a book and film in 1957 (see http: //en.wikipedia. org/wiki/The_Three_Faces_of_Eve). The split is dramatised in stories such as *The Strange Case of Dr Jekyll and Mr Hyde* by Robert Louis Stevenson, in which a doctor, experimenting with drugs and the occult, succeeds in separating himself into two alternating characters, one good, the other evil. This can be related to Jung's *beliefs* about an alter ego and his *principle of opposites*. This condition is often confused with *schizophrenia* in everyday language, but the conditions are quite different.

Diurnal/circadian rhythms: these are the daily biological rhythms which become established over roughly a regular 24-hour period. Diurnal refers specifically to the daytime period, the opposite of nocturnal or night-time. Circadian, from the Latin 'circa', round about, and 'dies', day, refers to approximately 24-hour cycles. When daily routine is altered, for example by travelling to a different time zone, starting shift work or going into hospital, the rhythms are disrupted. With long-term change, there is usually an adjustment period of around five days to two weeks during which new rhythms are established.

Divergent thinking: a style of *problem-solving* which is intended to find as many alternative solutions as possible. Divergent thinking may be the most important ingredient of the initial processes of problem-solving. The alternative solutions can be compared and then *convergent thinking* employed to select the most suitable solution for a particular case. See also *Creativity*, *Lateral thinking*.

Dopamine: this is one of the chief *neurotransmitters* that relate to psychological experiences. Dopamine is produced at the *synapses* between particular kinds of neurones, known as the dopamine neurones, which occur only in the *mid-brain*. One sub-group lies within the *basal nuclei*, which control co-ordination of movement. The other sub-group is in the *limbic system*, including the amygdala, which links with parts of the cortex dealing with the highest cortical functions, such as *memory*, intellect and personality. These dopamine neurones also receive impulses from regions of the *brain* involved in *motivation*, learning and rewarding mechanisms. In Parkinson's disease there is a shortage of natural dopamine in the basal nuclei, which results in a lack of control over motor activities, tremor and rigidity. There appear to be high levels of dopamine associated with *schizophrenia*. Antipsychotic drugs act on those areas of the brain that are associated with dopamine neurones.

Dreaming: sleep research shows that dreaming or REM sleep generally occurs as part of a personal pattern of *sleep cycles*, occupying roughly ten minutes in each period of an hour and a half. Most dreams are forgotten unless the person is wakened at the time. Dreams with emotional content that waken the sleeper are thus likely to be remembered best. Most people describe their dreams in terms of their visual images, but dreams can create fantasy situations with imagery in all sensory modes (Oswald, 1966, 1984). There are biological, behavioural, social, cognitive and *psychodynamic* explanations.

Biological explanations include the notion that *brain* activity during REM sleep is purely random, but if roused a person will try to make sense of the various snippets of thought and turn them into meaningful stories. Oswald (1966, 1984) believes that the dreaming period is allocated to growth and repair of the tissue of the brain although Horne (1988) believes that deep stage 4 sleep is also used for brain recovery. In the 1960s,

Christopher Evans, cited by Aldiss (1970) and Peter Evans (1991), believed that the main purpose of sleep was to allow us to dream; not to consciously explore ideas, but to enable the brain to sort out its new experiences and to put its files in order. Dreams, by this analogy, are the running through of the programmes and their reclassification. Evans believed the content is mostly trivial, and that we are aware only of the few sequences that are sufficiently emotional to wake us up. This theory, together with what is known of the switching mechanisms, provides an interesting explanation of *hallucinations*: that the brain becomes muddled and confused because of some interference with the procedure for going off-line, and sorting occurs while the person is awake. In addition, LSD might be activating the dream mechanism at unsuitable times when the brain is not off-line, and could well have permanent effects.

Psychoanalysis, and other *psychodynamic* approaches, assume that dreaming is a symbolic encoding of painful and disturbing unconscious material.

Dynamic memory theory: the approach of Schank (1982) who suggests a flexible model that allows for the changing dynamic aspects of *memory*. The model includes notions of *memory* organisation packets (MOPs) which define a way in which some items in memories are organised into plans, scenes, *schemas* (or scripts) and thematic organisation points (TOPs) which define a way in which some memories are organised into themes.

Electroconvulsive therapy (ECT): also known as ECS (electroconvulsive shock), this is a technique for treating a variety of mental disorders, particularly *depression*. An electric shock is given to the *brain* by applying a voltage between two electrodes placed on the surface of the scalp. *Anaesthesia* and muscle-relaxants reduce the risk of fracture or injury during the generalised seizure produced. ECT has the effect of temporarily disrupting normal activity in the brain and can be effective in reducing depression in many cases but its use is controversial as there is no theoretical basis to justify it and it may produce permanent *brain damage*, particularly loss of *memory* and *cognitive impairment* although there is little clear evidence (Gregory, 1987).

Electroencephalograph (EEG): the tracings of

brain activity obtained by attaching electrodes to the scalp and measuring the variations in voltage produced by the brain. These voltages are tiny compared with familiar electricity obtained from batteries or the domestic mains: they are in the range of approximately 0.000 05 volt (50 millionths of a volt or 50 μv).

Variations in the traces occur with the state of *arousal* of an individual and can be used to diagnose unusual or irregular brain activity such as seizure disorders and focal lesions. Their use is particularly noteworthy in *sleep* studies and in measures of *evoked potentials*. EEG has been used with *biofeedback*, in investigating *hypnosis*, in attempting to find correlations with *intelligence*, in measuring effects of tranquillisers and in investigating brain activity of all kinds. There has been some attempt to use these traces alongside *galvanic skin response* (GSR) in so-called lie-detector tests on the assumption that telling lies increases *arousal*, but such use is unreliable.

Efforts after meaning: a term used by Bartlett (1932) to indicate how people strive to make sense of what has happened, which involves making inferences or *deductions* about what could or should have happened, and may involve altering the content in order to make more sense. This process is often called search for meaning. See also *Redintegration*.

Ego: a term taken from the Latin for 'I' and used by Freud to refer to the self. The ego is active in learning and adapting to the environment, concerned principally with cognitive processes such as *perception* and *memory* and with the control of speech and intentions or volitions. Freud saw this as the 'executive' of the personality, balancing *id* and *superego*, weighing up the pros and cons of all activities and experiences. An imbalance between the demands of the id and superego can lead to anxiety, stress, tiredness or illness, and the *unconscious mind* may use *defence mechanisms* to try to protect the ego.

Egocentric: centred or focused on the self. According to Piaget, a newborn baby is totally egocentric, unable to make any distinction between itself and the outside world. The baby does not know that anything else exists, or that he or she exists. In the course of the *sensori-motor* period, the child

concepts

slowly manages to reduce this unawareness and begin to distinguish between self and the rest of the world (decentring). Egocentric *play* and an egocentric view may continue for several years until after a child has started school so the process of decentring can take some time. However, there is a problem with this approach as it is unlikely that a newborn baby is as lacking in experience as Piaget assumed. Moreover, observation of children indicates that although children may play alone, they are watching and copying each other.

Emotion: the word emotion derives from words meaning movement and suggests a stirring or agitation. Emotions can be seen as passions or disturbances and most words for emotions convey a sense of strong feeling. A person described as 'emotional' is someone who displays strong emotion. Early studies of emotion, such as that by Cannon (1929), concentrated on extreme or high emotions and emphasised peripheral physiological reactions, such as increased heart rate, sweating and goose-pimples. Lesser states may be labelled as *affect* or *mood*.

Several authors have classified emotions, based on various types of evidence, such as photographs of *facial expressions* or actors' demonstration. For example, Ekman and Friesen (1971) list six primary emotions, and Izard (1977), Oatley (1989) and Plutchik (1980) name eight. Five are common to all the lists:

> pleasure (happiness or joy)
> *anger*
> fear (or *anxiety*)
> distress (or sadness)
> disgust.

These five, in particular, seem to be basic emotions that are universally recognisable from *facial expressions* and postures. During evolutionary processes in which an organism was becoming capable of dealing with environmental emergencies, these would have formed a useful set of response patterns, directing an animal towards or away from situations with varying degrees of urgency. Moreover, it is possible to identify a corresponding underlying physiological system for each of the five. Each is linked to an area of the *limbic system* which has many connections upward into the cortex where cognitive processing takes place, and downward into the peripheral nervous

system and the effectors of bodily adjustment.

Pleasure can be viewed as linked to the 'pleasure centres' (see Olds in Part 4) of the *brain*; fear is linked with *anxiety* and *stress* to production of adrenaline; *anger* with *aggression* and the *hypothalamus* and amygdala; disgust to the centre that precipitates vomiting, and sadness to the system that precipitates tears. Furthermore, it has been claimed by Ekman and Oster (1979) that these are innate systems.

Other theories include:

> surprise
> pride
> guilt
> shame.

These also have characteristic facial expressions and bodily postures. It seems reasonable to suppose that basic emotions need not, and usually do not, act alone. Everyday experience is usually of mixtures or developments of these that are closely combined with *cognitions*.

Different parts of the brain are involved in true emotional expression and faking, but with practice and talent emotions can be faked or play-acted by adopting suitable *facial expressions* and other body language or verbal expression, in order to hide the true inner feelings. This makes explicit the realisation that the outward expression may not be the same as the inner feeling. In addition to deliberate acting we also find there can be considerable difference between what we feel inside and what we show to others, either because we have not developed sufficient social skills in recognising and displaying our emotions, or because the emotions are repressed. Conversely true feelings may 'leak' into facial expressions and body language despite attempts to hide them. See also Parts 2.2.3 and 2.2.4.

Emotional intelligence (EI): a popular but controversial and unsupported approach often measured as an emotional intelligence quotient or *EQ*, that describes an ability, capacity or skill to perceive, assess and manage the emotions of one's self, of others and of groups. Emotional intelligence theory draws on behavioural, emotional and communications theories, such as neurolinguistic programming (Bandler and Grinder, 1975, 1976), *Transactional Analysis*, and *empathy*; it was originally developed during the 1970s and 1980s by

concepts

Howard Gardner, Peter Salovey and John Mayer but was popularised by Daniel Goleman (1995).

Emotional intelligence is said to be relevant to organisational development and developing people, because the EQ principles provide a new way to understand and assess people's behaviours, management styles, attitudes, interpersonal skills and potential. Emotional intelligence is thus said to be an important consideration in human resources planning, job profiling, recruitment interviewing and selection, management development, customer relations and customer service, and more.

Arguments against the concept include those of Steve Hein, who says that emotional intelligence is the ability to feel good about doing whatever you are told, ordered, forced, convinced or expected to do. An emotionally intelligent leader, then, is one who can persuade others to do the same thing and to make them feel good about it (http: //equi.org/commdef.htm).

Empathy: an ability to understand another person's point of view and appreciate what it must feel like for that person in a particular situation. This involves a step beyond merely imagining what it would be like for you if you were in that situation since the other person will have different experiences and *perceptions*. This is a key *concept* in Carl Rogers' client-centred therapy, together with *congruence* and *unconditional regard* (see Part 2.3.13 'Humanistic psychology' and Part 4, Rogers).

Empowerment: strategies within organisations designed to enable individuals to participate in decision-making and exert more influence within the workplace. See also *Power*.

Enactive representation: the first of Bruner's three ways of describing mental representation of the environment in order to think or solve *problems* (see also *iconic* and *symbolic representation*). Enactive representation involves actions. For example if asked how many pieces you would get if you cut an apple across the middle, one way of finding the answer would be to get an apple and cut it. Bruner describes young children as using this mode as the main way of discovering how the world works, before developing the others. Bruner suggests that adults use a mixture of *enactive*, *iconic* and *symbolic representations*, moving between physical models, diagrams or plans, mental imagery and speech or writing.

Episodic or autobiographical memory: this refers to memories of personal experiences and events. This *memory* is difficult to research as it is rarely possible to check accuracy. Some studies indicate that young and old produce equal numbers of such memories. Early spontaneous reminiscences may be dimmer than recent memories but can become stronger if often rehearsed. Elderly people are generally slower to produce reminiscences (Rabbitt and Winthorpe, 1988). There is little clinical evidence to support the cliché that elderly people live in the past, but see also *reminiscence*. When considered alongside other aspects of *long-term memory*, this provides a more complex approach to memory than the early *multi-store* model.

Equilibration: a term from Piaget's work to describe the process by which a child tries to stay in balance, accommodating new information by changing *schemas* to suit new experiences or rejecting new information which will not fit.

Evoked potentials (EV): small variations in voltages in the *brain* and *nervous system* produced by incoming stimuli such as flashes of light or *touch*. These can be difficult to detect as they are usually masked by the overall brain activity (see for example, Springer and Deutsch, 1989) but can be isolated through computer averaging. Evoked potentials can be used to detect the specific areas in the brain that process incoming information and to measure the speed of transmission through the *nervous system*. This latter feature helps in the diagnosis and monitoring of conditions like multiple sclerosis where the loss of myelination slows down the transmission of action potentials along the nerves. Visual evoked potentials can also be used to assess visual function in apparently blind people (Towle et al, 1985).

Extinction: the diminishing in strength of a behaviour by withholding *reinforcement*s so that the behaviour eventually ceases. The rate at which extinction occurs depends on the *reinforcement schedule* used when the behaviour was learned.

Extroversion (or extraversion): a term used

concepts

by a number of theorists, particularly Jung and Eysenck (cited in Ryckman, 1989; Gross, 1996; and others), to describe people with an outgoing and relatively confident approach to life. In these theories, extroversion tends to be linked with an acceptance of conventions, a willingness to yield to peer pressure, shallowness of feeling with a change in emotions from one situation to another, pleasure-seeking and impatience. Jung identifies four extroverted types: extroverted feeling type, extroverted intuitive type, extroverted sensing type and extroverted thinking type. Eysenck identifies two extroverted types: stable extroverted (sanguine) and neurotic extroverted (choleric). Eysenck (1965), cited by Ryckman (1989), argues that extroverts have strong inhibitory processes in the *nervous system* and a large capacity to tolerate stimulation so that they seek out a greater variety of experiences. He found that when electric shocks are administered to participants, the pain tolerance of extroverts is greater than that of introverts. A contrary finding in practice is that sometimes people with extrovert tendencies make more display of emotions and pain behaviour.

Eye-witness testimony: an area of research (for example, Wells and Loftus, 1984) which involves laboratory studies, *recall* of details of films, simulations or real situations in a variety of conditions, in order to test the accuracy and reliability of memories.

Face recognition: *perception* of faces seems to be a special area of perception. Babies appear to have some recognition of faces very early in development. It is possible to have a loss of recognition of faces following *brain damage* even when other perceptual processes appear intact. Illusions involving faces tend to be very strong.

Fantz (1961) believes that new-born babies pay more *attention* to pictures of faces than to other complex figures. Hershenson et al (1965), however, did not find this difference until about four months of age if alternative figures of very similar complexity were used. Kleiner (1987) and others have found that new-born babies prefer abstract patterns while older babies prefer face-like patterns. These studies tend to suggest that face recognition is learned rather than innate but all seem to agree that to a baby several months old, faces are extremely interesting. See also Sternberg (1995: 416) and Fontana (1990: 82).

Facial expressions: the way in which the face is able to express *emotions* or the emotional 'colouring' of thoughts. The work of Thayer and Schiff (1969), illustrated in Gill and Adams (1998), with cartoon faces suggests that it is mainly the positioning of eyebrows and mouth that gives rise to different expressions. Most research supports the view that facial expressions relating to extreme forms of the basic *emotions* are universally recognisable, which would indicate that such expressions are innate rather than learned. However, this argument tends to be rather circular, since the identification of some of the basic emotions is based on responses to facial expressions. Complex mixtures of emotions, such as jealousy, fiendishness and sheepishness, or subtle or milder forms of emotion, are probably subject to cultural or individual variations, which may lead to misinterpretations. For example, there is a type of smile which can be recognised as indicating smouldering anger, and another smile which suggests fear or *appeasement*. Recognition may depend on whether the smiling person is making the expression deliberately and can therefore exaggerate the distinctive feature, and whether this is known and understood by the observer. Otherwise, an inadvertent smile may be taken at 'face value' as indicating pleasantness or friendliness and the hidden emotional message missed.

Factitious illnesses: a term for all illnesses in which there is thought to be an element of 'make-believe' on the part of the patient. This can be sub-divided into 'dissimulation' (in which the illness is false) and 'somatising' (which involves a belief that one is ill). 'Malingering' is a form of dissimulation in which symptoms or illness are exaggerated or faked in order to gain material benefits. Examples include prisoners who fake illness in order to go into hospital, where conditions are better, drug addicts who feign *pain* to obtain narcotics and those who fake illness to obtain social security benefits. There have been recent reports in the press of people faking conditions such as arthritis in order to obtain medication for their pets without having to pay the high veterinary fees. Munchausen's syndrome and Munchausen's by proxy are serious dissimulation conditions in which a person fakes illness in self or others so that this becomes the focus of life. These are thought to be related to deep-seated emotional disturbance. Somatising includes health anxiety, hypochondria and some aspects of *psychogenic* illness. A suspicion that a person is faking can create impatience and frustration on the part of carers, which may lead to a reduced quality of care. Understanding the underlying factors may lead to increased *empathy* and more choice of care options. This concept should not be confused with *psychogenic* illness or *psychosomatic* health care.

False awakening: there seem to be two types of false awakening. In one type, people believe they have woken up normally but then begin to doubt whether they are really awake and look around them trying to work out whether they are awake or not. Sometimes they realise they are not awake and then have a *lucid dream*. Some people experience repeated false awakenings and may imagine they have dressed and set out for work, only to 'wake' again a little later and find themselves still in bed. This can be repeated several times before the sleeper truly wakes. In the second type, the sleepers may believe they have woken normally but then have a sense of foreboding or excitement and may experience what appear to be *hallucinations*, before fully waking.

False consensus: this term has two important uses: first, that we have a tendency to see our own behaviour, feelings, beliefs and opinions as typical, that is, similar to those of others; and second, that we assume that everyone shares the same view when only a few have actually stated a view. This is related to the common finding that we expect much more consistency than actually occurs. It can lead to generalised assumptions such as 'Everyone else would have done the same', 'Everyone acts like this' and 'We all think the same', and to statements such as 'I know just how you feel'.

False consistency: a tendency to see people's behaviour as more consistent than it really is and to expect them to behave in much the same way on different occasions irrespective of the context. Nisbett and Ross (1980) suggest that this helps to make it easier to deal with people and predict

what they will do. In practice, it may lead to carers and patients being ill-prepared to cope with changes in behaviour due to medication or to changes in state of health, which can in turn lead to impatience and frustration. On the other hand, it can contribute to the *self-fulfilling prophecy* effect so that expectation of consistency may bring about such consistency.

False memory syndrome (recovered memories): these terms are usually used to refer to memories which arise under *hypnosis* but which are subsequently suspected of being false. Early *beliefs* included the assumption that *hypnosis* can free individuals from normal conscious constraints and facilitate accurate *recall*. This came from experiments with electrical stimulation (for example Penfield, 1958) that suggested that all experiences are stored somewhere in the *brain* in photographic fashion. The notion of recovered memories is also supported by *psychodynamic* theories of repression. Although some hypnotists hold strong *beliefs* that such memories are genuine, most cognitive researchers argue that such memories are as vulnerable to distortion, *efforts after meaning,* inferences and *reconstruction* as any others, if not more so because of the necessary element of *suggestibility* in *hypnosis*. In contexts other than *hypnosis*, the term pseudo memories may be used.

Fantasy play: Lucariello (1987) gives four dimensions of fantasy play (action, roles, objects and organisation), based on Piaget's stages of cognitive development. The list below is modified slightly to help avoid the notion of stages as a fixed sequence and integrate ideas from other theories:

> Action: *play* becomes more complex as a child becomes able to integrate a sequence of actions. Activities which at first are restricted to simple sensorimotor or *enactive* movements, babbling, manipulating objects and scribbling, later extends to include more elaborate use of artefacts, making and playing with three-dimensional action models, talking, drawing pictures, and later to writing.

> Roles: as children develop, the focus shifts from self to fantasies involving others and later to the creation of multiple roles. This kind of *play* becomes more elaborate as children

are exposed to an ever increasing variety of real-life situations and events and have greater opportunity for interaction with others. Solitary play may extend and enrich role-play with toys, telling stories to oneself, and later writing stories.

> Objects: children use objects at first in a way that is closely linked to the normal daily function. Later, substitute objects may be used to symbolically represent something else. For example, a cardboard tube may serve for a telescope. It can be argued that this simple *symbolic representation* and the realisation that one thing can stand for another even when it does not bear much resemblance, is essential to development of language, which, by its nature, is symbolic. Accurate miniature replicas (such as a realistic looking telescope) are, in some ways, less effective in helping this development than pure fantasy based on unrealistic substitutes. This may help to explain why small children are often more interested in playing with the cardboard box than the toy that came in it.

> Organisation: as children develop, planning and organisation of play becomes more complex and depend on elaborate sets of rules. Dynamics within a group become more complex; leaders may emerge. See also *Play*.

Fight or flight mechanism: the popular name for the *arousal* system of the sympathetic nervous system (SNS)-adrenal-medullary (or adreno-SNS) According to Cannon (1915, 1929) this 'sympathico-adrenal system' orchestrates changes in blood supply, sugar availability and the blood's clotting capacity such that when stress is sudden, the body reacts with a set of responses which prepare for physical action:

> A threat is perceived.
> Cortical activity triggers the *hypothalamus* which governs the SNS which in turn activates the adrenal medulla.
> Adrenaline is secreted from the adrenal medulla, stimulating the SNS (see Figure 3.3).
> Noradrenaline is released from SNS *synapses*.
> Noradrenaline continues to stimulate the SNS.

The adrenaline and noradrenaline (catecholamines) continue to circulate so that even if the stress is short-lived, SNS-adrenal-medullary

arousal will continue in a closed-loop self-perpetuating process, dying away only slowly unless physical activity dispels the catecholamines and the parasympathetic nervous system can restore normal activity. For this reason, a good brisk walk is recommended after driving in frustratingly slow traffic. Regular exercise and exposure to extremes of heat and cold can affect the rate at which the *arousal* system comes into effect and recovers (see *Toughness*). The amount of adrenaline and noradrenaline in the urine reflects the amount of SNS activity and correlates with how much stress a person reports experiencing. See Figure 3.1.

Figure–ground reversal: a number of drawings have been produced which illustrate how *perception* involves the processing of figure and background. The best known example is of Rubin's vase/two faces (for example, Gregory, 1971: 16; Gregory, 1990: 322; Gross, 1996: 218). In this, two interpretations are possible depending on what is selected as the figure, and what as the background. This illustrates how we make a mental decision about what we are seeing, not simply passively receiving a stimulus.

An intriguing example is given in Figure 3.9. If the black blocks are regarded as the figure against a white background, the arrangement looks simply like a pile of children's building blocks. If, however, a mental switch is made so that the black area becomes the background, a very different perception results! This can also be regarded as a *visual fiction*.

Five-factor model of personality: a comprehensive descriptive personality system developed from empirical research by Goldberg (1993) from earlier ideas by Thurstone (1933). The 'big five' factors are neuroticism, extroversion, agreeableness, conscientiousness and openness to experience.

Fixation: a state in which a person remains attached to objects or activities more appropriate for an earlier stage of psychosexual development.

Flashbulb memory: this refers to a type of *episodic memory* in which people *recall* vivid details of when and where they were and what they were doing when they heard some particularly important news. As with other memories, the details may not be accurate even though they appear vivid.

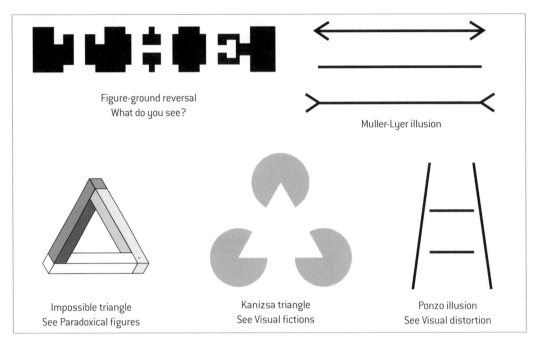

Figure-ground reversal
What do you see?

Muller-Lyer illusion

Impossible triangle
See Paradoxical figures

Kanizsa triangle
See Visual fictions

Ponzo illusion
See Visual distortion

Figure 3.9 Visual illusions

concepts

Forgetting: failure at any time to *recall* or recognise an experience or item, when attempting to do so or to perform any action previously learned. There are several broad categories of the theories of forgetting: decay theory, *interference* theory, *cue dependence*, inadequate processing during encoding or storage, *Gestalt theory* and motivated forgetting (repression).

Formal operations: the last of the stages of intellectual growth identified by Piaget (see also *concrete operations* and *sensori-motor*). Formal thinking is characterised by systematic experimentation, isolation of variables, looking for relationships and explanations, recognising contradictions, making logical *deductions*, reasoning with *abstracts*, and distinguishing between truth and logic. Piaget believes this does not start until adolescence and becomes the chief style of thinking of the intelligent adult. This notion of a stage is strongly criticised by other theorists who argue that children can use these operations at any age given appropriate conditions and that even intelligent adults do not think like this much of the time (for example Bryant, 1982; Wason and Johnson-Laird, 1968; see also Part 4). It is now considered more helpful to describe thinking and *problem-solving* throughout our lifespan in terms of different styles rather than stages.

Formative years: many *psychodynamic*, and other, theories stress that the first years of life, particularly the first five, are the most important ones because they determine what will follow. Some interpretations of these theories seem to suggest that early experiences are essentially important because a young child is more vulnerable or impressionable and that any damage done to the personality in early life is irrevocable and that it will always be too late to do anything about it. An alternative view is that the first few years of life are crucial, not because the experiences themselves are more important than later ones, but because they shape the ways in which later experiences will be perceived. In this view, self-awareness as an adult can help a person to develop a greater range of alternative *perceptions* and choices.

Frame problem: the frame problem arises if we consider a child to be a *blank slate* on which experience is written, such that the child develops into an adult equipped only with what has been learned. There appear to be many things that we just know, or can do, without being taught. These are the things that we think of as common sense and include the ability to distinguish between relevant and irrelevant implications of our actions (Pinker, 1998: 15 and 335). The frame problem did not come to light until researchers began programming computers (totally blank slates) and found that they could not programme for common sense. A computer can be programmed to select particular outcomes or it can be set to consider all possible outcomes but it cannot 'decide' which outcomes are relevant. Evolutionary psychology suggests that much of our common sense is built into our genes because the brain evolved in this way. This may be related to *value* and emotional colouring.

Free association: a technique pioneered by Jung and used within some *psychodynamic* therapies. The client is asked to say the first words that come into *consciousness* in response to a stimulus word. By looking at the pattern of responses, the therapist may find ways of directing the client along a fruitful line of enquiry. The game 'tennis–elbow–foot' uses free association without reference to hidden meanings.

Freudian slip: errors in speech or 'slips of the tongue' which seem to reveal some hidden thought that has contaminated what the person intended to say. Sometimes this contamination is merely mechanical due to similar sounds between what is intended and what is actually said. Sometimes there is a contraction of several sounds into one. Such slips have been recognised throughout history, and date back to ancient Greek civilisation. They were used widely in literature before Freud's time as a somewhat subtle way to reveal a character's inner thoughts.

Wording can be an excellent witticism, play on words or 'double entendre', or a blunder, depending on whether utterances are made with conscious or unconscious intention. Freud made use of slips that occurred during *psychoanalysis* to point towards associations that might reveal hidden emotional conflicts.

Functionalism: a theory of the mind in contemporary philosophy that developed as an alternative to behaviourism and the *identity theory of mind*. Mental states such as beliefs, desires and pain are considered solely in terms of their functional role in relation to sensory inputs (causes) and behavioural outputs (effects). Psychofunctionalism associated with Jerry Fodor and Zenon Pylyshyn views psychology as employing the same sorts of teleological or purposive explanations as the biological sciences. The role of mental states, such as belief and desire, is determined by the functional or causal role useful to an organism, such as in adapting to the environment, as described within scientific psychological theory. A third definition is the doctrine that the function of an object should determine its design and materials.

Fundamental attribution error: this expression was first used by Ross (1977) to refer to the tendency to attribute cause and blame to people rather than circumstances. Although almost all behaviour is the product of the person and the situation, it seems that there is a tendency to be biased towards attributing negative intentions and fault to the person. For example, if someone carrying drinks in a pub trips and spills some, many people tend to make the immediate assumption that the person is clumsy or drunk rather than look for an outstretched foot or stray bag. This bias gets worse with greater damage and when the onlooker making the judgement is involved. The difference in *perception* of an event from the point of view of the one involved and an onlooker has been called the actor–observer effect. See Jones and Nisbett (1971) and Nisbett et al (1973). The bias can be reduced by increased knowledge and understanding of the condition and the circumstances so that there is increased awareness of all the contributing factors. Zebrowitz (1990), cited by Gross (1996), shows that when participants are encouraged to empathise with the person displaying negative behaviours, attribution bias is less pronounced.

Galvanic skin response (GSR): a measure of the electrical conductivity of the skin, usually the palm of the hand. Moisture in the skin can conduct electricity and this alters with the saltiness or sweatiness of the skin. GSR has been widely used to study emotional reactions to stimuli, based on the assumption that a sudden emotional reaction will increase autonomic or sympathetic nervous system *arousal* (*fight or flight*) and hence the sweat and salt content of skin on the palms of the hands.

Gate control theory: Melzack and Wall (1965, 1982), Melzack and Dennis (1978) and Wall and Melzack (1984) developed the gate control theory in which they consider that pain messages carried by the specific nerve fibres (A-delta and C fibres) can be interrupted before reaching the brain by the action of other nerve fibres.

The model suggests the action of a gate in the dorsal horns of the spinal column where nerve fibres meet. Pain messages may be carried through the substantia gelatinosa of the dorsal horns to special T-cells in the spinal column, which relay pain messages to the brain. However, messages of heat, cold and pressure carried by large-diameter A-beta fibres may activate intervening nerves in the substantia gelatinosa, preventing the pain messages reaching the T-cells and thus closing the gate. This may explain why applying warmth or cold to a painful area, simple massage or TENS can act as counterirritants and reduce, mask or even replace pain (TENS – transcutaneous electrical nerve stimulation – applies tiny electrical impulses across the skin).

In addition, messages descending the spinal column from the brain can also close the gate. It appears that this process involves the production of natural pain-suppressing substances in the brain stem and spinal cord such as the endorphins, enkephalins and dynorphins (opioid peptides), which act in a similar way to morphine. This can be activated by memories of previous painful experiences that have been managed well, the perception of supportive surroundings and a positive meaning of pain, which lead to expectations that coping will occur again. In contrast, memories and expectations about poor pain control and factors such as boredom and anxiety can lead to opening the gate.

This theory can account for many of the psychological, anthropological and sociological data concerning individual and cultural differences in pain experience and behaviour. See also *Pain context*.

Gender: this term is commonly used interchangeably with *sex* to refer to biological characteristics, but in the social sciences is mostly used to describe the extent to which a person identifies with cultural constructions of femininity and masculinity, that is, has a sense of *gender identity*. In brief, sex is male/female whereas gender is masculine/feminine.

Gender Identity: the extent to which individuals conform to the cultural and social *norms* and ideals and think of themselves as masculine or feminine.

Throughout history, cultures have described what it means to be a typical or ideal man or woman. These descriptions can be seen either as archetypes (for example, Jung, 1964), the pure idealised form, or as stereotypes, which are over-simplified generalisations based on a few extreme examples.

Talcot Parsons in the 1950s described how, traditionally in Western society, masculinity and femininity are defined in terms of a dichotomy: instrumental versus expressive.

> Men are instrumental, aggressive, dominant, powerful, competitive, independent and self-assertive.
> Women are expressive, dependent, conformist, subjective, intuitive, sensitive, co-operative, tender and nurturing.

Until relatively recently, theories of personality and *self-concept* tended to categorise people as either masculine or feminine 'types' or as somewhere along a masculine–feminine continuum (for example, Eysenck and Wilson, 1976). In contrast, Sandra Bem (1981a) describes more recent thinking as rejecting the masculine–feminine continuum and describing individuals as having a measure of masculinity and a measure of femininity that are independent of each other: that is, a position on each of two separate scales. This has something in common with Jung's notion of both sexes having *anima and animus*. Yet others reject the whole notion of attributing *gender* labels to any of the above-listed characteristics and would like traits such as being expressive, nurturing, assertive and independent to be regarded as unrelated to *sex* or *gender*, being equally applicable to men or women and in any kind of mix.

There is ample evidence to suggest that *gender*-linked characteristics are encouraged from birth and are only rewarded when they are the 'right way round'. It is not at all clear whether this social *conditioning* causes the observable differences between males and females who would otherwise behave indistinguishably, or whether it merely fosters natural differences, in which case it creates problems for only a few non-conformists. The cultural notion of what is desirable and natural is constantly changing, and this can be seen as supporting the view that *conditioning* causes the differences. Images of men have undergone several transformations from male chauvinist to new man to reconstructed man and back to macho man. The image of women has moved from predominantly compliant, child-rearing and home-based to assertive and independent.

It could be argued that these changes either alter what is meant by masculine and feminine or support the notion that men and women are now expressing their opposite-gender characteristics more openly. In contrast, recent brain imaging seem to be revealing significant differences in brain function between male and female that could be related to genetic factors.

General adaptation syndrome (GAS) or adaptation level theory: Selye (1956) identified a second *arousal* system, after Cannon's *fight or flight* mechanism, and developed the general adaptation syndrome (GAS), which involves the pituitary-adrenal-cortical arousal system (see Figure 3.1). This has three stages:

> Alarm reaction: The noradrenaline triggers the pituitary gland, which produces ACTH (adrenocorticotrophic hormone or adrenocorticotrophin) which stimulates the outer part of the adrenal gland, the adrenal cortex. This in turn produces hormones, such as cortisol (a glucocorticoid), which control and conserve the amount of glucose in the blood. Sugar is freed from the reserves in the liver.

> Recovery or resistance: If the stressor is not removed the body begins to recover from the initial alarm reaction and cope with the situation. Increased activity of the pituitary-adrenal-cortical arousal system gradually brings blood sugar levels back to normal under continued moderate stress. Few outward signs of stress are visible though the ability to resist new stressors is impaired and vulnerability to health problems increases.

> Exhaustion: Under prolonged or extreme stress, the body's resources become depleted and the adrenal cortex no longer functions properly. Severe psychophysiological disorders may develop. The liver may deteriorate. Blood sugar levels drop and in extreme cases hypoglycaemia may result in death. See Figure 3.1.

Genes: sections of DNA each of which is a dis-

crete amino acid chain, containing up to 1,000 'bases' (adenine, cytosine, thymine and guanine) arranged in a specific order or code. Painstaking genetic labelling has resulted in identification of many genes at known positions on the relevant pairs of *chromosomes*. Genes may be dominant or recessive, the recessive gene remaining 'silent' when paired with a corresponding dominant or active gene. Each gene remains unchanged from generation to generation except where accidents or mistakes (mutations) happen during replication or repair or in cell division, but the mix of genes which any individual receives is unique. Each gene contributes something towards one particular feature in the *genotype* or overall pattern of inherited characteristics.

In order to explain the principles of inheritance, it is sometimes helpful to talk as if each gene contributes one characteristic on a one-to-one basis, but most characteristics are influenced by a combination of genes. Examples of single-factor inheritance involving recessive genes include red hair and red-green variations in colour *vision*. Eye colour is determined to some extent by single genes. This is illustrated in Figure 3.10. Conditions such as haemophilia can occur due to variations in any of the several genes responsible for blood coagulation.

Genetic counselling: in individual cases, genetic advice can help parents make decisions about the way they plan their family. This may entail testing a person for known genetic variations that are likely to create problems for any offspring and providing supportive counselling. There are considerable ethical problems associated with genetic counselling and parents, or prospective parents, face very difficult decisions related to whether to have children or to continue with a particular pregnancy. After conception, the foetus can be tested for the presence of particular *genes* to see whether the recognised condition will develop.

Genotype: the sum total of all the *genes*, the genetic constitution or inherited characteristics of an individual or group. These may or may not be outwardly apparent. For example where *genes* are recessive or 'silent' the related characteristics will not be outwardly visible. For example, a person may have brown hair but carry the gene for red hair. It is possible for two people with brown hair

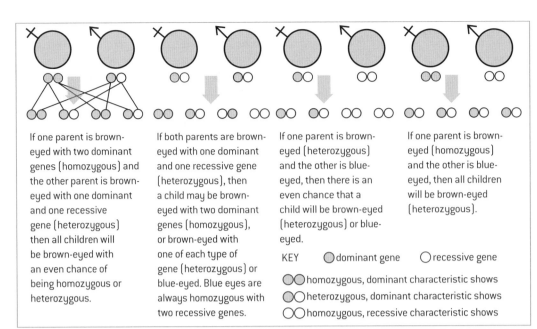

If one parent is brown-eyed with two dominant genes (homozygous) and the other parent is brown-eyed with one dominant and one recessive gene (heterozygous) then all children will be brown-eyed with an even chance of being homozygous or heterozygous.

If both parents are brown-eyed with one dominant and one recessive gene (heterozygous), then a child may be brown-eyed with two dominant genes (homozygous), or brown-eyed with one of each type of gene (heterozygous) or blue-eyed. Blue eyes are always homozygous with two recessive genes.

If one parent is brown-eyed (heterozygous) and the other is blue-eyed, then there is an even chance that a child will be brown-eyed (heterozygous) or blue-eyed.

If one parent is brown-eyed (homozygous) and the other is blue-eyed, then all children will be brown-eyed (heterozygous).

KEY ⬤ dominant gene ⭕ recessive gene

⬤⬤ homozygous, dominant characteristic shows
⬤⭕ heterozygous, dominant characteristic shows
⭕⭕ homozygous, recessive characteristic shows

Figure 3.10 Genes: inheritance of eye colour or other single-gene characteristic

concepts

to have a red-haired child, if the child inherits the recessive gene from each parent. See also *Phenotype*.

Glia cells: glia cells (also known as glial cells, neuroglia or satellite cells) are non-conducting and serve as support cells which provide substance and packing in between the *neurones* in the *brain*. They increase insulation between neurones and contribute to the carrying of nutrients within the brain, facilitate neural transmission, remove damaged and dead neurons, and prevent poisonous substances in the blood from reaching the brain. There are several different types, including Schwann cells, oligodendrocytes and astrocytes.

Grammatical representation: one of the four main formats of *representation* in the brain that arranges the different parts of language (nouns and verbs, phrases and clauses, stems and roots, phonemes and syllables) in meaningful hierarchical networks. These determine how we put sentences together and how we can communicate and play with language. For example we can play with normal or nonsense words in grammatically sound sentences, such as, 'Colourless green ideas sleep furiously' – one of the first nonsense sentences created in the game of 'cadavre exquis' started in 1925, and:

Twas brillig, and the slithy toves
Did gyre and gimble in the wabe:
All mimsy were the borogoves,
And the mome raths outgrabe.

from Jabberwocky by Lewis Carroll (from *Through the Looking-Glass and What Alice Found There*, 1872). In this, we can only guess what the words mean but we can follow the grammar properly. Conversely we can put normal words together in a non-grammatical way. For example 'put ran pencil arrange notwithstanding up sideways on the whole'. Without the grammar, we cannot bring any meaningful interpretation to the arrangement of words. It appears that the ability to follow rules of grammar may be 'hard-wired in the brain', whatever language we learn to speak. See also *Beliefs, Language centres*.

Grief: emotional experience of those who have been bereaved. Grief is a complex, individualised process that manifests itself in different ways at different times. Following a death, the nature of the reaction is influenced more by how great a part of someone's life the deceased occupied rather than by their emotional involvement (Marris, 1986). Grief may involve physical *pain* as well as psychological distress, which may precipitate uncharacteristic behaviour in the sufferer. For example, activities such as shopping which previously posed no threat may induce a panic attack after the *loss*. Feelings can be intense. These include *anger*, a sense of unfairness, guilt, rage, insecurity, *anxiety* and isolation. The physical impact of grief may be manifested in apathy, insomnia, loss of weight, palpitations, tightness of the chest or shortness of breath. If grief is unresolved it is known as pathological, complicated or unresolved grief. In such cases the grief may be excessive, delayed, absent or prolonged with disruption of ability to function as usual. Theoretical models focus either on the 'stages' or the 'tasks' of the grieving or mourning processes. Mourning is the expression of grief and may conform to well-established patterns or rituals.

Group development: a number of theories have been proposed which suggest that groups evolve and change over time. Most adopt a sequential approach in suggesting that groups pass through a number of developmental stages. Tuckman and Jensen (1977) suggest the following five:

> Forming – an initial period of caution.
> Storming – a period of conflict.
> Norming – members resolve conflict, settle arguments and develop acceptable forms of behaviour.
> Performing – energies become focused on the task.
> Adjourning – members prepare to part.

Further models provide lists for comparison, such as Johnson and Johnson (1994), Napier and Gershenfeld (1989) and Kiger (1995: 137).

Group initiation rituals: entry into a group may be marked by some kind of initiation ceremony or ritual which can range from a warm welcome to embarrassing mocking and teasing or even painful 'rites of passage'. For example 'rookie' recruits into the Fire or Ambulance Service or nursing are often sent on fools errands or ordered to carry out procedures which blatantly contradict rules, regulations or common-sense notions of health and safety. Coping successfully with the teasing marks the recruit as a real member.

Brown (1988) discusses some possible reasons for this. There may be a symbolic function for both the newcomer and the group and help in the process of identity transition. It can allow the

newcomer a reference point to recognise that he or she is no longer quite the same as before. It may introduce the recruit to the standards and norms of the group and perhaps go towards getting the recruit to feel and express some loyalty to the group. Aronson and Mills (1959) cited by Brown (1988) gave an interesting explanation for the painful rites inflicted by some groups, particularly where newcomers are in some doubt as to whether the group is worth joining, suggesting that having to overcome such a trial in order to join the group induces a belief that the group must be worthwhile if it is so difficult to become a member. The experimental findings have been linked to the notion of *cognitive dissonance* and *dissonance* reduction. Initiation rituals and teasing can also be seen as adult bullying (Randall, 1997) which serves to maintain hierarchical power relationships.

Group processes: how the group is functioning. Things to look for in groups include:

> participation
> influence
> styles of influence (see *Parenting styles*)
> decision-making procedures
> task functions
> maintenance functions
> group atmosphere
> membership
> expression of feelings
> norms.

The following unhelpful processes can be identified:

> Pairing: two group members usually sitting next to each other talk to each other rather than to the group. This can be a distraction to other group members. Alternatively, two group members form an exclusive relationship and support each other when one of them makes a contribution.
> Projection: a group member blames the group for the way he or she is feeling. This may stem from insecurity within the group or the individual's lack of self-awareness.
> Scapegoating: the group looks for someone to blame for the way the group is feeling or behaving, or the circumstances in which members find themselves. The scapegoat may be a quiet or vulnerable member on whom others vent feelings or an outside scapegoat,

concepts

for example employing organisation or professional body.

> Shutting down: a member may cut off from the rest of the group and become isolated. This often occurs when people cannot face or talk about their feelings.

> Rescuing: one person may constantly defend others from attack thus denying the attacked person the opportunity to learn how to cope with the situation.

> Flight: difficult issues or decisions are avoided by strategies such as changing the topic, making jokes, theorising or talking superficially.

See also *Bales interaction analysis*.

Group of displacements and reversibility: development of the *object concept* is closely tied up with the progressive organising of movements in space: the movements of the child and the movements of the objects. At first, the baby drops toys out of the pram and waits for an adult to pick them up. This is non-reversible action. Gradually, the child learns to make a group of displacements, moving herself or himself or the objects in a sequence of actions, taking objects from one place to another and retrieving them, or moving to another part of the room and returning. Piaget suggests this develops during the *sensori-motor* stage of development.

Habituation/sensory adaptation: becoming accustomed to a repeated stimulus so that it no longer registers and we cease to pay *attention* to it. This happens chiefly because the *nervous system* is 'programmed' to register a change in stimulus more strongly than continued stimulation. This is noticeable with the ticking of a clock. After continuous exposure to the ticking, we are no longer aware of it, although we can bring our attention back to it if we wish. However, if the clock suddenly stops, we immediately notice the change. This effect is necessary in protecting us from information overload; we can safely ignore anything which is not changing and use our resources to deal with new data which might be important. There is some suggestion that habituation (together with other selective *attention*al processes) does not function well in some people suffering symptoms of *schizophrenia* or *autism*. Habituation at the level of the *nervous system* can be compared with the

more complex processes of *desensitisation*. A related *concept* is tolerance, a term most often used in relation to drugs.

Hallucinations: the experience of an apparent perception of an object that is not present (*apparition*) and which is not related in any obvious way to sensory stimulation.

Hallucinations can occur in any of the sensory modes, *vision*, *hearing*, *touch*, *taste*, *smell*, *proprioception* or interoception. Visions and voices are the most commonly described experiences. Traditionally, hallucinatory experiences are regarded as mysterious or frightening and contribute to folklore and views of insanity. In contrast, we do not usually talk about the experience of the existence of a limb that has been amputated (phantom limb) as an hallucination, despite calling it phantom, presumably because the experience can be reasonably explained in terms of the neural activity and can be seen to be imagined. It may be that there is no justification for regarding a schizophrenic person's voices as physiologically different from the amputee's itchy foot. It is perhaps one person's realisation that the *sensation* must have been imagined, and another's conviction that it was real, that distinguishes between different mental states. Rankin and O'Carroll (1995) report that non-psychotic individuals who are disposed towards hallucination have more difficulty in cognitive tests in discriminating between memories of words they either heard or imagined hearing.

A negative hallucination is when a person fails to perceive something in the environment, such as not seeing an object one is looking for, only to find a moment later that it was there all the time. Such experiences are common and are probably responsible for belief in poltergeists, which are said to hide objects playfully. Under *hypnosis*, a person may respond to suggestion that an object is not present or not visible.

Halo and horns effects: an example of *attribution* in which positive or negative evaluation in one particular area leads to generalisations. That is, a halo effect arises when knowledge of one good characteristic leads to a perception that the person is also good in other areas about which nothing is yet known. The horns effect arises when being poor in one area generates beliefs that the person is also poor in other areas. This has repercussions for care. For example, Nordholm (1980) found that patients who are seen as physically attractive are often judged to have a better 'prognosis' and to be more intelligent and better motivated than their less attractive counterparts.

Hardiness: Maddi and Kobasa (1991) believe they have identified conditions in early life that will lead to hardiness or a hardy personality that is relatively resistant to stress. These include a family atmosphere of variety with many moderately difficult tasks, warm parental encouragement of attempts to succeed, and expression of individuality. They identify three main elements of psychological hardiness:

> a sense of commitment, rather than alienation
> control, not powerlessness
> challenge, rather than threat.

They argue that children brought up in a supportive family atmosphere will deal with demands in a non-stressful way. They add that these qualities of commitment, control and challenge are important throughout the lifespan, at school, college and in the workplace, and that it is possible for adults to develop them even if early experiences have been detrimental. See also *Parenting styles*.

Hearing (auditory sense): one of the five special *senses*, this can be described as an exteroceptor, telereceptor or mechano-receptor sense. The ears enable information to be picked up from a distance by the successive action of sound waves or pressure changes on the ear-drum, small bones in the ear and the small hairs (auditory receptors) in the cochlea. Movement of the auditory receptors creates action potentials, which travel via auditory pathways to the auditory areas of the *cerebral cortex* on both sides of the *brain* (Figure 3.4 and Figure 3.11). Auditory pathways from the ears to the cerebral auditory areas in the *brain* are partially crossed. Although each cerebral (cortical) hemisphere can receive input from both ears, the neural connections from one ear to the opposite hemisphere are stronger than the connections on the same side. When inputs compete, it is thought that the strong opposite side input inhibits the same side input. See also *Hemispherical specialisation*.

Hearing enables discrimination of the following variables:

> pitch
> loudness
> emphasis
> timbre or quality
> location (see *Auditory location*).

Hearing can be very important in the interpretation of *paralanguage*, and people with hearing loss may be insensitive to nuances of meaning conveyed by tone of voice.

Hemispheric specialisation: the two hemispheres of the *cerebral cortex* are mirror images but not exactly symmetrical.

Generally, motor and sensory pathways are crossed so that the left hemisphere controls movements on the right side of the body and vice versa (Figure 3.12). Thus the right hand, arm, leg and foot are controlled by the left hemisphere and the left hand, arm, leg and foot by the right hemisphere. However, some movements such as those of the trunk, shoulders and hips are controlled by either side.

With *vision*, information from the left field of view crosses to the right hemisphere and information from the right field of view crosses to the left hemisphere (Figure 3.22). For *hearing*, auditory pathways are partially crossed (Figure 3.11).

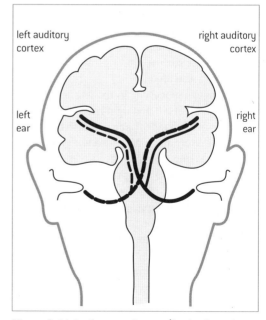

Figure 3.11 Auditory pathways (brain viewed from behind)

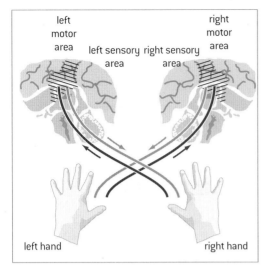

left motor area

right motor area

left sensory area

right sensory area

left hand

right hand

Figure 3.12 Motor and sensory pathways

In the majority of people, the left hemisphere is dominant, which results in the right hand being the preferred hand for many activities. The incidence of left-handedness is difficult to measure as it depends on how it is defined, and it seems to vary from society to society. Numbers vary from 4 per cent to 36 per cent (Gregory, 1987). Moreover, this dominance is not absolute and many people have mixed hand preference and foot preference across a variety of actions such as picking up an object, catching, throwing, grip strength, lifting, kicking and jumping. Once a preference has been established, it is likely to be reinforced by habit.

The right hemisphere controls certain skills like spatial abilities such as drawing, map reading and finding one's way around.

Language is processed in the left hemisphere in the majority of left and right-handed people. In a minority of left-handed people, whose brains are an exact mirror image of a typical right-handed person, the *language centres* are in the right hemisphere. See also *Topography*.

Heterozygous: this term is used in reference to a specific pair of *genes* on the corresponding pair of *chromosomes*, where the *genes* lead to different characteristics (the prefix hetero means 'other'). For example, a person can be called heterozygous for eye colour if the corresponding *genes* relate to different colour of eyes. That is a heterozygous brown-eyed person would have the gene for brown eyes (dominant) on one chromosome and

the gene for blue eyes (recessive or silent) on the corresponding chromosome in the pair. For most *genes*, the resulting characteristic will depend on which gene is dominant and whether several *genes* are involved in determining the characteristic. See also *Homozygous, Zygote*.

Hierarchical network model: a model by Collins and Quillian (1969, 1972) of *semantic memory*, which shows how we process some information according to meaningful hierarchies similar in some ways to scientific classification systems. However, unlike scientific systems the hierarchical schemas are often highly individual and we cannot always articulate them without prompting from others.

Hippocampus: the area of the *brain* most closely associated with specific memories for information, particularly the learning of new information. See Figure 3.5 for its location.

Homozygous: as with *heterozygous*, this term is used in reference to a specific pair of *genes* on the corresponding pair of *chromosomes*. In this case, it occurs as a result of the fertilisation of an ovum with a sperm which contain the same or matching *genes* for a particular characteristic (the prefix homo means 'same'). For example, a person can be called homozygous for eye colour if both corresponding *genes* relate to the same colour of eyes. That is, a homozygous brown-eyed person will have a gene for brown eyes on both *chromosomes* of the pair.

Hypnosis (hypnotism): the term hypnosis has several medical meanings. It may be used to refer to sleep induced by a sleep-promoting or hypnotic drug. Secondly, it may refer to a state of semi-*coma* induced by deliberate mild poisoning or intoxication such as 'barbiturate hypnosis'.

In common usage, hypnosis or hypnotism refers to a method of inducing deep relaxation or distraction by focusing *attention* on suggested specific emotional or physical experiences, or a condition in which one individual complies to an unusual extent with the suggestions of another, usually accompanied by the feeling that the experience is not quite the same as the normal state of *consciousness* and that the compliance is involuntary (Naish, 1986). Other names include mesmerism and animal magnetism. Some people experience this condition as a trance.

In 'trait' approaches it is argued that some people are more susceptible to hypnosis than others, and this is the generally held belief.

Many people also believe that hypnosis can be imposed against one's will. However, 'skills training' approaches, described by Naish (1986), argue that responses to hypnosis can be learned. Learned responses may include the willingness to comply and the ability to imagine vividly what is being suggested, which can improve with practice.

The experience will depend largely on what the individual expects to experience. If the individual expects hypnosis to feel trance-like or different in some way from normal *consciousness* and complies with suggestions, then this is what will happen. Similarly, if the individual complies with suggestions, while expecting his or her responses to feel involuntary, then this is what it will seem like. On the other hand, a person who expects things simply to happen, without any effort or willingness to comply, will not experience hypnosis. Someone who does not expect anything to happen and who makes no effort to comply is also unlikely to experience anything. Skills training approaches argue that hypnosis requires effort on the part of the hypnosee rather than the hypnotist.

Research into hypnosis continues and there are reliable scales that can measure a person's *suggestibility* (Fellows, 1988).

Hypnotherapy: the use of suggestion to help someone make changes to their lifestyle or state of being. In most cases, it involves suggesting that the client is in a state of deep *relaxation*, then talking through the client's *beliefs*, perhaps worries or fears, and aspects of self-concept or lifestyle. The therapist may make suggestions about improvements in habits or lifestyle, and the client may form an intention to carry out the suggested changes. Hypnotherapy may be used in attempts to treat eating disorders or stress or to give up smoking. Most hypnotherapists refer to the hypnotic state as deep relaxation rather than trance-like (see also *Hypnosis*).

Hypothalamus: the hypothalamus is below the thalamus (the prefix hypo means below or less than) in the *mid-brain* and has a specialised role

in the organisation of metabolism, control of body temperature, the production and circulation of hormones and the mechanisms of being awake or asleep and of *aggression*. It is also active in sexual behaviour and it controls the sympathetic and parasympathetic nervous systems in response to signals initiated by the cortex. See Figure 3.5 for its location.

Iconic representation (iconic imagery): the second of Bruner's modes of mental representation (see also *enactive* and *symbolic representation*). Iconic representation involves forming mental images of objects and activities. The term usually refers only to visual images but could be extended to cover all *senses*. It depends on having sufficient *memory* for the objects and activities to be held in the mind long enough for the activity to be thought through. This approach can be readily compared with Baddeley's ideas on *working memory* which he describes as using a visual 'sketch pad' or 'scratch pad' as part of the *short-term memory* processes designed to handle information which has been temporarily recalled from long-term storage (Baddeley, 1990).

Imagine a cube and think of cutting it in half and then half again. How easy you find this task may depend on how clear your iconic imagery is and how readily you can carry out this kind of activity in your mind. You might like to consider what your cube was made of and what colour it was, what you cut it with and so on. Many people do not make a particularly clear picture. Others imagine a specific material such as cheese or one with a distinct colour, which is different inside from outside, and may even evoke a smell and a taste. Others may imagine sawing a wooden cube with a power saw, complete with sound effects, the smell of the sawdust and the pull on the arm muscles. Notice how much easier this task becomes if you think of cutting an apple in half and half again. Your experience and memories of cutting apples into quarters is significantly greater than for cubes. Some people do not use iconic imagery in this sort of task but employ symbolic mathematical reasoning saying only that it requires two cuts and since one cut makes two pieces, two cuts will produce four pieces.

Barlow (in Barlow et al, 1990) makes a clear distinction between images in the outside world (before the eye) and those in the mind (behind the eye). Iconic images in the outside world include paintings, drawings, photographs, television and video pictures, films, shadows and reflections.

It is often difficult to communicate mental images and reproduce them in an outside world form. Differences in the ways in which people make use of iconic imagery can result in difficulties in communication, as two people may find they are just 'not on the same wavelength'. It is important in professional care to try to match descriptions and explanations of procedures to the kind of language and imagery the client uses. Much of cognitive, humanistic and *psychodynamic* therapy is concerned with helping people to develop the forms needed to articulate images and feelings. Music can have tremendous effect without the need for words; most other therapeutic techniques involve a combination of words and non-word forms. See also *Visual images*.

Iconic store: the term *iconic* may be used for any *memory*, mode of *representation* or cognitive process using visual or other images which resemble the actual object (for example, Bruner, 1964). This may refer to imagining an apple being cut in half, where the sound, appearance, smell, taste and feel of the apple and the act of cutting can be imagined. However, iconic store usually refers only to short-term sensory storage of visual stimuli in terms of physical features such as size, shape, colour and location but not meaning (Sperling, 1960, 1963).

Id: Freud used the word 'id', from the Latin for 'it', to stand for all biological aspects of the unconscious mind dealing with *psychosexual* needs. Freud viewed the id as natural, *instinct*ive and demanding instant gratification. He described it as having no logic or external reality and governed chiefly by the *pleasure principle*, while at the same time incorporating certain destructive elements.

Ideal self (ego-ideal or idealised self-image): this is one of the three components of *self-concept* identified by Rogers (1961) and included by Price (1990) in his approach to *body image*. In general, this would refer to the sort of person one would like to be. Specific features can also be identified, referring to particular desired attributes, such as length of hair, body shape, fitness, personality, lifestyle and occupation.

Identification: sharing or taking on the characteristics of another person to the extent that one's own identity is altered, such as in identification with an idol or role model.

Identity constancy: one type of *perceptual constancy*, this is being able to recognise an object as the same object even when viewed from a different angle or distance or under different lighting conditions. For example, you can still recognise a cup as the same cup even when someone is moving it around the room, despite the fact that your retinal image is continuously changing. You may lose this if you view an object from an unusual angle or can see only a tiny part of it: an effect exploited in the party game using close-up photographs of bits of familiar objects.

Identity theory of mind (monism): a theory, in philosophy of mind, which asserts that mental events are not separate from the brain but are type-identical to the physical events in the brain with which they are correlated.

Implicit personality theory: most introductory *psychology* texts describe how nearly all people have an individual way of categorising and pigeonholing characteristics in themselves and others. This idea has been extensively developed in *personal construct theory*.

Individuation: Jung used this term to refer to the process, which he saw in certain gifted people in the second half of life, of working towards the achievement of psychic wholeness or integration. This is an idea that Maslow (1943) adapted in his *concept* of self-actualisation. It is also used in a more general sense to refer to a sense of personal identity and leads to the notion of deindividuation in *crowds*, where some people lose their personal identity and follow along with mob behaviour.

Induction or inductive reasoning: reasoning from particular observations to a general belief, or, in more formal terms, from empirical data to a model, the opposite of *deduction*. Induction involves noticing commonalities and arriving at a general principle or *concept*. In most areas of life, despite sound reasoning, people are likely to arrive at only partial truths and faulty conceptions due to incomplete knowledge. It is helpful to realise that wrong answers are not usually due to an inability to think logically but merely to insufficient data. See also *Concept*.

Induced motion: an illusion in which a stationary point of light within a moving reference frame is seen as moving and the reference frame is perceived as stationary.

Information processing: an approach within cognitive science that developed through comparing the human mind with the way in which computers operate. Many psychologists see this as the 'dominant *paradigm* within cognitive psychology as a whole' (Gross, 1996: 262). Many explanations of *attention* and *memory* rely on the information processing approach and describe the carrying out of mental operations as *serial processing* or *parallel processing* or as *bottom-up* and *top-down processing*.

Insight: in the context of *problem-solving*, this term is used for a sudden solution to a problem where the steps involved in reaching the solution are not known. This may also be referred to as an 'aha' or 'Eureka' experience when a person has been struggling unsuccessfully to solve a *problem* and then abruptly sees what is needed. The term is also used in a wider sense to refer to deeper understanding of a situation, person or event.

Inspection time: a person's inspection time (IT) is an estimate of the time needed for presentation of a stimulus for a participant to make a given discrimination to a predetermined criterion of accuracy. The original and commonest form of the task involves presenting two parallel vertical lines of markedly different lengths to participants who are then asked to indicate, in their own time, which of the lines is longer (Vickers et al, 1972). The duration of the stimulus is manipulated by the experimenter to obtain an estimate of the minimum exposure time required by the participant to reach a given accuracy criterion. The relative lengths and inclination of the lines may then be varied. A similar study relates to hearing (Parker et al, 1999). The principal focus of interest in IT arises from claims that this biological measure is an indicator of the general factor (g) of *intelligence* (for example Brand and Deary, 1982; Deary and Stough, 1996).

Instinct: traditionally defined as an inherited and inborn predisposition to behave in a particular way in response to environmental cues. Very few aspects of human or animal behaviour are now regarded as instinctive and early psychoanalytical ideas based on instincts have been superseded. All evidence now suggests that opportunities for complicated learning processes may start to operate shortly after conception. This means that a new distinction has to be made between things that are present at birth (innate or inborn) or appear alongside maturational development and those that are genetically determined. A few human reflexes are present at birth, such as rooting and sucking and a walking response, but it is not yet at all clear how much subsequent behaviour can be attributed to inherited elements. Even with non-human animals many patterns of behaviour, like nest-building, that were assumed to be totally instinctive can be shown to involve learning.

Instrumental: a term used to denote behaviour which is goal-directed, that is intended to achieve something which is desired. In day-to-day communication this would refer to activities like shopping or working where we use speech and gestures to get things done. On a different (perhaps unconscious) level, a person may inflict self-injury to try to sustain a relationship that is floundering. Threatening another person may bring feelings of *power*.

Intellectualisation: thinking and reading about life events and giving theoretical explanations in preference to actually experiencing such events or acknowledging the relevance of individual experience. As with *asceticism*, Anna Freud added this term to her father's list of *defence mechanisms* in relation to adolescents who may adopt escapist behaviour because they are not coping well with the uncertainties of growing up.

Intelligence: an *abstract concept* relating to mental ability with no agreed definition – but, although we have trouble defining it, we generally recognise it when we see it. Alice Heim (1954) discussed over 40 definitions of intelligence. Some early definitions stressed rational, *convergent thinking*. For example, Guilford (1967) defines intelligence as ability in dealing with *problems* that require one, clearly-defined and correct answer. Others recognised the need to include imaginative *divergent* thinking.

Use of the term intelligence now usually refers to a person's ability to learn from experience, adapt to new situations and solve new problems. This may involve making decisions according to some set of rules, and wanting something and pursuing it in the face of obstacles. This view of intelligence appears to be related to the rate at which a person can assimilate information and the ease or effectiveness with which this can be related to previous knowledge, skills or experience.

It was commonly believed (for example Eysenck, 1962) that intelligence was determined by inheritance. However, much of what used to be regarded as intelligence can now be identified as *problem-solving* skills, which can be learned at any age.

Crystallised intelligence is associated with well-established patterns of thinking, habits, knowledge and skills. Fluid intelligence is concerned with responding to new situations and making use of previously learned knowledge and skills in new, creative and adaptive ways. Fluid and crystallised intelligence are sometimes abbreviated to 'wit and wisdom'.

There is now good agreement about the number and nature of human mental abilities. There is also clear evidence that a factor of general intelligence ('g') runs through virtually all tests that require thought for their successful completion, no matter how different the items are in content. *Concepts* such as mental speed (speed of processing and *inspection time*) and *working memory* are now central to research (for example Jensen, 2000). See also 'Triarchic intelligence' in Part 1.

Intelligence quotient (IQ): if you take an intelligence test you will be given a score that is compared with the average score for members of the population of different ages. This gives you a 'mental age'. Your IQ is then calculated by taking your mental age divided by your chronological age, expressed as a percentage. For example a $12\frac{1}{2}$-year-old who scores the same as an average 15-year-old will have an IQ of 15/12.5 x 100, that is, of 120. Although some intelligence tests have questionable *validity* (see Part 5), calculations assume that IQ gives a *normal distribution*, with a *mean* of 100 and a *standard deviation* of about 16.

This means that the average is 100 and two-thirds of the population have an IQ between 84 and 116. In fact the distribution is not quite normal, but is negatively *skewed* (the mean is lower than normal) because some people have low intelligence due to illness or a chromosomal difference such as Downs' Syndrome.

Interference or inhibition: any intervening activity that affects *retention* of learned material. Retroaction (retroactive interference or inhibition) is the effect of recent activity on previously learned material. 'Proaction' ('proactive' interference or inhibition) is the effect of past activity on future learning. Interference can be either positive (improving retention) or negative (hindering), but common usage, particularly of the term inhibition, may often refer only to *forgetting*.

Intersexuality: the term adopted by medicine during the 20th century for people (or other living organisms) who cannot be classified as either male or female because sex chromosomes, genitalia and/or secondary sex characteristics are either lacking or have biological characteristics of both the male and female sexes. The term hermaphrodite is usually reserved for organisms that are completely male and female and can reproduce sexually in either role. See also *Transgender*.

Introversion: a term complementary to *extroversion* in some theories of personality, particularly those attributable to Jung and Eysenck (cited in Ryckman, 1989; Gross, 1996; and others), to describe people with an inward-looking and seemingly quiet approach to life. In these theories, introversion tends to be linked with a strong conscience, reliance on personal *values* and a tendency to guilt and anxiety. Jung identifies four introverted types: introverted feeling, introverted intuitive, introverted sensing and introverted thinking. Eysenck identifies two introverted types: stable introverted (phlegmatic) and neurotic introverted (melancholic). Eysenck (1965), cited by Ryckman (1989), argues that introverts have weak inhibitory processes in the *nervous system* with a small capacity to tolerate stimulation. They avoid variety of experience. He found that when electric shocks are administered to participants, the pain tolerance of introverts is less than that of extroverts. Some people with introvert tendencies

concepts

may, however, hide their feelings and display less pain behaviour.

Kinaesthesia: the sense of movement and position felt through the sense receptors in the muscles. It is this sense that provides information about where all the parts of the body are and what they are doing at any particular moment, without having to look, and creates a kind of 'mental map' of the body. If you close your eyes, put both hands up in front of you, about a metre apart, with fists loosely clenched and forefingers extended and attempt to touch your forefingers together, you may find that your kinaesthetic sense is not particularly accurate! People who have *brain damage* that upsets this internal sense lose their 'body maps' and cannot tell what their body is doing. Sacks (1985) describes a few people who have learned to compensate for this by watching themselves in mirrors all the time. See also *Proprioception*.

Note that in neurolinguistic programming (Bandler and Grinder, 1975, 1976), the name Kinaesthetic (K) is used for a combination of *sensation* and emotion which is expressed in terms of how a person 'feels'.

Language centres: two language centres have been identified in the *brain*: Broca's area and Wernicke's area. In most people, including the majority of those who are left-handed, these language centres are situated in the left cortical hemisphere (see also *hemispheric specialisation*). Broca's area is towards the front of the brain, Wernicke's area further back. See Figure 3.4 for their location.

Damage to either of these areas causes aphasia or dysphasia, which means disruption of speech. This commonly follows a stroke affecting the left side of the brain and may be associated with right side paralysis of the body.

It appears that Broca's area processes use of grammar and the rules of language. Impairment is usually noticeable as an 'expressive' disorder. Speech may be slow and require enormous effort and sounds are poorly produced. Patients leave out the little words like 'if', 'but' and 'to', or lose endings like plurals or verb tenses so that sentences sound like a telegram. Writing may also be without grammatical rules. On the other hand, patients may be able to sing a melody well and may be able to sing words they cannot speak.

There may be failure to understand complicated sentences but in many patients understanding is not impaired. This adds support to the argument that potential for learning the rules of language is 'hard-wired' into the brain. That is, there seems to be a natural ability to learn language and follow rules in a way that is independent of *intelligence* or culture, even though the particular rules for different languages may bear little relation to each other. It is noticeable that this applies only to spoken language; learning the special rules for writing requires considerable *motivation* and effort.

In contrast, damage to Wernicke's area usually results in rather rapid speech with a normal flow and correct grammar but enormous difficulty in finding the right word, an experience commonly known as 'word-blindness'. Wernicke's area appears to be responsible for holding the bulk of vocabulary, rather like a dictionary, so that the right word for an object or action can be found when wanted.

Children who sustain damage to the left hemisphere before the age of about seven or eight usually develop or recover language. The right hemisphere has the potential for language and appears to take over.

Lateral thinking: thinking that does not follow logical (*deductive* or *inductive*) constraints but introduces novel solutions. This may involve shifting to another 'frame of reference' such that the answer belongs to a different set of expectations from what seems indicated by the task. Many jokes are based on a lateral thinking approach where the story seems to be leading in a certain direction but the punch line is a surprise. This kind of shift or surprise may evoke laughter, annoyance or puzzlement depending on whether the listener follows the lateral jump and considers it legitimate. Edward de Bono (1971) argues that lateral thinking produces a much richer set of possible solutions than pure logic and can be used productively to find the best solution. Lateral thinking represents the extreme in *divergent* approaches. In some *problem-solving* procedures, brainstorming or showering of a lateral kind can throw up many interesting and creative, often deliberately odd, ideas that in turn may give rise to a usable solution.

Leadership: the emergence of a leader in a group

can be studied in various ways. It may be seen from the point of view of personal leadership attributes, as an outcome of the structure of a group or as an interaction of the two. Leadership may also be regarded as a process of negotiation between leaders and followers. On the whole, leaders are seen as those people occupying high-status positions with a tendency to initiate ideas and activities in the group.

Brown (1988) suggests that leaders are those who influence others in the group more than they are themselves influenced. There are various methods by which a leader comes to be in that position, such as natural emergence, election, appointment, seniority or domination.

It is a common view that people who become leaders have natural qualities of leadership, hence the saying 'Leaders are born, not made'. In particular, political leaders are seen to share certain special traits. Conversely, a politician in a high-status position without these traits may be much criticised for lack of flair.

This can be contrasted with the view that anyone appointed to a leading position can acquire the necessary skills or that anyone aspiring to lead others can learn what is required. Current tendencies in management training are towards identifying skills that can be learned by all members of a group, including the leader, so that groups do not have to be dependent on having a naturally 'good' leader but can work towards developing effective methods. Brown (1988: 88) suggests that the objective of leadership training is to 'improve the fit' between the leader and the situation but that there is controversy over whether to change the leader, the situation or both. See also *Power*.

Leading questions: a form of question used in interviewing that suggests the answer that should be given. Apart from trapping people into giving certain answers, it is thought that some leading questions can actually affect how a person interprets and thus remembers an event (Loftus and Palmer, 1974). For example, asking a witness of an accident whether one of the cars involved was blue may lead the witness to visualise a blue car and subsequently confuse the imagined car with the *memory* of the accident. Other kinds of questions include *value*-laden, probing, confronting, closed and open (Adams and Bromley, 1998). See also *Eye-witness testimony*.

Leakage: a term used for the situation in which body language gives away clues to inner feelings where a person is trying to convey a different emotion or lack of emotion. Compare with *slippage*.

Learned helplessness: Seligman (1975) demonstrated that animals that were subjected to unpleasant experiences over which they had no control tended not to take action in other situations in which the outcome was in fact under their influence. He initially used these findings to explain the passivity of people who were depressed and did little to try to help themselves. He subsequently revised his ideas to include a cognitive element and ideas from *attribution theory*.

Learning theory: an early name for the basic behaviourist description of how learning takes place through a process of *conditioning*, either classical or operant. As there are now many learning theories, based on different theoretical concepts, the original usage is no longer very useful.

Levels of processing (LOP): a model proposed by Craik and Lockhart (1972) in which the durability of *memory* is seen as a direct function of the depth of processing rather than the structures of short and long term memory. Deeply processed items will be retained for a longer period of time. Two types of *rehearsal* are identified: maintenance rehearsal that simply repeats items in the form in which they were presented and which probably restricts them to short-term memory (STM), and elaborative rehearsal which includes additional associations and meanings and which can serve to transfer items into long-term memory (LTM). Three levels are suggested; structural or shallow level associated with visual physical appearance (with words this corresponds to the visual appearance of the word), phonetic or phonemic level associated with sounds (with words this corresponds to the sound of the word), and semantic level associated with meanings.

Libido: Freud used this term for the unconscious source of energy associated with *psychosexual* needs. Jung extended the meaning of the word to cover the whole of life-energy. In common usage it refers to sexual energy.

Lightness constancy: the tendency to perceive the whiteness, greyness or blackness of objects as constant across changing levels of illumination.

Limbic system: this consists of a number of structures around the central core of the *brain* and includes *thalamus*, *hypothalamus*, *hippocampus* and amygdala. It has a role in regulating emotional and sexual behaviour and often inhibits aggressive responses. Damage, surgery or cerebral atrophy may result in increased incidence of aggressive behaviour. See Figure 3.5 for the location.

Long-term memory (LTM): any memories that last for more than a few seconds can be described as long term. According to trace decay theories, *memory* seems to depend on how strongly a *structural trace* is developed in the *brain* and thus how likely it is to be reactivated at a later date either spontaneously or when required. According to the *levels of processing* theory, *retention* depends on how the information is processed rather than on different kinds of storage.

Long-term memory can be sub-divided as *episodic* (or autobiographical) *memory* and *semantic memory*, after Tulving (1972). *Procedural* and *remote* memories are also long term. Much long-term memory seems to be material specific and processed in associated areas of the brain. Changes to LTM can give rise to several identifiable types of memory loss. This may be due to problems in encoding, or with *retrieval* from long-term memory due to a faulty *central executive system*.

Loss: we can talk about people experiencing loss when there has been: a loss of a relationship through death or separation; failure, removal or alteration of body parts whether internal or external; or alteration in physical, psychological or social functioning such as intellectual capacity, income, roles, *self-esteem*, well-being, security, leisure or sporting activities. Such experiences may be acute or gradual and progressive, temporary or permanent, actual or potential, sudden or anticipated, obvious to others or possible to conceal. Loss and *grief* constitute one of the most important areas for concern in professional care.

Lucid dream: a dream in which the dreamer is aware that he or she is *dreaming*. It is thought that conscious awareness of dreaming is a learnable skill that enables dreamers to control the direction and content of their dreams

Mandala: a symbolic circular figure used as a religious symbol of the universe. Mandalas are associated particularly with Tantric Yoga, in which they are used as instruments of contemplation. Jung refers to the spontaneous appearance of mandalas in dreams, which he related to a search for completeness and self-unity.

Manifest content: in Freudian dream analysis, the surface content of a dream, which is assumed to mask the dream's deeper, or real meaning.

Means–end analysis: determining the differences between the current state of a *problem* and the goal state (differences between what the situation is now and what is required). It depends on problem-solvers having awareness of the means (operators) at their disposal for achieving the desired ends (Kahney, 1993). Examples can sound unappealingly pedantic and long-winded but means–end analysis is a powerful tool for breaking down a problem into goals and sub-goals until specific activities can be identified which can be used to solve the problem. Such task analysis underlies much of behaviour modification therapy where the individual steps need to be clearly identified.

Mediators: according to behaviourist theory, mediators come between a stimulus and a response. In *interference* theory of *memory* they refer to activities which affect whether *recall* will be hindered or enhanced.

Memory: a *concept* that refers to a variety of behaviours that appear to depend on cognitive processes similar to perception and include search for meaning and gap-filling. There are many different kinds of skills and information that can be remembered and it is accepted that memory is not a single process. Different aspects of memory can be found under the terms in italics in the list below:

> basic processes
>   – control
>   – registration
>   – storage
>   – *retrieval*

> areas of the brain
  - *hippocampus* (information)
  - Broca's and Wernicke's areas (*language centres*)
  - *cerebellum* (muscle or *procedural memory*)
> *structural components*
  - activity trace and *structural change* in neurones
  - *sensory* (for example *acoustic store*, persistence of vision/*after-image*, *modality-specific*)
  - *short-term* (primary or *immediate*)
  - *long-term* (*secondary*)
    anterograde (see *amnesia*)
    eidetic
    declarative (information such as facts and events)
    episodic (*autobiographical*)
    flashbulb
    muscle, enactive or procedural
    prospective
    remote
    retrograde (see *amnesia*)
    semantic
> strategies
  - *accessibility*
  - *availability*
  - *cue dependence* (context, state)
  - *efforts after meaning* and gap-filling
  - *false memory syndrome*
  - *metamemory*
  - *mnemonics*
  - *partial reports*
  - *prospective memory*
  - *recall*
  - *recognition*
  - *reconstruction*
  - *redintegration*
  - *rehearsal*
  - *relearning*
  - *reminiscence*
  - *retention*
  - span (capacity), backward span, subspan, supraspan
  - serial probe technique
  - *serial processing*
  - *serial reproduction*
  - *transfer*
  - *triggers*
  - verbal memory (meaningful words versus nonsense)

> theories
  - *dynamic memory theory* (Schank, 1982)
    memory organisation packets (plans, schemes, *schemas* or scripts)
    thematic organisation points
  - *hierarchical network model* (Collins and Quillian, 1969, 1972)
  - *levels of processing* (Craik and Lockhart, 1972)
    structural or shallow level
    phonetic or phonemic level
    semantic level
    maintenance rehearsal
    elaborative rehearsal
  - *multi-store* (dual process) model (Atkinson and Shiffrin, 1968, 1971)
    control processes (rehearsal, *pattern recognition*)
  - *signal-detection theory*
  - *working memory* (Baddeley and Hitch, 1974; Baddeley, 1990)
    central executive system
    slave systems (*visuo-spatial scratch-pad, phonological loop*).

See also *Amnesia* and *Forgetting*. Items not in italics may be located via the Index.

Memory span (span of apprehension or capacity): the longest list of to-be-remembered items the participant can reliably repeat back, usually after a single brief presentation. 'Digit span' denotes *memory* for numbers, 'word span' for word lists and so on. Most people can remember about seven random digits (Miller, 1956) but only about four or five random words or letters (McCarthy and Warrington, 1990). Miller (1956) produced the most well-known account of the limitations of memory span to the 'magic' number of seven, plus or minus two. Lists or material less than the participant's normal *memory span* are described as subspan, anything greater is supraspan. 'Backward span' is a test procedure where a participant is required to repeat a list of items in reverse order.

Mental modules/mental organs: terms used by Pinker (1998) and Chomsky (2004 and previously) for the different entities of the mind that have evolved to deal with different specialised problems. It is unlikely that these parts or faculties of the mind correspond to well-defined regions of the

concepts

brain (see *Topology*) but are most likely spread out through the fibres and are interconnected such that some regions act as a unit. Pinker (1998: 30) argues that 'each of our mental modules solves its unsolvable problems by a leap of faith about how the world works, by making assumptions that are indispensable but indefensible – the only defence being that the assumptions worked well enough in the world of our ancestors.'

Mentalese: one of the four main formats of *representation* in the brain, in which concepts and propositions are represented in the mind without words. Fodor (for example 1975) argues that mental states, such as beliefs and desires, can only be correctly explained in terms of a language of thought (LOT) in the mind and computation or information processing, which allows complex thoughts to be built up by combining simpler thoughts in various ways. This means that we can understand ideas and concepts independently of words or of the particular words in which we learned them. For example, a child can learn through play that some objects sink and others float. When we read a book, we can remember the story or the characters without having to memorise the exact words. We can paraphrase or translate a text, putting the same meaning in different words or a different language.

Metachoric experiences: experiences in which the normal field of perception is completely replaced by an hallucinatory one. Green and McCreery (1989) give waking dreams, *lucid dreams* and ordinary dreams as examples and point out that the hallucinatory environment may be an exact, or nearly exact, replica of a real one, as in a *false awakening* or an *out-of-the-body* experience.

Metacognition: an awareness of our own thinking processes. Improving metacognition involves understanding how to solve problems, becoming aware of planning strategies, perceptual processes and so on. The prefix 'meta' suggests a higher logical plane, a change of position or something beyond the regular condition.

Metacommunication: being aware of our own communication and how we appear to others, such as using body language (for example posture and gestures), pauses, silences, turn-taking and other skills in speaking, active listening and writing.

Metamemory: knowledge about our own *memory*; what its capacity is, how best to remember things, awareness of one's own memory abilities and limitations, a subdivision of metacognition. Although there seems to be no age difference in accuracy, it is reported that elderly people think their *semantic memory* has declined and have low confidence in their memories.

Mid-brain: if we cut the brain in half we can see the inner mid-brain, which is whitish in colour and contains the *limbic system*, the septum, the *thalamus*, the *hypothalamus*, the olfactory bulb, the pituitary, the mammiliary body, the *hippocampus* and the amygdala. See Figure 3.5.

Modality-specific: a term used either for *memory* storage which occurs in the sensory system that received the information which does not appear to be processed by some other location or central processing system (for example, Baddeley, 1990), or for storage in the cortex which is still closely related to the relevant sensory mode.

Modelling: an individual can learn many potential styles of response from observing and copying other people's behaviour. The person being copied is the 'model' or 'role-model'. The model need not be aware that copying has occurred. See also *Vicarious learning* and *Social learning theory*.

Mood: in the 1950s and 1960s, when the word *emotion* applied only to extreme states, mood was regarded as something less than emotion. For example, Drever (1964) defined mood as 'An affective condition or attitude, enduring for some time, characterised by particular emotions in a condition of subexcitability, so as to be readily evoked, for example, an irritable mood, or a cheerful mood'.

However, few modern textbooks list mood in the index and they do not discuss mood separately from emotion. It is probably most useful to simply define mood as the prevailing emotional state at any given time. Evidence suggests that mood influences perception and *memory* of events.

Motion parallax: the apparent relative motion of objects due to the motion of the observer. The simplest way to observe this is to line up two vertical objects, say two coffee mugs, at different distances from you, then close one eye and move your head from side to side. The nearer mug will appear to move from side to side relative to the distant mug. When travelling (by car, train and so on) nearer objects flash past more rapidly that distant ones. This relative movement gives clues to the distance of objects and contributes to *depth perception*. When two objects are at the same distance, they will appear to move together and are said to be in a position of 'no parallax'.

Motivation: in simple terms this means why we do something. Since this is not always conscious the formal definition is the process of starting, directing and maintaining physical and psychological activities; includes mechanisms involved in preferences for one activity over another and the vigour and persistence of responses. Explanations tend to fall into three main types:

> Rational explanation – reasons.
> Causal explanation – causes.
> Goal or endstate explanation – drives/needs.

It is generally accepted among psychologists that all behaviour is meaningful and purposeful, however unusual, incomprehensible or bizarre it may appear. Given this assumption, it should always be possible to find what motivated the behaviour and give a meaningful explanation for it.

Most people look for a rational explanation first, and it is nearly always possible to find some sort of plausible reason for ordinary behaviour. People know why they did something and can say so. It is, however, important to distinguish between admitted reasons and possibly different real reasons. People may lie or cover up their real reasons and give an explanation that they think is more socially acceptable.

When the reasons are not known, or seem inadequate or inappropriate, particularly where the person is distressed about his or her behaviour, it may be necessary to look for hidden causes, such as biological malfunction, early childhood experiences, *stress*, low *self-esteem* and so on. See also 'Level of enquiry' in Part 2.1.

Some psychologists regard all behaviour as striving towards the satisfaction of drives or needs to achieve a goal or comfortable end state. These needs may be purely biological in origin, such as needing food and water, or can be individual or social, such as needing approval, comfort or affection. Maslow (1943) devised a much-cited and much-debated hierarchy of needs to illustrate that everything people do can be described as fulfilling a need of some kind. Maslow argued that we do not concern ourselves with higher needs until the lower ones have been met. This is a modified version that sorts many needs into useful groups that includes some possibly damaging needs and does not imply a rigid hierarchy. Different elements may be uppermost or ignored at different times, such as neglecting to eat or sleep when fully absorbed in an activity:

> Physiological functioning related to the fundamental characteristics of living organisms – respiration, digestion, elimination, movement, irritability (sensitivity to surroundings) and reproduction – together with rest and *sleep*.
> Safety, freedom from physical and psychological harm (or challenging these).
> Social inclusion, sharing, love and belongingness, trust and acceptance(or power) in a group.
> Esteem and regard, for oneself and others, a sense of competence.
> Cognitive stimulation, through curiosity, exploration and learning.
> Aesthetic appreciation, of balance, order, form and beauty.
> Striving for wisdom or a sense of oneness with the world, or to reach one's full potential.

A useful distinction when talking about motivation is between intrinsic and extrinsic motivation. Intrinsic motivation includes all reasons, causes or needs that stem from within the person, such as eating healthily and exercising because it feels good. Extrinsic motivation includes all things that govern behaviour from outside the person, such as smoking to gain peer approval. These are things done in order to gain something else or to avoid unpleasant consequences.

Muller–Lyer illusion: this is one of the most commonly known *visual distortion*s or illusions, where lines of equal length appear different due to the presence of different arrow heads. A line with outward facing arrowheads appears shorter, and a line with inward-facing arrowheads appears longer than a comparison line with no arrowheads,

concepts

see Figure 3.9. The extent of this illusion appears constant within Western society, with most people seeing the same size difference. There have been many attempts to explain this illusion, but none is conclusive or universally accepted (see Gregory, 1971; Robinson, 1972).

Multi-store (dual process) model: this postulates two separate processes for short-term and *long-term memory* and suggests that *memory* is transferred from a short-term to a long-term store by *rehearsal* (for example, James, 1890/1981; Atkinson and Shiffrin, 1968, 1971). This early behavioural model has been superseded by more complex information-processing models such as *working memory*.

Myoclonic jerk: the commonest type is a sudden spasm, which may occur in the early stages of falling asleep, resulting from a tiny burst of activity in the *brain*. This may be linked to a missed heartbeat. It is sometimes associated with a brief dream image such as tripping over a step. It may be particularly noticeable in situations where a person is trying to stay awake, or appear as if awake, such as in lectures. See *Sleep cycles*. Other kinds of myoclonic jerk may occur in conditions such as epilepsy.

Narcolepsy: a chronic neurological disorder caused by the brain's inability to regulate the sleep switching mechanisms normally. It is a condition characterised by irresistible, usually brief, attacks of *sleep* or uncontrollable drowsiness, possibly with mumbled speech, double vision and stumbling. Attacks may be precipitated by boredom or when carrying out a monotonous or repetitive task. People with this disorder pass quickly into *dreaming sleep* without going through the usual stages and tend to report vivid dreams (Oswald, 1966). This condition is quite different from the sleepy sickness (encephalitis lethargica) reported by Oliver Sacks in *Awakenings* (1973/1999).

Nature–nurture debate: this is an ongoing discussion about whether characteristics are due to inheritance or to learning and environmental influences or a combination of both. A medical example to illustrate a simple combination is the likelihood of a child developing hip dysplasia (damaging spreading of the hips). This can be brought about by hip joints in which the ball and socket are loose, perhaps because the socket is shallow. It can also be brought about by carrying the child on the parent's back with the hips turned out. It is even more likely to occur in a child who has a loosely fitting joint and is carried repeatedly with the legs turned out. There is a combination effect when potential for a condition occurs in an environment that allows or encourages the condition to develop. Similar arguments can be applied to many physical and psychological health issues and to psychological characteristics such as intelligence and personality traits. Conversely, an environment that discourages a certain characteristic will reduce the likelihood of an inherited potential developing.

Necker cube: we normally perceive a two-dimensional drawing of a cube as three-dimensional. If we stare continuously at the drawing, it may appear to change perspective with the front face becoming the back face. If we continue to stare, it may change back or switch spontaneously from one interpretation to another. The *after-image* will also reverse spontaneously, indicating that the switching must occur in the *brain* and not in the retina. If a fluorescent wire cube is used in a darkened room, it can be a weird experience trying to touch the edges of the cube when the perception is reversed, as the brain is receiving conflicting information from the different *senses* of *vision* and *touch*. Some strange *motion parallax* effects can also be seen. We can compare this with people who gain sight after having been blind and who may experience similar confusion when they touch and look at objects. See also *Visual images*.

Nerve fibre: the axon of the nerve cell or *neurone* with its surrounding membrane. Large fibres may extend more than a metre between the spinal cord and the extremities of the body. A nerve fibre conducts a group or volley of electrical impulses in one direction only by exchanging positive and negative ions across the membrane. While at rest, there is a small *resting potential* across the membrane. The nerve impulse is a sudden rapid short-lived change in the membrane that allows ions to cross through the membrane, creating an action potential. A change in the next part of the membrane occurs just ahead of an action potential and thus the impulse moves along the nerve fibre.

There are two main types of nerve fibre, myelinated and unmyelinated. Myelinated fibres have layers of myelin, a lipoprotein, folded around the axon. The myelin sheath is not continuous but has little gaps at intervals, called the nodes of Ranvier where interchange of ions can take place. One effect of the myelin sheathing is to increase the speed and efficiency with which action potentials can travel along the nerve and prevent accidental connections with other nerves. In multiple sclerosis, the myelin is progressively destroyed.

Nervous system: the nervous system consists of the *brain* and all the nerves that make up the communication system within the body. It is usual to call the brain and spinal cord the central nervous system (CNS) and everything else the peripheral nervous system.

The peripheral nervous system comprises 43 pairs of sensory and motor nerves. Sensory nerves carry messages from the sense receptors towards the brain (afferent = to) and the motor nerves carry messages away from the brain (efferent = from) to muscles, internal organs and glands.

The cell bodies of most *neurones* lie within the brain or the spinal cord with only the extensions spread out through the rest of the body. The nerve supplying an arm or leg muscle, for instance, has its cell body and nucleus inside the spinal cord, with the axon extending down the limb. Within the spinal cord, the only way the peripheral nerves can connect with the central nerves is via chemical *synapses* as there is no physical connection. Nerves serving the muscles can be called somatic (soma = body) and are experienced as being under voluntary control. The nerves serving the internal organs and glands (endocrine system) make up the *autonomic nervous system* (ANS) which is not normally voluntarily controlled.

The *autonomic nervous system* (see Figure 3.3) is separated into the sympathetic and parasympathetic systems and the enteric nervous system. The parasympathetic nervous system maintains or restores normal functioning such as heart rate, digestion, emptying of bladder and sexual activity, whereas the sympathetic nervous system (SNS) prepares the body for sudden action (*fight or flight*) at times of *stress*.

Neurone (neuron): neurones are actively conducting nerve cells. Each has a cell body with a nucleus and many extensions. The main

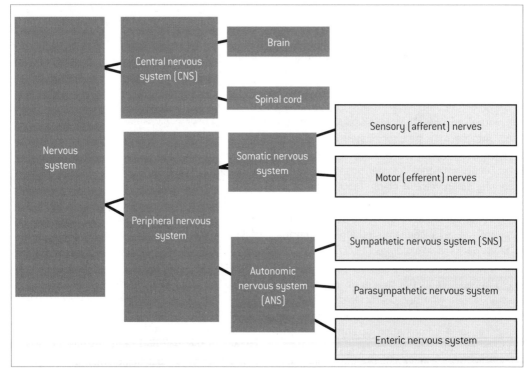

Figure 3.13 The nervous system

extension is the axon, the others are dendrites. In motor (efferent) nerves, the axon is usually involved in carrying impulses away from the cell body, away from the CNS (*brain* and spinal cord), towards the next neurone while the dendrites pick up in-coming signals from surrounding neurones. In sensory (afferent) nerves the direction is in reverse, the axon normally carries impulses to the cell body, towards the CNS, and the dendrites pass on signals to surrounding nerves. Individual brain cells fire electrical impulses, or action potentials, intermittently.

The action potentials are normally triggered by change in the environment. An action potential in one nerve can either excite or inhibit the next nerve, depending on the nature of the *synapse* between them. Many factors have an influence on the firing of a neurone including its threshold of excitability, the local chemical environment and the sum of excitatory and inhibitory impulses it receives at any time.

There are various different kinds of neurones and all possible directions of signal are possible. Neurones continually manufacturing new protein, which is continually lost or destroyed, and can increase the number and strength of the connections and the likelihood of impulses travelling down particular pathways. According to some sources, nearly all the protein in the brain is renewed every three weeks. See also *Structural change*.

Neurotransmitters: chemicals that carry messages across the *synapses* between *neurones*. Different cells use different transmitters. These include noradrenaline, *serotonin*, *dopamine*, GABA (gamma-amino butyric acid) and acetylcholine. Alteration to neurotransmitter systems and their receptors are thought to account for some illnesses, for example schizophrenia.

Non-verbal communication: in common usage, this refers to the combination of body language, paralanguage and silence that complements spoken words. In this sense, the abbreviation NVC is often used. These non-verbal signs can carry information about emotion. For example, fidgety hand movements, together with silence, rapid speech or a loud voice, may indicate anxiety. Where this is unintentional, it may be referred to as leakage. NVC has been identified by Argyle (1983) and others as:

> eye contact and gaze
> facial expression
> posture
> gesture
> orientation (angle of the body, particularly towards others)
> *touch* and bodily contact
> proximity (closeness to others)
> territoriality and personal space
> clothes and appearance
> *paralanguage*
> *silence*.

Since many people find it difficult to express emotions in words, either because the feeling is new and they simply do not know how to find the words, or because they believe they should not complain, non-verbal signs can be important clues to how a person is feeling. Books on non-verbal communication, such as that by Weitz (1979), indicate how non-verbal signs can be identified and what sort of interpretations are most likely.

In a wider sense, the term 'non-verbal communication' refers to anything that does not require words or which is used alongside words. This can include drawing, painting, music, dance, mime, flag signals and so on in addition to body language. This formal distinction between verbal (word) and non-verbal (non-word) draws attention to the wide range of media available for communication that are not dependent on words. Non-verbal means of communication are more accessible between people of different cultures, do not require an ability to read and write, and are independent of the capacity for speech. Some non-verbal forms, such as dance, mime and the visual arts, are independent of hearing. Other non-verbal forms, such as music and *touch*, are independent of sight.

Norms: according to Brown (1988: 50), 'all groups evolve systems of norms which define the limits of acceptable and unacceptable behaviours.' As with social consensus, these norms may be subject to change but can be highly stable over a period of time. Norms can provide a way of regulating or controlling the behaviour of members, help each member to make sense of the social environment and predict what is likely to happen. How much each member is expected to conform to the normative limits depends on how important a particular norm is to the group and on the status of the individual within the group.

concepts

Obedience: engagement in behaviours determined and demanded by those who are perceived to have *power* and where the expectation exists that those who possess the power may exercise it by administering *punishment* for a failure to obey. Milgram's (1963, 1965, 1974; see also Part 4) experiments indicated the extent to which participants would obey commands given by an authority figure and how *peer group* support enabled participants to defy an authority figure.

Object concept: according to Piaget and others, there is a stage of development in children during which they develop a sense of a world of objects that are independent of themselves and their actions. For example, a young baby learns the difference between being able to control movements of hands into field of view and not being able to control toys hanging on the cot. Gradually the baby comes to know things can go on existing when he or she cannot see them or sense them in any way.

Piaget tested this stage by hiding a toy behind a pillow. Up to six months, the young baby loses interest as soon as the toy disappears. At a slightly later stage, the baby waits for it to re-appear. However, personal experience has shown that babies, apparently at the earlier stage, show surprise if the object reappears from the 'wrong' place. This indicates a more sophisticated object concept than Piaget assumed.

Ontological insecurity: a term borrowed from philosophical *paradigms* to refer to feeling unsure of what is real about one's self or one's being.

Operant (instrumental) conditioning: the terms 'operant' and 'instrumental' are equivalent. The Latin word *opus* (plural *opera*) means 'work'. Instrumental means doing something in order to gain whatever is wanted. In this type of *conditioning*, some work or action is involved in order to gain something that satisfies a need. Like *classical conditioning*, the process is seen as happening without conscious effort or will to learn, but unlike classical conditioning, which can be completely passive, operant conditioning is an active process.

The early researchers (for example, Watson, Thorndike and Skinner, see Part 4) observed that animals have a tendency to repeat actions that have been followed by, for example, food or freedom. Animals were placed in cages having a lever. At first, the animal might happen to hit the lever only by chance, but if the lever opened the door or delivered a piece of food, the animal would, either immediately or after a few trials, go straight to the lever and press it. Thorndike spoke in terms of trial and error but Skinner says emphatically that 'the rat was not 'trying' to do anything when it first hit the lever and did not learn from 'errors' (see 7.2 for website).

Following on from discoveries within *classical conditioning*, each associated stimulus and response was identified and linked in stimulus–response (S–R) pairs or units. For example, the lever would be seen as the conditioned stimulus that evoked the conditioned response of pressing; the food or freedom was seen as *reinforcement*. Experiments were concerned with quantifying states of need such as hunger, measuring how many trials were required before the S–R unit became established and the action became conditioned (see Figure 3.14), how many trials were needed to shape behaviour or how many were needed before *extinction*.

Out-of-the-body (ecsomatic) experiences: experiences in which the person continues to act normally but seems to be perceiving what is going on from a position which is not the same as where the actual body is, such as feeling as if one is walking a few paces behind oneself, or watching oneself in bed from beside or above the bed.

Overlearning: material is regarded as underlearned when it has not been learned sufficiently for one perfect repetition and overlearned when the participant is required to go on with the learning trial after one perfect repletion has been achieved. Early studies, for example Kreuger (1929), showed that the greater the original overlearning, the slower the rate of *forgetting*.

Pain: an unpleasant subjective experience generally associated with tissue damage. Some writers, like Sternbach, Wall and Melzack, believe that pain may represent a threat and result in some kind of reaction or response, but this seems to apply only to acute pain for which the cause is known and which does seem to be acting as a warning signal. With chronic pain, the cause is often not known and it no

concepts

longer seems to serve any purpose. There are some kinds of sensation of pain that are not disliked. This suggests that it is the meaning of the pain for a person, not just the sensation, which has significance. See also *Gate control theory, Pain context, Pain management, Psychogenic illness, Reward, Touch*.

Pain context: intuitive experience and research indicate that the context in which an injury or potential pain-producing event occurs can greatly affect the amount of *pain* experienced. Toothache is less noticeable when busy. Injury during sport, particularly matches, may be ignored. Rough horseplay with children is not seen as painful whereas similar treatment in another context would be. Injuries sustained in war appear less painful than similar civilian injuries (Beecher, 1959).

Pain management: pharmacological and other approaches may be used to treat the cause of *pain* or alter perception or sensation. This may reduce pain or, where pain cannot be eliminated, help people learn to live with and cope with their pain in a constructive way. Strategies are designed to *empower* the person by confronting *learned helplessness* and may generate a sense of optimism. Non-drug measures include: radiotherapy, surgery, nerve blocks, TENS, traction, acupuncture, physiotherapy, occupational therapy, *relaxation*, massage, aromatherapy, talking and listening.

Paired-associate learning: the participant is presented with items in pairs, the task being to learn the second item of the pair as a response to the first. On subsequent trials, the participant is presented with the first stimulus and required to produce the response item. Learning a language often uses this method.

Paradigm: an example or pattern or representative set. In psychology, the term is mainly used for a viewpoint or way of looking at natural phenomena that is based on a particular set of philosophical assumptions. For example, one of the main paradigms for enquiry into the relationship between the mental experience and physiological processes is the Cartesian (from Descartes) idea of dualism, which considers that the mind and body are separate entities. There is always considerable debate about the most useful or appropriate paradigm to be used to guide a line of research,

or whether it is preferable to start without making any assumptions. See also Part 5 'Research Methods'.

Within communication studies, the term paradigm is used for a set of signs from which one or more can be chosen to contribute to a 'syntagm'. For example, shapes form one paradigm and colours another, from which the particular shapes and colours (syntagm) of the Union Flag can be chosen.

Paradoxical figures: specially contrived drawings that break the rules of perspective or 'play games' with visual perception. Perhaps the best known example is Penrose's 'impossible triangle' (see Figure 3.9) in which each apex looks correct but the triangle as a whole cannot exist as a joined three-dimensional solid. Robinson (1972: 176) cites Penrose (1958), Schuster (1964) and Fisher (1968) as having produced a whole range of such figures. The artist M. C. Escher has incorporated many of these figures into his paintings. William Hogarth (for example, an engraving in 1754) has also played extensively with the rules of perspective. Together with visual illusions, impossible figures help with our understanding of perception. See Gregory (1971: 51–3).

Paralanguage: use of the voice to convey meaning alongside the words themselves or even in the absence of words. Features include stress, intonation, pitch, tone, quality, loudness, speed of talking, clarity and all the ums, ers, grunts, whistles and gasps. When listening to someone speaking or singing in an unknown foreign language, much of the meaning of the speaker can be inferred from the paralanguage. Absence of this kind of paralanguage in written forms is one reason why written texts need to follow grammatical rules more precisely than speech in order to convey subtleties of meaning accurately and avoid ambiguity. Paralanguage and body language both contribute to *non-verbal communication*.

Parallel processing: a way of carrying out a complicated process in which several operations are carried out at the same time. Often known as concurrent processing when referring to doing two tasks at the same time, such as maintaining a *memory* and doing another *attention*-demanding task at the same time. According to the *working memory* model, the *central executive* helps to co-ordinate these tasks in the *slave systems*. Contrast with *serial processing*.

Paranormal: outside the normal range of scientific investigation.

Parenting skills: parents can develop strategies for involving children in activities that are rewarding for parents and children, and help to prevent the development of problem behaviour. Jenner (1993) recommends:

> letting children choose games or toys from a safe selection
> talking to them about what they are doing and letting them talk
> ignoring minor naughtiness
> reducing commands and instructions
> restricting factual teaching
> reducing questions
> avoiding criticism
> avoiding saying 'No' except when necessary for safety and health
> avoiding competition with children.

Parenting styles: Baumrind (1967, 1980), cited in Pitts and Phillips (1991) and Bee (1997), describes three styles of parenting:

> Authoritarian: children are expected to obey unquestioningly.
> Authoritative: control is exerted, explanations are given, and *obedience* and *conformity* are valued, as are independence and self-direction.
> Permissive: few regulations are imposed and an accepting, non-evaluative role is adopted.

A fuller list, gathered from various sources and also relevant to styles of caring, is as follows:

> coercive/bullying
> authoritarian
> persuasive
> authoritative
> directive/advice-giving
> didactic/teaching
> non-directive/information-giving
> facilitative/active listening
> befriending/buddy
> laissez faire/allowing/permissive
> neglecting.

Coopersmith (1967) cited in Gross (1996), found that children of parents who had clear definitions of authority tended to exhibit high *self-esteem*. Those with parents who seemed unclear about standards and expectations, and whose discipline was unpredictable and inconsistent, or who fluctuated between overstrictness and overpermissiveness, tended to have low self-esteem.

Bee (1997) cites Liebert and Harris (1992), who found little difference between the children of authoritarian and permissive parents. Both of these groups were less motivated to achieve, less independent and more disoriented, distrustful and self-centred. In contrast, authoritative parents 'produced' more successful children, who were responsible, self-reliant and friendly. These qualities can be compared with the development of *hardiness*. See also *Leadership* and *Power*.

Pattern recognition: an idea from the *multi-store model* that information will be transferred from sensory to *short-term memory* accompanied by a verbal label from *long-term memory* if a match occurs between a pattern in *long-term memory* and the incoming sensory data.

Peer group: those of the same status as, and associated with, a person; commonly used to refer to those of the same age group. An important concept in relation to peer group pressure and influence.

Perception: this is the study of how we bring meaning to the information received by our *senses*, that is, the way in which we make sense of our world, external and internal. Our senses are continuously receiving data about the environment and ourselves and sending signals in the form of action potentials to the *brain*. Our minds or brains monitor most of this incoming information unconsciously so that much of our behaviour and all of our physiological processes is automatic. However, we pay conscious *attention* to some of it and can talk about what we identify and make conscious decisions about what we do. It is often said that we see what we want to see or what we expect to see and it is realised (for example Gregory, 1971, 1990) that these processes are not just a passive 'picking up' of sensory messages but involve a great deal of 'gap-filling' and hypothesising from incomplete data.

In the processes of perception, the physical object in the world is the distal stimulus, as distinct from the proximal stimulus or optical image on the retina.

Perceptual constancy: the tendency to judge things as the same even though the retinal image has altered due to different conditions. The main examples are *identity*, *size*, *shape*, location, orientation, brightness, *lightness and colour constancy*.

Perceptual disorders: specific disorders of *perception* may occur due to illness or following a stroke. Examples are:

> actual sensory *loss* leading to reduced perception
> *visual neglect*
> visual interference patterns (such as spots, wavy lines or blank spaces in the visual field, sometimes found during a migraine or as a silent, optical or visual migraine when under stress)
> auditory interference patterns (such as the ringing due to tinnitus)
> exaggerated *visual illusions* or *hallucinations* which may occur where there is sensory loss, *sensory deprivation or overload*.

Perceptual changes may cause *anxiety* where the cause is not known to the individual as they may be interpreted as being a mental disorder. Conditions such as *schizophrenia* may give rise to perceptual disorders where there is biochemical imbalance but most perceptual disorders can be linked to alterations in the *senses*, or to minor biochemical changes in the *brain* and *nervous system*, or to damage to the brain.

Perceptual set: a tendency to notice certain familiar aspects of what is around, rather than novel or unexpected things. This is part of the selection and interpretation process, which directs *attention* to things of importance and protects from overload. In familiar terms, this refers to the judgement that we see what we expect to see or what we want to see. This may be strongly influenced by the language we use to refer to things or people. For example, most British people do not notice or believe there is blue-green (cyan) in the rainbow or white-light spectrum until it is pointed out to them as this is not mentioned in most books on

colour or in popular mnemonics for the rainbow (Adams, 1989).

Person (interpersonal) perception: in many situations, particularly when meeting a person for the first time, most people sum up the characteristics of the other person and tend to retain this initial judgement on subsequent occasions. Burton and Dimbleby (1995) give the following reasons for this process:

> to remember information
> to make sense of the other person's behaviour or to predict others' behaviour
> to organise social understanding
> to plan communication
> to maintain sense of self and reality to reduce anxiety
> to satisfy needs of inclusion, control, affection and so on.

This process, although useful, can lead to significant errors and interfere with more open awareness of what other people are like in different circumstances.

Burton and Dimbleby (1995) list the following errors of judgement that interfere with social interaction:

> *fundamental attribution error or bias*
> *false consensus*
> *false consistency*
> *primacy and recency effects*
> *halo and horns effects*
> *self-fulfilling prophecy*
> stereotyping.

Persona: a term used by Jung to refer to the part of the personality that people make accessible to other people, the outward mask, allowing them to express feelings in ways they believe will be acceptable to others. See also *Body image*.

Personal construct theory: a theory originating from Kelly (1955) and further developed by Bannister over a number of years (for example 1968, 1986). They believe that all people build their ideas of the world in a complex hierarchical network of bipolar constructs, similar in some ways to scientific classification systems. Constructs related to perceptions of people form a person's *implicit personality theory*. Constructs such as good—bad, polite—rude and happy—sad can be

concepts

used in a predictive way to judge how people will behave. Constructs are essentially individual; different opposites, or different shades of meaning, may be used. For example, one person may construe others as being either friendly or withdrawn, another might judge in terms of friendly versus aggressive. Unlike scientific systems, this is not normally done in a conscious way. Kelly and Bannister (see Fransella, 1990) developed a *repertory grid* technique for revealing constructs. It is particularly known for the way in which it can be used to reveal individuals' implicit notions about personality. It has many uses in therapy, education and research for exploring peoples' ideas and helping them to manage their lifestyles effectively.

Personality: a term widely used in attempts to classify people or explain individual differences but with little agreement about what is meant by the word. Ryckman (1989) says that despite the plethora of definitions, there is basic agreement among investigators that personality is an abstraction that includes the person's unique learning history and genetic background and the ways in which the person responds to certain stimuli in the environment. Theories tend to fall into a few basic kinds:

> *personality types* (for example Sheldon, Kretschmer, Hans Eysenck, Myers-Briggs)
> *personality traits* (for example Cattell's 16pf, MMPI)
> 'ideo' or individual (for example Carl Rogers, Kelly/Bannister *Personal Construct Theory*)
> *psychodynamic* (for example Freud, Horney).

Allport distinguishes between different kinds of definitions:

> Mask definitions focus on the external stimulus value of the person as presented to the world, usually associated with behavioural approaches (see also *Body Image*, *Persona*).
> Essence definitions focus on the concept that true personality is connected to some essential inner entity or quality that makes us uniquely human, usually associated with psychodynamic approaches.
> Omnibus or holistic definitions include all there is to know about our past, present, and future as a person, usually associated with humanistic and/or phenomenological approaches.

Allport gives his own definition: 'personality is the dynamic organization within the individual of those psychophysical systems that determine his unique adjustments to his environment' (1937: 48).

The *concept* of personality seems to encompass descriptions variously called '*temperament*' and '*character*', and may overlap with other such concepts as *attitudes*, *intelligence*, *motivation*, interests, skills (particularly social and communication skills) and lifestyle. Like attitudes, personality may be seen as having *cognitive*, *affective* and *behavioural* components, although the emphasis is often on the behaviour alone. Focus on behaviour is usually considered within a social or interpersonal context, but some approaches also include solitary behaviour. Explanations range from the purely biological to the purely social; most are a mixture.

Despite these differences, definitions of personality are consistent in referring to enduring characteristics or patterns of behaviour rather than fleeting *mood*s or fluctuations in behaviour (although the frequency of mood changes might in itself be regarded as contributing to a personality trait).

In health psychology it can be useful to distinguish between normal and abnormal personality patterns; see Millon and Everly (1985: 32–3) as cited in Adams and Bromley (1998).

Personality traits: Cattell (1965) cites Allport and Odbert as having found over 3,000 trait words for describing personality but suggests that, of these, there are a limited number of traits that can be identified by factor analysis as natural, unitary structures in personality. Allport (1962) refers to cardinal, central and secondary traits and warns against 'pseudo-traits'. William Stern (1912), mentioned by Holt (1962), emphasised that particular traits, however precisely described, are meaningful only in the context of the whole person.

According to Allport (1962), there are personality traits of major significance and traits of minor significance. A person's central traits are those few that stand out and can be readily distinguished. Allport suggests that these are what are normally included in letters of reference, in some rating scales or in brief descriptions of a person. Less conspicuous traits are said to be secondary. Cattell distinguishes source or underlying traits from surface traits and developed the commonly used 16 Personality Factor (16PF) Questionnaire.

Another well-known example used for screening candidates for high-risk public safety positions is the MMPI (Minnesota Multiphasic Personality Inventory) that that identifies ten trait scales relating to disorders.

Personality types: a way of classifying people into a small number of distinct groups. This is a popular way of pigeonholing people and is common in management training, in selection for careers options and in magazines and horoscopes. Its usefulness as an approach depends on the thoroughness with which trait analysis has been carried out. This should determine the clusters of traits involved in each type. It also depends on whether a typology attempts to provide a general theory of personality or a 'narrow-band' picture concerned with a more specific and restricted content area. A popular psychometric model is the Myers-Briggs Personality Type that sorts people into 16 types according to a set of assumed bipolar pairs: introversion–extroversion, intuition–sensing, thinking–feeling and judging–perception.

Phenomenon (plural phenomena): in the strict sense this means a thing which can be detected by the senses: an object, an event. Hence the phrase 'visual phenomena' refers to ordinary things which can be seen. However, common usage is broadened to cover things and events which are experienced without obvious sensory input, such as in the expression 'mental phenomena'. In common usage the term is further extended to also include things which can be imagined or supposed, or are thought to have been seen, and is used for events or happenings which are unusual or remarkable or for which there is no material evidence as in the phrase 'supernatural phenomena'.

Phenotype: the sum total of all the observable characteristics of appearance and behaviour, whatever their origins, of an individual or group. At a basic level of inheritance of genes, there may be a genetic difference between people with identical outward characteristics. For example two people with brown eyes may have different genes: one may have a homozygous arrangement with both genes contributing to brown eyes, the other may be heterozygous with the dominant gene for brown

eyes on one chromosome in the pair but the recessive gene for blue eyes on the other. A person with blond hair may appear blond partly because of the genes that determine fair hair and partly because of natural or artificial bleaching, or wholly through artificial bleaching.

With other characteristics such as personality, intelligence and mental health disorders, the distinction is not clear. Such complex characteristics are most likely determined by the interaction of genetic inheritance with upbringing and experience. Where similarities are seen across families or cultural groups, speculation arises as to the extent to which the observable phenotype is due to shared inheritance or cultural patterns of behaviour. This kind of speculation has given rise to the Nature–Nurture debate. The phenotype is what shows; the genotype is all the genes, visible and 'silent'.

Phi phenomenon: the simplest form of apparent motion, the movement illusion in which one or more stationary lights going on and off in succession are perceived as a moving light, as exploited in decorative lighting.

Phonological (articulatory) loop: this is the name given to the mental process that deals with the sounds of words. It is one of the four main formats of representation in the brain and is one of the slave systems suggested by Baddeley and Hitch (1974). Activity traces of the sounds of words in the phonological store are assumed to fade and become irretrievable after one and a half to two seconds but can be refreshed by subvocal rehearsal or inner speech, which feeds back into the store. When starting to speak we can play the sounds in our mind like a tape loop, planning the mouth movements and imagining what the syllables will sound like. We can look up a phone number and silently repeat it just long enough to dial the number. The memory span will be determined by how many items can be refreshed before they fade away. This plays an important role in learning to read.

Phonological (articulatory) suppression: an experimental task used to lend support to the working model of memory. A participant repeats meaningless data aloud at the same time as trying to carry out another task (parallel processing). The meaningless data uses up the resources of the *phonological loop* so that it cannot perform other functions.

Pineal body (pineal gland): a small cone-shaped piece of tissue attached by a stalk deep in the brain at the top of the brain stem that secretes a hormone, melatonin, which influences rhythms of *sleep* and activity as part of the *sleep switching mechanisms*. It appears to be sensitive to light as it receives information from the eyes and in some lower vertebrates it develops a rudimentary lens and retina, which show it to be related to an eye. See Figure 3.5 for its location.

Placebo effect: a placebo is a harmless, inactive preparation in the same form as a drug under test. The word 'placebo' comes from the Latin for 'I shall be acceptable.' It is frequently found that people given placebos obtain relief similar to that given by active drugs. This indicates that beliefs and expectations about outcomes can bring about change. This is known as an expectancy effect and can be compared with the *Hawthorne Effect*.

Play: traditionally, play has been generally considered any activity that does not appear to serve a 'useful' purpose or satisfy basic physiological needs. However, it is now believed that play can contribute to many facets of cognitive and emotional development at all ages.

Fantasy play can be helpful in exploring *emotions*. Relaxation of logical constraints and 'playing with ideas' can be a significant part of *problem-solving*.

Department of Health (1991), Bee (1997), Harvey and Hales-Tooke (1972), Newman and Newman (1991) and Slade (1995) identify many types of play and how these can be used in psychological settings. For example, stages of play can be seen, relating to ideas from Piaget, Bruner and *Social Learning Theory*.

> sensorimotor play (infancy)
> first pretend play (from 12 months)
> constructive play (approximately two years)
> substitute pretend play (two to three years)
> sociodrama (preschool)
> awareness of the roles (six years and above)
> games with rules.

At any given age, the child (or adult) may engage in a variety of play activities, drawing on whatever is available in his or her current repertoire and exploring and experimenting with new things. Many therapeutic approaches use creative arts to encourage adults to take part in child-like play in order to give new expression to *emotions* and bring release from stress. See also *Fantasy play*.

Pleasure principle (Eros): Freud believed that the *id* operates in terms of pleasure obtained through immediate gratification of *psychosexual* needs. The name Eros comes from the ancient Greek god of love. When basic needs cannot be met, energy and tension build up which have to be released in some other way such as *catharsis, compensation, displacement* or *sublimation*.

Post-traumatic stress disorder: it has been increasingly recognised since the 1980s that symptoms following a personal or major disaster may have psychological rather than organic origins. The DSM IV (American Psychiatric Association, 1994) includes post-traumatic stress disorder alongside *anxiety* and *depression* as a clinical syndrome. It is felt that the disorder is a normal or naturally occurring response to abnormal events.

Treatment generally consists of a structured cognitive-behavioural programme of therapy (Scott and Stradling, 1992). Brief counselling may be given immediately following a disaster. Those involved may be advised to seek help if symptoms appear at a later date. There is ongoing debate about the effectiveness and appropriateness of therapy.

Power: 'Social power is the potential influence that one person exerts over another. Influence is defined as a change in the *cognition, behaviour* or *emotions* of that second person which can be attributed to the first' (Huczynski and Buchanan, 1991: 192).

Most groups have a power structure, and whenever power is exercised, it can act as a significant motivating force promoting group functioning and goal achievement. Although power is a neutral concept, it is often viewed negatively, probably because of the way in which it can be abused. French and Raven (1959) propose six kinds of power:

> legitimate
> reward
> coercive

> expert
> referent
> informational.

It is possible for one person to use different types of power in different contexts and at different times. To a large extent, the power of a leader depends on the beliefs of the followers. Although a leader may have expert knowledge and be able to control *rewards* and *punishments*, if the subordinates do not believe that the leader has these attributes, they may not be willing to be led. See also *Authoritarian personality, Empowerment*.

Preconception: a term used by Piaget and in education and health care to refer to an idea or notion that can be articulated (unlike a schema) but is 'incorrect' in relation to the formal concept that is being taught. Teachers need to take into consideration the various preconceptions that learners bring to the learning situation so that notions can be explored and understanding developed. For example, many children and adults believe that heavy objects always fall faster than light objects and that there is no gravity on the moon. Unless these preconceptions are aired and explored so that contradictions are revealed it can be difficult for the learner to understand the scientific *concept* of gravity.

Preconscious: a term used by Freud to identify the part of the unconscious mind that holds and processes information that we can readily bring into *consciousness*.

Primacy effects: the improved memory for items at the start of a list. Also used for the tendency to judge others in terms of first impressions.

Principle of opposites: a key *concept* in Jungian analytical psychology that is based on the idea that personality arises from the relative expression of opposite qualities such as masculinity and femininity. Jung suggested that one half of a pair is expressed strongly through the *ego* or *persona*, while the other half is repressed as the alter-ego or shadow. To achieve a sense of personal integration or wholeness, Jung argues that the repressed parts need to be recognised and expressed.

Problem-solving: according to Bransford and Stein (1993: 7) a problem exists when there is a discrepancy between an initial state and a goal state, and there is no ready-made solution for the problem-solver.

Bartlett (1958) suggests two processes of problem-solving:

> closed-system thinking, characterised by the application of a particular solution which is already known to similar problems (compare with *convergent thinking*)
> adventurous thinking, characterised by a new formulation of a problem and obtaining a solution by original or creative thinking (compare with *creativity, divergent* and *lateral thinking*).

An early behaviourist, Thorndike (1931), suggests that problem-solving is an aspect of trial and error learning. His experiments with cats in a 'puzzle-box' generally seemed to support this view. This was strongly challenged by the Gestalt psychologists, especially Kohler (1925), who emphasised that solutions to problems were sometimes reached quickly and not gradually by trial and error. This explanation utilised the *concept* of *insight*, which refers to a sudden reorganisation of a problem and completion of a solution without trying out all possible alternatives.

Some of these ideas were put forward by Thomson (1959) and later developed by Bransford and Stein (1993):

> Decide what the central problem really is.
> Explore the situation, trying out various things, by trial and error, handling materials, play and so on.
> Analyse the problem, construct a plan, systematically work through (*formal operations*); if this does not work, then it is necessary to restate the problem and search again.
> Then attack; sometimes this can lead to immediate or '*insight*ful' solutions, sometimes to more trial and error, sometimes following the plan, usually a mixture.
> Review, reflect and learn.

All these states are affected by prior knowledge and emotional factors such as *anxiety*, tension, disappointment, *anger*, boredom, satisfaction, relief, according to success or failure and previous experience of success or failure.

Bruner suggests that a sequence of *enactive, iconic* and *symbolic representations* is needed when faced with a new problem. That is, three-dimensional action models can be made which can be handled and experimented or played with. Then the problem can be represented as drawings and diagrams. Finally, the problem and possible solutions can be talked and written about, possibly with mathematical or other *symbolic representations*. This sequence can be repeated as needed.

Problem-solving abilities often depend on specialised knowledge in a discipline. Bransford and Stein (1993: 4) point out that the same individual may be both good and poor at *problem-solving*, depending on the nature of the problem: a brain surgeon may be brilliant in the operating theatre but unable to solve a plumbing problem. When assessing people's problem-solving abilities (including one's own), it is important to ask whether the problem is relatively routine or non-routine for the problem-solver. See also 'Capability' in Part 1.

Procedural memory (PM): includes *memory* of activities that we know how to do but cannot readily describe, and corresponds to muscle memory or Bruner's (1964) *enactive* mode of representation. This kind of memory seems to be handled in the *cerebellum* of the *brain* and can remain intact even if other kinds of memory are lost through *brain damage*. Activities such as playing a musical instrument, juggling, riding a bicycle and driving seem to involve this kind of memory.

Projection: an unconscious process of attributing to people qualities that you have, or which are possessed by other people you have known. This might include liking someone because they unconsciously remind you of someone else. It also applies to disliking someone because of something you perceive in them, when that quality or behaviour is something you do, which you are not aware of, but unconsciously dislike about yourself. In a general sense, it refers to bringing or projecting personal interests and concerns into *perception* of any stimuli.

Projective techniques: standardised procedures for exploring a person's cognitive and emotional world. Stimuli are deliberately vague and can allow a wide variety of interpretations. Normative data are available for some tests. Examples include the *Rorscharch* inkblots and the *Thematic apperception test (TAT)*.

Proprioception: this is a general term used for the combination of all internal body *senses* which give information about the body's position and movement. It includes both the muscle (*kinaesthetic*) sense of where all the parts of the body are and the sense of balance in the inner ear (*vestibular sense*) which tells about movement in relation to the horizontal and vertical. Proprioception gives complete information about position and motion in the external world. It depends on the basic physical principles of gravity and inertia and allows a person to know how much and how rapidly to move in order to re-position or move one part of the body without disturbing other parts or losing balance. For example, proprioception enables the source of an itch to be located and scratched without falling over. Anyone watching babies or toddlers will appreciate that proprioception is often learned the hard way!

Prospective memory: the use of *memory* to remember to do something in the future.

Psychoanalysis: the particular style of analysis developed by Freud and used by psychoanalysts who adhere closely to his interpretative model. The more general terms *psychodynamic* or depth psychology are used for approaches that involve theories of the unconscious mind but are not strictly Freudian. See Part 2 'Approaches in psychology'.

Psychodrama: a technique involving role-play enactment, role reversal and alter-ego support. It was first developed by Moreno (for example, 1946) who believed that working through problematic relationships and events would lead to *insight* and *catharsis*. This is a particular form of drama that involves Freudian and Jungian analytical interpretations. The term is sometimes used loosely for other uses of drama and role-play in which psychoanalytical *concepts* like *ego* and alter-ego are not given any value.

Psychogenic illness: an illness which is believed to be emotional or mental in origin, such as some forms of back *pain*, stomach ulcer, thyroid disorder and asthma, thought to have been brought about by chronic emotional upset or stress, rather than any recognisable medical cause or trauma. The pain, discomfort or organic change is real. Treat-

concepts

ment may consist of a combination of medical and psychological interventions to deal with the physical manifestations of the problem as well as the emotional precipitants. See also *Psychosomatic*.

Psychoneuroimmunology: a study of the interrelationship between psychological, neuroendocrine and immunological factors. Research includes investigation of the effects of stressors on the immune system. For example, Cohen et al (1991) found a positive correlation between the degree of stress participants experienced and their susceptibility to the common cold. In describing how the immune system responds to psychological challenge, Evans et al (1997) use the terms 'up-regulation' and 'down-regulation' in preference to the more common terms of enhanced or suppressed immunity. They cite a number of studies that suggest that the effects of short-term acute stress and profound chronic stress can differ greatly. The immune system responds with down-regulation to major stressors such as bereavement, marital disharmony and caring for a relative with Alzheimer's disease. The immune response is one of up-regulation to short-term acute stressors such as having to give an assessed oral presentation. Evans et al (1997) suggest that these differences in immune response may be influenced by perceived coping ability rather than simply by the nature of the stressor. See also *Physiological arousal systems*.

Psychosexual stages: Freud tends to be best known for his description of the psychosexual stages of child development, which he named as oral, anal, phallic, latent and genital. He suggested that tensions arising from conflict between *id* and *superego* during these stages, if not properly resolved, result in lasting emotional disturbance. This has given rise to the notion of people becoming 'fixated' at a particular stage. In many modern *psychodynamic* approaches, a focus on interpersonal relationships replaces Freud's model.

Psychosomatic: the psychosomatic model of health and disease developed in the 1930s by Helen Flanders Dunbar is concerned with the inter-relationship of mind and body in all states of health and illness. The term refers to the health care approach, not to the illness.

The term is often confused with *psychogenic* and both terms may be used in a derogatory or dismissive way where the concepts are not understood.

Psychotropic (psychoactive) drugs: drugs that affect *mood* or other psychological state or experience: mind altering substances ('tropic' as a suffix means bending or altering). This group includes everything from food to legal and illegal substances that have an effect on the central nervous system and affect mental processes. Psychoactive drugs interfere in three main ways with the processes by which brain cells pass messages across the *synapses*: by mimicking natural *neurotransmitters*, by increasing endogenous neurotransmitter release or by blocking natural neurotransmitters, or a combination of these.

Moon and Karb (1993)list psychotropic medications as antipsychotic, antianxiety, antidepressant and antimanic agents.

Punishment: anything perceived as intended to be unpleasant and in recognition of undesired behaviour. This is usually carried out with the explicit intention that it should *extinguish* the undesired behaviour or decrease the probability of its occurring again on future occasions. However, punishment may also contain elements of retribution or revenge, and since this contains cognitive and social factors, it cannot be explained in terms of behavioural principles alone. The principles of behaviourism would suggest that punishment is ineffective in reducing unwanted behaviour but rather that new behaviours may emerge which circumvent the discomfort (avoidance learning). With people, this may involve deceit.

Crucially, a child's *perception* of punishment will determine whether its behaviour is reinforced or extinguished. For example, if the punishment involves providing more attention, the child may increase the naughty behaviour. Alternatively, a child may avoid punishment by pretending to be good or blaming another child. Hence, punishment sometimes works and sometimes does not.

Q technique: a technique developed by Stephenson (1953) for studying *attitudes* by means of *questionnaires,* cited and adapted for the study of *self* by Butler and Haigh (1954). See also Brown (1986).

Rationalisation: giving a rational explanation for something that is not really explainable, 'inventing' a plausible explanation for irrational behaviour or when the reasons are not known. We can see this most clearly with post-hypnotic suggestion when participants who carry out 'daft' activities tend to offer sensible-sounding explanations. We can view this as a face-saving activity or avoidance or as a *defence mechanism*. People often use rationalisations to cover embarrassment or where it is difficult to recognise and express underlying *emotions*.

Reaction formation: a *defence mechanism* in which behaviour patterns express an emotion opposite to the one that is unconsciously felt. Freud described how some of his patients who unconsciously feared their fathers expressed strong feelings of love and devotion. In a more general sense, the term can be used for unconscious or partly conscious devices, which may or may not be transparent to another person. This could include insisting that visitors stay longer, when you really wish they would go, or protesting that you intensely dislike someone whom you secretly or unconsciously fancy. This type of behaviour was used by Shakespeare in *Much Ado About Nothing*, with humorous effect.

Reality orientation: the strategy of reality orientation is sometimes used for people with *dementia* or who are disoriented. This involves helping the person to orientate to time, place and person by use of clocks, calendars, signs and labels for rooms and so on. This can, however, appear confrontational and upsetting if the person is contradicted, and needs to be used with sensitivity.

Recall: demonstration of *retention* and *retrieval* of *memory* in which the participant reproduces (in words or in *concrete* images, pictures, sounds and so on) what has previously been learned; the external evidence that an item or list of items has been learned.

Recency effects: the improved memory for items at the end of a list. Also used for the tendency to judge others in terms of their latest words or actions.

Recognition: perceiving (or recalling) an object accompanied by a feeling of familiarity, or the conviction that the same object has been perceived before. The recognition method requires the participant to learn certain items (the targets) and then point out those items in a given list, which may include items that were not in the original list (the distracters). This kind of test may be adapted to distinguish between items a participant has actually handled, and those only thought about.

Reconstruction: the idea that mis-remembering may be due to memories being transformed or distorted at the time of *retrieval* due to *leading questions*, subsequent information, *emotions* or other *interference* effects, (for example, Loftus and Palmer, 1974). See also *Redintegration* and *Serial reproduction*.

Redintegration: the word redintegration, now rare, means restoring or re-establishing in a united or perfect state. An alternative term would be re-integration. According to the *Shorter Oxford English Dictionary* (1983), it was first used in *psychology* by Sir William Hamilton in 1836, in his Law of Redintegration or Totality to indicate that thoughts which had previously been part of the same total act of *cognition* later suggest each other. It is now used to indicate a search of *memory*, or *efforts after meaning*, started by a few cues, leading to some kind of coherent whole. Since processes of interpretation, *interference*, confabulation and *suggestibility* also have to be taken into account, the integrated wholeness which is perceived may be substantially different from the original *perception*.

Reductionism: an approach, like early structuralism, that attempts to explain complex patterns or systems in terms of simpler elements or sub-systems. In psychology this usually refers to belief that all mental experience and activity will eventually be explained in terms of the activity of the brain and nervous system and thus reduced to basic physical and chemical processes.

Regression: a term used by Freud to refer to people who exhibit behaviour associated with the childhood stages of *psychosexual* development as a *defence mechanism*. In more general terms, it is now used to describe any behaviour that is childish or considered more appropriate to a younger age group. It may be used in a health care context when an anxious patient becomes angry and shouts in a way associated with childish temper tantrums, or when adults in *pain* rock themselves to *sleep* or seek comfort in cuddly toys.

Rehearsal (or repetition): repeating to oneself the items that are to be *recall*ed. This is a common tactic for memorising a telephone number for long enough to dial it. The *levels of processing* model distinguishes between maintenance rehearsal and elaborative rehearsal.

Reinforcement: in *operant conditioning*, the probability of a response is seen as being altered by its consequences, as shown in Figure 3.14. Anything that increases the probability of a response is called reinforcement. The reinforcement (sometimes called a reinforcer) does not have to be perceived as pleasant or as a *reward* but merely has to increase the incidence of the responses to a stimulus. In general, reinforcement works automatically without free will or choice and occurs when the consequences meet a 'need' of the recipient.

Positive reinforcement involves the addition of something that meets a need, for example giving a child attention. In negative reinforcement, the removal of something meets a need.

Reinforcement schedules: the timing of the association between behaviour and the *reinforcement* is crucial. Different response rates and *extinction* rates will be found according to whether the reinforcement is regular and predictable or intermittent and unpredictable. Findings from early work with animals can be roughly compared with different jobs or activities which give financial reward. Simplified assumptions are summarised in Figure 3.15. In practice, of course, there are many more needs and interests that are served by these activities, and the real relationship is far from simple.

Relativism: the claim, especially in ethics or aesthetics, that there is no knowledge independent of an individual and that all knowledge is created within a cultural system so that conceptions of truth and moral values are not absolute but are relative to the persons or groups holding them and we can only understand and evaluate beliefs and behaviours in terms of their historical or cultural context.

Relaxation training: this is one of the central interventions in *stress management*. There are a number of different procedures, such as:

> progressive muscle relaxation
> yoga
> meditation
> autogenic relaxation training
> *biofeedback*
> *hypnosis* or self-hypnosis
> quiet drifting, with or without specially designed music or visual imagery.

It is often assumed that the body mechanisms respond in the same ways in all relaxed states, but this may not be so.

Relearning: it is often easier to relearn something even if the original material seems to have been forgotten, as in relearning a foreign language. Ebbinghaus (1885) identified relearning as one of the four measurable types of *memory*, alongside *recall*, *recognition* and *reconstruction*. Even severely brain-damaged patients who show little

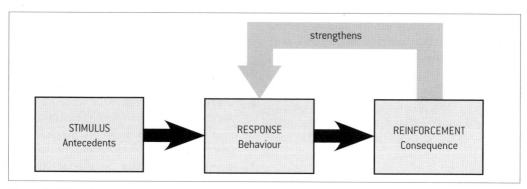

Figure 3.14 Reinforcement of the S–R unit in operant conditioning

Schedule	Example	Response rate	Extinction
Continuous every response is reinforced	Vending machine	steady, slow	quick
Fixed ratio reinforcement is given for a fixed number of responses	Pay for piece work	high, with a pause after reinforcement	fairly quick
Fixed interval reinforcement given after a fixed amount of time if response has occurred	Being paid regularly for work	slow, speeds up when reinforcement is due	fairly quick
Variable ratio reinforcement given on average for a fixed number of responses	Gambling	steady, high	very slow
Variable interval reinforcement given on average for a fixed amount of time, each trial is a different time, but overall average time may be set in advance	Self employed people receiving payment irregularly.	steady, builds up with time after last reinforcement	very slow

Figure 3.15 Reinforcement schedules

concepts

awareness of learning new information some-times show relearning abilities and improved relearning savings.

Relearning savings: in laboratory tasks, the number of trials needed to relearn material is compared with the original number of trials and the saving is expressed as a percentage.

REM sleep: rapid eye-movement *sleep* associated with *dreaming* that occurs regularly throughout the *sleep cycle*. It was called 'paradoxical' sleep early on in the research with cats, before the association with dreaming was understood, because it was obviously deep sleep, but the *brain* patterns were like waking.

Reminiscence: *recall* which is passive rather than active; that is, appearing spontaneously and without effort, often after a period of rest.

Remote memory: is sometimes used to refer to *long-term memory* of non-autobiographical events that have occurred within a person's lifetime such as events in the news or the names of famous people.

Repertory grid: the repertory grid was invented by George Kelly (1955) as a therapeutic tech-nique, and further developed by Bannister (for example, Bannister and Fransella, 1986) as part of *personal construct theory*. It is a way of collecting data from individuals that preserves their individual personal constructs or *beliefs* of how they see their world, without imposing any theoretical *concepts* or constructs. It combines *cognitive* and phenomenological principles. It is formally structured, following a set pattern of collecting responses to questions, but content-free. The simplest technique is to ask the participant to list about 20 familiar people. Three of these are selected, the participant then naming one way in which two of the three are similar but the third different. A bipolar label is then chosen for this similarity–difference construct and applied to all other people in the list. Three different names are then selected and the process repeated. This continues until a grid of constructs has emerged.

Representation: this term is used in a number of different contexts, for example:
> Representation formats in the brain: it appears that the brain uses four distinct formats of representation – *visual image, phonological loop, grammatical representation* and *'mentalese'*.
> Representation modes: an expression used in relation to Bruner's approach to thinking – *enactive, iconic* and *symbolic*.

Repression (motivated forgetting): this is an example of a defence mechanism, and is a *psychodynamic* term used to describe memories that are unconsciously hidden because they are disturbing. According to Freud, much *forgetting* is unconsciously motivated in some way. Some memories can be difficult to uncover, but psychodynamic therapies encourage a client to bring them to light, in the belief that such recovery will eventually lead to improved mental health. On the other hand, repression may be a beneficial coping mechanism and unless there are *problems*, too much pressure to seek out recent hidden memories may not be helpful.

Resistance: a term used in psychoanalysis for the inability or unwillingness of a patient to discuss certain ideas, desires or experiences.

Resting potential: the electrical potential across the membrane of a *nerve fibre* while it is not firing.

Retention: the persisting activity trace left behind as an after-effect by an experience; the neurological indication that an item has been learned and is in the *memory*.

Retrieval: reproduction of a retained *memory* or location of items in the memory, one's own knowledge or experience that an item has been learned.

Reward: something given as a consequence of behaviour that is perceived as intended to be pleasant and in recognition of a desired behaviour. A reward is not the same as *reinforcement* and may or may not result in the behaviour being repeated on another occasion. The term is essentially a *cognitive* one as it depends on beliefs and expectations and, as such, has no place in behaviourism. However, where something is given which meets a need of the recipient, it may both be perceived as a reward and serve as a *reinforcement* of the linked behaviour.

Bruner points out that praising or otherwise rewarding good behaviour in children rarely results in exactly the same good behaviour being reinforced, but in the children exploring new behaviours. As soon as cognitive processes are involved, basic behavioural principles no longer apply.

Rorscharch psychodiagnostic test: this is perhaps the best known of the *projective* techniques. It consists of a set of apparently random designs or 'inkblots'. The final set was selected from a large number used in pilot investigations as these designs proved to be particularly useful. The tester invites the patient or client to look for recognisable patterns, pictures or objects, in the same way that many people like to look for meaningful shapes in clouds. A counsellor may use the inkblots in a client-centred way as a convenient device for helping the client to talk freely. Alternatively, a therapist may use the client's responses in a structured way and develop interpretations according to a theoretical model, directing the client towards fruitful lines of enquiry. Clinical psychologists or psychiatrists may use the test to examine cognitive patterns and help towards diagnosis of *cognitive impairment*. Standardised data are available.

Saccadic eye movements (saccades): perpetual, apparently random, rapid and relatively large movements of the eye that are essential in the process of centralising a target on the fovea, the most sensitive part of the retina. Centralising in this way provides the greatest acuity. Cornsweet (1970) showed that if there were no movement, images would tend to stay in exactly the same place on the retina; inability to renew the chemicals needed for *vision*, and natural *habituation* of the receptors would then result in a lack of visual sensitivity.

The movement is most clearly noticeable in a darkened room in which a spot of light is projected onto a wall. The spot appears to move, jumping about irregularly and the effect is termed autokinetic. The amount of movement varies from person to person but can also be influenced by suggestion and by a tendency to conform to group *norms*. This effect has been used by Sherif (1935), cited by Alexander et al (1970), in some classical studies of group *norms* and social influences. Initially diverse judgements would gradually become more like the others and converge towards a group norm.

Schema (plural schemas or schemata): a term used by Piaget in the 1920s to refer to internalised *representation* or *cognitive* frameworks built up from experience for organising, interpreting and recalling information. A schema is personal and individualistic, not always readily articulated and thus less definite than a *concept*, which can be verbally expressed.

The process of developing schemas starts in the *sensori-motor* stage, where each schema is simply a mental representation of a sequence of actions. Through the processes of *assimilation* and *accommodation*, a child adapts to the environment and develops schemas that are more complex. The term is also used in models of *problem-solving* and *memory*, such as *top-down processing*, *dynamic memory theory* and the *hierarchical network model*.

Schizophrenia: the word is derived from the Greek words for split and brain. The common misperception is that schizophrenia means split personality. However, *dissociative identity disorder* (formerly multiple or dual personality) is an extremely rare disorder quite different from schizophrenia. Schizophrenia affects one in every hundred or so people at some time in their lives, and the name comes from the perception that people seem split off from reality or that there is a split between thoughts and feelings. The term was first introduced in 1912, gradually replacing the term Dementia Praecox, which dates from 1891, and was used to label young people who developed symptoms.

Characteristic symptoms include paranoia, delusions, hallucinations (particularly voices that torment and persecute), and believing that their own thoughts can be heard by others. Behaviour ranges from explosive *anger* and *aggression* to extreme withdrawal and unresponsive states of immobility (catatonia). Causes are not properly known. There appears to be a genetic component with a few biological advantages, sometimes linked with high *creativity* (Hoffer, 1983, cited by Howe, 1990).

Evidence suggests that delusions and *hallucinations* may occur because the person's brain is overwhelmed by sensory information, perhaps because the brain is unable to filter out unnecessary information and allow for selective *attention* processes. Srivastava (Barbeau et al, 1995) indicates that there is a lack of the protein PSA-NCAM, which gives healthy people's brains the flexibility needed to filter large amounts of sensory information. There also appear to be high

levels of *dopamine* associated with schizophrenic symptoms and it is known that disruption of the *hippocampus* can stimulate the overproduction of dopamine. An alternative opinion is that the levels of dopamine may be within normal limits but cannot be tolerated. It is not clear whether the altered brain chemistry is a cause or effect of symptoms.

Earlier approaches to schizophrenia indicated that patterns of communication within families might exacerbate the condition. R. D. Laing (1967) described a 'double bind' situation that he believed contributes to the cause. This takes place when a parent or other significant person imposes conflicting demands on a child so that whatever the child does, it will be judged to be wrong. It is now more widely held that awkward or faulty patterns of communication are likely to arise either because the person with schizophrenic tendencies responds in non-standard ways, or because other members of the family also have some schizophrenic tendencies but these are not marked enough to have been diagnosed as such.

The book *Welcome Silence* (North, 1987) and the film *A Beautiful Mind* help to give some insight into what it feels like to be schizophrenic.

Secondary representation system: the way in which words are used to describe the world as it has been perceived. This term has been refined by the founders of neurolinguistic programming (Bandler and Grinder, 1975, 1976) in their attempt to describe accurately the difference between what we perceive and how we communicate these *perceptions* to each other. In NLP, this difference is called 'slippage'. Much of therapy is concerned with assisting the client to develop appropriate language for articulating experience.

At all times, we are constrained by the language we have and by what we have developed historically as a whole for our society. Further constraint is applied in each individual's choice of language on a day-to-day basis. There is a further 'slippage' between those words that are known and those that are regularly used. Therapy can assist either in recognising the language used by the client and in linking this to *cognition* and *emotions* that have been so far unexplored, or by increasing the range of language available and introducing new *concepts*.

Self-concept: in general, our self-concept is

concepts

what we think, feel and want about all aspects of ourselves. Carl Rogers (1961) discusses three separate components of self-concept:

> descriptive (*self-image*)
> comparative (*ideal self*)
> evaluative (*self-esteem*).

Rogers emphasises that it is not just how we describe ourselves that matters but the assessment we make, how we feel about ourselves and whether or not we like what we are. Rogers suggests that how we feel depends on whether we believe we measure up to our personal and cultural expectations and ideals. His work suggests that, when there is a gap between self-image and ideal self, the size of this gap contributes to self-esteem (Figure 3.16). The greater the gap, the lower the self-esteem. Interventions can work in two ways: either focusing on the self-image to see if there are distortions in *perception*, or focusing on the ideal self to see whether this is realistic and attainable. Counselling would aim to reduce the gap by facilitating the adjustment of both self-image and ideal self until they are closer.

Self-efficacy: the belief in one's ability to achieved desired *goals*. This can be expressed as 'I personally have the capability to do something' (Schwarzer, 1992). For example, 'I am confident that I can perform a planned exercise even if I am tired, friends are visiting, the weather is bad and so on.' Schwarzer identifies three components – self-efficacy, outcome expectancy and risk perception – as contributing to the adoption and maintenance of health behaviours. We imagine outcomes, and what we imagine depends on what we think we can do and the risks involved.

Self-esteem: feelings of self-worth. This is the evaluative part of *self-concept*, the judgement of how we feel about ourselves and whether we like what we are and whether we live up to others' expectations. See also *Altered body image, Attitudes, Body image, Cognitive distortion, Cognitive impairment, Cognitive therapy, Depression, Loss, Motivation, Parenting styles, Self-image, Stress management*.

Self-fulfilling prophecy: Burton and Dimbleby (1995) summarise this as: 'What you want is what you get.' Behaving in a particular way that indicates that a particular outcome is expected is likely to bring about that outcome. This can refer to our expectations about ourselves or about others. For example, if a parent, teacher or carer repeatedly praises a child for being brave, careful or thoughtful, the child is likely to develop those attributes more strongly. Conversely, if a child is constantly in trouble for lack of ability, laziness or clumsiness, these traits are likely to become more noticeable.

Self-image: using Rogers' (1961) definitions, this is the purely descriptive aspect of *self-concept*. This includes anything we would say about ourselves if asked to define who we are without making any comparisons with other people or with an ideal or any judgement or evaluation. For example,

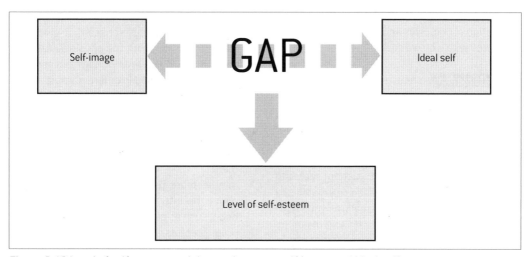

Figure 3.16 Level of self-esteem and the gap between self-image and ideal self

I might say I am female, five foot seven, a mother and grandmother and a teacher and writer. This objective description does not say whether I like these things about myself.

If I said I felt too tall or was a bad mother but loved being a grandmother, these comparisons and evaluations would indicate that I felt taller than some ideal height and had some concept of what it means to be a good mother or grandmother. My judgement of myself would be part of my wider *self-concept* and contribute to *self-esteem*. In practice, when asked to describe themselves most people give a mixture of description, comparison and evaluation and would have difficulty distinguishing between self-image and self-concept.

The following six areas, derived from several existing models, for example James (1890) and Kuhn and McPartland (1954), help to sort the different aspects of what might be included in perception of self. The same categories can also be applied to perception of others:

> *Body image*: physical appearance and state of fitness and health.
> *Sexuality*: *sex*, *gender identity,* sexual orientation and identity.
> Roles: *social roles*, occupational and family positions.
> Interpersonal behaviour: *personality*, *emotions*, *temperament* and *character.*
> Spiritual: educational, intellectual, aesthetic and moral attributes and *values*.
> Lifestyle: activities, skills, interests and possessions.

This list could usefully be compared with Maslow's hierarchy of needs (see *Motivation*) as our description of ourselves and what we do is closely connected with why we do it.

Semantic memory: a term used for items independent of personal experiences such as use of language, general knowledge and academic learning. Some semantic *memory* may require significant effort in encoding information so that it can be retrieved at will, but can usually be retrieved independently of context. Semantic memory seems to survive ageing and can be related to crystallised *intelligence*. Older people are usually as good as or better than younger people at recalling meaningful facts and information. In a general sense in communication theory the word semantic refers to 'meaning'.

Sensation: a term used in physiology and *psychology* to refer to information received by the *senses*. It is linked to the notion of irritability, used in biology, which indicates how parts of the body are responsive to the environment and can provide information about the surroundings. Irritability and sensation are defined as essential differences between living and non-living organisations of matter and energy, and the need for sensory input appears to be fundamental to living creatures. Although rarely mentioned specifically, it is helpful to include it in lists such as Maslow's (1943) hierarchy of needs, alongside the other basic physiological needs such as nutrition and respiration.

Senses: there are five 'special senses' that have specific sense organs and have been recognised from the time of Aristotle and provide information about the outside world:

> seeing (*vision* or visual sense))
> *hearing* (auditory sense)
> *touch*ing (haptic and passive)
> tasting (gustation)
> *smell*ing (olfaction).

In the early 1800s, Bell added a sixth sense, muscle or kinaesthetic sensation. This tells us where all the parts of the body are and how they are moving in relation to the outside world. It is now also recognised that the balance organ in the inner ear provides information about the body's orientation and movement, and this is referred to as the *vestibular sense*. The kinaesthetic and *vestibular senses* are usually known collectively as proprioceptors.

There are also various senses that give information to the brain about the physiological state of the body but these are not normally *sentient*. Senses can be classified in different ways.

Gross (1992) cites Sherrington (1906) who names three groups of senses:

> exteroceptors (the five 'special senses' which give information about the external environment)
> interoceptors (pass information to the *brain* about the internal physiological state of the body, such as blood glucose levels)
> proprioceptors (kinaesthetic and *vestibular senses*).

concepts

An alternative classification is given by Messenger (1979) who argues that the location of the stimulus is a key distinction:

> exteroceptors (limited to receptors which pick up data at the surface of the body, such as hairs which respond to *touch*)
> interoceptors (inside the body)
> proprioceptors (mainly muscles, some are at the joints)
> telereceptors (sound, sight and *smell*, which can pick up signals distant from the body).

Messenger makes a further classification according to the kind of signal that can be processed:

> mechano-receptors (pressure, tension, vibration, sound, involved in *touch*, balance and *hearing*)
> chemo-receptors (chemicals involved in *smell* and *taste*)
> thermo-receptors (warmth, cold and changes in temperature)
> electro-receptors (not specialised in humans, but there is a generalised response to electrical stimulation, such as in TENS, and electric shock)
> photo-receptors (sensitivity to light, mainly *vision*, but also thought to occur in other ways which affect the pineal gland and responses to daylight).

Through all these senses, a complete mental map is built up in relation to the environment. Damage to any of these senses, or to the *nervous system*, which carries messages to the *brain*, or to the brain itself results in limited or faulty information. People can compensate through greater use of other senses, new ways of interpreting data or other complex individual strategies.

Sensitisation: the process by which emotions become associated with particular objects or events. See also *Classical conditioning*. Compare with *Desensitisation* and *Habituation*.

Sensori-motor: the first stage of intellectual growth or cognitive development identified by Piaget (see also *Concrete* and *Formal operations*). The period can be summarised by the expression 'Thought is internalised action'. During this period, the baby is gaining experience through all the *senses* and absorbing it in patterns of behaviour. By using a combination of *assimilation* and *accommodation*, the baby adapts to the environment in such a way as to achieve success. Lasting roughly from birth to 18 months, it includes reduction in *egocentricity*, development of *object concept*, *group of displacements* and *reversibility* and beginnings of language.

Sensory deprivation/overload: too much or too little incoming information from the *senses* can disturb the smooth organisation of *perception* and lead to symptoms of stress and even to *hallucinations*, confusional states and susceptibility to suggestion (Heron, 1957).

Sensory memory: according to Baddeley (1990), this is the initial registration of information in the *senses*, lasting up to 100 milliseconds, and represents a stage of *memory* before the *brain* processes the information, such as the *persistence of vision*. Other writers may use the term sensory memory for storage in the *cerebral cortex*, which is short lived and associated with the related sensory modality.

Sentience/sentient experiences/qualia: being conscious or consciously aware of objects or other information received via the senses.

Serial probe technique: an experimental task in *memory* research in which a sequence of digits is presented and then one of the digits is selected as the probe and the participant is asked to *recall* the digit that follows the probe (for example, Waugh and Norman, 1965).

Serial processing: a step-by-step sequence in any cognitive process, for example *perception*, *memory* or *problem-solving*, in which the steps of the process are carried out separately, one after the other.

Serial reproduction: developed by Bartlett (1932) for investigating *reconstruction*, this early technique examines the way in which a message may be progressively altered when an account is reproduced from *memory* on a number of successive occasions. It can be compared with the *Gestalt theory* of *forgetting*.

concepts

Seriation (serial order): putting things in order or a series according to some rule. An activity for children in the intuitive or pre-school stage would include putting beakers, building blocks or saucepan lids in order of size.

Serotonin: also called 5-HT or 5-Hydroxytryptamine. This is a neurotransmitter that is found in the *pineal body*, blood platelets, the digestive tract and the *brain* and is active as part of the *sleep switching mechanism*. Changes in serotonin levels can alter mood and are thought to be implicated in *depression* and seasonal affective disorder, and possibly in sudden infant death syndrome (cot death). Medications that affect the level of serotonin are used to treat depression.

Set (fixity) in problem-solving: once a person has found a suitable procedure for solving a *problem*, there is a tendency to keep to this procedure for all similar problems. This can be a successful technique and may save time and effort. However, a simpler solution may sometimes be missed. Moreover, as a habit, it will not lead to novel or creative solutions.

Sex: the biological designation of male or female. In most cases this is decided at birth based on visible physical characteristics (morphology).

The basic biological determinant of sex is the arrangement of *chromosomes*. Generally, males have two different sex chromosomes, XY; females have two similar ones, XX. These come one from the mother, the other from the father and since all ova have only an X but spermatozoa can be either X or Y it is the father who contributes the basic sex to the fertilised embryo. However, hormones also influence development of the embryo. The XY embryo will only develop male characteristics if there is sufficient androgen in the uterus. Hence a baby which is chromosomally male could develop (morphologically) as a female (for example, Ruse, 1990, Ch. 5).

Genes for male and female characteristics may be scattered throughout all the *chromosomes*. Secondary sexual characteristics such as a bass voice, beard and muscular physique in males, breasts and wide pelvis in females, are not the result of sex-linked genes but the different expression of the same genes present in both sexes. Both sexes carry genes controlling the growth of hair, mammary glands and penis, but in the presence of male or female hormones they have different effects.

A person with partially developed male and female physical characteristics may be referred to as *intersexual*, hermaphrodite or sometimes bisexual.

Some rare chromosome variations arise because the sex chromosomes fail to separate during meiosis (Simpkins and Williams, 1987: 380) so that instead of XX or XY, there may be XO, XXY, XXXY, or XYY with corresponding characteristics.

Sexuality: in popular usage and the mass media, the term 'sexuality' is generally restricted to mean either sexual activity or sexual orientation/preference. In the social sciences and professional usage, sexuality has a much wider meaning and includes all aspects of experience and expression that have anything to do with *sex*, *gender identity*, sensuality and attractiveness. Thelan et al (1994: 111) define sexuality as:

> a unique, highly individual expression and experience of the self as a sexual, erotic being. It is an holistic experience in that it encompasses both the mind and the body and a part of the *character* of a person also termed the *personality*.

Components of sexuality can be listed as follows (adapted from various sources):

> ❯ Biological *sex*: male, female or intersex, defined by genetic coding, sex *chromosomes*, hormones, visible sexual characteristics and functioning sexual organs.
> ❯ Core sex identity: an inner sense of being male or female.
> ❯ Gender identity: *conformity* to the cultural and social *norms* and ideals corresponding to masculinity and femininity.
> ❯ Sexual orientation: an inner sense of being homosexual, heterosexual or bisexual.
> ❯ Sexual identity: adopting the lifestyle and sharing characteristics of a particular group, such as heterosexual, homosexual, bisexual or *transvestite*.
> ❯ Sexual behaviour: the communication, expression and action of sexual feelings and beliefs.
> ❯ Sexual thoughts: desires, fantasies, frustrations and anxieties.
> ❯ Attractiveness: the self-perception of how

concepts

one looks to other people; this can apply in all social interaction but has particular relevance in finding and relating to partners and the perceived ability to meet their needs.

> Personal boundaries: the limits of what is found to be acceptable sexual behaviour, including attitudes to abuse, harassment and rape.

Other sources (for example, Webb, 1985, 1994) give lists that can usefully be compared.

Shape constancy: like other forms of *perceptual constancy*, this refers to the perceptual interpretation remaining constant even when the viewer and object move relative to each other. For example, a round plate continues to be seen as a circle even when placed at an angle to the viewer so that the retinal image is not circular but oval (elliptical).

Short-term memory (STM): usually refers to storage of a few seconds, involving higher mental processes in the cortex of the *brain*, such as remembering a telephone number for long enough to dial it. Changes in short-term *memory* are very varied. Studies of short-term memory loss distinguish between capacity and duration. There can be significant changes in some tasks with no noticeable difference in others. For example, a person may have difficulty recalling words presented aurally, but no difficulty with visual presentations. Baddeley and Hitch (1974) explain this in terms of their *concept* of *working memory*. Simple short-term *memory span* shows little or no decline with age. However when extra demands are placed on participants, the age effects generally become apparent. Backward span procedure and concurrent or *parallel processing* indicate that elderly people are significantly worse at these tasks. Baddeley (1982) suggests the *central executive* is the prime cause of this age-related decline.

Signal detection theory (signal detectability theory): a theory, fashionable in the 1960s and 1970s, which is useful in the study of *sensation*, *perception* and *memory*. It is based on the measurable responses to varying levels of stimulation and shows how weak signals can be detected even when there are distracting stimuli. According to Robinson (1996) its main achievement was to separate a participant's sensitivity to a stimulus from the mental 'preparedness' to acknowledge

it. Participants were more likely to detect a signal when they were expecting it or when they attached some *value* to detecting it.

Silence: in normal conversation, gaps of silence are usually a sign that one person has finished speaking and is waiting for a response from the other. There are unwritten 'rules' for how long the silence should be allowed to last. French (1994) suggests that each knows when it is someone else's turn to speak. People with poor communication skills may be less aware of turn-taking cues. Many health-care professionals and patients feel uncomfortable when faced with a period of silence. Bradley and Edinberg (1990) found that people who have not had time to build up a relationship or good rapport are uncomfortable with as little as five to ten seconds of silence. In well-established relationships, silences may be tolerated with more ease and comfort. Those involved can use silence positively as a sign of trust and acceptance or to contemplate and formulate ideas. Conversely, silence may be a sign of anxiety, *depression*, boredom or preoccupation, or it may be used negatively to convey anger or frustration. The task for the professional carer is to create an atmosphere in which silence can be accepted and used positively and in which different kinds of silence can be accurately identified.

Size constancy: this refers to our *perception* that objects and people remain the same size when we are moving towards or away from them, or when they have moved. The image on the retina is changing, so the judgement about lack of change is a mental one. It is thought that babies have to learn this *perceptual constancy* but that it is present by 18 weeks (for example, Slater, 1989).

It is found by most people that size constancy has not been learned in a vertical direction as most visual experience takes place in a horizontal plane. When looking down from a tall building or an aeroplane, things no longer look the right size but often give the impression of toy cars and people below. It seems that aeroplane pilots soon lose this effect as they develop new size constancy in the vertical direction.

Slave systems: according to the *working memory* model of Baddeley and Hitch (1974) and their later work, *short-term memory* consists of a *central* *executive system* and subsidiary slave systems that handle *modality-specific* information. Two such slave systems are the *phonological loop* and the *visuo-spatial* sketchpad or scratchpad.

Sleep: a recurrent healthy state of inertia and unresponsiveness (Oswald, 1966). It appears most likely that sleep is needed for brain repair and recovery (Horne, 1988). Human growth hormone (hGH) is released during sleep (Calder, 1970). Cell division (mitosis) and somatomedin (a protein) *synthesis* occur at night and are inhibited by cortisol, glycogen and catecholamines produced during the day. Adam and Oswald (1983) concluded that much of healing takes place at night, or during resting and sleeping, and this remains a widely held view. However, Horne (1988) argues that the conditions of night-time, resting and sleeping need to be considered separately. Cell repair takes place most efficiently during wakeful resting and is reduced during sleep. Human growth hormone is released at night but this continues to occur during *sleep deprivation* and is likely to be associated with circadian rhythms rather than sleep as such; its function in adults is not understood.

See also: *Dreaming, Narcolepsy, REM sleep, Sleep cycles, Sleep Deprivation, Sleep duration, Sleep paralysis, Sleep switching mechanisms.*

Sleep cycles: *sleep* is commonly sub-divided into:

> *REM sleep*, during which *dreaming* occurs (previously known as *paradoxical*)
> SWS slow wave sleep (non-REM or orthodox), which can be further sub-divided.

Sleep occurs in a series of cycles (see Figure 3.17) throughout the night, on average four or five cycles of about an hour and a half each. Different stages of sleep can be identified through observation of visible signs, difficulty of waking and characteristic EEG traces (see Figure 3.18). Small irregular traces when awake (beta waves) are similar to REM sleep. During 'orthodox' sleep the waves gradually become slower and bigger from threshold (alpha waves) to stage I and on to Stage IV (delta waves). Each person has a unique style and timing; so much so, that experimenters watching the EEG recorder can predict what is about to happen.

Typically, each cycle consists of a gradual descent through Stage I, Stage II, Stage III to Stage IV, which is deep or delta sleep, followed by *dreaming* or REM sleep. After about ten minutes of dreaming, the first REM period ceases. The person may turn over in bed, begin the cycle again, down through stage II to Stage IV, and have another REM dream. The entire cycle is repeated four or five times. Towards morning, the person no longer sinks to the bottom in delta sleep, and REM periods are longer. Sleep becomes lighter; the body temperature begins to rise and body chemistry changes, ready for waking. On awakening, a fragment of dream may be recalled. It is extremely rare for anyone to recall enough to account for all the time spent in REM sleep. See also Oswald in Part 4.

Sleep deprivation: under experimental conditions, deprivation of slow wave, deep or delta *sleep* (SWS) tends to lead to physical symptoms, aches and *pains*, *depression* and apathy. Deprivation of REM sleep may lead to *mood* changes, hostility, irritation, *anxiety* and behaviour changes, which may be perceived as changes in *personality*. When deprived of all sleep, delta sleep is made up first. When deprived only of REM sleep, volunteers tend to lapse into REM sleep almost as soon as they are allowed to close their eyes (Oswald, 1966). No physiological effects of short-term sleep deprivation have been reliably found and psychological effects are felt to be due more to levels of *motivation* rather than impairment up to about three days of deprivation. After this time, there are measurable changes in *cognitive* function and this suggests that sleep is essential for brain repair and restoration.

Sleep duration: most people have an idea of what they consider to be the right amount of *sleep* – and do their best to make their children conform to that norm. The usual figure given is seven to eight hours a night, more for young children, and considerably more for babies. There are some, particularly older people, who complain of insomnia, because they are not having a regular eight hours sleep, even if they do not have any other symptoms. 'Good' sleepers generally fill in questionnaires to the effect that they take about seven minutes to get to sleep, and have about

Stage	Brain waves	Behaviour and sensations	Depth of sleep	Physiological changes	Dreams
Awake	beta: small irregular waves	concentrated thought, activity			coherent thoughts
Threshold	alpha: small, even rhythm 9–13 per sec	serene relaxation, no concentrated thought	relaxed wakefulness		fragments of thought
Myoclonic jerk	tiny burst	a sudden spasm	momentary arousal		
I	small, pinched, irregular, changing	floating, drifting sensation, idle thoughts	can still be woken easily	muscles relaxing, pulse even, breathing regular, temperature falling	little fragments of images and thoughts
II	growing larger quick bursts	if eyes are open, will not see	needs modest sound to awaken	eyes roll slowly from side to side	low intensity dreams, rarely recalled
III	large, slow waves, one per second	removed from the waking world	takes louder noises	muscles relaxed, breathing even, heart rate slow, temp down, blood pressure down	as II
IV	delta: very large slow waves	period of bed-wetting, sleep-walking, or oblivion	most difficult to waken	temperature and blood pressure at lowest	poor recall, apparent oblivion
REM	irregular, small, similar to awake	rapid eye movements as if watching	hard to bring to surface and reality	low muscle tone, limp, irregular pulse, blood pressure and breathing, twitching	very vivid dreams, 85% of the time
The entire cycle is repeated roughly every 90 minutes, or about four or five times in a night					

Figure 3.17 Sleep cycles

seven or eight hours of sleep a night. 'Poor' sleep-ers think they take an hour to fall asleep, wake at least three times in the night, and only have a few hours sleep (McGhie and Russell, 1962). Labora-tory findings suggest that people's *beliefs* about how long they sleep can be widely inaccurate.

Horne (1988) suggests that a useful division is into:

> essential or core sleep
> optional or behaviourally learned sleep.

He suggests that core sleep takes place during the

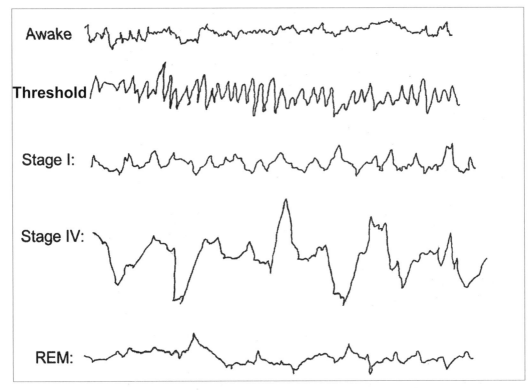

Figure 3.18 EEG wave traces in sleep

first part of sleep and that about five hours (three *sleep cycles*) are necessary for most people on a long-term basis. Extra sleep is used to conform to social patterns, occupy the dark hours of the night and provide a surplus that allows for coping readily with short-term *sleep deprivation*.

Sleep paralysis: unpleasant dreams in which the dreamer struggles to escape some impending danger but is unable to move. *EEG* records show that the main muscles are indeed paralysed, as during all *dreaming sleep*, but there may be facial twitching and strangled cries.

Sleep switching mechanisms: various parts of the *brain* are interconnected and responsible for controlling sleeping and waking. The *pineal body* (see Figure 3.5), is the part of the brain that controls the biological clock – the *diurnal* rhythms. One of its functions is to receive information indirectly from the eyes, and it responds to darkness by producing melatonin. The melatonin affects those brain cells that produce *serotonin* and this,

in turn, affects the switching mechanisms. In the brain-stem, there are three distinct 'switches':

> the reticular activating system for waking
> the raphe system for deep *sleep*
> locus coerulus for *dreaming* sleep.

At the same time as the raphe system is switching on to permit sleep, the reticular activating system switches off and information from the sense organs and other parts of the brain do not reach the higher centres of the cortex. If the raphe system is destroyed, the owner becomes incapable of sleep, however tired. The locus coerulus (from the Latin – blue region) is important in *dreaming* or *REM sleep* as it prevents the dreamer getting up and acting out the dream. Sleepwalking tends to occur during periods of deep delta sleep and is rarely associated with *dreaming*.

Smell (olfaction): this is defined by Messenger (1979) as a distant chemical sense. The receptors in the nose and nasal passages respond to air-borne and water-borne stimuli even in very low concentrations. In western cultures, smell is a neglected area of study and little has been known until recently. For most people the *perception* of smell is largely unconscious except in response to strong smells. For many smells *habituation* is quite rapid. It is often found that smell plays a significant part in the detection of certain health conditions and many nurses and doctors are alerted to changes in a patient's state of health by a change in smell, even if they cannot name the change or describe to an observer what they are noticing. The olfactory bulb is the centre where odour-sensitive receptors send their signals, located just below the frontal lobes of the cortex.

Social construction: according to the school of constructionist thought, a social construction or social construct is a concept or practice which may appear to be natural and obvious to those who accept it, but in reality is an invention or artefact of a particular culture or society.

Social learning theory: an extension and development of *behavioural* principles that takes social interaction into consideration. Observational learning or *modelling* can lead to imitation or identification.

Bandura (1965, 1977) drew attention to the difference between learning and behaviour. Not all learning results in observable actions. In pure behaviourism, it is believed that *reinforcement* works automatically with no element of free will; the human or animal is not required to assess or evaluate the effects of the behaviour.

In contrast, Bandura believes that reinforcement serves as information and *motivation*. By 'informative', he means that the consequences of the behaviour tell the person in what circumstances it would seem wise to try a particular behaviour in the future; they improve the prediction of whether a given action will lead to pleasant or unpleasant outcomes in the future (see Figure 3.19). People can learn from observing others (*modelling* and *vicarious learning*) since watching others can provide information on which kind of behaviour leads to which consequences. By '*motivation*', Bandura means that more attempts will be made to learn the modelled behaviour if the consequences are *valued*. This approach implies that people can weigh up the disadvantages and advantages of behaviour and have a choice about what they actually do. Some people are concerned about the undue influence on children of violence portrayed in the media. However, as Pinker (1998: 51) argues, we cannot attribute all of human history and ethnography to toy guns and superhero cartoons. Many of our desires and fears are inherited and social learning can go some way towards understanding these and choosing more appropriate behaviour.

Social roles: positions we occupy within groups or society as a whole, either by choice or by circumstances. Roles can be roughly classified as follows:

> family/partner relationships and positions
> neighbourhood relationships
> educational/professional/occupational positions
> clubs and group memberships and positions of responsibility
> age, *gender identity, sexual orientation or identity* and ethnic identity.

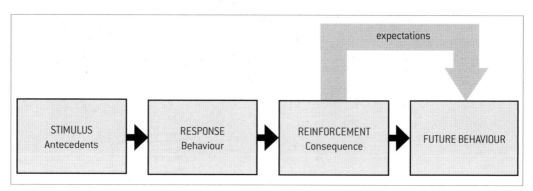

Figure 3.19 Social learning theory

How people act within each role depends to a large extent on expectations about what it means to be a member of that group. What does it mean to be a mother, neighbour, manager or counsellor? Moreover, what does it mean to be a good mother, good neighbour, good manager or good counsellor? Rogers' (1961) model of *self-concept* helps to identify any gap between a person's perception of himself or herself in a particular role and what he or she thinks is required of the role in order to be seen as 'good'.

Sociograms: a visual means for recording the patterns of interactions between members of a group. These may range from a simple tally of the number of times each person makes a contribution, to a complete map showing the number and direction of all contributions, see Figure 3.20. Sociograms are useful in conjunction with analysis of the content of interaction, such as *Bales interaction analysis* and can be employed as part of the analysis of *broken information games*. Sociograms may be used in clinical practice to identify communication problems within a dysfunctional family.

Split-brain: it is possible to separate the two hemispheres of the *cerebral cortex* by cutting the corpus callosum. This operation has been performed on a few patients since the 1940s in attempts to reduce the effects of epileptic seizures. The few detectable changes are very interesting and

contribute to the debate about where *consciousness* resides. One patient reported that when she intended to reach for an object with her right hand, her left hand might suddenly take control and grab something different even though she knew this was unsuitable (Gilling and Brightwell, 1982). Experiments indicate that, in most cases, only images in the right visual field (Figure 3.22), available to the left brain, can be named, since the language centres are on the left (Figure 3.4). An image in the left visual field (processed in the right hemisphere) is not apparently recognised, although it can sometimes be drawn by the left hand (controlled by the right hemisphere). It is only after making such a drawing and viewing it with both sides of the field of view that the patient can name the stimulus object. It appears that the image can be mentally processed and a drawing made without any conscious awareness – similar to *blindsight*. This may indicate that our experience of *consciousness* is closely connected with our capacity for language but it is not possible to derive any general conclusions from a few isolated and unusual cases. See also Sperry in Part 4.

Stress: stress is a general label for a vast, complex, interdisciplinary area of interest and study, much of which is health-related. Commonly, stress is associated with over-arousal of physiological reactions, which are seen to be harmful, and much stress-reduction is centred around

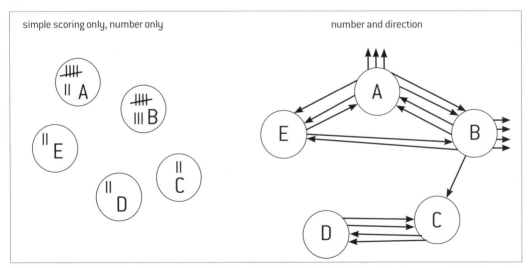

Figure 3.20 Sociogram to show the number and direction of communications between members of a group

calming and soothing activities such as *relaxation* and meditation. Selye (1974) differentiates between good stress (eustress) and bad stress (distress). Eustress involves growth-enhancing reaction, with stressors perceived as opportunities and associated with strength and resistance (see *Hardiness* and *Toughness*). Distress involves stress overload, with stressors associated with weakness and vulnerability.

The inverted U-curve, or curvilinear relationship, adapted from Yerkes–Dodson (1908) shows a fuller relationship between demands, performance and stress (see Figure 3.21). It illustrates how either too much or too little in the way of perceived demands can lead to discomfort, disturbance, or low performance. Unemployment, sensory loss and physical disability can all be stressful because there are too few demands. Often, friends and relatives try to help by taking over difficult tasks, leaving even less to strive for.

Similarly, Lazarus (1966) talks about the balance of demands and resources. When there is an even balance, the perceived demands are healthy, but when they exceed the perceived resources, the person experiences distress.

A distinction is usually made between 'symptoms' which the sufferer notices and 'signs' which others can use as an indication of stress. These can be grouped according to whether they are predominantly physiological or psychological. Psychological indicators can be sub-divided into the three main domains of *cognitive*, *affective* and *behavioural* (*see* Adams and Bromley, 1998).

See also: *Anger management, Arousal systems, Autonomic nervous system, Catharsis, Cognitve appraisal, Cognitive therapy, Coping styles, Fight or flight mechanism, General adaptation syndrome, Hardiness, Hypnotherapy, Motivation, Nervous system, Perceptual disorders, Post-traumatic stress disorder, Psychogenic illness, Psychoneuroimmunology, Psychosomatic, relaxation training, Sensory deprivation/overload, Stress management, Stressors, Toughness, Type A behaviour pattern (TAPB).*

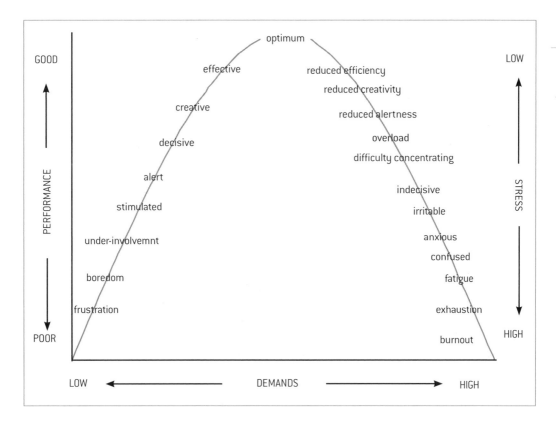

Figure 3.21 Stress, demands and performance

Stress management: management of *stress* can be seen in terms of making alterations to the personal stressors (perceptions of self), *environmental stressors* (perception of events) and response (physiological *arousal* and behaviour). Changes can be effected through *relaxation training*, stress inoculation in the form of progressive desensitisation or flooding, personal *coping styles*, group sessions, organisational strategies and the use of drugs. There is no special category of stress-reducing drugs; treatment will depend on what combination of symptoms is present.

Stressors: situations, events and demands that contribute to *stress* and can be described in terms of duration, quality, quantity and type:

> Duration: (Elliot and Eisdorfer, 1982)
>   – acute, time limited, such as interview, visit to dentist
>   – sequences or series of events that occur over an extended period of time as the result of an initiating stress trigger, such as divorce which brings multiple residential, financial, job, parental and social changes
>   – chronic intermittent stressors such as periodic arguments with a partner, weekly project meetings
>   – chronic stressors such as permanent disabilities and long-term marital strife.
> Quality: (Lazarus and Cohen, 1977)
>   – major changes, often cataclysmic and affecting large numbers of people such as war, earthquake, economic depression
>   – major changes affecting one or a few persons such as bereavement, divorce
>   – daily hassles such as running out of coffee and arguing about who was supposed to buy it.
> Quantity: (Holmes and Rahe, 1967; Yerkes–Dodson, 1908)
>   – the accumulation of stressors is significant in stress-related disorders
>   – both desirable and undesirable changes can have stressful effects
>   – both too much and too little in the way of demands can be stressful (see Figure 3.21).

> Type: (Holmes and Rahe, 1967)
>   – environment/society such as war, earthquake, financial depression, noise, heat, air pollution, wind, crowding, housing conditions, the city, discrimination
>   – personal circumstances such as bereavement, divorce, marriage, responsibilities, changes at work, pregnancy, arguments, changes in diet, changes in health, daily hassles.

Structural change or trace/engram: changes in the form of growth of *synapses* or the dendrites of the *neurone,* which (possibly) facilitates neural connections and therefore the firing of a particular sequence on a later occasion, related to *long-term memory*. Theories of *memory* based on this notion used to rely more on supposition than on physiological evidence. However, there is now increasing evidence that denser growth corresponds to areas connected with repeated physical activity. For example, there is some evidence that a person who regularly practises playing the violin will have a correspondingly greater number of nerve connections related to control of the muscles in the fingers.

Structural components: *sensory memory*, short-term store (STS) and long-term store (LTS) are referred to as structural components in the *multi-store* model. Control processes such as *rehearsal* serve to transfer memories from one structure to another.

Structuralism: an early form of structuralism was the study of the structure of mental experience and behaviour as a combination of simple elements or events that could be identified by introspection, associated with Wilhelm Wundt and Edward B. Titchener (see Part 4) and abandoned when it was realised that introspection could not be examined scientifically in the same way as the physical sciences. Later structuralism as a field of academic interest began around 1958 and peaked in the late 1960s and early 1970s. It refers to various theories across the humanities, social sciences and economics that share the assumption that structural relationships between concepts vary between different cultures and languages and that these relationships can reveal how meaning is produced within a particular person, system or culture.

Subconscious: a popular term for the unconscious mind, but not used in Freudian or other *psychodynamic* theories. Freud distinguishes between the *preconscious* that can readily be brought into *consciousness* and the deeply unconscious that is difficult to access.

Subjective: an individual personal viewpoint which depends on one's own emotions and capacities or imaginary elements which are separate from the objective reality.

Subjectivity: the philosophical claim that consciousness and mental states cannot be studied objectively because they cannot be independent of any descriptions or interpretations offered by any subjects. See also discussion in Part 2.1.

Sublimation: a form of displacement in which a highly regarded socially acceptable activity such as artistic expression is used for the expression of *psychosexual* energy. An example would be painting or sculpting nudes, or going to galleries to view them.

Subliminal perception: *perception* of a stimulus below the normally measured limit or threshold of perception. This is said to occur when a stimulus is very brief or at very low intensity. It is thought that under some circumstances, even though a stimulus has been considered too small to be registered, a person may none the less be influenced by unconscious mental processing of the information. Evidence for this is conflicting.

Suggestibility (malleability): willingness to be led by another person, for example in *hypnosis* or giving *eye-witness testimony* that may be inadvertently distorted in response to certain kinds of questioning such as *leading questions*. Some people may be more prone to this than others and factors such as vividness of imagination may be as important as compliance.

Superego: the term used by Freud to describe the aspect of the mind that is constantly in conflict with the *id*, attributing praise to good behaviour

and guilt and blame to bad behaviour. The 'super-ego' is partly conscious and partly unconscious, and is learned through social constraints. It forms the core of conscience and adult morality.

Syllogism: a simple three-part representation of a sequence of logical *deduction*. A syllogism consists of two premises and a conclusion. The syllogism can be examined in a number of ways to see whether the conclusion follows logically from the premises, whether both premises are true and whether the conclusion is true. Representing a logical argument in the form of a syllogism can help distinguish between truth and logic and help in identifying what has led to faulty conclusions. Compare the following two statements:

- Miss Smith must be able to read minds if she is a psychology student.
- We can assume Mr Brown is a psychology student if he writes essays.

The first has correct logic, but is based on a false premise. The second, is based on true premises, but uses faulty logic. The syllogisms would be:

(All) Psychology students can read minds Miss Smith is a psychology student Therefore Miss Smith can read minds.	Psychology students write essays Mr Brown writes essays Therefore Mr Brown is a psychology student.

Symbolic interactionism: a sociological perspective that is important in social psychology. It is associated with the work of George Herbert Mead, who argued that people's selves, while being individually purposive and creative, are social products. Symbolic interaction uses hermeneutics (see Part 5) by emphasising how people perceive the world through their individual constructions of reality: that is, if people define situations as real, they are real in their consequences. We relate to each other and to the world largely on the basis of our perceptions, rather than merely the objective features of a given situation. See also *Social constructionism*.

Symbolic representation: the third of Bruner's

(1964) ways of describing mental representation of the environment in order to think or solve *problems* (see also *enactive* and *iconic representation*). Symbolism means using one thing to stand for another even when it does not look like it. This can include using a cardboard tube as a telescope, putting symbols on a map to show the positions of churches and using words to stand for objects, activities and *concepts*. Where the object or mark looks like the thing it stands for, as in a model telescope or a drawing of a church, it is referred to as an icon rather than a symbol. Symbols belong to a system that has been agreed by people who wish to use them for communication and the meanings have to be learned. All words are symbols, and use of language depends on a fundamental understanding that something can stand for something else, and it is felt that symbolic imaginative *play* with children accelerates language development. See also *Fantasy play*.

Synaesthesia: an apparently rare but interesting phenomenon first described by Francis Galton (1822–1911). Certain individuals seem to get an overlap between two or more *senses*, which gives them a very different *perception* of the world from the majority, such as colours interfering with numbers or shapes having distinctive tastes (for example Cytovic, 1994).

Synapse: the microscopic area between *neurones* in which messages pass from one cell to another in the form of chemicals. When the action potential in one neurone reaches the synapse, the pre-synaptic cell endings manufacture and release a chemical substance that diffuses across the gap to the next cell (post-synaptic) where it is taken up.

Each nerve cell has thousands of synapses and each synapse connects between many cells. According to Simpkins and Williams (1987) there are about $10^{2,783,000}$ synapses in an average *brain*. The synapses which converge on a cell all contribute to whether the cell will fire or not. Some are excitatory, which would cause the cell to fire; others are inhibitory, which would prevent it firing. The synapse serves as a selective routing mechanism and as an intermediate station where a power step-up or step-down can occur.

Synthesis: the putting together of parts or elements to make up a complex whole – the converse of analysis. In *thinking* processes, it normally refers to putting ideas together in a new arrangement or relationship, which produces a new 'whole'.

Taste (gustation): this is a 'chemotactile' sense where a large number of chemoreceptors are present in humans in a special region of the mouth and tongue (Messenger, 1979). It used to be thought, from early psychological experimentation, that only four types of receptors were present on the tongue, responding to saltiness, sweetness, sourness and bitterness. These areas can be clearly mapped out on the tongue in simple taste tests. It was believed that all other aspects of what we consider taste when responding to the flavours of foods were due to the sense of *smell*. A person who loses the sense of smell, either through damage or through applying a clip or clothes-peg to the nose, cannot readily distinguish between the taste of pieces of apple and onion. However, it is now acknowledged that taste may be more complex than formerly realised. Ageing, illness, *mood*, experience and hormonal changes such as in pregnancy can all affect the sense of taste. It is well known that some bitter tastes must be 'acquired', and in some situations individuals may find they can no longer tolerate previously liked foods.

Teleology: the doctrine or study of ends or causes, especially in relation to the belief that everything in nature has been designed according to some purpose. In the context of health beliefs and lifestyle, a teleological approach is based on the concept that a person's current behaviour is driven or motivated by goals. Adler took a teleological approach to personality and believed that an understanding of personality was only possible if an individual's goals were known. He believed that people strive towards fulfilment of their own personal potential; this can be compared with Maslow's (1943) notion of self-actualisation and his hierarchical model of needs (see *motivation*).

Temperament/disposition: terms used for aspects of behaviour or personality that are regarded as fundamental characteristics, usually viewed as innate rather than acquired, and related to levels of energy and physiological responsiveness to the environment (Buss and Plomin, 1975). However, It is argued that all aspects of physiological responsiveness can be strongly influenced by lifestyle.

Thalamus: this is the hub of communications for the whole *brain*, with a busy traffic of impulses flowing in all directions. See Figure 3.5.

Thematic apperception test (TAT): this is a well-known *projective* test and consists of a set of pictures which can be used to determine a person's patterns of thought and emotional concerns. The pictures, mostly of people, are deliberately vague and ambiguous and the client is invited to talk about the picture or tell a story.

Theory of mind (ToM): an expression taken from Kant and Descartes, used in relation to autism and schizophrenia. It describes the ability (or lack of ability) to sense the state of mind of another person, to appreciate another point of view and be able to see the world through another person's eyes. If you have ToM then you will understand that just because you know something it doesn't mean that I will know it too. People who lack ToM assume you know what they know and they often open conversations with statements that seem to come from the middle of a conversation without giving the background to establish the context. See also *Animism, Autism, Computational theory of mind, Identity theory of mind, Consciousness* and 'Primatology' in Part 2.3.4.

Thinking: thinking involves processing of information gathered from sensory experience and memory. This requires energy, and the technique of functional brain imaging (PET) depends on the fact that the brain consumes more glucose from the blood when it is working.

See *Abstract thinking, Bottom-up processing, Concrete operations, Convergent thinking, Creativity, Deduction, Divergent thinking, Formal operations, Induction, Intelligence, Lateral thinking, Metacognition, Play, Problem-solving, Representation modes, Syllogisms; Synthesis*, and Parts 2.2.3 and 2.2.4.

Time out: removing a person from a problem situation to prevent his or her behaviour receiving *rein-*

forcement. For example, this can involve sending a child to another room, such as a bedroom, or using a 'naughty chair'. The child is held in the naughty chair, by force if necessary, until he or she promises to join in activities 'properly'. This procedure avoids smacking and is recommended in family therapy where a child is persistently naughty. See also *Parenting skills* and *Parenting styles*.

Top-down processing: a *concept* that refers to starting with a higher mental process, hypothesis or *schema* and working downwards towards recognising the basic elements or examples. In *thinking* and *problem-solving* this can be compared with *deductive* processes. In *perception*, it refers to identifying an object by reference to a previously formed *synthesis* or *concept* of a class of objects or expectations. It is also known as concept-driven (or conceptually-driven) processing. See also *Bottom-up processing*.

Topography: the study of the areas of the *brain*. The word comes from 'topology' a branch of mathematics concerned with the properties of figures, surfaces and spaces. Some areas of the cortex, for example the motor control area, or motor strip, are said to be arranged topographically such that particular functions can be related to specific areas in a clearly mapped out and unchanging way, (Blakemore, in Barlow et al, 1990). Similarly, deeper inside the brain, it is possible to label distinct areas and give an indication of their main functions in relation to psychological experiences. However, localisation does not exactly match the visible shapes and there is increasing evidence that other areas can take over functions. Although such labelling is useful as an introduction to brain function, there is an increasing trend away from a topographical approach. See Figure 3.4 and 3.5. See also *Computational theory of mind, Hemispheric specialisation*.

Touch: sense receptors in the skin respond to pressure, warmth and cold, and can also detect chemical or electrical stimulation. These receptors activate specific *nerve fibres*, which may be activated singly or in parallel. Neural processing takes place within the spinal cord, in the brain-stem and in the *thalamus* on the way to the somatosensory area of the *cerebral cortex*. Motor and sensory pathways are crossed so that the left hemisphere

concepts

controls the right side of the body, see Figure 3.12 and *hemispheric specialisation*.

> Haptic touch is active exploration, especially with the fingers or tongue, that makes use of single neural channels.
> Passive touch is all other kinds of touch that make use of *parallel processing* of neural channels when external objects press on the skin on any part of the body.

Toughness: Dienstbier (1989) takes a positive attitude to *stressors* and *stress*, arguing that proper management of stress can lead to greater toughness and improved physical and mental health, through:

> passive toughening (exposure to extremes of heat and cold)
> active toughening (physical fitness).

The SNS-adrenal-medullary (*fight or flight*) arousal system adjusts to a low base rate with fast recovery after arousal. See also *Hardiness*.

Transactional Analysis (TA): a multifaceted system of psychotherapy developed by Eric Berne (1910–1970) that stems from *psychodynamic* theories but uses a humanistic approach.

Like others, Berne (1964) believes that life is basically hard and that everyone feels anxious. He suggests that various unconscious conversational devices or 'games' may be used to maintain control of a situation. These include adopting the positions of 'parent', 'adult' and 'child', which have developed out of childhood experiences. In particular, each of us may respond to a distressing situation by adopting a childlike or helpless position, or by attempting to be parent-like and controlling. By understanding our own responses, we can learn to be more balanced and adult-like.

Some sources mistakenly refer to transactional analysis as if it offers a quick way of interpreting other people's behaviour. The greatest danger lies in imposing one's own idea of what the terms 'parent' and 'child' stand for instead of appreciating that these are different for every individual.

Transfer: the effect (positive or negative) of learning one task upon the learning of another. Positive transfer refers to improved performance as a result of solving a number of similar *problems*.

Negative transfer occurs when previous experience interferes with the solution to a current problem. Kahney (1993) gives the example that motorists would soon learn new traffic light signals if the green were changed to blue since these are similar, but would have frequent accidents if the red and green were reversed. In theories of *memory*, the term refers to transfer from one *structural component* to another. See also *Interference*.

Transference: in therapy, clients may unconsciously treat the therapist in the same way they have responded to a significant figure from the past, typically a parent or sibling. This may lead to resistance to therapy or to over-dependence or exaggerated feelings of *attachment*. The therapist can make use of this by helping clients look at patterns of behaviour and relate this to past experiences. Counter-transference can occur when the therapist loses sight of professional objectivity and begins to respond to the relationship in a personal way because of unresolved emotional difficulties.

Transgender/transsexual: a person whose biological *sex* and *gender identity* are not the same (Ruse, 1990: 3). This can happen by accident, when a baby whose sexual characteristics are not well defined is wrongly 'sexed' at birth. Such a person may have to make a choice of whether to continue with the accustomed *gender identity* or to develop a new one.

Other individuals feel deeply that they are the wrong biological sex, that is, they have an inner sense of being male or female that does not correspond with their visible characteristics, and living as the wrong sex can become unbearable.

The Department of Health provide a leaflet of support that says that this discomfort is not a mental illness but a recognised condition (known as gender dysphoria) for which medical treatment is appropriate in some cases. The condition is increasingly understood to have its origins before birth (see Part 7.2).

Transvestite: someone who dresses in the clothing the culture considers proper to a member of the opposite *sex* in order to achieve some kind of erotic arousal. If no erotic arousal is intended, the

concepts

person is better known as a cross-dresser (Ruse, 1990), whether this is a regular behaviour or a temporary one for a party or pantomime.

Traps: Ryle and Cowmeadow (1992: 105) define traps as certain kinds of thinking and acting which result in a 'vicious circle' when, however hard we try, things seem to get worse instead of better. Trying to deal with feeling bad about ourselves, we think and act in ways that tend to confirm our badness. They argue that people often get trapped because they confuse *aggression* with *assertiveness*. Believing that aggression is wrong, many people bottle up aggression or *anger* until they cannot help letting it out in a burst of childish behaviour. Seeing themselves acting childishly or causing harm confirms their belief that the aggression is wrong. They do not easily see that being assertive and asking for their rights is acceptable.

Triggers: items which act as *memory* cues that set off a train of memories. In everyday experience, snatches of songs or certain *smell*s can trigger vivid memories. See also *Reconstruction*, *Cue dependence* and *Redintegration*.

Twins: babies that develop together in the uterus. Twins can be either:

> monozygotic (from one *zygote* or fertilised ovum which has divided into two within one amniotic membrane) or

> dizygotic (two separate zygotes in separate amniotic membranes).

Monozygotic twins are identical and necessarily the same *sex*, whereas dizygotic twins are no more alike than any siblings and can be either the same or different sex. See also *Zygote*.

Twin studies: studies of twins are useful in *psychology* as they contribute to the nature–nurture debate and help to distinguish between characteristics that are more likely to be due to *genotype* or to upbringing and personal experience. The basic pattern of research is to compare twins who have lived together with those that were separated at birth. Behaviour patterns that are alike in separated twins are likely to have been inherited rather than learned. Some of these similarities might be expected, such as intelligence and personality traits but others can be quite startling, such as unusual habits or preferences for particular clothes or brand of toothpaste.

Type A behaviour pattern: Rosenman et al (1964) identified a type of person who responded in a particular way to *stress* and was susceptible to coronary heart disease. TABP is the behaviour of a competitive, achievement-orientated person who possesses a sense of time urgency and impatience and who is both easily aroused and hostile or angry.

TABP is a controversial area of research. Criteria for deciding how many of the observable characteristics should be included, or the strength of these, are variable, making it difficult to compare studies. There is a wealth of research in this area, including continuing refinements to the profiles and alternative models, and search for specific factors, rather than the general profile, which put the person most at risk. See also *Personality*, *Temperament*.

Unconditional regard (unconditional positive regard): Rogers (1980) wrote that: 'the therapeutic phenomenon seems most likely to occur when the therapist feels, very genuinely and deeply, an attitude of acceptance of and respect for the client as he is, with the potentialities inherent in his present state.' Words such as warmth, caring, acceptance, respect or 'prizing' may also be used to convey regard but the essential feature is that these are 'unconditional'. It is considered important that the client must not be made to feel that the carer's warmth or caring is conditional or dependent on some change taking place as a result of the relationship or therapy (Murgatroyd, 1985). Neither should any views about whether the client is a 'nice' or 'good' person be allowed to interfere with therapy. Real help will only occur when the therapist is not trying to make the client change. See also *Congruence* and *Empathy*, and Part 4, Rogers and Part 2.3.13 'Humanistic psychology'.

Value: the judgement that a person places on the desirability, worth or utility of obtaining some outcome. People are guided by emotions and moods and are only partly rational in decision-making. See *Emotion* and Part 2.2.3.

Vestibular sense: the *sense* of balance in the inner ear, which provides information about movement in relation to the horizontal and vertical. Gravity and inertia cause fluid in the semi-circular canals to move in response to movements of the head so that the amount, direction and speed of movement can be 'calculated' mentally. See also *Proprioception*.

Vicarious learning: a term used in *social learning theory* to refer to the ways in which people can learn by observing what happens to others. For example, a toddler may learn not to break plates by observing that a sibling is punished for doing so, or a young child learns to help in laying the table through noticing that a friend is praised for doing so. Vicarious learning differs from simple *modelling* in which any behaviour may be copied as it includes the assumption that the outcome of the behaviour (usually perceived as *reward* or *punishment*) has been observed. The terms 'modelling' and 'vicarious learning' may, however, be used interchangeably where outcomes are taken into account.

Vision: this can variously be described as an exteroceptor, telereceptor or photo-receptor sense, see *senses*. The eyes enable us to pick up information from a distance by the action of light on receptors in the retina. The human retina consists of a mosaic of rods and cones, each receptor having its separate nerve. The rod nerves encode information in dim light, the cone nerves encode bright light and colour. Rod signals and cone signals coexist all the time and are combined in varying degrees depending on conditions. Rods contain a pigment (rhodopsin, or visual purple) which responds to low levels of illumination. Cones contain a range of pigments which respond to different colours or frequencies of light, see *Colour Vision*. Changes in the chemical nature of the pigments create action potentials, which travel via the optic nerve to the visual cortex at the back of the *brain*. Information from one side of the visual field travels to the opposite hemisphere, see Figure 3.22. Gregory (1971) argues that the eye and brain developed simultaneously during evolution to allow processing of the information. Vision is normally the dominant sense and most imagery is described in visual terms, which

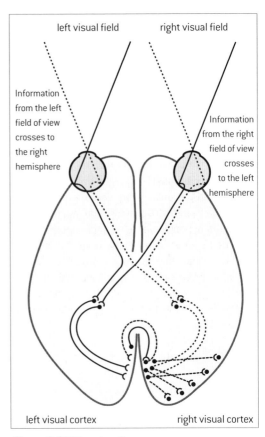

Figure 3.22 Visual pathways

socially disadvantages those with limited or no vision.

Visual distortions: a type of visual illusion in which we judge something as a different length or shape from what it actually is. We genuinely make a mistake, usually because there are distracting surroundings. Examples of standardised distortions used to illustrate this are the '*Muller–Lyer*' lines and the '*Ponzo*' effect where equal lines appear to be different (See Figure 3.9). In day-to-day situations, this kind of distortion is common although it rarely causes major problems. Most people learn the hard way that if they wish to move a heavy piece of furniture from one corner of the room to another, to fit it into a convenient space, it is wise to measure the space first.

Visual fictions (embedded figures): a type of illusion in which we see something that is not there, usually created out of a 'space' with apparent boundaries formed by other parts of the figure. A widely cited example is the Kanizsa triangle in which the illusion is not a simple space but cuts across other parts of the figure, see Figure 3.9. Art students are trained to look at negative spaces in order to help with the relative positioning of lines and angles and much art is created with special *attention* to these spaces.

Visual illusions: the *perception* of something that does not actually exist, but which, unlike an *apparition*, is related to specific visual stimuli, see Figure 3.9. Robinson (1972) gives a detailed account of illusions. Illusions can be classified as:

> *ambiguous figures*
> *paradoxical figures*
> *visual distortions*
> *visual fictions*
> *movement illusions.*

Visual images: one of the four main formats of *representation* in the brain. The visual system uses a two-dimensional (2-D or 2¹/₂-D) picture-like sketch of visible surfaces that can indicate depth, slant (forwards or backwards), tilt (left or right), colour, texture, boundaries or edges, valleys and ridges. We do not immediately see objects as such but have to interpret the surface information in the light of previous experience – hence the expression 'we see what we expect to see' and the occurrence of *visual illusions*. The image is a mosaic of elements that represent points in the visual field. The elements are set out in two dimensions so that neighbouring elements in the array stand for neighbouring points in the visual field. The expression 2¹/₂-D was coined by David Marr (for example, 1982) to make a distinction between a true 3-D object, which has solidity, and the mental representation that only partially re-creates the third dimension. See also *Iconic imagery, Visuo-spatial scratchpad*.

Visual neglect: a lack of *attention* or *perception* of parts of the body or of the surrounding environment. Visual neglect is an inability to perceive objects in part of the visual field. The term 'hemianopia' is used where half of the visual field appears to be lost. This may occur together with paralysis of one side of the body (hemiplegia). This can occur after a stroke. Hemianopia may be

a temporary symptom of migraine. Sacks (1984) gives a vivid description of how he 'lost' one side of the visual field during a migraine following an accident. The most striking effect is that the sufferer usually has no awareness that there is anything missing. This may also be associated with a change in spatial awareness, which can be revealed by observation of behaviour and of drawings made by the person. The person may be seen to continually move the head to one side and may end up continually lying on one side, staring at the wall, unaware that there is anything else to look at or that there is any point in turning the other way. Drawings may show information that the person knows about all heaped up on one side of the drawing, such as the numbers of a clock all placed around a half circle, or all the features of a face on one side. Curiously, the drawings do not necessarily look wrong to the person who drew them, although it is possible, with hard work and feedback, for an individual to learn to produce near 'normal' drawings.

Visuo-spatial sketchpad (scratchpad): this is one of the subsidiary *slave systems* suggested by Baddeley and Hitch (1974) and refers to the rehearsing of items as visual images in terms of how and where they would occur in the normal visual field. Examples would be remembering the moves in a football game in order to describe it to someone else or visualising a room that you are planning to re-decorate. Visual memories would also be used in imagining a similar situation, such as imagining a football game while listening to a radio broadcast. This kind of visual memory can be compared with Bruner's iconic mode of representation.

Weapons effect: the realisation (for example, Dixon, 1987) that the mere presence of weapons can lead to violent behaviour.

Working memory: Baddeley and Hitch (1974) and Baddeley (1990) suggest that *short-term memory* functions as a set of sub-systems, which act as temporary working memory systems enabling us to perform a range of cognitive tasks. Baddeley and Hitch conceive the working memory as consisting of a controlling *central executive system* and a number of subsidiary *slave systems*. Two such slave systems are the *phonological (sound) loop* and the *visuo-spatial sketchpad*. The sub-systems appear to be independent and are assumed to be processed in different parts of the brain.

When someone is trying to solve a *problem*, visual and sound memories are brought into *consciousness* or short-term working memory where they can be continuously rehearsed via the sketchpad or sound loop. Other sensory memories may also be involved in different slave systems. These processes are organised by the *central executive system* until the problem is solved and the solution committed either to paper or to *long-term memory*.

X-rays and gamma (γ) rays: these are short wavelength, high-frequency, high-energy invisible rays belonging to the extreme end of the electromagnetic or light spectrum. They cover a range of frequencies known as 'soft' or 'hard'. They can penetrate solid matter and the different frequencies may be used for taking photographs of bones or other organs within the human body (soft rays) or for irradiating and destroying tumours (hard rays). CT scans use X-rays; PET scans involve gamma rays.

X-rays and gamma rays are identical except for the precise range of frequencies. The distinction is made for historical reasons as they were identified separately and come from different parts of the atom. Gamma rays are produced naturally from the nuclei of atoms in radioactive materials such as Cobalt-60. They are also produced by the collision of positrons and electrons. X-rays are generated by very high voltage X-ray machines that stimulate the electron shells of atoms. X-rays are also naturally radiated from the Sun, but are absorbed by the atmosphere before reaching Earth.

Zygote: the initial stage in fertilisation when male and female gametes fuse, that is when the sperm first joins with the ovum. After fertilisation, the zygote undergoes cell division and growth and develops into an embryo and later a foetus. *Twins* are described as monozygotic or dizygotic and all genetic characteristics can be identified as *heterozygous* or *homozygous*.

Adler, Alfred (1870–1937) [224] ¦ Adorno, Theodor W. (1903–1969)
[224] ¦ Ainsworth, Mary D. Salter (1913–1999) [225] ¦ Allport,
Floyd Henry (1890–1971) [225] ¦ Allport, Gordon Willard (1897–
1967) [226?] ¦ Aronson, Elliot (current) [226] ¦ Asch, Solomon
E. (1907–1996) [226] ¦ Atkinson Richard C. and Shiffrin Richard
M. (current) [226] ¦ Baddeley Alan D. and Hitch Graham (current)
[227] ¦ Bales, Robert Freed (1916–2004) [228] ¦ Bandura, Albert
(current) [228] ¦ Baron-Cohen, Simon (current) [229] ¦ Bartlett,
Frederic Charles (1886–1969) [229] ¦ Bem, Sandra Lipsitz
(current) [229] ¦ Berne, Eric (1910–1970) [230] ¦ Bernstein, Basil
(1924–2000) [230] ¦ Bettelheim, Bruno (1903–1990) [231] ¦
Bion, Wilfred Ruprecht (1897–1979) [231] ¦ Blakemore,
Colin (current) [231] ¦ Bowlby, John (1907–1990) [232] ¦
Broadbent, Donald E. (1926–1993) [232] ¦ Bruner, Jerome S.
(current) [232] ¦ Bryant, Peter (current) [233] ¦ Burt, Cyril Lodowic
(1883–1971) [233] ¦ Cannon, Walter Bradford (1871–1945) [233] ¦
Cattell, Raymond Bernard (1905–1998) [233] ¦ Chomsky, Avram
Noam (current) [234] ¦ Craik, Fergus I. M. and Lockhart, Robert
S. (current) [234] ¦ Damasio, Antonio R. (current) [235] ¦ De
Bono, Edward (current) [235] ¦ Dennett, Daniel Clement (current)
[235] ¦ Deutsch, J. Anthony and Deutsch, Diana (current) [235] ¦
Donaldson, Margaret (current) [236] ¦ Ebbinghaus, Hermann
(1850–1909) [236] ¦ Elliot, Jane (current) [236] ¦

4 key theorists and studies

theorists

Ellis, Albert (1913–2007) [237] ¦ Erikson, Erik Homberger (1902–1994) [237] ¦ Eysenck, Hans. J.
(1916–1997) [237] ¦ Festinger, Leon (1919–1989) [238] ¦ Feyerabend, Paul (1924–1994) [238] ¦
Freud, Anna (1896–1982) [238] ¦ Freud, Sigmund (1856–1939) [238] ¦ Friedman, Meyer (1910–
2001) and Rosenman, Ray H. (1957–1964) [239] ¦ Fromm, Eric (1900–1980) [239] ¦ Gibson,
Eleanor (Jackie) (1910–2002) and Walk, Richard, D. (retired) [239] ¦ Gilligan, Carol (current) [240] ¦
Goodall, Jane (current) [240] ¦ Gregory, Richard (current) [240] ¦ Harlow, Harry Frederick (1905–
1981) [240] ¦ Hebb, Donald Olding (1904–1985) [240] ¦ Holmes, Thomas and Rahe, Richard H.
(current) [241] ¦ Horney, Karen Danielsen (1885–1952) [241] ¦ Hubel, David H. and Wiesel, Torsten
N. (current) [241] ¦ James, William (1842–1910) [242] ¦ Jung, Carl Gustav (1875–1961) [242] ¦
Kahneman, Daniel (current) [242] ¦ Kelley, Harold H. (1921–2003) [243] ¦ Kelly, George Alexander
(1905–1967) [243] ¦ Klein, Melanie (1882–1960) [243] ¦ Kohlberg, Lawrence (1927–1987) [244] ¦
Kohler, Wolfgang (1887–1967) [244] ¦ Kraepelin, Emil (1856–1926) [244] ¦ Kuhn, Thomas S.
(1922–1996) [245] ¦ Labov, William (current) [245] ¦ Lacan, Jacques-Marie-Émile (1901–1981)
[245] ¦ Laing, Ronald David (1927–1989) [245] ¦ Lakatos, Imre (1922–1974) [246] ¦ LaPiere,
Richard T. (1899–1986) [246] ¦ Latané, Bibb (current) [246] ¦ Lazarus, Richard S. (1922–2002)
[247] ¦ Loftus, Elizabeth F. (current) [247] ¦ Lorenz, Konrad Zacharias (1903–1989) [247] ¦

Luria, Alexander Romanovich (1902–1977) [248] ¦ Maslow, Abraham (1908–1970) [248] ¦ Mead, George Herbert (1836–1931) [248] ¦ Milgram, Stanley (1933–1984) [248] ¦ Miller, George A. (current) [248] ¦ Mollon, J. D. (current) [249] ¦ Olds, James (1922–1976) [249] ¦ Osgood, Charles E. (1916–1991) [249] ¦ Oswald, Ian (current) [250] ¦ Pavlov, Ivan Petrovich (1849–1936) [250] ¦ Penfield, Wilder Graves (1891–1976) [250] ¦ Peris, Frederick (Fritz) Salomon (1893–1970) [250] ¦ Piaget, Jean (1896–1980) [250] ¦ Pinker, Steven (current) [251] ¦ Rogers, Carl Ransom (1902–1987) [252] ¦ Rorschach, Hermann (1884–1922) [252] ¦ Rose, Stephen (current) [252] ¦ Rutter, Michael (current) [252] ¦ Sacks, Oliver Wolf (current) [253] ¦ Sapir, Edward (1884–1939) and Whorf, Benjamin Lee (1897–1941) [252] ¦ Schachter, Stanley (1922–1997) and Singer, Jerome L. (current) [253] ¦ Seligman, Martin E. P. (current) [254] ¦ Selye, Hans (Hugo Bruno) (1907–1982) [254] ¦ Sheldon, William H. (1898–1977) [254] ¦ Sherif, Muzafer (1906–1988) [254] ¦ Shiffrin, Richard M. (current) [254] ¦ Skinner, Burrhus Frederic (Fred) (1904–1990) [254] ¦ Sperry, Roger Walcott (1913–1994) [254] ¦ Tajfel, Henri (1919–1982) [255] ¦ Thorndike, Edward Lee (1874–1949) [255] ¦ Tinbergen, Nikolaas (1907–1988) [255] ¦ Tolman, Edward Chace (1886–1959) [256] ¦ Treisman, Anne (current) [256] ¦ Triandis, Harry C. (current) [256] ¦ Tulving, Endel (current) [257] ¦ Turing, Alan (1912–1954) [257] ¦ Vygotsky, Leo Semyonovich (1896–1934) [257] ¦ Wason, Peter Cathcart (1924–2003) and Johnson-Laird, Philip (current) [257] ¦ Watson, John Broadus (1878–1958) [258] ¦ Weiss, Samuel (current) [259] ¦ Winnicott, Donald Woods (1896–1971) [259] ¦ Wundt, Wilhelm Maximilian (1832–1920) [259] ¦ Yerkes, Robert Mearns (1876–1956) [259] ¦ Young, Thomas (1773–1829), von Helmholtz, Hermann (1821–1894) and Maxwell, James Clerk (1831–1879) [259] ¦ Zimbardo, Philip G. (current) [260] ¦

theorists

4.1 History and philosophy of psychology

This section provides a quick romp through the development of ideas in philosophy and psychology.

Early philosophy: mind and reason

Modern psychology has many strands, all of which are influenced in one way or another by early ideas of magic, superstition, myth, religion, science, philosophy, healing and medicine.

In the Western world, the first written accounts of significant influence were those of Hippocrates, Plato and Aristotle in the 5th and 4th centuries BC. These were in turn based on early Egyptian, other North African, Indian and other influences.

Hippocrates, remembered now in the Hippocratic Oath of modern medicine, was a physician who described temperament in medical terms and was among the first to think of epilepsy as an illness resulting from natural causes rather than divine inspiration. This idea was later suppressed during the dark ages and was not fully appreciated until the 20th century.

Plato (427–347 BC) was concerned with the teaching of philosophy in order to achieve the ideal state. He emphasised that the purpose of education was not to put knowledge or thoughts into the pupils' minds but to make them think for themselves. He demonstrated that conventional morality was often muddled and inadequate, and he attempted to analyse the elements of the human mind to show that its well-being, full development and happiness are to be secured by doing right and not doing wrong. He distinguished between doing right through deliberate choice, generous impulse and acting on animal appetite. He outlined the various arguments concerning whether we do something right because we know it is right or because there is some sort of reward. Plato followed Socrates' teaching that doubt was the most important feature of human thought and that knowledge of one's own doubts and limitations was the basis of real wisdom. These ideas are periodically lost and re-established throughout history.

Aristotle (*c*. 384–322 BC) was interested in the relationship between mind and reason. He was concerned with the concept of the association of ideas in the mind, and notions of similarities and differences. He distinguished between our knowledge of the world derived from the senses and the power of rational thought, explaining desire in terms of the pleasure, or its reverse, gained from the senses. He defined five senses: sight, hearing, taste, smell and touch. Aristotle's ideas are derived from intuition and are often unsupported by observation (what we call armchair philosophising). They remained largely unchallenged for centuries and have profoundly influenced thinking. Much of what Aristotle described is similar to what people today tend intuitively to believe until introduced to more rigorous and scientific education.

The Stoic philosophers overrode Aristotle's neutral stance towards our biology by distinguishing between universal reason, which they considered to be pure and good, and man's often irrational nature, which by definition must be impure and bad. This led to passions and feelings being regarded as vile. Early Christian teachings, notably those of St Augustine (AD 354–430), took this further and thought of man as a pure rational soul temporarily using an impure, mortal, earthly body. They denounced the senses as evil sources of satisfaction and desire, while continuing to teach that all knowledge derives from them. Sexual feelings were particularly condemned and, more often than not, women were blamed for leading men astray, as is portrayed in the Biblical story contained in the Book of Genesis.

The Reformation, the Inquisition and witchcraft: the separation of mind and body, and the suppression of doubt

Confusion between mind and reason, and value judgements of mind versus body, coloured late Roman and medieval thought. For hundreds of years, theology was inextricably drawn into the psychological strands of philosophy, and new ideas were suppressed.

Not until the 13th century did new ideas begin to emerge. St Thomas Aquinas (1224–1274) revived Aristotelian philosophy. He regarded the soul as immortal but made respectable and non-heretical the revival of Aristotle's biological intellectualism, which did not condemn the senses and biological functions.

Over the next four centuries, the deadening influence of religious orthodoxy was beginning to be challenged in many spheres: political, economic, medical and philosophical. Important advances in medicine, notably Harvey's demonstration of the circulation of the blood, were made. The supreme authority of the Church to sway people's minds regarding all questions of moral conduct and personal responsibility was challenged.

In a desperate attempt by religious orthodoxy to hold onto its power, the Inquisition and its teachings about witchcraft and heresy led to extensive witch-hunts and purges. Until doubt and enquiry could be acknowledged as legitimate human responses to times of profound change, doubt was logically regarded as the ultimate of all heretical evils and must therefore be due to demonic possession. The body was seen as something gross that could be inhabited by any spirit craving a lodging. Witches, mostly women, were recognisable as those who expressed or led others to express excessive sexual appetite or who were hysterical or psychotic people. Burning and other inhuman treatment of the mere body was justified in terms of the purifying effect on the soul.

Johannis Weyer (1515–1588), city physician at Arnhem, deserves credit for insight and moral courage in asserting that the illnesses attributed to witchcraft came from natural causes. Weyer has been called the first clinical psychiatrist, both for his humanity and for his factual approach to psychological phenomena.

René Descartes (1596–1650) attempted to resolve the mind–body dilemma by postulating that the body worked on mechanical, physical lines but was controlled by the soul, which he thought had its seat in the pineal gland in the middle of the brain. The soul, operating via the pineal, regulated the flow of 'animal spirits' along the nerves and blood vessels like an elaborate plumbing system. Descartes' (or Cartesian) theory is of mind–body interaction, with a firm distinction drawn between the two entities. Thenceforth, philosophers and theologians could mostly devote themselves to the problem of mind, leaving it to the physical scientists to puzzle out the relationship between the mind and the nervous system.

The empiricist philosophers of the late 17th and 18th centuries (Locke, Hume, Berkeley and others) again revived the Aristotelian concept of the association of ideas, which seemed to fit the increased knowledge of the nervous system and its connection with mental phenomena. Immanuel Kant (1724–1804) proposed the division of mental faculties into knowing, feeling and willing (cognition, affection and conation). Kant insisted on the unity of perception and on the experience of an active self that organises experience.

Positivism, the brain, and the beginnings of scientific psychology

Auguste Comte (1798–1857), who is also credited with the founding of sociology, introduced a style of philosophy known as positivism, which advocates the study of man by the methods of science, marking the beginning of the demise of armchair philosophising and the start of systematic observation.

Concurrently with all these advances, physiologists had been busy adding knowledge about the nervous system and the brain. Thomas Willis (1621–1675) studied brain structures and postulated that the nerves were not tubes through which animal spirits flowed but fibres by which some influence passed from brain to body. In the 1790s Galvani found that muscle contraction in frogs resulted from electrical discharge. In the early 1800s Bell and Magendie showed that the motor and sensory nerves were distinct and that each individual nerve fibre served only one function. Bell added a sixth sense – muscle or kinaesthetic sensation – to Aristotle's original five. Pierre Flourens, c.1824, published evidence that there existed in pigeons a general correspondence between certain major divisions of the brain and various levels of bodily activity.

The stimulus given to experimental work on the animal brain, and its possible application to the human brain, was largely derived from Charles Darwin's theory of evolution published in 1859. It was gradually becoming clear that human pre-eminence was due to the greater growth and complexity of the cortex of the brain.

In 1861 Pierre Broca discovered the site of the centre for speech in the left hemisphere of the human brain. Hughlings Jackson in 1775 described the function of the nervous system as hierarchical, and the concept of levels of mental functioning was developed. Marshall Hall (1790–1857) described the difference between voluntary action and reflex action in the nervous system. Hermann Helmholtz (1821–1894) measured the speed of the nerve impulse and later developed his theories of vision and hearing (see entry in 4.2). Gustav Fechner (1801–1887) can be considered to be the founder of experimental psychology through his attempts to apply the laws of mathematics to the physiology of sensation and develop psychology as a science with a mathematical base.

The appearance of psychology as a subject discipline in its own right is generally dated at 1879, when Wilhelm Wundt (1832–1920) founded the first laboratory for experimental psychology at Leipzig. The institute's researches added to knowledge about problems of sensation and reaction time. Wundt also attempted to develop a psychological theory that, while acknowledging the importance of introspection as a method of direct observation of oneself, laid stress upon the importance of experimentation and measurement in psychology (see entry in 4.2).

William James (1842–1910) published *Principles of Psychology* in 1890, which established him as one of the most influential thinkers of his time. His work advanced the principle of functionalism in psychology, removing psychology from its traditional place as a branch of philosophy and establishing it among the laboratory sciences based on experimental method (see entry in 4.2).

By 1882 Stanley Hall had founded America's first psychological laboratory at Johns Hopkins University, and ten years later there were 15 such laboratories in the United States. In Britain, after some smaller beginnings, a psychological laboratory was founded at Cambridge in 1913 under the direction of C. S. Myers.

Psychoanalysis, behaviourism and humanistic psychology

At the same time, new discoveries were being made in psychological medicine. Ancient ideas of divine and demoniacal possession had persisted despite attempts to contradict them, and it was still largely believed that the abnormal behaviour of the mentally ill was the product of some external influence or physical agent. Jean Charcot (1825–1893) was the first to demonstrate that hysterical phenomena could be induced and even relieved by suggestion. Further work by Pierre Janet, Bernheim and Liebeault began to uncover the mind's unconscious dynamics but these early discoveries were soon overshadowed by the work of Sigmund Freud (1856–1939).

Freud used the methods of hypnosis and free association and the study of his own dreams to evolve his theories about unconscious mental striving, largely based on sexual repression and defence mechanisms. Psychoanalysis became both a mode of treating patients and a system of psychology (see entry in 4.2). Carl Gustav Jung (1875–1962) differed from Freud in rejecting the theory of infantile sexuality, introducing the notion of collective unconscious and considering all people as a mixture of masculine and feminine characteristics. He considered the libido not as exclusively sexual but as a generalised life energy or will to live (see entry in 4.2).

By the 1920s introspection as a method of enquiry was being seriously questioned. Observation and measurement of behaviour was considered more reliable, in particular by John B. Watson (1878–1958). A new brand of psychology – behaviourism – emerged. Watson believed that, to be a science, psychology must adopt only objective methods (see entry in 4.2). The study of inaccessible, private, mental processes was to have no place in a truly scientific psychology. Behaviourism (in one form or another) was to remain the dominant force within psychology for the next 30 years or so, especially in the United States and to a lesser extent in Britain. The emphasis on learning, in the form of conditioning, was to make that topic one of the central areas of research in psychology as a whole. Behaviourist theories of learning are often referred to as stimulus–response or S–R theories because of their attempt to analyse all behaviour into stimulus–response units, no matter how complex the behaviour. In contrast to Freudian analysis, behaviourism gave rise to a form of therapy for neuroses based on a use of conditioning and deconditioning to the relevant stimuli.

Purposive or hormic psychology developed as a reaction to behaviourism. William McDougall (1871–1944) rejected the mechanistic views of behaviourism and held that the mind has an element of free will and that purposive striving played a decisive role in mental activity, behaviour being the resultant of mind–body interaction. Like Freud, however, McDougall believed that social organisation developed from inborn drives or instincts.

Carl Rogers (1902–1987) and Abraham Maslow (1908–1970) rejected both the psychoanalytic and the behaviourist approaches (see entries in 4.2). They emphasised the individual's uniqueness and freedom to choose a particular course of action and are the leading proponents of humanistic or phenomenological psychology. Central themes of the theory and psychotherapy are self-concept and self-actualisation. The psychodynamics of the individual are not considered to have fixed or generalised interpretations. Humanistic therapy is client centred or person centred (rather than analyst or theory centred): the therapist does not offer any explanations or use theory-based interpretations but instead assists clients in exploring and finding their own meanings.

Gestalt psychology, cognitive development and social learning theory

Another reaction against behaviourism came in the form of the Gestalt school of psychology, which emerged in the 1920s and 1930s in Austria and Germany. The Gestalt view is that 'the whole is more than the sum of its parts' and focuses attention on the organising functions of the nervous system. Gestalt principles can also be applied to learning, showing that insight is often more important than trial and error. After 1920 the Gestalt movement spread to America, where Kurt Lewin (1890–1947) developed his field theory, in which he viewed the mind as a dynamic tension system and behaviour as the means of reducing or abolishing tension. The aim of the individual is to attain a tension-free state of equilibrium. This links with the homeostatic principles of the time, in which the ideal state is seen as quiescent and free from disturbance.

Freud's dynamic concept of the mind links up with educational theories from Plato to Rousseau (1712–1778) and Froebel (1782–1852) that children are individuals in their own right and that education should develop innate qualities and not merely be an implanting of adult precepts.

The work of Freud and the evolutionary theories of Darwin combined to bring about the growth of interest in child development. Sir Francis Galton (1822–1911) is usually regarded as the father of the mental test, using statistical methods in correlating mental traits. His work was continued in Britain by Karl Pearson, Cyril Burt (see entry in 4.2), Godfrey Thomson, William Brown and C. E. Spearman. In the United States, J. M. Cattell (1860–1944) carried out independent studies, while in Paris Alfred Binet (1857–1911) studied the problem of backwardness in schoolchildren. Mental testing of all sorts became widespread in schools, in the armed forces and for job selection.

In the mid-1920s social psychology research began to take a firm hold in psychology. An important publication was *Social Psychology* by Floyd Allport (1924), see 4.2. Psychologists continued to emphasise the individual in society rather than the structure of society itself, which was largely left to sociologists.

Jean Piaget (1896–1980), working on various tests, became concerned with underlying mental structures and outlined his theory of cognitive development. Piaget believed that children think in a concrete way that is fundamentally different from that of adults and that they have to develop through a series of stages before they can reach formal adult or abstract thinking (see entry in 4.2). This was later disputed by, for example, Peter Bryant and Margaret Donaldson (see entries in 4.2), who believed that adults and children alike use a mixture of concrete and abstract thinking, according to context and individual interests, and that differences are due more to differing concepts, memory and concentration span.

A development of behaviourism arose in social learning theory, in the United States in the 1940s and 1950s, as an attempt to reinterpret certain aspects of Freud's psychoanalytic theory in terms of conditioning theory. This was carried on in the 1960s and 1970s, notably

theorists

by Albert Bandura, who emphasised learning through watching and imitating others (see entry in 4.2).

Jerome Bruner was greatly influenced both by Piaget and social leaning theory; rather than describing stages of growth, he was concerned with ways of representing the world (enactive, iconic and symbolic), the need for language for the development of logical thought and the ways in which social interaction lead to the acquisition of language (see entry in 4.2). These theories of cognitive development and social learning have led to significant changes in education and health-care practice, the emphasis now being on providing plenty of concrete examples and the opportunity to explore concepts through play and the age-appropriate use of language.

Brain imaging, cybernetics and modern psychology

Fresh lines of investigation into the mode of brain functioning were opened up in the 1960s in the use of the electroencephalogram (EEG). Together with newer forms of brain imaging – computerised axial tomography (CAT or CT), positron emission tomography (PET) and magnetic resonance imaging (MRI) – this allows study of the structure and activity of the brain without interference or damage. Another modern approach to investigating brain function is the science of cybernetics, which attempts to explain human thinking and behaviour using computer simulations, artificial intelligence, feedback and communication systems.

Although many definitions can be found, modern psychology is best defined as the scientific study of behaviour and experience. Psychology is not a single subject but a complex mosaic: a vast collection of individual studies with the common aim of using scientific methods to describe, understand, predict and influence (or control) human behaviour and experience.

Underlying all modern psychology is the still unresolved relationship between mind (or consciousness) and neurological processes, in particular brain activity. Many psychologists recognise the importance of the brain and nervous system but are inclined to think of physiological activity as being separate from mental experience. Others regard psychology and physiology as fully integrated. Those who believe that all mental experience will eventually be explained in terms of the brain and nervous system are referred to as reductionists. Evolutionary psychologists avoid the dichotomy by saying the mind is not the brain but what the brain does, and that different entities or modules of the mind evolved to solve our ancestors' particular problems. We inherit a range of desires and fears and strategies for adapting to new environments and solving new problems.

From fixed models of the normal child and adult to lifespan development and human diversity in cultural and environmental contexts

New approaches to psychology are developing all the time as psychologists look for new types of explanation or seek new applications to meet the problems of the current world situation.

Innovations include evolutionary psychology that seeks to explain human potential in terms of how our minds evolved to deal with solving problems; cultural, environmental, and ecological approaches that argue that people can only be considered fully within the context in which they live; the move away from noticing and studying only men (or

theorists

assuming that what was true for men would also be true for women) to including the psychology of women; and away from making rigid assumptions about what we should consider normal and desirable.

Concepts such as cognitive development, intelligence, thinking and creativity that used to be seen as limited by inheritance and fixed to particular age groups are now regarded as lifelong growth patterns that we can influence by our attitudes and behaviour.

Approaches to 'abnormal psychology' are changing and even the concept of 'abnormality' is in question. In some contexts, the emphasis has shifted away from the medical model of mental illness towards more flexible notions of mental health. There is fierce debate as to whether diagnostic categories, such as autism, can be regarded as extensions of normal behaviour and it is recognised that many variations, such as dyslexia, have advantages as well as disadvantages. Differences between individuals and the whole range of human diversity can be seen as something to welcome and celebrate rather than pigeon-holed as normal or abnormal.

theorists

4.2 Alphabetical list of key theorists and studies

The biographical information given here was correct at the time of submitting for publication, to the best of the author's ability. However, some individuals may have since died or changed affiliations or work in a field that has moved on so that the text is not necessarily current.

The length of each item does not reflect the importance of the individual within psychology but rather the nature of the work and whether it requires more explanation; whether it is dealt with elsewhere in this book and whether it can be found easily in basic textbooks.

Adler, Alfred (1870–1937)

Alfred Adler was an Austrian doctor who turned to psychiatry and joined Freud's Wednesday Psychological Society, later called the Vienna Psychoanalytic Society. He resigned due to growing differences in their respective theories. In particular, Adler disputed Freud's assertion that sex or libido is the fundamental drive which determines human behaviour.

Adler developed a psychodynamic approach to personality, based on detailed case histories, which he named 'Individual psychology'. This is the psychology of the unique, undivided personality and was influenced by Adler's belief in the social equality of all human beings, regardless of race, position, class or gender. He used early recollections, dream analysis and knowledge of birth order to analyse childhood experiences. A key principle is that faulty response patterns have developed to safeguard the person from the burden of excessive feelings of inferiority. In particular, the theory focuses on the idea that personality is influenced by birth order, with particular characteristics being linked to this. Adler (1927) proposes four major personality types: the Ruling Type, the Getting Type, the Avoiding Type and the Socially Useful Type. Ryckman (1989) suggests Adler offered this typology reluctantly as he strongly believed that each individual is unique, but found it useful in explaining the nature of healthy and unhealthy personalities.

In the last 11 years of his life, he devoted most of his time to teaching, lecturing and travelling in Europe and the United States, where he eventually settled.

Adorno, Theodor W. (1903–1969)

Theodor W. Adorno was an important philosopher and social critic in Germany after the Second World War and best known for the interdisciplinary character of his research and as a member of the Frankfurt School. Born Theodor Ludwig Wiesengrund, he adopted 'Adorno', his mother's surname, by which he is best known.

Although Adorno is of more importance to political studies, sociology, philosophy and related disciplines, he is recognised within psychology for his description of the authoritarian personality (see also Part 3), in relation to the political concepts of domination and hegemony (acceptance of domination). The Frankfurt School was a group of thinkers employed by the Institute for Social Research in Frankfurt, Germany, with ideas based on the work of Karl Marx. Other members included Max Horkheimer, Walter Benjamin and Herbert Marcuse. Adorno was also influenced by Hegel, Kant, Heidegger and Lukacs.

These intellectuals developed and practised

theorists

a mode of understanding called critical theory, which contrasts with critical rationalism. Whereas critical rationalism views society as a collection of autonomous individuals, critical theory views society as a totality in which each individual 'is determined by its mediation within that totality' (O'Connor, 2000: 174). These two theories of sociology disagree over the use of empirical research techniques. Critical rationalists believe that identifying and analysing the opinions of individuals within a society leads to an understanding of the society, but critical theorists believe that empirical research techniques cannot give insight into society because they will merely reflect the ideologies that society imposes on individuals.

According to Horkheimer and Adorno, people believe they will be free of fear only when there is no longer anything unknown and are trapped by an irrational fear of the unknown into a pattern of blind domination:

> domination of nature by human beings
> domination of nature within human beings
> domination of some human beings by others.

These concepts can usefully be compared with psychodynamic theories that seek to understand anxiety.

Ainsworth, Mary D. Salter (1913–1999)

Mary Ainsworth was an American developmental psychologist known for her work in early emotional attachment with 'The Strange Situation' as well as her work with John Bowlby in the development of Attachment Theory.

She married Leonard Ainsworth in 1950 and moved from Toronto to England, joining the research team at Tavistock Clinic investigating the effects of maternal separation on child development. Comparison of disrupted mother–child bonds with normal mother–child relationships showed that a child's lack of a mother figure leads to 'adverse development effects'. In 1954, she went to Africa, where she carried out her longitudinal field study of mother–infant interaction.

In the 1960s, she and her colleagues developed the Strange Situation Procedure, which is a widely used method of assessing an infant's pattern and style of attachment to a caregiver.

Two aspects of the child's behaviour are observed:

> the amount of exploration (for example playing with new toys) the child engages in throughout
> the child's reactions to the departure and return of its caregiver.

On the basis of their behaviour, the children can be categorised into three groups each of which reflects a different kind of attachment relationship with the mother:

> Secure attachment. The child will explore freely while the mother is present, engage with strangers, be visibly upset when the mother departs and happy to see the mother return.
> Anxious-ambivalent insecure attachment. The child is anxious of exploration and of strangers, even when the mother is present. When the mother departs, the child is extremely distressed. The child will be ambivalent when she returns, seeking to remain close to the mother but resentful, and also resistant when the mother initiates attention.
> Anxious-avoidant insecure attachment. The child will avoid or ignore the mother, showing little emotion on departure or return. The child will not explore much or display much emotional range regardless of who is there. Strangers will not be treated very differently from the mother.

Allport, Floyd Henry (1890–1971)

Floyd Allport was a psychologist in the combined psychology and philosophy department at Harvard until 1922, then professor for social psychology and political psychology at Syracuse University's Maxwell School of Citizenship and Public Affairs and visiting professor at University of California, Berkeley. He is considered the founder of social psychology as a scientific discipline. Floyd Henry Allport was the brother of Gordon Willard Allport.

He focused his dissertation research on a comparison of the performance of individuals acting alone and in groups, undertook an analysis of personality and discussion of the individual by describing the nature and measurement of innate traits (intelligence, motility, temperament) and acquired traits (drive, compensation, extroversion/introversion, insight, ascendance/submission; expansion/reclusion, sociality) and strongly influenced the development of social psychology.

theorists

Allport, Gordon Willard (1897–1967)

Gordon Allport was an American psychologist, youngest brother of Floyd Henry Allport, and an important figure at Harvard University from 1930 to 1967.

Allport has had a profound and lasting influence on the field of psychology, particularly with regard to his ideas on rumour, prejudice, religion and personality traits. Among his students were Anthony Greenwald, Stanley Milgram, Leo Postman, Thomas Pettigrew and M. Brewster Smith.

Allport was one of the first psychologists to focus on the study of personality. After an encounter with Freud in 1920 (see Allport, 1961), he rejected both psychoanalytic approaches to personality, which he thought went too deep, too quickly, and behavioural approaches, which did not go deep enough. He emphasised the uniqueness of each individual and the relative importance of conscious experience of the present context compared with past history and unconscious memories. See Part 3 *Personality* and *Personality traits*.

Aronson, Elliot (current)

Elliot Aronson is Professor Emeritus in Social Psychology at the University of California in Santa Cruz. He is known for his work on prejudice and racialism. In 1971, Aronson and colleagues in Austin, Texas, developed the 'jigsaw classroom technique' to encourage co-operation rather than competition between students. Each child in a jigsaw classroom works as a member of a small team with individual responsibility for researching and learning one particular aspect of a class project. All students are then brought together for presentation of their items and discussion and all the material presented is used towards a class quiz. This technique can lead to academic and social improvements. Aronson continues his research interests in social influence and attitude change, cognitive dissonance, research methodology, and interpersonal attraction.

Asch, Solomon E. (1907–1996)

Dr Solomon E. Asch was an Emeritus Professor of Psychology at Penn University and is best known for the 1950s Asch experiment, a study of conformity.

Asch showed diagrams of bars (see website) to male college students in groups of eight to ten. He told them he was studying visual perception and that their task was to choose the bar from three on the right that was the same length as the one on the left and give their answers aloud. He repeated the procedure with 18 sets of bars. Only one student in each group was a genuine participant, all the others were confederates who had been instructed to give incorrect answers on 12 of the 18 trials. Asch arranged for the real participant to be the next-to-the-last person in each group to announce the answer so that he would hear most of the confederates' incorrect responses before giving his own. While most participants answered correctly, many showed extreme discomfort. Control participants with no exposure to a majority view had no trouble giving the correct answer.

Asch was surprised and disturbed by these results and as a consequence of these and other studies, social psychologists have come to distinguish between two different types of social influence: informational and normative (see also *Conformity* in Part 3). Informational influence occurs when group members are persuaded by the content of what they read or hear to accept a particular opinion; Sherif's study (see below and in Part 3) appears to be an example. Normative influence occurs when group members are persuaded by the knowledge that a majority of group members take a particular position. Normative influence should not be confused with compliance, which occurs when group members are not persuaded but merely voice the opinions of the group majority. Although some of the participants in the Asch studies who conformed admitted that they had complied, the ones mentioned above who believed the majority to be correct are best considered to have been persuaded through normative influence.

Atkinson, Richard C. and Shiffrin, Richard M. (current)

Richard C. Atkinson is President of the University of California. Richard M. Shiffrin is Luther Dana Waterman Professor of Psychology at the University of Indiana. Their early work together at Stanford University contributed to behavioural models of memory.

Earlier behavioural models of memory (for example, James, 1890/1981; Hebb, 1949; Broadbent, 1958; Waugh and Norman, 1965) distinguished only between short-term (STM) and long-term memory (LTM) and suggested that memories go into a long-term memory store (LTS) from the short-term memory store (STS) after a process of rehearsal. Atkinson and Shiffrin (for example 1971) added sensory memory as a preliminary stage.

Models based on these simple ideas are known as multistore, gateway or dual-process models. Diagrams imply that memory resembles a set of boxes and that there is a simple progression through the stages of storage. This idea was based on experimental data involving regulated tasks of memorising. Alternative views of memory are given by the levels of processing approach of Craik and Lockhart (1972) and Neisser (1976), the dynamic memory theory of Schank (1982) and the concepts of working memory and central executive system (Baddeley and Hitch, 1974). Information-processing approaches have led to short-term and long-term processes being viewed as much more complicated than behavioural experiments could reveal.

As with other 'stages' models throughout psychology, the pioneering ideas have been superseded but these theories of human memory were influential in shaping research in the field and helped clarify the relationship between brain structures and psychological phenomena, the effects of drugs on memory and the formulation of techniques that optimise the learning process. See also Part 3.

Baddeley, Alan D. and Hitch, Graham (current)

Alan Baddeley and Graham Hitch are professors of psychology at York University.

According to Baddeley (1990), sensory memory is the initial registration of information in the senses, lasting up to 100 milliseconds and representing a stage of memory before information is processed by the brain, for example the *persistence of vision*. Short-term memory (STM) usually refers to storage of a few seconds, involving higher mental processes in the cortex of the brain, such as remembering a telephone number for long enough to dial it.

Baddeley and Hitch (1974) and Baddeley (1990) suggest that short-term memory functions as a set of subsystems acting as temporary working memory systems and enabling us to perform a range of cognitive tasks. Baddeley and Hitch conceive the working memory as

consisting of a controlling central executive system and a number of subsidiary slave systems. When concurrent processing is required (that is, maintaining a memory and doing another attention-demanding task at the same time), the central executive helps to co-ordinate these tasks in the slave systems. Two such slave systems are the phonological (sound) loop and the visuo-spatial sketchpad. The visuo-spatial sketchpad or scratchpad refers to the rehearsing of items as visual images in terms of how and where they would occur in the normal visual field. An example would be imagining a football game while listening to a radio broadcast. When someone is trying to solve a problem, visual and sound memories are brought into consciousness or short-term working memory, where they can be continuously rehearsed via the visual sketchpad or sound loop. Memory traces of the sounds of words in the phonological store are assumed to fade and become unretrievable after 1.5–2.0 seconds but can be refreshed by subvocal rehearsal or inner speech, which feeds back into the store. The memory span will be determined by how many items can be refreshed before they fade away. This plays an important role in learning to read. Other sensory memories may also be involved in different slave systems. If there are too many items for the slave systems to cope with, some items can be transferred to long-term memory, which acts as a back-up. These processes are organised by the central executive system until the problem is solved and the solution committed to either paper or long-term memory.

LTM can be subdivided into episodic or auto-biographical, and semantic. This separates things remembered in the context in which they were first encountered and those remembered independently of how they were learned. Procedural and remote memories can also be regarded as distinct systems. Baddeley and Hitch (1974) propose that there is transfer in both directions between short-term and long-term memory. Procedural memory (PM) was defined by Tulving (1985), Anderson (1985) and others as information from long-term memory that cannot be readily articulated. It includes memories of activities that we know how to do but cannot readily describe and corresponds to muscle memory or Bruner's (1964) enactive mode of representation. This kind of memory seems to be handled in the *cerebellum* of the brain and can remain intact even if other kinds of memory are lost through brain damage (for an example, *see* the description of Clive Wearing, in Blakemore, 1988; Baddeley, 1990; Gross, 1996). Activities such as playing a musical instrument, juggling, riding a bicycle and driving seem to involve this kind of memory.

Changes in STM are very varied. Studies of STM loss distinguish between capacity and duration. It is found that there can be significant changes in some tasks with no noticeable difference in others. For example, a person may have difficulty recalling words presented aurally but no difficulty with visual presentations. This can be explained in terms of Baddeley and Hitch's (1974) concept of working memory. The subsystems appear to be independent and are assumed to be processed in different parts of the brain. Investigations also show that a person may have no trouble recalling single items, presented either aurally or visually, but will make errors with two or more items. Or there may be severe difficulty in recalling more than one item presented as either an aural or a visual stimulus, but less difficulty when both types of presentation are given simultaneously for each item (Warrington and Shallice, 1969). Simple STM span shows little or no decline with age. However, when extra demands are placed on participants, the age effects generally become apparent. Backward span procedure and concurrent processing indicate that elderly people are significantly worse at these tasks. Baddeley (1982) suggests that the central executive is the prime cause of this age-related decline.

Bales, Robert Freed (1916–2004)

Robert Bales was Professor Emeritus of Social Relations at Harvard University and a member of the Harvard Project with Talcott Parsons, Gordon W. Allport, Henry A. Murray and Clyde M. Kluckhohn. He published the first important research study of small group communication in a series of books and articles in the early and mid-1950s (for example, Bales, 1950, 1953; Bales and Strodtbeck, 1951). This research entailed the *content analysis* of discussions within groups making decisions about human relations problems (vignettes about relationship difficulties within families or organisations).

Bales made a series of important discoveries. First, group discussion tends to shift back and forth relatively quickly between the discussion of the group task and discussion relevant to the relationship among the members. He believed that this shifting was the product of an implicit attempt to balance the demands of task completion and group cohesiveness, under the presumption that conflict generated during task-relevant discussion causes stress among members, which must be released through positive relational talk. Second, task-relevant group discussion shifts across time from an emphasis on opinion exchange through attentiveness to values underlying the decision to making the decision itself. This implication that group discussion goes through the same series of stages in the same order for any decision-making group is known as the *linear phase model*. Third, the most talkative member of a group tends to make between 40 and 50 per cent of the comments and the second most talkative member between 25 and 30, no matter the size of the group. As a consequence, large groups tend to be dominated by one or two members to the detriment of the others.

He developed the Bales interaction process analysis and the SYMLOG system. SYMLOG is an acronym for System for the Multiple Level Observation of Groups. See Part 3.

Bandura, Albert (current)

Canadian born, Albert Bandura is David Starr Jordan Professor of Social Science in Psychology at Stanford University. His main area of focus is personality. One line of research concerns how people regulate their own motivation, thought patterns, affective states and behaviour through beliefs of personal and collective efficacy (see also *Self-efficacy* in Part 3). Other research examines the role of self-regulatory mechanisms relying on internal standards and self-influence in human self-development, adaptation and change. This work is related to sociocognitive development, 'affect' regulation, health promotion and disease prevention, organisational functioning and collective action for social change.

He is best known for his 'bobo doll' studies (Bandura and Walters, 1963) on observational learning and modelling of aggression, in which children tended to copy the aggressive behaviour of a 'model' adult without direct reinforcement.

Bandura had previously observed aggression in adolescents and concluded that they learned vicariously from watching their parents and other influences rather than through reinforcement of behaviour or punishment. Rejecting behavioural and psychoanalytical approaches, he developed a social learning theory and then in the 1980s, social cognitive theory. He was one of the first to develop ideas about self-efficacy. In his view, people are self-organising, planning, self-reflecting and self-regulating, not just reactive organisms shaped by environmental forces or driven by concealed inner impulses. Human functioning is the product of a dynamic and reciprocal interplay of personal, behavioural and environmental influences.

Baron-Cohen, Simon (current)

Simon Baron-Cohen is Professor of Developmental Psychopathology at the University of Cambridge and a fellow at Trinity College, Cambridge. He is Director of the Autism Research Centre (ARC) in Cambridge.

Theory of mind suggests that autism is due to an inability to infer the mental states of others, and that people with autism have difficulty performing tasks where they must infer another person's mental state (Baron-Cohen, 2000). People with Asperger's syndrome cope with simple tasks about the beliefs of others, but appear to do so through using conscious, effortful strategies, rather than normal automatic processing.

Research on the cognitive deficits and neurology of individuals with autism suggests the presence of abnormalities in a number of areas and it is extremely difficult to point to one particular area of the brain and say that damage to that one structure causes autism. Evidence indicates multiple deficits in the structure and function of the brain in individuals with autism. There is strong evidence supporting one of the major theories of autism, known as the limbic system theory, which suggests that damage to the amygdala and the frontal cortex contributes highly to what appears to be the primary symptom of autism, social impairment. Research on the neurobiology of autism shows some promising leads, but it is a difficult subject to pin down, and more research in all areas is needed in order to develop a fuller understanding of autism.

He is author of the DVD-ROM *Mind Reading: an interactive guide to emotions* (Jessica Kingsley Ltd, 2003).

Bartlett, Frederic Charles (1886–1969)

Sir Frederic Charles Bartlett was a British cognitive psychologist between the World Wars, when memory had only just started to be considered a psychological rather than a philosophical subject. From 1922 to 1952 at Cambridge University, Bartlett was Reader in Experimental Psychology, Director of the Psychology Laboratory, succeeding C. S. Myers, and first Professor of Experimental Psychology. He was elected a Fellow of the Royal Society in 1932 and knighted in 1948 for services to the Royal Air Force, on the basis of his wartime work in applied psychology.

Bartlett influenced the course of British psychology as an administrator and an educator and is best known for his studies of memory and social psychology. He is still the foremost figure in the constructivist school of memory research, which holds that we do not retain a perfect copy of events that we experienced, but have to reconstruct them when we want to remember them, an approach that conflicted with the behaviourist approach dominant in American psychology at that time.

In Bartlett's most famous experiment, his participants read a Native American story about ghosts and retold the tale later. He observed that recall was not duplicative but represented a reconstruction of the original story or picture based on memories of key details. The participants' backgrounds were different from the cultural context of the story, so they changed details that were unfamiliar or that they could not understand.

Bartlett's findings led him to propose 'schema': the cultural and historical contexts of memory, which have important implications for eyewitness testimony, false memory syndrome and for artificial intelligence. He noted the essential role that affect or emotion plays in cognition, claiming that affect serves as the basis for thinking and remembering. More recently, Susan Fiske, (2004) with her concept of schema-triggered affect, builds on Bartlett's work. (See also Damasio, below.)

Bem, Sandra Lipsitz (current)

Sandra Bem is Director of Women's Studies and Professor of Psychology at Cornell University.

In 1971 she created the Bem Sex Role Inventory (BSRI) in which she states that her instrument measures both feminine and masculine traits in men and women, giving a score on two scales, unlike other tests which tend to use a single scale from masculine to feminine. Bem asserts that these traits that are commonly linked to one gender can apply to either and argues that:

> The concept of psychological androgyny implies that it is possible for an individual to be both compassionate and assertive, both expressive and instrumental, both feminine and masculine, depending upon the situational appropriateness of these various modalities. And it further implies that an individual may even blend these complementary modalities in a single act, such as the ability to fire an employee, if the circumstances warrant it, but with sensitivity for the human emotion that such an act inevitably produces.

Bem Sex Role Inventory Manual

The BSRI contains 60 personality characteristics or trait names. Twenty of the characteristics are stereotypically feminine (for example, affectionate, gentle, understanding, sensitive to the needs of others), 20 are stereotypically masculine (for example, ambitious, self-reliant, independent, assertive) and the remaining 20 are gender neutral or filler items (for example, truthful, happy, conceited). Individuals rate themselves as possessing the characteristic on a *Likert-type* scale from one to seven, including never or almost never true to always or almost always true. If individuals score high on both the feminine and masculine scales they are seen as androgynous. If the individual's scores are below the median of 4.5 on both the feminine and masculine characteristics they are seen as undifferentiated (1974). Along with the belief that masculinity and femininity are separate, Bem also believed androgynous individuals who possessed both masculine and feminine traits were 'truly effective and well functioning' (O'Connell and Russo, 1990: 33). The BSRI was designed for conducting empirical research on psychological androgyny. It is also used for workshops and counselling on gender awareness.

Lenses of Gender (Bem, 1993), examines the concepts of masculinity and femininity. She begins (1993: 1) by stating what she sees as western society's main beliefs concerning men and women, including:

> that they have fundamentally different psychological and sexual natures
> that men are inherently the dominant or superior sex
> that male–female differences and male dominance are natural, either God-given or as a natural product of human evolution.

These ideas, according to Bem, shape our everyday lives. She labels these beliefs as:

> Androcentrism or 'male-centredness' describes how society is structured. Male experiences are seen as the norm and female experiences as not the norm, that is men are treated as people and women as 'other'.
> Gender polarisation uses the differences between men and women to structure society such that the masculine way of doing something is usually seen as the correct way.
> Biological essentialism argues that since men and women are biologically sexually different, then they must play different roles in life.

The social structure that is created as a result of these beliefs separates men and women unequally and because these beliefs are taught through socialisation, many individuals continue to reinforce them while living by them.

Berne, Eric (1910–1970)

Eric Berne was born in Canada, trained in psychiatry and worked at the Psychiatric Clinic of Yale University School of Medicine, then at Mt Zion Hospital, New York City, until 1943 when he went into the Army Medical Corps. He began training as a psychoanalyst in 1941 at the New York Psychoanalytic Institute and underwent analysis with Paul Federn and later with Erik Erikson. He wanted to add something new to psychoanalysis and developed the concept of ego states and the separation of 'adult' from 'child', later introducing the tripartite scheme of parent, adult and child, with a series of three-circle diagrams to illustrate different patterns of interaction that became known as *transactional analysis*. According to Dr Berne, games are ritualistic transactions or behaviour patterns between individuals that can indicate hidden feelings or emotions.

Bernstein, Basil (1924–2000)

Basil Bernstein was professor and head of the

sociological research unit at the Institute of Education in London.

In his most cited work, he argued (Bernstein, 1973) that children's use of language is partly determined by the social environment in which they grow up. He distinguished between two styles or patterns of speech that he called restricted and elaborated code. The restricted code is relatively simple and descriptive, relating to concrete examples that are context dependent. The elaborated code is more complex and involves abstract concepts that can be understood without knowledge of the context. He believed that language is necessary for thinking and held that children with access only to a restricted code would not be able to think in abstract terms. Since the restricted code was found in lower-class situations, this implied that lower-class children would be disadvantaged in an education system that used elaborated code and abstract concepts. This approach is disputed by William Labov, see below.

Bettelheim, Bruno (1903–1990)

Bruno Bettelheim taught psychology at the University of Chicago (1944–73) and directed the Chicago-based Orthogenic School for children with emotional problems, placing special emphasis on the treatment of autism.

Bettleheim, who had spent time in a Nazi concentration camp, believed he saw parallels between the behaviour of some camp prisoners and autistic children. He believed that autistic children had been raised in unstimulating environments during the first few years of their lives, when language and motor skills were developing, and suggested that autism was a psychological disturbance arising from detached and 'frigid' mothering – similar to the way prisoners reacted to the cold authority of camp guards. This led to the concept of the 'refrigerator mother' which was adopted by medical orthodoxy for many years, blaming autism on the mother's failure to bond with her child. In his later work he used Winnicott's concept of 'good enough mothering'.

In his book, *The Uses of Enchantment* (1976), Bruno Bettleheim discusses from a Freudian perspective the importance of fairy tales to the healthy development of young children. Bettleheim believes that fairy tales are expressions of our cultural heritage and represent 'in imaginative form what the process of healthy human development consists of … [and] make great and positive psychological contributions to the child's inner growth'. A child's preference for a certain fairy tale is a result of 'what the tale evokes in his conscious and unconscious mind' in terms of his 'needs of the moment'.

His theories on autism have been discredited but he authored a number of influential works on child development.

Bion, Wilfred Ruprecht (1897–1979)

W. R. Bion was Director of the London Clinic of Psycho-Analysis (1956–62) and President of the British Psycho-Analytical Society (1962–5). From 1968 he worked in Los Angeles.

Bion was trained by Melanie Klein and developed ideas relating to the carer as *'container for emotions'*. He considered 'no mother is bad at everything', an idea related to Winnicott's description of 'good enough mothering'. Other ideas associated with Bion include the need to know when to stop digging, the recognition that it can sometimes be helpful to give back feelings, and the separation of person and behaviour, which helps people to clarify attributions. These ideas are developed in humanistic approaches. He is particularly well known for his studies of groups, during which he took the role of passive observer and waited to see what would happen. This upset many participants who did not know how to respond positively to a non-directive approach. Their complaints and other behaviour led him to identify three types of group behaviour: fight–flight, dependent and pairing (Bion, 1961).

Blakemore, Colin (current)

Colin Blakemore is a British neurobiologist specialising in vision, and Chief Executive of the British Medical Research Council (MRC). He studied at Cambridge and the University of California in Berkeley. He was on the staff of Cambridge University from 1967 until 1979, when he became professor of physiology at Oxford.

His research has focused on vision, the early development of the brain and Huntington's and Alzheimer's disease. In his early experimental work, Blakemore showed that cells in the visual cortex of the brain of a newborn kitten are able to detect visual outlines. If, at a critical period, the kitten is kept in a restricted environment with, say, only vertical lines, it will later prove to have in the cortex only cells that can recognise these patterns and not others. Other work has involved rearing kittens without any visual experience. Blakemore has stated that the work on cats is directly applicable to humans and that thanks to it, and similar research, we now know why conditions like amblyopia (the most common form of child blindness) occur and are now able to tackle it and think of ways of preventing it.

Throughout his career he has made television programmes and delivered public lectures intended to further the understanding and acceptance of science. He has called for reform of the education system, including a broader curriculum to replace A-levels and allow sixth-formers to study both science and the arts, as they do in most of Europe and the United States. As an academic adviser to the government Blakemore has worked on the health implications of mobile telephones and advised the Home Office and the Police Federation on telecommunications.

He is known to the public as the target of a long-running animal-rights campaign. Blakemore is outspoken in his support of the use of animal testing in medical research but has publicly denounced animal testing for cosmetics.

He was director of the MRC Centre for Cognitive Neuroscience for eight years and, in 1989, was awarded the Royal Society's Michael Faraday Prize for excellence in communicating science to UK audiences. He has also served as president of the Biosciences Federation, British Neuroscience Association, the Physiological Society, and President and Chairman of the British Association for the Advancement of Science.

Bowlby, John (1907–1990)

Bowlby, a paediatrician, was a British developmental psychologist in the Freudian psychoanalytic tradition, noted for his pioneering work in attachment theory. (See also Ainsworth above.) In 1945, Bowlby became Head of the Children's Department at the Tavistock Clinic, then Deputy Director, and from 1950, Mental Health Consultant to the World Health Organisation.

He studied mother–child relationships and considered the effects on a child's behaviour when bonds are prematurely broken, unduly strained or not properly formed. According to the gender norms of the time, Bowlby believed that mothers were the primary attachment figure in children's lives. He is associated with explanations of juvenile and adult delinquency in terms of the problem of the 'unwanted child'. His work (for example, 1953, 1988) has had a powerful influence on the hospital practice of allowing parents to stay with their children.

Broadbent, Donald E. (1926–1993)

Donald E. Broadbent was an influential British experimental psychologist who focused on what became cognitive psychology. He became Director of the Applied Psychology Research Unit at the University of Cambridge which had been set up by the UK Medical Research Council (MRC).

He developed theories of selective attention and short-term memory. His Filter Model proposed that people focus attention on only a single audible message according to the physical characteristics (for example, pitch, loudness) and irrelevant messages are filtered out before the stimulus information is processed for meaning. These characteristics are referred to as 'early selection' and 'single channel'.

Bruner, Jerome S. (current)

Jerome Bruner is Research Professor of Psychology and Senior Research Fellow in Law at New York University. He is interested in the various institutional forms by which culture is passed on.

In the 1960s, Bruner became interested in the processes by which a child progresses. He suggests there are no distinct stages but a gradual development of competence in mental representation and integration. Bruner (1964) identifies three ways of mentally representing recurrent regularities of the environment: enactive, iconic and symbolic. At first the child thinks only through actions, but gradually develops the ability to hold mental images in the form of pictures of objects and activities and then use substitute objects and language to symbolically stand for the objects and activities. Bruner suggests that all activity is intentional and that the child learns to make links between an intention to do something, the activity itself and the feedback it receives about the success of the activity. This happens more readily if surprising and conflicting events are observed. Bruner believes concepts can only develop if attention is paid to language. That is, language comes before thinking. He recommends a spiral curriculum in which students revisit topic areas according to a carefully planned timetable so that the same content is covered repeatedly at new levels of understanding and language. He argues that early development will be assisted if education does not try to introduce logical reasoning at an early age but centres on guided discovery learning in which the teacher makes full use of language and introduces opportunities for observing similar and contrasting situations. In a clinical or educational setting, this might mean introducing a child to some of the language associated with activities but without attempting rational explanations.

Vocabulary associated with Bruner includes: skilled activity (intention, activities, feedback), *representation* (enactive, iconic, symbolic), integration (comparing and contrasting, sorting), spiral curriculum.

Bryant, Peter (current)

Peter Bryant is Visiting Professor of Psychology at Oxford Brookes University, and Emeritus Fellow of Wolfson College, Oxford. Like Margaret Donaldson (see below), Bryant is indebted to Piaget for setting the scene, since the controversies arising from the early theory have led to much exciting and productive exploration of children's and adults' minds (Bryant, 1982). Bryant rejects Piaget's conclusions about why children fail in certain set tasks and argues that children can think logically providing they know what is being asked and can concentrate and remember for long enough. He has demonstrated that children use different strategies at different times and, like Donaldson, suggests that education needs to take account of individual differences. His ideas can be compared with those of Wason (see below and for example Wason and Johnson-Laird, 1968) who has demonstrated that adults also use different strategies in different situations and for different tasks. Wason argues that adults pay more attention to the overall meaning of a situation than to the rules of pure logic. When given a task which is removed from social reality, adults make the same logic errors as children and give an answer which is personally meaningful rather than strictly logical. The differences between children and adults, both Wason and Bryant would agree, are due to experience and to attention span and memory, not to a fundamental difference in choice of strategy or ability to think logically.

Burt, Cyril Lodowic (1883–1971)

Sir Cyril Burt was a British educational psychologist, Professor and Chair of Psychology at University College, London, and a member of the London School of Differential Psychology.

Burt was interested in psychometrics and was a consultant with the committees that developed the 11-Plus examinations. He supported eugenics and was a member of the British Eugenics Society. He was influenced by Francis Galton, William McDougall, Charles Spearman and Sir Charles Sherrington, and in turn influenced Raymond Cattell and Hans Eysenck.

Some of his work was controversial for its conclusions that genetics substantially influences mental and behavioural traits. After his death, he was accused of scientific fraud when data concerning his twin studies were shown to be unreliable. Many of Burt's supporters believe the discrepancies were mostly caused by negligence rather than deliberate deception.

Cannon, Walter Bradford (1871–1945)

From 1906, W. B. Cannon was George Higginson Professor of Physiology and chair of the Harvard Department of Physiology. Cannon is remembered for his work (1915, 1929) with animals that showed that when strongly aroused, the sympathetic division of the autonomic nervous system combines with the hormone adrenaline to mobilise the animal for an emergency response of 'flight or fight' (see Part 3). He coined the term 'homeostasis' for the maintenance of steady states in the body and the physiological processes through which they are regulated. Cannon turned increasing attention to the clinical implications of his physiological discoveries, becoming a major authority in the emerging research field of *psychosomatic* medicine (Cannon, 1945).

He is often cited for the Cannon–Bard theory of emotion, which suggests that people feel emotions first and then act upon them. These actions may include physiological changes in muscular tension and perspiration. This theory contrasts with the James–Lange theory of emotion of the 1800s (see Part 3), which suggested that emotion results from perception of the reaction or physiological change.

Cattell, Raymond Bernard (1905–1998)

Raymond B. Cattell moved to the United States

from Britain, becoming Professor of Psychology at the University of Illinois in 1945 and then Emeritus Professor in 1974.

Cattell was interested in psychological measurement and mainly concerned with the concepts of intelligence and personality. Following the work of Charles E. Spearman and L. L. Thurstone, who used *factor analysis* to try to determine whether intelligence consisted of one general factor or several primary mental abilities, Cattell, together with Philip E. Vernon, suggested that mental abilities are hierarchical.

At the top of the hierarchy is Spearman's 'g' or general factor, then successive levels of gradually narrowing abilities, then specific abilities such as Thurstone's seven primary mental abilities of verbal comprehension, verbal fluency, number, spatial visualisation, *inductive reasoning*, *memory* and perceptual speed (*inspection time*) that are related to particular tests.

Cattell further suggested that general ability can be subdivided into fluid and crystallised intelligence, sometimes abbreviated to wit and wisdom. Fluid abilities (wit) are the reasoning and problem-solving abilities measured by tests such as analogies, classifications and series completions, and these increase early in life but decline with age. Crystallised abilities (wisdom) are derived from fluid abilities and include specific knowledge, vocabulary and general information, and these continue to increase over the life span.

In the field of personality, Cattell used factor analysis in an attempt to reduce the several thousand words that represent traits to the smallest possible number of trait clusters. He developed the 16 personality factor test of personality (now available as 16PF Fifth Edition), which covers 16 bipolar dimensions of personality. This test is widely used by psychologists and counsellors for occupational guidance, personnel selection, clinical diagnosis, marital counselling and student counselling.

In *Personality and Learning Theory* (1979–80) he proposes an integrated theory of human development that includes intellect, temperament and dynamic aspects of personality in the environmental and cultural context.

Chomsky, Avram Noam (current)

Noam Chomsky is the Institute Professor Emeritus of Linguistics at the Massachusetts Institute of Technology, specialising in linguistic theory, syntax, semantics and philosophy of language. He contributed to the cognitive revolution in psychology through his review of B. F. Skinner's *Verbal Behavior*, in which he challenged the behaviourist approach to the study of mind and language dominant in the 1950s. His naturalistic approach to the study of language has also affected the philosophy of language and mind.

He argues that children have an innate ability to learn languages, similar steps are followed by children all across the world when learning languages, and children make certain characteristic errors as they learn their first language, whereas other seemingly logical kinds of errors never occur. According to Chomsky, human language is a 'biological object' and should be analysed using the methodology of the sciences.

He is known for his distinction between the deep structure and the surface structure of language. That is, we can give the same meaning (deep structure) using different words (surface structure). For example, Wordsworth's 'I wandered lonely as a cloud' has the same deep structure as 'I walked about a bit on my own, feeling lonely'. See also *Beliefs*, *Grammatical representation*, *Mentalese*.

Craik, Fergus I. M. and Lockhart, Robert S. (current)

Fergus I. M. Craik (from Scotland) and Robert S. Lockhart (from Sydney) are professors in psychology at the University of Toronto.

Craik and Lockhart (1972) proposed a 'levels of processing' (LOP) model of memory in which the durability of memory is seen as a direct function of the depth of processing rather than of the structures of short and long-term memory. Items that have been more deeply processed will be retained for a longer period of time. Two types of rehearsal are identified:

> maintenance rehearsal, which simply repeats items in the form in which they were presented and which probably restricts them to short-term memory

> elaborative rehearsal, which includes additional associations and meanings and which can serve to transfer items into long-term memory.

Three levels are suggested:

> structural or shallow level, associated with visual physical appearance (with words this corresponds to the visual appearance of the word)

> phonetic or phonemic level, associated with sounds (with words this corresponds to the sound of the word)

> semantic level, associated with meanings. (See also *semantic memory* in Part 3.)

Damasio, Antonio R. (current)

Antonio Damsio is David Dornsife Professor of Neuroscience, Neurology and Psychology at the University of Southern California, where he directs the new Brain and Creativity Institute. He is also adjunct professor at the Salk Institute and at the University of Iowa. His research interests include the neurobiology of the mind; specifically, the understanding of the neural systems which subserve memory, language, emotion, and decision-making. His clinical interests are disorders of behaviour and cognition and movement disorders.

He became particularly well known for his book *Descartes' Error*, in which he discusses the relationship between emotion and cognition. He challenges traditional ideas about the connection between emotion and rationality, arguing that emotions are not silly or a luxury but essential to rational thinking and to normal social behaviour as they enable us to give *value* to decisions.

De Bono, Edward (current)

Edward de Bono is a psychologist and writer who has held appointments at the universities of Oxford, London, Cambridge and Harvard and is now involved with a number of organisations to promote the skills of thinking, including the Cognitive Research Trust, Cambridge (Director since 1971), and the Supranational Independent Thinking Organization (Secretary-general since 1983).He is regarded by many to be the leading authority in the world in the field of creative thinking and the direct teaching of thinking as a skill. He coined the term *lateral thinking*, which treats creativity as the behaviour of information in any self-organising information system, for example the neural networks in the brain.

Dennett, Daniel Clement (current)

Daniel C. Dennett is Austin B. Fletcher Professor of Philosophy and Co-director of the Centre for Cognitive Studies at Tufts University, Medford, Massachusetts.

Like Damasio (above) and others, he challenges Descartes' dual notion of the mind and observer. Dennett sets out methods for studying consciousness and built a model of consciousness as a cognitive system, and discusses whether there is a difference between how a mental state functions in us and how it feels to us (qualia or felt quality), what 'self' might be and the neural implementation of consciousness. He claims that language enables us to have the kind of mind that can co-operate with other minds and record the results of co-operation for others to build on.

A core idea relevant to psychology is that, when describing, explaining and predicting behaviour, we can choose to view it at varying levels of abstraction. The most concrete is the physical stance, where we are concerned with measurable physical or chemical quantities such as mass, length, time, energy, velocity and chemical composition. More abstract is the design stance, which is concerned with things such as purpose, function and design, as found in biology and engineering. Most abstract is the intentional stance, which concerns belief, thinking and intent, as in software and minds.

Deutsch, J. Anthony and Deutsch, Diana (current)

J. Anthony Deutsch is Emeritus Professor and Diana Deutsch is Professor of Psychology at University of California, San Diego. Her research interests include perception and memory for sounds, particularly music. Their most frequently cited works concern selective attention, from studies carried out at Stanford.

Comparing Broadbent (1958), see above, and Treisman (1960), see below, they say that perhaps it was after all the central nervous system that was doing the selecting underlying attention. They sought to explain how the central nervous system could select a perceptual stream after it had sorted and analysed all the incoming information. The mechanism they postulated compared the various arriving signals with a shifting reference standard that took up the level of the most pertinent arriving signal. Only the signal reaching the level of this reference standard switched in further processes, such as motor output, memory

theorists

storage and other correlates of awareness. They assumed that this stage of awareness is only reached after a decision is made to deal with a percept that is already formed:

> The reason why our paper has been so widely cited is probably two-fold. The first is that it gave a clear alternative to Filter theory, and therefore stimulated a great deal of discussion and experimental work. The second is that it was written in a field which was small at the time but which has since expanded enormously. While the distinction between perceptual and attentional processes no longer seems as clear as it once was, many of the problems that were there when the paper was written are still with us and still challenge experimental ingenuity.
>
> (www.garfield.library.upenn.edu/, accessed June 2007.)

Donaldson, Margaret (current)

Margaret Donaldson is Emeritus Professor of Psychology at Edinburgh University. Donaldson greatly respects Piaget's work but rejects certain features. She has investigated why some children find school work difficult or boring and strongly believes that education based on Piaget's theory of stages severely underestimates children's capacity for rational thought. She has shown that if children are in a meaningful setting and able to use language that makes sense to them in ordinary human terms, they are very often able to perform tasks and explain what they are doing in ways which Piaget would have thought impossible. Donaldson (1978) recommends that teachers should take account of children's conceptions by listening carefully to each child's explanation and then build on what the child already knows. For example, when trying to explain a procedure, the teacher must listen carefully to how a child describes what happens. What the teacher then says or does will depend on each individual child's preconceptions. Explanation should encourage reasoning and problem-solving skills carefully linked to concrete examples using appropriate language. Tasks can be devised which assist attention and concentration, memory and imagination. Donaldson also stresses the importance of reading in the development of language and thinking. The teacher should be clear about the intentions of

a task so the child understands what is expected. It is also important for the teacher to give 'real' explanations, based on thorough understanding of the concepts, not something superficial, learned by rote, muddled up with faulty preconceptions or using 'baby' language that obscures meaning. In a health-care setting, this would mean listening carefully to each individual child to discover what preconceptions he or she has and what kind of language the child uses. Play preparation might involve interacting closely with the child, building on previous knowledge and understanding, encouraging the child to work out explanations, introducing useful language and guiding towards appropriate concepts.

Ebbinghaus, Hermann (1850–1909)

Hermann Ebbinghaus was a German experimental psychologist and professor at Berlin and Breslau. Ebbinghaus gave psychology a quantitative and experimental basis and developed the first scientific approach to the study of memory. He introduced the use of nonsense syllables in learning and memory research and was the first to describe the 'learning curve': that is, increasing the amount of material to be learned usually dramatically increases the amount of time it takes to learn it.

His experiments demonstrated that meaningless stimuli are more difficult to memorise than meaningful stimuli, that relearning is easier than initial learning, and that it takes longer to forget material after each subsequent re-learning. Ebbinghaus's work also suggested that learning is more effective when repetitions are spaced out over time.

Elliot, Jane (current)

Jane Elliott is an internationally known teacher, lecturer and diversity trainer, and recipient of the National Mental Health Association Award for Excellence in Education.

In 1968, as a teacher in a small all-white Iowa town, Jane tried a direct exercise to bring the truth home about racial discrimination.

On the first day Jane Elliott told her pupils that people with blue-eyes were cleverer, quicker, more likely to succeed. They were superior to people with brown eyes, who were untrustworthy, lazy and stupid. She marked the 'inferior' brown-eyed children with ribbons, and frequently praised the

theorists

blue-eyed children, giving them extra classroom privileges while being negative to the browns. Jane Elliott was amazed at the rapid transformation in her class. The superior blue-eyed children became arrogant, bossy and unpleasant to their brown-eyed class mates. The brown eyes quickly became cowed and timid. Much more astonishing was the difference academically. Blue-eyed children improved their grades and speed with mathematical and reading tasks but the brown eyes deteriorated.

On the following day, Jane Elliott told her class that she had the information the wrong way round, and swapped the colour superiorities over. The brown-eyed children tore off their now-hated ribbons, and the situations quickly reversed.

Jane Elliott showed – more dramatically than she had ever thought possible – how much discrimination is absorbed unconsciously, by both the oppressor and the oppressed. She treated them differently but she had not told her pupils to treat each other differently, only that they *were* different; and yet they developed the characteristic responses of discrimination. Jane Elliott felt that they did this because they had already learned discriminatory behaviour from their parents and other adults. On the plus side, she also showed that racism can be unlearnt. She had also found an excellent way of demonstrating what it feels like to be the object of discrimination.

After the exercise the children went home and told their parents that racism was wrong, and it was a lesson that stayed with them. Reunions and interviews have shown that the children remember the exercise and are positively affected by it, feeling that it makes them more empathic and sensitive.

As news of her exercise spread, she was invited to appear on television shows, and repeat the exercise in professional training days for adults. In the 1980s she left schoolteaching to become a full-time 'diversity trainer'. She takes the Brown Eyes/Blue Eyes exercise, and other work, out to colleges and government, professional and community groups across the world.

Ellis, Albert (1913–2007)

Albert Ellis was an American cognitive-behavioural therapist who developed Rational Emotive Behaviour Therapy (REBT) in the 1950s. Ellis founded and was the President Emeritus of the Albert Ellis

Institute (AEI) in New York City, formerly known as the Institute for Rational-Emotive Therapy.

As a psychoanalyst, Ellis had found it helpful to give his own opinions about how people could improve their lives, based on his reading of principles derived from the works of Epictetus, Marcus Aurelius, Spinoza and Bertrand Russell, and by 1955 he abandoned Freudian psychoanalysis. REBT is a humanistic action-oriented cognitive-behavioural therapy that encourages individuals to examine their own thoughts, beliefs and actions, identify dysfunctional emotions and behaviours and replace those that are self-defeating with more rational alternatives.

Erikson, Erik Homberger (1902–1994)

Erik Erikson was a clinician and psychiatric consultant at Mount Zion Hospital in San Francisco. He developed a psychodynamic theory of psychosocial development, identifying eight stages. This can be compared with Freud's psychosexual stages but Erikson puts emphasis on social influences rather than sexual causes of conflict, and extends the stages beyond adolescence to the whole of the lifespan. The fundamental feelings and approach to life that a person develops at each of the eight stages can be summarised as being either:

> basic trust versus mistrust
> autonomy versus shame and doubt
> initiative versus guilt
> industry versus inferiority
> identity versus role confusion
> intimacy versus isolation
> generativity (growth) versus stagnation
> integrity versus despair.

Therapy using this model is not limited to psychodynamic analysis but involves social and cognitive elements aimed at helping clients understand their emotional development and cope with problem areas.

Eysenck, Hans. J. (1916–1997)

H. J. Eysenck was a German-born British psychologist, founder of the Psychology Department, University of London Institute of Psychiatry, and Professor Emeritus (1983–97). He is one of the world's most prolific and frequently cited psychologists, both for his defence of the argument that racial differences in intelligence are partially attributable to genetic factors, and his highly influential, rigorous, measurement-based approaches to personality research.

Eysenck was a proponent of the theory of human intelligence proposed by Donald Hebb and elaborated by Philip Vernon (see below). Hebb identified two levels of intelligence: Intelligence A, which is the biological potential for cognitive ability, and Intelligence B, which is generated when Intelligence A interacts with environmental influences. Vernon added Intelligence C, which is what can be measured in tests of cognitive ability. Intelligence tests vary to the degree that they reflect Intelligence A or B. Eysenck believed that culturally bound tests and tests of educational attainment are likely to capture Intelligence B, whereas physiological measures such as positron emission tomography (PET) and electroencephalography (EEG) held more potential as possible tools for capturing Intelligence A.

Eysenck approached personality through factor analysis and measured two dimensions of personality: introversion–extroversion and stability–instability (neuroticism).

Festinger, Leon (1919–1989)

Leon Festinger was a social psychologist from the New School for Social Research in New York City. During his years at Stanford in the 1950s and 1960s, he was at the height of his influence and became famous for his *Theory of Cognitive Dissonance* (Festinger, 1957). Festinger studied under Kurt Lewin, who is often considered the father of social psychology.

The theory appears counterintuitive as it proposes that actions can influence subsequent beliefs and attitudes rather than be the result of them. Cognitive dissonance theory is based on three fundamental assumptions:

> We recognise when we have inconsistencies between actions and beliefs.
> Recognition of this inconsistency will cause dissonance, and will motivate us to resolve the dissonance.
> We can resolve the dissonance in one of three basic ways:
>   – change beliefs
>   – change actions
>   – change perception of action.

Feyerabend, Paul (1924–1994)

Paul Feyerabend is known as an influential and maverick philosopher of science. He studied science at the University of Vienna and moved into philosophy and philosophy of science, first supporting and later rejecting Karl Popper's 'critical rationalism'. He became a critic of philosophy of science itself, particularly of reductionism and 'rationalist' attempts to lay down or discover rules of scientific method. He studied and worked at the London School of Economics (LSE), University of Bristol, University of Sussex, University of Auckland, New Zealand, University of California, Berkeley and Zurich among others.

Freud, Anna (1896–1982)

Anna Freud, daughter of Sigmund, became Director of the Vienna Psychoanalytical Training Institute in 1935 and later moved to England where she founded the Hampstead Clinic, renamed the Anna Freud Centre, and became Honorary President of the International Psychoanalytical Association.

In England the conflict between her approach and Melanie Klein threatened to split the British Psychoanalytical Society. This was resolved through a series of war-time 'Controversial discussions' that ended with the formation of parallel training courses for the two groups. Klein differed from Anna Freud as to the timing of the development of object relations and internalised structures; also she put the oedipal stage much earlier, and considered the death drive to be of fundamental importance in infancy.

Anna Freud was particularly interested in defence mechanisms, and added asceticism and intellectualisation as relevant to adolescent coping. Later, she became more concerned with the practical ways of helping children than with the theoretical analysis.

Freud, Sigmund (1856–1939)

Sigmund Freud was a professor in Vienna and co-founded the Vienna Psychoanalytical Society and the International Psychoanalytic Association. He worked briefly with Carl Jung, and set up a practice in neuropsychiatry, with the help of Joseph Breuer. He emigrated to England just before the Second World War.

Freud developed a method of psychoanalysis based on a predominantly biological approach to mental functions. He believed that eventually

theorists

psychology would be explained in purely biological terms. However, he used a mental model to explain clinical observations that biology could not account for. He used it for treating patients whose symptoms could not, at that time, be explained in terms of organic disorders. He labelled three distinct aspects of mental activity. He used the term 'id' for biological instincts related to psychosexual gratification. The 'ego' is what is normally thought of as the conscious mind. The 'super-ego' or basis of conscience is partly conscious and partly unconscious.

Freud believed that anxiety can be traced to unconscious conflict between id and superego. When anxiety becomes very great, the superego may operate through defence mechanisms to repress memories, fantasies or thoughts because they are too painful to dwell on. However, the distressing emotions remain and may be expressed through dreams and other disguised or symbolic representations.

Through examination and interpretation of dreams and defence mechanisms, the client may become aware of the repressed material and, as an adult, find a way of resolving the conflict and dispelling the anxiety.

Vocabulary associated with Freud includes id, ego, superego, libido, death-wish (Thanatos), pleasure principle (Eros), psychosexual stages, complex, penis envy, defence mechanisms.

Friedman, Meyer (1910–2001) and Rosenman, Ray H. (1957–1964)

Meyer Friedman and Ray H. Rosenman were cardiologists at the Harold Brunn Institute Mount Zion Hospital and Medical Center in San Francisco, California. Friedman founded the Meyer Friedman Institute that supports research on the physiological consequences of stress.

Friedman and Rosenman (1974) linked behaviours such as those that are immensely competitive, overachieving, time-pressured, fast-moving, inconsiderate, aggressive and hostile with an increased risk of heart disease and described the 'Type A' person.

Type A is no longer considered a personality type and is usually given as Type A behaviour pattern (TABP). Continuing research suggests that hostility is the only significant predictor of heart disease and that a high degree of hostility also predicts a range of other diseases, including atherosclerosis, hemorrhagic stroke and Type 2 diabetes, and higher rates of mortality with these diseases. There is some debate as to whether there is an underlying disease that causes the behaviour pattern, rather than the other way around.

Fromm, Eric (1900–1980)

Eric Fromm was a German psychoanalyst who helped to establish the South German Institute for Psychoanalysis in Frankfurt before opening his own practice in Berlin. He emigrated to the United States and was employed at the Institute for Social Research in New York.

Fromm believed that the strongest motivating force for all people is a need to find a reason for existence. He argued than humans have lost a sense of 'one-ness' with nature and listed a number of needs which help us not to feel isolated:

> transcendence
> rootedness
> identity
> frame of reference and devotion
> excitement and stimulation.

Fromm (1947) lists a number of different personality types related to whether people find satisfaction from stimuli within themselves or in the external environment. He suggests (1942, 1956) that problems arise from faulty social relationships and a fear of true freedom.

Gibson, Eleanor (Jackie) (1910–2002) and Walk, Richard, D. (retired)

Eleanor (Jackie) Gibson was Professor Emeritus of Psychology at Cornell University. Richard Walk served on the faculty of Cornell University prior to going to George Washington University where he served as Director of the Doctoral Programme in Cognitive and Perceptual Development and Department Chair.

Gibson and Walk (1960) placed infants of various ages on a glass (or plexiglass) surface over a check-patterned runway that ran across the centre of a table designed with a visual cliff, that is a drop from shallow to deep. On one side the cloth is placed immediately beneath the glass, and on the other, it is dropped about four feet below. Since the glass would easily support the infant, this is a visual cliff rather than an actual cliff. The

theorists

majority of infants who had begun to crawl refused to venture onto the seemingly unsupported surface, even when their mothers beckoned encouragingly from the other side, which suggest they could perceive the drop. Gibson and Walk also report on depth perception and locomotion in other species.

The main drawback with this experiment is that it cannot be used until the infants are able to crawl. Anecdotal evidence suggests that much younger babies who are carried in front of a parent may show a startle reaction as the adult begins to walk down a flight of steps.

Gilligan, Carol (current)

Gilligan is professor for the Harvard Graduate School of Education and is currently co-ordinating the formation of the new Harvard Center on Gender and Education. She was invited (1992–4) to the University of Cambridge in England as a Pitt Professor of American History and Institutions.

Gilligan began teaching at Harvard in 1967 with Erik Erikson. In 1970 she became a research assistant for Lawrence Kohlberg. Gilligan's area of academic expertise is in human development and psychology. She is considered to be a pioneer of gender studies and particularly in the psychological and moral development of girls.

Goodall, Jane (current)

Jane Goodall is Scientific Director of the Gombe Stream Research Center in Tanzania and founder of the Jane Goodall Institute in Arlington, VA.

Jane Goodall is the world's foremost authority on chimpanzees, having closely observed their social behaviour for the past quarter century in the jungles of the Gombe Game Reserve in Africa, living in the chimps' environment and gaining their confidence.

Her work can usefully be compared with that of Dian Fossey. See 7.2 for DVDs.

Gregory, Richard (current)

Richard Gregory FRS is Emeritus Professor of Neuropsychology at the University of Bristol. He is frequently cited and is well known for his many scientific papers and talks, especially on perception and visual illusions. The *Oxford Companion to the Mind*, which he edited, is a valuable source of information for all psychologists.

Cognitive approaches involve the realisation

that much, perhaps nearly all, of our mental activity takes place without awareness, and that we engage in very sophisticated *information-processing* without being able to give any account of what we are doing. We can think and solve problems while functioning on a sort of 'autopilot' but we do not know how we do this. Gregory (1981) describes consciousness as a kind of moving beam of light searching and illuminating facets of the mind. Current consciousness consists of whatever is being lit by the patch of light of the beam and there is a great deal more around it which is not lit for the moment, and some that is never lit.

Harlow, Harry Frederick (1905–1981)

Harlow was an American psychologist best known for his work with rhesus monkeys on maternal-deprivation and social isolation. He conducted most of his research at the University of Wisconsin-Madison, where he worked for a time with humanistic psychologist Abraham Maslow.

In the frequently cited series of experiments conducted between 1963 and 1968, Harlow removed baby rhesus monkeys from their mothers, and provided only surrogate mothers, one made of terrycloth, the other of wire. He observed that the baby monkeys who were able to cling to the cloth mothers appeared to thrive better and exhibited more curiosity behaviour than those with only the wire mother. Critics have argued that clinging is a matter of survival in young rhesus monkeys, but not in humans, and have suggested that his conclusions, when applied to humans, overestimated the importance of contact comfort. His work continues to influence the care of both humans and nonhuman primates.

Hebb, Donald Olding (1904–1985)

D. O. Hebb was a Canadian psychologist who became Chancellor of McGill University in Montreal.

Hebb conducted research on brain-damaged patients with Wilder Penfield (see below) at the Montreal Neurological Institute (1937–39) and his central concern as a psychologist was to develop his neurophysiological theory of such mental functions as thought, imagery, volition, attention and memory. He frequently engaged in debates which attracted the attention of the mass media and the general public, and is considered the father of cognitive psychobiology.

Holmes, Thomas and Rahe, Richard H. (current)

Thomas Holmes is a psychiatrist at the University of Washington medical school. Richard Rahe is currently psychiatric consultant to the US Army Medical Corps, concerned with combat stress.

In 1967, Holmes and Rahe adapted the Hawkins et al (1957) Schedule of Recent Experience into the Social Readjustment Rating Scale, which assigned numeric values to life events to quantify the probability that someone would become ill. Death of a spouse, for example, was worth 100 points (life change units), whereas trouble with a supervisor was worth 23 points. Prospective studies subsequently showed that 80 per cent of persons who had a score of more than 300 points developed a serious illness within two years compared with only 30 per cent of those with a score of less than 150 points. This scale is still widely in use.

Horney, Karen Danielsen (1885–1952)

Karen Horney was a German-born American psychoanalyst who believed that every human being has an innate drive toward self-realisation and that neurosis is essentially a process obstructing this healthy development.

Horney participated in many international congresses in which Sigmund Freud was the leading figure, and taught at the New York Psychoanalytic Institute, but she increasingly questioned some of Freud's ideas, particularly those concerning male-oriented concepts such as penis envy, and moved away from the Freudian group in 1941.

She took the lead in founding the Association for the Advancement of Psychoanalysis, the American Institute for Psychoanalysis and the *American Journal of Psychoanalysis*. Horney is sometimes described as a neo-Freudian member of 'the cultural school', a group that also included Erich Fromm, Harry Stack Sullivan, Clara Thompson, and Abram Kardiner.

Karen Horney stressed that cultural and social conditions, rather than sexual instincts, contribute to neurosis and sexual disturbances. Horney suggests that basic anxiety is common to all people and that extreme or neurotic anxiety comes about as a result of disturbed relationships between parents and children and that all children are anxious owing to the difficult nature of childhood. She saw anxiety as originating in:

the feelings a child has of being isolated and helpless in a potentially hostile world.

A wide range of adverse factors in the environment can produce this insecurity in a child: direct or indirect domination, indifference, erratic behaviour, lack of respect for the child's individual needs, lack of real guidance, disparaging attitudes, too much admiration or the absence of it, lack of reliable warmth, having to take sides in parental disagreements, too much or too little responsibility, overprotection, isolation from other children, injustice, discrimination, unkept promises.

(Horney, 1945: 41.)

She proposes that there are a number of neurotic strategies that people use to cope with feelings of basic anxiety. In particular, she lists ten neurotic needs (Horney, 1942: 54–60). These are for:

> affection and approval
> a partner to take over one's life
> restriction of one's life within narrow borders
> power
> exploitation of others
> social recognition and purpose
> personal admiration
> personal achievement
> self-sufficiency and independence
> perfection and unassailability.

These ten needs can be classified into three basic types:

> compliant (moving towards others)
> aggressive (moving against others)
> detached (moving away from others).

Most people can identify elements of these needs in normal personality patterns. It is only when they become overly rigid, distressing or destructive, that they would be classed as neurotic. As an adult, a client can be helped to understand these anxieties and work through them. This list can be compared with those used in cognitive and rational-emotive therapy.

Hubel, David H. and Wiesel, Torsten N. (current)

David Hubel is John Enders University Professor of Neurobiology, Emeritus at Harvard University, and is interested in learning how the activation of brain cells is related to an animal's environment and behaviour. He studies the primary visual cortex of macaque and squirrel monkeys. Torsten N. Wiesel is President and Vincent and Brook Astor

theorists

Professor at The Rockefeller University, where he established a new Laboratory of Neurobiology and is concerned with the circuitry of the primary visual cortex.

Hubel and Wiesel worked together at Johns Hopkins Medical School and Harvard Medical School, and with Roger W. Sperry (see below) were awarded the Nobel Prize in Physiology or Medicine 1981 for their discoveries concerning information processing in the visual system in cats and monkeys. By recording electrical activity in individual brain cells, they could determine how the brain responded to pictures of lines in different orientations.

James, William (1842–1910)

William James was a professor at Harvard University and studied at Harvard's Lawrence Scientific School and the School of Medicine.

He was an original thinker and his *The Principles of Psychology* (1890) combines physiology, psychology, philosophy and personal reflection, together with the beginnings of pragmatism and phenomenology, and influenced generations of thinkers in Europe and America, including Edmund Husserl, Bertrand Russell, John Dewey and Ludwig Wittgenstein. Later, in *Pragmatism* (1907), he presents a systematic set of views about truth, knowledge, reality, religion and philosophy.

In psychology he is known for the expression 'the stream of thought', also known as the 'stream of consciousness'; the newborn baby's impression of the world 'as one great blooming, buzzing confusion'; the James–Lange theory of emotions (see Part 3); the concept of *attention* (see Part 3) as the ability to select part of the information available in the environment for further processing; the notion of several selves (see *self-concept* in Part 3); and the concept of 'soft *determinism*' in which we appear to be only lightly constrained by the environment so that our behaviour appears to be voluntary and we think we have free will.

He is often quoted for having said (in 1870) 'my first act of free will shall be to believe in free will.'

Jung, Carl Gustav (1875–1961)

C. G. Jung is known as the founder of analytical psychology. He became Professor of Psychology at the Federal Institute of Technology in Zurich (1933–41) and was appointed Professor of Medical Psychology at the University of Basel in 1943.

He and Freud worked closely for several years; Jung edited the *Jahrbuch für psychologische und psychopathologische Forschungen* and was made president of the International Psychoanalytic Society in 1911. However, after much correspondence, he moved away from Freud as he disagreed with Freud's emphasis on sexual trauma as the basis for all neurosis and with the literal interpretation of the Oedipus complex.

Jung uses much of the same language as Freud but defines the terms rather differently. For example he takes libido to mean life energy in the broadest sense, not just sexual energy. His principal concern is with people who have been separated from their parents. He considers that people are striving towards psychic wholeness or integration, an idea also developed by Maslow (1962) from a phenomenological perspective. One of the key elements in Jungian therapy can be the recognition and integration of opposite attributes of the self (for example, masculine and feminine) which have previously been repressed. Jung called his method analytical psychology, to distinguish it from Freudian psychoanalysis.

Vocabulary associated with Jung includes extravert and introvert, psyche, principle of opposites, libido, archetype, persona, shadow, alterego, anima and animus, individuation, mandala, collective unconscious.

Kahneman, Daniel (current)

Daniel Kahneman is Eugene Higgins Professor of Psychology, Professor of Psychology and Public Affairs at the Woodrow Wilson School, Princeton University, and the winner of the Sveriges Riksbank Prize in Economic Sciences in Memory of Alfred Nobel 2002. Kahneman shared the award with American economist Vernon L. Smith. He is married to Anne Treisman (see below).

In order to increase understanding of how people make economic decisions, Kahneman drew on cognitive psychology in relation to the mental processes used in forming judgements and making choices. Kahneman's research with Amos Tversky, based on surveys and experiments, showed that participants were not capable of analysing complex decision situations when the future consequences were uncertain but relied on heuristic or rule-of-thumb strategies. They formulated a new branch of economics that they called prospect theory (Kahneman and Tversky, 1979).

This challenges mainstream economists' assumptions that people are rational and motivated by self-interest when making financial decisions, but rather suggests that psychological motives, including emotions and biases, determine our economic behaviour. Their work has influenced the study of judgement and decision-making in related disciplines such as economics, finance, marketing, law and medicine. Useful comparisons can be made with the earlier work of Wason and Johnson-Laird (1968), who demonstrated that adults as well as children rarely use pure logic in problem-solving but search for familiar meanings (see below) and with Damasio who stresses the importance of emotion in giving value to decisions (see above).

Kelley, Harold H. (1921–2003)

H. H. Kelley was a social psychologist, particularly interested in group behaviour and group problem-solving. He was Emeritus Professor of Psychology, at the University of California, Los Angeles (UCLA). He collaborated with Kurt Lewin, Carl Hovland, Irving Janis and John Thibaut. He is often cited for his study showing that people are particularly influenced by the words warm and cold when giving their first impressions of a person (Kelley, 1950).

Kelley (1967) proposed that people are 'intuitive scientists' and suggested that inferences we make about other people or events are based on a principle he termed covariation, that can be measured statistically using the analysis of variance (ANOVA, see Part 5). Kelley proposed three information variables and devised a three-dimensional model, known as the 'Kelley cube':

> Consistency: the extent to which the observed person's behaviour is consistent with past behaviours.
> Distinctiveness: the degree to which differences in context surround the behaviour.
> Consensus: the extent to which others in the same situation behave in the same way.

The interaction of these three variables gives a measure of stability or instability to the observed behaviour.

Kelly, George Alexander (1905–1967)

George Kelly was Professor and Director of Clinical Psychology at the Ohio State University.

As psychologist, therapist and teacher, he is best known for developing *personal construct psychology*, a key concept in the psychology of individual differences (see Part 3).

He described how people develop a set of personal constructs in order to make sense of themselves, other people and the world. The constructs are bipolar or dichotomous, that is, they consist of two opposites, and vary from one person to another. He suggests that each of us has a whole 'repertoire' of constructs such as warm–cold, empathetic–distant, thoughtful–thoughtless, strict–easy-going, honest–dishonest, which we apply to the people around us. When something turns out not to be true, we revise the construct. We are likely to attach more value to some constructs than others.

To illustrate how each person's individual construct system worked, Kelly developed what became known as a *repertory grid*. Each client thinks about a small number of people and finds words to describe them. The easiest way to do this is to think of three people and choose something that two of them have in common but the third does not share and express this as a pair of opposites. The main bipolar constructs are then arranged in a grid and the client can then assess other significant people according to each pair. By seeing if certain constructs tended to cluster together, the therapist could come to see if the client had distinctive ways of understanding the world.

Personal construct psychology (PCP) developed mostly in the UK, promoted by Donald Bannister and by Professor Fay Fransella (of London University). who founded the Centre for Personal Construct Psychology in London, but is now gaining in international popularity.

Klein, Melanie (1882–1960)

Melanie Klein was an Austrian psychoanalyst who was accepted by the British Psychoanalytic Society: she was a member of the Training Committee, a training analyst, and leader of the Kleinian group, which included for a while John Bowlby and Donald Winnicott.

Melanie Klein worked predominantly with children. As a substitute for Freud's free association, Klein developed the technique of play therapy to uncover children's unconscious motivations. She believed that strong emotions are present in children from an early age but that these are not always adequately expressed. She developed her theory in terms of the positions a child must move through in order to accept its mother as a whole separate person and struggle to move from dependence to independence. This can involve ambivalence and unresolved feelings of love, hate, fear and concern. She suggested that it is possible to detect and interpret these by observing play and she undertook to analyse children's problems at a much earlier age than anyone had thought possible or necessary. Her most significant contribution is her insistence that children adopt 'positions' rather than go through 'stages'. She disagreed with Freud that children pass through a sequence of psychosexual stages and found, rather, that childhood represents a time of development of a particular way of approaching the world. She identified two main kinds of problematic positions, paranoid-schizoid and depressive. The paranoid-schizoid position involves splitting the external world into extreme opposites, a form of dichotomous reasoning, so that some things are seen as very good, others as very bad, with little in between. The depressive position represents a turning-in on oneself and internal conflict. A key principle of Kleinian therapy is that a carer can act as *container* for the child's distressing emotions (see also Part 3).

Kohlberg, Lawrence (1927–1987)

Lawrence Kohlberg was a professor at the University of Chicago and at Harvard University. He is known for his research on moral development and his stage theory of moral development, justice and rights.

Kohlberg's work reflects and extends Jean Piaget's theory of cognitive development (see below) and in turn Kohlberg's work has been further extended and modified by Carol Gilligan (see above) and James Rest.

His model of moral reasoning, the basis for ethical behaviour, has six developmental constructive stages, grouped into three levels: pre-conventional, conventional and post-conventional.

> Level 1. Pre-conventional (right and wrong determined by rewards and punishment):
>   – Stage 1. Obedience and punishment.
>   – Stage 2. Self-interest and rewards.
> Level 2 Conventional (views of others matter):
>   – Stage 3. Good intentions and conformity.

> – Stage 4. Obedience to authority and maintaining social order.
> Level 3 Post-conventional (abstract notions of justice):
>   – Stage 5. Distinction between moral and legal right. Understanding that rules could or should sometimes be broken.
>   – Stage 6. Universal ethical principles and individual principles of conscience.

Kohler, Wolfgang (1887–1967)

Wolfgang Kohler was a German psychologist who became a professor at Swarthmore College, Pennsylvania, and a key figure in the development of *Gestalt psychology*, which describes learning, perception and other components of mental life as structured wholes (see also Part 3).

He is particularly remembered for his work (1925) with chimpanzees in which he sought to demonstrate that primates show 'insight' in problem-solving, reaching a solution suddenly after a period of inactivity following previous trial and error. The ongoing debate is whether insight is a useful concept or whether all learning can be shown to occur by trial and error and reinforcement provided sufficient detail is known of the previous experience.

Kraepelin, Emil (1856–1926)

Emil Kraepelin was Professor of Psychiatry at the University of Dorpat, Heidelberg (1891) and Münich (1903) and can be regarded as the founder of modern scientific psychiatry, psychopharmacology and psychiatric genetics. Kraepelin believed that psychiatric diseases are mainly caused by biological and genetic disorders and opposed the approach of Sigmund Freud, who regarded and treated psychiatric disorders as caused by psychological factors. Kraepelin was the first to distinguish between manic-depressive psychosis (now known as bipolar disorder) and dementia praecox (now known as schizophrenia), His classification of mental disorders served as the foundation for the *Diagnostic and Statistical Manual* (DSM), now in its fourth edition (DSM-IV), and the *International Classification of Diseases* (ICD), the standard reference texts used by psychiatrists today.

The DSM-IV is the manual published by the American Psychiatric Association that covers all mental health disorders for both children

theorists

and adults. It also lists known causes of these disorders, statistics in terms of gender, age at onset and prognosis, as well as some research concerning the optimal treatment approaches.

Kuhn, Thomas S. (1922–1996)

Thomas Kuhn was a professor of philosophy and history of science. In 1983 he was named Laurence S. Rockefeller Professor of Philosophy at Massachusetts Institute of Technology (MIT).

He is remembered for his discussions concerning the social and cultural nature of science and the use of *paradigms* (see also Part 3). In particular, he suggests (Kuhn, 1970) that psychology is pre-scientific as it does not follow a generally accepted paradigm.

Note that Thomas Kuhn should not be confused with the Kuhn and McPartland (1954) study on self-concept.

Labov, William (current)

William Labov is Professor of Linguistics at Pennsylvania University, with a particular interest in non-standard variations of English. He used the expression verbal deprivation theory (Labov, 1969), also used by Bernstein (see above). Labov criticised Bernstein's view that lower-class English was restricted, arguing that Bernstein did not recognise the subtleties of non-standard English.

Lacan, Jacques-Marie-Émile (1901–1981)

Jaques Lacan was a French psychoanalyst and psychiatrist. According to Bowie (1991: 7) Lacan believed that 'Freud was right but not right enough, or not right in quite the right way.' Lacan's theoretical approach is derived directly from Freudian analysis but is developed according to linguistic models, for example those of Levi-Strauss, Saussure and Jakobson. Lacan asserts that the unconscious mind is structured like a language. Bowie (1991) suggests that for Lacan, psychoanalysis is concerned primarily with understanding human speech: an idea which reappears in *beliefs*, *grammatical representation*, *mentalese* and neurolinguistic programming (Bandler and Grinder, 1975, 1976). Lacan's ideas can be difficult to understand and Lacan (1977) says he deliberately makes his writings obscure so that the reader must bring his or her own ideas into making sense of them and must not expect any simple or ready-made answers. This is in line with postmodernist ideas in which the reader's meaning of a text is considered as important as the writer's meaning.

He is known for several catchphrases, such as 'a letter never reaches its destination'. This can have several interpretations including the meaning of the word 'letter' either as the letter 'a', or as mail, and is linked to the notion that if the reader brings a different interpretation then the writer's intended meaning is never received.

He used the term 'jouissance' in various senses, including orgasm or as a kind of gaiety, roguishness or 'bloody-mindedness' of the unconscious mind, or some other meaning according to context.

One of the ideas that Lacan developed is that we are constantly striving towards the things we desire, but as soon as we achieve them we want something else. This ancient concept is associated with St Augustine (354–430) who said 'our heart is restless till it finds its rest in thee.' (*Confessions*, Book 1, Chapter 1)

This theme has also been developed by Baudelaire in his poem 'The Voyage' (1859). Baudelaire's poem is a metaphor for the journey through life. He describes an insatiable desire to travel and gain new experiences, mixed with ideas of a voyage towards death. Baudelaire uses imagination of a wonderful world seen with a childlike naivety interwoven with disillusionment, jaded experience and an obscure catalogue of horrors and says:

> desire, that great elm, fertilised by lust. . .
> why are you always growing taller?

Lacan is associated with feminist writings and his views are widely used in the interpretation of creative arts.

Laing, Ronald David (1927–1989)

Ronald (Ronnie) Laing was a Scottish psychiatrist who worked at the Tavistock Clinic, trained as a psychoanalyst at the Institute of Psychoanalysis and founded the Philadelphia Association in Kingsley Hall in London's East End. He wrote about the experience of psychosis from the individual's point of view. He was influenced by existentialism, a philosophical movement that asserts that individual human beings have full responsibility for creating the meanings of their own lives.

He believed that the often bizarre or apparently meaningless behaviour or random speech (word salad) of a person diagnosed as undergoing a psychotic episode, represented a valid point of view or an attempt to communicate worries and concerns, often in situations where this was not possible or not permitted.

Laing believed that society, and particularly the family, played a fundamental role in the development of madness. He argued that individuals found themselves put in impossible situations, where they were expected to conform to conflicting expectations, leading to a 'lose–lose situation' and immense mental distress. Madness could be interpreted as an expression of the distress and valued as a cathartic and transformative experience. Gregory Bateson (Bateson et al, 1956) described a related pattern of double bind situations in which a member of a family is faced with having to make impossible choices (see also Part 3). In these cases, although only one member of the family is diagnosed as having schizophrenia, it is possible that others have a similar condition that leads to distorted communication. This approach supported the general view in the 1960s and 1970s that parents 'cause' mental illness in their children (see also Bettleheim, above). Laing was critical of orthodox psychiatry and belief in the biological basis of mental illness, and is often associated with the anti-psychiatry movement.

Lakatos, Imre (1922–1974)

Imre Lakatos was a Hungarian philosopher of mathematics who came to Cambridge and then the London School of Economics, where he was a popular lecturer in the philosophy and history of mathematics and science. Like Feyerabend (above) he was seen as a maverick, critical of all mainstream thought. He questioned the mainstream philosophical account of 'the mathematical knowledge of an individual, something that would reveal how people are justified in believing what they do quite independently of their society or the history of that society's inquiries' (see 7.2 for website).

LaPiere, Richard T. (1899–1986)

Richard T. LaPiere was Professor Emeritus of Social Psychology at Stanford University. He queried the validity of using questionnaires to measure social attitudes when he found that although responses to questionnaires were generally consistent they tended to show what people thought they believed rather than their actual behaviour. In his classic study he (white Caucasian) travelled around the United States with a young Chinese couple and recorded how the two Asians were treated in hotels and restaurants. At the time prejudice against Asians was widespread and there were no laws against racial discrimination. They stayed at hotels, motels and restaurants and, with one exception, were served without difficulty. Later, LaPiere wrote to all of the establishments asking if they would refuse to serve Asians. Of the 128 replies received, over 90 per cent said they would refuse.

Latané, Bibb (current)

Bibb Latané is a social psychologist and Chair of Psychology at Florida Atlantic University.

Darley and Latané (1968) and Latané and Darley (1970) explored the behaviour of bystanders in emergency settings. They used field experiments which placed people in emergency settings, such as hearing someone apparently having an epileptic seizure, or falling off a ladder, or sitting in a room which begins to fill with smoke. Their findings were that the more people who witness an emergency event, the less likely each individual is to help. This became known as 'the bystander effect'. The experimental work was preferred to questionnaires, as with LaPiere, above, as it deals with real intervention behaviour, not beliefs about intentions.

They developed a theory of social impact (Latané, 1981), now called dynamic social impact theory (Latané, 1996). Social impact means any of the number of changes that might occur in an individual (physiological, cognitive, emotional or behavioural) due to the presence or action of others, who are real, imagined or implied. Dynamic social impact theory views society as a self-organising complex system in which individuals interact and influence each others' beliefs. There are three basic principles:

> The impact depends on the number and social status or influential position of the people present.
> The rate of impact increases to some extent but not in mathematical proportional with the number of others added. That is, doubling the audience does not produce twice the effect.
> Each person influences others, but as the audience size increases the individual influence decreases.

theorists

Lazarus, Richard S. (1922–2002)

Richard S. Lazarus was a Professor Emeritus of psychology at the University of California, Berkeley.

He is cited in health psychology for his work on stress, which he defined as resulting from an imbalance between demands and resources. Instead of focusing on the physiological stress response he focused on the way the people think about what is happening to them. Lazarus and Susan Folkman, his former student who is now on the faculty of UC San Francisco, argued that people suffer stress when they believe they lack the resources to deal with difficult events, but that they do not suffer stress if they believe that they have such resources (Lazarus and Folkman, 1984).

When faced with a stressor (a demand made by the internal or external environment that upsets balance), a person evaluates the potential threat (primary appraisal) and assesses coping resources and options (secondary appraisal). Actual coping efforts aimed at regulation of the problem give rise to outcomes of the coping process.

Lazarus (1994/1991) showed how patterns of appraisal enter into the generation of emotions. He demonstrated that *cognitive appraisal theory* explains the meaning of a person's emotional behaviour; how a single response, like a smile, can be used in many different emotional responses and how totally different responses, such as retaliation or passive aggressiveness, can be related to the same emotion.

Loftus, Elizabeth F. (current)

Elizabeth Loftus is a professor in departments of psychology, criminology, law and social behaviour and Fellow of the Center for the Neurobiology of Learning and Memory at the University of California, Irvine and Affiliate Professor of psychology and law at the University of Washington.

Her main area of study is human memory, how memories can be changed by things that we are told, such as facts, ideas, suggestions and other forms of post-event information, and applications in the legal field. She is particularly known for her work on *eyewitness testimony* and *recovered memories*.

Lorenz, Konrad Zacharias (1903–1989)

Konrad Lorenz was an Austrian zoologist and ethologist at the Max Planck Institute for Behavioural Physiology in Seewiesen, Germany and was professor at the University of Maryland, College Park Campus towards the end of his life. Lorenz may be regarded as one of the founders of modern ethology, the study of animals in their natural habitat (see also Part 2).

Lorenz studied instinctive behaviour in animals and is most often cited for his description of imprinting in geese. When the goslings hatch they tend to follow the first moving object that they see. In the natural world this would usually be the mother but Lorenz experimented with various objects and has various photographs of the geese following himself.

He also asserted that aggressive impulses serve a number of evolutionary purposes and are to a degree innate in humans as well as animals, a point of view that gives rise to considerable controversy.

Lorenz was awarded the Nobel Prize in Physiology or Medicine 1973, together with Karl von Frisch and Nikolaas Tinbergen (see below) for their discoveries concerning organisation and elicitation of individual and social behaviour patterns.

Luria, Alexander Romanovich (1902–1977)

A. R. Luria was a Georgian neuropsychologist and developmental psychologist at the Moscow State University, where he was head of the Departments of Pathopsychology and Neuropsychology, concerned with the effects of brain damage.

Like his teacher Vygotsky (see below), he believed that even the most basic functions of brain and mind were not only biological in nature but related to experiences and social influences, and he is associated with cultural-historical psychology and psychological activity theory (see Part 2).

Luria is best known for his two main case studies that provide excellent introductions to the topic of brain structure and function: S. V. Shereshevskii, a Russian journalist with apparently unlimited memory and synaesthesia (see Luria and Bruner, 1987), and Zazetsky, who sustained massive brain damage when severely wounded by shell fragments. He lost his ability to read, write and speak, and suffered impaired *vision*, *memory*, *proprioception* and other functions with constantly shifting images (1972). Luria's work is cited and discussed by Jerome Bruner (see above) and Oliver Sacks (see below).

Maslow, Abraham (1908–1970)

Abraham Maslow became Chair of the Psychology Department at Brandeis University, MA, from 1951 to 1969 and a resident fellow of the Laughlin Institute in California.

He was particularly influenced by anthropologist Ruth Benedict, Gestalt psychologist Max Wertheimer and Kurt Goldstein, who had originated the idea of self-actualisation (Goldstein, 1934). He was an important proponent of humanistic psychology and is known for his Hierarchy of Needs (Maslow, 1943), which can be found in many introductory textbooks and websites (see also *Motivation* in Part 3).

Mead, George Herbert (1836–1931)

George Herbert Mead became a professor at the University of Chicago. He is a major figure in the history of American philosophy and one of the founders of pragmatism along with Charles Sanders Peirce, William James, James Hayden Tufts and John Dewey.

Mead's theory of the emergence of mind and self out of social processes has become the foundation of the symbolic interactionist school of sociology and social psychology. Mead's writings also include significant contributions to the philosophy of nature, the philosophy of science, philosophical anthropology, the philosophy of history, and 'process philosophy' (an aspect of metaphysics) from the days when the lines between philosophy and psychology were not sharply drawn.

Mead was interested in the social context in which children learn, rather than in the precise nature of logical thought. He discussed how children develop a sense of self and others through interactions with others (Mead, 1934). His work indicates how children can see things from another's point of view and are not purely egocentric in the way Piaget describes. His approach influences other psychologists who have analysed why children fail in a task like the 'three mountains' (Piaget and Inhelder, 1956) but cope well with similar tasks that are more obviously related to normal social experience.

Milgram, Stanley (1933–1984)

Stanley Milgram was a social psychologist at Yale University, Harvard University and the City University of New York. While at Harvard, he conducted the small-world experiment (Milgram, 1967) and while at Yale, he conducted his well-known experiment on obedience to authority (Milgram, 1963, 1974). He also introduced the concept of familiar strangers (Milgram, 1972). Two main influences were Max Wertheimer and Stanley Asch.

In the obedience to authority study, participants were instructed to give a supposed student electric shocks in response to incorrect answers on a test of learning. They were informed that the student had a severe heart condition and that the highest-level shocks could prove fatal. The unexpected results showed that a high percentage of the participants continued to the highest level, despite experiencing distress. No electric shocks were actually given but even after debriefing some participants continued to feel distress. This study is perhaps one of the most cited of all psychological experiments and has given rise to considerable debate.

The small-world experiment refers to Milgram's series of letters sent from one person to another to examine the average path length for social networks of people in the United States. The research revealed that human society is a small-world-type network characterised by shorter-than-expected path lengths. The experiments are often associated with the term 'six degrees of separation', although Milgram did not use this term himself. Six degrees of separation is the theory that anyone on the planet can be connected to any other person on the planet through a chain of acquaintances that has no more than five intermediaries. The theory was first proposed in 1929 by the Hungarian writer Frigyes Karinthy in a short story called 'Chains'.

A familiar stranger is an individual who is recognised from regular activities, but with whom one does not normally interact. However, if such individuals do meet in an unfamiliar setting, for example while travelling, they are more likely to introduce themselves than would perfect strangers, since they have a background of shared experiences. This has become an increasingly popular concept in research about social networks.

Miller, George A. (current)

George A. Miller is the James S. McDonnell Distinguished University Professor of Psychology, Emeritus, at Princeton University. He is best known for his 'magical number seven' (Miller, 1956).

Miller (1956) demonstrated that short-term memory could only hold between five and nine chunks of information (seven plus or minus two, 7 ± 2), where a chunk is any meaningful unit of information. A chunk could refer to words, numerals, game positions, or people's faces. The concept of chunking and the limited capacity of short term memory have become basic features of all subsequent theories of memory.

He is also known for the TOTE (Test–Operate–Test–Exit) concept (Miller et al, 1960), suggesting that TOTE is more useful than the stimulus–response (S–R) unit as the basic unit of behaviour. In a TOTE unit, a goal is tested to see if it has been achieved and if not an operation is performed to achieve the goal; this cycle of test–operate is repeated until the goal is eventually achieved or abandoned. The TOTE concept has provided the basis of subsequent theories of problem-solving

Mollon, J. D. (current)

J. D. Mollon is Professor of Visual Neuroscience and Fellow and Lecturer in Experimental Psychology at the University of Cambridge. His interests include sensation, perception and information processing; colour vision and colour blindness; primate vision; molecular genetics of mental disorder; cognition during sleep and the history of psychology.

Colour vision is usually described in terms of trichromacy, that is three types of cones in the retina that respond to overlapping ranges of frequencies of light. Mollon's work illustrates the basic principles and the many variations that occur in human and animal colour vision, including the addition of a fourth cone. It appears that some people may have four types of cones and be able to discriminate more finely than usual, particularly in the green and blue region of the spectrum. Moreover, women who have these four kinds of cone may be carriers of other types, and their sons may inherit a deficiency.

Olds, James (1922–1976)

James Olds was a psychobiologist who studied and worked at Harvard University, McGill University, the Brain Research Institute at the University of California, Los Angeles, the University of Michigan and the California Institute of Technology, where he held the position of Bing Professor of Behavioural Biology.

James Olds was an important psychologist of the 20th century who is best known for his discovery of the 'reward' system (pleasure centres) in the brain. He found that rats would continue to press a lever that activated an electrical impulse connected to the septal area of the limbic system in the brain (Olds, 1956). The rats would press the lever up to thousands of times per hour and in preference to receiving food or water. In humans, stimulation of this area produces a pleasurable sensation (see Penfield, below). Olds' discovery led to a much-increased understanding of the brain bases and mechanisms of substance abuse and addiction. Olds was also a pioneer in the study of neural substrates of learning and memory and the first to show that neurons in the hippocampus become substantially engaged in basic associative learning. Main influences include Talcott Parsons and Donald Hebb (see above).

Osgood, Charles E. (1916–1991)

Charles E. Osgood was Professor of Communications and Psychology and Director of the Institute of Communications Research at the University of Illinois.

His concern was with semantics (meanings in language and communication) and, with Suci and Tannenbau (Osgood et al, 1957), he devised a method known as the semantic differential to plot connotations for different words and indicate links between attitudes and behaviour. This can be adapted to a wide variety of problems in such areas as clinical psychology, social psychology, linguistics, mass communications, aesthetics and political science. They used a Likert-type scale (see Part 5) with pairs of opposite terms (bipolar constructs that can be compared with Kelley, see above). These included: angular–rounded, weak–strong, rough–smooth, active–passive, small–large, cold–hot, good–bad, tense–relaxed, wet–dry, fresh–stale. Participants were asked to indicate a position on the scale how each construct applied to a given example. Even when some of these constructs do not really seem to apply to a given example word, such as 'aeroplane', participants are apparently able to give sufficient responses to provide a usable profile.

Osgood is also known for his two-way model of interpersonal communication that provided a

theorists

useful comparison with the earlier one-way model of Shannon and Weaver (see also Gill and Adams, 1998).

Oswald, Ian (current)

Ian Oswald is a retired psychiatrist and sleep researcher who worked at the Maudsley hospital, St Bartholomew's Medical School and the University of Edinburgh.

He is best known for his early work on sleep that identified the stages of normal sleep and REM (rapid eye movement) or dreaming sleep and demonstrated the different EEG waves.

Sleep research continues at various establishments including the Sleep Research Centre in Loughborough where the Director is Professor Jim Horne.

Pavlov, Ivan Petrovich (1849–1936)

Ivan Pavlov was a Russian physiologist who studied and worked in St Petersburg at the university and the Imperial Medical Academy, where he became professor, and then Director of the Oldenburgski Institute of Experimental Medicine.

He was awarded a Nobel Prize for Physiology or Medicine in 1904 for his discovery of the physiology of digestion. Pavlov studied conditioned reflexes in animals and his work has had a great impact on behavioural theory and learning theory (see also Part 2 and Part 3).

In the course of physiological research into dog's production of saliva in response to putting meat powder into their mouths, Pavlov found that his results became 'contaminated' when the dogs began to salivate in response to various cues such as seeing or smelling the food before the meat powder was actually given. He then systematically tested this type of response by deliberately pairing a cue or stimulus (such as ringing a bell) with giving the meat powder. He found that dogs would then salivate to the sound of the bell alone. This apparent learning of the pairing of stimulus and response is known as *classical conditioning*.

In classical conditioning the learning is passive, requiring no effort or action on the part of the learner. This can be compared with operant or instrumental conditioning (see Skinner, below).

Penfield, Wilder Graves (1891–1976)

Wilder Penfield was a Canadian neurosurgeon who studied and worked at Oxford University, Johns Hopkins Medical School, Peter Bent Brigham Hospital in Boston, the National Hospital in London, Columbia University, McGill University and the Royal Victoria and Montreal General Hospitals. He became the founder and director of the Montreal Institute of Neurology.

In the 1950s, he pioneered the technique of applying electrodes to different areas of the brain to create direct stimulation while the patient was awake and able to speak. He demonstrated that the entire surface of the body is 'mapped' on to corresponding areas of the brain's surface and that stimulation of the temporal lobes produced what seemed to be vivid memories.

Perls, Frederick (Fritz) Salomon (1893–1970)

Frederick Perls was a German-born psychiatrist who became resident psychiatrist at the Esalen Institute at Big Sur, California where he organised and conducted 'dream workshops' in which participants could discuss their dreams and engage in role-playing exercises. With his wife Laura, he was a founder and the most influential practitioner of Gestalt psychotherapy. Gestalt therapy is recognised as one of several standard approaches or as part of an eclectic approach to modern therapy.

Trained as a Freudian, Perls modified some of Freud's theories to develop a more holistic approach with the focus on present influences and experience, the 'here and now', rather than past experiences going back to early childhood.

Piaget, Jean (1896–1980)

Jean Piaget was a Swiss zoologist and child psychologist with an interest in child intelligence, sociology and history of science. He studied and worked at the University of Neuchâtel, the University of Zürich, the Ecole de la rue de la Grange-aux-Belles (a boys' institution created by Alfred Binet and then directed by De Simon), became Director of Studies at the J.-J. Rousseau Institute in Geneva and created and directed the International Centre for Genetic Epistemology in Geneva.

Piaget observed that children give answers to problems that are different from those given by adults. They do not seem to think logically. They get things wrong. Piaget reasoned that children think differently from adults (for example, 1926, 1929, see 1989, 1990). He believed that children are unable to reason logically or abstractly but pass through a series of stages, involving sensori-motor and concrete operations, after which logical thinking emerges if the right information has been correctly absorbed. However, see Bryant and Donaldson, above, and Wason (below) for ideas on adult logic.

Piaget recommends that education should not introduce reasoning at an early age. He believes that thinking comes before language (the opposite of Bruner, see above) and that the main educational method at early stages should be unguided discovery learning which provides experience with handling objects and observing events, allowing the formation of concepts that will lead naturally to development of language.

The most well-known tasks include the three mountains, and conservation of length, number, volume, mass and area. In the three mountains tasks, a child is shown a model of three mountains and asked to pick out from a set of pictures, the picture that represents the child's view of the mountains. Most children can do this well from pre-school age. The child is then shown a doll climbing the mountains to go to the other side and asked to pick out the picture that represents what the doll can see. Many children continue to pick out the picture that shows their own point of view. Piaget said that this illustrated egocentricity, an inability to see things from another's point of view.

However, other researchers, for example Bryant and Donaldson, argue that most children simply do not understand what they are being asked or what the model of mountains represents. By asking similar questions in a familiar context, many children can respond correctly despite 'failing' on the three mountains. The most familiar conservation task is the one concerning volume. Children are shown coloured water being poured into two identical glasses (or something similar). Water from one of the glasses is then poured into a different shape of glass, either tall and thin or short and fat. The child is then asked whether the new glass has more, or less, or the same amount of liquid. Many children give an answer of less or more. Piaget asserted that these children cannot 'conserve' volume. That is, they cannot work out or reason that the volume stays the same when the shape is changed.

Current researchers argue that the children either do not understand the question, do not know the meaning of more or less, cannot concentrate on the task, forget what was shown

to them or give an answer that they think the researcher must be expecting. In an informal piece of research with conservation of number, this writer found one child who always said 'more' biscuits when five or more biscuits were used, whether they were spread apart or moved closer, and always responded 'less' if only three biscuits were used. In conversation later, the child explained that she was allowed to help herself to four biscuits from the tin at home. She could 'conserve' perfectly! Five biscuits were more than she was allowed, three were less, and, despite limited use of language, she could see this did not change when they were moved around.

Problems with Piaget's approach include: that his set tasks are obscure and remote from reality, that children cannot pay attention or remember for long enough, particularly when they are confused about expectations, it is not clear how children move from one stage to the next, children are found to use logic in many contexts, and even intelligent adults do not stick precisely to formal logic on most occasions. Comparisons can be made with Bruner, Bryant, Donaldson and Vygotsky.

Vocabulary associated with Piaget includes: *schema, assimilation, accommodation, equilibration, sensori-motor, concrete operations, formal operations, egocentricity, conservation.*

Pinker, Steven (current)

Steven Pinker is a Canadian-American experimental psychologist, cognitive scientist, and popular science writer known for his advocacy of evolutionary psychology and the computational theory of mind. He is the Johnstone Family Professor in the Department of Psychology at Harvard University, previously Professor of Psychology and Director of the Center for Cognitive Neuroscience at the Massachusetts Institute of Technology (MIT). He was educated at McGill and Harvard, and taught at Harvard and Stanford before moving to MIT. He conducts research on language and cognition, writes for publications such as the *New York Times*, *Time* and *Slate*, and is the author of several books.

He is inclined to talk as if evolution produced types of mind and behaviour that were 'designed to solve certain problems' rather than always reminding us that evolution could not be responsible for designing with purpose, but only resulted in changes that happened to enable our ancestors to solve problems effectively and therefore become more successful in continuing to reproduce.

Rogers, Carl Ransom (1902–1987)

Carl Rogers is known as a founder of the humanistic psychology movement and one of the most influential psychotherapists of the 20th century. He studied and worked at the University of Chicago and the University of Wisconsin-Madison. He became the first President of the American Academy of Psychotherapists and joined the Western Behavioral Sciences Institute (WBSI) before helping to found the Center for Studies of the Person in La Jolla, California.

Carl Rogers' client-centred approach to therapy is described as humanistic and phenomenological, based on his deep belief that all people have worth, dignity and the capacity for self-direction regardless of any opinions or judgements that other people might make. He prompted clients to seek their own interpretations of their behaviour and rejected behaviourism and psychodynamic theories. He says:

> it is the client who knows what hurts, what directions to go, what problems are crucial, what experiences have been deeply buried. It began to occur to me that unless I had a need to demonstrate my own cleverness and learning, I would do better to rely upon the client for the direction of movement in the process (1961: 11).

Vocabulary associated with Rogers includes: empathy, unconditional regard, congruence (genuineness), confrontation, active listening, non-directed or facilitative therapy, client-centred, person-centred. See also Part 2.3.13 and Part 3.

Rorschach, Hermann (1884–1922)

Hermann Rorschach was a Swiss psychiatrist who became associate director of the asylum at Herisau. He was interested in psychoanalysis, particularly Jung's approach, and the interpretation of art works by people diagnosed as psychotics and neurotics, and in their abilities to paint.

He is best known for the Rorschach test, a set of ten cards with bilaterally symmetrical inkblots that are presented to clients who are invited to describe what they see. The test is generally considered to be projective, such that people are expected to project unconscious fears and conflicts onto the inkblots so that their description should shed some light on their personality, particularly the unconscious elements. However, the test can be used in a variety of ways from an open-ended or non-directed way that allows a client to explore thoughts and feelings, to a measured or scored approach that can be compared with statistical norms in order to determine brain damage, specific mental health problems or creativity.

Rose, Stephen (current)

Stephen Rose is Visiting Professor in Biochemistry and Neuroscience for the Open University. He is a popular speaker and writer, best known for research into the molecular and cellular processes which occur during memory formation. According to the Open University website:

> We use the young chick as a model, with a variety of behavioural paradigms, notably one-trial passive avoidance training. We employ a number of techniques, including behaviour, pharmacology, neuroanatomy, biochemistry, molecular biology and immunocytochemistry, to elucidate the cascade of events required for long-term memory formation, beginning with synaptic transients and culminating in the remodelling of synapses. Most recently our laboratory programme has centred on the molecular processes involved in reconsolidation, and on the development of a cognitive enhancer intended as a potential therapeutic agent in Alzheimer's Disease.
>
> (http://www.open.ac.uk/science/biosci/ research/rose/rose.htm, accessed 24 July 2007)

Rutter, Michael (current)

Michael Rutter is an Emeritus Professor in Child and Adolescent Psychiatry and Developmental Psychopathology at the Institute of Psychiatry, Kings College, at the Maudsley in London. His research interests include autism, neuropsychiatric disorders, depression, antisocial behaviour, reading difficulties, deprivation syndromes and hyperkinetic disorder. He is frequently cited for his work on maternal deprivation (Rutter, 1981) in which he reassesses the findings of Bowlby (see above).

theorists

Sacks, Oliver Wolf (current)

Oliver Sacks is Clinical Professor of Neurology at the Albert Einstein College of Medicine in New York. He is well known for his collections of case histories of people with conditions such as Tourette's syndrome, autism, Parkinson's, musical hallucination, phantom limb syndrome, schizophrenia and Alzheimer's disease. His books explore the ways in which people are able to survive and adapt to different neurological diseases and conditions and what their experiences tell us about the human brain and mind. His book *Awakenings* (1973), about the treatment of patients with L-dopa, inspired the 1990 Hollywood movie with Robert de Niro and Robin Williams.

Sapir, Edward (1884–1939) and Whorf, Benjamin Lee (1897–1941)

Edward Sapir was anthropologist and linguist at the Universities of Pennsylvania, Chicago and Yale and Chief of Anthropology for the Canadian National Museum. Benjamin Lee Whorf began studying linguistics at Yale University under Sapir. Together, they are known for the Sapir–Whorf hypothesis of linguistic *determinism*, which is concerned with how our language shapes our thinking and our perceptions.

The usual examples that are given relate to cultures that have a particular need for an increased vocabulary in relation to some particular topic. For example, the Inuit have individual words for different kinds of snow and an increased awareness of their different properties. Racehorse breeders have individual terms for the ages and types of 'horse' and enhanced awareness of their abilities.

In the UK, the colour names that we learn for the rainbow determine what we see. Listing only a few colours means that we tend to see the rainbow in bands rather than a gradual merging of one hue into the next, even though we are capable of distinguishing several hundred different hues. Moreover, in the UK we normally use Isaac Newton's names red, orange, yellow, green, blue, indigo and violet and have difficulty distinguishing between the blue and the indigo. However, Newton probably intended the word blue or 'blew' to refer to the bright blue-green we now call cyan and knowing this enables us to see cyan in the rainbow or white light spectrum, where we would normally not notice it.

Schachter, Stanley (1922–1997) and Singer, Jerome L. (current)

Stanley Schachter was a social psychologist who studied and worked at Yale University, MIT, University of Minnesota, University of Michigan and the University of Columbia.

His wide range of research interests lay in the study of communication and social influence, group processes, sources of the affiliation motive, intellectual and temperamental correlates of birth order (see also Adler, above), nature of emotional experience, people's ability to correctly attribute the causes of their behaviour to external versus internal factors, causes of obesity and eating behaviour disorders, the addictive nature of nicotine, psychological reactions to events that affect stock market prices (see also Kahneman, above), and the proper interpretation of paralanguage such as filled pauses (uh, er) in speech. His main influences included Clark Hull, Leon Festinger and Kurt Lewin.

Jerome L. Singer is Professor Emeritus at the University of Pennsylvania. His research is concerned with development of systematic, rigorous, replicable methodologies to study features of human personality and conscious experience as reflected in an ongoing stream of thought, fantasies and daydreams, interior monologues, and the more general issues of imagination, emotion and nocturnal dreaming.

Together with Bibb Latané (see above), and Ladd Wheeler, Schachter and Singer (1962) carried out an experiment that showed that people who are aroused from some unknown source (for example, from an injection containing adrenaline) can be influenced to experience anger, euphoria or fear, depending on the situation in which they are placed. This suggested to them that elements of both the James–Lange (see Part 3) and Cannon–Bard (see above and Part 3) theories are factors in the experience of emotion and they developed a theory of emotion, now known as the Schachter–Singer two-factor theory, that proposes that both bodily changes and a cognitive label are needed to experience emotion. Schachter argued that the physiological substrate of all strong emotion may be the same. It is the appraisal of situations, often aided by cues from other people, that determines precisely which emotion will be experienced. This idea is taken further by Lazarus in his cognitive-appraisal model (see above and Part 3). The work on the attribution of emotions was part of the research on causal attribution, which dominated the field of social psychology in the 1970s.

Seligman, Martin E. P. (current)

Martin Seligman is Fox Leadership Professor of Psychology at the University of Pennsylvania. He is best known for his theories of *learned helplessness* and learned optimism.

Seligman has developed an interest in what he calls 'positive psychology', moving away from his earlier research programme of studying what can go wrong with the human condition. He now argues that psychology should focus on strength as well as weakness, and be concerned with improving the lives of normal people as well as healing problems.

Selye, Hans (Hugo Bruno) (1907–1982)

Hans Selye was an Austrian physician who worked at McGill University in Montreal and became Director of the Institute for Experimental Medicine and Surgery at the French-language University of Montreal.

He is best known for identifying a second arousal system, after Cannon's fight or flight mechanism, and developing the general adaptation syndrome (GAS), which involves the pituitary-adrenal-cortical arousal system (see Part 3).

Sheldon, William H. (1898–1977)

William Sheldon was a physician at the College of Physicians and Surgeons in New York City. He studied the body shapes of men and described and coined the word somatotype and names of the three components: endomorphy (fat shape), mesomorphy (muscular shape) and ectomorphy (thin shape). These components were rated on seven-point scales such that each man would be assigned three scores, indicating the relative quantity of each component. Sheldon claimed that the components were derived from embryonic layers and that the somatotype was permanent. He went on to relate body type to temperament, asserting that endomorphy was associated with viscerotonia, mesomorphy with somatotonia and ectomorphy with cerebrotonia (Sheldon and Stevens, 1942).

Sherif, Muzafer (1906–1988)

Muzafer Sherif is known as one of the founders of social psychology. He was a Turkish professor in the fields of psychology and sociology at Harvard University, Berlin, Columbia University, Ankara University and then Princeton, where he was a fellow of the US State Department.

Sherif's research provides a base for most of the understanding we have today about the nature of groups and its members. He is best known for his realistic conflict theory which describes inner group conflict, negative prejudices, and stereotypes as a result of actual competition between groups for desired resources. His most famous experiment is The Robber's Cave. When boys on a summer camp were separated into groups and encouraged to compete for valued prizes, they demonstrated prejudice and aggression towards the competing group. When, later, they were directed to co-operate on tasks for mutual benefit, the prejudice reduced. (See also Tajfel, below)

Shiffrin, Richard M. (current)

Richard M. Shiffrin is Luther Dana Waterman Professor of Psychology at Indiana University. His research area in cognitive science includes memory and perception.

He is frequently cited for early work on a multi-store (dual process) model of memory (Atkinson and Shiffrin, 1968, 1971) that includes the control processes of rehearsal and pattern recognition (see Part 3). This has formed an important basis for subsequent work on memory.

Skinner, Burrhus Frederic (Fred) (1904–1990)

B. F. Skinner was Edgar Pierce Professor of Psychology at Harvard University.

Using cages, now known as Skinner boxes, with a lever that delivered pellets of food when pressed, Skinner discovered that the rate with which the rat pressed the bar depended not on any preceding stimulus but on what followed the bar presses. This contradicted the ideas of Watson (below) and Pavlov (see above) and modified those of Thorndike (see above). Unlike the reflexes that Pavlov had studied, this kind of behaviour operated on the environment and was controlled by its effects. Skinner named it operant behaviour. It is also known as *operant or instrumental conditioning* and involves actions and is not dependent on trial and error.

Sperry, Roger Walcott (1913–1994)

Roger Walcott Sperry studied and worked at

theorists

Oberlin College, in Ohio, University of Chicago, Harvard University, the Yerkes Laboratory for Primate Biology in Florida and the California Institute of Technology (Caltech) where he held the Hixon Professorship of Psychobiology. He was awarded the Nobel Prize in 1981 'for his discoveries concerning the functional specialization of the cerebral hemispheres'.

Sperry disproved a widely accepted theory (of Paul Weiss) that the neural network that connects the sense organs and muscles to the brain starts as an undifferentiated and unspecified mesh of randomly connected nerve fibres and, under the influence of experience and learning, is later transformed into a highly co-ordinated, purposeful system. Plasticity and interchangeability of function were the key ideas.

Sperry showed that the circuits of the brain are largely hardwired, in the sense that each nerve cell gains its own chemical individuality early in embryonic development so that the function of the cell is fixed and is not modifiable thereafter.

In his *split-brain* work, Sperry and his students showed that if the two cerebral hemispheres of the brain are separated by severing the corpus callosum (the large band of fibres that connects them), the transfer of information between the hemispheres ceases, and the person behaves as if there are now two functionally different brains. By means of ingenious tests, Sperry was able to show that a conscious mind exists in each hemisphere but that the person can only articulate that consciousness or *sentience* when the left hemisphere (with the language centres) has access to the information.

Tajfel, Henri (1919–1982)

Henri Tajfel was a social psychologist at Oxford University and then Chair of Social Psychology at the University of Bristol.

Tajfel like Sherif (see above) believes that the personality approach is inadequate in explaining prejudice and uses a social psychological approach. Moreover, Tajfel et al (1971) argue that 'competition' is not a necessary condition for intergroup conflict and hostility. In the minimal groups experiments (1970), participants were divided arbitrarily into two groups. Members of both groups began to identify themselves with their group, preferring other members of their group (their in-group) and behaving antagonistically to members of the other group (their out-group). Tajfel does not deny the importance of competition between groups, or of personality types as explanations for the origins of prejudice, but argues that mere perception of the existence of another group can itself produce discrimination. The theory of social identity asserts that people have an inbuilt tendency to self-categorise themselves into one or more in-groups, building a part of their identity on the basis of membership of that group and enforcing boundaries with other groups, and the very act of categorisation produces conflict and discrimination.

Thorndike, Edward Lee (1874–1949)

Edward Lee Thorndike was an American pioneer in comparative psychology at the Teachers College, Columbia University and became President of the American Association for the Advancement of Science and William James Lecturer at Harvard University

He studied animal intelligence and is known for his 'cats in a puzzle box' experiments on trial and error and stimulus–response association and for his three primary laws:

> Law of effect – responses to a situation which are followed by a rewarding state of affairs will be strengthened and become habitual responses to that situation. Responses that reduce the likelihood of achieving a rewarding state (punishments, failures) will decrease in strength.

> Law of readiness – a series of responses can be chained together to satisfy some goal which will result in annoyance if blocked.

> Law of exercise – connections become strengthened with practice and weakened when practice is discontinued.

He went on to say:

> Transfer of learning occurs because of previously encountered situations.

> Intelligence is a function of the number of connections learned.

Tinbergen, Nikolaas (1907–1988)

Nikolaas Tinbergen was a zoologist at the University of Oxford and was awarded the Nobel Prize for Physiology or Medicine in 1973 (with Konrad Lorenz, see above, and Karl von Frisch) for his work on ethology and stress diseases in relation to individual and social behaviour patterns.

He is often cited for his early work on instinctive behaviour in sticklebacks, where he demonstrated that female fish that normally follow the red belly of the male as part of the mating procedure will also follow any similar red object. The red stimulus can be referred to as a 'trigger' for the normal instinctive behaviour. Tinbergen also demonstrated displacement behaviour, which refers to behaviour patterns which appear to be unrelated to the behaviour which closely precedes or follows them and occur in three situations: motivational conflict, frustration of sexual acts and physical thwarting of performance.

Tolman, Edward Chace (1886–1959)

Edward Chace Tolman studied at Massachusetts Institute of Technology and Harvard University and was a professor of psychology at the University of California, Berkeley. He is known for his studies on behavioural psychology, particularly learning in rats using mazes. He is particularly noted for his use of the term *cognitive map* to refer to the mental representation of spatial relationships in the environment in order to say what is happening when a rat learns to run through a maze to obtain a reward.

Tolman was not such a radical behaviourist as Skinner (see above) and set out to demonstrate that animals did not merely learn automatic responses to environmental stimuli but could use their learning in a flexible manner. This led the way to the development of cognitive psychology and problem-solving approaches.

Treisman, Anne (current)

Anne Treisman studied at Cambridge and Oxford Universities and is a highly influential Professor of Psychology at Princeton University. She is married to Daniel Kahneman (see above).

Her research laboratory is concerned with visual attention, object perception and memory, exploring the nature of the limits to human perception, the information-processing that results in the perception of objects and events, and the nature of the representations that underlie both conscious experience and implicit memory. They study patients with *brain damage*, and collaborate in studies using *brain imaging* or *evoked potentials*.

Treisman is often cited for her early model (1969) of selective *attention*. Instead of a single filter, as in Broadbent's model (see above), Treisman's model has a hierarchy of tests, including one for physical properties of words, and others for syllable patterns, grammar, and finally semantic meaning. Messages that fail various tests became attenuated (less noticeable), which reduces interference with the preferred message, but are not discarded until the final filter, which examines the semantic meaning of the messages.

More influential is her feature integration theory of attention (1980) that describes how early vision encodes features such as colour, form, orientation and others in separate 'feature maps', and that without spatial attention these features can bind randomly to form illusory conjunctions and deficits in selection.

In one classic study, participants are shown a display of coloured shapes, like Xs and Os, and instructed to press a button if they see a specified shape. If the search target is an O and the display shows only one O in an array of Xs, the participant responds quickly. However many Xs there are, the O seems to 'pop out'. The expression 'pop-out' is now used for this effect, which illustrates unconscious parallel processing. Similarly, where only two colours are used, an O in one colour pops out from an array of Os in the other colour. However, if the participant is asked to find a shape that is both green and an O in a display that contains red Os and green Xs, the participant must consciously search the array, letter by letter. See also *Attention* in Part 3.

Triandis, Harry C. (current)

Harry C. Triandis is Professor Emeritus at the University of Illinois.

His research focuses on links between behaviour and attitudes, norms, roles and other elements of subjective culture in different kinds of cultures, including individualistic cultures found in Europe and North America, and collectivist cultures found in most other parts of the world. The links have implications for social behaviour, personality, work behaviour, intergroup relations, prejudice, attitude change and cultural training. These approaches can be applied to intercultural training for successful interaction in other cultures.

His early work on attitudes and attitude change (1971) provides reasons for why we tend to hold settled attitudes (see Part 3).

Tulving, Endel (current)

Endel Tulving studied at Harvard and is currently Professor of Psychology concerned with cognitive neuroscience studies of memory processes and memory systems at the University of Toronto (see also Craik and Lockhart, above).

Tulving is often cited for his early work on episodic memory. According to episodic theory (Tulving, 1972, 1976; Tulving and Thomson, 1973), a unique episodic memory trace is formed at the time of input, and whether a retrieval cue will be effective depends on the relation between the cue and this episodic trace. If the information in the retrieval cue matches the information in the episodic trace the item will be remembered. The term ecphory refers to the process by which retrieval information provided by a cue is correlated with the information stored in an episodic memory trace.

Turing, Alan (1912–1954)

Alan Turing was a mathematician at Cambridge University and one of the Bletchley Park code-breakers working on Enigma during the Second World War. He is best known for his concept of the Turing machine (Turing, 1936/37) and the Turing test (Turing, 1950).

Turing machines are not physical objects but mathematical ones. They are simple abstract computational devices intended to help investigate the extent and limitations of what can be computed. We now think of them as computer software, but Turing's ideas date from before computers were commonplace.

The Turing test refers to a situation in which a person takes part in communication, usually through a keyboard, not knowing whether there is another person involved in giving responses or only a machine. If it is only a machine but the person cannot tell whether the responses have been generated by another person or a machine then it is considered reasonable to describe the machine as 'thinking' or having intelligence. This important notion has given rise to much controversy in the field of artificial intelligence.

Vygotsky, Leo Semyonovich (1896–1934)

Leo Vygotsky was a Russian developmental psychologist who promoted the socio-cultural idea that the intellectual development of children is a function of human communities, rather than of individuals.

Unlike Piaget (see above) who believes that children learn best from unguided discovery, Vygotsky believes that the individual child's development depends on learning from others and that children can often complete tasks with the help of others that they could not accomplish independently. He refers to the zone of proximal development (ZPD) which is related to the difference between the range of skill that can be developed with adult guidance or peer collaboration and what can be attained alone, and the time taken to minimise this difference. Vygotsky argues that at any given time in development children are on the verge of being able to solve certain problems and they learn best with full social interaction that includes structure, clues, reminders, help with remembering details and encouragement.

In comparison with Piaget and Bruner, Vygotsky argues that language and thinking are inter-related. This supports common-sense notions and anecdotal evidence that children (and adults) can think conceptually without having the language to express their ideas and that acquisition of relevant language brings about clarity and refinement of the concepts and the ability to share the ideas with others.

See also Bernstein, Chomsky, Dennett, Donaldson, Labov and Sapir for arguments relating to linguistic *determinism*, and George Herbert Mead for *symbolic interactionism*.

Wason, Peter Cathcart (1924–2003) and Johnson-Laird, Philip (current)

Peter Cathcart Wason was a cognitive psychologist at University College, London. Philip Johnson-Laird is Stuart Professor of Psychology at Princeton University and has studied and worked at UCL, University of Sussex, Cambridge University, Darwin College and Stanford University. They have collaborated on the psychology of thinking and reasoning.

Wason designed logical problems and tests to demonstrate and explain why people make certain consistent mistakes in logical reasoning, for example the THOG problem, the Wason selection task and the 2–4–6 task. These can be compared with the logical tasks that Piaget gave to children. Piaget believed that children are significantly different from adults because they do not think logically; he did not realise that the majority of adults make similar errors in abstract logical tasks.

For the THOG problem, participants are shown four shapes: a black square, a black circle, a white square and a white circle. The experimenter says 'I am thinking of one colour (black or white) and one shape (square or circle). Any figure that has either the colour I am thinking of, or the shape I am thinking of, but not both, is a THOG. Given that the black square is a THOG what, if anything, can you say about whether the other figures are THOGS?' (Answer below.)

In the Wason selection task, participants are given four situations or shown four cards with various symbols on the front and back and have to turn over the appropriate cards to disprove a rule. See some of the websites for examples. Most people do not choose sufficient cards or choose a wrong one, mainly because they are focusing on proving an imagined (more meaningful) rule, rather than disproving the given one.

In the standard form of the 2–4–6 task participants are asked to discover a rule (known to the experimenter) that generates sequences of three numbers (referred to as triples). The experimenter provides an example triple of 2–4–6 as being one that fits the rule. Participants are then asked to generate further triples that the experimenter classifies as either fitting or not fitting the to-be-discovered rule. Participants are encouraged to produce triples until they reach a point where they are confident that they know the rule, at which point they announce it. Despite the apparent simplicity of the 2–4–6 task actual success rates for first time announcements are very low. Incorrect announcements are typically restricted versions of the rule such as 'numbers increasing with intervals of two'.

The rule is actually 'ascending triples'. That is any three ascending numbers. These can be related or not, such as 1–2–3 or 78–99–526. Most people try triples that are similar to 2–4–6 and give only examples that fit their restricted notion and do not explore further.

In all these cases, participants provide their own meanings for the tasks and, for people not trained in logic, the meaning is much more important than the abstract logic.

Answer to THOG problem: If the black square is a THOG then the experimenter is thinking of a shape that is either black or square, that is the black circle or the white square. This means that those two shapes cannot be THOGS as each would have both qualities (or neither). The only shape that is

a THOG is the white circle as it has either the white (for the white square) or the circle (for the black circle). Most people do not answer this correctly, choosing instead one or both of the shapes that the experimenter must be thinking of and losing sight of the logic.

Watson, John Broadus (1878–1958)

John B. Watson was professor and director of the psychological laboratory at Johns Hopkins, Baltimore. Watson emphasised the study of observable behaviour and rejected introspection and theories of the unconscious mind and is known as the founder of behaviourism (see Part 2), which he defined as an experimental branch of natural science aimed at the prediction and control of behaviour. Watson's work influenced B. F. Skinner in his studies of operant conditioning, and had a major impact on the development of behaviour therapy.

He is often quoted (or misquoted) for his exaggerated reference to a child being a blank slate or *tabula rasa* that can be trained in any required manner:

> Give me a dozen healthy infants, well-formed, and my own specified world to bring them up in and I'll guarantee to take any one at random and train him to become any type of specialist I might select – doctor, lawyer, artist, merchant-chief and, yes, even beggar-man and thief, regardless of his talents, penchants, tendencies, abilities, vocations, and race of his ancestors. I am going beyond my facts and I admit it, but so have the advocates of the contrary and they have been doing it for many thousands of years.
>
> (Watson, 1930)

He defined personality in terms of organised habits, instincts, emotions, their combinations, plasticity (capability of new habit formation or altering of old habits), and retention (readiness of established habits to function after disuse). Watson argues that healthy personality consists of clean-cut and definite habit systems, and instincts and emotions that have yielded to social control. Psychopathology, on the other hand, is habit distortion; failure to eliminate old, unworkable habits and the emotions connected with them as situations change, and hence, Watson believed, able to be cured.

In a highly controversial experiment Watson conditioned 11-month-old 'little Albert' to fear furry objects; demonstrating, he argued, that complex behaviour develops out of simple unlearned responses by conditioning.

Weiss, Samuel (current)

Samuel Weiss is a professor in the Department of Cell Biology and Anatomy/Pharmacology and Therapeutics in the University of Calgary and Director of the Hotchkiss Brain Institute.

He is at the forefront of brain research. He is cited for his important breakthrough in 1992 when he found that brain cells could regenerate. According to his website (see 7.2):

> Our research has generated two new and important perspectives in the study of developmental neurobiology. First, neural development continues throughout the lifetime of adult mammals. Second, insights into ongoing adult cell production may allow for the use of stem cells to repair neural tissue and allow for functional recovery from brain and spinal cord injury or disease.

Winnicott, Donald Woods (1896–1971)

Donald Winnicott was a paediatrician and psychoanalyst at Paddington Green Children's Hospital in London and President of the British Psychoanalytical Society.

Greatly influenced by Melanie Klein (see above), he analysed how children develop attachment bonds with the mother and how these bonds loosen as the child grows. The mother can assist in this process by allowing the child to choose continuously between feeling independent and acknowledging dependence. Winnicott (for example, 1960) suggests that an 'ordinary devoted mother' who offers 'good enough mothering' will allow the child rights over precious feelings of dependence and unity with the mother and will not interfere with the sense of security this brings.

Wundt, Wilhelm Maximilian (1832–1920)

Wilhelm Wundt was a German philosopher and psychologist, Professor of Inductive Philosophy at Leipzig University, where he established the world's first experimental laboratory in psychology. He is often referred to as the Father of Experimental Psychology and the Founder of Modern Psychology.

Wundt combined philosophical introspection with laboratory techniques, influenced by his physiological studies with Helmholtz (see above, and Young–Helmholtz below).

Yerkes, Robert Mearns (1876–1956)

Robert M. Yerkes was an American comparative psychologist who studied and worked at Harvard, John Hopkins and Yale University, where he was Professor of Psychobiology and founded and directed the first non-human primate research laboratory in the United States. The Yerkes National Primate Research Centre located in Atlanta, Georgia at Emory University conducts multidisciplinary medical research primarily aimed at development of vaccines and medical treatments.

Yerkes is well known for his work on instinctive behaviour and intelligence in animals and humans. He is cited, particularly in health psychology, for the Yerkes–Dodson law (1908) concerning the relationship between physiological arousal and performance. This is an inverted U-curve relationship which shows that when the demands on a person are right for that person, arousal, and hence performance, will be at an optimum level. It is only when arousal increases beyond the optimum, or falls too far below, that the person feels distress and suffers a drop in performance. This is important for work on stress levels as it suggests that too little arousal is as harmful as too much. See also Part 3.

Young, Thomas (1773–1829), von Helmholtz, Hermann (1821–1894) and Maxwell, James Clerk (1831–1879)

These three scientists are often cited together for what is usually called the Young–Helmholtz trichromatic theory of colour vision that proposed that the human retina contains three types of light receptors (known as cones) sensitive to bright light. See also Mollon, above, and colour *vision* in Part 3.

Thomas Young was an English physician and physicist who established the principle of interference of light and thus resurrected the century-old wave theory of light.

Hermann von Helmholtz was a German scientist and philosopher who made fundamental contributions to physiology, optics, electrodynamics,

theorists

mathematics and meteorology (http://www.britannica.com/eb/art-35724?articleTypeId=1). He is best known in physics for his statement of the law of the conservation of energy, and in psychology for his contribution to the measurement of the speed of the nerve impulse and his theories of vision and hearing.

James Clerk Maxwell was a Scottish mathematician and physicist at Cambridge and the University of London. Among his many achievements, he demonstrated the electromagnetic properties of light and contributed to theories of colour vision. He confirmed Young's theory that the eye has three kinds of receptors sensitive to different colours, and showed that colour 'blindness' is due to 'defects' in the receptors. He spun disks painted with sectors of red, green and blue to mix those primary colours into other colours and explained (to some extent) how the addition and subtraction of primary colours produces other colours.

Zimbardo, Philip G. (current)

Philip G. Zimbardo is Professor Emeritus of Psychology at Stanford University. According to his website, his research interests include prisons, time, shyness, madness, violence, persuasion, hypnosis, dissonance, political psychology and terrorism.

Zimbardo is best known for the 1971 Stanford Prison Experiment in which students took the roles of prisoners and prison guards. The simulation was realistic and the experiment was remarkable for the changes that took place in the participants. Zimbardo says that after only six days the planned two-week study had to be stopped because the guards had taken over and some were behaving sadistically and the prisoners had become withdrawn and isolated, like prisoners of war or hospitalised mental patients. Even the 'good' guards felt helpless to intervene. See 7.2.

theorists

5 research methods

research

A–B–A design [271] ¦ Analysis of qualitative data [271] ¦ Analysis of variance (ANOVA) [271] ¦ Bar chart/bar graph [271] ¦ Baseline observations [271] ¦ Bias [271] ¦ Bimodal (bi-modal) distribution [271] ¦ Binomial test and binomial sign test [271] ¦ Bonferroni correction [272] ¦ Box-and-whisker display/five-number summary [272] ¦ Case study [272] ¦ Causality (question of) [272] ¦ Central tendency [272] ¦ Chi-square (χ^2) measure of association [273] ¦ Confounding variable [274] ¦ Content analysis [274] ¦ Context of discovery [274] ¦ Context of justification [274] ¦ Contingency table [274] ¦ Control group/condition [275] ¦ Control procedures [275] ¦ Correlation [275] ¦ Correlation coefficient [275] ¦ Cramer's phi [275] ¦ Cross-sectional study [275] ¦ Cumulative frequency [275] ¦ Data (singular datum) [275] ¦ Degrees of freedom (df) [275] ¦ Dependent variable (DV) [276] ¦ Descriptive statistics [276] ¦ Deviation score [276] ¦ Discourse analysis [276] ¦ Dispersion (variability or spread) [276] ¦ Double-blind design [276] ¦ Errors [277] ¦ Experience-sampling method [277] ¦ Experimental conditions [277] ¦ Experimenter effect [277] ¦ Exploratory data analysis [277] ¦ Factor analysis and factorial design [277] ¦ Focus group interview [277] ¦ Focused (semi-structured) interview [277] ¦ Frequency distribution [277] ¦ Frequency polygon [278] ¦ Friedman test [278] ¦ Graphical representation [278] ¦ Grounded theory [278] ¦ Hawthorne effect [278] ¦ Hermeneutics [278] ¦ Heuristics [279] ¦ Histogram [279] ¦ Hypothesis/experimental hypothesis [279] ¦ Hypothetico-deductive [280] ¦ Idiographic [280] ¦ Independent variable (IV) [280] ¦ Inference [280] ¦ Inferential statistics/tests of statistical significance [280] ¦ Kendall's coefficient of concordance [280] ¦ Kruskal–Wallis test [280] ¦ Kurtosis [280] ¦ Law [280] ¦ Level of data [281] ¦ Likert-type scale [281] ¦ Linear regression [281] ¦ Longitudinal study [283] ¦ Mann–Whitney U test [283] ¦ Model [283] ¦ Naturalistic observation [284] ¦ Nomothetic [284] ¦ Normal (Gaussian) distribution [284] ¦ Null hypothesis [285] ¦ Objective [285] ¦ Operational definitions [285] ¦ Opportunity sample [285] ¦ Parameter [286] ¦ Parametric and non-parametric tests [286] ¦ Participant [286] ¦ Participant observation [286] ¦ Participant (subject) variables [286] ¦ Pie chart [286] ¦ Population [286] ¦ Post-hoc comparisons [286] ¦ Protocol analysis [287] ¦ Psychometric tests/psychometrics [287] ¦ Q technique [287] ¦ Qualitative and quantitative variables [287] ¦ Qualitative research methods [287] ¦ Quantitative research [288] ¦ Questionnaire [288] ¦ Randomised controlled trial [288] ¦ Rank order [288] ¦ Range [288] ¦ Rate [288] ¦ Raw data [288] ¦ Related/within groups design [289] ¦ Reliability [289] ¦ Repeated measures design [289] ¦ Retrospective and prospective studies [289] ¦ Sample [290] ¦ Sampling bias [290] ¦ Scattergram/scatterplot [290] ¦ Significance level [290] ¦ Skew [291] ¦ Spearman's rho [291] ¦ Standard deviation (s, or σ 'sigma') [291] ¦ Stem-and-leaf display [292] ¦ Subjective [293] ¦ Subjects [293] ¦ Symbolic interaction [293] ¦ Tally [293] ¦ Tests of proportions [293] ¦ T-test (Student's t-test or Student–Fisher t-distribution) [294] ¦ Theory [294] ¦ Thesis [294] ¦ Two-tailed hypothesis [294] ¦ Unrelated/between groups design [294] ¦ Validity [294] ¦ Variable [295] ¦ Variance [295] ¦ Wilcoxon test [295] ¦ Z-scores [295] ¦

This part includes outlines of research design and method with statistics needed for interpreting results, in order to introduce terminology or serve as a refresher or revision aid. The length of each item bears no relation to its importance.

There are many specialist statistic textbooks available with varying levels of 'readability' and plenty of accessible material on the Internet. Statistical formulae are given by the BPS on the website for the qualifying examination, see Part 7. Tables of significance are given in most specialist texts e.g. Clegg (1982).

See Part 1 for the section on 'Write an essay, report, dissertation or article'.

See also Part 2.1 Ways of Looking – Scientific nature of enquiry.

Table 5.1 English and Greek letters used in statistical notation

n or N	Number of values or scores in a set.
d or D	Difference between two values, e.g. difference between ranks.
x	Values in a set.
y	Instead of x where there is a second set of values.
|x| and |y|	Numerical value of x and y, ignoring the positive (+) or negative sign (−).
$\bar{x}$ (x bar) and $\bar{y}$ (y bar) or μ (Greek small letter mu)	Mean of a set of values, where $\bar{x} = \Sigma x/N$, that is the sum of all the x values divided by the number of values.
$(x - \bar{x})$	Deviation score or the difference between value x and the mean.
Σ (Greek capital letter sigma)	Sum, or total of a set of values, e.g. Σx, that is the sum of all the x values.
ρ (Greek small letter rho) or r	Correlation coefficient. For example, Spearman's rho, $\rho = 1 - 6\ \Sigma D^2/N(N^2 - N)$
σ (Greek small letter sigma) or s	Standard deviation, where $\sigma = \sqrt{(\Sigma(x - \bar{x})^2/N)}$, that is the square root of the sum of all the squares of the deviation scores divided by the number of values.

5.1 Methodology and ethical issues

QAA research methods in psychology: research design, the nature and appropriate statistical analysis of data, psychometrics and measurement techniques, and quantitative and qualitative methods. It should be noted that qualitative methods are understood broadly here, and might include protocol analysis, interviews, grounded theory and discourse analysis.

(Reproduced with permission from *Subject Benchmark Statement: Psychology 2007*. © The Quality Assurance Agency for Higher Education, 2007.)

BPS PAPER 5: RESEARCH DESIGN AND QUANTITATIVE METHODS IN PSYCHOLOGY

Section 1: Research issues

Problem definition and hypothesis formulation. Independent and dependent variables: their identification and selection. Experimental manipulation, control and internal validity: the roles of random allocation, matching, and counterbalancing in independent groups, related samples and repeated measure designs. The experimental manipulation of more than one independent variable in factorial designs: the contribution of interaction effects. The role of random sampling in psychological research: external validity. Quasi-experimental studies of pre-existing groups: the question of causality. The particular strengths and weaknesses of "single-participant" designs and case studies.

Observational approaches. Survey research: sampling and the problem of non-response; descriptive versus explanatory surveys; attitude scale construction; different questioning methods, e.g. postal, telephone, face-to-face. Methods of controlling for participants' expectations and experimenter effects. Inter-rater reliability. Critical evaluation of the methods employed to collect data in psychological research. The theory of psychological measurement: standardisation; reliability and the standard error of measurement; validity. The collection of qualitative data: observation, participant observation, techniques for the collection of verbal protocols. The analysis of qualitative data: content analysis, discourse analysis, grounded theory and protocol analysis. The ethics of research with humans and animals.

Section 2: Quantitative methods

Descriptive and summary statistics: measures of central tendency and dispersion; skew and kurtosis; frequency distributions; graphical methods including frequency histograms and cumulative frequency plots; exploratory data analysis including stem-and-leaf and box-and-whisker displays. Probability theory: rules for assigning and combining probabilities; the OR rule with mutually exclusive and non-mutually exclusive events; the AND rule with independent and non-independent events; the binomial distribution (and its normal approximation). The normal distribution: z scores and areas under the curve; the sampling distribution of the sample mean. Statistical inference: significance testing (including the null and alternative hypothesis, type 1 and type 2 errors, significance level, power and sample size);. Confidence intervals: for the population mean; for the difference between two population means. Mean and error bar graphs. Non-parametric alternatives to t-tests: the sign test; Wilcoxon matched-pairs signed ranks test; Mann–Whitney test. Tests of proportions: chi-squared tests for goodness of fit and for contingency tables. Cramer's Phi as a measure of association in contingency tables. McNemar's test of change. Bivariate correlation and linear regression: scatterplots; Pearson's correlation coefficient; partial correlation; the significance of a correlation coefficient; the linear regression equation and its use in prediction; the accuracy of prediction; Spearman's and Kendall's rank order correlation coefficients. The analysis of variance: one factor independent and repeated measures designs; two factor independent, repeated measures and mixed designs; main effects and interaction effects (including graphical presentation); planned (including trend) comparisons; the Bonferroni correction; post hoc comparisons (including the choice between methods); the analysis of simple effects. Non-parametric alternatives to one factor analyses of variance: Kruskal–Wallis, Friedman and Cochran's Q tests. The choice of an appropriate statistical analysis: the issue of level of measurement (nominal, ordinal, interval and ratio scales); test assumptions (e.g. normality, homogeneity of variance, linearity); transformations of the dependent variable in an attempt to meet assumptions; robustness; power efficiency.

(Reproduced with permission.)

Approaches in psychological research

Research can be *quantitative* or *qualitative*, scientific or non-scientific.

Quantitative research involves countable or measurable quantities such as length, weight or number of visits. These numbers can be analysed using statistical tests. *Parametric tests* can be used where the data can be compared with data that has already been amassed for the normal population. *Non-parametric tests* must be used where there is no normal population for comparison. The chief *experimental investigations* related to health professions are the *randomised controlled trial* and *hypothetico-deductive* research.

Qualitative research tends to be exploratory, based on *research questions* rather than hypotheses, does not involve *experiments* and is less rigid.

Traditionally, only quantitative research has been regarded as scientific, being seen as systematic, objective, based on clearly defined *hypotheses*, examining cause and effect, seeking general *laws*, using *statistical analysis* when necessary and seeking to have *reliability* and *validity*. (See *Research process* and Figure 5.1). However, as qualitative approaches are gaining in reliability and respectability this position may change.

Research criteria

To qualify as scientific, studies are expected to follow natural science methods and satisfy accepted criteria for good theory and research practice. These criteria include:

> falsifiability or refutability
> validity or truth value
> clarity
> ability to predict
> internal consistency or coherence
> simplicity or economy of ideas

> fertility or generating of ideas
> aesthetic or intuitive appeal
> practical guidance
> impact on our self-concept.

Scientific method and the research process

Investigations or projects may involve the following components:

> research rationale or project justification, decision about area of interest, aims and purposes, ethical aspects, costs
> choice of research *paradigm*
> examination of personal assumptions, beliefs and expectations
> information gathering, search of relevant publications, consultation, general, pilot or preliminary work
> detailing and categorisation, essential factors, similarities, differences, relationships, hierarchies
> selection of variables, sorting the dependent and independent variables
> formulation of hypotheses, expression of each expectation clearly as an experimental hypothesis or null hypothesis
> selection of research questions
> project design, choosing or setting up situations for observation, experiments or surveys and identification and control of variables
> systematic and methodical collection of data with regard to safety, resources and ethical considerations
> statistical analysis of the data
> evaluation to ensure objectivity and conclusions
> theories, laws and models, reasons behind findings, confirmation of hypotheses
> publication and debate, follow-up work
> consideration of allied fields and applications of findings.

Figure 5.1 summarises the possible steps in the research process, or scientific method.

Research ethics (see also Ethics in Part 1)

All research has to meet the highest standards in design and implementation.

BPS guidelines can be found at www.bps.org.uk (follow the links from the Society in the main menu).

Francis (2004: 51–4) gives a clear discussion of the need for a code of conduct that sets out expectations in writing since any researcher might not think of all relevant aspects. Guidelines help each individual to evaluate every piece of work and avoid the pressures of competition, including communication with other researchers, record keeping, presentation and discussion, publication and the possible replication of the research by others.

Responsibility lies with both individuals and the institutions where they work. Issues include:

> accuracy
> honesty and commitment to truth

> confidentiality
> care and avoidance of harm (physical and psychological)
> authorship and right to publish.

1. Decide topic, research the literature
2. Think through hunches and guesses
3. Select variables
4. Formulate hypotheses, including null hypothesis
5. Conduct pilot study
6. Re-think and prepare
7. Experiment/ observe/ survey
8. Draw conclusions
9. DESCRIBE : similarities and differences/categories/ hierarchies/ relationships
10. EXPLAIN: formulate theory / laws/ models
11. PREDICT outcome in similar circumstances
12. Re-test
13. Evaluate for reliability, validity
14. Publish and critically debate
15. 'support, improve, disprove'
16. CONTROL – apply findings in practice

Figure 5.1 Some steps in the scientific method

Statistics and statistical tests

Statistics is concerned with scientific methods for collecting, organising, summarising, presenting and analysing data, as well as drawing valid conclusions and making reasonable decisions on the basis of this analysis (Hannigan, 1982: 1). A distinction is made between *descriptive statistics* and *inferential statistics*.

Research design

Experimental Investigation: in a 'true' experiment, the relationship between two variables is investigated under conditions in which all variables are controlled, except the one being investigated (the *dependent variable*). There are three defining characteristics of the true experiment:

> randomisation
> control
> manipulation.

In a 'quasi' experiment, one or two of the three defining characteristics are not present.
Five basic experimental designs can be identified:

> *single-group* or single participant
> *independent-groups* or independent participants
> *matched-groups* or matched participants
> *repeated measures*
> complex designs.

research

By deliberately producing a change in one variable at a time (the *independent variable*), it can be determined whether a change in an independent variable brings about a change in the dependent variable. By manipulating only one independent variable at a time and eliminating the possible effects of other variables, it may be possible to conclude that one change is the cause of the other, rather than merely being observed as a correlation. In the social sciences it is difficult to identify and control all extraneous variables, so that even where experiments are possible and are considered ethically appropriate, conclusions must be cautiously drawn.

Choosing a design

When designing psychological experiments, remember that the more complicated the design, the more complicated will be the statistical analysis. It is best to keep the design simple, with clear objectives and related to simple, straightforward statistical tests.

You can choose between:

> Descriptive statistics
   - frequency distributions (bar chart, histogram, frequency polygon or line graph, pie chart, box and whiskers, stem and leaf)
   - measures of central tendency (mean, median, mode)
   - measures of dispersion (range, standard deviation).
> Inferential statistics
   - correlational studies:
     Kendall's rank order correlation coefficient
     Linear regression equation and line of best fit
     Pearson's product-moment
     Scatterplots
     Spearman's rho.
   - Parametric tests:
     analysis of variance (ANOVA)
     normal distribution
     t-tests (matched pairs or independent measures).
   - non-parametric statistical tests:
     Mann–Whitney U-test (independent measures)
     Wilcoxon test (matched pairs).
> Qualitative research methods:
   - ethnography
   - *grounded theory research*
   - *hermeneutics*
   - empirical phenomenology
   - *heuristics.*

The design you choose will depend on what you are trying to investigate. Find as many examples of other people's research as you can. When you find something similar to what you want to do, you can look at the design and the statistical tests and see if it is possible for you to replicate the method.

Calculator and information technology (IT) skills

Unless you are going to laboriously work out everything the hard way and draw all your diagrams by hand, you will need to become familiar with the available computer software. Rest assured it is much, much easier in the long run and repays all your effort.

Calculator

The most useful type of calculator is one with scientific notation and statistics. There are several different sorts and you will need to follow the instructions.

The procedure for finding mean, *variance* and *standard deviation* is usually quite straightforward. Working out the answers for other formulas can take a bit of practice.

Check whether it is programmed for standard or scientific use. Computer calculators usually offer a choice in the 'view' menu. The scientific ones are set up with algebraic logic and notation. You may know this as BODMAS (brackets, of, divide, multiply, add, subtract) or some variation. This means that the calculator will do the operations in a special order. To test your calculator, try the following, without putting in any brackets or hitting the 'equals' button' before the end.

Put the numbers and signs in as they are written:

$$3 + 2 \times 5 =$$

The key presses look like this:

$$\boxed{3}\,\boxed{+}\,\boxed{2}\,\boxed{\times}\,\boxed{5}\,\boxed{=}$$

What answer do you get? If your calculator gives 25, then it is standard. If, on the other hand it gives 13, it is a scientific calculator using algebraic logic. Algebraic logic is much better for statistics so it is well worth finding out how to use this efficiently if you have forgotten.

Try the following calculation for Spearman's rho from Figure 5.15.

The formula is
$$r_s = 1 - \frac{6\Sigma D^2}{N(N^2 - 1)}$$

Putting the values in gives
$$r_s = 1 - \frac{6 \times 8}{5(5^2 - 1)} \quad \text{where } \Sigma D^2 = 8 \text{ and } N = 5$$

You just need to remember that everything under the dividing line is to be divided, so you will use a 'divide' sign before the bracket, not a 'multiply' sign.

Think of it as 'one, minus six times eight, divided by five and divided by five squared minus one (in a bracket)'.

$$1 - 6 \times 8 / 5 / (5\verb|^|2 - 1) =$$

The key presses look like this (where ^2 is the 'square' key):

$$\boxed{1}\,\boxed{-}\,\boxed{6}\,\boxed{\times}\,\boxed{8}\,\boxed{/}\,\boxed{5}\,\boxed{/}\,\boxed{(}\,\boxed{(}\,\boxed{5}\,\boxed{^2}\,\boxed{-}\,\boxed{1}\,\boxed{)}\,\boxed{=}$$

This should give the answer $r_s = 0.6$

If you have difficulty, find someone to help you: it is usually much easier to understand a person than written instructions.

Spreadsheets and databases

It helps to become familiar with software such as Microsoft Excel, Lotus or Mac. You can use this for drawing pie charts, bar charts, histograms, frequency distributions and so on. As you progress you will find many ways of storing and manipulating data.

SPSS (originally Statistics for Social Sciences)

SPSS is a comprehensive package for all statistical calculations and data handling and will run on Windows, Mac or Linus. It will almost certainly be available as part of your course. See Part 7 for a website.

research

5.2 Key terms and concepts in research methods and statistics

A–B–A design: experimental design in which participants first experience the baseline condition (A), then experience the experimental treatment (B), and then return to the baseline (A).

Analysis of qualitative data: see under separate entries:

› Content analysis
› Discourse analysis
› Grounded theory
› Protocol analysis.

Analysis of variance (ANOVA): this is a parametric method based on variance for comparing samples to see whether there is any significant difference between them which can be attributed to the different experimental conditions. It is used for tackling problems where the simple t-test is not sufficient, because there are more than two variables, and can reveal whether sampling errors are confusing the results. Like the t-test, ANOVA is only useful for data which are selected from approximately normal (Gaussian) distributions. Special tables are used to compare values with normative data. Calculations can be complicated and it is now usual to employ computer software, such as SPSS. As with all complicated procedures, however, we recommend that students devise a simple set of results and analyse these in the long way by hand before using the computer, in order to understand the various steps. See also Kruskal–Wallis, Friedman and Kendall tests.

Bar chart/bar graph: visual representation of nominal level of data, in which columns are used to show how many scores are obtained for each category. Data may be actual frequencies or percentages. The bars may be drawn vertically or horizontally, and in two or three dimensions but in academic work it is common to put them vertically and two-dimensionally as in a histogram, see Figures 5.2 and 5.6. Since the categories are nominal and not part of a continuous scale of measurement, the bars are drawn with gaps in between.

Baseline observations: initial measurements of physical and psychological factors, taken before intervention and against which the effectiveness of the intervention can be evaluated.

Bias: a tendency to influence results in one way rather than another. There are several kinds:

› experimenter bias, see Experimenter effect
› participant bias, see Experimenter effect
› sampling bias.

Bimodal (bi-modal) distribution: a set of numbers which has two modes. When shown as a diagram or graph, a bimodal distribution has two humps.

Binomial test and binomial sign test: use the binomial test when there are two possible and mutually exclusive outcomes, such as flipping a coin which can be heads or tails, and with related groups design. Count each kind of outcome (often called 'success' and 'failure') that occurred in your experiment. Work out your hypothesis for what the probability of 'success' is. For example, if you flip a coin once, the probability of heads (success) is 0.5. If you flip it twice, the probability of at least one head is three out of the four possibilities or 0.75, that is, both heads, first head then tail, first tail then head, both tails, and so on for successive flips. Compare your experimental results with the theoretical probabilities and estimate the significance.

The sign test is the special case of the binomial case where the hypothesis is that the two outcomes have equal probabilities.

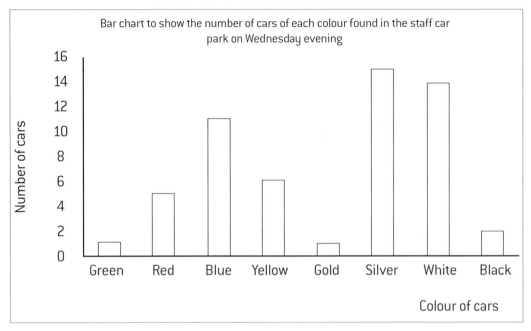

Figure 5.2 Bar chart

Bonferroni correction: this is a safeguard against multiple tests of statistical significance on the same data falsely giving the appearance of significance, due to chance. It was developed by Italian mathematician Carlo Emilio Bonferroni and states that if an experimenter is testing n dependent or independent hypotheses on a set of data, then the statistical significance level that should be used for each hypothesis separately is 1/n times what it would be if only one hypothesis were tested. An example of this is the significance level for the two-tailed hypothesis (that is, n=2), which is half that of the one-tailed (n=1).

Box-and-whisker display/five-number summary: box-and-whisker plots show only certain statistics rather than all the data and can be useful for handling many data values and allowing people to explore data and draw informal conclusions when two or more variables are present. The five-number summary consists of:

> the lowest value
> the first quartile, that is the median of the lower part of the data
> the second quartile or median of the entire set of data

> the third quartile, that is the median of the upper part of the data
> the greatest value.

Quartiles separate the original set of data into four equal parts. Each of these parts contains one quarter of the data. Figure 5.3 shows how to construct the box and whisker from the data. Immediate visuals of a box-and-whisker plot are the centre, the spread and the overall range of distribution.

Case study: intensive observation of a particular individual or small group of individuals.

Causality (question of): when two sets of data are found to have a correlation it is dangerous to assume that one caused the other. We can only infer that they occur together. It is possible that they have a common cause or that there is some unknown factor.

Central tendency: the formal mathematical term for an average or typical value in a set. There are three main types, each of which is an attempt to summarise the whole set of figures in one representative figure:

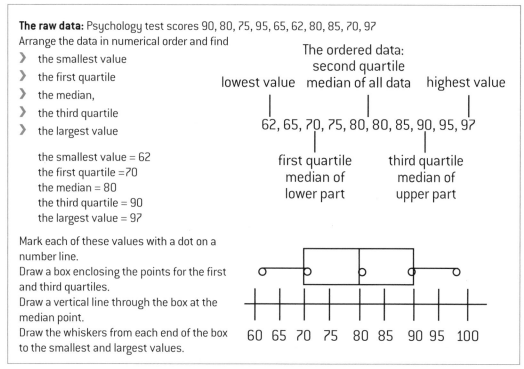

The raw data: Psychology test scores 90, 80, 75, 95, 65, 62, 80, 85, 70, 97
Arrange the data in numerical order and find

> the smallest value
> the first quartile
> the median,
> the third quartile
> the largest value

the smallest value = 62
the first quartile = 70
the median = 80
the third quartile = 90
the largest value = 97

The ordered data:
second quartile
lowest value   median of all data   highest value

62, 65, 70, 75, 80, 80, 85, 90, 95, 97

first quartile   third quartile
median of   median of
lower part   upper part

Mark each of these values with a dot on a number line.
Draw a box enclosing the points for the first and third quartiles.
Draw a vertical line through the box at the median point.
Draw the whiskers from each end of the box to the smallest and largest values.

60 65 70 75 80 85 90 95 100

Figure 5.3 Box and whisker display

> Mean: the arithmetical average of a range of scores. This is represented by x̄ (pronounced x bar), where x̄ = Σx/N. That is the sum of all the values divided by the number of values.

> Median: the score in the middle of a group of ranked scores, with an equal number of higher and lower values.

> Mode: the most frequently occurring value in a set of scores. In a distribution graph, this would show as the peak of the curve.

Although they are all called a measure of central tendency, they may not actually occur at the midpoint of a distribution graph. The choice of which to use depends on the nature of the figures and the purpose of the study.

The mean is most useful where the numbers cluster closely around a central value, but is misleading where there is a large spread or uneven distribution. The median is useful for small samples and likely to be more stable than the mean, particularly where the values at each end (outliers) change dramatically. That is, if the mean and median are calculated for a set of figures and then one or two more values are added to the sample

which are at the extreme ends of the scale, the mean will change noticeably but the median will stay roughly the same. The median can be time-consuming to calculate or a nuisance to use with large samples or where the middle values move. The mode is rarely used in statistical analysis but can be useful in everyday situations if decisions will be based on the most commonly occurring values.

Chi-square (χ^2) measure of association: a group of tests based on the calculation of χ^2, where χ is the Greek letter chi (pronounced ky, to rhyme with my). These tests provide numbers to show relationships between variables in groups of observations and can be used to test the null hypothesis. It is useful where data can be arranged in a contingency table where each cell represents a variable. This is used at the nominal level of data where variables are named descriptions, not numbers.

For example, the simple chi-square test could be used to indicate whether there is a relationship between body weight and susceptibility to heart attack. In this case there might be four cells arranged in a 2 x 2 table, that is overweight/underweight x have/have not had a heart attack (Clegg, 1982: 94). Just as in a t-test, there is a particular formula for calculating the chi-square test statistic. We can compare this statistic with a chi-square distribution with known degrees of freedom in order to arrive at the p-value. We then use the p-value to decide whether or not we can reject the null hypothesis.

Like tests of correlation, the chi-square measure does not indicate whether one thing precedes or causes another, only that the data show an association. The chi-square test cannot say whether relationships are certain, but can put a number on their degree of certainty.

Confounding variable: a stimulus other than the variable an experimenter explicitly introduces into a research setting that affects a participant's behaviour.

Content analysis: a research method that identifies key items in the message content of any text, compares them with other items and compares them with equivalent statistics gathered from society at large. It is usually a straightforward technique of seeing what is included in a piece of text, according to some scheme of intention or purpose. Sometimes only the content is counted; sometimes there is a wider brief. For example, content analysis of this book according to Lasswell's (1948) model of communication would identify:

> WHO: information about the author and her sources.
> SAYS WHAT: label and classify the different kinds of content and count how many times each occurred.
> IN WHICH CHANNEL: the type of mass media

involved, that is, print through educational publishing for a limited readership (narrow-casting).
> TO WHOM: the readership it is intended for, and who actually reads it.
> WITH WHAT EFFECT: this could include benefits (or otherwise) to the author and publisher as well as the readership. (See Gill and Adams, 1998).

This book could then be compared with other psychology books and with books in general or with other forms of media such as journals and websites.

Context of discovery: the initial phase of research, in which observations, beliefs, information and general knowledge lead to a new idea or a different way of thinking about some phenomenon.

Context of justification: the research phase in which evidence is brought to bear on hypotheses.

Contingency table: also known as a cross-classification table, this is a way of presenting data so that the frequencies of two variables can be cross-tabulated. Polit and Hungler (1995: 387) give an example of participants' gender and their responses to a question asking whether they are non-smokers, light smokers or heavy smokers. The raw data is presented as a table which lists participants and shows whether each one is male or female and non-smoker, light smoker or heavy smoker. This can then be arranged as cells in a 3 x 2 contingency table (see Figure 5.4). Data may be presented as frequencies or percentage frequencies. Totals may also be given. When presented in this way, data in each of the sub-groups or cells can be compared to see whether there

Contingency table for the number of male and female non-smokers, light smokers and heavy smokers using the college bar regularly.

	female	male
non-smoker	56	23
light smoker	12	37
heavy smoker	1	5

Figure 5.4 Contingency table

are significant relationships. Common statistical calculations for determining significance are the chi-square measure of association and Cramer's phi.

Control group/condition: a group or condition which is used for comparison in an experimental investigation. The control group does not receive any intervention or treatment.

Control procedures: consistent procedures for giving instructions, scoring responses, and holding all other variables constant except those being systematically varied.

Correlation: a measure of the relationship between two variables, that is when one variable increases, so does the other. For example, we might expect a correlation between height and weight such that taller people are heavier, across the whole population. We could measure height and weight for a representative sample, plot a scattergram and apply a simple test of correlation to obtain the correlation coefficient and see if there is a relationship. Tests for correlation include Spearman's rho and Pearson's product-moment calculation. A correlation only shows that two variables are related. It does not indicate that one causes the other. See also *Degrees of freedom* and *Validity*.

Correlation coefficient: this is the probability of correlation and is a number between zero and one which represents the degree of relationship between two variables. A high coefficient, for example, 0.8 or 0.9, indicates a high level of relatedness. A low coefficient indicates the variables are not noticeably related. A negative correlation indicates an inverse relationship: that is, when one value increases, the other decreases . Either the letter r or the Greek letter ρ (rho) is usually used to denote the correlation coefficient.

Cramer's phi: is used as a measure of association in contingency tables when the chi-squared matrix is bigger than a 2 x 2 matrix. The end result is interpreted like a correlation coefficient (Pearson r).

Cross-sectional study: an investigation for comparing performance at different ages, which is carried out at a single point in time, based on groups of different age or development. For example, investigations of how memory changes with age might compare groups of 20-year-old, 40-year-old, 60-year-old and 80-year-old people. Difficulties with this approach include problems with isolating or compensating for differences in education, familiarity with measuring equipment such as computers, and use of language, all of which will affect individuals' responses and may yield misleading data.

Cumulative frequency: a cumulative frequency distribution table looks almost the same as a frequency distribution table but it has added columns that give the cumulative frequency and the cumulative percentage of the results. In each new row, the new value is added to the previous total. These cumulative values can be plotted to give a cumulative frequency graph.

Data (singular datum): data are things which are known or assumed to be known as a basis for inference. Statistics is concerned with the systematic collection of numerical data or facts, and their interpretation.

Degrees of freedom (df): this is the number of items you need to know before you can calculate the remaining items. For example, if I told you that the sum of five numbers is 16 and that four of these numbers are 1, 5, 4, and 3, you can calculate the remaining number. If I only told you three of the numbers, you would not be able to calculate either of the remaining two numbers. In this case of five numbers, you always need to know four of them, that is one less than the number of items. That is, $df = n - 1$.

Usually the number of degrees of freedom is n − 1, that is one less than the number of values in a sample. Where there is more than one sample, the smallest sample is used.

In working out the degrees of freedom for the t-test, there is a difference between the matched pairs test and the independent measures test. For matched pairs, we need the total number of pairs minus one, since the pairs can be seen as units. For the independent measures, we need the number of items in each set minus one, that is, the total number of items minus two.

research

In other tests, degrees of freedom may be calculated in different ways. Degrees of freedom represent the number of factors which have to be taken into account when calculating correlations and affect the way findings are interpreted.

Dependent variable (DV): the 'effect' variable; the outcome that is being observed and measured to see whether the independent variable has any effect on it, that is, whether it is dependent on the conditions. For example in a simple experiment to test the effect of alcohol on performance (for example reaction times), the dependent variable is the performance of the participant. The independent variable (manipulated by the experimenter) is the consumption of alcohol by the participant.

Descriptive statistics: 'statistical methods which summarize, organize, and describe data, providing an organized visual representation of the data collected.' (Talbot, 1995: 653). These include,

> frequency distributions
> measures of central tendency (mean, median and mode)
> measures of dispersion (range and standard deviation).

See also *Inferential statistics*.

Deviation score: the difference between an individual value and the mean. Where each value is symbolised by x and the mean is x̄, each deviation score is $(x - \bar{x})$. This would be the same numerically as $(\bar{x} - x)$ and the order does not matter so long as you are consistent. See *Standard deviation*.

Discourse analysis: a method of investigating the meaning of everyday conversations. The starting point for analysis is a written transcript of what has been said. Transcribing a tape of a conversation or statement can be a long and laborious task and there are certain conventions for the paralanguage or non-verbal elements of speech. In the following example:

> the numbers in brackets indicate pauses timed to tenths of a second.
> (.) represents a pause that is too short to be measured.

> Underlining shows emphasis.
> Upward and downward arrows indicate rising and falling intonation (pitch).
> Colons: signal elongation of the previous sound (the more colons, the longer the elongation).

so:: did you ↑hear (.2) about the ↓ Conways (.) their car was stolen last night (.5) you can't trust kids these days they've got no <u>respect</u>'

The next stage in the process is to code the transcribed material. This involves searching for themes so that passages can be organised under various headings. Discourse analysts examine people's speech for the functions it is designed to serve. The simple description and comment in the example above establish the speaker as a concerned (or nosey) and observant neighbour who wishes to be distinct from the sort of people who steal cars and who makes quick assumptions about the causes of events, probably according to prevailing stereotypes.

Discourse analysis does not record facial expressions or posture and gesture and so may miss important clues about the speakers. See also *Protocol analysis*.

Dispersion (variability or spread): the degree to which values in a set of scores are widely different. A small dispersion would indicate that the scores are clustered closely around the mean. A large dispersion would indicate that the scores are widely spread or dispersed. Dispersion can be shown visually in a frequency distribution graph or curve. Measures of dispersion include the range, mean deviation, standard deviation and variance.

Double-blind design: in order to avoid bias and experimenter effect as much as possible a double-blind method may be used. In this method, where an experimental condition is compared with a control condition, neither the experimenter nor the participant knows who is in which group. For example in testing the effects of a new drug, one group is given the drug, the other group is given a placebo (see Part 3). Neither the experimenter nor the participants know who has been given the drug. In this way, the experimenter has less chance of affecting observations by anticipating or expecting certain effects, and the participant has less chance of inadvertently behaving differently because of beliefs or expectations about the drug. Only when all the observations have been made and correlated, is it revealed who was in each group.

Errors:
> Sampling bias.
> Interpretation errors
  – Type one error: rejecting the null hypothesis, claiming that results are significant when they are only due to chance.
  – Type two error: accepting the null hypothesis, believing the results are due to chance when they are in fact significant.
> Experimenter effects.
> Expectancy effects (for example *Hawthorne effect* and *Placebo effect*).

Experience-sampling method: an experimental method that assists researchers in describing the typical contents of consciousness; participants are asked to record what they are feeling and thinking whenever signalled to do so.

Experimental conditions: in simple experiments, two conditions are normally compared. One condition is usually a control. The other 'test' condition introduces the independent variable which is to be tested. For example in order to test the effects of alcohol on performance in a task, in the 'test' condition, the performance is measured once with and once without alcohol and in the 'control' condition twice without alcohol. This makes sure that other variables such as practice do not confuse the results.

Experimenter effect: there are at least two main kinds of effects an experimenter has on an experiment, the first to do with the way in which the experimenter sees the experiment, the second to do with the way in which the participant sees the experimenter. As Medawar (1963), cited by Wright et al (1970: 29), asserts: 'There is no such thing as unprejudiced observation.' Every experimenter chooses what to look for on the basis of his or her own interests and experiences and will interpret all observations in the light of those interests and

experiences. It is difficult to be truly objective. Moreover, the mere presence of an experimenter may affect the behaviour of participants and it is impossible to know what the behaviour would have been like if it had not been observed. To try to avoid some of these effects a double-blind design is used if possible. See also *Hawthorne effect*.

Exploratory data analysis:
> box-and-whisker display
> stem-and-leaf display.

Factor analysis and factorial design: a technique for examining a large number of variables and looking for interrelationships. Items which can be seen to be closely correlated can be gathered into a smaller number of variables. These can then be compared to see whether they can be interpreted according to known concepts, or give rise to new concepts or constructs.

Focus group interview: a type of group interview which is becoming increasingly used in health research. A small group of people is gathered together and guided by the interviewer in a discussion according to a prepared set of questions. In this way the interviewer can gather a number of different people's views in a short time. Disadvantages are that not everyone is likely to contribute equally to the discussion and some people are reluctant to discuss their views in a group.

Focused (semi-structured) interview: an interview in which the researcher or interviewer prepares a list of questions or a topic guide but encourages participants to talk freely about all the questions or aspects of the topic without being closely guided. Interviews are generally recorded so that they can be analysed in depth later.

Frequency distribution: the number of scores occurring for each value. In descriptive statistics, the raw data are grouped into categories and the frequency is then the number of values or occurrences in each category. The distribution can be represented as a tally, a table, a histogram, frequency polygon (or line graph), pie chart, bar chart or frequency distribution curve and compared with the normal distribution curve, depending on the type of data. See also *Cumulative frequency*.

research

Frequency polygon: from a histogram, a frequency polygon can be constructed by marking the frequency at the mid-point of each interval and then joining these points. In some contexts (for example Microsoft Excel) this may be called a line graph but line graphs have many other uses with all sorts of data. Where there is a large amount of data the lines of the polygon can be smoothed out into a curve to give a frequency distribution curve and for normal samples, a normal distribution curve as shown in Figure 5.5.

Friedman test: this is two-way analysis of variance by ranks for mixed modal situations with a procedure of setting out the different experimental conditions and the participants in ranked rows and columns and then arriving at a chi-square value.

Graphical representation: a chart or pictorial or graphical representation of data will demonstrate the characteristics and overall pattern of a distribution more clearly and be more appealing to the eye than mere tables of values. Particular advantages are that the mode and range will be immediately apparent and any interesting clusters will be revealed so that comparisons between similar sets of data can be made. Types include:

> pie chart
> bar graph
> histogram
> frequency polygon or line graph
> normal distribution and its variations.

Grounded theory: A qualitative research methodology developed by Glaser and Strauss (1967) based on symbolic interaction. This can be used when there is little known about the subject matter at first. During initial data analysis, the researcher develops working hypotheses which are tested through the collection of further data. Through further careful analysis of data, a theory can be developed. Rather than using random sampling, the researcher initially uses purposive sampling. As categories begin to emerge from the data a move is made to using theoretical sampling (see *Sample*). Glaser and Strauss (1967) used this strategy for looking at types of awareness of impending death (see Part 3). Another example might be looking at health-care professionals' perceptions of an aspect of their practice which has not been previously researched from the same perspective.

Hawthorne effect: an important example of an observer or experimenter effect which has been found in industrial research where increases in productivity may be found to occur in response to the mere fact that attention is being paid by the investigator, irrespective of what changes in practice are actually implemented. It is named after

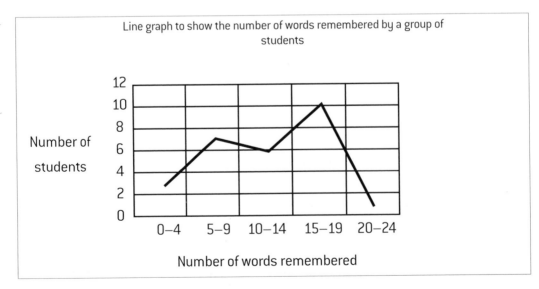

Figure 5.5 Frequency polygon or line graph

research

a study in 1927–9 in the Hawthorne plant of the Western Electric Company in Chicago (Gregory, 1987: 303) when a series of studies on the productivity of factory workers varied conditions such as light levels and rest breaks and found that productivity always rose following a change, even when returning to original conditions. Like the placebo effect, this is known as an expectancy effect.

Hermeneutics: the interpretation and understanding of social events by analysing their meanings to people and to their culture in the context in which it takes place. It was prominent in the 1960s and 1970s, more in sociology than psychology, and emphasises the importance of the content as well as the form of social behaviour. For example, putting a piece of paper in a box has one meaning in the context of democratic elections, where it is the action of putting a ballot paper in a box, and another if it refers to someone putting money in a shoe box to hide under the bed. Writers may refer to the 'hermeneutic circle': that is, relating the whole to the part and the part to the whole.

Heuristics: heuristic strategies are (usually imperfect) rules of thumb that people use without instruction when trying to solve problems, often used as short cuts in solving a complex task (Kahney, 1993: 49).

Histogram: a visual representation of interval level data. It is usual to put the intervals of the scale for the variable that you are measuring (for example the number of words remembered in a test) along the horizontal x-axis. Then put the value or number of scores or frequency in the vertical y-axis. Each column is the same width so the area of each column is proportional to the number of cases it represents. The total of all columns equals the whole sample. Note that unlike in a bar chart, the intervals come next to each other with no gaps, indicating that the data is continuous along a scale. If a gap is present it indicates there is no score for that interval. However, in many business applications, the word histogram may be used instead of bar chart for representations of nominal level data.

Hypothesis/experimental hypothesis: an idea or hunch, or a prediction made on the basis of a theory, about the kinds of results which may be expected from an investigation: for example, that a relationship between variables might exist, expressed as a statement of an expected relationship between the dependent and independent variables, which it is possible to investigate systematically. For example it has been hypothesised that people chose partners who are similar to themselves in attractiveness (Murstein, 1972). In quantitative research, it is usual to identify one

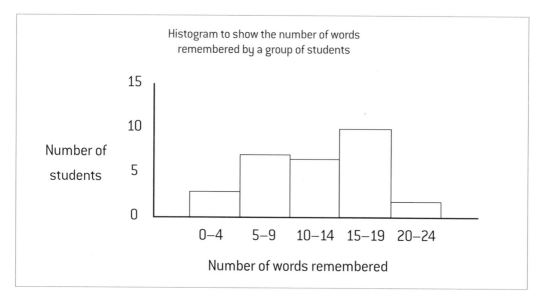

Figure 5.6 Histogram

or more hypotheses from previous experimental work and then test these systematically. In qualitative research, hypotheses may emerge as data is being collected and analysed. The word hypothesis is derived from 'hypo', less than or under, and thesis. See also *Null hypothesis*.

Hypothetico-deductive: a shorthand term for referring to the highly structured type of research which is based on one or more hypotheses and uses processes of logical deduction for deriving conclusions. It is usually contrasted with more open phenomenological methods.

Idiographic: studies and theories which consider each individual as an individual rather than looking for statistical norms and general laws and hence include all members of a population, not only those who behave according to the norm. The idiographic approach can be just as systematic, and hence considered as scientific, as nomothetic studies but yields a very different type of description and analysis of behaviour.

Lazarus (1976) argues that both nomothetic and idiographic approaches are needed for a full picture and that they should be considered supplementary rather than contradictory approaches.

Independent variable (IV): the causal variable. The IV is the variable that the experimenter controls or manipulates. That is, the factor that is being systematically altered to see if it has any effect on behaviour. For example in a simple experiment to test the effect of alcohol on performance, the independent variable (manipulated by the experimenter) is the consumption of alcohol by the participant; the dependent variable is the performance of the participant.

Inference: an idea that can be concluded from what has gone before. It is not as definite as a logical deduction or induction but 'picked up' from what appears to be valid.

Inferential statistics/tests of statistical significance: statistical tests that involve complex calculations that arrive at a figure, such as the t-test, from which inferences can be drawn concerning the nature of the relationships. These include correlational studies and parametric and non-parametric statistical tests which are used for testing hypotheses. These are not as definite as descriptive statistics but give an indication of trends.

Kendall's coefficient of concordance: this is a measure of agreement, for example between judges where a number of judges place a number of individuals in rank order. The ranks are scored and the variances compared with the maximum possible variance. This can be compared directly with Friedman's test but they have different purposes and the rows and columns are interchanged.

Kruskal–Wallis test: this is one-way analysis of variance by ranks for several independent groups with varying numbers of cases per group. Scores are ranked in ascending order with the lowest score given the rank of 1, and the sum of rank scores is found for each group. A formula is then applied and the significance of the value assessed from tables.

Kurtosis: a measure of whether the frequency distribution for data is peaked (high kurtosis) or flat (low kurtosis) relative to the bell shape of a normal distribution.

Law: a statement of a relationship which is always found to exist under certain conditions and which will stand even if a more sophisticated investigation shows there are limits to its applicability which had not been known about. So long as the conditions are specified under which the relationship can be observed, the law still stands. Laws and general principles are common in the physical sciences. In the social sciences there are few relationships which can be stated as laws: most social science statements are better referred to as confirmed hypotheses. There are approaches which are described as nomothetic, seeking general laws and principles, but at best, social science is based on statistical analysis rather than absolute numbers and the general principles can only be roughly applied to a percentage of the population. Findings cannot be used to predict individual cases, but used only to estimate how many examples are likely to be found in any given sample.

It would be inappropriate to publish as a law the

conclusion that partners are similar in attractiveness, since this finding is not always replicated for different samples, the conditions under which it does apply cannot be firmly established, and it cannot be applied to individual cases. Murstein (1972) felt that the evidence he collected confirmed his hypothesis that partners are similar in attractiveness more than would be expected by chance.

Level of data: a useful distinction can be made between the following different levels:

> Nominal level: observations that can be named but are not necessarily assigned a numerical or ordinal value. That is, a level of data by categorisation alone, into separate, discrete categories, with no quantitative element. Examples would be qualitative data such as the colour and make of cars, or signs and symptoms of an illness. Descriptive statistics show how many values fall into each category. Inferential tests at nominal level include the binomial sign test for related measures and chi-square test for unrelated measures.

> Ordinal level: values placed in rank order.

> Interval level: a scale of measurement that uses equal intervals for example minutes, numbers of words counted. To define the intervals, you check all the raw data and see what the range is and then choose suitable intervals to split the data into a convenient number of piles or groups. You then sort the raw data into the intervals, counting how many go into each interval. This will give you a frequency distribution. Each interval is given between lower and higher values, for example 0 to 4, 5 to 9, 10 to 14. Or you could have 1–5, 6–10, 11–15 and so on, being careful not to duplicate the boundaries. If you then plot the histogram, you will see whether the intervals you have chosen are suitable for what you want to show, or whether you need fewer groups or more groups. Interval level is the most useful level of data and permits the use of histograms, line graphs, distribution or frequency graphs and parametric tests. Tests at interval level include the parametric t test for related measures (within groups) and the parametric t test for unrelated measures (between groups).

> Ratio level: interval level data that start from zero. This is straightforward for measurements such as length, weight, time or counting responses, that have an obvious zero. It is less obvious in temperature where the zero is an arbitrary point, such as the melting point of ice on the Celsius scale. Some measurements cannot have a meaningful zero, for example IQ. In most tests this distinction is not particularly important and interval and ratio level data are treated in the same way.

Likert-type scale: a commonly used type of scale for recording responses to a questionnaire. The scale is constructed and tested in preliminary studies from about 100 statements that are evaluated for how positive or negative they are towards the attitude object. Items are selected that achieve consistent scores (internal validity), and reduced to a convenient list with an equal number of positive and negative statements.

The respondent is usually given an odd number of boxes (usually three, five or seven) from which to choose one response to each statement. The boxes may be numbered in either ascending or descending order of importance, or may be labelled from 'true' to 'false' or from 'strongly agree' to 'strongly disagree' or may use some other relevant wording. The middle choice is usually arranged to be of neutral importance, for example, 'neither agree nor disagree'. A choice of 'not applicable' may be placed in the middle or at one end. A variety of arrangements is in common use; examples are given in Figure 5.8. In any of these, the boxes can be assigned a numerical value so that scores can be calculated. Problems may be found in collecting data in this way. Since the format can vary, the order of importance may not be immediately apparent and respondents may misinterpret the boxes. Pilot studies should reveal most of these difficulties so that the instructions can be made clear and unambiguous.

Linear regression: a method for obtaining the line of best fit through points on a graph, for example a scatterplot. The simple linear regression equation is also called the least squares regression equation.

There are many straight lines that could be drawn through the data. One approach would be to

research

Raw data	
Participants	Score on test of how many words remembered out of 24
Mary	5
John	12
Fred	6
Joan	20
Susan	7
Bill	1
Ali	15
Kamal	10
Lu Wong	13
Dan	4
Alastair	17
Frank	17
Matthew	16
Maria	5
Andrew	0
Renny	19
William	6
Davina	16
Kirsty	15
Adam	9
Tiruven	19
Jess	16
Christopher	11
Andy	8
Charlie	11
Lisa	13
Helene	15
Number of participants, N = 27	

Range	Score, in intervals	Number of participants in each interval (Frequency)
	0–4	3
	5–9	7
	10–14	6
	15–19	10
	20–24	1
0–20		N = 27

Figure 5.7 Interval level data derived from raw data

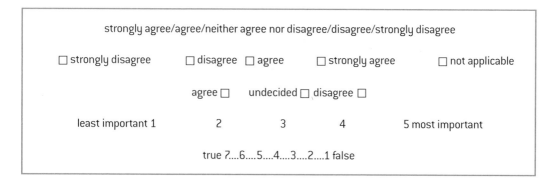

strongly agree/agree/neither agree nor disagree/disagree/strongly disagree

☐ strongly disagree   ☐ disagree ☐ agree   ☐ strongly agree   ☐ not applicable

agree ☐   undecided ☐ disagree ☐

least important 1   2   3   4   5 most important

true 7....6....5....4....3....2....1 false

Figure 5.8 Likert-type scales

think of drawing the best line by eye, with equal numbers of points on each side of the line or a balance of points on each side that allows for some of the points to be more widely scattered, then calculate the differences (residuals) between each point and the line and square these residuals. It is then possible to minimise the differences and calculate the line of best fit. That is, the least squares regression equation is the line for which the sum of squared residuals $\Sigma(x - \bar{x})^2$ is a minimum. In practice this is done by calculation only, using calculus, without drawing an approximate line first. A line gives a good fit to a set of data if the points are close to it.

Figure 5.9 shows an imaginary scatterplot for dependent variable against independent variable and the linear regression or line of best fit. Notice that the analysis is always described as 'the re-gression of the response (dependent variable) on the carrier (independent variable)'.

Longitudinal study: a study of a group or groups of people which takes place over a number of years, following the individuals. This has some advantages over a cross-sectional study as real changes in individual people can be measured, but it is time consuming.

Mann–Whitney U test: a test for comparing two sets of values which are not matched or which do not contain the same number of values and cannot be put into pairs. See also *Tests for statistical significance*.

Model: a device that helps to organise thoughts. A model may be a series of statements, a diagram, a

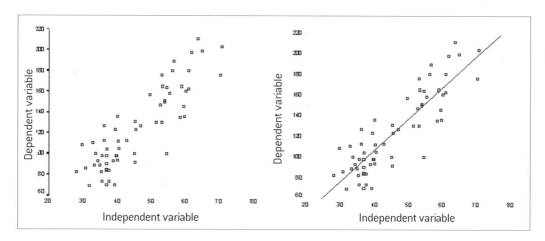

Figure 5.9 Linear regression: the line of best fit through a scatterplot

physical construction or a mathematical formula. It represents an ideal, or simplified, or scale version of the real thing. It can show the relationships and patterns between constituent parts, indicate similarities and differences, and can be used to describe, explain, predict and influence events. For example, the London tube map is a model of the underground system. It is not to scale and does not follow the actual path of the tunnels but it shows the relationship between the stations and helps you plan your journey. In psychology, Piaget's stages of cognitive development and subsequent alternative explanations can be seen as models of child development that enable educators to plan appropriate activities. Similarly, we have a number of models of attention and information processing, see Part 3, which illustrate the stages and processes and help with understanding.

Naturalistic observation: here no deliberate attempt is made to manipulate variables – rather it involves observing and recording behaviour in its natural setting.

Methods for recording data include checklists or tally charts or using a rating scale and can include the following:

> Time interval sampling: observing and recording what happens in a series of fixed time intervals.
> Time point sampling: observing and recording the behaviour which occurs at a series of given points in time.
> Event sampling: observing and recording a complete event each time it occurs.

The observer may adopt one of a number of roles:

> Non-participant observer: the researcher remains external to those being observed.
> Undisclosed (covert) participant observer: the researcher actually joins in the activities of the observed group. The group themselves are not informed that research is being conducted and that their behaviour is under observation.
> Disclosed (overt) participant observer: the researcher joins in the activities of the observed group, who are informed that they are being studied.

Each of these roles has different implications in

terms of validity of the observations, interpretation of the data and ethical considerations.

Observation is useful where behaviour might be difficult to recreate in a laboratory setting, either for practical reasons or for ethical reasons. Observational studies can rarely assert causation or be used in hypothesis testing. However, they are often used as a preliminary to laboratory studies and for the generation of hypotheses.

Naturalistic observations pose ethical problems if the participants do not realise that their behaviour is being observed. Important examples include the use of one-way mirrors and the observation of people in public places. In these circumstances they obviously cannot give their informed consent to be involved in the study. There can also be problems regarding confidentiality. For example, an observation takes place in a particular school and the published findings indicate that many of the children are badly behaved. Even if the name of the school is not mentioned, many of the people reading it will probably be able to identify it because they know that researchers were conducting an observational study there.

Nomothetic: the term comes from the Greek nomos meaning law, and refers to research which seeks general laws or principles. This is done by studying samples and applying statistical tests to compare these with the general population, looking for normal distributions and establishing what most people do under certain conditions. These studies are inclined to ignore the percentage of the population which falls outside of the norm. Nomothetic approaches can be contrasted with idiographic ones.

Normal (Gaussian) distribution: a smooth bell-shaped curve that represents the way in which values in a normal population are distributed, see Figure 5.10. It is derived from a histogram in the same way as a frequency polygon or line graph, as shown in Figure 5.11.

Its main features are that it is symmetrical so that data falls equally on either side of the mean, and the mean, median and mode all have the same value and lie in the same place at the centre. The areas under the curve correspond to the number of values occurring within a specified number of standard deviations. As shown in Figure

5.10, about two-thirds of the population lie within one standard deviation either side of the mean (z-score = 1), while 95 per cent lie within two standard deviations (z-score = 2) and 99.7 per cent (almost all) lie within three standard deviations (z-score = 3).

As an alternative to the standard deviation markers, vertical lines called percentiles can be drawn at intervals of 1 per cent across the curve. The 50th percentile would be at the centre, indicating that 50 per cent of the population fall below this line. The 99th percentile, or top percentile, represents the position above which 1 per cent of the population occur, for whatever measure is under consideration. Quartiles may also be used, see *Box and whisker*.

To be 'normal' the curve must be a true bell shape which conforms closely to the mathematical formula derived by Gauss. Normality is often assumed but real-life variations can be taller or flatter than the normal (kurtosis), or skewed, bi-modal, multi-modal or irregular.

Null hypothesis: a null hypothesis makes a statement of no difference between scores in the different conditions of the variable tested. It is the statement of no expected relationship between

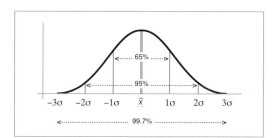

Figure 5.10 Normal distribution curve

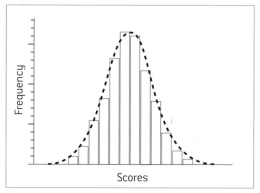

Figure 5.11 Histogram for normal distribution

two variables. This can be thought of as the restating of an hypothesis such that no effect is expected more than by chance. In Murstein's (1972) study the null hypothesis would state that there is no correlation between the attractiveness of partners more than would be expected by chance. Clegg (1982: 60) suggests that the best approach to take to any analysis of statistical data is to assume that 'the experiment has not worked' and that the independent variable has not affected the dependent variable. This can help to avoid bias due to expectations about the results that are wanted by the experimenter in order to prove a point.

Objective: describes a viewpoint which sticks as closely as possible to the observable and measurable reality and which is the same for all observers, uncoloured by feelings or opinions. In other contexts an objective is something to strive for. In education theory objectives are the skills a student will be able to demonstrate after completing the course.

Operational definitions: before an idea for an experiment can be made into an actual experiment, the independent and dependent variables must be carefully defined. An operational definition is stated in terms of the steps or operations that have to be carried out in observing or measuring whatever it is that is being defined. It is necessary to specify the procedure that is carried out to distinguish between two experimental conditions, and the exact nature of the tasks and exactly what is being measured. For example in a simple experiment to determine the effects of alcohol on performance, the type and quantity of alcohol must be defined as well as the task to be performed and how the performance is to be measured. This allows different experiments to be compared more meaningfully. For example the effects of alcohol could be different according to whether beer or spirits are consumed and care is needed in comparing experiments in which different types of alcohol are used.

Opportunity sample: participants who just happen to be available, for example in the college canteen.

Parameter: the thing that is being measured; any quantity whose value varies with circumstances or individuals, such as radius of a circle, reaction time, inspection time, intelligence quotient (IQ).

Popular usage includes a boundary or limit as in the phrase 'within certain parameters' but this is not the proper usage in experimental psychology.

Parametric and non-parametric tests: parametric statistical tests can be used when the parameters (values) for the population are known, that is where there is already data available for the population as a whole so that the new experimental data for the sample can be compared with the normal results. But remember that data for the population never refers to the whole population, merely to inferences from previous samples. Parametric tests usually assume that the scores conform to a normal distribution. Examples are the two t-tests and analysis of variance.

Non-parametric tests are used where the normal parameters are not known, and where the data is qualitative rather than quantitative; that is, they require only ordinal, or is some cases only nominal, data. Examples are the Wilcoxon test and Mann–Whitney U test.

Participant: a person taking part in an observation, survey or experiment. This name is now preferred to the previously used the word subject. See also *Subjects*.

Participant (subject) design: As with groups, there are two types:

> same participant twice (within participants design)
> different participants (between participants design).

Participant observation: an observation where the investigator takes a part in the activity being observed. This is often used in observation of children where the observers interact with the children, observing the children's responses to their interventions as well as other behaviour. See *Naturalistic observation*.

Participant (subject) variables: it is possible that differences between groups may be due to differences between participants rather than the independent variable. The solution is to use matched participants or within participants design.

Pie chart: visual representation of nominal level data, in which slices of the pie are used to show how many scores are obtained for each category. Values are usually given as percentages; the larger the slice, the greater the percentage. This provides an alternative to the bar chart if showing the relationship of each category to the whole is desirable.

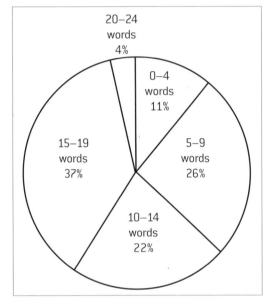

Figure 5.12 Pie chart

Population: all the existing members of the group to be tested; the entire set of people or objects with a common characteristic which is under investigation. For example, you might pick all the students in your college as your population for a study. Or all men between the ages of 20 and 25 in your city. Or all women of childbearing age in Dorset. As it is impossible to study all the people in the chosen population, you will need to pick a representative sample.

Post-hoc comparisons: comparisons made after some procedure for a particular purpose. (Ad-hoc is sometimes used as if it means decided on the spur of the moment but actually means for a particular, usually exclusive, purpose made in advance, as in ad-hoc appointment.)

Protocol analysis: in common usage a protocol is a set of rules, formalities or etiquette; in computing, a protocol is the convention that allows data transfer between two systems. In psychology research the term protocol usually refers to an interview transcript so that protocol analysis, like content analysis and discourse analysis, involves the identification of basic concepts, values, purposes or tasks within a transcript. A verbal protocol usually refers to spoken, rather than written, information.

Psychometric tests/psychometrics: tests for measuring psychological traits or attributes such as:

> developmental assessment
> mental ability
> neuropsychological assessment
> personality (for example 16pF, MMPI, Myers–Briggs)
> projective techniques (for example Rorschach ink blots, TAT)
> social behaviour
> family relations
> visual perception
> language dysfunction
> motor skills.

Tests provide an objective measure that can be compared with normative data. We can ask the same questions of everybody and compare the answers. Unfortunately, we do not much like being tested and tend to think of the answers in terms of pass or fail. In some styles of testing, where a 'good' result will lead to a desired outcome, people may tend to give the answers that they think will lead to a 'pass'. In more effective testing, the results provide information that enables each person to make an informed choice about the best possible personal outcome. Tests must meet the proper standards of reliability and validity.

Q technique: a technique developed by Stephenson (1953) for studying attitudes by means of questionnaires (see, for example, Brown, 1986); more complicated than the Likert-type scale.

Qualitative and quantitative variables: variables are called qualitative when they are described without being given a number value, that is, types rather than measurements. When a measurement is made so that a numerical value is recorded, the variable is quantitative.

For hospital treatment, descriptions of satisfaction and comfort are qualitative while waiting-list time, cost and length of stay can be quantified. Sometimes a qualitative variable can be assigned a numerical value on a rating or Likert-type scale so that quantitative comparisons can be made. For example, satisfaction with care could be assigned a rating on a scale from 1 to 5, going from least satisfied to most satisfied.

Qualitative research methods: qualitative research tends to be exploratory, based on research questions rather than hypotheses, does not involve experiments and is less rigid than quantitative research. At least five models of qualitative research can be identified:

> ethnography
> grounded theory research
> hermeneutics
> empirical phenomenology
> heuristics.

These methods focus on the wholeness of experience, searching for individual meanings and essences of experience rather than quantitative measurements and abstract explanations.

Polit and Hungler (1995: 16) suggest that qualitative research generally:

> attempts to understand the entirety of some phenomenon rather than focus on specific concepts
> has few preconceived hunches; stresses the importance of people's interpretation of events and circumstances, rather than the researcher's interpretation
> collects information without formal, structured instruments
> does not attempt to control the context of the research but, rather, attempts to capture it in its entirety
> attempts to capitalise on the subjective as a means for understanding and interpreting human experiences
> analyses narrative information in an organised, but intuitive, fashion.

research

Quantitative research: research which involves the measurement of variable quantities and the systematic collection of this numerical data which can be analysed using statistical methods. Polit and Hungler (1995: 15) suggest that quantitative research generally:

> focuses on a relatively small number of specific concepts
> begins with preconceived hunches about how the concepts are interrelated
> uses structured procedures and formal instruments to collect information
> collects the information under conditions of control
> emphasises objectivity in the collection and analysis of information
> analyses numerical information through statistical procedures.

Questionnaire: a set of questions or statements, usually presented in written form, which can be used to collect standardised data on a particular research topic. Unlike an objective test, questionnaires do not involve respondents in exercising skill, only in stating a point of view. Most commonly, questionnaires are used to measure attitudes, lifestyles or levels of satisfaction. Responses to statements are usually given according to a Likert-type scale ranging from true to false or strongly agree to strongly disagree. Statements need to be carefully designed to ensure they are not ambiguous or impossible to answer. A choice can be made between closed and open-ended questions depending on the design. A pilot study is essential. The following criteria from Edwards (1957) can be useful in constructing statements:

> Avoid statements that refer to the past rather than the present.
> Avoid statements that are factual or capable of being interpreted as factual.
> Avoid statements that may be interpreted in more than one way.
> Avoid statements that are irrelevant to the psychological object under consideration.
> Avoid statements that are likely to be endorsed by almost everyone or no one.
> Select statements that are believed to cover the entire range of the affective scale of interest.

> Keep the language of the statements simple, clear and direct.
> Statements should be short, rarely exceeding 20 words.
> Each statement should contain only one complete thought.
> Avoid universals such as all, always, none, never.
> Words such as only, just, merely ... should be used with care and moderation in writing statements.
> Whenever possible, statements should be in the form of simple sentences, rather than compound or complex sentences.
> Avoid the use of words that may not be understood.
> Avoid the use of double negatives.

Randomised controlled trial: the most important type of research in medicine. When testing the effectiveness of a new treatment, groups are selected randomly as far as possible then one group is given the treatment and compared with a control group. A double-blind design is usually employed.

Rank order: placing scores (ordinal data) in order according to size, or some other dimension.

Range: the spread of scores. That is, the difference between the top score and the bottom score in a group of scores.

Rate: the frequency with which something occurs. In the physical sciences, this can be measured in a number of ways, according to how many items occur in a certain mass, length, area, volume or time. In statistical analysis, most commonly the rate is given with time, that is how many (or how much) per second, per hour or per year and so on.

Particularly in social matters, for example the 'birth rate', the standard way of expressing the rate is to give the occurrence per 100,000 in a population for the year in question. Expressing rates or frequencies in this way enables comparisons to be made between groups. Raw data of this kind need to be treated with caution and should never be taken out of context.

Raw data: all the information that has been

collected in a research study before any analysis has been undertaken. Raw data is not given in an experiment report, see Part 1.

Related/within groups design: an experimental design where the same group is used in both conditions (repeated measures or test–retest) or the participants in the two groups are paired together, for example, for age, gender, IQ, social background (matched pairs).

Reliability: To be of any use, any measuring device (whether weighing scales or psychometric test) should always measure the same characteristic or produce the same value or score if it is used to measure the same thing on two separate occasions. This assumes, of course, that the thing being measured is stable – that it has not changed between the first and second measurement, or that if it has changed then the test will be able to detect this change. The degree to which a measuring instrument achieves reproducible measurements is called its reliability. Reliability can be statistically defined as a measure of the accuracy with which it measures the 'true' scores. Apart from the self-explanatory test–retest reliability, there are several different ways of assessing reliability, such as delayed-equivalence, equivalent-form and split-half reliability:

> Test–retest reliability: the same test is given on different occasions to the same individuals.
> Equivalent-form reliability: two equivalent forms of the same test are used with the same individuals with very little time delay between tests. This avoids the administrative problems of retesting at different times and the likelihood that the individuals will themselves have changed between tests.
> Delayed-equivalence reliability: this procedure takes into account changes in the individuals taking the test and changes in the test items introduced in the retest, and counts both of these as errors. Only lasting general factors are regarded as true variance. It is less frequently used than simple test–retest or equivalence reliability.
> Split-half reliability: as Wright et al (1970: 460) point out, it is not possible to administer equivalent forms of a test to the same individuals at the same time, and there must

always be some delay even in equivalent-form assessing, so there may be some change in the individuals taking the tests (for example practice, boredom, tiredness). To avoid this problem the items of a test are compared by splitting the test in half and comparing the results on one half with the results on the other half. In practice, the items making up the two split halves are usually selected on an odd–even basis. Thus the scores obtained on the odd items are correlated with the scores obtained by the same participants on the even items. Split-half reliability is different from other reliability measures in that it examines the homogeneity, or internal consistency, of a test rather than its reliability from one occasion to another. It is more clearly part of test construction than the other procedures and may be used more often during that process.

> Cronbach's Alpha: a commonly used assessment of reliability that depends on item analysis. The correlation coefficient (the strength of the relationship) is measured between each individual score on all questions and the score on the test overall. According to this approach, if participants vary a lot on individual items, relative to how much they vary on the overall test, then a low value of Alpha is achieved and the test is considered unreliable.
> Kuder–Richardson method: this is based on the same principles as Cronbach's Alpha but is used when the scale has dichotomous test items, that is, pass/fail or yes/no answers.

A test which is reliable may still not be valid, in the sense that it may give similar scores under different conditions but not actually measure what it is intended to measure. See also *Validity*.

Repeated measures design: the same group of participants is used in both conditions of the experiment. The advantage of this design is that only one group is needed and any measured changes must be due to experimental conditions not to differences between groups. The disadvantage is that changes may be due to practice.

Retrospective and prospective studies: retrospective studies are those which look back to see whether anything in the past can be linked to effects which are currently noticeable.

Prospective studies start with investigation of what is happening currently and then follow through into the future to see if there is any link with what is observed later.

Sample: a sub-set of the population. The sample contains the tested participants of the population. It is usually desirable for an investigation to give results that would be applicable to the population as a whole. A sample that is unbiased, in the sense that each member of the population has an equal chance of appearing in the sample, is known as a random sample. In principle, therefore, a random sample is representative of the whole population. Where a sample is not random, the way in which it was selected must be stated. Several types of sampling can be identified, such as:

> random sampling
> probabilistic sampling
> opportunity or convenience sampling
> quota sampling
> purposive sampling
> snowball sampling
> theoretical sampling.

A random or probabilistic sample is one in which every member of the population has an equal chance or probability of being included in the study.

Opportunity or convenience sampling uses people who are readily available.

Quota sampling aims to produce samples which reflect the broader population on some agreed criteria, without a random selection of cases. It is used widely in market research as it is quicker and cheaper than probability sampling, but it does not ensure absence of bias or allow any assessment of bias.

Participants in a purposive sample are chosen for their relevance to the information being sought because they are judged to be typical of some category of interest to the research, such as recent service users.

Snowball sampling is a type of purposive sampling. It involves identifying one or more people from the population who can then identify other members of the population who, in turn can identify further members and so on. In this way a substantial number of people can be identified and approached to take part in the research. Snowball

sampling is also known as 'network sampling' and is particularly useful when it is difficult to identify members of a population, as may be the case when researching hard-to-reach groups.

Theoretical sampling (Glaser and Strauss, 1967) is often confused with purposive sampling but relates specifically to the selection of what or whom to study on the basis of emerging analysis, ideas or theory.

Sampling bias: if one category is over represented within the sample, there is said to be sampling bias.

Scattergram/scatterplot: visual representation of pairs of values, for example height and weight, for a sample, in order to show whether there is a relationship or correlation. When two variables are displayed in a scatterplot and one can be thought of as a response to the other (one produces the other), standard practice is to place the dependent variable on the vertical (or Y) axis. The names of the variables on the X and Y axes vary according to the field of application. Some of the more common usages are :

X-axis	Y-axis
independent variable	dependent variable
predictor	predicted
carrier	response
input	output

Different types of correlation are shown in Figure 5.13. Where the regression line or line of best fit (see Linear regression) is straight or a simple curve, Spearman's rho can be calculated, but arched or U-shaped curves are too complex for Spearman's rho.

Significance level: many statistical tests (for example correlation) have tables giving the level of significance, expressed as a numerical probability. This is a measure of how likely the result could have occurred by chance. Three levels are normally used, 0.05 (5 per cent), 0.01 (1 per cent) and 0.001 (0.1 per cent).

> 0.05 (5 per cent): commonly accepted within the social sciences as being an acceptable

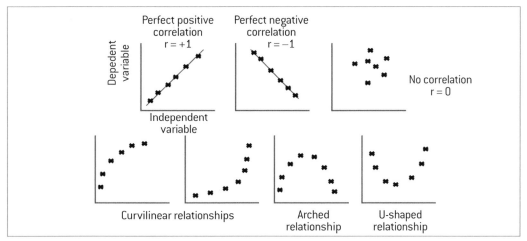

Figure 5.13 Scattergrams/scatterplots for correlation

level. This means that you have a 1 in 20 probability that your results did not happen by chance. You can be reasonably confident that you have shown a significant difference between your experimental condition and the control condition and can reject the null hypothesis.

> 0.01 (1 per cent): a better level of significance. At this level you have a 1 in 100 chance of being wrong to reject the null hypothesis on the basis of your findings.

> 0.001 (0.1 per cent): an excellent significance level. You have a 1 in 1,000 chance of the results happening by chance.

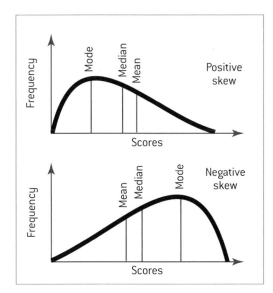

Figure 5.14 Skewed distributions

Tables of significance for each of the different statistical tests can be found in most books on statistics (for example Clegg, 1982). Tables usually give values for 5 per cent and 1 per cent. A probability level of more than 0.05 is not acceptable; the hypothesis must be rejected and the null hypothesis accepted. The level of significance to be accepted should be stated before conducting the research.

Skew: where scores fall mainly below the mean the distribution is said to be positively skewed (the mean is towards the positive direction of the axis). Where scores fall mainly above the mean, the skew is negative.

Spearman's rho: Spearman's rho is a measure of the linear relationship between two variables. It is a way of calculating a correlation coefficient by placing two sets of values in rank order and comparing whether they appear in the same order in both sets. It differs from Pearson's correlation only in that the calculations are done after the numbers are converted to ranks. The lowest value in each set is given the rank of 1 and so on. Spearman's rho is an example of a rank-randomisation test.

Spearman's rho is calculated by comparing the rank values according to a procedure using the formula given in Figure 5.15. The value will always be between −1 and +1. The significance of rho is found from a table of critical values.

Standard deviation (s, or σ 'sigma'): a measure of the variability or spread of the scores. It is the average distance away from the mean score or

Consider the following fictitious X-Y pairs of values:			Assigning these a rank order would result in the following:		Differences between ranks D and the square of the differences D²	
	Maths mark (x)	Music mark (y)	Rank (X)	Rank (Y)	D	D²
Amanda	53	72	4	5	1	1
Amy	91	57	5	3	2	4
Andrew	49	58	3	4	1	1
Alex	45	36	2	1	1	1
Andrea	17	40	1	2	1	1
The X value of 17 is assigned a 1 since it is the lowest. The X value of 45 is assigned a 2 because 42 is the second lowest value of X and so on. The Y value of 36 is first in rank and so on. The two sets of ranks are then compared and Spearman's rho can be calculated, and its significance determined from a table of critical values.					$\Sigma D^2 = 8$ $N = 5$	
Formula for Spearman's rho $$r = 1 - \frac{6\Sigma D^2}{N(N^2 - N)}$$ Where ΣD^2 = the sum of the squared values of the differences between the ranked scores, N = the number of paired scores Use tables to find whether answer is significant.					$r = 1 - \dfrac{6 \times 8}{5(5^2 - 5)}$ $= 1 - 0.4$ $= 0.6$ This is not significant. For this small number of values, rho would have to be more than 0.9	

Figure 5.15 Spearman's rho

the average amount of deviation of values from the mean. The bigger the standard deviation, the wider the spread around the mean. Where the standard deviation is large, this indicates a wide spread of scores and the distribution graph is wide. Where the scores are all very close to the mean, the bell shape is narrow and the standard deviation is small.

To quickly find an average deviation, it is possible to use a numerical mean deviation, $\Sigma[|x - \bar{x}|]/N$, that is, ignoring whether each deviation is positive or negative, summing all the deviations and dividing by the number of values.

However, it is not possible to calculate a true algebraic mean deviation taking into consideration the sign of each deviation, since roughly half the values are above the mean and half below and this would always come to zero. To allow for this, the deviations are squared to make them all positive. They are then summed and the mean is calculated. This is known as the variance. The square root of this answer is taken to give the standard deviation, $\sigma = \sqrt{(\Sigma(X - \bar{x})^2/N)}$. The procedure of squaring the values is derived from the equation

defining the 'bell curve' and is related in various ways to the area under the curve. See also *Normal distribution*.

Stem-and-leaf display: a stem-and-leaf plot shows the shape and distribution of data. Each datum value is split into a 'stem' and a 'leaf'. The 'leaf' is usually the last digit, in the place farthest to the right in the number. The 'stem' consists of the other digits to the left in the number that remain when the leaf is dropped. The number 175 would be split as:

Figure 5.16 shows how to construct the stem-and-leaf display from a set of data. As can be seen a stem-and-leaf plot resembles a histogram turned sideways, if you think of the stem values as the intervals of a histogram and the leaf values as the frequency for each interval. The display shows a distribution around the 70 per cent values. One advantage to the stem-and-leaf plot over the

Raw data	Fictitious psychology test scores: 91, 83, 52, 74, 74, 65, 65, 62, 80, 73, 85, 40, 40, 70, 75%
Ordered data	40, 40, 52, 62, 65, 65, 70, 73, 74, 74, 75, 80, 83, 85, 91%
Separate each number into a stem and a leaf. Since these are two digit numbers, the digit on the left (tens column) is the stem and the digit on the right (units column) is the leaf.	The number 75 is represented by Stem ¦ Leaf 7 ¦ 5
Group the numbers with the same stems. List the stems in numerical order. Title the graph and add a key (legend) to explain the stem and leaf.	Stem and leaf display for psychology test marks Key: 4 ¦ 0 represents 40%

Stem	Leaf
4	0, 0
5	2
6	2, 5, 5
7	0, 3, 4,4, 5
8	0,3, 5
9	1

Figure 5.16 Stem-and-leaf display

histogram is that the stem-and-leaf plot displays not only the frequency for each interval, but also displays all of the individual values within that interval.

Subjective: an individual personal viewpoint which depends on one's own emotions and capacities or imaginary elements which are separate from the objective reality. See also Subjectivity in Part3 and discussion in Part 2.1.

Subjects: until recently the people or animals taking part in a psychology experiment were referred to as subjects. The symbol S was used to indicate a subject. The term participant is now preferred. The British Psychological Society (BPS) occasionally prints reminders (for example, July 1997) that the term subject is no longer acceptable in their publications when referring to people.

Symbolic interaction: a theoretical paradigm based on the idea that people 'act towards things on the basis of the meanings that the things have for them' (Blumer, 1969). The actions of individuals are guided by the way they define and interpret what is happening in their environment. Meanings given to events derive from social interaction and are shaped by personal experiences.

In grounded research and other approaches using this paradigm, it is expected that individuals will behave differently, according to their own particular meanings. The research focuses on these individual differences, and is not concerned with looking for general laws and principles.

Tally: a simple way of counting how many scores occurs for any category. It is particularly useful when events happen serially, that is one after another, as with people attending an exhibition and filing through a turntable. A single stroke is made for each score and it is customary to cluster the tallies in groups of five, with a horizontal stroke for the fifth, to make it easier to add the total. For example, ~~////~~ ~~////~~ ~~////~~ /// gives a total tally of 18.

Tests of proportions:
- chi-squared
- Cramer's phi.

T-test (Student's t-test or Student–Fisher t-distribution): a test devised by W. S. Gossett in 1908, writing under the pen name of Student. There are two types of t-test, the matched t and the independent t. These are parametric tests that are used to compare two sets of data that follow a normal distribution. The matched t corresponds to the non-parametric Wilcoxon test and is used with matched pairs. The independent t test corresponds to the non-parametric Mann–Whitney U test and is used where sets of scores are not matched. The test gives a number that, in its relation to the numbers of values in the data, allows the probability of correlation to be estimated.

Theory: a coherent system of ideas or statements which can either be a hypothesis which has been confirmed by observation or experiment or an attempt to explain a group of observations or experimental data. A theory can only stand until it is improved or disproved by further study. It was an interesting hypothesis of Murstein (1972) that marriage partners are of similar attractiveness, which he found was confirmed by his data and which he developed into a theory by linking together appropriate explanations for his findings. His work is open to question and would be easily disproved if someone accumulated convincing data to show there is no relationship between the attractiveness of partners more than would be expected by chance. A rival theory could be developed which introduced arguments and explanations for why a person is not likely to marry someone of similar attractiveness. Alternatively, it might be confirmed in repeated observations that partners are of similar attractiveness but a new theory developed, giving different explanations for this.

Thesis: a proposition stated as a theme to be discussed; an understanding of the matter being investigated, to be proved or maintained against attack. A thesis can be stated when an experimental hypothesis has been confirmed and can be related to a law, model or theory.

Two-tailed hypothesis: a hypothesis that can have more than one outcome, that is you do not know in advance which outcome is more likely. For example, whether males or females will score more highly on tests of extroversion. If you already knew the direction of the outcome, there would probably be no need to do the research, for example whether males are taller than females (overall), but given that kind of situation you would use a one-tailed test. The null hypothesis is always two-tailed. The one-tailed probability is exactly half the value of the two-tailed probability. See also *Bonferroni correction*.

Unrelated/between groups design: also known as independent groups design, independent participants or independent subjects. Different participants take part in each condition. The advantage of this design is that there are no effects due to practice. However, as the groups are not matched it is not possible to eliminate effects due to differences between the participants. Also, as the two groups may be tested on different occasions, there may be differences in experimental conditions.

Validity: validity is concerned with what is being measured or investigated and whether the research or psychometric test is true or meaningful. Talbot (1995: 661) defines validity in quantitative research as the extent to which an instrument measures what it purports to measure, and validity in qualitative research as the extent to which the research findings represent reality.

With psychometric tests, it is not possible to guarantee that the final test will actually measure what was intended. Evidence is needed to show what it does test and how well. Validity cannot be defined statistically but 'relates to the appropriateness and justifiability of the things we say about scores on a test and the justification we have for making inferences from such scores to other measures' (Bartram, in Beech and Harding, 1990). There are many ways in which the term validity is used, including: face validity, content validity, construct validity, predictive validity, criterion-related validity, concurrent validity, internal and external validity.

> Face validity: this refers to the degree to which the test-taker sees the test as being reasonable and appropriate for a given situation. In practice, high face validity has no necessary relationship with what a test measures, nor how its scores may be justifiably used.

However, it may have indirect results in aiding co-operation between the test-taker and the administrator. People are more likely to take seriously activities which seem reasonable and which they feel they understand.

> Content validity: this refers to the degree to which the test is judged to be appropriate by 'professionals', and the extent to which a group of experts agree, for example, whether the items cover sufficient breadth. Such judgements are best seen as part of the process of test development, as an indication that the testers are on the right track.

> Construct validity: many tests are constructed to measure traits that are hypothetical. For example 'intelligence' does not exist in any physical or tangible form, nor do 'extroversion', 'spatial ability' or 'mechanical reasoning ability', yet tests have been created to measure all these qualities. Such physically non-existent qualities are often called constructs, rather than concepts, as they have been deliberately constructed as a means of trying to describe and explain patterns of differences between people's behaviour. There is no one piece of evidence that can prove construct validity. In practice, the construct validity is gradually built up as more and more evidence accumulates about its usefulness. Each test should have positive correlations with other tests of the same construct and it should correlate with real-world measures that are known to involve the construct. It should not correlate with situations known to be independent of the construct. Good test manuals contain a range of detailed information about correlates of a test. Ultimately, construct validity relates to how well it is known and understood what a test score means. This knowledge may be gained inductively from individual instances or deductively from general principles. It should allow practical predictions to be made about real-world behaviour if the test is to be any use.

> Predictive validity: this involves using scores from psychometric tests to predict future performance. For example, in developing a new test, an ability test may be given to students before they start their college course and the scores later compared with their final academic marks and practice assessments. It can then be calculated how well the test scores correlate with performance in real tasks. A variety of statistical methods can then be used with subsequent cohorts to make predictions from their test scores about the likely scores new students will achieve at the end of their course. These predictions may be used to assist in deciding which applicants to accept. At the time of writing there are no standardised predictive tests for psychology education: selection is made according to academic qualifications and interview, neither of which have proven predictive validity.

> Criterion-related validity (also known as empirical validity): some tests are designed to predict specific aspects of behaviour, for example degree of success in a course. In this case, it is not so important what is measured but how well it predicts a criterion. For example if students are given a whole range of tests before, during and after a diploma course, their scores can be compared with their success rates on the course. A test which correlates well with success could be considered criterion-related even if there is no obvious connection between the questions and success. Such a test is not given an overall score for criterion-related validity since it might be good for indicating success on one course (high validity coefficient) but not on another (low validity coefficient). Criterion-related validity is typically measured either predictively or concurrently or both. There is no clear cut distinction between construct validity and criterion-related validity in many cases since construct validity is related to making predictions as to what real-world criteria it should correlate with.

> Concurrent validity: when the criterion and the predictor measures are obtained at the same time, the correlation is concurrent. Thus, if an ability test is administered to a sample of students at the end of their college course and their scores compared with final academic marks and practice assessments, then the correlation will give a measure of the concurrent validity.

> Internal and external validity: these two concepts are used in judging the value of

research

scientific research, particularly when considering information presented in a popular format, such as statistics provided by newspapers.

- Internal validity refers to the bias that may arise from the way in which the data are collected. For example, in surveys bias may result from the way the questions are asked, or the way the sample is selected.
- External validity refers to the relevance that data have to a particular situation. A piece of research may have been well conducted (have good internal validity) but the circumstances under which the data were collected may or may not apply to the situation in which you want to apply the information.

A big problem in reporting scientific research is that reporters often consider only its apparent external validity, or apparent relevance to certain circumstances, without considering whether it is internally valid. To be interpreted and applied correctly, information must be both internally and externally valid.

Variable: any characteristic or attribute of an object or person that varies within the population being studied. That is, something that can have different values for each of the observations taken, for example age, height, amount of alcohol consumed, attractiveness, marital status.

Variance: distance away from the mean of scores; a measure of dispersion or variability. It is the mean of sum of the squares of the deviations, $v = \Sigma(x - \bar{x})^2/N$, and is the square of the standard deviation. If you assume that the variance within each of the populations is equal, this is known as the assumption of homogeneity of variance. This assumption underlies analysis of variance (ANOVA) although ANOVA can work well even when this is not true unless there are unequal numbers of participants in the various groups. If the variances are not homogeneous, they are said to be heterogeneous.

Wilcoxon test: a non-parametric test which can be used to see if one set of scores is significantly different (for example, higher) than a paired set of scores. The scores are kept in pairs and the differences compared.

Z-scores: a measure of how many standard deviations a score lies above or below the mean for a set. A z-score of 1 indicates that a score lies within one standard deviation either side of the mean. A z-score of 2 indicates that a score lies within two standard deviations and a z-score of 3 indicates that a score lies within three standard deviations.

6 career pathways

next

6.1 Further study, accreditation and transferable skills

You will need more than your academic qualifications to survive in the world of graduate employment. You will need to demonstrate a wide range of transferable skills – skills that can be transferred directly into the work place. You will have acquired many of these and, if you have been keeping a portfolio, or transcript of personal development (see Part 1) you will have evidence to show a prospective employer and will have spent time working out just exactly what it is you have to offer. Recruitment managers are looking for the most impressive personal skills in creativity, flexibility and communication with enthusiasm and drive. See also *capability* in Part 1.

Registering as a chartered psychologist

Why register as a chartered psychologist?

A member of the public who 'consults or employs a Chartered Psychologist can be assured that the person is properly trained, fully qualified and answerable to an independent authority for professional actions' (Extract from BPS publication available from www.bps.org.uk).

How to become a chartered psychologist

In order to obtain employment as a professional psychologist further postgraduate study and supervised training are required, normally lasting a further three years. At the end of this time it is possible to become a Chartered Psychologist specialising in one of the areas of professional psychology such as clinical, educational, occupational, health, counselling or forensic psychology.

In order to proceed to postgraduate training in professional psychology, a student's first degree must be accredited by the British Psychological Society as conferring eligibility for the Graduate Basis for Registration. Graduates from non-accredited courses can achieve the Graduate Basis for Registration by taking the Society's Qualifying Examination or an accredited conversion course. Regular reviews are conducted by the British Psychological Society to ensure that accredited degrees continue to reach the necessary standards.

http://www.qaa.ac.uk/academicinfrastructure/benchmark/statements/Psychology07.pdf (accessed 3 July 2008) with permission from *Subject Benchmark Statement: Psychology 2007*. © The Quality Assurance Agency for Higher Education, 2007.

next

See Part 2 for information about the content of these approaches.

For careers go to http://www.bps.org.uk/careers/careers_home.cfm and follow links to Careers and Qualifications>Areas of Psychology>

For available jobs in the UK go to www.direct.gov.uk.

The BPS booklet *So you want to be a Psychologist* and leaflets about the Society and courses are also available from the BPS Leicester office (see Part 7).

Clinical psychology, for mental health problems, in hospitals, health and care settings:

Work Experience as an assistant psychologist/research assistant plus postgraduate accredited training course (three years full-time) to gain a doctorate in clinical psychology.

A clearing house scheme operates for all applications. Information is available from the BPS.

As places are in short supply a first or upper-second-class degree is required with relevant research or care experience.

Counselling psychology, in private practice and commercial settings:

Either accredited MSc/Diploma/Certificate in Counselling Psychology (three years full-time or equivalent part-time) or The Society's Qualification in Counselling Psychology (three years full-time independent study/practice)

Postgraduate training is normally self-financed but funding may be available.

Educational psychology, in local education authorities, schools and special schools:

In UK except Scotland, teacher training (for example PGCE) plus two years teaching plus PG accredited training course (one year full-time) to gain MSc.

In Scotland, no need to teach but MSc course is two years plus supervised practice as an educational psychologist for one year.

Prospective students are encouraged to combine a National Curriculum subject (for example maths, English) with psychology for a joint/combined Honours degree in order to meet requirements.

A clearing house system operates for the PG training, which can also advise on funding.

Forensic psychology, in penal establishments, special hospitals and with young offenders:

Either accredited MSc (one year full-time) in forensic psychology plus completion of Stage 2 of the Society's Diploma in Forensic Psychology or completion of Stages 1 and 2.

Applicants are required to attend a national assessment centre for assessing interpersonal and professional skills and further interviews to demonstrate a range of competencies and knowledge of current issues in the Probation and Prison service and the role of the psychologist in criminal justice.

Health psychology, in hospitals, health authorities and health research departments:

Either accredited MSc (one year full-time) in health psychology plus completion of Stage 2 of the Society's Diploma in Health Psychology or completion of Stages 1 and 2.

next

Neuropsychology, helping people with neurological disease or brain injury:

Specialised training in neuropsychology is based on prior training in one of the other areas of applied psychology, particularly clinical or educational psychology, followed by a minimum of two years formal supervised practice together with assessment and professional examinations.

Neuropsychologists require general clinical skills and knowledge of the broad range of mental health problems as well as specialist knowledge in the neurosciences. There is a serious shortage of neuropsychologists, particularly paediatric, and prospects for professional advancement are good.

Occupational psychology, in management, personnel, training, selection and careers services:

Either accredited MSc in occupational psychology (one year full-time) plus two years supervised work experience or at least three years full-time supervised work experience, with the Society's Postgraduate Certificate in Occupational Psychology.

Mature entrants are encouraged and graduates can go straight into employment.

Research and teaching, in institutions of higher education:

Either PhD in Psychology or for teachers at least three years full-time experience as teacher of psychology including the Society's Diploma in the Applied Psychology of Teaching.

To teach psychology in a state school it is necessary to have a Postgraduate Certificate in Education (PGCE). It may be difficult for psychology graduates to find places on PGCE courses as psychology is not a National Curriculum subject so prospective students should select a National Curriculum subject for joint or combined honours.

Psychotherapy and sports psychology are not yet accredited by the BPS and prospective applicants are warned to be careful in choosing a training course.

next

6.2 Psychology-related careers

Psychology students proceed into a variety of careers. Three months after graduation two-thirds of psychology graduates are in paid employment with another quarter undertaking postgraduate study. A significant number (though less than one-fifth of the overall number of graduates) ultimately gain employment as professional psychologists. Many of the remainder work in teaching, industry, social services, the media, information technology, computing, marketing and government agencies.

Because of the wide range of generic skills and the rigour with which they are taught, a training in psychology is widely accepted as providing an excellent preparation for a number of careers. In addition to subject skills and knowledge, graduates also develop skills in communication, numeracy, teamwork, critical thinking, computing, independent learning and many others, all of which are highly valued by employers.

http://www.qaa.ac.uk/academicinfrastructure/benchmark/statements/Psychology07.pdf (accessed 3 July 2008) with permission from *Subject Benchmark Statement: Psychology 2007*. © The Quality Assurance Agency for Higher Education, 2007.

Besides those already mentioned, other careers for psychology graduates include entertainment, politics and the following:

Armed forces:
http://www.army.mod.uk, www.raf.mod.uk, www.royalnavy.mod.uk
Although there is no recognised military psychology in the UK (at the time of writing) there are openings for psychology graduates. Website searches for the army and RAF may not give any response to 'psychology' or 'psychologist' so you may have to hunt a bit to find something relevant to you. The Royal Navy has an Applied Psychology Team which carries out a wide range of hands-on research and consulting activities in the areas of occupational psychology and health psychology.

Civil Service:
http://www.gchq.gov.uk and http://www.careers.civil-service.gov.uk/
The Civil Service communication and intelligence branch (GCHQ) has a graduate management trainee scheme. Careers may involve helping people with special needs, attitude surveys, training, and programme evaluation. The second website gives information about all careers.

Clinical auditor:
This position involves assessing the quality of care and treatment in clinical settings and is suited to someone with some clinical experience.

Defence Evaluation and Research Agency:

http://www.dera.gov.uk, split into http://www.dstl.gov.uk/ and http://www.qinetiq.com/.

Qinetiq offer work experience and summer placements but do not specifically mention psychology. DSTL list psychology under their careers and say 'individuality thrives; smart thinking is rewarded; innovation and creativity are valued.'

Foreign and Commonwealth Office:

http://www.fco.gov.uk/en/

http://www.fco.gov.uk/en/about-the-fco/working-for-us/work-experience/

The FCO offers work experience and placement programme for those interested in a career.

Home Office:

http://www.homeoffice.gov.uk/about-us/working-for-us/

http://www.careers.civil-service.gov.uk/

Career opportunities in the Home Office can be found through the Civil Service.

Management consultancy:

Many management consultancy firms offer psychology related work such as personnel selection, job analysis and human resources and might be useful either for work placements or a career.

Market research:

This often involves questionnaires and individual and group interviews. The general approach of psychology is of real benefit. Advertising also attracts psychology graduates.

Ministry of Defence:

http://www.mod.uk

The Ministry of Defence is the organisation that enables the armed services to do their job, from providing supplies to making international defence policy by implementing the government's wishes. The website leads to careers for civilians as well as each of the armed forces.

NHS hospital trusts:

http://www.nhscareers.nhs.uk/

The NHS website lists all available careers including those for psychologists.

Organisational psychology:

This is related to, but not the same as, occupational psychology and may involve organisational structures, job planning, leadership, group processes, teamwork, stress management, negotiation and conflict resolution. In a practical way organisational psychologists can assist with organisational effectiveness and deal with redundancy, retirement, redeployment and disciplinary problems. Personnel managers may also have a psychology background.

The police:

http://www.police-information.co.uk/Docs/policejobsandvacancies/

There are a number of openings for graduates. A police psychologist is essentially an organisational psychologist who may also give advice on public order training, promotion assessment, selection procedures for firearms officers, crime analysis and the accreditation of intelligence officers.

7 Learning resources

resources

7.1 Bibliography

Comprehensive reading lists are included in the website for the BPS qualifying examination (see 7.3); a few examples from them are noted here.

Abraham, C. and Shanley, E. (1992) *Social Psychology for Nurses: Understanding interaction in health care*. London: Edward Arnold.

Adam, K. and Oswald, I. (1983) Protein synthesis, bodily renewal and the sleep-wake cycle, *Clinical Science*, **65**: 561–7.

Adams, B. (1989) *Colour Physics in the Curriculum: A comparison of the ways in which colour theory is taught in art and science*. MSc. dissertation, Reading University.

Adams, B. and Bromley, B. (1998) *Psychology for Health Care*. Basingstoke: Macmillan.

Adams, N. (2008) Reparative Reasoning, *Modern Theology*, **24** (3): 447–57.

Ader, R. (1980) Psychosomatic and psychoimmulogic research, *Psychosomatic Medicine*, **42** (3): 307–21.

Adler, A. (1927) *The Practice and Theory of Individual Psychology*. New York: Harcourt Brace Jovanovich.

Adorno, T. W., Frenkey-Brunswick, E., Levinson, D. J. and Sanford, R. N. (1950) *The Authoritarian Personality*. New York: Harper and Row.

Ainsworth, M., Blehar, M., Waters, E. and Wall, S. (1978) *Patterns of Attachment*. Hillsdale, NJ: Erlbaum.

Ainsworth, M. and Bowlby, J. (1965) *Child Care and the Growth of Love*. London: Penguin Books.

Alcock, J. (2001) *Animal behaviour: An evolutionary approach, 7th edn*. Sunderland: Sinauer Associates (recommended by BPS).

Aldiss, B. W. (1970) *The Shape of Further Things: Speculations on change*. London: Faber.

Alexander, C. N., Zucker, L. G. and Brady, C. L. (1970) Experimental expectations and autokinetic experiences: consistency theories and judgmental convergence, *Sociometry*, **33**: 108–22.

Allport, F. H. (1924) *Social Psychology*. Boston: Houghton Mifflin.

Allport, F. H. (1974) Floyd H. Allport. In G. Lindzey (ed.), *A History of Psychology in Autobiography* (Vol. VI). Englewood Cliffs, NJ: Prentice-Hall, pp. 3–29.

Allport, G. W. (1937) *Personality: A psychological interpretation*. New York: Holt, Reinhart and Winston.

Allport, G. W. (1947) *The Use of Personal Documents in Psychological Science*. London: Holt, Rinehart and Winston.

Allport, G. W. (1954) *The Nature of Prejudice*. Reading, MA: Addison-Wesley.

Allport, G. W. (1955) *Becoming: Basic considerations for a psychology of personality*. New Haven: Yale University Press.

Allport, G. W. (1961) *Pattern and Growth in Personality*. New York: Holt, Rinehart and Winston.

resources

Allport, G. W. (1962) The general and the unique in psychological science. In R. S. Lazarus and E. M. Option Jr (1967) *Personality: Selected readings*. Harmondsworth: Penguin.

American Psychiatric Association (1994) *Diagnostic and Statistical Manual of Mental Disorders, 4th edn*. Washington DC: American Psychiatric Association.

Anastasi, A. and Urbina, S. (1997) *Psychological Testing, 7th edn*. Englewood Cliffs, NJ: Prentice Hall (recommended by BPS).

Anderson, C. A. (1987) Temperature and aggression: effects on quarterly, yearly and city rates of violent and nonviolent crime, *Journal of Personality and Social Psychology*, **52**: 1161–73.

Anderson, J. R. (1985) *Cognitive Psychology and its Implications, 2nd edn*. New York: Freeman.

Argyle, M. (1983) *The Psychology of Interpersonal Behaviour*. Harmondsworth: Penguin.

Argyle, M. and Trower, P. (1979) *Person to Person*. London: Harper and Row.

Aronson, E. (1992) *The Social Animal, 6th edn*. San Francisco: W. H. Freeman and Co.

Aronson, E. (2007) *Mistakes Were Made (But Not by Me): Why we justify foolish beliefs, bad decisions, and hurtful acts*. Oxford: Harcourt.

Aronson, E., Blaney, N., Stephin, C., Sikes, J. and Snapp, M. (1978) *The Jigsaw Classroom*. Beverly Hills, CA: Sage Publishing Company.

Aronson, E. and Osherow, N. (1980) Co-operation, prosocial behaviour and academic performance: experiments in the desegregated classroom. In L. Bickman (ed.), *Applied Social Psychology Annual*, Vol. 1. Beverly Hills, CA: Sage.

Aronson, E. and Patnoe, S. (1997) *The Jigsaw Classroom: Building cooperation in the classroom, 2nd edn*. New York: Addison Wesley Longman.

Asch, S. E. (1956) Studies of independence and conformity: 1. A minority of one against a unanimous majority. *Psychological Monographs*, **70** (9), Whole #416.

Asch, S. E. and Rock, I. (1990) *The Legacy of Solomon Asch: Essays in cognition and social psychology*. Hillsdale, NJ: Lawrence Erlbaum Associates.

Atkinson, R. C. and Shiffrin, R. M. (1968) Human memory: a proposed system and its control processes. In K. W. Spence and J. T. Spence (eds), *The Psychology of Learning and Motivation: Advances in research and theory* (Vol 2). New York: Academic Press, pp. 89–195.

Atkinson, R. L., Atkinson, R. C., Smith, E. E., Bem, D. J. and Nolen-Hoeksema, S. (1996) *Hilgard's Introduction to Psychology, 12th edn*. London: Harcourt Brace Jovanovich.

Atkinson, R. L. and Hilgard, E. R. (1990) *Introduction to Psychology, 10th edn*. London: Harcourt Brace Jovanovich.

Atkinson, R. L. and Shiffrin, R. M. (1971) The control of short-term memory, *Scientific American*, **224**: 82–90.

Ausubel, D. P., Novak, J. D. and Hanesian, H. (1968) *Educational Psychology: A cognitive view*. New York: Holt, Rinehart and Winston.

Ayer, A. J. (1963) *The Concept of a Person and Other Essays*. London: Macmillan.

Baddeley, A. D. (1976) *The Psychology of Memory*. New York: Basic Books.

Baddeley, A. D. (1982) *Your Memory: A user's guide*. Harmondsworth: Penguin.

Baddeley, A. D. (1987) *Working Memory*. Oxford: Oxford University Press.

Baddeley, A. D. (1990) *Human Memory: Theory and practice*. London: Lawrence Erlbaum.

Baddeley, A. D. and Hitch, G. J. (1974) Working memory. In G. A. Bower (ed.), *The Psychology of Learning and Motivation: Advances in research and theory* (Vol. 8). New York: Academic Press, pp. 47–89.

Bales, R. F. (1950) *Interaction Process Analysis: A method for the study of small groups*. Chicago: University of Chicago Press.

resources

Bales, R. F. (1953) The equilibrium problem in small groups. In T. Parsons, R. F. Bales and E. A. Shils (eds), *Working Papers in the Theory of Action*. Glencoe, IL: Free Press, pp. 111–61.

Bales, R. F. (1999) *Social Interaction Systems: Theory and measurement*. Piscataway, New Jersey: Transaction Press.

Bales, R. F. and Cohen, S. P. (1979) *SYMLOG: A system for the multiple level observation of groups*. New York: The Free Press.

Bales, R. F. and Strodtbeck, F. L. (1951) Phases in group problem-solving, *Journal of Abnormal and Social Psychology*, **46**: 485–95.

Bandler, R. and Grinder, J. (1975) *The Structure of Magic*. Palo Alto, CA: Science and Behaviour Books.

Bandler, R. and Grinder, J. (1976) *The Structure of Magic II*. Palo Alto, CA: Science and Behaviour Books.

Bandura, A. (1965) Influence of models' reinforcement contingencies on the acquisition of imitative responses, *Journal of Personality and Social Psychology*, **1**: 589–95.

Bandura, A. (1969) *Principles of Behaviour Modification*. New York: Holt, Rinehart and Winston.

Bandura, A. (1977) *Social Learning Theory*. Englewood Cliffs, NJ: Prentice Hall.

Bandura, A. (1973) *Aggression: A social learning analysis*. Englewood Cliffs, NJ: Prentice-Hall.

Bandura, A. (1986) *Social Foundations of Thought and Action: A social cognitive theory*. Englewood Cliffs, NJ: Prentice- Hall,

Bandura, A. (ed.) (1995) *Self-Efficacy in Changing Societies*. New York, NY: Cambridge University Press.

Bandura, A. (1997) *Self-Efficacy: The exercise of control*. New York: W. H. Freeman and company.

Bandura, A. (2006) Autobiography. In M. G. Lindzey and W. M. Runyan (eds), *A History of Psychology in Autobiography* (Vol. IX). Washington DC: American Psychological Association.

Bandura, A. and Walters, R. H. (1959) *Adolescent Aggression*. New York: Ronald Press.

Bandura, A. and Walters, R. H. (1963) *Social Learning and Personality Development*. New York: Holt, Rinehart and Winston.

Bannister, D. and Fransella, F. (1986) *Inquiring Man: the theory of personal constructs, 3rd edn*. Harmondsworth: Penguin. (Original edition 1971.)

Bannister, D. and Mair, J. M. M. (1968) *The Evaluation of Personal Constructs*. London: Academic Press.

Barbeau,D., Liang, J.J., Robitaille,Y., Quirion, R., and Srivastava, L.K. (1995) Decreased expression of the embryonic form of the neural cell adhesion molecule in schizophrenic brain. *Proceedings of the National Academy of Science*, USA, **92**: 2785–9.

Barker, R. G. and Wright, H. F. (1955) *Midwest and its Children: The psychological ecology of an American town*. New York: Harper and Row.

Barlow, H. B., Blakemore, C. and Weston-Smith, M. (1990) *Images and Understanding*. Cambridge: Cambridge University Press.

Barlow, H. B. and Mollon, J. D. (eds) (1982) *The Senses*. Cambridge: Cambridge University Press.

Baron-Cohen, S. (1989) The autistic child's theory of mind: a case of specific developmental delay, *Journal of Child Psychology and Psychiatry*, **30**: 85–297.

Baron-Cohen, S. (1993) *Autism: The Facts*. Osford: Oxford University Press.

Baron-Cohen, S. (1995) *Mindblindness*. Cambridge, MA: MIT Press.

Baron-Cohen, S. (1997a) *Synaesthesia*. Oxford: Wiley/Blackwell.

Baron-Cohen, S. (1997b) *The Maladapted Mind*. Hillsdale, New Jersey: Erlbaum.

Baron-Cohen, S. (1998) *Tourette Syndrome: The facts*. Oxford: Oxford University Press.

Baron-Cohen, S. (2000) Autism and theory of mind. In J. Harley and A. Braithwaite (eds), *The Applied Psychologist*. Buckingham: Open University Press.

Baron-Cohen, S. (2001) *Understanding Other Minds*. Oxford: Oxford University Press.

Baron-Cohen, S. (2003) *The Essential Difference: Men, Women and the Extreme Male Brain*. Harmondsworth: Penguin UK/Basic Books.

Barron, F. (1965) The psychology of creativity. In *New Directions in Psychology II*. London: Holt, Rinehart and Winston.

Bartlett, F. C. (1932) *Remembering: A study in experimental and social psychology*. Cambridge: Cambridge University Press.

Bartlett, F. C. (1958) *Thinking*. New York: Basic Books.

Bateson, G., Jackson, D. D., Haley, J. and Weakland, J. (1956) Toward a theory of schizophrenia, *Behavioral Science*, **1**: 251–64.

Baumeister, R., Bratslavsky, E., Muraven, M. and Tice, D. (1998) Ego depletion: is the active self a limited resource? *Journal of Personality and Social Psychology*, **74** (5): 1252–65.

Bee, H. (1997) *The Developing Child, 8th edn*. London: Addison-Wesley.

Bee, H. L. and Mitchell, S. K. (1984) *The Developing Person*. New York: Harper and Row.

Beech, J. R. and Harding, L. (eds) (1990) *Testing People; A practical guide to psychometrics*. Windsor: NFER-NELSON.

Beecher, H. K. (1959) *Measurement of Subjective Responses: Quantitative effects of drugs*. Oxford: Oxford University Press.

Bem, D. J. (1970) *Beliefs, Attitudes and Human Affairs*. Belmont, CA: Brooks Cole.

Bem, S. L. (1974) The measurement of psychological androgyny, *Journal of Consulting and Clinical Psychology*, **42**: 155–62.

Bem, S. L. (1981a) Gender schema theory: a cognitive account of sex-typing, *Psychological Review*, **88**: 354–64.

Bem, S. L. (1981b) The BSRI and gender schema theory: a reply to Spence and Helmreich. *Psychological Review*, **88**: 369–71.

Bem, S. L. (1993) *The Lenses of Gender: Transforming the debate on sexual inequality*. New Haven, CT: Yale University Press.

Berkowitz, L. (1962) *Aggression: A social psychological analysis*. New York: Academic Press.

Berkowitz, L. (1983) The experience of anger as a parallel process in the display of impulsive 'angry' aggression. In R. G. Geen and E. I. Donnerstein (eds), *Aggression: Theoretical and Empirical Reviews, 2: Issues in research*. New York: Academic Press.

Berkowitz, L. (1993) *Aggression, Its Causes, Consequences and Control*. New York: McGraw-Hill.

Berlo, D. K. (1960) *The Process of Communication: An introduction to theory and practice*. London: Holt, Rinehart and Winston.

Berne, E. (1964) *Games People Play*. Harmondsworth: Penguin.

Bernstein, B. (ed.) (1973) *Class, Codes And Control*, (Vol 2), *Applied studies towards a sociology of language*. London: Routledge.

Berry, A., Mulhall, P., Gunstone, R. and Loughran, J. (1999) Helping students learn from laboratory work, *Australian Science Teachers Journal*, **45**: 27–32.

Bersoff, D. N. (2003) *Ethical Conflicts in Psychology*. New York: American Psychological Association (recommended by BPS).

Bettleheim, B. (1976) *The Uses of Enchantment: The meaning and importance of fairy tales*. New York: Random House.

Bettleheim, B. (1987) *Good Enough Parent: A book on child rearing*. New York: Random House.

Bion, W. R. (1961) *Experiences in Groups and Other Papers*. London: Routledge.

Blakemore, C. (1977) *Mechanics of the Mind*. Cambridge, UK: Cambridge University Press.

Blakemore, C. (1988) *The Mind Machine.* London: BBC Publications.

Blass, T. (ed.) (2000) *Obedience to Authority: Current perspectives on the Milgram paradigm*. NJ: Lawrence Erlbaum Associates.

Bloom, B. S., Engelhart, M. D., Furst, E. J., Walker, H. H. and Krathwohl, D. R. (1956) *Taxonomy of Educational Objectives. Handbook 1: Cognitive domains*. London: Longman.

Blumer, H. (1969) *Symbolic Interactionism: Perspective and method.* Englewood Cliffs, NJ: Prentice Hall.

Boakes, R. A. (1984) *From Darwin to Behaviourism*. Cambridge: Cambridge University Press.

Bowie, M. (1991) *Lacan: An introduction*. London: Fontana.

Bowlby, J. (1951) *Maternal Care and Mental Health.* Geneva: World Health Organisation.

Bowlby, J. (1953) *Child Care and the Growth of Love.* Harmondsworth: Penguin.

Bowlby, J. (1969) *Attachment and Loss, I: Attachment*. London: Hogarth.

Bowlby, J. (1973) *Attachment and Loss II: Separation, anxiety and anger*. London: Hogarth.

Bowlby, J. (1980) *Attachment and Loss III: Loss, sadness and depression.* London: Hogarth.

Bowlby, J. (1988) *A Secure Base: Clinical applications of attachment theory.* London: Tavistock/ Routledge.

Bradley, J. C. and Edinberg, M. A. (1990) *Communication in the Nursing Context*, 3rd edn. Norwalk, CT: Appleton and Lange.

Brand, C. R. and Deary, I. (1982) Intelligence and inspection time. In H. J. Eysenck (ed.), *A Model for Intelligence*. New York: Springer.

Bransford, J. D. and Stein, B. S. (1993) *The Ideal Problem Solver: A guide for improving thinking, learning and creativity, 2nd edn*. New York: W. H. Freeman.

Breggin, P. (1993) *Toxic Psychiatry: Drugs and electroconvulsive therapy: the truth and the better alternatives.* London: Fontana.

British Association of Counselling (1990) *BAC Code of Ethics and Practice for Counsellors.* Rugby: BAC.

Broadbent, D. E. (1958) *Perception and Communication.* London: Pergamon Press.

Brody, R., Hayes, N., Newton, J. and Sanders, P. (1982) *Handbook for Psychology Students*. Association for the Teaching of Psychology.

Bromley, D. B. (1966) *The Psychology of Human Ageing.* Harmondsworth: Penguin.

Brown, R. J. (1988) *Group processes: Dynamics within and between groups, Revised edn.* London: Basil Blackwell (recommended by BPS).

Brown, R. J. (1995) *Prejudice: Its social psychology.* Oxford: Basil Blackwell (recommended by BPS).

Brown, S. R. (1986) Q technique and method. In W. D. Berry and M. S. Lewis-Beck (eds), *New Tools for Social Scientists*, Beverly Hills, CA: Sage,

Bruce, V. Green, P. and Georgeson, M. (2003) *Visual perception: Physiology, psychology and ecology, 4th edn*. Hove: Psychology Press (recommended by BPS).

Bruner, J. S. (1960) *The Process of Education.* Cambridge, MA: Harvard University Press.

Bruner, J. S. (1964) The course of cognitive growth, *American Psychologist,* **19**: 1–15.

Bryant, P. (1982) *Piaget: Issues and experiments.* Leicester: BPS.

Buckman, R. (1988) *I Don't Know What to Say: How to help and support someone who is dying.* London: Macmillan Papermac.

Burnard, P. and Morrison, P. (1991) Client-centred counselling: a study of nurses' attitudes, *Nurse Education Today,* **11**: 104–9.

Burt, C. L. (1949) An autobiographical sketch, *Occupational Psychology*, **23**: 9–20.

resources

Burt, C. L. (1958) The inheritance of mental ability, *American Psychologist*, **13**: 1–15.

Burt, K. (1995) The effects of cancer on body image and sexuality, *Nursing Times*, **91** (7): 36–7.

Burton, G. and Dimbleby, R. (1995) *Between Ourselves, 2nd edn*. London: Edward Arnold.

Buss, A. H. (1961) *The Psychology of Aggression.* New York : John Wiley and Sons.

Buss, A. H. and Plomin, R. (1975) A *Temperament Theory of Personality Development.* New York: John Wiley and Sons.

Butler, J. M. and Haigh, G. V. (1954) Changes in the relation between self-concepts and ideal concepts consequent upon client-centred counseling. In C. R. Rogers and R. F. Dymond (eds), *Psychotherapy and Personality Change.* Chicago: University of Chicago Press.

Buzan, T. (1988) *Use Your Head.* London: Pan.

Buzan, T. (1993) *The Mind Map Book*. London: BBC.

Byrne, M. S. and Johnstone, A. H. (1987) Critical thinking and science education, *Studies in Higher Education*, 12: 325–39.

Calder, N. (1970) *The Mind of Man.* London: BBC Publications.

Calev, A., Gaudino, E. A., Squires, N. K., Zervas, I. M. and Fink, M. (1995) ECT and non-memory cognitions: a review, *British Journal of Clinical Psychology,* **34** (4): 505–15.

Campbell, A. and. Muncer, S. (1998) *The Social Child*. Hove: The Psychology Press (recommended by BPS).

Cannon, W. B. (1915) *Bodily Changes in Pain, Hunger, Fear and Rage*. New York, NY: D. Appleton and Company.

Cannon, W. B. (1927) The James-Lange theory of emotion: a critical examination and an alternative theory, *American Journal of Psychology*, **39**: 10–124.

Cannon, W. B. (1929) *Bodily Changes in Pain, Hunger, Fear and Rage.* Boston: Branford. (Original work published in 1915.)

Cannon, W. B. (1945) *The Way of an Investigator: A scientist's experiences in medical research*. New York, NY: W. W. Norton.

Cardwell, M., Clark, L. and Meldrum, C. (1996) *Psychology for A Level.* London: Harper-Collins.

Carlson, N. R. (2004) *Physiology of Behaviour, 8th edn*. Boston: Allyn and Bacon (recommended by BPS).

Carter, R. (1998) *Mapping the Mind*. London: Weidenfeld and NIcholson.

Cattell, R. B. (1965) Personality structure: the larger dimension. In R. S. Lazarus and E. M. Option Jr (1967), *Personality: Selected Readings*. Harmondsworth: Penguin.

Cattell, R. B. (1979, 1980) *Personality and Learning Theory* (Vols 1 and 2), New York: Springer.

Cattell, R. B., Cattell, A. K. and Cattell, H. E. P. (1996) *16PF Fifth Edition*. NCS Pearson Inc.

Chalmers, D. J. (1995) The puzzle of conscious experience, *Scientific American,* December: 62–8.

Chase, T. (1987) *When Rabbit Howls.* New York: Jove.

Child, D. (1986) *Psychology and the Teacher, 4th edn*. London: Cassell.

Chomsky, N. (2004) *Language and Politics*. London: AK Press.

Clarkson, P. and Gilbert, M. (1990) Transactional Analysis. In W. Dryden (ed.), *Individual Therapy: A handbook*. Milton Keynes: Open University Press.

Clegg, C. (1986) *Biology for Schools and Colleges, 2nd edn*. London: Heinemann Educational.

Clegg, F. (1982) *Simple Statistics: A course book for the social sciences.* Cambridge: Cambridge University Press.

Cohen, S., Tyrrell, D. A. J. and Smith, A. P. (1991) Psychological stress and susceptibility to the common cold, *New England Journal of Medicine,* **325**: 606–12.

Coleman, J. C. and Hendry, L. B. (1999) *The Nature of Adolescence, 3rd edn*. London and New York: Routledge (recommended by BPS).

resources

Coles, M. (1995) *A Student's Guide to Coursework Writing.* Stirling: University of Stirling.

Collingwood, R. G. (1998) *An Essay on Metaphysics, revised edn.* Oxford: Oxford University Press.

Collins, A. M. and Quillian, M. (1969) Retrieval time for semantic memory, *Journal of Verbal Learning and Verbal Behaviour,* **8**: 240–7.

Collins, A. M. and Quillian, M. (1972) How to make a language user. In E. Tulving and W. Donaldson (eds), *Organisation of Memory.* New York: Academic Press.

Collinson, D., Kirkup, G., Kyd, R. and Slocombe, L. (1992) *Plain English, 2nd edn.* Buckingham: Open University Press.

Colman, A. M. (ed.) (1995) *Controversies in Psychology.* London: Longman (recommended by BPS).

Concise Oxford Dictionary (1982) *7th edn.* Oxford: Clarendon Press.

Cooper, C. (2002) *Individual Differences, 2nd edn.* London: Arnold (recommended by BPS).

Cooper, C. L. and Sutherland, V. (2006) Stress and the changing nature of work. In D. Clements-Croome (ed.), *Creating the Productive Workplace.* Abingdon: Taylor and Francis.

Cornsweet, T. N. (1970) *Visual Perception.* New York: Academic Press.

Cosmides, L. and Tooby, J. (2001) *Universal Minds: Human nature and the science of evolutionary psychology.* Blaine, WA: Phoenix .

Cottrell, S. (2003) *The Study Skills Handbook, 2nd edn.* Basingstoke: Palgrave Macmillan.

Cox, D. F. and Bauer, R. A. (1964) Self-confidence and persuasability in women, *Public Opinion Quarterly,* **28**: 453–66.

Craik, F. I. M. and Lockhart, R. S. (1972) Levels of processing: a framework for memory research, *Journal of Verbal Learning and Verbal Behavior*, **11**: 671–84.

Cramer, D. (1998) *Close relationships.* London: Arnold (recommended by BPS).

Crammond, W. A. (1970) Psychotherapy of the dying patient, *British Medical Journal,* **15** (4): 389–93.

Crowe, M. and Ridley, J. (1990) *Therapy with Couples.* Oxford: Blackwell.

Curzon, L. B. (1985) *Teaching in Further Education. An outline of principles and practice, 3rd edn.* London: Holt, Rinehart and Winston.

Cytovic, R. E. (1994) *The Man Who Tasted Shapes.* London: Abacus.

Damasio, A. R. (1994) *Descartes' Error: Emotion, reason and the human brain.* New York: Grosset/Putnam.

Damasio, A. R. (1999, 2000) *The Feeling of What Happens: Body and emotion in the making of consciousness.* New York: Harcourt Brace.

Damasio, A. R. (2001) Fundamental feelings, *Nature,* **413**: 781.

Darley, J. and Latané, B. (1968) Group inhibition of bystander intervention in emergencies, *Journal of Personality and Social Psychology*, **10**: 215–21.

Dawkins, R. (1989) *The Selfish Gene, 2nd edn.* Oxford: Oxford University Press (recommended by BPS).

Deary, I. J. and Stough, C. (1996) Intelligence and inspection time: achievements, prospects and problems, *American Psychologist*, 51: 599–608.

De Bono, E. (1971) *The Use of Lateral Thinking.* Harmondsworth: Penguin.

De Bono, E. (2000) *Lateral Thinking: A textbook of creativity, new edn.* Harmondsworth: Penguin.

de Certeau, M. (1984) *The Practice of Everyday Life.* London: University of California Press.

Deliege, I. and Sloboda, J. (eds) (1996) *Musical Beginnings: Origins and development of musical competence.* Oxford: Oxford University Press.

Dennett, D. C. (1991) *Consciousness Explained.* London: Allen Lane/Penguin.

Dennett, D. C. (1987) *The Intentional Stance.* Cambridge, MA: MIT Press/A Bradford Book.

resources

Department of Health (1991) *Welfare of Children and Young People in Hospital.* London: HMSO.

Department of Health (1992) *The Health of the Nation.* London: HMSO.

Deutsch, J. A. and Deutsch, D. (1963) Attention: Some theoretical considerations, *Psychological Review,* **70**: 80–90.

Deutsch, J. A. and Deutsch, D. (1967) Comments on selective attention: perception or response, *Quarterly Journal of Experimental Psychology,* **19**: 362–7.

Dienstbier, R. A. (1989) Arousal and physiological toughness: implications for mental and physical health, *Psychology Review,* **96** (1): 84–100.

Dixon, N. (1987) *Our Own Worst Enemy.* London: Fontana.

Dollard, J., Doob, L., Miller, N. E., Mowrer, O. H. and Sears, R. R. (1939) *Frustration and Aggression.* New Haven, CT: Yale University Press.

Donaldson, M. (1978) *Children's Minds.* Glasgow: Fontana/Collins.

Donaldson, M. (1992) *Human minds.* Harmondsworth: Penguin (recommended by BPS).

Drabman, R. S. and Thomas, M. H. (1974) Does media violence increase children's tolerance of real-life aggression? *Developmental Psychology,* **10**: 418–21.

Drever, J. (1964) *A Dictionary of Psychology.* Harmondsworth: Penguin.

Drew, S. and Bingham, R. (1997) *The Student Skills Guide.* Aldershot: Gower.

Dunn, J. (1988) *The Beginnings of Social Understanding.* Oxford: Basil Blackwell (recommended by BPS).

Eagly, A. and Chaiken, S. (1975) An attribution analysis of the effect of communication characteristics on opinion change: the case of communicator attractiveness, *Journal of Personality and Social Psychology,* **32**: 136–44.

Ebbinghaus, H. (1885/1962) *Memory: A contribution to experimental psychology.* New York: Dover.

Edwards, A. L. (1957) *Techniques of Attitude Scale Construction.* New York: Appleton-Century Croft.

Ekman, P. and Friesen, W. V.(1971) Constants across cultures in the face and emotion, *Journal of Personality and Social Psychology,* **17**: 124–9.

Ekman, P. and Oster, H. (1979) Facial expressions of emotion, *Annual Review of Psychology,* **30**: 52 7–54.

Elliot , G. R. and Eisdorfer, C. (eds) (1982) *Stress and Human Health.* New York: Springer.

Ellis, A. W. (1993) *Reading, Writing and Dyslexia: A cognitive analysis, 2nd edn.* Hove: Erlbaum (recommended by BPS).

Emmons, R. (1986) Personal strivings: an approach to personality and subjective well-being, *Journal of Personality and Social Psychology,* **51**: 1058–68.

Entwistle. See Raaheim, K., Radford. and Wankowski, J. (1991) *Helping Students Learn: Teaching, counselling, research, 2nd Rev Edn.* Buckingham: SRHE and Open University Press.

Erikson, E. H. and Erikson, J. M. (1987) *The Life Cycle Completed.* New York: Norton.

Erikson, E. H., Erikson, J. M.; and Kivnick, H. Q. (1986) *Vital Involvement in Old Age.* New York: W. W. Norton.

Evans, P. (1991) Symbol clash, *Listener,* January 3: 7.

Evans, P., Clow, A. and Hucklebridge, F. (1997) Stress and the immune system, *Psychologist,* **10** (7): 303–7.

Evans, P. and Deehan, G. (1988) *The Keys to Creativity.* London: Grafton Books.

Ewing, T. N. (1942) A study of certain factors involved in changes of opinion, *Journal of Social Psychology,* **16**: 63–8.

Eysenck, H. J. (1947) *Dimensions of Personality: A record of research carried out in collaboration with H. T. Himmelweit.* London: Kegan Paul.

resources

Eysenck, H. J. (1962) *Know Your Own IQ.* Harmondsworth: Penguin/Pelican.

Eysenck, H. J. (1985) Personality, cancer and cardiovascular disease: a causal analysis, *Personality and Individual Differences,* **6**: 535–56.

Eysenck, H. J. (1990/1997) *Rebel with a Cause: The autobiography of Hans Eysenck.* New Brunswick, NJ: Transaction Publishers.

Eysenck, H. J. (1994) Cancer, personality and stress: prediction and prevention, *Advances in Behaviour Research and Therapy,* **16** (3): 167–215.

Eysenck, H. J. and Wilson, G. (1976) *Know Your Own Personality.* Harmondsworth: Penguin/Pelican.

Eysenck, M. W. (1994) *Perspectives on Psychology.* Hove: L. Erlbaum (recommended by BPS).

Eysenck, M. W. (2003) *Psychology for AS Level.* London: Psychology Press Ltd.

Eysenck, M. W. and Keane, M. T. (2000) *Cognitive Psychology: A student's handbook, 4th edn.* Hove: Erlbaum (recommended by BPS).

Fairbairn, G. J. and Winch, C. (1991) *Reading, Writing and Reasoning: A guide for students.* Buckingham: Open University Press.

Fantz, R. L. (1961) The origin of form perception, *Scientific American,* **204** (5): 66–72.

Fazio, R. H. and Zanna, M. D. (1978) Attitudinal qualities relating to the strength of the attitude-behaviour relation, *Journal of Experimental and Social Psychology,* **14**: 398–408.

Fellows, B. (1988) The use of hypnotic susceptibility scales. In M. Heap (ed.), *Hypnosis, Current Clinical Experimental and Forensic Practices.* London: Croom Helm.

Ferster, C. B. and Skinner, B. F. (1957) *Schedules of Reinforcement.* Reprinted by the B. F. Skinner Foundation in 1997.

Feshbach, S. (1964) The function of aggression and the regulation of the aggressive drive, *Psychological Review,* **71**: 257–62.

Festinger, L. (1957) *A Theory of Cognitive Dissonance.* Evanston, IL: Row and Peterson.

Festinger, L. and Carlsmith, J. M. (1959) Cognitive consequences of forced compliance, *Journal of Abnormal and Social Psychology,* **5**8: 203–10.

Feyerabend, P. and J. Preston (eds) (1999) *Knowledge, Science and Relativism: Philosophical papers* (Vol. 3). Cambridge: Cambridge University Press.

Fiske, S. T. (2004) *Social Beings: A core motives approach to social psychology.* New York: Wiley.

Fodor, J. A. (1975) *The Language of Thought.* Cambridge, MA: Harvard University Press.

Fontana, D. (1990) *Your Growing Child: From birth to adolescence.* London: Fontana.

Fossey, D. (2000) *Gorillas in the Mist.* New York: Mariner Books.

Foucault, M. (1978) *History of Sexuality,* Vol. 1. New York: Pantheon.

Fouts, R. (1997) *Next of Kin.* New York: Morrow.

Francis, R. D. (2004) *Becoming a Psychologist.* Basingstoke: Palgrave Macmillan.

Franken, R. (2002) *Human Motivation, 5th edn.* Belmont, CA: Wadsworth (recommended by BPS).

Fransella, F. (1990) Personal construct theory. In W. Dryden (ed.), *Individual Therapy: A handbook.* Milton Keynes: Open University Press.

Fransella, F., Bell, R. and Bannister, D. (2003) *A Manual for Repertory Grid Technique, 2nd edn.* Chichester, UK: John Wiley and Sons.

French, J. R. and Raven, B. (1959) The bases of social power. In D. Cartwright (ed.), Studies in social power, *Journal of Applied Communication,* **11** (2): 23–5.

French, P. (1994) *Social Skills for Nursing Practice, 2nd edn.* London: Chapman and Hall.

Freud, A. (1998) *Normality and Pathology in Childhood,* NY: International Universities Press.

Freud, S. (1938) *Psychopathology of Everyday Life.* Harmondsworth: Penguin/Pelican.

Freud, S. (1999) *The Interpretation of Dreams*, newly translated by J. Crick, with introduction and notes by R. Robertson. Oxford: Oxford University Press (original publication 1899).

Friedman, M. and Rosenman, R. H. (1974) *Type A Behavior and Your Heart.* New York: Knopf.

Fromm, E. (1942) *Fear of Freedom*. London: Routledge and Kegan Paul. Also (2001) Routledge Classics.

Fromm, E. (1947) *Man for Himself: An enquiry into the psychology of ethics.* New York: Rinehart. Also (2003) Routledge Classics.

Fromm, E. (1948, 1956) *The Art of Loving*. London: Routledge and Kegan Paul. Also (1995) HarperCollins Publishers; New edn.

Gardner, H. (1975) *The Shattered Mind*. New York: Knopf.

Gardner, H., Kornhaber, M. and Wake, W. (2001) *Intelligence: Multiple perspectives*. Fort Worth: Harcourt Brace (recommended by BPS).

Garnham, A. and Oakhill, J. (1994) *Thinking and Reasoning*. Oxford: Basil Blackwell.

Garrod, S. and Pickering, M. (eds) (1999) *Language Processing*. Hove: Psychology Press (recommended by BPS).

Geen, R. G. (1990) *Human Aggression.* Milton Keynes: Open University Press.

Gibson, E. J. (1994) Has psychology a future? *Psychological Science* **5**: 69—76.

Gibson, E. J. and Walk, R. D. (1960) The visual cliff, *Scientific American*, **202**: 64—71.

Gibson, J. J. (1950) *The Perception of the Visual World*. Boston: Houghton Mifflin.

Gill, D. and Adams, B. (1998) *ABC of Communication Studies, 2nd edn.* London: Nelson.

Gilligan, C. (1982) *In a Different Voice: Psychological theory and women's development.* Cambridge, MA: Harvard University Press.

Gilling, D. and Brightwell, R. (1982) *The Human Brain*. London: Orbis Publishing/BBC.

Gilovich, T. Griffin, D. and Kahneman, D. (eds) (2002) *Heuristics and Biases: The psychology of intuitive judgement*. Cambridge, UK: Cambridge University Press,

Glaser, B. G. and Strauss, A. L. (1965) *Awareness of Dying*. Chicago: Aldine.

Glaser, B. G. and Strauss, A. L. (1967) *The Discovery of Grounded Theory: Strategies for qualitative research.* Chicago: Aldine.

Glass, D. C. and Singer, J. E. (1972) *Urban Stress: Experiments on noise and social stressors.* New York: Academic Press.

Glassman, W. E. (1979) The biological approach. In J. Medcof and J. Roth (eds), *Approaches to Psychology.* Milton Keynes: Open University Press.

Gleick, J. (1988) *Chaos*. London: Sphere.

Goldberg, L. R. (1993) The structure of phenotypic personality traits, *American Psychologist*, 48: 26–34.

Goldstein, K. (1934/1995) *The Organism: A holistic approach to biology derived from pathological data in man.* New York: Zone Books, 1995.

Goleman, D. (1995) *Emotional Intelligence: Why it can matter more than IQ*. London: Bloomsbury Publishing.

Goodall, J. (1986) *The Chimpanzees of Gombe: Patterns of behavior.* Cambridge, MA: Harvard University Press.

Goodall, J. (2000) *In the Shadow of Man*, revised edn. New York: Mariner Books.

Green, C. and McCreery, C. (1989) *Apparitions.* Oxford: Institute of Psychophysical Research.

Green, S. (1994) *Principles of Biopsychology.* Hove: Lawrence Erlbaum Associates.

Greenberg, M. and Littlewood, R. (1995) Post-adoption incest and phenotype matching: experience, personal meanings and biosocial implications, *British Journal of Medical Psychology,* **68** (1): 29–44.

Greene, J. and Coulson, M. (1995) *Language Understanding: Current issues, 2nd edn.* Milton Keynes: Open University Press (recommended by BPS).

Gregory, R. L. (1971) *The Intelligent Eye.* London: Weidenfeld and Nicolson.

Gregory, R. L. (1981) *Mind in Science: A history of explanations in psychology and physics.* Harmondsworth: Penguin.

Gregory, R. L. (ed.) (1987) *The Oxford Companion to the Mind.* Oxford: Oxford University Press.

Gregory, R. L. (1990) How do we interpret images? In H. Barlow, C. Blakemore and M. Weston-Smith (eds), *Images and Understanding.* Cambridge: Cambridge University Press.

Gross, R. D. (1992) *Psychology, the Science of Mind and Behaviour, 2nd edn.* London: Hodder and Stoughton.

Gross, R. D. (1996) *Psychology, the Science of Mind and Behaviour, 3rd edn.* London: Hodder and Stoughton.

Gross, R. D. (2003) *Themes, Issues and Debates in Psychology.* London: Hodder and Stoughton (recommended by BPS).

Gross, R. D. (2005) *Psychology, the Science of Mind and Behaviour, 5th edn.* London: Hodder Arnold.

Guilford, J. P. (1967) *The Nature of Human Intelligence.* New York: McGraw Hill.

Hall, E. T. (1969) *The Hidden Dimension: Man's Use of Space in Public and Private.* London: Bodley Head.

Hampson, P. J. and Morris, P. E. (1996) *Understanding Cognition.* Oxford: Basil Blackwell (recommended by BPS).

Hampton, S. J. (2009) *Essential Evolutionary Psychology.* London: Sage.

Hannigan, T. J. (1982) *Mastering Statistics.* London: Macmillan.

Harley, T. A. (2001) *The Psychology of Language, 2nd edn.* Hove: Psychology Press (recommended by BPS).

Harlow, H. F. (1958) The nature of love, *American Psychologist,* 13: 573–685.

Harlow, H. F. (1959) Love in infant monkeys. In *Frontiers of Psychological Research: Readings from Scientific American.* London: W. H. Freeman and Co.

Harvey, S. and Hales-Tooke, A. (1972) *Play in Hospital.* London: Faber and Faber.

Hawkins, N. G., Davies, R. and Holmes, T. H. (1957) Evidence of psychosocial factors in the development of pulmonary tuberculosis. *American Review of Tubercular and Pulmonary Disease,* **75**: 768–80.

Hayes, N. (1994) *Foundations of Psychology: an introductory text.* London: Routledge.

Hearnshaw, L. (1979) *Cyril Burt: Psychologist.* Ithaca, NY: Cornell University Press.

Hebb, D. O. (1949) *Organization of Behaviour: A neuropsychological theory.* New York: John Wiley and Sons.

Hebb, D. O. (1958) *A Textbook of Psychology.* Philadelphia: Saunders.

Heider, F. (1958) *The Psychology of Interpersonal Relations.* New York: John Wiley and Sons.

Heider, F. and Simmel, M. (1944) An experimental study of apparent behaviour, *American Journal of Psychology,* **57**: 243–59.

Heim, A. (1954) *The Appraisal of Intelligence.* London: Methuen (1970 edn NFER).

Hein, E. C. and Nicholson, M. J. (eds) (1994) *Contemporary Leadership Behaviour: Selected readings, 4th edn.* London: Lippincott.

Hendin, H. (1964) *Suicide and Scandinavia.* New York: Grune and Stratton.

Hendry, L. B. and Kloep, M. (2002) *Lifespan Development: Resources, challenges and risks.* London and New York: Thompson (recommended by BPS).

Heron (1957) The pathology of boredom. In *Frontiers of Psychological Research: Readings from Scientific American.* London: WH Freeman.

resources

Hershenson, M., Munsinger, H. and Kessen, W. (1965) Preference for shapes of intermediate variability in the newborn human, *Science,* **147**: 630–1.

Hindmarch, C. (1993) *On the Death of a Child.* Oxford: Radcliffe Medical Press.

Hinton, J. M. (1972) *Dying, 2nd edn.* Harmondsworth: Penguin.

Hinton, J. M. (1980) Whom do dying patients tell? *British Medical Journal,* **281**: 1328–30.

Hinton, J. M. (1984) Coping with terminal illness. In R. Fitzpatrick, J. M. Hinton, S. Newman, S. Scambler and J. Thompson (eds), *The Experience of Illness.* London: Tavistock.

Hirschorn, P. (1979) The behaviourist approach. In J. Medcof and J. Roth (eds), *Approaches to Psychology.* Milton Keynes: Open University Press.

Hobson, R. P. (1993) *Autism and the Development of Mind.* Hove: Lawrence Erlbaum Associates.

Hock, R. (1995) *Forty Studies that Changed Psychology: Explorations into the history of psychological research.* London: Prentice-Hall (recommended by BPS).

Hogg, M. A. and Vaughan, G. M. (1998) *Social Psychology, 2nd edn.* London: Prentice Hall (recommended by BPS).

Hollin, C. R. and Howells, K. (1989) An introduction to concepts, models and techniques. In K. Howells and C. R. Hollin (eds), *Clinical Approaches to Violence.* Chichester: John Wiley and Sons.

Holmes, T. H. and Rahe, R. H. (1967) The social readjustment rating scale, *Journal of Psychosomatic Research,* **11**: 213–18.

Holt, R. R. (1962) Individuality and generalisation in the psychology of personality. In R. S. Lazarus and E. M. Option Jr (1967) *Personality: Selected readings.* Harmondsworth: Penguin.

Homans, G. C. (1961) *Social Behaviour: Its elementary forms.* New York: Harcourt Brace Jovanovich.

Hopson, B. (1981) Response to papers by Schlossberg, Brammer and Abrego. *Counselling Psychology,* **9**: 36–9.

Horne, J. (1988) *Why We Sleep: The functions of sleep in humans and other mammals.* Oxford: Oxford University Press.

Horne, J. (2006) *Sleepfaring: A journey through the science of sleep.* Oxford: Oxford University Press.

Horney, K. (1942) *Self-analysis.* New York: W. W. Norton.

Horney, K. (1945) *Our Inner Conflicts.* New York: W. W. Norton.

Hovland, C. I. and Weiss, W. (1951) The influence of source credibility on communication effectiveness, *Public Opinion Quarterly,* **15**: 635–50.

Howard, G. (1997) *The Macmillan Good English Handbook.* London: Macmillan.

Howe, G. (1990) *Schizophrenia: A fresh approach, 2nd edn.* London: David and Charles.

Hubel, D. H. and Wiesel, T. N. (1962) Receptive fields, binocular interaction and functional architecture in the cat's visual cortex, *Journal of Physiology,* **160**: 106–54.

Hubel, D. H. and Wiesel, T. N. (1979) Brain mechanisms of vision, *Scientific American,* **249**: 150–62.

Huczynski, A. and Buchanan, D. (1991) *Organisational Behaviour: An introductory text, 2nd edn.* New York: Prentice Hall.

Hunter, I. M. L. (1957) *Memory.* Harmondsworth: Penguin.

Huxley, J. and Lorenz, K. Z. (2002) *On Aggression.* London: Routledge Classics.

Insko, C. A. (1967) *Theories of Attitude Change.* New York: Appleton-Century-Croft.

Irwin, D. and Ross, B. (eds) (2003) *Cognitive vision: The psychology of learning and motivation, Vol 42.* San Diego: Elsevier Science (USA) (recommended by BPS).

Izard, C. E. (1977) *Human Emotions.* NewYork: Plenum.

James, W. (1979) *Pragmatism*. Cambridge, MA: Harvard University Press. Originally published in 1907.

James, W. (1981/1890) *The Principles of Psychology*. Cambridge, MA: Harvard University Press. Originally published in 1890 by Holt.

Janis, I. L. (1982) *Groupthink: Psychological studies of policy decisions and fiascos, 2nd edn*. Boston: Houghton Mifflin.

Janis, I. L. and King, B. (1954) The influence of role-playing on opinion change, *Journal of Abnormal and Social Psychology,* **49**: 211–18.

Janis, I. L. and Mann, L. (1965) Effectiveness of emotional role-playing in modifying smoking habits and attitudes, *Journal of Experimental Personality Research,* **1**: 84–90.

Jenkins, C. D., Zyzansk, S. J. and Rosenman, R. H. (1979) *The Jenkins Activity Survey for Health Prediction.* New York: Psychological Corporation.

Jenner, S. (1993) *QED: The Family Game*. London: BBC Education.

Jensen, A. R. (2000) The ubiquity of mental speed and the centrality of working memory, *Psycholoquy,* **11** (38) (Article 37 on Intelligence g factor).

Johnson, D. W. and Johnson, F. P. (1994) *Joining Together: Group Theory and Group Skills, 5th edn*. Boston: Allyn and Bacon.

Johnson-Laird, P. N. (1998) *Computer and the Mind: An introduction to cognitive science*. Cambridge, MA: Harvard University Press.

Johnson-Laird, P. N. (2006) *How We Reason*. Oxford: Oxford University Press.

Jones, E. E. (1979) The rocky road from acts to dispositions, *American Psychologist,* **34**: 107–17.

Jones, E. E. and Nisbett, R. E. (1971) *The Actor and the Observer: Divergent perceptions of the causes of behaviour.* Morristown, NJ: General Learning Press.

Jorgensen, E. and Jorgensen, H. (1984) *Eric Berne, Master Gamesman*. New York: Grove Press.

Jouve, N. W. (1980) *Baudelaire: A fire to conquer darkness.* London: Macmillan.

Joynson, R. B. (1989) *The Burt affair*. New York: Routledge.

Jung, C. G. (1916) The structure of the unconscious. *Collected Works, Vol. 7*. London: Routledge and Kegan Paul.

Jung, C. G. (1923) Psychological types. *Collected Works, Vol. 6*. London: Routledge and Kegan Paul.

Jung, C. G. (ed.) (1964) *Man and his symbols.* London: Picador.

Jung, C. G. and Jaffe, A. (ed.) (1995) *Memories, Dreams, Reflections*. Fontana Press; New edn (Original work 1962).

Kahneman, D. and Tversky, A. (1979) Prospect theory: an analysis of decision under risk, *Econometrica,* **47** (2): 263–97.

Kahney, H. (1993) *Problem Solving: Current issues, 2nd edn*. Buckingham: Open University Press (recommended by BPS).

Kanner, A. D., Coyne, J. C., Schaeffer, C. and Lazarus, R. S. (1981) Comparison of two models of stress measurement: daily hassles and uplifts versus major life events, *Journal of Behavioural Medicine,* **4**: 1–39.

Kaplan, R. M. and Saccuzzo, D. (2005) *Psychological Testing: Principles, applications and issues, 6th edn.* Belmont, CA: Wadsworth (recommended by BPS).

Kasl, S. V. and Cobb, S. (1966) Health behaviour, illness behaviour and sick-role behaviour, *Archives of Environmental Health,* **12**: 246–66, 531–41.

Kelly, G. A. (1955) *The Psychology of Personal Constructs* (2 vols). New York: W. W. Norton.

Kelley, H. H. (1950) The warm–cold variable in first impressions of people, *Journal of Personality,* **18**: 431–9.

Kelley, H. H. (1967) Attribution theory in social psychology. In D. Levine (ed.), *Nebraska Symposium on Motivation* (Vol. 15). Lincoln, NE: University of Nebraska Press, pp. 192–238.

Kennell, J. H., Voos, D. K. and Klaus, M. H. (1979) Parent–infant bonding. In J. D. Osofsky (ed.), *Handbook of Infant Development*. New York: John Wiley and Sons.

Kermis, M. D. (1983) *The Psychology of Human Aging: Theory, research and practice*. Boston: Allyn and Bacon.

Kerns, R. D., Turk, D. C. and Rudy, T. E. (1985) The West Haven-Yale Multidimensional Pain Inventory (WHYMPI), *Pain,* **23**: 345–56.

Kesey, K. (1976) *One Flew Over the Cuckoo's Nest*. London: Picador/Pan.

Kiger, A. M. (1995) *Teaching for Health, 2nd edn*. Edinburgh: Churchill Livingstone.

Kinzel, A. F. (1970) Body buffer zone in violent prisoners, *American Journal of Psychiatry,* **127**: 59–64.

Klein, M. (1997) *Envy and Gratitude*. (Contemporary Classics). Vintage; New edn.

Klein, M. (2002) *Love, Guilt and Reparation: and other works 1921–1945* (*The Writings of Melanie Klein, Vol. 1*). New York: Free Press.

Kleiner, A. (1987) Amplitude and phase spectra as indices of infants' pattern preferences, *Infant Behaviour and Development,* **10**: 49–59.

Kohlberg, L. (1976) Moral stages and moralization: the cognitive-developmental approach. In T. Lickona (ed.), *Moral Development and Behavior: Theory, research and social issues*. New York: Rinehart and Winston.

Kohlberg, L. (1981) *Essays on Moral Development, Vol. I: The philosophy of moral development*. San Francisco: Harper and Row.

Kohler, W. (1925) *The Mentality of Apes*. New York: Harcourt Brace Jovanovich.

Kohler, W. (1947) *Gestalt Psychology: An introduction to new concepts in modern psychology*. Chicago: Liveright.

Kolb, B. and Whishaw, I. Q. (2003) *Fundamentals of Human Neuropsychology, 5th edn*. New York: Freeman (recommended by BPS).

Kraepelin, E. (1927) *Textbook of Psychiatry, 9th edn*. Leipzig: Barth.

Krebs, J. R. and Davies, N. B. (1993) *An Introduction to Behavioural Ecology, 3rd edn*. Oxford: Blackwell Scientific (recommended by BPS).

Kreuger, W. C. F. (1929) The effect of overlearning on retention, *Journal of Experimental Psychology,* **12**: 71–8.

Kubler-Ross, E. (1970) *On Death and Dying*. London: Tavistock.

Kuhn, M. H. and McPartland, T. S. (1954) An empirical investigation of self-attitudes, *American Sociological Review,* **19**: 68–76;

Kuhn, T. S. (1970) *The Structure of Scientific Revolutions, 2nd edn*. Chicago: Chicago University Press.

Labov, W. (1969) The logic of nonstandard English. *Georgetown Monographs on Language and Lingusitics,* **22**: 1–22, 26–31.

Labov, W. (1972) *Language in the Inner City: Studies in Black English vernacular*. Philadelphia: Falmer Press.

Labov, W., Ash, S. and Boberg, C. (2006) *Atlas of North American English: Phonology and phonetics*. Berlin: Mouton/de Gruyter. Print and interactive CD, also available online.

Lacan, J. (1977) *Ecrits, A Selection,* trans. Alan Sheridan. London: Tavistock Publications/Norton.

Lacan, J. (2006) *Ecrits,* trans. Bruce Fink. New York: W. W. Norton and Co. (complete edition).

Laing, R. D. (1960) *The Divided Self: An existential study in sanity and madness*. Harmondsworth: Penguin.

Laing, R. D. (1967) *The Politics of Experience and the Bird of Paradise*. Harmondsworth: Penguin.

Laing, R. D. (1969) *Self and Others*, 2nd edn. Harmondsworth: Penguin Books.

Laing, R. D. (1970) *Knots*. Harmondsworth: Penguin.

Lakatos, I. (1976) *Proofs and Refutations*. Cambridge: Cambridge University Press.

Lakatos, I. (1978) *Mathematics, Science and Epistemology: Philosophical Papers* (Vol. 2), Cambridge: Cambridge University Press.

Lakatos, I. (1978) *The Methodology of Scientific Research Programmes: Philosophical Papers* (Vol. 1), Cambridge: Cambridge University Press.

LaPiere, R. T. (1934) Attitudes versus actions, *Social Forces,* **13** (2): 230–7.

Lasagna, L. (1970) Physicians' behaviour toward the dying patient. In O. G. Brim, H. E. Freeman, S. Levine and N. A. Scotch (eds), *The Dying Patient.* New York: Russell Sage Foundation.

Lasswell, H. D. (1948) The structure and function of communication in society. In L. Bryson (ed.), *The Communication of Ideas*. New York: Harper and Row.

Latané, B. (1981) The psychology of social impact, *American Psychologist,* **36**: 343–56.

Latané, B. (1996) Dynamic social impact: the creation of culture by communication, *Journal of Communication* **4**: 13–25.

Latané, B. and Darley, J. M. (1970) *The Unresponsive Bystander: Why doesn't he help?* New York: Meredith Corporation.

Latané, B. and Wolf, S. (1981) The social impact of majorities and minorities, *Psychological Review,* **88**: 438–53.

Lazarus, A. A. (1981) *The Practice of Multi-modal Therapy: Systematic, comprehensive and effective therapy.* New York: McGraw Hill.

Lazarus, R. S. (1966) *Psychological Stress and the Coping Process.* New York: McGraw-Hill.

Lazarus, R. S. (1976) *Patterns of Adjustment, 3rd edn.* New York: McGraw Hill.

Lazarus, R. S. (1982) Thoughts on the relations between emotion and cognition, *American Psychologist*, **37**: 1019–24.

Lazarus, R. S. (1994/1991) *Emotion and Adaptation, reprint edition.* Oxford University Press. First published in 1991.

Lazarus, R. S. and Cohen, J. B. (1977) Environmental stress. In L. Altman and J. F. Wohlwill (eds), *Human Behaviour and the Environment: Current Theory and Research* (Vol. 2), New York: Plenum.

Lazarus, R. S. and Folkman, S. (1984) *Stress, Appraisal and Coping.* New York: Springer-Verlag.

Leach, R. (2008) *The Politics Companion*. Basingstoke: PalgraveMacmillan.

LeDoux, J. (1998) *The Emotional Brain*. London: Phoenix Press (recommended by BPS).

Lefebvre, M. F. (1981) Cognitive distortion and cognitive errors in depressed psychiatric and low back pain patients, *Journal of Consulting and Clinical Psychology,* **49**: 517–25.

Leiber, J. (1991) *An Invitation to Cognitive Science.* Oxford: Basil Blackwell.

Levin, S. (2000) Undergraduate education in political psychology, *Political Psychology,* **21** (3): 603–20 (published by Blackwells Synergy).

Levine, F. M. and de Simone, L. L. (1991) The effects of experimenter gender on pain report in male and female subjects, *Pain,* **44**: 69–72.

Lewis, C. S. (1940) *The Problem of Pain.* London: Century Press.

Liebert, R. and Liebert, L. L. (1998) *Personality: Strategies and issues, 8th edn.* Belmont, CA: Wadsworth (recommended by BPS).

Lilienfeld, S. O. (1995) *Seeing Both Sides: Classic controversies in abnormal psychology.* Pacific Grove CA: Brooks/Cole (recommended by BPS).

resources

Loftus, E. F. (1996) *Eyewitness Testimony*. Cambridge, MA: Harvard University Press (revised edition of 1979 book).

Loftus, E. F. (2004) Memories of things unseen, *Current Directions in Psychological Science*, **13**: 145–7.

Loftus, E.F. and Davis, D. (2006) Recovered memories. *Annual Review of Clinical Psychology*. **2**, 469–98.

Loftus, E. F. and Palmer, J. C. (1974) Reconstruction of automobile destruction: an example of the interaction between language and memory, *Journal of Verbal Learning and Verbal Behaviour*, **13**: 585–9.

Loftus, E. F. and Ketcham, K. (1991) *Witness for the Defense: The accused, the eyewitness and the expert who puts memory on trial*. New York: St. Martin's Press.

Loftus, E. F. and Ketcham, K. (1994) *The Myth of Repressed Memory :False memories and allegations of sexual abuse*. New York: St. Martin's Press.

Lorenz, K. Z. (1966) *On Aggression*. London: Methuen.

Lorenz, K. Z. (1974) *Civilized Man's Eight Deadly Sins*. New York: Harcourt Brace.

Lorenz, K. Z. (1988) *King Solomon's Ring*. Gloucester, MA: Peter Smith Pub. Inc. Original work 1943.

Lucariello, J. (1987) Spinning fantasy: themes, structure, and the knowledge base, *Child Development*, **58** (2): 434–42.

Luria, A. R. (1972) *The Man with a Shattered World: The history of a brain wound*. New York: Basic Books.

Luria, A. R. (1973) *The Working Brain*. New York: Basic Books.

Luria, A. R. with Bruner, J. (1987) *The Mind of a Mnemonist: A little book about a vast memory*. Cambridge, MA: Harvard University Press.

Maccoby, E. E. (1980) *Social Development: Psychological growth and the parent–child relationship*. New York: Harcourt Brace Jovanovich.

Mackean, D. G. (1973) *Introduction to Biology, 5th edn*. London: John Murray.

Mackintosh, N. (1995) *Cyril Burt – Fraud or Framed?* Oxford University Press.

Maddi, S. R. and Kobasa, S. C. (1991) The development of hardiness. In A. Monat and R. S. Lazarus (eds), *Stress and Coping, 3rd edn*. New York: Columbia University Press.

Manning, M., Heron, J. and Marshall, T. (1978) Styles of hostility and social interactions at nursery, at school and at home. In L. A. Hersov and M. Berger (eds), *Aggression and Antisocial Behaviour in Childhood and Adolescence*. Oxford: Pergamon Press.

Marks, I. M. (1986) *Behavioural Psychotherapy: Maudsley pocket book of clinical management*. Bristol: Wright.

Marr, D. (1982) *Vision*. San Francisco: Freeman.

Marris, P. (1986) *Loss and Change*. London: Routledge and Kegan Paul.

Maslow, A. (1943) A theory of human motivation, *Psychological Review*, **50**: 370–96.

Maslow, A. (1962) *Towards a Psychology of Being*. New York: van Nostrand.

Mason, J. W. (1975) Emotion as reflected in patterns of endocrine integration. In L. Levi (ed.), *Emotions: Their Parameters and Measurement*. New York: Raven Press.

Masters, W. H. and Johnson, V. E. (1966) *Human Sexual Response*. Boston: Little, Brown.

Mathews, K. E. and Cannon, L. K. (1975) Environmental noise level as a determinant of helping behaviour, *Journal of Personality and Social Psychology*, **32**: 571–7.

Mayo, S. (1996) Symbol, metaphor and story; the function of group art therapy in palliative care, *Palliative Medicine*, **10**: 209–16.

McCarthy, R. A. and Warrington, E. K. (1990) *Cognitive Neuropsychology: A clinical introduction*. London: Academic Press.

McGarrigle, J. and Donaldson, M. (1974) Conservation accidents, *Cognition,* **3**: 341–50.

McGhie, A. and Russell, S. M. (1962) The subjective assessment of normal sleep patterns, *Journal of Mental Science,* **108**: 642.

McGinn, C. (1993) *The Problem of Consciousness.* Oxford: Blackwell.

McGuire, W. (1974) *The Freud–Jung Letters: The correspondence between Sigmund Freud and C. G. Jung.* Princeton, NJ: Princeton University Press.

McLeod, J. (1993) *An Introduction to Counselling.* Buckingham: Open University Press.

Mead, G. H. (1934) *Mind, Self and Society.* Chicago: University of Chicago Press.

Melzack, R. (1973) *The Puzzle of Pain.* New York: Basic Books.

Melzack, R. (1975) The McGill pain questionnaire: major properties and scoring methods, *Pain,* **1**: 277–99.

Melzack, R. and Dennis, S. G. (1978) Neurophysiological foundations of pain. In R. A. Sternbach (ed.), *The Psychology of Pain.* New York: Raven Press.

Melzack, R. and Wall, P. D. (1965) Pain mechanisms: a new theory, *Science,* **150**: 971–9.

Melzack, R. and Wall, P. D. (1982) *The Challenge of Pain.* Harmondsworth: Penguin.

Merskey, H. (1979) Pain terms: a list with definitions and notes on usage, *Pain,* **6**: 249–52.

Messenger, J. B. (1979) *Nerves, Brain and Behaviour.* London: Edward Arnold.

Milgram, S. (1963) Behavioural study of obedience, *Journal of Abnormal and Social Psychology,* **67**: 371–8.

Milgram, S. (1965) Liberating effects of group pressure, *Journal of Personality and Social Psychology,* **1**: 127–34.

Milgram, S. (1967) The small-world problem, *Psychology Today,* **1**: 61–7.

Milgram, S. (1972/1992) The familiar stranger: an aspect of urban anonymity. In J. Sabini and M. Silver (eds), *The Individual in a Social World: Essays and experiments,* 2nd edn. McGraw-Hill, 1992: 68–71. (First published in the *Division 8 Newsletter,* Division of Personality and Social Psychology, Washington: American Psychological Association, July 1972.)

Milgram, S. (1974/2004) *Obedience to Authority: An experimental view.* New York: Harper and Row. (2004, New York: HarperCollins).

Miller, G. A. (1956) The magical number seven, plus or minus two: some limits on our capacity for processing information, *Psychological Review,* 63: 81–97.

Miller, G. A. (1962) *Psychology: The science of mental life.* Harmondsworth: Penguin.

Miller, G. A., Galanter, E. and Pribram, K. H. (1960) *Plans and the Structure of Behavior.* New York: Holt, Rinehart and Winston.

Miller, L., Rustin, M., Rustin, M. and Shuttleworth, J. (eds) (1989) *Closely Observed Infants.* London: Duckworth.

Miller, S. M. (1987) Monitoring and blunting: validation of a questionnaire to asses style of information-seeking under threat, *Journal of Personality and Social Psychology,* **52** (2): 345–3.

Miller, S. M. (1989) Coping style in hypertensive patients: nature and consequences, *Journal of Consulting and Clinical Psychology,* **57** (3): 333–7.

Miller, S. M. and Mangan, C. (1983) Interacting effects of information and coping style in adapting to gynaecological stress: should the doctor tell all? *Journal of Personality and Social Psychology,* **45** (1): 22 3–5.

Millon, T. and Everly, G. S. Jr (1985) *Personality and its Disorders: A biosocial approach.* Chichester: John Wiley and Sons.

Milner, B., Corkin, S. and Teuber, H. L. (1968) Further analysis of the hippocampal amnesic syndrome: 14–year follow-up study of H.M., *Neuropsychologia,* **6**: 215–34.

Mischel, W., Shoda, Y. and Smith, R. E. (2004) *Introduction to Personality, 7th edn*. New York: John Wiley (recommended by BPS).

Mitchell, P. (1997) *Introduction to Theory of Mind*. London: Arnold (recommended by BPS).

Miyake, A. and Shah, P. (eds) (1999) *Models of Working Memory*. New York: Cambridge University Press (recommended by BPS).

Mollon, J. D. (1990) The tricks of colour. In H. Barlow, C. Blakemore and M. Weston-Smith (eds), *Images and Understanding*. Cambridge: Cambridge University Press.

Mollon, J. D., Pokorny, J. and Knoblauch, K. (2003) *Normal and Defective Colour Vision*. Oxford: Oxford University Press.

Mollon, J. D. and Sharpe, L. T. (1983) *Colour Vision: Physiology and psychophysics*. New York: Academic Press.

Monat, A. and Lazarus, R. S. (1991) *Stress and Coping, 3rd edn*. New York: Columbia University Press.

Montgomery, S. A. (1990) *Anxiety and Depression*. Petersfield: Wrightson Biomedical Publishing.

Moon, E. G. and Karb, V. B. (1993) Psychotropic medication. In R. P. Rawlins, S. R. Williams and C. K. Beck (eds), *Mental Health – Psychiatric Nursing: A holistic life-cycle approach, 3rd edn*. St Louis: C. V. Mosby.

Moos, R. H. (1986) *Coping With Life Crises: An integrated approach*. New York: Plenum.

Moreno, J. L. (1946) *Psychodrama* (Vol. 1), New York: Beacon House.

Morgan, C. T. and King, R. A. (1971) *Introduction to Psychology*. London: McGraw Hill.

Morison, M. (1990) *Psychology Essays and Practicals: A guide for students*. Harlow: Longman.

Morris, B. (1987) *Anthropological Studies of Religion*. Cambridge: Cambridge University Press.

Morris, D. (1978) *Manwatching: A field guide to human behaviour*. St Albans: Triad/Panther.

Moyer, K. E. (1976) *The Psychobiology of Aggression*. New York: Harper and Row.

Mueller, C. W. (1983) Environmental stressors and aggressive behaviour. In R. G. Geen and E. I. Donnerstein (eds), *Aggression: Theoretical and empirical reviews* (Vol. 2), *Issues in Research*. New York: Academic Press.

Murgatroyd, S. (1985) *Counselling and Helping*. Leicester/London: BPS/Routledge.

Murstein, B. I. (1972) Physical attractiveness and marital choice, *Journal of Personality and Social Psychology*, **22** (1): 8–12.

Myers, D. and Lamm, H. (1975) The group polarization phenomenon, *Psychological Bulletin*, **83**: 602–27.

Naish, P. L. N. (1986) *What is Hypnosis? Current theories and research*. Milton Keynes: Open University Press.

Napier, R. W. and Gershenfeld, M. K. (1989) *Groups: Theory and experience, 4th edn*. Boston: Houghton Mifflin.

Neisser, U. (1976) *Cognition and Reality*. San Francisco: W. H. Freeman.

Newcomb, T. (1953) An approach to the study of communication acts, *Psychological Review*, **60**: 393–404.

Newman, B. M. and Newman, P. R. (1991) *Development Through Life*. London: Brooks/Cole.

Nisbett, R. E., Caputo, C., Legant, P. and Maracek, J. (1973) Behaviour as seen by the actor and as seen by the observer, *Journal of Personality and Social Psychology*, **27**: 154–65.

Nisbett, R. E. and Ross, L. (1980) *Human Inference: Strategies and shortcomings of social judgement*. Englewood Cliffs, NJ: Prentice-Hall.

Niven, N. (1994) *Health Psychology: An introduction for nurses and other health care professionals, 2nd edn*. London: Churchill Livingstone.

Nordholm, L. (1980) Beautiful patients are good patients: evidence for the physical attractiveness stereotype in first impressions of patients, *Social Science and Medicine,* , **14**: 81–3.

North, C. (1987) *Welcome Silence: My triumph over schizophrenia.* London: Arrow Books.

Novaco, R. W. (1975) *Anger Control: The development and evaluation of an experimental treatment.* Lexington, MA: D. C. Heath.

Novaco, R. W. (1978) Anger and coping with stress. In J. P. Foreyt and D. P. Rathjen (eds), *Cognitive Behavior Therapy.* New York: Plenum Press.

Novaco, R. W. and Welsh, W. N. (1989) Anger disturbances: cognitive mediation and clinical prescriptions. In K. Howells and C. Hollin (eds), *Clinical Approaches to Violence.* Chichester: John Wiley and Sons.

Oatley, K. (1989) *Cognitive Science and the Understanding of Emotions.* Hove: Psychology Press Ltd.

Ochs, P. (1998) *Peirce, Pragmatism and the Logic of Scripture.* Cambridge: Cambridge University Press.

O'Connell, A. N. and Russo, N. F. (1990) *Women in Psychology: A biographic sourcebook.* New York: Greenwood Press.

O'Connor, B. (ed.) (2000) *The Adorno Reader.* Oxford: Blackwell Publishers.

Olds, J. (1956) Pleasure centres in the brain. In *Frontiers of Psychological Research: Readings from Scientific American.* London: W. H. Freeman.

Olds, J. (1977) *Drives and Reinforcements: Behavioral studies of hypothalamic functions.* New York: Raven Press.

Olds, J. and Milner, P. (1954) Positive reinforcement produced by electrical stimulation of septal area and other regions of the rat brain, *Journal of Comparative and Physiological Psychology,* **47**: 419–27.

Ornstein, R. E. (ed.) (1973) *The Nature of Human Consciousness: A book of readings.* New York: W. H. Freeman.

Osgood, C. E. (1956) *Method and Theory in Experimental Psychology.* Oxford: Oxford University Press.

Osgood, C. E., Suci, G. J. and Tannenbau, P. H. (1957) *The Measurement of Meaning.* Urbana IL: University of Illinois Press.

Osgood, C. E. and Tzeng, O. (eds) (1990) *Language, Meaning, and Culture: The selected papers of C. E. Osgood.* Westport, CT: Praeger.

Oswald, I. (1966) *Sleep.* Harmondsworth: Penguin.

Oswald, I. (1984) *Sleep, 4th edn.* Harmondsworth: Penguin.

Owusu-Bempah, K. and Howitt, D. (2000) *Psychology beyond Western Perspectives.* London: BPS Blackwell (recommended by BPS).

Palfai, T. and Jankiewicz, H. (1996) *Drugs and Human Behaviour, 2nd edn.* Madison: Brown and Benchmark (recommended by BPS).

Paritsis, N. C. and Stewart, D. J. (1983) *A Cybernetic Approach to Colour Perception.* London: Gordon and Breach.

Parker, D. M., Crawford, J. R. and Stephen, E. (1999) Auditory inspection time and intelligence: a new spatial localisation task, *Intelligence,* **27** (2): 131–9.

Parkes, C. M. (1996) *Bereavement, 3rd edn.* London: Routledge.

Parliamentary Office of Science and Technology (1996) *Common Illegal Drugs and Their Effects.* London: POST.

Partlett, M. and Page, F. (1990) Gestalt therapy. In W. Dryden (ed.), *Individual Therapy: A handbook.* Milton Keynes: Open University Press.

Partridge, E. (1958) *Origins. An etymological dictionary of modern English*. London: Routledge.

Pavlov, I. P. (1927) *Conditioned Reflexes*. London: Routledge and Kegan Paul.

Pearce, J. M. (1996) *Animal Learning and Cognition: An introduction*. Hove: Lawrence Erlbaum (recommended by BPS).

Peck, D. and Whitlow, D. (1975) *Approaches to Personality Theory*. London: Methuen.

Penfield, W. (ed.) (1958) *Neurological Bases of Behaviour*. Boston: Little, Brown.

Penfield, W. (1975) *The Mystery of the Mind: A critical study of consciousness and the human brain*. Princeton, NJ: Princeton University Press.

Penfield, W. (1977) *No Man Alone: A surgeon's life*. Boston, MA: Little, Brown.

Perez, A. G. (2001) Political psychology as discipline and resource, *Political Psychology*, **22** (2): 347–56 (published by Blackwells Synergy).

Perls, F. S. (1947) *Ego, Hunger, and Aggression: A revision of Freud's theory and method*. London: Allen and Unwin.

Perls, F. S. (1969/1992) *Gestalt Therapy Verbatim*. New York: Bantam. Gestalt Journal Press; Revised edition (1992).

Perls, F. S., Goodman, P. and Hefferline, R. (1951) *Gestalt Therapy: Excitement and growth in the human personality*. New York: Julian Press.

Pervin, L. A. and John, O. P (2001) *Personality: Theories and research, 8th edn*. New York: John Wiley (recommended by BPS).

Peters, T. (1989) *Thriving on Chaos: Handbook for a management revolution*. London: Pan Books.

Peters, W. (1987) *A Class Divided, Then and Now, expanded edition*. Yale University Press.

Phillips, K. C. (1979) Biofeedback as an aid to autogenic training. In B. A. Stoll (ed.), *Mind and Cancer Prognosis*. Chichester: John Wiley and Sons.

Phillips, K. C. (1991) Biofeedback. In M. Pitts and K. Phillips *The Psychology of Health: An introduction*. London: Routledge.

Piaget, J. (1952) *The Child's Conception of Number*. London: Routledge and Kegan Paul.

Piaget, J. (1953) *The Origins of Intelligence in Children*. London: Routledge and Kegan Paul.

Piaget, J. (1989) *The Language and Thought of the Child*. London: Routledge (original publication 1926).

Piaget, J. (1990) *The Child's Conception of the World*. Distributed by Eurospan Group (original publication 1929).

Piaget, J. and Inhelder, B. (1956) *The Child's Conception of Space*. London: Routledge and Kegan Paul.

Pickren, W. A. and Dewsbury, D. A. (2002) *Evolving Perspectives on the History of Psychology*. New York: American Psychological Association (recommended by BPS).

Pinel, J. P. J. (1997) *Biopsychology, 3rd edn*. London: Allyn and Bacon.

Pinker, S. (1995) *The Language Instinct: The new science of language and mind*. London: Penguin (recommended by BPS).

Pinker, S. (1998) *How the Mind Works, new edn*. London: Penguin Books.

Pinker, S. (2000) *Words and Rules, new edn*. London: Phoenix.

Pinker, S. (2003) *The Blank Slate: The modern denial of human nature, new edn*. London: Penguin Books Ltd.

Pinker, S. (2007) *The Stuff of Thought: Language as a window into human nature, 1st edn*. London: Allen Lane.

Pitts, M. (1991) Personality. In J. Radford and E. Govier (eds), *A Textbook of Psychology, 2nd edn*. London: Routledge.

Pitts, M. and Phillips, K. (1991) *The Psychology of Health: An introduction*. London: Routledge.

Plomin, R., DeFries, J. C., McClearn, G. E. and Rutter, M. (1997) *Behavioural Genetics*. New York: Freeman (recommended by BPS).

Plutchik, R. (1980) A general psychoevolutionary theory of emotion. In R. Plutchik and H. Kellerman (eds), *Emotion: Theory, Research, and Experience* (Vol. 1), *Theories of emotion* (pp. 3–33). New York: Academic Press.

Polit, D. F. and Hungler, B. P. (1995) *Nursing Research: Principles and Methods, 5th edn*. Philadelphia: J. B. Lippincott.

Power, M. and Dalgleish, T. (1997) *Cognition and Emotion*. Hove: Psychology Press Ltd.

Price, B. (1986) Mirror, mirror on the wall . . ., *Nursing Times*, **24**: 30–2.

Price, B. (1990) *Body Image: Nursing concepts and care*. London: Prentice Hall.

Pritchard, C. (1995) *Suicide: The ultimate rejection? A psycho-social study*. Buckingham: Open University Press.

Prochaska, J. O., DiClemente, C. C. and Norcross, J. C. (1992) In search of how people change: applications to addictive behaviours, *American Psychologist*, **47**: 1102–14.

Raaheim, K. Radford and Wankowski, J. (1991) *Helping Students Learn: Teaching, counselling, research, 2nd rev edn*. Buckingham: SRHE and Open University Press (for Entwistle).

Rabbitt, P. M. A. and Winthorpe, C. (1988) What do old people remember? The Galton Paradigm reconsidered. In M. M. Grunberg, R. E. Morris and R. N. Sykes (eds), *Practical Aspects of Memory, Vol. 2*. Chichester: John Wiley and Sons.

Radcliffe-Brown, A. R. (1952) *Structure and Function in Primitive Society*. London: Cohen and West.

Randall, P. (1997) *Adult Bullying: Perpetrators and victims*. London: Routledge.

Rankin, P. M. and O'Carroll, P. J. (1995) Reality discrimination, reality monitoring and disposition towards hallucination, *British Journal of Clinical Psychology*, **34**: 517–28.

Rapoport, R. and Rapoport, R. (1980) *Growing Through Life*. London: Harper and Row.

Rau, M. T. (1993) *Coping with Communication Challenges in Alzheimer's Disease*. San Diego: Singular Publishing Group.

Reeve, J. M. (2005) *Understanding Motivation and Emotion, 4th edn*. New York: John Wiley (recommended by BPS).

Retterstol, N. (1990) *Suicide, A European Perspective*. Cambridge: Cambridge University Press.

Review Panel on Coronary Prone Behaviour and Coronary Heart Disease (1981) Coronary prone behaviour and coronary heart disease: a critical review, *Circulation*, **63**: 1199–215.

Reynolds, B. A. and Weiss, S. (1992) Generation of neurons and astrocytes from isolated cells of the adult mammalian central nervous system, *Science*, **255**: 1707–10.

Richards, G. (2002) *Putting psychology in its place, 2nd edn*. London: Routledge (recommended by BPS).

Richardson, K. (1998) *The origins of human potential*. London: Routledge (recommended by BPS).

Robbie, E. (1988) Neuro-linguistic programming. In J. Rowan and W. Dryden (eds), *Innovative Therapy in Britain*. Milton Keynes: Open University Press.

Robertson, S. I. (2001) *Problem Solving*. Hove: Psychology Press (recommended by BPS).

Robinson, J. O. (1972) *The Psychology of Visual Illusion*. London: Hutchinson University Library.

Robinson, J. O. (1996) *An Emotional View of Cognition*. Unpublished manuscript.

Robinson, R. (1992) Sex and sexuality, *Cancer Topics*, **9** (2): 13–14.

Rogers, C. R. (1961) *On Becoming a Person: A therapist's view of psychotherapy*. Boston: Houghton Mifflin.

resources

Rogers, C. R. (1965) *Client-centred Therapy.* Boston: Houghton Mifflin.

Rogers, C. R. (1975) Empathic: an appreciated way of being, *Counselling Psychologist,* **5** (2): 2–10.

Rogers, C. R. (1980) *A Way of Being.* Boston: Houghton Mifflin.

Rogers, C. R. and Russell, D. E. (2003) *Carl Rogers: The quiet revolutionary: An oral history.* Roseville, CA: Penmarin Books.

Rogers, R. W. (1975) A protection motivation theory of fear appeals and attitude change, *Journal of Psychiatry,* **91**: 93–114.

Rokeach, M. (1960) *The Open and Closed Mind.* New York: Basic Books.

Rokeach, M. (1968) *Beliefs, Attitudes and Values.* San Francisco: Jossey-Bass.

Rorschach, H. (1975) *Psychodiagnostics 9th edn.* Bern: H Huber Verlag.

Rose, S. (2003) *The Making of Memory.* London: Bantam Press (recommended by BPS).

Rose, S. (2005) *Lifelines: Life beyond the gene.* Vintage.

Rose, S. (2006) The *21st Century Brain: Explaining, mending and manipulating the mind, new edn.* New York: Vintage.

Rose, S. (2006) *The Future of the Brain: The promise and perils of tomorrow's neuroscience, new edn.* Oxford: Oxford University Press.

Rosenberg, M. J. and Hovland, C. I. (1960) Cognitive, affective and behavioural components of attitude. In M. J. Rosenberg, C. I. Hovland, W. J. McGuire, R. P. Abelson and J. W. Brehm (eds), *Attitude Organization and Change: An analysis of consistency among attitude components.* New Haven, CT: Yale University Press.

Rosenblum, L. A. and Harlow, H. F. (1963) Approach-avoidance conflict in the mother surrogate situation, *Psychological Reports,* **12**: 83–5.

Rosenman, R. H., Brand, R. J., Jenkins, C. D. et al. (1975) Coronary heart disease in the western collaborative group study, *Journal of the American Medical Association,* **233**: 872–7.

Rosenman, R. H., Friedman, M., Straus, R. *et al.* (1964) A predictive study of coronary heart disease, *Journal of the American Medical Association,* **189**: 103–10.

Rosenstock, I. M. (1974) The health belief model and preventative health behaviour, *Health Education Monographs,* **2**: 354–86.

Rosnow, R. L. and Rosenthal, R. (1997) *People Studying People: Artefacts and ethics in behavioural research.* New York: Freeman (recommended by BPS).

Ross, L. (1977) The intuitive psychologist and his shortcomings. In L. Berkowitz (ed.), *Advances in Experimental and Social Psychology* (Vol. 10), New York: Academic Press.

Roth, S. and Cohen, L. J. (1986) Approach, avoidance and coping with stress, *American Psychologist,* **41**: 813–19.

Rotter, J. B. (1954) *Social Learning and Clinical Psychology.* Englewood Cliffs, NJ: Prentice Hall.

Rotter, J. B. (1966) Generalized expectancies for internal versus external control of reinforcement, *Psychological Monographs,* **30** (1): 1–26.

Rotter, J. B. (1975) Some problems and misconceptions related to the construct of internal versus external control of reinforcement, *Journal of Consulting and Clinical Psychology,* **43**: 56–67.

Rowan, J. (1988) Primal integration therapy. In J. Rowan and W. Dryden (eds), *Innovative Therapy in Britain.* Milton Keynes: Open University Press.

Rowe, D. (1983) *Depression: The way out of your prison.* London: Routledge.

Rule, B. G., Taylor, B. R. and Dobbs, A. R. (1987) Priming effects of heat on aggressive thoughts, *Social Cognitions,* **5**: 131–43.

Rumsey, N. (1991) Counselling and disfigurement. In H. Davis and L. Fallowfield *Counselling and Communication in Health Care.* Chichester: John Wiley and Sons.

Runco, M. A. and Albert, R. S. (1990) *Theories of Creativity*. London: Sage.

Ruse, M. (1990) *Homosexuality*. Oxford: Basil Blackwell.

Rutter, M. (1979) Maternal deprivation 1972–1978: New findings, new concepts, new approaches, *Child Development*, **50**: 283–305.

Rutter, M. (1981) *Maternal Deprivation Reassessed (2nd edn)*. Harmondsworth: Penguin.

Rutter, M. and O'Connor, T. G. (1999) Implications of attachment theory for child care policies. In J. Cassidy and P. Shaver (eds), *Handbook of Attachment Theory and Research*. New York: Guilford Press, pp. 823–44.

Ryckman, R. M. (1989) *Theories of Personality, 4th edn*. Pacific Grove, California: Brooks/Cole.

Ryle, A. and Cowmeadow, P. (1992) Cognitive-analytic therapy (CAT.) In W. Dryden (ed.), *Integrative and Eclectic Therapy: A handbook*. Milton Keynes: Open University Press.

Sacks, O. (1970/1985/1998) *The Man who Mistook his Wife for a Hat and Other Clinical Tales*. New York: Touchstone.

Sacks, O. (1973/1999) *Awakenings*. New York: Vintage.

Sacks, O. (1984/1998) *A Leg To Stand On*. New York: Vintage.

Sacks, O. (1989/2000) *Seeing Voices: A journey into the world of the deaf*. New York: Vintage.

Sacks, O. (1993/1998) *The Island of the Colorblind*. New York: Vintage.

Sacks, O. (1996) *An Anthropologist On Mars: Seven paradoxical tales*. New York: Vintage.

Sander, L. and Thompson, P. (1989) *Epilepsy: A practical guide to coping*. Marlborough: Crowood Press.

Sapir, E. (1929): The status of linguistics as a science. In E. Sapir (1958): *Culture, Language and Personality* (ed. D. G. Mandelbaum). Berkeley, CA: University of California Press.

Sarafino, E. (1990) *Health Psychology: Biopsychosocial interactions*. New York: John Wiley and Sons.

Schachter, S. and Singer, J. (1962) Cognitive, social, and physiological determinants of emotional state, *Psychological Review*, **69**: 379–99.

Schaffer, H. R. (1977) *Mothering*. London: Fontana.

Schaffer, H. R. (1990) *Making Decisions About Children: Psychological questions and answers*. Oxford: Basil Blackwell (recommended by BPS).

Schank, R. C. (1982) *Dynamic Memory: A theory of reminding and learning in computers and people*. Cambridge: Cambridge University Press.

Schauss, A. G. (1979) Tranquilizing effect of color reduces aggressive behavior and potential violence, *Journal of Orthomolecular Psychiatry*, **8** (4): 218–21.

Schauss, A. G. (1985) The physiological effect of color on the suppression of human aggression: research on Baker-Miller Pink, *International Journal of Biosocial Research*, **7** (2): 55–64,

Schildkraut, D. J. (2004) All politics is psychological; a review of political psychology syllabi, *Perspectives on Politics*, **2**: 807–19. Cambridge University Press.

Schneidman, E. S. (1978) Some aspects of psychotherapy with dying persons. In C. A. Garfield (ed.), *Psychological Care of the Dying Patient*. New York: McGraw Hill.

Schramm, W. (1970) *Men, Messages and Media*. New York: Harper and Row.

Schramm, W. (1982) *Men, Women, Messages and Media, 2nd edn*. New York: Harper and Row.

Schreiber, F. R. (1974) *Sybil: The true story of a woman possessed by sixteen separate personalities*. Harmondsworth: Penguin.

Schwartz, G. E. (1977) Psychosomatic disorders and biofeedback: a psychobiological model of disregulation. In J. D. Maser and M. E. P. Seligman (eds), *Psychopathology: Experimental models*. San Francisco: W. H. Freeman.

Schwarzer, R. (ed.) (1992) *Self-efficacy: Thought control of action*. Washington DC: Hemisphere.

resources

Scott, J., Williams, J. M. G. and Beck, A. T. (1991) *Cognitive Therapy in Clinical Practice.* London: Routledge.

Scott, M. J. and Stradling, S. G. (1992) *Counselling for Post-Traumatic Stress Disorder.* London: Sage.

Searle, J. (1989) *Minds, Brains and Science.* Harmondsworth: Penguin.

Seligman, M. E. P. (1975) *Helplessness: On depression, development and death.* San Francisco: W. H. Freeman.

Seligman, M. E. P. (1994) *What You Can Change and What You Can't.* New York: Knopf.

Seligman, M. E. P. (1998) *Learned Optimism, 2nd edn.* New York: Pocket Books (Simon and Schuster).

Seligman, M. E. P. (2002) *Authentic Happiness: Using the new positive psychology to realize your potential for lasting fulfilment.* New York: Free Press/Simon and Schuster.

Selye, H. (1956) *The Stress of Life.* New York: McGraw-Hill.

Selye, H. (1974) *Stress Without Distress.* Toronto: McClelland and Stewart.

Sheehy, N. (2004) *Fifty Key Thinkers in Psychology.* London: Routledge (recommended by BPS).

Sheldon, W. H. Dupertuis, C. W. and McDermott, E. (1954) *Atlas of Men.* New York: Harper and Brothers.

Sheldon, W. H., Lewis, N. D. C. and Tenney, A. S. (1969) Psychotic patterns and physical constitution. In D. V. Siva (ed.), *Schizophrenia, Current Concepts and Research.* Hicksville, New York: PJD Publications, pp. 839–911.

Sheldon, W. H. and Stevens, S. S. (1942) *The Varieties of Temperament.* New York: Harper and Brothers.

Sheldon, W. H. Stevens, S. S. and Tucker, W. B. (1940) The *Varieties of Human Physique.* New York: Harper and Brothers.

Sherif, M. (1935) A study of some social factors in perception, *Archives of Psychology,* **27** (187): 1–60.

Sherif, M., Harvey, O. J., White, B. J., Hood, W. R. and Sherif, C. W. (1954/1961) *Intergroup Conflict and Cooperation: The Robbers Cave Experiment.* Middletown, CT: Wesleyan University Press.

Sherman, P. D. (1981) *Colour Vision in the Nineteenth Century : The Young-Helmholtz-Maxwell theory.* Bristol: Adam Hilger (foreword by W. D. Wright).

Silverstone, L. (1993) *Art Therapy the Person-Centred Way.* London: Autonomy Books.

Simon, H. A. (1974) How big is a chunk?, *Science,* **183**: 482–8.

Simpkins, J. and Williams, J. I. (1987) *Advanced Human Biology.* London: Unwin Hyman.

Skevington, S. M. (1995) *Psychology of Pain.* Chichester: John Wiley and Sons.

Skinner, B. F. (1938) *The Behavior of Organisms: An Experimental Analysis.* Reprinted by the B. F. Skinner Foundation, 1991 and 1999.

Skinner, B. F. (1957) *Verbal Behavior.* New York: Appleton-Century-Crofts. Reprinted by the B. F. Skinner Foundation in 1992 and 2002.

Skinner, B. F. (1976) *Particulars of My Life: Part one of an autobiography.* New York: Knopf and New York University Press.

Skinner, B. F. (1979) *The Shaping of a Behaviorist: Part two of an autobiography.* NewYork: Knopf. New York University Press (1984).

Skinner, B. F. (1983) *A Matter of Consequences: Part three of an autobiography.* Hardcover, New York: Knopf; paperback, New York University Press.

Skinner, B. F. (2006) *Walden Two,* read by B. F. Skinner on DVD.

Slade, P. (1995) *Child Play: Its importance for human development.* London: Jessica Kingsley.

Slater, A. (1989) Visual memory and perception in early infancy. In A. Slater and G. Bremner (eds), *Infant Development*. Hove: Lawrence Erlbaum Associates.

Smith, P., Cowie, H. and Blades, M. (1998) *Understanding Children's Development, 3rd edn*. Oxford: Basil Blackwell (recommended by BPS).

Smyth, M. M., Collins, A. F., Morris, P. E. and Levy, P. (1994) *Cognition in Action, 2nd edn*. Hove: Erlbaum (recommended by BPS).

Sperling, G. (1960) The information available in brief visual presentation, *Psychological Monographs*, **74**: 1–2 9.

Sperling, G. (1963) A mode for visual memory tasks, *Human Factors*, **5**: 19–31.

Sperry, R. W. (1968) Hemispheric disconnection and unity in conscious awareness, *American Psychologist*, **23** (10): 723–33.

Sperry, R. W. (1969) A modified concept of consciousness, *Psychological Review*, **76** (6): 532–6.

Sperry, R. W. (1970) An objective approach to subjective experience: further explanation of a hypothesis, *Psychological Review*, **77** (6): 585–90.

Spielberger, C. D. (1977) *Stress and Anxiety, Vol. 4*. Washington DC: Hemisphere.

Spielberger, C. D., Gorsuch, R. L. and Lushene, R. (1968) *Self-evaluation Questionnaire*. Palo Alto, CA: Consulting Psychologists Press.

Spielberger, C. D., Krasner, S. S. and Solomon, E. P. (1988) The experience, expression and control of anger. In M. P. Janisse (ed.), *Health Psychology: Individual differences and stress.* New York: Springer-Verlag.

Springer, S. P. and Deutsch, G. (1989) *Left Brain, Right Brain*. New York: W. H. Freeman.

Springer, S. P. and Deutsch, G. (1993) *Left Brain, Right Brain, 2nd edn*. New York: W. H. Freeman.

Stayton, D. J. and Ainsworth, M. D. S. (1973) Individual differences in infant response to brief, everyday separation as related to other infant and maternal behaviours, *Developmental Psychology*, **9**: 226–35.

Steiner, I. D. (1972) *Group Process and Productivity*. New York: Academic Press.

Stephenson, W. (1953) *The Study of Behaviour: Q technique and its methodology.* Chicago: University of Chicago Press. (See also Wright et al., 1970.)

Steptoe, A. (1989) Psychophysiological interventions in behavioural medicine. In G. Turpin (ed.), *Handbook of Clinical Psychophysiology.* Chichester: John Wiley and Sons.

Stern, W. (1912) *The Psychological Methods of Testing Intelligence* (translated by G. M. Whipple, Baltimore, MD: Warwick and York, 1914).

Sternbach, R. A. (1968) *Pain: A Psychophysiological Analysis.* New York: Academic Press.

Sternberg, R. J. (1995) *In Search of the Human Mind.* London: Harcourt Brace.

Sternberg, R. J. (2003) *Cognitive Psychology, 3rd edn*. Brimont, CA: Wadsworth (recommended by BPS).

Sternberg, R. J., Lautrey, J. and Lubart, T. I. (eds) (2003) *Models of Human Intelligence*. New York: American Psychological Association (recommended by BPS).

Stevens, R. (1975) The functions of communication. In *Communication. Social Sciences, A Foundation Course: Making sense of society, D101 Block 3 Units 7, 8, 9 and 10.* Milton Keynes: Open University Press.

Storr, A. (1973) *Jung*. London: Fontana Modern Classics.

Storr, A. (1983) *Jung: Selected writings*. London: Fontana.

Stratton, P. and Hayes, N. (1993) *A Student's Dictionary of Psychology, 2nd edn*. London: Edward Arnold.

Stroebe, M. S., Stroebe, W. and Hanson, R. (eds) (1993) *Handbook of Bereavement*. New York: Cambridge University Press.

Stroebe, W. and Stroebe, M. S. (1995) *Social Psychology and Health*. Buckingham: Open University Press.

Strunk, W. and White, E. B. (1979) *The Elements of Style, 3rd edn.* New York: Macmillan.

Stuart-Hamilton, I. (1991) *The Psychology of Ageing: An introduction.* London: Jessica Kingsley.

Stuart-Hamilton, I. (1994) *The Psychology of Ageing: An introduction, 2nd edn*. London: Jessica Kingsley.

Sugarman, L. (1986) *Life-span Development*. London: Routledge (recommended by BPS).

Suinn, R. M. (1990) *Anxiety Management Training: A behaviour therapy.* New York: Plenum.

Sutherland, V. J. and Cooper, C. L. (1990) *Understanding Stress: A psychological perspective for health professionals.* London: Chapman and Hall.

Tait, H., Entwistle, N. J. and McCune, V. (1998) ASSIST: a re-conceptualisation of the *Approaches to Studying Inventory.* In C. Rust (ed.), *Improving Students as Learners.* Oxford: Oxford Brookes University, Centre for Staff and Learning Development, pp. 262–71.

Tajfel, H. (1970) Experiments in intergroup discrimination, *Scientific American,* **223**: 96–102.

Tajfel, H., Billig, M., Bundy, R. P. and Flament, C. (1971) Social categorization and intergroup behaviour, *European Journal of Social Psychology,* **2**: 149–78.

Tajfel, H. and Fraser, C. (1978) *Introducing Social Psychology.* Harmondsworth: Penguin.

Tajfel, H. and Turner, J. C. (1986) The social identity theory of inter-group behavior. In S. Worchel and L. W. Austin (eds), *Psychology of Intergroup Relations*. Chigago: Nelson-Hall.

Talbot, L. (1995) *Principles and Practice of Nursing Research.* New York: C. V. Mosby.

Tamm, M. E. (1993) Models of health and disease, *British Journal of Medical Psychology,* **66**: 213–28.

Tan, S. Y. (1982) Cognitive and cognitive-behavioural methods for pain control: a selective review, *Pain,* **12**: 201–28.

Taylor, S. E., Peplau, L. A. and Sears, D. O. (1999) *Social psychology*. Boston: Prentice Hall (recommended by BPS).

Teigen, K. H. (1994) Yerkes-Dodson: a law for all seasons, *Theory and Psychology,* **4** (4): 525–47.

Thelan, L. A., Davie, J. K., Urden, L. D. and Lough, M. E. (1994) *Critical Care Management, 2nd edn*. New York: C. V. Mosby.

Thibaut, J. W. and Kelley, H. H. (1959) *The Social Psychology of Groups.* New York: Wiley.

Thomas, A. and Chess, S. (1977) *Temperament and Development.* New York: Brunner Mazel.

Thomson, R. (1959) *The Psychology of Thinking.* Aylesbury: Pelican.

Thorndike, E. L. (1931) *Human Learning.* New York: Century.

Thurstone, L. L. (1934) The vectors of the mind, *Psychological Review,* **41**: 1–32.

Thurstone, L. L. (1948) *Primary Mental Abilities.* Chicago: Chicago University Press.

Ticklenberg, J. R. and Ochberg, F. M. (1981) Patterns of adolescent violence. In D. A. Hamburg and M. B. Trudeau (eds), *Biobehavioural Aspects of Aggression.* New York: Alan Liss.

Tinbergen, N. (1951/89) *The Study of Instinct.* Oxford: Oxford University Press.

Tolman, E. C. (1932) *Purposive Behavior in Animals and Men*. New York: Century.

Tolman, E. C. (1948) Cognitive maps in rats and men, *Psychological Review,* **55**: 189–208.

Towle, V. L., Sutcliff, E. and Sokol, S. (1985) Diagnosing functional visual deficits with the P300 component of the visual evoked potential, *Archives of Ophthalmology,* **103**: 47–50.

Treisman, A. M. (1960) Contextual cues in selective listening. *Quarterly Journal of Experimental Psychology,* **12**: 242–8.

Treisman, A. M. (1969) Strategies and models of selective attention, *Psychological Review,* **76**: 282–299.

resources

Treisman, A. M. and Gelade, G. (1980) A feature integration theory of attention, *Cognitive Psychology*, **12**: 97–136.

Triandis, H. C. (1971) *Attitude and Attitude Change*. London: John Wiley and Sons.

Triandis, H. C. (1995) *Individualism and Collectivism*. Boulder, CO: Westview Press.

Truss, L. (2003) *Eats, Shoots and Leaves: The zero tolerance approach to punctuation*. London: Profile Books.

Tuckman, B. W. and Jensen, M. A. C. (1977) Stages of small-group development revisited, *Group and Organizational Studies,* **2** (4): 419–27.

Tulving, E. (1972) Episodic and semantic memory. In E. Tulving and W. Donaldson (eds), *The Organization of Memory*. New York: Academic Press.

Tulving, E. (1974) Cue-dependent forgetting, *American Scientist*, **62**: 74–82.

Tulving, E. (1976) Ecphoric processes in recall and recognition. In J. Brown (ed.), *Recognition and Recall*. London: Wiley, pp. 37–73.

Tulving, E. (1985) How many memory systems are there? *American Psychologist,* **40**: 385–98.

Tulving, E. (2002) Episodic memory: from mind to brain, *Annual Review of Psychology*, **53**: 1–25.

Tulving, E. and Thomson, D. M. (1973) Encoding specificity and retrieval processes in episodic memory, *Psychological Review*, **80**: 352–73.

Turing, A. M. (1936/37) On computable numbers with an application to the *Entscheidungproblem*. *Proceedings of the London Mathematical Society*, Series 2, Vol. 42: 230–65.

Turing, A. M. (1950) Computing machinery and intelligence. *Mind*, **LIX** (236, October): 433–60.

Tursky, B. (1976) The development of a pain perception profile: a psychological approach. In M. Weisenberg and B. Tursky (eds), *New Perspectives in Therapy and Research*. New York: Plenum Press.

Tversky, A. and Kahneman, D. (1974) Judgement under uncertainty: heuristics and biases, *Science*, **185**: 1124–31.

Tversky, A. and Kahneman, D. (1981) The framing of decisions and the psychology of choice, *Science*, **211**: 453–8.

Twaddle, V. and Scott, J. (1991) Depression. In W. Dryden and R. Rentoul (eds), *Adult Clinical Problems*. London: Routledge.

Ursin, H., Baade, E. and Levine, S. (eds) (1978) *Psychobiology of Stress: A study of coping men*. New York: Academic Press.

Vaillant, G. (1977) *Adaptation to Life*. Boston: Little, Brown.

Valentine, E. R. (1992) *Conceptual Issues in Psychology, 2nd edn*. London: Routledge (recommended by BPS).

van Wynsberghe, D., Noback, C. R. and Carola, R. (1995) *Human Anatomy and Physiology, 3rd edn*. New York: McGraw Hill.

Vickers, D., Nettelback. T. and Wilson, R. J. (1972) Perceptual indices of performance: the measurement of 'inspection time' and 'noise' in the visual system, *Perception*, **I**, 263–95.

Vygotsky, L. S. (1962) *Thought and Language*. Cambridge, MA: MIT Press.

Vygotsky, L. S. (1978) *Mind in Society*. Cambridge, MA: Harvard University Press.

Wall, P. D. and Melzack, R. (eds) (1984) *Textbook of Pain, 2nd edn*. Edinburgh: Churchill Livingstone.

Wallas, G. (1926) *The Art of Thought*. New York: Harcourt Brace.

Warrington, E. K. and Shallice, T. (1969) The selective impairment of auditory verbal short-term memory, *Brain,* **92**: 885–96.

Warrington, E. K. and Shallice, T. (1972) Neuropsychological evidence of visual storage in short-term memory tasks, *Quarterly Journal of Experimental Psychology,* **14**: 30–40.

Wason, P. C. and Johnson-Laird, R. N. (1968) *Thinking and Reasoning.* Harmondsworth: Penguin.

Wason, P. C. and Johnson-Laird, P. N. (1972) *Psychology of Reasoning: Structure and content* Harvard University Press.

Watson, J. B. (1913) Psychology as the behaviorist views it, *Psychological Review,* **20**: 158–77.

Watson, J. B. (1919) *Psychology from the Standpoint of a Behaviorist.* Ann Arbor, MI: University of Michigan. Digitized 12 June 2006.

Watson, J. B. (1925/1930) *Behaviorism,* Revised edition. Chicago: University of Chicago Press.

Watson, J. B. (1928) *The Ways of Behaviorism.* New York, NY: Harper and Brothers.

Watson, J. B. (1928/1972) *Psychological Care of Infant and Child.* New York: Arno Press.

Watson, J. B. (1936) John Broadus Watson. In C. Murchison (ed.), *A History of Psychology in Autobiography* (Vol. III). Worcester, MA: Clark University Press, 271–81.

Watts, F. (1992) Applications of current cognitive theories of the emotions to the conceptualization of emotional disorders, *British Journal of Clinical Psychology,* **31** (2): 153–67.

Waugh, N. C. and Norman, D. A. (1965) Primary memory, *Psychological Review,* **72**: 89–104.

Webb, C. (1985) *Sexuality, Nursing and Health,* Chichester: John Wiley and Sons.

Webb, C. (1994) *Living Sexuality.* London: Scutari Press.

Weinstein, N. D. (1988) The precaution adoption process, *Health Psychology,* **7**: 355–86.

Weinstein, N. D. and Sandman, P. M. (1992) A model of the precaution adoption process: evidence from home radon testing, *Journal of Health Psychology,* **11** (3): 170–80.

Weitz, S. (ed.) (1979) *Nonverbal Communication: Readings with commentary, 2nd edn.* New York: Oxford University Press.

Welch, S. and Booth, A. (1975) The effect of crowding on aggression, *Sociological Symposium,* **14**: 105–27.

Wells, G. L. and Loftus, E. F. (1984) *Eyewitness Testimony: Psychological perspectives.* Cambridge: Cambridge University Press.

Whittaker, J. O. and Meade, R. D. (1967) Sex and age variables in persuasability, *Journal of Social Psychology,* **73**: 47–52.

Whorf, B. L. (1940): Science and linguistics, *Technology Review, 42* (6): 229–31, 247–8. Also in B. L. Whorf (1956): *Language, Thought and Reality* (Ed. J. B. Carroll). Cambridge, MA: MIT Press.

Williams, D. (1992) *Nobody Nowhere.* London: Corgi Books/Bantam.

Williams, J. M. G., Watts, F. N., Macleod, C. and Matthews, A. (1988) *Cognitive Psychology and Emotional Disorders.* Chichester: John Wiley and Sons.

Wingard, L. B., Brody, T. M., Larner, J. and Schwartz, A. (1991) *Human Pharmacology.* New York: Mosby Year Book.

Winnicott, D. W. (1960) The theory of the parent-infant relationship, *International Journal of Psychoanalysis,* **41**: 585–95.

Winnicott, D. W. (1988) *Babies and Their Mothers.* London: Free Association Books.

Winnicott, D. W. and Rodman, F. R. (ed.) (1987) *The Spontaneous Gesture: Selected letters of D. W. Winnicott.* London: Karnac Books.

Wood, D. (1998) *How Children Think and Learn, 2nd edn.* Oxford: Basil Blackwell (recommended by BPS).

Worchel, S. and Teddle, C. (1976) The experience of crowding: a two-factor theory, *Journal of Personality and Social Psychology,* **34**: 30–40.

World Health Organisation (1992) *The ICD-10 Classification of Mental Behavioural Disorders: Clinical Descriptions and Diagnostic Guidelines.* Geneva: WHO.

Wright, B. (1996) *Sudden Death: A research base for practice, 2nd edn*. London: Churchill Livingstone.

Wright, D. S., Taylor, A., Davies, D. R. *et al*. (1970) *Introducing Psychology: An experimental approach*. Harmondsworth: Penguin.

Wright, L. (1991) The Type A behaviour pattern and coronary artery disease: quest for the active ingredients and the elusive mechanism. In A. Monat and R. S. Lazarus (eds), *Stress and Coping, 3rd edn*. New York: Columbia University Press.

Wundt, W. (1863) *Lectures on Human and Animal Psychology*. London: Allen (English translation 1896).

Wundt, W. (1874) *Principles of Physiological Psychology*. London: Allen. English Translation 1893/1904.

Wundt, W. (1897) *Outlines of Psychology*. Tr. Judd, C. H. St Clair Shores, MI: Scholarly Press.

Yerkes, R. M. and Dodson, J. D. (1908) The relation of strength of stimulus to rapidity of habit-formation, *Journal of Comparative and Neurological Psychology,* **18**: 459–82.

Young, T. (1793) *Observations on Vision.* Philosophical Transactions, **83**: 169–81.

Young, T. (1802) On the theory of light and colours. *Philosophical Transactions*, **92**: 12–48.

Zander, A. (1982) *Making Groups Effective*. San Francisco: Jossey Bass.

Zebrowitz, L. A. (1990) *Social Perception*. Milton Keynes: Open University Press (recommended by BPS).

Ziesler, A. A. (1993) Art therapy: a meaningful part of cancer care, *Journal of Cancer Care,* **2**: 107–11.

Zimbardo, P. G. (2004) A situationist perspective on the psychology of evil: understanding how good people are transformed into perpetrators. In A. G. Miller (ed.), *The Social Psychology of good and evil*. New York: Guilford Press, pp. 21–50.

Zimbardo, P. G. (2007) *The Lucifer Effect: Understanding how good people turn evil*. USA and UK: Random House.

Zimbardo, P. G., Maslach, C. and Haney, C. (2000) Reflections on the Stanford Prison Experiment: genesis, transformations, consequences. In T. Blass (ed.), *Obedience to Authority: Current perspectives on the Milgram paradigm*. Mahwah, N.J.: Erlbaum, pp. 193–237.

Zimmerman, B. J. and Schunk, D. H. (eds) (2002) *Educational Psychology: A century of contributions*. Mahwah, NJ: Erlbaum.

resources

7.2 Website references

All the websites mentioned in this book have been accessed by the author between August 2007 and July 2008. Some websites may have changed or no longer be available. If the full address does not work, try the first part (for example, up to .com or .edu/) to locate the home page and follow links.

Where to find information on website and blogs

Any individual, group or organisation can set up websites or blogs.

A website is a collection of linked web pages with text, images, videos or other material that can be stored digitally. All publicly accessible websites form the World Wide Web, usually referred to as the Internet, which is the umbrella term for the whole system. To access websites you need to have access to a web server. You can subscribe to one for your home computer and arrange access via a modem connected to your telephone line or via broadband. Broadband also uses the telephone line but is much faster and more efficient than a modem and works particularly well with wireless connections. Alternatively you can use computers in public libraries, Internet cafes or other facilities.

A blog (from web log) is a personal website, either used to keep track of a particular subject or as a personal diary. A typical blog combines text, images and links to other blogs, web pages and other media related to its topic. Readers may be able leave comments in an interactive format.

You will find websites listed in almost everything you read (if published recently) and links to other websites on every website. Using a search engine will lead you to a range of possible sites. You only need to type one or more words relevant to what you want to find out then choose the most likely site and go on searching until you find what you want.

Search engines

There are many search engines which can be accessed via their own websites. Among the most popular ones for the UK are:

http://uk. altavista.com
http://uk.ask.com
http://www.google.co.uk
http://www. msn.com
http://uk.yahoo.com.

In addition, putting 'search engines' into your favourite one will give a list of many others.

resources

Reliable and unreliable websites

Since websites can be established by anyone there is often no control over the content and you will find that many sites giving information relevant to psychology are personal opinions. This means you have to always check information with official sites or go to primary sources.

Wikipedia is a very popular encyclopaedia site. It is easy to use and you will find most material readily available. It is good but there are likely to be errors, particularly in dates and names in reference lists, and some of the language is awkward and not easy for a new student to follow. You always need to double check, but it is an excellent place to start any search, particularly as so many links are given to other items.

Unwanted links

Many website owners make money by providing links to commercial sites. Each time a reader clicks on one of these sites, the owner gets a small commission. Much of the time the links are useful and related to the content of the original site. But occasionally you may find you are given links to unwanted material so care is needed.

Have-to-pay sites

Some websites require a subscription to access some or all of their content. Examples of subscription sites include academic journal sites. If you would like to access these sites, check with the library to see if they have a subscription.

Copyright and plagiarism

As with printed material, copying of official website material is permitted only under very strict rules. Look for the copyright policy. Normally you may use material for your personal educational work. However, if you use it in your essays be careful to avoid plagiarism. Use it sparingly and always paraphrase and reference the sources. If you wish to use material directly in a publication you will need to gain permission.

Item	Website
Part 1	**Studying psychology**
How to use the Internet for psychology	http://www.vts.intute.ac.uk/he/tutorial/psychologist
BPS Code of Ethics	http://www.bps.org.uk/ Go to The Society in the menu bar and follow links.
Applying for financial help	http://www.direct.gov.uk/en/EducationAndLearning/ UniversityAndHigherEducation/StudentFinance/index.htm or http://www. direct.gov.uk/en/index.htm and follow links.
Choosing and applying for a university and course	http://www.ucas.com/ http://www.merlinhelpsstudents.com/studentlife/beforeuniversity/ choosing/choosingauniversity.asp http://www.direct.gov.uk/en/EducationAndLearning/ UniversityAndHigherEducation/DecidingWhereToStudy/DG_4017763 http://education.guardian.co.uk/netclass/parents/links/0,,70515,00. html http://www.qaa.ac.uk/students/guides/bestcourse/default.asp http://education.guardian.co.uk/chooseadegree http://www.thesite.org/workandstudy/studychoices/whatcourse http://www.prospects.ac.uk/cms/ShowPage/Home_page/For_parents/ Choosing_a_course_at_university/p!eikakd
Access courses	www.learndirect.co.ukwww.ucas.com/students/beforeyouapply/access_ programmes/www.britishcouncil.org/learning-infosheets-choosing-an- access-course.pdf
Open and distance learning	http://www.open.ac.uk http://www.odlqc.org.uk
English for university entrance	http://www.englishforuniversity.com
Studying	http://www.bbc.co.uk http://www4.ncsu.edu/unity/lockers/users/f/felder/public/ILSdir/styles. htm http://condor.admin.ccny.cuny.edu/ffhhartman/Sternberg.ppt www.icherney.com/Teaching/Courses/Intelligence/Argument%20Papers/ Brandon_Bashong.doc http://www.uwsp.edu/Education/lwilson/learning/STERNB1.htm http://www.uwsp.edu/Education/lwilson/brainintro.htm http://www.aare.edu.au/06pap/abd06289.pdf (Dweck) http://news-service.stanford.edu/news/2007/february7/dweck-020707. html http://news-service.stanford.edu/news/2007/february7/videos/179_ flash.html (Dweck) http://itc.conversationsnetwork.org/shows/detail1011.html (Dweck) http://www.londonmet.ac.uk/deliberations/ocsld-publications/islass- entwistle.cfm http://www.newhorizons.org/future/Creating_the_Future/crfut_entwistle. html http://www.tlrp.org/acadpub/Entwistle2000.pdf http://www.re-skill.org.uk/grads/cc_grdid.htm (competence and capability)

Referencing and Primary and secondary sources	http://www.apastyle.org/ http://www.liu.edu/cwis/cwp/library/workshop/citapa.htm http://www.bma.org.uk/ap.nsf/Content/LIBReferenceStyles http://owl.english.purdue.edu/owl/resource/557/01/ http://library.carlow.edu/ResearchGuides/Mlastylepth.pdf http://portal.surrey.ac.uk/portal/page?_pageid=734,200347&_dad=portal&_schema=PORTAL http://www.usq.edu.au/library/help/ehelp/ref_guides/harvardonline.htm http://www.library.jcu.edu.au/LibraryGuides/primsrcs.shtml http://tutorial.lib.umn.edu/infomachine.asp?moduleID=10&lessonID=74&pageID=237 http://www.unf.edu/library/guides/citationguide.pdf
Part 2	**Approaches in psychology**
Traditional perspectives	http://en.wikipedia.org/wiki/Psychology#Schools_of_thought
APA divisions and topics	http://www.apa.org/about/division.html?imw=Y
Bio- and neuro-psychology	http://www.bps.org.uk/don/about.cfm
Cognitive psychology	http://psychology.about.com/od/cognitivepsychology/f/cogpsych.htm
Social psychology	http://en.wikipedia.org/wiki/Social_constructionism http://en.wikipedia.org/wiki/Symbolic_interactionism
Clinical psychology	http://bps.org.uk
Coaching psychology	http://www.bps.org.uk/coachingpsy/coachingpsy_home.cfm http://www.coachingnetwork.org.uk/resourcecentre/WhatAreCoachingAndMentoring.htm http://www.centreforcoaching.com/ http://www.city.ac.uk/psychology/research/CoachPsych/CoachPsych.html
Comparative psychology and ethology	http://www.tiscali.co.uk/reference/encyclopaedia/hutchinson/m0008040.html http://www.usask.ca/wcvm/herdmed/applied-ethology/ http://www.applied-ethology.org/
Consciousness and experiential psychology	http://www.bps.org.uk/conex/consciousness-experiential_home.cfm http://consciousness.arizona.edu/
Counselling psychology	http://www.bps.org.uk/dcop/dcop_home.cfm http://www.bps.org.uk/careers/areas/counselling.cfm#what%20they%20do http://www.bacp.co.uk/
Cultural psychology	http://www.learner.org/discoveringpsychology/26/e26expand.html http://en.wikipedia.org/wiki/Distributed_cognition http://www.sapdesignguild.org/editions/edition7/distrib_cognition.asp http://www.answers.com/topic/cultural-historical-psychology http://en.wikipedia.org/wiki/Activity_theory http://carbon.cudenver.edu/ffmryder/itc_data/activity.html http://www.edu.helsinki.fi/activity/

Ecological psychology and ecopsychology	http://en.wikipedia.org/wiki/Ecological_psychology http://jhp.sagepub.com/cgi/content/abstract/41/2/25 http://www.port.ac.uk/departments/academic/psychology/research/ecologicalpsychology/ http://members.shaw.ca/jscull/ecointro.htm
Environmental psychology	http://en.wikipedia.org/wiki/Environmental_psychology http://www.surrey.ac.uk/Psychology/EPRG/ http://www-personal.umich.edu/ffrdeyoung/envtpsych.html http://web.ed.ntnu.edu.tw/ffminfei/groupdynamicreading-14.htm
Evolutionary psychology	http://www.epjournal.net/ http://www.psych.ucsb.edu/research/cep/primer.html
Forensic psychology	http://www.bps.org.uk/dfp/dfp_home.cfm http://www.nhscareers.nhs.uk/details/Default.aspx?Id=451 http://www.surrey.ac.uk/Psychology/MScForensicPsychology.htm
Health psychology	http://www.bps.org.uk/health http://www.bps.org.uk/sub-sites$/dhp/dhp_home.cfm?&redirectCount=0 http://www.amazon.co.uk/gp/reader/0335204309/ref=sib_rdr_ex/202-5795604-2068648?ie=UTF8&p=S00C&j=0#reader-page
History and philosophy of psychology	http://www.bps.org.uk/hopc/hopc_services/hopc_services_home.cfm http://www.bps.org.uk/history/history_home.cfm
Lesbian and gay psychology	http://www.bps.org.uk/lesgay/lesgay_home.cfm http://www.groups.psychology.org.au/glip/ http://www.dh.gov.uk/en/Publicationsandstatistics/Publications/PublicationsPolicyAndGuidance/DH_081579
Military psychology	http://www.enotes.com/gale-psychology-encyclopedia/military-psychology http://www.apa.org/divisions/div19/images/StratPlan2007_2012_DOC.pdf http://www.apa.org/about/division/div19.html
Occupational psychology	http://www.bps.org.uk/sub-sites$/dop/about-the-division/about-the-division_home.cfm http://www.psychometrics.co.uk/what.htm
Political psychology	http://www.psych.ubc.ca/ffpsuedfeld/PoliPsy.html http://www.blackwell-synergy.com/doi/abs/10.1111/0162-895X.00243?journalCode=pops http://journals.cambridge.org/action/displayAbstract?fromPage=online&aid=266193
Psychology of women	http://www.bps.org.uk/pows/pows_home.cfm http://www.blackwellpublishing.com/journal.asp?ref=0361-6843&site=1 http://www.apa.org/divisions/div35/
Psychotherapy	http://www.bps.org.uk/ps/ps_home.cfm
Sport and exercise psychology	http://www.bps.org.uk/careers/areas/sport.cfm
Teaching and researching	http://www.bps.org.uk/dtrp/about.cfm
Transpersonal psychology	http://www.transpersonalpsychology.co.uk/

resources

Part 3	Key terms and concepts
General information	http://en.wikipedia.org http://chiron.valdosta.edu/whuitt/index.html
Basic psychology introductory and AS and A2 level	http://www.s-cool.co.uk http://www.intute.ac.uk http://www.queendom.com (psychometric tests) http://www.cwu.edu/ffcwuchci/ (chimpanzees) http://psychclassics.yorku.ca http://www.simplypsych.com http://www.questia.com http://www.abdn.ac.uk/ffpsy086/dept/WEBPUB_dev.HTM
Abnormal	http://ccvillage.buffalo.edu/Abpsy/lecture1.html (useful but unreferenced)
Attention and perception	http://asj.gr.jp/2006/data/kashi/index.htm http://www.lifesci.sussex.ac.uk/home/Chris_Darwin/SWS/ http://www.psych.ubc.ca/ffrensink/flicker/download/index.html
Broca's area	http://www.youtube.com/watch?v=ra6ZKHiFM2g http://www.youtube.com/watch?v=f2liMEbMnPM&NR=1
Conation	http://chiron.valdosta.edu/whuitt/col/regsys/conation.html
Colour	http://bacweb.the-bac.edu/ffmichael.b.williams/baker-miller.html
Emotional Intelligence	http://eqi.org/commdef.htm http://www.businessballs.com/eq.htm http://www.danielgoleman.info
Intelligence	http://www.michna.com/intelligence.htm
Leadership	http://www.nwlink.com/ffdonclark/
Personality	http://www.pearsonassessments.com/tests/sixtpf_5.htm
Pineal	www.tiscali.co.uk/reference/encyclopaedia/hutchinson (pineal)
Split-brain	http://www.youtube.com/watch?v=ZMLzP1VCANo&mode=related&search=
Subjectivity	http://www.chass.utoronto.ca/ffsousa/subjectivity.html
Transgender/ transsexual	http://www.dh.gov.uk/en/Publicationsandstatistics/Publications/PublicationsPolicyAndGuidance/DH_081579
Wernicke's area	http://www.youtube.com/watch?v=aVhYN7NTIKU
Part 4	Key theorists and studies
Adler	http://www.adleriansociety.co.uk/ http://www.alfredadler.edu/ http://ourworld.compuserve.com/homepages/hstein/homepage.htm http://www.quotemonk.com/authors/alfred-adler/biography-profile.htm
Adorno	http://www.adorno-archiv.de/ http:///wbenjamin.org/links4.html http://www.gseis.ucla.edu/faculty/kellner/Illumina%20Folder/index.html http://www.members.aol.com/eandcw/adorno.htm http://www.uta.edu/huma/illuminations http://plato.stanford.edu/cgi-bin/encyclopedia/archinfo.cgi

Ainsworth	http://www.psy.pdx.edn/PsiCafe/Key theorists/Ainsworth.htm
	http://www.webster.edu/ffwoolflm/ainsworth.html
	http://www.richardatkins.co.uk/atws/person/1.html
	http://en.wikipedia.org/wiki/Mary_Ainsworth
Allport, F.H.	http://www.brynmawr.edu/Acads/Psych/rwozniak/allport.html
Allport, G.W.	http://www.stolaf.edu/people/huff/misc/Allporttalk.html
	http://en.wikipedia.org/wiki/Gordon_Allport
	http://web.bmoyne.edu/ffhevern/nr-theorists/allport_gordon_w.htm/
	#biography
	http://www.ship.edu/ffcgboeree/perscontents.html
	http://www.wjh.harvard.edu/psych/history.html
	http://www.sruweb.com/ffwalsh/psychology100.html
Aronson	www.jigsaw.org/about.htm
	www.ucsc.edu/currents/02-03/09-02/aronson.html
	www.library.wwu.edu/ref/subjguides/psychology/aronsonmain.htm
Asch	http://www.cultsock.ndirect.co.uk/MUHome/cshtml/socinf/conform.
	html
	http://www.age-of-the-sage.org/psychology/social/index.html
	http://en.wikpedia/wiki/Asch_conformity_experiments
	http://www.upenn.edu/almanac/
	http://thinkorthwim.com/index.php?tag=research (contains video)
Atkinson and Shiffrin	http://www.ucop.edu/ucophome/pres/atprofil.html
	http://www.indiana.edu/ffpsych/faculty/shiffrin.html
Baddeley and Hitch	http://www.york.ac.uk/depts/psych/www/people/biogs/ab50.html
	http://www.york.ac.uk/depts/psych/www/people/biogs/gjh3.html
Bales	http://www.symlog.com/internet.what_is_symlog/what_is_symlog-01c.htm
	http://en.wikipedia.org/wiki/Small-group_communication
Bandura	http://www-psych.stanford.edu/faculty/bandura.html
	http://www.des.emory.edu/mfp/bandurabio.htm
	http://www.ship.edu/ffcgboeree
	http://www.psy.pdx.edu/PsiCafe/KeyTheroists/Bandura.htm
	Filmed interviews with Professor Bandura:
	Title: Social Cognitive Theory. Davidson Films, Inc.
	Title: Albert Bandura. Insight Media
	Title: AABT Archives Videotapes: Bandura. Association for
	Advancement of Behaviour Therapy
Baron-Cohen	http://www.autismresearchcentre.com/arc/staff_member.asp?id=33
Bartlett	http://cogprints.org/666/00/110.htm
	http://en.wikipedia.org/wiki/Frederic_Bartlett
	http://io.uwinnipeg.ca/ffepritch1/ltm2000.html
	http://jac.gsu.edu/jac/11.2/ReaderResponse/3.htm
	http://ntgateway.com.cob-web.org:8888/weblog/2003/12/sir-frederic-bartlett-war-of-ghosts.html
	http://pages.slc.edu/ffebj/bartlett.html
	http://www.artsci.wustl.edu/ffphilos/MindDict/bartlett.html
	http://www.bbc.co.uk/radio4/science/mindchangers3.shtml
	http://www.bethel.edu/ffjohluc/history-resource/memory.html
	http://www.bookrags.com/biography/frederic-charles-bartlett-sir

Bartlett (continued)	http://www.bookrags.com /research/bartlett-frederic-1886-1969-lmem-01 http://www.columbia.edu /ffch2020/exam/theories2.html http://www.factbites.com http://www.fathom.com /contributors/4141.html http://www.forbesbookclub.com /BookPage.asp?prod_cd=I3TNE http://www.textbookx.com /product_detail.php?detail_isbn=0415201721 http://www.todayinsci.com /10/10_20.htm http://www.usabilityviews.com /uv006295.html http://www-bartlett.sps.cam.ac.uk /BartlettAutobio.htm
Bem	http://www.cornell.edu/search/index.cfm?tab=people&netid=slb6&q=sandra%20bem http://en.wikipedia.org/wiki/Sandra_Bem http://spsp.clarion.edu/mm/topss/tptn7052.htm http://www.awc.cc.az.us/psy/dgershaw/lol/androgyny.htm http://www.garysturt.free-online.co.uk/ http://www.webster.edu/ffwoolflm/sandrabem.html
Berne	http://en.wikipedia/wiki/Eric_Berne http://www.answers.com/topic/eric-berne http://www.businessbalss.com/traqnsact.htm http://www.ericberne.com/Games_PeoplePlay.htm http://www.itaa-net.org/ta/index.htm http://www.quotationspage.com/quotes/Eric_Berne
Bernstein	http://www.ioe.ac.uk/library/archives/bbb.html http://evolution.massey.ac.nz/emural/descrip.htm#welcome http://www.guardian.co.uk/obituaries/story/0,3604,373772,00.html
Bettelheim	http://www.gwu.edu/ffolktale/GERM232/rapunzel/bettleheim.htm http://www.pbs.org/pov/pov2002/refrigeratormothers/aboutthefilm.html
Bion	http://www.psyctc.org/bion97/biobiblio.htm http://www.oxforddnb.com/index/101051057/
Blakemore	http://en.wikipedia.org/wiki/Colin_Blakemore http://observer.guardian.co.uk/uk_news/ http://timesonline.co.uk/ http://www.education.guardian.co.uk/higher/ http://www.law.cornell.edu/uscode/17/107.shtml http://www.mrc.ac.uk http://www.publications.parliament.uk/ http://www.royalsoc.ac.uk/ http://www.telegraph.co.uk/ http://www.the-scientist.com/news http://www.vega.org.uk/video/series/2
Bowlby	http://www.personalityresearch.org/papers/lee.html http:// en.wikipedia.org/wiki/Attachment_theory
Broadbent	http://en.wikipedia.org/wiki/Donald_Broadbent http://arts-sciences.cua.edu/psy/csl/csln996.htm http://www.questia.com/library/psychology/psychologists/donald-broadbent.jsp

Bruner	http://eric.ed.gov/ERICWebPortal/Home.portal?_nfpb=true&_pageLabel=RecordDetails&ERICExtSearch_SearchValue_0=EJ213831&ERICExtSearch_SearchType_0=eric_accno&objectId=0900000b800a302a http://www.psych.nyu.edu/bruner/
Bryant	http://www.edstud.ox.ac.uk/research/childlearning/learningliteracy.html http://ssl.brookes.ac.uk/psych/profile.asp?ident=303 http://www.primaryreview.org.uk/Printable_Sections/People_Print_All.html
Burt	www.indiana.edu/ffintell/burt.shtml www.muskingum.edu/ffpsych/psycweb/history/burt.htm www.answers.com/topic/cyril-burt www.abelard.org/burt/burt-ie.asp www.cartage.org.lb/en/themes/Biographies/MainBiographies/B/Burt/1.html
Cannon	http://www.pubmedcentral.nih.gov/ http://www.kli.ac.at/theorylab/AuthPage/C/CannonWB.html http://www.the-aps.org/publications/classics/originals.htm
Cattell	http://www.pearsonassessments.com/tests/sixtpf_5.htm http://www.cattell.net/devon/rbcmain.htm http://www.indiana.edu/ffintell/rcattell.shtml
Chomsky	http://web.mit.edu/linguistics/people/faculty/index.html http://en.wikipedia.org/wiki/Noam_Chomsky http://chomsky.info/
Craik and Lockhart	http://tip.psychology.org/craik.html www.revision-notes.co.uk/revision/863.html www.simplypsychology.pwp.blueyonder.co.uk/levelsofprocessing.html http://www.st-andrews.ac.uk/psychology/teaching/resources/proj797.pdf http://talks.cam.ac.uk/show/index/5382 www.erin.utoronto.ca/ffw3cihrsc/Cihr/html/fergus.htm http://abigail.psych.utoronto.ca/psych/grad/gradpercep.asp?pg=res
De Bono	http://www.edwdebono.com http://www.debonothinkingsystems.com/ http://www.gurteen.com/gurteen/gurteen.nsf/id/edward-de-bono
Dennett	http://ase.tufts.edu/cogstud/incbios/dennettd/dennettd.htm http://ase.tufts.edu/cogstud/incbios/griffinr/datapubs/Griffin&BC-Dennett.pdf http://www.kli.ac.at/theorylab/AuthPage/D/DennettDC.html http://en.wikipedia.org/wiki/Intentional_stance www.consciousentities.com/dennett.htm
Deutsch & Deutsch	http://www.ucsd.edu/ http://psy.ucsd.edu/ffdeutsch/ http://philomel.com/pdf/Psych_Rev-1963_70_80-90.pdf http://www.apa.org/archives/psyimaged.html http://www.garfield.library.upenn.edu/classics1981/A1981LE35000001.pdf

Donaldson	http://www.authortracker.ca/author.asp?a=authorid&b=uk_1532 http://www.ed.ac.uk/ http://www.psy.ed.ac.uk/department/ http://www.scimednet.org/people.htm http://www.spokenword.ac.uk/record_view.php?pbd=gcu-a0a2r2-a
Ebbinghaus	http://www.indiana.edu/ffintell/ebbinghaus.shtml http://www.answers.com/topic/hermann-ebbinghaus http://www.britannica.com/eb/article-9031847/Hermann-Ebbinghaus http://en.wikipedia.org/wiki/Hermann_Ebbinghaus
Elliott	http://www.janeelliott.com/ http://www.bbc.co.uk/dna/h2g2/A1132480 Films are available, e.g. A Class Divided.
Ellis	http://www.albertellisinstitute.org/aei/index.html http://www.psychnet-uk.com/psychotherapy/psychotherapy_rational_emotive_behaviour_therapy.htm
Erikson	http://www.muskingum.edu/ffpsych/psycweb/history/erikson.htm http://www.rlc.dcccd.edu/MATHSCI/anth/P101/DVLMENTL/ERIKSON.HTM http://www.childdevelopmentinfo.com/development/erickson.shtml http://www.d.umn.edu/ffmeberhar/ref/psy/psychologists/erikson.htm http://www.ces.ncsu.edu/depts/fcs/pub/aging.html
Eysenck	http://www.psychnet-uk.com/training_ethics/psychologists.htm http://www.indiana.edu/ffintell/eysenck.shtml
Festinger	http://web.umr.edu/ffpsyworld/cognitive_dissonance.htm http://en.wikipedia.org/wiki/Leon_Festinger
Feyerabend	http://plato.stanford.edu/entries/feyerabend/ http://www.humboldt.edu/ffjlw47/fe041502.html
Freud, Anna	http://www.annafreudcentre.org/ http://www.webster.edu/ffwoolflm/annafreud.html http://www.geocities.com/mhrowell/anna_freud.html
Freud, Sigmund	http://users.iafrica.com/m/mw/mwivansm/freud.htm http://en.wikipedia.org/wiki/Sigmund_Freud http://www.answers.com/topic/sigmund-freud?cat=health
Friedman & Rosenman	http://www.ucsf.edu/daybreak/1999/08/09_friedman.html http://www.psychosomaticmedicine.org/cgi/reprint/28/3/283.pdf http://daily.stanford.org/article/2005/2/17/typeANotJustAPersonalityTrait http://www.makingthemodernworld.org.uk/learning_modules/psychology/02.TU.01/?section=7 http://www.acc.org/membership/cca/pdfs/newsletter_mar05.pdf
Fromm	http://allpsych.com/personalitysynopsis/fromm.html http://www.spartacus.schoolnet.co.uk/USAfromm.htm http://www.d.umn.edu/ffmeberhar/ref/psy/psychologists/fromm.htm
Gibson and Walk	http://www.wadsworth.com/psychology_d/templates/student_resources/0155060678_rathus/ps/ps05.html www.webrenovators.com/psych/EleanorGibson.htm http://www.gwu.edu/ffpsycdept/view.cfm?page=walk_fund

Gilligan	http://www.stolaf.edu/people/huff/classes/handbook/Gilligan.html http://www.psy.pdx.edu/PsiCafe/KeyTheorists/Gilligan.htm http://www.webster.edu/ffwoolflm/gilligan.html
Goodall	http://pin.primate.wisc.edu/idp/idp/entry/377 http://www.wic.org/bio/jgoodall.htm http://www.janegoodall.org/?gclid=CKrZ2vPX_owCFQMIHgodOQ7Y-g http://www.janegoodall.org/africa-programs/programs/gombe-stream-research-center.asp http://www-rcf.usc.edu/ffstanford/chimphunt.html DVD Wild Chimpanzees (Jane Goodall) and DVD Gorillas in the Mist (about Dian Fossey).
Gregory	http://www.richardgregory.org
Harlow	http://en.wikipedia.org/wiki/Harry_Harlow http://www.ycc.ac.uk/yc/new/HUMSOC/psycho/unit1/harlow.htm http://oacu.od.nih.gov/regs/primate/ref.htm
Hebb	http://www.mcgill.ca/hebb/biographies/ http://www.questia.com/library/psychology/psychologists/d-o-hebb.jsp
Holmes and Rahe	http://www.statcan.ca/english/studies/11-008/feature/star2003068000s1a01.pdf http://news.bbc.co.uk/cbbcnews/hi/teachers/pshe_11_14/subject_areas/health_influences/newsid_1868000/1868691.stm http://www.bupa.co.uk/members/asp/tng/parents/stress/ http://en.wikipedia.org/wiki/Holmes_and_Rahe_stress_scale http://www.annals.org/cgi/content/full/124/7/673 http://www.drrahe.com/ http://www.psychosomaticmedicine.org/cgi/content/abstract/64/2/278
Horney	http://www.answers.com/topic/karen-horney?cat=health
Hubel and Wiesel	http://nobelprize.org/nobel_prizes/medicine/laureates/1981/wiesel-autobio.html http://nobelprize.org/nobel_prizes/medicine/laureates/1981/index.html http://hubel.med.harvard.edu/index.html http://www.nature.com/nature/journal/v299/n5883/abs/299515a0.html
James	http://psychclassics.yorku.ca/James/Principles/index.htm http://plato.stanford.edu/entries/james/ http://www.des.emory.edu/mfp/james.html
Jung	http://www.cgjungpage.org/ http://www.answers.com/topic/carl-jung?cat=health
Kahneman	http://www.marshallsociety.com/events.php/?id=12&archive=1 http://www.tandf.co.uk/journals/titles/13546783.asp http://www.thinking-and-reasoning-arena.com/ http://nobelprize.org/nobel_prizes/economics/laureates/2002/kahneman-autobio.html http://webdb.princeton.edu/dbtoolbox/query.asp?qname=facultydetail&ID=kahneman

Kelley	http://www.leaonline.com/doi/abs/10.1207/s15324834basp2004_4 http://reasoninglab.psych.ucla.edu/CHENG%20pdfs/C&N.1990.pdf http://www.agsm.edu.au/eajm/0209/pdf/ashkanasy.pdf http://www.scottsdalecc.edu/ricker/psy101/readings/Section_5/5-4.html http://www.universityofcalifornia.edu/senate/inmemoriam/HaroldH.Kelley.htm
Kelly	http://www.oikos.org/vincpcp.htm http://www.cultsock.ndirect.co.uk/MUHome/cshtml/index.html http://en.wikipedia.org/wiki/George_Kelly_(psychologist) http://ksi.cpsc.ucalgary.ca/PCP/Kelly.html http://www.social-psychology.de/do/pt_kelly.pdf http://pages.cpsc.ucalgary.ca/ffgaines/pcp/
Klein	http://www.psych.yorku.ca/femhop/Melanie%20Klein.htm http://www.webster.edu/ffwoolflm/klein.html
Kohlberg	http://faculty.plts.edu/gpence/html/kohlberg.htm http://www.psy.pdx.edu/PsiCafe/KeyTheorists/Kohlberg.htm http://en.wikipedia.org/wiki/Lawrence_Kohlberg http://en.wikipedia.org/wiki/Kohlberg's_stages_of_moral_development
Kohler	http://www.britannica.com/eb/article-9045891/Wolfgang-Kohler http://www.cambridge.org/uk/catalogue/catalogue.asp?isbn=9780521646277 http://psychclassics.yorku.ca/index.htm http://psychclassics.yorku.ca/Kohler/today.htm http://www.dushkin.com/connectext/psy/ch04/bio4.mhtml
Kraepelin	http://www.answers.com/topic/emil-kraepelin?cat=health
Kuhn	http://www.des.emory.edu/mfp/Kuhnsnap.html http://www.des.emory.edu/mfp/Kuhn.html
Labov	http://www.ling.upenn.edu/ffwlabov/ http://www.npr.org/templates/story/story.php?storyId=5220090 http://www.degruyter.com/rfiles/p/9783110167467More%20Information.pdf
Lacan	http://www.answers.com/topic/jacques-lacan?cat=health http://www.iep.utm.edu/l/lacweb.htm
Laing	http://en.wikipedia.org/wiki/R._D._Laing http://www.laingsociety.org/ http://www.philadelphia-association.co.uk/R_D_Laing.htm http://lainginstitut.ch/
Lakatos	http://www-history.mcs.st-andrews.ac.uk/Biographies/Lakatos.html http://www.timesonline.co.uk/tol/incomingFeeds/article778413.ece http://en.wikipedia.org/wiki/Imre_Lakatos
LaPiere	http://histsoc.stanford.edu/pdfmem/LaPiereR.pdf http://links.jstor.org/sici?sici=0037-7732(193412)13%3A2%3C230%3AAVA%3E2.0.CO;2-B http://www.gerardkeegan.co.uk/index.htm http://www.gerardkeegan.co.uk/aboutgerard.htm http://www.cultsock.ndirect.co.uk/MUHome/cshtml/psy/consist.html http://www.psych.uncc.edu/UJOP17.pdf

Latane	http://www.blackwellpublishing.com/sociology/docs/BEOS_S1413.pdf http://www.psych.lancs.ac.uk/people/uploads/MarkLevine20050211T153928.pdf http://www.muskingum.edu/ffpsych/psycweb/history/latane.htm
Lazarus	http://www.tcw.utwente.nl/theorieenoverzicht/Theory%20clusters/Health%20Communication/transactional_model_of_stress_and_coping.doc/ http://www.berkeley.edu/news/media/releases/2002/12/04_lazarus.html
Loftus	http://faculty.washington.edu/eloftus/ http://www.soceco.uci.edu/faculty/loftus/
Lorenz	http://nobelprize.org/nobel_prizes/medicine/laureates/1973/lorenz-autobio.html http://nobelprize.org/nobel_prizes/medicine/laureates/1973/ http://www.oeaw.ac.at/klivv/ http://www.mpg.de/english/portal/index.html
Luria	http://litmed.med.nyu.edu/Annotation?action=view&annid=12247 http://litmed.med.nyu.edu/Annotation?action=view&annid=202 http://luria.ucsd.edu/ http://www.pubmedcentral.nih.gov/articlerender.fcgi?artid=433397
Maslow	http://webspace.ship.edu/cgboer/maslow.html http://www.maslow.com/ http://www.pbs.org/wgbh/aso/databank/entries/bhmasl.html (Public Broadcasting Service, USA).
Mead	http://www.iep.utm.edu/m/mead.htm http://www.csudh.edu/dearhabermas/mead.htm http://www.brocku.ca/MeadProject/ http://www.bartleby.com/65/me/Mead-Geo.html
Milgram	http://www.stanleymilgram.com/ http://www.cba.uri.edu/Faculty/dellabitta/mr415s98/EthicEtcLinks/Milgram.htm http://www3.niu.edu/acad/psych/Millis/History/2003/stanley_milgram.htm http://psychologytoday.com/articles/pto-20020301-000037.html http://en.wikipedia.org/wiki/Stanley_Milgram
Miller	http://wordnet.princeton.edu/ffgeo/ http://www.musanim.com/miller1956/ http://tip.psychology.org/miller.html
Mollon	http://www.psychol.cam.ac.uk/pages/staffweb/mollon/ www.psychol.cam.ac.uk/vision/ http://vision.psychol.cam.ac.uk/jdmollon/
Olds	http://books.nap.edu/readingroom/books/biomems/jolds.html http://www.dushkin.com/connectext/psy/ch02/earlymethods.mhtml http://www.mrw.interscience.wiley.com/ecs/articles/s00466/frame.html
Osgood	http://web.library.uiuc.edu/ahx/ead/ua/1305020/1305020f.html http://www.cultsock.ndirect.co.uk/MUHome/cshtml/introductory/semdif.html http://www.answers.com/topic/charles-e-osgood

Oswald	http://www.lboro.ac.uk/departments/hu/groups/sleep/
Pavlov	http://encyclopedia.farlex.com/Pavlov,+Ivan+Petrovich http://en.wikipedia.org/wiki/Ivan_Pavlov http://www.ivanpavlov.com/default.htm http://www.us.oup.com/us/catalog/general/subject/HistoryOther/ HistoryofScience/?view=usa&ci=9780195105148 http://nobelprize.org/medicine/educational/pavlov/ http://www.dur.ac.uk/robert.kentridge/comp2.html http://www.epic.co.uk/content/resources/email_newsletter/pavlov. htm
Penfield	http://etcweb.princeton.edu/CampusWWW/Companion/penfield_wilder. html http://en.wikipedia.org/wiki/Wilder_Penfield http://www.histori.ca/minutes/minute.do?id=10211
Perls	http://www.gestalt.org/fritz.htm http://findarticles.com/p/articles/mi_g2699/is_0005/ai_2699000582 http://www.britannica.com/eb/topic-452176/Frederick-S-Perls http://www.psychedfilms.com/FritzandGestalt.htm http://www.aagt.org/
Piaget	http://www.piaget.org/aboutPiaget.html http://www.indiana.edu/ffintell/piaget.shtml http://en.wikipedia.org/wiki/Jean_Piaget http://www.questia.com/library/book/the-origins-of-intelligence-in- children-by-jean-piaget-margaret-cook.jsp
Pinker	http://pinker.wjh.harvard.edu/about/index.html http://video.google.com/videoplay?docid=3554279466299738997
Rogers	http://www.ahpb.org.uk/ http://www.nrogers.com/carlrogers.html http://www.infed.org/thinkers/et-rogers.htm http://www.sonoma.edu/users/d/daniels/rogers.html
Rorschach	http://www.whonamedit.com/doctor.cfm/1232.html http://www.phil.gu.se/fu/ro.html http://www.rorschach.com/
Rose	http://www.open.ac.uk/science/biosci/research/rose/rose.htm http://www.edge.org/3rd_culture/rose/rose_p1.html
Rutter	http://www.iop.kcl.ac.uk/staff/profile/default.aspx?go=10273 http://www.richardatkins.co.uk/atws/person/289.html http://www.youngminds.org.uk/magazine/54/carr.php http://www.acscd.ca/acscd/public/bios.nsf/0/ 3d9c4a770aa3e7d688256b960072d99d?OpenDocument http://www.alicevanderpas.demon.nl/pages/intsub1.html
Sapir	http://www.aber.ac.uk/media/Documents/short/whorf.html http://en.wikipedia.org/wiki/Linguistic_determinism http://www.mnsu.edu/emuseum/information/biography/pqrst/sapir_ edward.html
Sacks	http://www.oliversacks.com/ http://search.barnesandnoble.com/booksearch/results. asp?ATH=Oliver%20Sacks

Schachter and Singer	http://books.google.com/books?id=6mu3DLkyGfUC&pg=PA418&lpg=PA418&dq=schachter+singer+theory&source=web&ots=yNfbkZtpHv&sig=lb_KvgS3d5LQo5MI2qhc38hT9H8#PPA418,M1 http://books.nap.edu/readingroom/books/biomems/sschachter.html http://www.yale.edu/psychology/FacInfo/Singer.html
Seligman	http://www.psych.upenn.edu/ffseligman/ http://www.swarthmore.edu/SocSci/bschwar1/helplessness.pdf http://www.curedisease.com/Perspectives/vol_1_1989/Learned%20Helplessness.html
Selye	http://www.garfield.library.upenn.edu/classics1977/A1977DM03500001.pdf http://www.allbiographies.com/biography-HansHugoBrunoSelye-28828.html
Sheldon	http://www.somatotype.org/history.php http://home.tiscali.nl/knmg0234/7variety.htm
Sherif	http://www.muskingum.edu/ffpsych/psycweb/history/sherif.htm http://psychclassics.yorku.ca/Sherif/index.htm http://links.jstor.org/sici?sici=0190-2725(199012)53%3A4%3C283%3ASCOMST%3E2.0.CO%3B2-%23
Shiffrin	http://www.indiana.edu/ffpsych/faculty/shiffrin.html http://rumelhartprize.org/richard.htm
Skinner	http://www.bfskinner.org/ http://tip.psychology.org/skinner.html http://ww2.lafayette.edu/ffallanr/early.html
Sperry	http://nobelprize.org/nobel_prizes/medicine/articles/sperry/index.html
Tajfel	http://www.eaesp.org/activities/own/awards/tajfel.htm http://www.holah.karoo.net/tajfestudy.htm
Thorndike	http://www.indiana.edu/ffintell/ethorndike.shtml http://www.muskingum.edu/ffpsych/psycweb/history/thorndike.htm http://psychclassics.yorku.ca/Thorndike/Animal/
Tinbergen	http://nobelprize.org/nobel_prizes/medicine/laureates/1973/tinbergen-lecture.pdf http://users.rcn.com/jkimball.ma.ultranet/BiologyPages/I/InnateBehavior.html
Tolman	http://psychclassics.yorku.ca/Tolman/Maps/maps.htm http://cogprints.org/3705/
Treisman	http://weblamp.princeton.edu/ffpsych/psychology/research/treisman/index.php http://www.psychologicalscience.org/awards/james/citations/treisman.cfm
Triandis	http://www.ac.wwu.edu/ffculture/triandis1.htm
Tulving	http://www.utoronto.ca/neurosci/faculty/tulving.html http://www.psych.utoronto.ca/ffmuter/Abs1978.htm http://www.garfield.library.upenn.edu/classics1987/A1987K827500001.pdf

Turing	http://plato.stanford.edu/entries/turing-machine/ http://www.aaai.org/AITopics/html/turing.html http://www.turing.org.uk/turing/ http://en.wikipedia.org/wiki/Turing_test
Vygotsky	https://www.cs.tcd.ie/crite/lpr/teaching/constructivism.html http://www.stanford.edu/ffroypea/RoyPDF%20folder/A117_Pea_04_JLS_Scaffolding.pdf
Wason and Johnson-Laird	http://en.wikipedia.org/wiki/Peter_Cathcart_Wason http://en.wikipedia.org/wiki/Philip_Johnson-Laird http://pages.slc.edu/ffebj/minds/THOG.html# http://www.psych.lancs.ac.uk/people/uploads/LindenBall20050808T160059.pdf http://coglab.wadsworth.com/experiments/WasonSelection.shtml http://www.psych.ucsb.edu/research/cep/socex/wason.htm http://education.guardian.co.uk/obituary/story/0,12212,943315,00.html
Watson	http://www.muskingum.edu/ffpsych/psycweb/history/watson.htm http://www.brynmawr.edu/Acads/Psych/rwozniak/watson.html http://en.wikipedia.org/wiki/John_B._Watson
Weiss	http://www.hbi.ucalgary.ca http://www.cell.ucalgary.ca/s_weiss.html http://www.hbi.ucalgary.ca/sections.php?sid=1&cid=54
Winnicott	http://www.winnicott.net/ingles/html/biogr.asp http://www.karnacbooks.com/searchbasic.php?Keywords=winnicott&searchbutton.x=37&searchbutton.y=15&SearchIn=Author
Wundt	http://www.indiana.edu/ffintell/wundt.shtml http://plato.stanford.edu/entries/wilhelm-wundt/ http://psychclassics.yorku.ca/Wundt/Outlines/ http://serendip.brynmawr.edu/Mind/Consciousness.html
Yerkes	http://www.indiana.edu/ffintell/yerkes.shtml http://www.yerkes.emory.edu/
Young, Helmholtz and Maxwell	http://www.britannica.com/eb/article-9106281/Hermann-von-Helmholtz http://www-history.mcs.st-andrews.ac.uk/Biographies/Helmholtz.html http://www.britannica.com/eb/article-9078063/Thomas-Young http://www.studyworld.com/james_clark_maxwell.htm
Zimbardo	http://www.zimbardo.com/ http://www.prisonexp.org/slide-1.htm
Part 5	**Research methods**
Just a few of the available sites that help you through the concepts and calculations	http://en.wikipedia.org/wiki/Statistics http://math.about.com/od/statistics/Statistics_Tutorials_and_Resources.htm http://www.stats.gla.ac.uk/steps/glossary/index.html http://www.graphpad.com/quickcalcs http://www.ling.ed.ac.uk/ffastrid/stat99l4.html http://www.stat-help.com/
SPSS	http://www.spss.com/SPSS/

7.3 Psychology organisations and institutions

The Directory of British Associations and Associations in Ireland (CBD Research Ltd; 18 revised edition,15 January 2007) is a comprehensive guide to professional bodies.

An Internet search will give rise to many organisations and institutions throughout the world. Here are just a few of the important and readily accessible ones.

British Psychological Society (BPS)

http://www.bps.org.uk/
The British Psychological Society, St Andrews House, 48 Princess Road East LE1 7DR, UK.
Tel: 0116 254 9568
Fax: 0116 247 0787
Email: students@bps.org.uk

The British Psychological Society is the representative body for psychology and psychologists in the UK. . . . It has responsibility for the development, promotion and application of pure and applied psychology for the public good. The British Psychological Society has approximately 45,000 members in the UK and overseas, and maintains a Register of Chartered Psychologists. The Society's structure and organisation enables outside bodies and advertisers to target the entire membership or a specific group, either by what the psychologists do or where they work

(BPS website, accessed July 2008).

Within the BPS divisions, sections, special groups and support groups have been established to meet the needs of psychologists, see Figure 7.1. On the home page click the link to Member Networks.

The History of Psychology Centre is the main repository for the British Psychological Society's archive collections. Work is ongoing to create a major history of psychology research resource on the website.

The Student Members Group (SMG) is part of the British Psychological Society and is run by students for students. When you join the Society as an undergraduate psychology student, you automatically become a member of the SMG, qualifying you for many benefits.

The SMG provides you with access to a network of psychology students across the UK and brings you into closer contact with leading professional psychologists. It gives you the opportunity to get involved and shape the future of the discipline. The SMG works to develop new services for students, improve connections with international networks and represent students throughout the Society to ensure that your voice is heard.

BPS Divisions	BPS Sections
Division for Teachers and Researchers in Psychology Division of Clinical Psychology Division of Counselling Psychology Division of Educational and Child Psychology Division of Forensic Psychology Division of Health Psychology Division of Neuropsychology Division of Occupational Psychology Division of Sport and Exercise Psychology Scottish Division of Educational Psychology Divisions exist to further members' professional interests. Focused on training and practice, their aim is to develop psychology as a profession and as a body of knowledge and skills. http://www.bps.org.uk/networks/divisions/divisions$.cfm	Cognitive Psychology Section Consciousness and Experiential Psychology Section Development Psychology Section History and Philosophy of Psychology Section Lesbian and Gay Psychology Section Mathematical, Statistical and Computing Section Psychobiology Section Psychology of Education Section Psychology of Women Section Psychotherapy Section Qualitative Methods in Psychology Section Social Psychology Section Transpersonal Psychology Section Sections exist to further members' specialised scientific interests. They aim to promote psychological research and the exchange of ideas. http://www.bps.org.uk/networks/sections/sections$.cfm
BPS Special Groups	BPS Support Groups
Special Group of Psychologists and Social Services Special Group in Coaching Psychology Special Groups provide a forum for members working in particular specialist fields, and help promote standards. http://www.bps.org.uk/networks/special-groups/special-groups$.cfm	The Student Members Group (SMG) Psychology Postgraduate Affairs Group (PsyPAG) Division of Clinical Psychology Pre-Qualification Group College of Fellows Support Groups for members at undergraduate, postgraduate, training practitioner and fellowship levels. http://www.bps.org.uk/networks/support/support-groups_home$.cfm

Figure 7.1 BPS divisions, sections, special groups and support groups

The SMG gets involved in events specifically aimed at students, such as the London and Edinburgh Lectures, and each year holds an Annual Conference alongside the main BPS Conference, where you even get the chance to present your own research! The SMG also provides a close link with the European Federation of Psychology Students' Associations (EFPSA), publishes a quarterly magazine called *Psych-Talk*, and releases regular newsletters and information through student representatives at each university. http://www.bps.org.uk/smg/smg_home.cfm.

The BPS Qualifying Examination is intended for people who are graduates but who do not hold an honours degree in psychology recognised by the Society and who are therefore not yet eligible for the Graduate Basis for Registration. The website gives details of the syllabus with reading lists, statistical formulae and other useful information relevant

resources

to undergraduate courses in psychology. http://www.bps.org.uk/careers/society_qual/qualifying.cfm.

Quality Assurance Agency for Higher Education (QAA)

http://www.qaa.ac.uk.
http://www.qaa.ac.uk/academicinfrastructure/benchmark/statements/Psychology07.asp

The Quality Assurance Agency for Higher Education was established in 1997 to provide an integrated quality assurance service for UK higher education. Each university and college of higher education is responsible for ensuring that appropriate standards are being achieved and a good-quality education is being offered. It is QAA's responsibility to safeguard the public interest in sound standards of higher education qualifications, and to encourage continuous improvement in the management of the quality of higher education. They achieve this by reviewing standards and quality, and providing reference points that help to define clear and explicit standards.

QAA is an independent body funded by subscriptions from universities and colleges of higher education, and through contracts with the main higher education funding bodies. They are governed by a board, which has overall responsibility for the conduct and strategic direction of our business.

Follow the links for academic infrastructure to find the benchmark statements concerning psychology courses. This gives detailed descriptions of what courses should contain, including teaching and learning skills and resources.

American Psychological Association (APA)

http://www.apa.org/
Based in Washington, DC, the American Psychological Association (APA) is a scientific and professional organisation that represents psychology in the United States. With 148,000 members, APA is the largest association of psychologists worldwide. The aims of the American Psychological Association are to advance psychology as a science and profession and as a means of promoting health, education and human welfare.

There are 53 professional divisions in the APA. Go to http://www.apa.org/about/division.html for a complete list. This site also contains a list of the divisions organised by topic area. This is a useful website for all aspects of psychology.

[Note that the American Psychiatric Association is also abbreviated to APA. http://www.psych.org/about_apa/ (accessed 30 August 2007)]

The Australian Psychological Society (APS)

http://www.psychology.org.au/
The Australian Psychological Society is the largest professional association for psychologists in Australia, representing more than 16,500 members. The APS is committed to advancing psychology as a discipline and profession, and serves as advocate for psychologists at all levels of government. It spreads the message that psychologists make a difference to people's lives, through improving scientific knowledge and community well-being. This is a useful website for all aspects of psychology.

The Canadian Psychological Association (CPA)

http://www.cpa.ca/

The Canadian Psychological Association was organised in 1939 and incorporated under the Canada Corporations Act, Part II, in May 1950. Its objectives are to improve the health and welfare of all Canadians; to promote excellence and innovation in psychological research, education and practice; to promote the advancement, development, dissemination and application of psychological knowledge; and to provide high-quality services to members. This is a useful website for all aspects of psychology.

British Association of Counselling and Psychotherapy (BACP)

http://www.bacp.co.uk/about_bacp/profile_history.html

The British Association for Counselling and Psychotherapy (BACP) changed its name in 2000 from the British Association for Counselling, which grew from the Standing Conference for the Advancement of Counselling, a grouping of organisations inaugurated in 1970 at the instigation of the National Council for Voluntary Organisations. BACP is a company limited by guarantee and a registered charity. Members are not usually psychologists but trained in counselling, psychotherapy or counselling skills. The website may be of interest to psychology undergraduates who are thinking of counselling or psychotherapy as a career but do not necessarily wish to become chartered psychologists.

Through its work BACP ensures that it meets its remit of public protection whilst also developing and informing its members. Its work with large and small organisations within the sector ranges from advising schools on how to set up a counselling service, assisting the NHS on service provision, working with voluntary agencies and supporting independent practitioners. BACP participates in the development of counselling and psychotherapy at an international level.

BACP operates specialist interest divisions and forums that focus on informing members and the public in the following areas:

> children and young people
> health care
> workplace
> higher and further education
> spiritual and pastoral
> independent and group practice
> equality and diversity
> voluntary sector.

7.4 Educational organisations and institutions

The following websites (listed alphabetically) provide background information concerning all levels of education and may be of interest to A-level students as well as psychology undergraduates, particularly mature students returning to education.

Websites for international students planning to study in the UK are given at the end.

Association of Commonwealth Universities – ACU

http://www.acu.ac.uk/
The Association of Commonwealth Universities is an inter-university network. Its concerns are that higher education is more international than ever before and the market for students and staff is a global one. Research funds are increasingly allocated on an international, collaborative basis and academic reputations are based on global connections.

The Association of Graduate Recruiters – AGR

http://www.agr.org.uk/
The Association of Graduate Recruiters, is an independent, not-for-profit organisation dedicated to supporting employers in all aspects of graduate recruitment.

The Association for the Teaching of Psychology (ATP and ATPS)

http://www.theatp.org/ and www.atps.org.uk (accessed 11 september2007).
The ATP is a voluntary body run by psychology teachers for psychology teachers.

It provides a variety of services for members, including a telephone help-line, help via email, ethics advice for practicals and coursework, a magazine, journals, and economically priced one-day and weekend courses for teachers new to psychology.

The **ATPS**, the Scottish branch of the ATP, is a support organisation for all teachers and lecturers of psychology in Scotland.

The British Council

http://www.britishcouncil.org/
The British Council connects people with learning opportunities and creative ideas from the UK to build lasting relationships around the world.

Centre for Higher Education Research and Information at the Open University (CHERI)

http://www.open.ac.uk/cheri/index.htm
The Centre informs higher education policy by providing research, intelligence and analysis to policy makers at institutional, national and international levels. The focus is on

the relationship between higher education and society which is under radical change in many parts of the world today.

Awarding bodies for GCSE, AS and A2

http://www.theatp.org/awardingbodies/index.html (accessed 11 September 2007)
There are four main UK awarding bodies that cover the teaching of psychology in England and Wales (AQA, Edexcel, OCR and WJEC) and one for Scotland (SQA). These websites are useful for students as well as teachers.

> AQA: http://www.aqa.org.uk/
> Edexcel: http://www.edexcel.org.uk/home/
> OCR (Oxford Cambridge and RSA Examinations) http://www.ocr.org.uk/
> WJEC: (Welsh Joint Education Committee) http://www.wjec.co.uk/
> SQA: (The Scottish Qualifications Authority) http://www.sqa.org.uk/sqa/CCC_FirstPage.jsp.

The Department for Education and Skills (dfes)

http://www.dfes.gov.uk/ (accessed 13 September 2007)
www.direct.gov.uk/uni (accessed 17 June 2008)
http://www.direct.gov.uk/en/EducationAndLearning/UniversityAndHigherEducation/index.htm.

The Department now has three educational departments, set up by the Prime Minister on 28 June 2007:

> Department for Children, Schools and Families (DCSF)
> Department for Innovation, Universities and Skills (DIUS)
> Department for Business, Enterprise and Regulatory Reform (DBERR).

Department of Education for Ireland – DENI

http://www.deni.gov.uk/ (accessed 13 September 2007)
DENI is responsible for the central administration of all aspects of education and related services in Northern Ireland – excepting the higher and further education sector, responsibility for which is within the remit of the Department for Employment and Learning.

The devolved Government for Scotland

http://www.scotland.gov.uk/About/ (accessed 10 October 2007)
This is responsible for most of the issues of day-to-day concern to the people of Scotland, including health, education, justice, rural affairs and transport. The Government was known as the Scottish Executive when it was established in 1999 following the first elections to the Scottish Parliament. The current administration was formed after elections in May 2007. The Scottish Government is led by a First Minister who is nominated by the Parliament and in turn appoints the other Scottish Ministers who make up the Cabinet. Civil servants in Scotland are accountable to Scottish ministers, who are themselves accountable to the Scottish Parliament.

resources

Higher Education Wales – HEW

http://www.hew.ac.uk/ (accessed 10 October 2007)
Higher Education Wales represents all the vice-chancellors and principals of the Higher Education Institutions in Wales.

Higher Education Funding Council for England – HEFCE

http://www.hefce.ac.uk/
The Higher Education Funding Council for England promotes and funds high-quality, cost-effective teaching and research, meeting the diverse needs of students, the economy and society.

Higher Education Funding Council for Wales – HEFCW

http://www.hefcw.ac.uk/
The HEFCW promotes higher education in Wales, for the benefit of individuals, society and the economy, in Wales and more widely.

Higher Education Reform Network – HERN

http://www.srhe.ac.uk/HERN/index.htm
This thematic network is supported by the European Union and is a collaborative partnership to explore, disseminate and advise on the future development of the university in relation to societal change and lifelong learning needs and in the context of EU enlargement.

Higher Education Academy

http://www.heacademy.ac.uk/
The Academy's mission is to help institutions, discipline groups and all staff to provide the best possible learning experience for their students.

The Learning and Skills Council – LSC

http://www.lsc.gov.uk/
The Learning and Skills Council is responsible for planning and funding high-quality education and training for everyone in England other than those in universities in order to make England better skilled and more competitive.

National Union of Students – NUS

http://www.nusonline.co.uk/
NUS is a voluntary membership organisation of local student representative organisations in colleges and universities throughout the United Kingdom and Northern Ireland. NUS provides research, representation, training and expert advice for individual students and students' unions.

Oxford Centre for Staff Learning and Development – OCSLD

http://www.brookes.ac.uk/services/ocsd/
The Oxford Centre for Staff and Learning Development provides staff development and

resources

educational development for higher education, supporting the university as an employer as well as a service provider.

Scottish Higher Education Funding Council – SFC (SHEFC)

http://www.sfc.ac.uk/
The Scottish Funding Council distributes funds to Scotland's colleges and universities for teaching and learning, research and other activities in support of Scottish government priorities.

SfE

http://www.sfe.co.uk
An education and training organisation that provides courses for teachers. They are part of the Tribal Group (www.tribalgroup.co.uk) and work with Quality Education and Development (QED), www.qedcoaching.co.uk.

Society for Research into Higher Education (SRE)

http://www.srhe.ac.uk/index.asp (accessed 13 September 2007)
http://www.srhe.ac.uk/networks.sen.asp (accessed 13 September 2007)
http://www.srhe.ac.uk/links.ed.org.asp (accessed 13 September 2007)
This is an independent society which aims to improve the quality of higher education through the encouragement of debate and publication on issues of policy, on the organisation and management of higher education institutions and on the curriculum, teaching and learning methods.

The Student Experience Network brings together students, teachers, researchers and those working in various capacities of student support.

Staff and Educational Development Association – SEDA

http://www.seda.ac.uk/
SEDA is the professional association for staff and educational developers in the UK, promoting innovation and good practice in higher education.

SEDA's activities are clustered into five main areas:

> professional development
> conferences and events
> publications
> research
> services to members.

Standing Conference of Principals – SCOP

http://www.scop.ac.uk/Scop.asp
The Standing Conference of Principals is the representative body for higher education colleges in England and Northern Ireland for the Heads of publicly-designated colleges and institutions of HE and some universities in England and Northern Ireland.

Standing Conference on University Teaching and Research in the Education of Adults – SCUTREA

http://www.scutrea.ac.uk/
SCUTREA is a professional network that provides a focus and meeting place for institutions, departments and individuals engaged in the education and training of adults and/or research in the broad field of continuing education.

UCAS

http://www.ucas.ac.uk/
The organisation responsible for managing applications to higher education courses in the UK. They provide online tools for students and colleges to manage applications and offers. They also organise conferences, education fairs and conventions across the UK and produce a wide range of publications. These are all aimed at helping students to make informed decisions about higher education and to guide them, their parents and advisers through the application process.

UKCGE

http://www.ukcge.ac.uk/
The UK Council for Graduate Education advances graduate education in all academic disciplines throughout the UK through activities such as the organisation of conferences, workshops and discussion forums debating and reflecting on topical postgraduate issues, and the publication of reports and newsletters. UKCGE also promotes and conducts research surveys and investigations into postgraduate education, as well as providing postgraduate data and information to both members and other interested parties.

Universities Scotland

http://www.universities-scotland.ac.uk/
Universities Scotland exists to represent, promote and campaign for the Scottish higher education sector. Through this work, it seeks to assist the sector to deliver its essential contribution to the economic, social and cultural needs of Scotland, and to the enhancement of Scotland's international reputation.

Universities UK

http://www.universitiesuk.ac.uk/
Universities UK has arisen from the Committee of Vice-Chancellors and Principals of the Universities of the United Kingdom (CVCP) and works to a vision of UK universities that are autonomous, properly funded from a diversity of sources, accessible to all, delivering high quality teaching and learning, and at the leading edge of research of regional, national and international significance.

Information for international students planning to study in the UK

The British Council
http://www.educationuk.org/pls/hot_bc/page_pls_all_homepage.
Department for Education and Skills(dfes) (formerly DfEE)

http://www.direct.gov.uk/uni (and follow links for funding and 'not from England').
UKCISA (formerly UKCOSA) – The Council for International Student Affairs
http://www.ukcisa.org.uk/student/fees_student_support.php (accessed June 2008).
HERO – Higher Education and Research Opportunities
http://www.hero.ac.uk and follow links HERO homepage > Studying > International Students' Guide.

Index

Note: Page numbers shown in **bold type** refer to specific entries and those in *italics* refer to sources in the bibliography and website sections.

2-4-6 task, 257, 258
16pF, 184, 185, 234, 287, 312

A

A-B-A design, **271**
abnormal, 68, 78, **123**, 138, 140, 184, 220, 223, *321, 341*
abstract for scientific report, 45, 46
abstract thinking, 20, **123**, 145, 146, 158, 235, 250, 288
accessibility (memory), **124**, 174
accommodation
   of the eye, 124, 150
   Piaget, **124**, 129, 194, 197, 251
   student services, 16, 18
accreditation by BPS, 1, **299**
acoustic store, **124**, 174
action potential, 154, 165, 177, 179, 182, 208, 212
activity theory, 97, 247, *339*
activity trace, 174, 185, 193
actor-observer effect, 131, 159
adaptation
   dark, **148**
   level theory/GAS, 127, 128, **161**, 254
   sensory (habituation), 129, 164, 193
Adler, A., 112, 208, **224**, *307, 342*
adolescence, 74, 158, 237, *312, 315, 322*
Adorno, T., 131, **224**, *307, 325, 342*
adrenaline, 128, 133, 141, 153, 157, 233, 253
adrenocorticotrophic hormone (ACTH), 128, 161
adult bullying, 125, 163, 182, *327*
affect, **124**, 130, 153, 228, 229

affective domain/condition, 4, 131, 149, 175, 184, 198, 228, 288, *328*
affordances, **124**
after-image, **124**, 174, 177
ageing, 74, 75, **125**, 149, 196, 208, *311, 320, 331, 346*
aggression, **125**, 126, 127, 129, 153, 167, 228, 308–34
Ainsworth, M., 129, **225**, 232, *307, 331, 342*
Allport, F., 81, 221, **225**, *307, 342*
Allport, G., 59, 135, 150, 184, **226**, 228, *307, 308, 342*
altered body image, **125**
altered state of consciousness (ASC), 67, 93, **125**
alter-ego, 151, 187, 188
altruism, 111, **126**, 148
ambiguous figures, 71, **126**, 213
amnesia, **126**, 174
amygdala, 151, 153, 173, 175, 229
analysis of qualitative data, 4, 264, 271
analysis of variance (ANOVA), 243, 265, 268, **271**, 278, 280, 286, 296
analytical psychology, 10, 112, 187, 242
androgyny, 230, *310, 343*
anger, **126**, 142, 150, 153, 155, 163, 187, 194, 199, 211, *310, 311, 324, 331*
anger management, **126**, 139, 205
anima and animus, **126**, 145, 160, 242
animism, **126**, 131
anticathexis, 139
anticipation, **127**, 148
anxiety, 124, 126, **127**, 149, 150, 153, 160, 199, 239, 241, *311, 324, 331*
APA Guidelines for referencing, 25, 26, 27, 30, *339*
apparition, **127**, 164, 213, *316*
appeasement, **127**, 155
arbitrary inference, 142

archetype, **127**, 145, 242

Aristotle, 60, 63, 138, 196, 217

Aronson, E., 81, 163, **226**, *308, 342*

arousal systems, **127**, 128, 157, 161, 204, 254, *314*

articulatory loop and suppression, 185

artificial intelligence, 70, 71, 93, **128**, 142, 222, 257

Asperger's syndrome, 229

asceticism, **128**, 148, 169, 238

Asch, S., 146, **226**, 248, *308, 342*

assertiveness, **129**, 211

assimilation, **129**, 194, 197, 251

ASSIST (Entwistle), **21**, 22, 54, *314, 327, 332, 338*

Atkinson and Shiffrin, 174, 177, **226**, 227, 254, *308, 342*

attachment and bonding, **129**, 210, 225, 232, 259, *307, 311, 319, 328, 344*

attention, 71, **129**, 169, 181, 182, 183, 235, 236, 242, 256, *314, 332, 341*

attitude, 82, **130**, 226, 238, 249, 256, *310–32*

    development, **131**

    questionnaire, **131**, 189, 246, 264, 268

attribution, 82, **131**, 164, 231, 253, 254, *314*

    fundamental error, **159**, 183

    theory, **131**, 172, *319*

auditory

    inspection time, **169**, 179, 234, 286, *311, 313, 325*

    interference patterns, 183

    location, **131**, 165

    memory (acoustic, phonological, sounds, speech), 124, 174, 185, 190, 192, 200, 214, 227, 235, 333

    sense (hearing), cortex and pathways, 71, **165**, 196

    sign or signal, 90, 134

authoritarian

    parenting style, 182

    personality, 131, 187, 224, *307*

autism, 69, 123, 126, **132**, 164, 209, 223, 229, 231, 252, 253, *309, 318, 343*

autobiographical (episodic) memory, 71, **154**, 173, 174, 227

autogenic relaxation training, 126, 132, 191, *326*

autohypnosis (self hypnosis), 125, 191

autokinetic effect (saccadic eye movements), 193, *307*

autonomic nervous system, 69, **132**, 133, 178, 205, 233

availability (memory), 124, **132**, 174

aversion therapy, 134

avoidance

    behaviour/coping style, **132**, 147, 148, 149, 190, *329*

    learning, 134, 189, 252

axons, 136, 177, 178, 179

B

backward span (memory), 174, 199, 228

Baddeley and Hitch, 139, 174, 185, 199, 213, 227, *308, 342*

Bales Interaction Process Analysis, **132**, 138, 204, 228, *308*

Bales, R., 132, 138, 204, **228**, *308, 309, 342*

Bandura, A., 62, 84, 127, 203, 222, **228**, *309, 343*

bar chart/bar graph, 268, 270, **271**, 272, 277, 279, 286

Baron-Cohen, S., 132, **229**, *309, 310, 343*

Bartlett, F., 152, 187, 197, **229**, *310, 343*

basal nuclei, **133**, 151

baseline observations, **271**

behaviour

    modification/shaping, 85, **133**, 134, *309*

    modification therapy, 134, 173

    therapies, **134**

beliefs, **134**, *308, 310, 328*

Bell, A., 68, 196, 219

Bem, S., 160, **229**, 230, *310, 343*

Berne, E., 210, **230**, *310, 319, 344*

Bernstein, B., **230**, 231, 245, 257, *310, 344*

Bettelheim, B., 132, **231**, 246, *310, 344*

between groups design, 281, 286, 288, 289, **294**

bias

    cultural, 14

    experimenter, 276, 285

    participant, 276

    sampling, 277, 290

bimodal distribution, **271**, 285

Binet, A., 221, 250

binomial test, 264, **271**, 281

biofeedback, 69, 132, **134**, 152, 191, *326, 329*

Bion, W., 147, **231**, *310, 344*

colour
> constancy, **143**, 183
> of rainbow, 183, 253
> of surroundings, **143**
> vision, **143**, 212, 249, 259, 260, *324, 330*
> vision variations/blindness, 143, 183, 249, 253

coma, **144**, 166
compensation, **144**, 148, 186
competence, 13, 15, 21, 23, 124, 176, 232, *313, 338*
complexes, 126, **145**
complexity theory, **145**
computational theory of mind, 92, **145**, 251
Comte, A., 219
conation, **145**, 219, 341
conative domain/behaviour, 4, 64, 70, 72, 78, 140
concept, **145**, 187
concrete operations, **146**, 158, 251
concurrent processing, 139, 181, 199, 227, 228
conditioned response, stimulus, 85, 140, 141, 180
confabulation, 190
conformity, 82, **146**, 182, 198, 226, 244, *308, 342*
confounding variable, **274**
confrontation, 107, 252
confusional state, 14, 197
congruence, 107, **146**, 154, 211, 252
conservation, **146**, 147, 251, *322*
constancy, 183
> colour, **143**
> identity, **168**
> lightness, **173**
> shape, **199**
> size, **199**
container for emotions, **147**, 231, 244
content analysis, 228, 264, 271, **274**, 287
context
> dependence, *see* cue dependence
> of discovery, **274**
> of justification, **274**
> pain, **181**
contingency table, 265, 273, **274**, 275
control
> condition/group, **275**, 276, 277, 291
> procedures, **275**

convergent thinking, 20, 76, **147**, 151, 169, 187, 209
coping styles, **147**, 205, 206
core approaches, 67, 86, 95
correlation, 46, 265, 268,272, **275**, 280, 290, 291, 294, 295
> coefficient, 263, 265, 268, 275, 289, 291
counter conditioning, 141
counter transference, 148, 210
counselling psychology, 11, 66, **95**, 108, **300**, 339, 355
covariation, 243
covert participant observer, 284
Craik and Lockhart, 172, 174, 227, **234**, 257, *313, 345*
Cramer's Phi, 265, **275**, 293, *313*
creativity, 74, **147**, 235, 252, 299, *310, 311, 313, 314, 328*
critical theory, rationalism, 225, 238
Cronbach's alpha, 289
cross-classification table *see* contingency table
cross-sectional study, **275**, 283
crowds, **148**, 149, 168
cue dependence, **148**, 158, 174, 211
cultural psychology, 4, 66, 81, **97**, 111, 114, *339*
cultural-historical psychology, 97
culturally bound, 14, 238
cumulative frequency, 264, **275**, 277
cybernetics, **70**, 222, 325
cycle of violence, 125

D

Damasio, A., 72, 229, **235**, 243, *313*
dark adaptation, **148**
Darwin, C., 68, 75, 78, 100, 219, 221, *311*
data, **275**
De Bono, E., 75, 171, **235**, *313, 345*
death-wish (thanatos), **148**, 239
decay (trace decay), 158, 173
deduction and deductive reasoning/processes, **148**, 158, 168, 171, 207, 209, 280, 295
defence mechanisms, 112, 147, **148**,149, 152,169, 220, 238, 239
degrees of freedom, 274, **275**, 276
dementia, 67, 69, 126, **149**, 190, 194, 244
denial, 129, 132, 148, **149**
Dennett, D., **235**, 257, *313, 345*

theory of mind, 159, **168**, 209
idiographic, 77, **280**, 284
immediate memory, 174
implicit
    memory, 71, 256
    personality theory, **168**, 183
    theory of intelligence scale (ITIS), 21
independent variable, 130, 266, 276, 279, **280**,
    283, 290, 291
individual psychology, 112, 224, *307*
individuation, 149, **168**, 242
induced motion, **169**
inferences, 130, 152, 156, 243, 280, 286, 294
inferential statistics, 267, 268, **280**
information
    overload, 129, 142, 164
    processing, 71, 75, 92, 101, 126,145, **169**,
        175, 177, 227, 240, 242, 249, 256
    technology, 268, 302
inhibition, **170**
insight (in problem-solving), 75, 90, **169**, 187,
    221, 244
insomnia, 163, 200
inspection time, **169**, 170, 234, 286, *311, 313,*
    325, 333
instinct, 129, **169**,220, 239, 241,247, 256, 258,
    259, *326, 332*
instrumental conditioning, *see* operant
    conditioning
intellectualisation, 149, **169**, 238
intelligence, **170**
    artificial, 70, 71, 73, 93, **128**,142, 222, 229,
        257
    crystallised, 125, 170, 196, 234
    emotional, **153**
    fluid, 170, 234
    implicit theory of (ITIS), 21
    quotient (IQ), **170**
    triarchic, **20**, 170
interference, **170**, 173, 190, 256
interpersonal perception, *see* person perception
intersexuality, **170**, 198
interval level, 279,281, 282
intrinsic, 84, 176
introversion, **170**,185, 225, 238

Jackson, H., 219
James, W., 9, 72, 196, 219, 226, 233, **242**, *312,*
    318, 348
Janet, P., 220
jargon, 42
jigsaw classroom technique, 226, *308, 342*
Jung, C., 126, 127,143, 160, **242**, 252, *319, 322,*
    331, 348

Kahneman, D., **242**, 253, 256, *316, 319, 333, 348*
Kant, I., 64, 72, 145, 209, 219,224
Kelley, H., **243**, 249, *319, 332, 348*
Kelly, G., 183, 184, 192, **243**, *319, 348*
kinaesthesia, **171**
Klein, M., 11, 147, 231, 238, **243**, 259, *320, 348*
Kohlberg, L., 76, 240, **244**, *320, 348*
Kohler, W., 187, **244**, *320, 349*
Kraepelin, E., **244**, *320, 349*
Kuder-Richardson method, 289
Kuhn, T., 105, **245**, *320, 349*
kurtosis, 264, **280**, 285

Labov, W., 231, **245**, *320, 349*
Lacan, J., **245**, *311,320, 349*
Laing, R., 194, **245**, *320, 349*
Lakatos, I., 105, **246**, *320, 321, 349*
language
    animal, 90
    centres in the brain, 166, 171, 174, 204, 255
    communication and culture, 71, 81, 93, 162,
        194, 206, 235, 310-334
    consciousness, 204, 255
    development, 74, 76, 157, 197, 208,
        234
    and thinking, 183, 222, 231, 232, 236, 251,
        253, 257, *326, 333*
    of thought, 175, *315*
LaPiere, R., **246**, *321, 349*
Latané, B., **246**, 253, *313, 321, 349*
lateral thinking, 75, **171**, 187, 235, *313*
law(s), 60,68, 265, 266, **280**, 284
Lazarus, R., 72, 141, 205, **247**, 253, *319, 322,*
    324, 349
L-dopa, 253

motor nervous system, 69, 133, 136, 165, 166, 178, 209, 219

mourning, 163

movement illusions, 175, 185, 169, 213, 327

Muller-Lyer illusion, 158, **176**

multiple personality, *see* dissociative identity disorder

multi-store model, 154, 174, **177**, 182

Myers, C., 220, 229

Myers–Briggs, 184, 185, 287

myoclonic jerk, **177**, 201

N

narcolepsy, **177**

naturalistic observation, **284**

nature–nurture debate, 5, 140, **177**, 185, 211

Necker cube, **177**

negative
  affect, 124
  after image, 124
  hallucination, 164
  reinforcement, 191

nerve fibre, **177**

nervous system, **178**

neurolinguistic programming (NLP), 107, 194

neurone, 136, 139, 145, 151, 162, 174, 177, **178**, 179, 206, 208

neuroscience, *see* cognitive neuroscience

neurotransmitters, 68, 128, 151, **179**, 189

nominal level, 265, 271, 273, 279, **281**, 286

nomothetic, 77, 280, **284**

non-parametric tests, 265, 268, 280, **286**, 294, 296

non-participant observer, 284

non-verbal communication, 111, 130, **179**, 181, 276

normal (Gaussian) distribution, 123, 268, 278, 280, **284**, 285, 286

norms, 79, 81, 82, 148, 163, **179**, 193, 198

null hypothesis, 46, 265, 266, 267, 277, **285**, 291, 294

O

obedience, 81, 82, **180**, 182, 244, 248, *311, 323,* 335

object concept, 164, **180**, 197

objective, **285**, *331*

Oedipus complex, 145, 242

Olds, J., **249**, *325, 350*

olfaction, *see* smell

ontological insecurity, **180**

operant conditioning, 131, 133, **180**, 191, 254, 258

operational definitions, **285**

opportunity sample, **285**, 290

ordinal level, 265, 281, 286, 288

orientation
  body, 196
  constancy, 183
  NVC, 179
  reality, 37, **190**
  sexual, 114, 196, 198, 203

Osgood, C., **249**, *325, 350*

Oswald, I., 151, 200, **250**, *307, 325, 350*

out-of-the-body experiences, 175, **180**

outliers, **273**

overgeneralisation, 142

overlearning, **180**, *320*

overt participant observer, 284

P

pain
  context, **181**
  management, **181**
  tolerance, 155

paired-associate learning, **181**

paradigm, 4, 93, 169, **181**, 245, 266, 293

paradoxical
  figures, 158, **181**, 213
  sleep, 192, 200

paralanguage, 165, 179, **181**, 253, 276

parallel processing, 130, 139, 169, **181**, 185, 210, 256

parameter, **286**

parametric tests, 265, 268, 280, 281, **286**, 294

paranormal, 33, 182

parenting
  skills, **182**
  styles, **182**

partial reports, 174

participant
  bias, 271, 272
  design, 264, 267, **286**
  observation, 264, 284, **286**

147, 151, 169, 170, 171, **187**, 197, 198, 209, 244, 249, 256, *309, 319, 327*
procedural memory (PM), 137, 139, 173, 174, **188**, 227
progressive desensitisation, 134, 141, 206
projection (defence mechanism), 126, 149, 163, **188**
projective techniques, **188**, 193, 209, 252, 287
proprioception, 164, **188**, 247
prospect theory, **242**, *319*
prospective
    memory, 174, **188**
    studies, **289**
protocol analysis, 264, 271, **287**
pseudodementia, 149
psyche, 2, 9, 145, 242
psychoactive drugs, 67, 126, **189**
psychoanalysis, 11, 112, 113, 115, 152, 159, **188**, 193, 220
psychoanalytical psychology, 4, 10, 78, 221
psychodrama, 139, **188**, *324*
psychodynamic psychology, 65, **112**, 129
psychogenic illness, 156, **188**, 189
psychology of women, 66, 108, **114**, 223, *340, 355*
psychometric tests/psychometrics, 14, 79, 86, 95, 233, 264, **287**, 294, *310, 340, 341*
psychoneuroimmunology, 128, **189**
psychosexual stages, 157, **189**, 190, 237, 239, 244
psychosomatic, 156, **189**, 233, *307, 346*
psychotherapy, 66, 95, 106, **115**, 301, *312, 313, 322, 327, 340, 346, 355, 352*
psychotropic drugs, 67, 126, **189**, *324*
punishment, 84, 85, 180, **189**, 212, 244, 255
puzzle box, 255

Q technique, 131, **189**, 287, *311, 331*
Qualia, 197, 235
qualitative
    research methods, 4, 66, 264, 265, 268, 271, **287**, *316, 355*
    variables, **287**
quantitative
    research methods, 4, 236, 264, 265, 279, **288**
    variables, **287**
quartile, 272, 273, 285

questionnaire, 131, 189, 246, 264, 287, **288**

R

random sample, 290
randomised controlled trial, 265, **288**
range, 268, 272, 276, 278, 281, **288**
rank order, 265, 268, 280, 281, **288**, 291
rapid eye movement (REM) sleep, 151, **192**, 200, 201, 202, 250
rate, **288**
ratio level, **281**
rational-emotive therapy, 143, 237, 241, *346*
rationalisation, 149, *190*
raw data, 46, 135, 273, 274, 277, 281, 282, **288**, 293
reaction formation, 148, **190**
realistic conflict theory, 254
reality orientation, 37, **190**
recall, 148, 155, 156, 157, 173, 174, **190**, 192, 197, 229, 333
recency effects, 131, 183, **190**
recognition, 135, 155, 174, 182, **190**, 191, 254, 333
reconstruction, 156, 174, **190**, 191, 197, 229, *321*
recovered memories, **156**, 247, *349*
redintegration, 174, **190**
reductionism, 5, **190**, 238
referencing, Harvard system, 25, 26, 30, 31, 53
regression
    defence mechanism, 149, **190**
    linear, 265, 268, **281**, 283, 290
rehearsal, 172, 174, 177, 185, **191**, 206, 227, 234, 254
reinforcement, 84, 131, 133, 154, 180, **191**, 193, 203, 209, 228, 244, *309, 315*
    schedules, **191**, 192
related groups design, **284**
relativism, **191**, *315*
relaxation training, 132, **191**, 206
relearning, 174, **191**, 236
    savings, **192**
reliability, 5, **289**
REM sleep, 151, **192**, 200, 201, 202, 250
reminiscence, 126, 154, 174, **192**
remote memory, 173, 174, **192**, 227
repeated measures design, 46, 264, 265, 267, **289**
repertory grid, 184, **192**, 243, *315*